Words Their Way

Word Study for Phonics, Vocabulary, and Spelling Instruction

Third Edition

Donald R. Bear
University of Nevada, Reno

Marcia Invernizzi
University of Virginia

Shane Templeton
University of Nevada, Reno

Francine Johnston
University of North Carolina at Greensboro

PEARSON

Merrill
Prentice Hall

Upper Saddle River, New Jersey
Columbus, Ohio

Library of Congress Cataloging-in-Publication Data

Words their way : word study for phonics, vocabulary, and spelling instruction / Donald R. Bear ... [et al.].—3rd ed.
 p. cm.
 Includes bibliographical references and index.
 ISBN 0-13-111338-0
 1. Word recognition. 2. Reading—Phonetic method. 3. English language—Orthography and spelling. I. Bear, Donald R.
 LB1050. 44 .B43 2004
 372.46'2—dc21   2002040995

Vice President and Executive Publisher: Jeffery W. Johnston
Senior Editor: Linda Ashe Montgomery
Development Editor: Hope Madden
Production Editor: Mary M. Irvin
Design Coordinator: Diane C. Lorenzo
Production Coordination: Amy Gehl, Carlisle Publishers Services
Cover Designer: Ali Mohrman
Cover Image: Jean Claude Lejeune
Production Manager: Pamela D. Bennett
Director of Marketing: Ann Castel Davis
Marketing Manager: Darcy Betts Prybella
Marketing Coordinator: Tyra Poole
Photo Credits: Marcia Invernizzi, pp 1, 249; Donald Bear, pp. 3, 138, 180; Jean-Claude Lejeune, pp. 31, 59, 218; Anthony Magnacca/Merrill, p. 94.
Text Illustrations: Francine R. Johnston

This book was set in Palatino by Carlisle Communications, Ltd., and was printed and bound by Courier Kendallville, Inc. The cover was printed by Phoenix Color Corp.

Pearson Education Ltd.
Pearson Education Singapore Pte. Ltd.
Pearson Education Canada, Ltd.
Pearson Education—Japan

Pearson Education Australia Pty. Limited
Pearson Education North Asia Ltd.
Pearson Educación de Mexico, S.A. de C.V.
Pearson Education Malaysia Pte. Ltd.

10 9 8 7 6 5 4 3 2 1
ISBN 0-13-111338-0

This book is dedicated to our families and friends.

We wish you and your students happy sorting!

Donald R. Bear
Marcia Invernizzi
Shane Templeton
Francine Johnston

About the Authors

Donald R. Bear

Donald Bear is director of the E. L. Cord Foundation Center for Learning and Literacy in the College of Education at the University of Nevada, Reno. As a former preschool, third, and fourth grade teacher, Donald extends his experience working with children who experience difficulties learning to read and write both in the center and in numerous outreach programs. His recent research includes the study of literacy development in different

languages and the influence of first language and literacy knowledge in learning to read in another language. He and his colleagues work with many schools and districts to conduct literacy instruction workshops.

Shane Templeton

Shane Templeton is Foundation Professor of Curriculum and Instruction at the University of Nevada, Reno, where he is Program Coordinator for Literacy Studies. A former elementary and secondary teacher, his research focuses on the development of orthographic knowledge. He has written several books on the teaching and learning of reading and language arts and is a member of the Usage Panel of the *American Heritage Dictionary*. He is author of the "Spelling Logics" column in *Voices from the Middle*, the middle school journal of the National Council of Teachers of English.

Marcia Invernizzi

Marcia Invernizzi is a professor of reading education at the Curry School of Education at the University of Virginia. Marcia is also the director of the McGuffey Reading Center, where she teaches the clinical practica in reading diagnosis and remedial reading. Formerly an English and reading teacher, she works with Book Buddies, Virginia's Early Intervention Reading Initiative (EIRI), and Phonological Awareness Literacy Screening (PALS).

Francine Johnston

Francine Johnston is a former first grade teacher and reading specialist who learned about word study during her graduate work at the University of Virginia. She is now an associate professor in the School of Education at the University of North Carolina at Greensboro, where she teaches courses in reading, language arts, and children's literature. Francine frequently works with regional school systems as a consultant and researcher. Her research interests include current spelling practices and materials as well as the relationship between spelling and reading achievement.

Preface

Words Their Way: Word Study for Phonics, Vocabulary, and Spelling Instruction, Third Edition, provides a practical way to study words with students. Based on research on developmental spelling and word knowledge, the framework of this text is keyed to five stages and instructional levels. Ordered in this way, *Words Their Way* complements the use of any existing phonics, spelling, and vocabulary curricula.

The third edition of our text broadens and strengthens an already acute vision of today's classrooms. We provide more support for upper elementary, middle, and secondary students and their teachers, and add a new focus on English Language Learners. Issues of classroom management are also examined in every chapter, beginning with a deep focus in Chapter 3.

SPECIAL FEATURES

 New! ELL Teaching Notes throughout chapters help you to adapt your word study lessons to better suit English Language Learners.

 New! CD-ROM integration. Notes throughout each chapter point to ways to integrate the materials found on the free CD-ROM with chapter content.

 New! Companion Website margin notes integrate this great online supplement with the text, leading you to additional related content to be found on our Companion Website, available at http://www.prenhall.com/bear

 This symbol indicates activities that can be adapted to other developmental levels.

TEXT ORGANIZATION

We have organized this text so that it can be easily used in a number of ways. To explore the nature of word study and the type of classroom organization and environment that enhances implementation of word study, we suggest you begin reading this text at the beginning—with Chapter 1. If you want to jump right in and explore word study activities with your students, we recommend that you skim Chapters 3 through 8, look for activities related to the developmental levels of your students, and examine a few closely. Then try one or two out with a small group of students. Remember that additional materials are available on the free CD-ROM enclosed in the text.

Chapter 1: The first chapter presents an overview of how words are learned, a discussion of reading, spelling, and writing development, and a rationale for word study phonics, spelling, and vocabulary instruction in the classroom.

Chapter 2: The second chapter presents the assessment process in a step-by-step manner to administer, score, and analyze students' spelling. There are now nine inventories, including a Spanish spelling inventory, and based on our recent research we made refinements in the word lists and scoring guides to make instructional planning easier. Guidelines for interpreting spelling errors by English language learners are presented.

Chapter 3: In this chapter we clearly present ways to organize word study in a classroom setting. The planning activities integrate word study into reading and language arts programs.

Chapters 4 through 8 focus on particular stages of literacy development. We hope you will be pleased to see a more explicit scope and sequence of word study instruction for each developmental stage. Sections of developmentally appropriate activities, tabbed in color for easy location, accompany each of these chapters. Often presented in a game-like format, these activities are actually minilessons that draw upon what students are learning concurrently in developmental reading and writing.

We have included activities that are especially interesting to students and can be easily integrated into the many contexts in which reading and writing activities occur. In each activity, students examine words and their **sound and spelling** patterns, and they reflect on how words are organized, how they are spelled, and what they mean.

Chapter 4: This chapter is dedicated to **Word Study for Learners in the Emergent Stage.** The accompanying activities address phonological awareness and vocabulary development as well as alphabet knowledge and concepts about print and the orthography.

Chapter 5: Chapter 5 examines **Word Study for Beginners in the Letter Name-Alphabetic Stage.** Here we present a systematic scope and sequence for phonics instruction appropriate for beginning readers, including explicit directions for teacher-directed word sorts and suggestions for more open-ended explorations.

Chapter 6: In this chapter we focus on **Word Study for Transitional Learners in the Within Word Pattern Stage.** The sequence of word study for this stage focuses on vowel patterns, and the accompanying activities support the development of automatic word recognition and fluency.

Chapter 7: This third edition includes an even stronger focus on intermediate and advanced readers and writers. In this chapter we look at **Word Study for Intermediate Readers and Writers: The Syllables and Affixes Stage.** We outline a systematic curriculum for vocabulary and spelling instruction of multisyllabic words. The activities begin with consonant doubling and end with the study of the basic prefixes and suffixes.

Chapter 8: Chapter 8 is strengthened to include even more on **Word Study for Advanced Readers and Writers: The Derivational Relations Stage.** Throughout this chapter, the spelling-meaning connection is the fundamental principle we use to teach students Greek and Latin bases and roots. The scope and sequence is clearly described, and the activities will advance students' vocabularies.

Appendix: In the Appendix you will find all of the reproducible materials in one place. It begins with the assessment materials that were discussed in Chapter 2. We have added more games, assessments, word lists, and sorts to this edition, all of which are available, along with game templates, in the Appendix. These pages are perforated for your convenience.

SUPPLEMENTS

This edition hosts a complement of *Words Their Way* materials that help tremendously to begin and maintain word study in the classroom, teaching in small groups, and tutoring.

Words Their Way **CD***: An Interactive Resource:* This free CD supplement contains word sorts and games for each developmental level, ready to print. Templates for many new games and favorites from *Words Their Way* are included. A Spanish word study program for English language learners and Spanish foreign language learners is also presented.

Companion Website: This free supplement contains valuable material, including word study activities for each developmental level, additional spelling inventories for grades 1-3 and for secondary students, resources for using word study with students who speak Spanish, links to websites relating to word study, as well as news about new supplementary materials and word study events. You can link to this site at http://www.prenhall.com/bear

Words Their Way Video (ISBN: 0-13-022183-X). We present seven teaching segments that cover the entire developmental continuum. This instructional video presents classrooms in action, where teachers show us how they conduct word study in small reading groups. You'll see how to present word sorts at each developmental level. The authors present brief overviews of instruction and the assessment process, and we go on a room tour to study classroom organization. Priced inexpensively for students and schools, this video can be purchased through your Prentice Hall sales representative or your local bookstore. For more information on purchasing this or other supplements, please visit our Companion Website at http://www.prenhall.com/bear

Words Their Way: Word Sorts for Letter Name-Alphabetic Spellers (ISBN: 0-13-183813-X). This text is the first in a series of sorts and activities for each developmental level, allowing you to extend your word study throughout the school year. Keep an eye out for each new text in the series. Their publication will be announced on our Companion Website at http://www.prenhall.com/bear

ACKNOWLEDGMENTS

We would like to thank the following people for their contributions: Tamara Baren, Washoe County School District; Marla Bussey, Washoe County School District; Mary Fowler and the Book Buddy Coordinators in Charlottesville, Virginia; Sandra Madura, Washoe County School District and the University of Nevada, Reno; Shari Nielsen, Washoe County School District; Wanda Nomura, Washoe County School District; Diane Olds, Washoe County School District; and Terry Purcell, Cleveland State University.

We also thank the reviewers of the third edition for their comments and insights: Phyllis Y. Coulter, Eastern Mennonite University; Lori Helman, University of California, Santa Cruz; Cheryl A. Melton, University of LaVerne; and Leslie Smith, Santa Cruz New Teacher Project.

Brief Contents

Contents

CHAPTER 6

Word Study for Transitional Learners in the Within Word Pattern Stage   180

CHAPTER 7

Word Study for Intermediate Readers and Writers: The Syllables and Affixes Stage   218

CHAPTER 8

Word Study for Advanced Readers and Writers: The Derivational Relations Stage   249

Note: Every effort has been made to provide accurate and current Internet information in this book. However, the Internet and information posted on it are constantly changing, so it is inevitable that some of the Internet addresses listed in this textbook will change.

Introduction

WHY WORD STUDY?

Literacy is like a braid of interwoven threads. The braid begins with the intertwining threads of oral language and stories. As children experiment with putting ideas on paper, a writing thread is intertwined as well. As children move into reading, the threads of literacy begin to bond. Students' growing knowledge of spelling or **orthography**—the correct sequences of letters in the writing system—strengthens that bonding. The size of the threads and the braid itself become thicker as orthographic knowledge grows.

During the primary years word knowledge is fundamentally aural. From the oral language that surrounds them (e.g., world experiences and stories), children develop a rich speaking vocabulary. As children have opportunities to talk about and to categorize

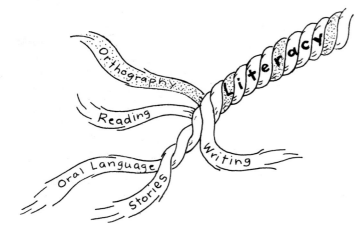

FIGURE I-1   Braid of Literacy

their everyday experiences, they begin to elaborate what they know and to expand their oral vocabulary. As children observe parents, siblings, and caregivers writing for many purposes, they begin to experiment with pen and paper, gradually coming to understand the forms and functions of written language. The first written words students learn are usually their own names, followed by those of significant others. Words such as *Mom, cat, dog,* and *I love you* represent people, animals, and ideas dear to their lives.

As students mature as readers and writers, they learn vocabulary from written language that they have not heard in their aural language. Print becomes a critical medium for conceptual development. When purposeful reading, writing, listening, and speaking take place, words are learned along the way. Even more words are acquired when they are explicitly examined to discover the orthographic relationships among words—their sounds, spelling patterns, and meanings.

The aim of this book is to demonstrate how an exploration of orthographic knowledge can lead to the lengthening and strengthening of the literacy braid (Figure I-1). To do this, teachers must know a good deal about the way in which these threads join to create this bond so that they can direct children's attention to "words their way."

There are similarities in the ways learners of all ages expand their knowledge of the world. It seems that humans have a natural interest to find order, to compare and contrast, and to pay attention to what remains the same despite minor variations. Infants learn to recognize Daddy as the same Daddy with or without glasses, with or without a hat or whiskers. Through such daily interactions, we categorize our surroundings. Our students expand their vocabularies by comparing one concept with another. Gradually, the number of concepts they analyze increases, but the process is still one of comparing and contrasting.

FIGURE I-2   Student Sorting Words by Sound

Word study, as described in this textbook, occurs in hands-on activities that mimic basic cognitive learning processes; comparing and contrasting categories of word features and discovering similarities and differences within and between categories. For example, students often misspell words that end with the /k/ sound, spelling the word *snake* as SNACK or even SNACKE. By sorting words that end in *ck* and *ke* into two groups by sound, as the student is doing in Figure I-2, students discover the invariant pattern that goes with each (*ck* only follows a short vowel). The system is laid bare when words are sorted into categories.

During word study, words and pictures are sorted in routines that require children to examine, discriminate, and make critical judgments about speech sounds, word structures, spelling patterns, and meanings. The activities that we present build on what students do on their own. Just as *Math Their Way* (Baretta-Lorton, 1968) uses concrete manipulatives to illustrate principles of combining and separation, so *Words Their Way,* Third Edition, uses concrete pictures and words to illustrate principles of similarity and difference.

Word Study and the Development of Orthographic Knowledge

1

T he Rosetta Stone, which reveals the hidden logic behind students' invented spellings, was first discovered by Charles Read in 1971. Read investigated preschoolers' invented spellings and discovered that their attempts were not just random displays of ignorance and confusion. To the contrary, Read's linguistic analysis exposed a window through which teachers could ascertain the children's tacit understanding of English phonology (Read, 1971, 1975). Read's study uncovered a systematic, phonetic logic to preschoolers' categorizations of English speech sounds. His insight led Edmund Henderson and colleagues at the University of Virginia to look for similar logic in students' spellings across time and grade levels (Beers & Henderson, 1977; Gentry, 1980; Henderson, Estes, & Stonecash, 1972). The Virginia spelling studies corroborated and extended Read's findings upward through the grades and resulted in a comprehensive model of developmental word knowledge (Henderson, 1990; Templeton & Bear, 1992a; Templeton & Morris, 2000). The power of this model lies in the diagnostic information contained in students' spelling inventions that reveal their current understanding of how written English words work (Invernizzi, Abouzeid, & Gill, 1994). An informed analysis of students' spelling attempts can cue timely instruction in phonics, spelling, and vocabulary features—instruction that is essential to move students forward in reading and writing. By using students' invented spellings as a guide, teachers can differentiate efficient, effective instruction in phonics, spelling, and vocabulary. We call this instruction **word study.**

WHY IS WORD STUDY IMPORTANT?

Becoming fully literate is absolutely dependent on fast, accurate recognition of words in texts, and fast, accurate production of words in writing so that readers and writers can focus their attention on making meaning. Letter-sound correspondences, phonics, spelling patterns, high frequency word recognition, decoding, word meanings, and other word attributes are the basis of written word knowledge. Designing a word study program that explicitly teaches students necessary skills and engages their interest and motivation to learn about how words work is a vital aspect of any literacy program. Indeed, how to teach students these basics in an effective manner has sparked controversy among educators for nearly a century.

Commercial phonics, spelling, and vocabulary programs are often characterized by explicit skill instruction, a systematic scope and sequence, and repeated practice. Unfortunately, much of the repeated practice consists of rote drill, so students have little opportunity to manipulate word concepts or apply critical thinking skills. Although students need explicit skill instruction within a systematic curriculum, it is equally true that "teaching is not telling" (James, 1958).

> **"Teaching Is Not Telling"**
> *William James*

Students need hands-on opportunities to manipulate word features in a way that allows them to generalize beyond isolated, individual examples to entire groups of words that are spelled the same way (Juel & Minden-Cupp, 2000). Excelling at word recognition, spelling, and vocabulary is not just a matter of memorizing isolated rules and definitions. The best way to develop fast and accurate perception of word features is to engage in meaningful reading and writing, and to have multiple opportunities to examine those same words out of context. The most effective instruction in phonics, spelling, and vocabulary links word study to the texts being read, provides a systematic scope and sequence of word-level skills, and provides multiple opportunities for hands-on practice and application. In a sense, word study teaches students how to look at words so that they can construct an ever-deepening understanding of how written words work. We believe that this word study is well worth the 10 to 15 minutes of time daily.

What Is the Purpose of Word Study?

The purpose of word study is twofold. First, through active exploration, word study teaches students to examine words to discover the regularities, patterns, and conventions of English orthography needed to read and spell. This knowledge is conceptual in nature and reflects what students understand about the *general* nature of our spelling system. Second, word study increases *specific* knowledge of words—the spelling and meaning of individual words.

General knowledge is what we access when we encounter a new word, when we do not know how to spell a word, or if we do not know the meaning of a specific word. The better our knowledge of the system, the better we are at decoding an unfamiliar word, spelling correctly, or guessing the meaning of a word. For example, if you have knowledge of short vowels and consonant blends, you would have no trouble attempting the word *crash* even if you have never seen it or written it before. The spelling is unambiguous, like so many single-syllable short-vowel words. Knowledge of how words that are similar in spelling are related in meaning, such as *compete* and *competition*, makes it easier to understand the meaning of a word like *competitor,* even if it is unfamiliar. Additional clues offered by context also increase the chances of reading and understanding a word correctly.

To become fully literate, however, we also need specific knowledge about individual words. Knowledge about the English spelling system provides us the tools to do the job correctly. The word *rain,* for example, might be spelled RANE, RAIN, or RAYNE—all are orthographically and phonetically plausible. However, only specific knowledge will allow us to remember the correct spelling. Likewise, only specific knowledge of the spelling of *which* and *witch* makes it possible to know which witch is which! The relationship between specific knowledge and knowledge of the system is reciprocal; that is, each supports the other. Ehri (1992) expressed the idea in the following manner.

> What students store in memory about specific words' spellings is regulated in part by what they know about the general system. Learners who lack this knowledge are left with rote memorization which takes longer and is more easily forgotten. Similarly, what students learn about the orthographic system evolves in part from the accumulation of experiences with specific word spellings. (p. 308)

The purpose of word study, then, is to examine words in order to reveal consistencies within our written language system and to help students master the recognition, spelling, and meaning of specific words.

WHAT IS THE BASIS FOR WORD STUDY?

Word study evolves from three decades of research in developmental aspects of word knowledge with children and adults (Henderson, 1990; Henderson & Beers, 1980; Templeton & Bear, 1992a). This line of research has documented the convergence of certain kinds of spelling errors that occur in clusters and reflect students' confusion over certain recurring orthographic principles. These clusters have been described in relationship to the types of errors noted, specifically (1) errors dealing with the alphabetic match of letters and sound (BAD for *bed*), (2) errors dealing with letter patterns (SNAIK for *snake,*) and (3) errors dealing with words related in meaning (INVUTATION for *invitation*). The same cluster types of errors have been observed among students with learning disabilities and dyslexia (Sawyer, Lipa-Wade, Kim, Ritenour, & Knight, 1997; Worthy & Invernizzi, 1989), students who speak in nonstandard dialects (Cantrell, 1990), and students who are learning to read in different alphabetic languages (Bear, Templeton, Helman, & Baren, 2003). Students and adult learners move from using but confusing elements of sound, to using but confusing elements of pattern, to using but confusing elements of meaning. Longitudinal and cross-grade-level research in developmental spelling has shown that this progression occurs for all learners of written English in the same direction and varies only in the rate of acquisition. The scope and sequence of word study instruction is based on research of linguistic logic underlying students' spelling as they progress in literacy.

Word study also comes from what we have learned about the orthographic structure of written words. Developmental spelling researchers have examined the three layers of English orthography (Figure 1-1) in relation to the historical evolution of English spelling as well as developmental progressions from alphabet to pattern to meaning among learners of English. Each layer provides information, and in mature readers and writers, there is interaction among the layers.

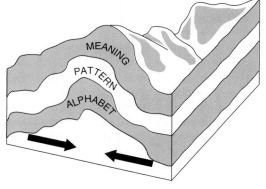

FIGURE 1-1   Three Layers of English Orthography

Alphabet

Our spelling system is **alphabetic** because it represents the relationship between letters and sounds. In English, this relationship is manifested in a left-to-right sequence. In the word *sat,*

 In teaching the alphabetic code to English Language Learners, teachers are sensitive to the English sounds that may not exist in students' native languages, and to letters that may be paired with different sounds in different orthographies.

clearly each sound is represented by a single letter; we blend the sounds for /s/, /a/, and /t/ to create the word *sat*. In the word *chin*, we still hear three sounds, even though there are four letters, because the first two letters, *ch*, function like a single letter, representing a single sound. So we can match letters—sometimes singly, sometimes in pairs—to sounds from left to right and create words. This **alphabetic layer of instruction** in English spelling is the first layer of information at work.

Pattern

What about words like *cape, bead,* and *light?* If we spelled these words with single letters, they would look something like CAP, BED, and LIT; but of course these spellings already represent other words. The **pattern layer of information** therefore overlays the alphabetic layer. English does not have a single sound for each letter under all conditions. Single sounds are sometimes spelled with more than one letter or are affected by other letters that do not stand for any sounds themselves. When we look beyond single letter-sound matchups and search for **patterns** that guide the groupings of letters, however, we find more consistency than expected.

Take for example the *-ape* in *cape;* we say that the final *-e* makes the preceding vowel letter, *a,* stand for a long or tense-vowel sound. The *e* does not stand for a sound itself, but it plays an important role. The *-ape* group of letters therefore follows a pattern: When you have a vowel, a consonant, and a silent *-e* in a single syllable, this letter grouping forms a pattern that usually will function to indicate a long vowel. We refer to this pattern as the consonant-vowel-consonant-silent e (CVCe) pattern, one of several high frequency, long-vowel patterns.

The notion of pattern helps us talk more efficiently about the alphabetic layer as well. In a CVC pattern (*sat, chin*), note that, regardless of how many consonant letters are on either side of the single vowel, the fact that there is but one vowel letter in that pattern means it will usually stand for a short vowel sound. (Later in the chapter we learn how the brain comes to operate in terms of these patterns rather than in terms of any specific letters. In the case of spelling, the brain can be much more efficient if it comes to understand how these patterns work.)

Words of more than one syllable also follow spelling patterns. These patterns are described with the same V and C symbols and also relate to the vowel sound within each syllable. Let us consider two of the most common syllable patterns. First is the VCCV pattern, such as in *robber* (the pattern is vowel and consonant in the first syllable and consonant and vowel in the second syllable). When we have this pattern, the first vowel is usually short. Knowledge of this pattern can help students figure out an unknown word when reading and correctly spell an uncertain word when writing. Second is the VCV syllable pattern, as in *radar, pilot,* and *limit.* This pattern will usually signal that the first vowel is long, but as in the case of *limit,* the first vowel also can be short (see Chapter 7 for more information). Overall, knowledge about patterns within single syllables, and syllable patterns within words, will be of considerable value to students in both their reading and their spelling.

 Older English Language Learners who already know how to read in their native script may have different expectations of patterns. For example, they may think that doubled consonants relate to consonant sounds or to grammatical function, as they do in Korean. Teachers must be clear that in written English, patterns refer to vowel sounds.

Meaning

The third layer of English orthography is the **meaning layer of information.** When students learn that groups of letters can represent meaning directly, they will be much less puzzled when encountering unusual spellings. Examples of these units or groups of letters are prefixes, suffixes, and Greek and Latin stems.

As one example of how meaning functions in the spelling system, think of the prefix *re-;* whether we hear it pronounced "ree" as in *rethink* or "ruh" as in *remove,* its spelling stays the same because it directly represents meaning. Why is *composition* not spelled COMPUSITION? It is related in meaning to *compose*—the spelling in the related

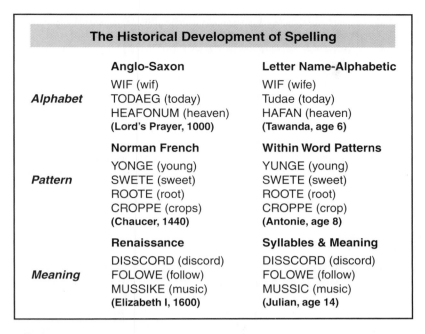

The Historical Development of Spelling		
	Anglo-Saxon	**Letter Name-Alphabetic**
Alphabet	WIF (wif) TODAEG (today) HEAFONUM (heaven) (Lord's Prayer, 1000)	WIF (wife) Tudae (today) HAFAN (heaven) (Tawanda, age 6)
	Norman French	**Within Word Patterns**
Pattern	YONGE (young) SWETE (sweet) ROOTE (root) CROPPE (crops) (Chaucer, 1440)	YUNGE (young) SWETE (sweet) ROOTE (root) CROPPE (crop) (Antonie, age 8)
	Renaissance	**Syllables & Meaning**
Meaning	DISSCORD (discord) FOLOWE (follow) MUSSIKE (music) (Elizabeth I, 1600)	DISSCORD (discord) FOLOWE (follow) MUSSIC (music) (Julian, age 14)

FIGURE 1-2 Historical Development of English Orthography: Sound, Pattern, and Meaning from Past to Present Adapted from "Using Students' Invented Spellings as a Guide for Spelling Instruction that Emphasizes Word Study" by M. Invernizzi, M. Abouzeid, & T. Gill, 1994, *Elementary School Journal, 95*(2), p. 158. Reprinted by permission of The University of Chicago Press.

words *compose* and *composition* stays the same even though the sound that the letter *o* represents changes. Likewise, the letter sequence PHOTO in *photograph, photographer,* and *photographic* signals family relationships among these words, despite the changes in sound that these letters represent.

By building connections between meaning parts and their derivations, we enlarge our vocabulary. Although few people recognize this powerful feature of English spelling, we will find that this interaction of spelling and meaning opens up a whole new frontier in exploring and learning about word meanings.

Alphabet, pattern, and meaning represent three broad principles of written English and form the layered record of orthographic history. Students' spelling attempts mirror the richness and layered complexity of this history. As students learn to read and write, they appear to literally reinvent the system as it was itself invented. As shown in Figure 1-2, beginners invent the spellings of simple words quite phonetically, just as the Anglo Saxons did in A.D. 1000. As students become independent readers, they add a second layer of complexity by using patterns, much as the Norman French did in the latter part of the 14th century. Notice the overuse of the silent -*e* at the end of all of Antonie's words, much like Geoffrey Chaucer! Intermediate and advanced readers invent conventions for joining syllables and morphemes, as was done in the Renaissance when English was first introduced to a Greco and Latinate vocabulary (Henderson, 1990). As Figure 1-2 shows, both Julian and Elizabeth I struggled with issues relating to consonant doubling where syllables meet.

By classifying student spellings as experimentations with sound, pattern, or meaning, teachers can steer students toward a more sophisticated written vocabulary. For students who are experimenting with the alphabetic match of letters and sounds, teachers can contrast aspects of the writing system that relate directly to the representation of sound. For students experimenting with pattern, teachers can contrast patterns as they relate to vowel sounds; and for students experimenting with conventions of syllables, affixes, and other meaning units, teachers can contrast the stability of base words, roots, and affixes across variations in speech.

 English Language Learners may find the meaning layer of English orthography the easiest to learn, because similarities in the spelling of related words make visually apparent what is otherwise obscured by pronunciation changes from one word form to another (invite/invitation).

What Students Need to Learn to Read and Spell English

Students invent and discover the basic principles of spelling—alphabet, pattern, and meaning—when they read good stories, write purposefully, and are guided by knowledgeable teachers in word study. Word study should give students the experiences they need to progress through these layers of information.

- Students need hands-on experience comparing and contrasting words by sound so that they can categorize similar sounds and associate them consistently with letters and letter combinations. This process is the heart of the alphabetic principle.

For example, words spelled with short *e* (*bed, leg, net, neck, mess*) are compared with words spelled with short *i* (*sit, list, pick, zip, with*).

- Students need hands-on experience comparing and contrasting words by consistent spelling patterns associated with categories of sound. They need opportunities to recognize these patterns in other words they encounter in text. For example, words spelled with *ay* (*play, day, tray, way*) are compared with words spelled with *ai* (*wait, rain, chain, maid*).

- Students need hands-on experience categorizing words by meaning, use, and parts of speech. When grouping words by broad categories of meaning, students can see that words with similar meanings are often spelled the same, despite changes in pronunciation. For example, *admiration* is spelled with an *i* because it comes from the word *admire*.

WORD STUDY IS DEVELOPMENTAL

When we say word study is developmental, we mean that the study of word features must match the level of word knowledge of the learner. Word study is not a one-size-fits-all program of instruction that begins in the same place for all students within a grade level. One unique quality of word study as we describe it lies in what we believe is the critical role of differentiating instruction for different levels of word knowledge. Research spanning over 20 years has established how students learn the specific *features* of words as well as the *order* in which they learn them. Knowledgeable educators have come to know that word study instruction must match the needs of the child. This construct, called **instructional level,** is a powerful delimiter of what may be learned. Simply put, we must teach to where a child "is at." To do otherwise results in frustration or boredom and little learning in either case. Just as in learning to play the piano students must work through book A, then book B, and then book C, learning to read and spell is a gradual and cumulative process. Word study begins with finding out what each child already knows about the cumulative aspects of English spelling and then starting instruction there.

One of the easiest ways to know what students need to learn is to look at the way they spell words. Students' spellings provide a direct window into how they think the system works. By interpreting what students do when they spell, educators can target a specific student's "zone of proximal development" (Vygotsky, 1962) and plan word study instruction that this student is conceptually ready to master. Further, by applying basic principles of child development, educators have learned how to engage students in learning about word features in a child-centered, developmentally appropriate way. When students are instructed within their own zone of proximal development—at their own level of word knowledge—they are able to build on what they already know, to learn what they need to know next, to move forward. With direct instruction and ongoing support, word features that were previously omitted or confused become amalgamated into an ever-increasing reading and writing vocabulary.

The Development of Orthographic Knowledge

Developmental spelling research describes students' growing knowledge of words as a continuum or a series of chronologically ordered phases of knowledge. The phases are differentiated by the kinds of cues used by the child when encountering words and by specific featural knowledge of how the English spelling system works. In this book, we use the word *stage* instead of *phase* as a metaphor to inform instruction. In reality, students grow in conceptual knowledge of the three general layers of information, and of specific word features, along a continuum. Students move hierarchically from easier, one-to-one correspondences between letters and sounds, to more difficult, abstract relationships between letter patterns and sounds, to even more sophisticated relationships between meaning units as they relate to sound and pattern. Stages are marked by broad, qualitative shifts in the types of spelling errors students commit as well as behavioral changes in their reading and writing. It is not the case that students abandon sound once they move to the more efficient use of patterns, or abandon patterns once they move to the more efficient use of morphology. Rather, the names of the stages capture the key capability that distinguishes them among the tiers of English orthography and among the levels of students' general knowledge of the orthography (Bryant & Bindman, 1997; Ehri, 1997; Templeton, 2003).

Because word study is based on students' level of orthographic knowledge, the word study activities presented in this book are arranged by stages of spelling. The principles of word study and the organization of word study in the classroom are discussed in depth in Chapter 3. Chapters 4 through 8 are devoted to instruction that is based on these stages. Knowing the stage of spelling of each of your students will determine your choices of appropriate word study activities. This chapter presents an overview of these stages (see Figure 1-3), which guides you to the instructional chapters arranged by stages.

The metaphor of stages is used to describe particular scenarios of students' orthographic development and to characterize the dominant approach to reading and spelling words at that general level of knowledge. Over the past 20 years we have established criteria to determine the stage of word knowledge where students are, and we have worked with numerous teachers in using the guidelines discussed in this chapter

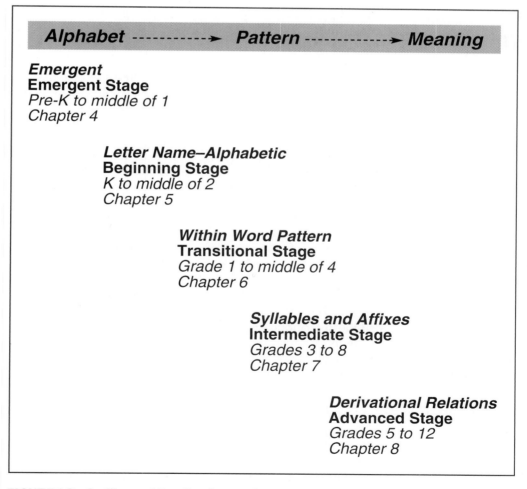

FIGURE 1-3 Spelling and Reading Stages, Grade Levels, and Corresponding Instructional Chapters

and the assessment procedures described in Chapter 2. By conducting regular spelling assessments, perhaps three times a year, teachers can track students' progress and development. An important prerequisite, however, is to know about the continuum of orthographic knowledge.

Levels of Learning

For each stage of learning, students' orthographic knowledge is defined by three functional levels that are useful guides for knowing when to teach what (Invernizzi et al., 1994):

1. What students do correctly—an independent or easy level
2. What students use but confuse—an instructional level where instruction is most helpful
3. What is absent in students' spelling—a frustration level where spelling concepts are too difficult

The following discussion of each stage describes spelling development according to these three functional levels. To determine what orthographic features and patterns to explore with each child, we focus on what the child uses but confuses, because this is where instruction will be of most benefit to a student. In Vygotskian (1962) terms again, we focus on the student's zone of proximal development. By studying the stages of spelling development, it becomes obvious what sequence the study of orthographic features should take.

STAGES OF SPELLING DEVELOPMENT

Henderson (1981) described six stages of spelling. A decade earlier, at the University of Delaware and later at the University of Virginia, Henderson examined the specific spelling features students use to spell when they write. He and his colleagues found that students' spelling errors are not random and that they evolve over time (Henderson et al., 1972). About the same time, in Boston, Chomsky (1971) and Read (1971, 1975) were also looking at preschoolers' invented spellings. There was a natural match in interests when Read and Henderson discovered each other. The discovery of Read's work in the linguistic arena helped Henderson and his students make sense of the spellings they had been collecting. Henderson and Read explored and identified the common errors students make as they learn more about the orthography. Subsequently, these patterns in spelling development have been observed across many groups of students, from preschoolers (Templeton & Spivey, 1980) through adults (Bear, Truex, & Barone, 1989; Worthy & Viise, 1993), as well as across socioeconomic levels, dialects, and other alphabetic languages (Cantrell, 2001). In addition, the analysis of students' spelling has subsequently been explored by other researchers (e.g., Treiman, 1985).

By 1974, Henderson had formulated a description of increasingly sophisticated phases, or stages, of orthographic knowledge. Since then, he and his students have refined the description of these stages and have reworked the labels to reflect their changing understanding of developmental word knowledge and to represent most appropriately what occurs at each level. The following stages describe students' spelling behavior and make it easier to remember the basic strategies that students use to spell.

Stages of Spelling
Emergent
Letter Name–Alphabetic
Within Word Pattern
Syllables and Affixes
Derivational Relations

Stage I: Emergent Spelling

Emergent spelling encompasses the writing effort of children who are not yet reading conventionally, and in most cases have not been exposed to formal reading instruction. This first stage, emergent literacy, refers to that period of time prior to conventional reading and writing; emergent spelling refers to that period prior to the conventional matching of letters and sounds in a left-to-right sequence.

Emergent spellers typically range in age from 0 to 5 years, although anyone not yet reading conventionally is in this stage of development. Most toddlers and preschoolers are emergent spellers, as are most kindergartners at the beginning of the year. Students who have not had many experiences with books and print may still be emergent in the first grade.

Emergent spelling may range from random marks to legitimate letters that bear no relationship to sound. Because of this lack of correspondence to sound, however, this stage of developmental orthographic knowledge is decidedly **prephonetic.** The characteristics of this stage in the developmental model are presented in Table 1-1.

Emergent spelling may be divided into a series of steps or landmarks. At the beginning of this stage, students may produce large scribbles that are basically drawings. The movement may be circular, and children may tell a story while they draw. At the earliest points in this stage, there are no designs that look like letters, and the writing is undecipherable from the drawing. As you can see in Figure 1-4A, Haley has drawn large scribble-like circles and simply called it writing, asserting that it says, "All the little birdies." There is little order to the direction in Haley's production; it goes up, down, and around, willy-nilly.

Gradually and especially when sitting next to other children or adults who write letters, children begin to use letters and something that looks like script to "tell" about the picture. This kind of pretend writing is separate from the picture, although there is still no relationship between letters and sound, and the writing may occur in any direction. In Figure 1-4B, the child labeled his drawing to the left of the picture as "Cowboy." About the time they are able to draw "tadpoles" for people (Figure 1-4C), children acquire the convention of **directionality** (left to right in English).

As teachers model the process of reading and writing, students begin to recognize the basic visual characteristics of written text—that writing moves from left to right and

TABLE 1-1 Characteristics of Emergent Spelling*

	What Students Do Correctly	What Students Use but Confuse	What Is Absent
Early Emergent (SƐ)	• Write on the page • Hold the writing implement	• Drawing and scribbling for writing	• Sound-symbol correspondence • Directionality
Middle Emergent BLZIB	• Horizontal movement across page • Clear distinction between writing and drawing • Lines and dots for writing • Letterlike forms	• Letters, numbers, and letterlike forms • Writing may wrap from right to left at the end of a line	• Sound-symbol correspondence
Late Emergent V for *elevator* D for *down*	• Consistent directionality • Some letter-sound match	• Substitutions of letters that sound, feel, and look alike: B/p, D/b	• Complete sound-symbol correspondence • Consistent spacing between words

*Characteristics of emergent spelling are discussed in depth in Chapter 4.

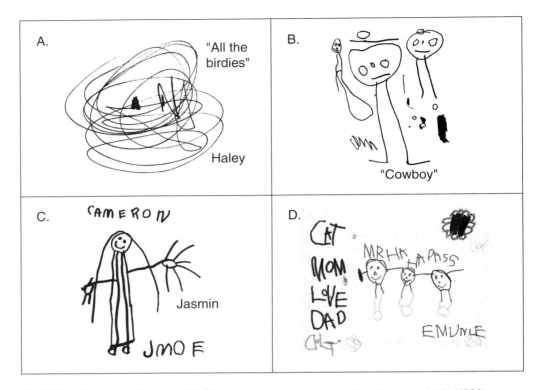

FIGURE 1-4   Early Emergent Writing Adapted with permission from Bloodgood, J.R. (1996).

top to bottom and that writing is somehow related to what they say through the use of letters. As children learn some letter-sound matches, they use this information to guide their fingers as they point to printed words in a memorized nursery rhyme or jingle. They begin to develop a speech-to-print match, or a **concept of word.** When children achieve this speech-to-print match, they are at the end of the emergent stage and at the beginning of the next stage of word knowledge.

Throughout the emergent stage, children begin to learn letters, particularly the letters in their own names. The writing by Carly in Figure 1-5 is characteristic of a child in the middle emergent stage of spelling. When asked to spell a series of words, Carly spelled the words by using the letters she knew best—those in her own name. This child is beginning to use letters to represent words, but has no sound-symbol correspondence between what she writes and the sounds of the word.

Gradually, and as children are encouraged to illustrate their ideas and stories through drawing and to tell about them in writing, they begin to write the most prominent phonetic features of a word or two. At first, only the foremost or most salient sound in a word may be represented, which may or may not correspond to the initial one, as shown in the spelling of V for the word *elevator* in the bottom left corner of Table 1-1. When emergent students are exposed to directed instruction that is developmentally appropriate, their writing starts to reflect this influence and attention to beginning sounds becomes apparent. The ability to make a few letter-sound matches is evident in Figure 1-4C where *Jasmin* is spelled JMOE. The movement from this stage to the next stage hinges on learning the **alphabetic principle:** Letters represent sound, and words can be segmented into sequences of sound from left to right. Toward the end of emergent spelling, as students acquire a concept of word, they even start to memorize some words and write them repeatedly, such as the *cat, Mom, love,* and *Dad* in Figure 1-4D.

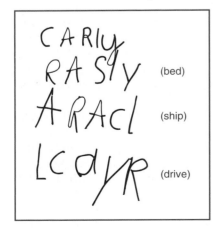

FIGURE 1-5   Middle Emergent Writing

During the emergent stage, teachers teach students to recognize and write the letters of the alphabet and they play with the sounds in words and letters. Most of the sound play focuses on beginning and rhyme sounds. You will see in Chapter 4 that toward the end of the emergent stage, students are introduced to picture sorts in which they categorize words by beginning consonants or by rhyming sounds.

 Beginning consonant picture sorts for learners in the emergent stage, such as the *B, R,* and *S* sort, can be found in the Emergent Stage on the accompanying CD-ROM.

Stage II: Letter Name–Alphabetic Spelling

The **letter name–alphabetic spelling stage** is the second stage in the developmental model and encompasses that period of time during which students are formally taught to read, typically during the kindergarten and first-grade years and extending into the middle of second grade. True letter name–alphabetic spellers are between the ages of 5 and 8 years, although a beginning reader at age 55 also can be a letter name–alphabetic speller (Viise, 1996). The name of this stage reflects students' dominant approach to spelling; that is, they use the *names* of the letters in combination with the alphabetic principle when they spell (Read, 1975).

We divide this letter name–alphabetic stage into early, middle, and late periods because of the rapid and dramatic growth during this time. Throughout this stage, students learn to divide sound sequences within words and to match the appropriate letters or letter pairs to those sequences. They move from partial to full **phoneme segmentation** and spellings are correspondingly more complete (see Table 1-2).

Early Letter Name–Alphabetic Spelling

Students who are early in the letter name–alphabetic stage apply the alphabetic principle primarily to consonants. Modern psycholinguistic research has shown that consonants are the "noise" and vowels are the "music" of language (Crystal, 1987). Spellers in the early part of the letter name–alphabetic stage attend to the noise and use the alphabetic principle to find letter names in the alphabet to spell the most prominent features in words—the consonants. Sometimes strong vowels draw students' attention; for example, the long vowel at the beginning of *ice* may lead the child to spell *ice* as I or IS. Often, students spell the first sound and then the last sound of single-syllable words. For example, *bake* may be spelled B or BK. The middle elements of syllables, the vowels, are usually omitted. Typically, only the first sound of a two-letter consonant blend is represented, as in FT for *float*. Early letter name–alphabetic writing often lacks spacing between words, but because these spellings represent the beginning and ending sounds of words, the writing is usually decipherable. This type of writing is **semiphonetic.**

When early letter name–alphabetic students use the alphabetic principle, they find matches between letters and the spoken word by how the sound is made or articulated in the mouth. For example, students may substitute a /b/ sound for a /p/ sound, because they are made with the lips in the same way except for one feature: In making the /p/ sound, air comes out of the mouth in an explosive way, whereas with the /b/ sound, there is no accompanying explosion of air. A less obvious example is the substitution of an *f* for a *v* to spell *dive* as DF. Given that *f* is a much more familiar letter, students often choose it to represent the /v/ sound. Nevertheless, a student's relative experience will also influence his or her choice; so a child named Virginia would perhaps learn the /v/ sound first and, as a result, begin *face* with a *v.*

TABLE 1-2   Characteristics of Letter Name–Alphabetic Spelling*

	What Students Do Correctly	What Students Use but Confuse	What Is Absent
Early Letter Name–Alphabetic B, BD for *bed* S, SHP for *ship* Y for *when* L, LP for *lump* U for *you* R for *are* FT for *float*	• Represent most salient sounds, usually beginning consonants • Directionality • Most letters of the alphabet • Clear letter-sound correspondences • Partial spelling of consonant blends and digraphs	• Letters based on point of articulation: J, JRF for *drive* • Often long vowels by letter name	• Consistency in beginning and end of syllables • Some spacing between words • Vowels in syllables
Middle Letter Name–Alphabetic BAD for *bed* SEP or SHP for *ship* FOT for *float* LOP for *lump*	• Most beginning and ending consonants • Clear letter-sound correspondences • Frequently occurring short-vowel words	• Substitutions of letter name closest in point of articulation for short vowels • Some consonant blends and digraphs	• Preconsonantal nasals: LOP for *lump*
Late Letter Name–Alphabetic *lump* spelled correctly FLOT for *float* BAKR for *baker* PLAS for *place* BRIT for *bright*	• All of the above plus: • Regular short-vowel patterns • Most consonant blends and digraphs • Preconsonantal nasals • Some common long-vowel words: *time, name*	• Substitutions of common patterns for low frequency short vowels: COT for *caught*	• Most long-vowel markers or silent vowels • Vowels in unstressed syllables

*Characteristics of letter name–alphabetic spelling are discussed in depth in Chapter 5.

Middle Letter Name–Alphabetic Spelling

Middle letter name–alphabetic spellers continue to use a phonetic spelling strategy in which they focus on the letter-sound matches. By the middle of the letter name–alphabetic stage, spellers also have learned to segment and represent the middle vowel sound within words. Whereas the early letter name–alphabetic speller would spell the word *baker* as BKR, students in the middle part of this stage would use the letter name of the long vowel in the stressed syllable and spell *baker* as BAKR. Students' growing knowledge of short vowels allows them to remember words they have read many times out of context. Words that contain frequently occurring short vowels are often spelled from memory correctly. Other short vowels are phonetically represented with the letter name that feels most like the targeted short-vowel sound in the mouth. As you will learn in Chapter 5, the short-vowel substitutions of the middle letter name–alphabetic speller are phonetically logical, letter-name substitutions that rely on the feel of sounds as they are articulated or produced in the vocal tract. Middle letter name–alphabetic spellers also spell the more difficult consonant blends and digraphs by using the names of the letters of the alphabet as their guide. Because middle letter name–alphabetic spellers can segment and represent most of the sound sequences within single-syllable words, their spelling is described as **phonetic.** However, subtle sounds that are not fully articulated, such as *m* in *bump* or *lump,* are often still omitted.

Late Letter Name–Alphabetic Spelling

Students in the late letter name–alphabetic spelling stage not only represent beginning, middle, and ending sounds within words, but they also learn to deal with more ambiguous sounds. Over the course of the letter name–alphabetic stage, students make the match between short-vowel sounds and the standard or correct short-vowel spellings. With plenty of reading, they also learn the odd spellings of high frequency words such as *were* and *come*. Lower frequency vowel sounds, such as the /aw/ sound in the word *caught*, are spelled phonetically by analogy to a known short-vowel sound, resulting in spellings like COT (rhymes with *hot*). At this point, the vowel substitutions are not as dependent on the names of the letters and begin to show evidence of using the strategy of analogy to other letter sounds and patterns.

By the end of this stage, late letter name–alphabetic spellers are able to represent most regular short-vowel patterns, consonant digraphs, and consonant blends correctly. Instruction during the late letter name–alphabetic stage focuses on the finer distinctions of the more difficult consonant blends and on the inclusion of nasals before final consonants. In fact, a hallmark of a student who is moving from the letter name–alphabetic stage to the next stage, within word pattern spelling, is the correct spelling of words with *m* or *n* before the final consonant in words like *bump* or *bunch*. The letters *n* and *m* are referred to as **nasals.** Their sound is made by air passing through the nasal passage. Words like *bump* have a **preconsonantal nasal** because the *m* (or *n* in *bunch*) occurs in front of another consonant. Henderson (1990) recognized that the correct spelling of the preconsonantal nasal was a reliable and important watershed event that heralds the onset of the next stage of orthographic knowledge (see Table 1-2). By the end of the letter name–alphabetic stage, students have mastered the basic orthographic elements of the alphabetic layer of English orthography. Throughout this stage of learning students have omitted letters that have no sound, but at the end of this stage, they will begin to use but confuse silent long-vowel markers such as the silent *-e*.

 For tools for instruction during the late letter name stage, (the *-ing*, *-amp*, and *-ink* Sort, for example) visit the Letter Name–Alphabetic Stage on the accompanying CD-ROM.

Stage III: Within Word Pattern Spelling

Students entering the **within word pattern spelling stage** have a sight reading vocabulary of 200 to 400 words. In addition, students' automatic knowledge of letter sounds and short-vowel patterns allows them to read new material independently, without the support of predictable or familiar texts. This level of orthographic knowledge typically begins as students transition to independent reading toward the end of first grade, and expands throughout the second and third grades, and even into the fourth grade. While most students move into the within word stage in the second grade, students who have struggled with learning to read and write may not reach this level of orthographic knowledge until much later. Although most within word pattern spellers typically range in age from 7 to 10 years, many adult, low-skilled readers remain in this stage. Regardless, this period of orthographic development lasts longer than the preceding one, because the vowel patterning system of English orthography is quite extensive.

As shown in Table 1-3 under "What Students Do Correctly," the within word pattern stage begins when students can correctly spell most single-syllable, short-vowel words correctly—with or without consonant blends, digraphs, or preconsonantal nasals. Since these basic phonics features have been mastered, within word pattern spellers work with the orthography and the writing system at a more abstract level than letter name–alphabetic spellers can (Zutell, 1994). They move away from the linear, sound-by-sound approach of

TABLE 1-3   Characteristics of Within Word Pattern Spelling*

	What Students Do Correctly	What Students Use but Confuse	What Is Absent
Early Within Word Pattern FLOTE for *float* PLAIS for *place* BRIET for *bright* TABL for *table*	• Initial and final consonants • Consonant blends and digraphs • Regular short-vowel patterns and preconsonantal nasals • Good accuracy on *r*-influenced single-syllable short-vowel words: *fur, bird* • Some infrequently used short-vowel and frequently used long-vowel words: *like, see*	• Long-vowel markers: SNAIK for *snake*, FELE for *feel*	• Consonant doubling: SHOPING for *shopping*, CAREES for *carries* • Vowels in unaccented syllables
Middle Within Word Pattern SPOLE for *spoil* DRIEV for *drive*	• All of the above plus: • Slightly more than half of the long-vowel words in single-syllable words: *hike, nail*	• Long-vowel markers: NITE for *night* • Consonant patterns: SMOCK for *smoke* • Inventive substitutions in frequent, unstressed syllable patterns: TEACHAUR for *teacher* • *-ed* and other common inflections: MARCHT for *marched*, BATID for *batted*	
Late Within Word Pattern CHUED for *chewed*	• All of the above plus: • Single-syllable long-vowel words • May know some common Latin suffixes: *inspection*	• Low frequency long-vowel words: HIEGHT for *height* • *-ed* and other common inflections • Common Latin suffixes are spelled phonetically: ATENSHUN for *attention*	• Consonant doubling • *e* drop: AMAZEING for *amazing*

*Characteristics of within word pattern spelling are discussed in depth in Chapter 6.

the letter name–alphabetic spellers and begin to include patterns or chunks of letter sequences that relate to sound and meaning. Within word spellers can think about words in more than one dimension; they study words by sound and pattern simultaneously. As the name of this stage suggests, within word pattern spellers take a closer look at vowels within syllables and begin to examine long-vowel patterns (Henderson, 1990). Within word pattern spellers are often referred to as being in the **transitional stage of literacy development,** transitioning from the alphabetic layer to the meaning layer of English orthography through patterns. Knowledge of within word patterns affords greater efficiency and speed in reading and writing than previous levels.

Because the focus for instruction is on what students use but confuse, teachers involve students in exploring long-vowel patterns. At first, students may overgeneralize common long-vowel patterns, spelling *drain* as DRANE, for example. Teachers begin with one vowel and spend time having students examine the various patterns of that long vowel. Next, they teach similar patterns in another long vowel. Comparisons are made across the two long-vowel patterns, for example, the CVCe patterns in *name* and *line*. After these comparisons, students examine some of the special patterns for the vowel being studied, as in *child* and *kind* when they study the long -*i*. An important new feature throughout this stage is that students develop **word study notebooks** (see Chapter 6) in which they enter groups of words that they have sorted or have found to follow particular patterns.

 For materials to use when instructing within word pattern spellers, including many long-vowel games, visit the Within Word Pattern Stage on the accompanying CD-ROM.

During the early part of the within word stage, teachers focus their instruction on the most commonly occurring long-vowel patterns. In the middle part of the within word stage, teachers direct students' attention to lower frequency long-vowel patterns and to consonant patterns that also signal whether the vowel is long or short. Toward the end of the within word stage, students examine other low frequency vowel patterns and ambiguous vowel sounds that are difficult to categorize (see Table 1-3).

With changes in the ability to reflect and to use abstract patterns, students also begin to think more about their spoken vocabulary. They can play with words in meaning sorts in the same way that they may arrange baseball cards. To foster this analysis, students keep lists of words arranged by type or topic. For example, they might make lists of **homophones,** words that sound the same but have different meanings, and consequently spelling patterns every time they hear one. One student listed over 100 homophones such as *bear* and *bare, deer* and *dear, hire* and *higher.* In this way, student interest in vocabulary is easily expanded upon in the next two stages of spelling development where the spelling-meaning connection is explored.

Stage IV: Syllables and Affixes Spelling

The **syllables and affixes stage** is typically achieved in the intermediate grades of upper elementary and middle school years, when there is greater emphasis on content area reading. Students in this fourth stage are most often between 9 and 14 years, though again, many adults may be found in this stage. As noted in Table 1-4, students in the syllables and affixes stage of spelling already spell most one-syllable short- and long-vowel words correctly, so the locus of their experimentation shifts to the orthographic conventions of preserving pattern-to-sound relationships at the place where syllables meet. As the name of the stage suggests, in addition to syllables, students grapple with meaning units such as prefixes and suffixes.

The syllables and affixes stage represents a new point in word analysis when students consider where syllables and meaning units meet at their **juncture.** In the previous stages, students examined single-syllable words and patterns. In this stage, they examine multisyllabic words and patterns. The analysis of multisyllabic words is more complicated, for there is more than one perceptual unit to consider. For example, a two-syllable word such as *dungeon* may be divided into *dun* and *geon.* For easy words, and especially where the text gives plenty of contextual clues, this analysis is done at an unconscious or tacit level. The analysis of unfamiliar multisyllabic words will call on students to divide words into syllables and then see how the syllables fit together.

Table 1-4 under "What Students Use but Confuse" signals where to begin instruction. Word study in this stage begins with the English convention for preserving vowel sounds across syllables: the consonant-doubling principle. A frequently occurring word

TABLE 1-4   Characteristics of Syllables and Affixes Spelling*

	What Students Do Correctly	What Students Use but Confuse	What Is Absent
Early Syllables and Affixes SHOPING for *shopping* CATEL for *cattle* KEPER or KEPPER for *keeper*	• Initial and final consonants • Consonant blends and digraphs • Short-vowel patterns • Most long-vowel patterns • *-ed* and most inflections	• Consonant doubling: HOPING for *hopping* • Long-vowel patterns in accented syllables: PERAIDING or PERADDING for *parading* • Reduced vowel in unaccented syllables: CIRCUL for *circle* • Doubling and *e* drop: AMAZZING for *amazing*	• Occasional deletion of middle syllables: CONFDENT for *confident*
Middle Syllables and Affixes SELLER for *cellar* DAMIGE for *damage* FORTUNET for *fortunate*	• All of the above plus: • Consonant doubling: *shopping, cattle* • Double and *e* drop: *stopping, amazing*	• Syllables that receive less stress: HOCKY for *hockey*, FAVER for *favor* • Spell sounds at syllable junctures like single-syllable words: PUNCHUR for *puncture*, ATTENSHUN for *attention*	• Assimilated prefixes: ILEGAL for *illegal* • Root constancies in derivationally related pairs: CONDEM for *condemn*
Late Syllables and Affixes CONFEDENT for *confident*	• All of the above plus: • Long-vowel patterns in accented syllables: *compose/composition* • Double and *e* drop (except where overlaps with assimilated prefixes)	• Some suffixes and prefixes: ATTENSION for *attention*, PERTEND for *pretend* • Vowel alternation in derivationally related pairs: COMPUSITION for *composition* • Consonant alternations in derivationally related pairs: SPACIAL for *spatial*	

*Characteristics of syllables and affixes spelling are discussed in depth in Chapter 7.

such as *stopped* may require little processing time; recognition of this frequent word may be close to automatic; however, a word like *clopped* may call for slightly more analysis. Beyond consonant doubling for suffixes (*-ed* and *-ing*), students examine consonant doubling in words such as *settle, success,* and *occasion.* When students understand why some consonants are doubled, they begin to think about and study the meaning of prefixes.

It is often at this time that teachers and students study plurals, where the link between syntax and spelling is also obvious. They examine the various spelling changes for the plural, as in *funnies* and *foxes.* Toward the middle of this stage, students come to see the convention of *-tion* and *-sion* as affixes for changing verbs into nouns. They also study other syntactic and semantic affixes such as *-er, -or,* and *-ian.*

 For tools to address plural endings, as well as other inflectional endings, visit the Syllables and Affixes Stage on the accompanying CD-ROM.

As word study proceeds in this stage, the examination of accent or syllable stress becomes a more central interest, and the meaning connection is made with numerous language systems. For example, notice how a change in accent can affect the syntactic and semantic function of the word *contract:*

You signed the contract for a year.
He may contract the disease.

Beginning in the syllables and affixes stage, and throughout the next stage, the derivational relations stage, students study the **spelling-meaning connections** (Templeton, 1983). As you will see briefly in the discussion to follow, and in depth in Chapters 7 and 8, students learn about English spelling at the same time that they study to enrich their vocabularies.

Stage V: Derivational Relations Spelling

The **derivational relations spelling stage** is the last stage in the developmental model. Although some students may move into the derivational stage as early as grade 4 or 5, most derivational relations spellers are found in middle school, high school, and college. The derivational relations stage of learning continues throughout adulthood, when individuals continue to read and write according to their interest and specialty. Word study for the derivational relations stage both builds on and expands a wide vocabulary.

Derivational relations learners spell most words correctly (see Table 1-5). The few errors that they do commit have to do with using but confusing issues of consonant doubling with issues of prefix absorption (the convention of changing the last consonant of a prefix to the first consonant of the root, e.g., in + mobile = immobile) and other aspects of affixation and root constancy across related words. This stage of orthographic knowledge is known as derivational relations, because this is when students examine how words share common derivations and related roots and bases. They discover that the meaning and spelling of parts of words remain constant across different but derivationally related words (Henderson & Templeton, 1986; Henry, 1988). Word study in the derivational relations stage depends on and expands knowledge of a Greco and Latinate vocabulary.

After the common prefixes and suffixes are examined, students begin to look at the meaning of bases and roots and the classical origin of polysyllabic words or the study of derivational morphology. For example, it is not a big jump from seeing what *trans* means in exemplars such as *transportation, transport, transplant,* and *transmit* to looking deeper at some of the basic English bases like *ten* in *tennis, tendency, tenet, tenant,* and *pretend.* Throughout this stage students learn about the history of words and their derivations. With plenty of reading, writing, and word study, students' vocabularies continue to grow and branch out into specialized disciplines and interests.

 For specific Latin and Greek root word study tools, visit the Derivational Relations Stage on the accompanying CD-ROM.

In word study, teachers show students how to consider both the spelling of a word and its meaning. Students begin to see how spelling tells them about meaning and how pronunciation can blur meaning. A student who misspells *competition* as COMPOTITION may see the correct spelling more easily by going back to a base or root, as in *compete* where the long vowel gives a clear clue to spelling. When a student spells *composition* as COMPUSITION, the spelling can be clarified by referring to the long *-o* in the related word *compose.*

The aim of word study in this fifth stage is to teach students how to examine words for their related histories. One exciting aspect about word study sessions at these advanced stages is that teachers do not always know the meaning connections themselves, and so there is a freshness that comes with the word study explorations. Here, word study is managed with the assumption that together students and teachers can explore

TABLE 1-5   Characteristics of Derivational Relations Spelling*

	What Students Do Correctly	What Students Use but Confuse	What Is Absent
Early Derivational Relations OPPISITION for *opposition*	• Spell most words correctly • Most vowel and consonant alternations	• Unaccented or *schwa* sounds misspelled: BENAFIT for *benefit* • Some silent consonants: CONDEM for *condemn* • Some consonant doubling: AMMUSEMENT for *amusement* • Some suffixes and prefixes: APPEARENCE for *appearance,* PERTEND for *pretend* • Some vowel alternation in derivationally related pairs: COMPUSITION for *composition*	• Silent letters related to derivation: TERADACTIL for *pterodactyl*
Middle Derivational Relations	• Spell most words correctly • Common Latin suffixes: *attention*	• Some silent letters: EMFASIZE for *emphasize,* INDITEMENT for *indictment*	• Same as above plus: • Some reduced vowels: PROHABITION for *prohibition*
Late Derivational Relations	• Spell most words correctly	• Assimilated prefixes: ACOMODATE for *accommodate* • Unfamiliar derived forms, Greek & Latin forms, and foreign borrowings	• Some uncommon roots: EXHILERATE for *exhilarate*

*Characteristics of derivational relations spelling are discussed in depth in Chapter 8.

the histories of words and that words are interesting. Word study sessions throughout these stages can begin with the basic question: Did you find any interesting words in your reading? And so, together the group is off exploring, studying the words students bring to the session. Teachers show their excitement to students about what can be learned in the area of words, language, and ideas.

The word study activities in Chapter 8 are ordered in terms of development, but there is some flexibility in the exact order in which the affixes and roots are studied. Sometimes the words that students examine are familiar but fascinating in their histories, and as the students study words they add a new dimension to their vocabularies. As an example, a student brought the word *panacea* to the group because its meaning was unclear to her. What was fascinating was how the word study came around to a simple word—*company*. The students and the teacher could see that both words had *pan* in them, and over the course of the session, students began to wonder if *pan* represented the same meaning in both words. Subsequently, they found out that there are four different meanings of *pan. Company* can literally mean "to break bread with," because *com* means "with," and *pan* in this word means "bread." At the beginning of this word study session, no one knew that *company* would be studied or that such a charming word story would appear. The history of the English language has many wonderful stories to tell. It takes on more importance during the derivational relations stage, as students learn the meanings behind the vocabularies in specialized areas of study.

THE SYNCHRONY OF LITERACY DEVELOPMENT

The scope and sequence of word study instruction that is presented in Chapters 4 through 8 is based on a synchronous developmental foundation. When teachers conduct word study with students, they are addressing learning needs in all areas of literacy, because development in one area relates to development in other areas. This harmony in the timing of development has been described as the **synchrony** of reading, writing, and spelling development (Bear, 1991b; Bear & Templeton, 1998). This means that development in one area is observed along with advances in other areas. All three advance in stagelike progressions that share important conceptual dimensions.

The synchrony of literacy development may also be seen in the congruence of stages of spelling development, the developmental benchmarks just described, and the phases of reading acquisition described by other researchers (Chall, 1983; Ehri, 1997; Frith, 1985; Juel, 1991). There is converging evidence that reading, writing, and spelling development are integrally related. Figure 1-6 lists stages of word knowledge in relation to developmental stages of reading, and compares other researchers' descriptions of reading development.

Working independently, these researchers have described a remarkably similar progression of reading stages that cover the range from prereading to highly skilled, mature

FIGURE 1-6 Spelling and Reading Stages

reading. Individuals may vary in their rate of progression through these stages, but most tend to follow the same order of development. Overall, the stages can be divided into three major levels corresponding to the three layers of English orthography—alphabet, pattern, and meaning. The following discussion centers on this overall progression with an emphasis on the synchronous behaviors of reading and writing with spelling.

Emergent Readers

During the emergent stage, the child may undertake reading and writing in earnest, but adults will recognize their efforts as more pretend than real. For this reason, Chall (1983) called this stage of development *prereading*. Students may write with scribbles, letterlike forms, or random letters that have no phonetic relationship with the words they confidently believe they are writing. These students may call out the name of a favorite fast food restaurant when they recognize its logo or identify a friend's name because it starts with a *t,* but they are not systematic in their use of any particular cue. During the emergent stage, children lack an understanding of the alphabetic principle or show only the beginning of this understanding. Ehri (1997) designated this as the *prealphabetic phase;* children's use of logos led Frith (1985) to name it the *logographic stage.* Juel (1991) uses the term *selective cue* to describe how children select nonalphabetic visual cues like the two *o*s in *look* to remember a word.

During the emergent stage, children can become quite attached to selected letters that they notice in their name. Upon entering preschool, Lee noticed that other children's names on their cubbies used some of the same letters that she used in her name. Perplexed and somewhat annoyed, she pointed to the letters that were also in her name. "Hey, that's MY letter!" she insisted. Children in the emergent stage also begin to see selected letters in their names in environmental print. Walking around the grocery store, Lee pointed to the box of Cheer detergent and said, "Look Mommy, there's my name." Lee's special relationship with the letters in her name is a living embodiment of the prealphabetic, logographic, and selective-cue strategy these researchers describe.

Beginning Readers

The understanding of the alphabetic nature of our language is a major hurdle for readers and spellers. The child who writes *light* as LT has made a quantum conceptual leap, having grasped that there are systematic matches between sounds and letters that must be made when writing. This early letter name–alphabetic speller is a beginning reader who has moved from pretend reading to real reading. Just as early attempts to spell words are partial, so too, beginning readers initially have limited knowledge of letter sounds as they identify words by phonetic cues. Ehri (1997) describes these readers and writers as being in the *partial alphabetic phase.* The kinds of reading errors students make during this phase offer insights into what they understand about print. Using the context as well as partial consonant cues, a child reading about good things to eat might substitute *candy* or even *cookie* for *cake* in the sentence, "The cake was very good to eat." Readers in this stage require much support in the form of predictable, memorable texts, and much teacher guidance in the form of prompts and strategies to use for decoding.

As readers and writers acquire more complete knowledge of letter sounds in the later part of the letter name–alphabetic stage, they will include but often confuse vowels in the words they write and read. Students who spell BAD for *bed* may make similar vowel errors when they read *hid* as HAD in "I hid the last cookie." These students resemble Ehri's (1997) *full alphabetic* readers who begin to use the entire letter string to decode and store sight words. Nevertheless, the reading of letter name–alphabetic spellers is often disfluent and word by word, unless they have read it before or are otherwise familiar with the passage (Bear, 1992). If you ask such spellers to read silently, the best they can do is to whisper. They need to read aloud to vocalize the letter sounds. Readers in this stage continue to benefit from repeated readings of predictable texts, but also from the reading of text with many phonetically regular words. These "decodable" texts will support the development of decoding strategies and the acquisition of sight words (Juel & Roper/Schneider, 1985). Not surprisingly, Chall (1983) referred to this stage as a period of *initial reading and decoding.*

Transitional Readers

Transitional readers and spellers move into the within word pattern spelling stage where single letter-sound units are consolidated into patterns or larger chunks and other spelling regularities are internalized. Longitudinal research on spelling development has identified the progressive order in which students appear to use these larger chunks. After automating basic letter sounds in the **onset** position (initial consonants, consonant blends, and consonant digraphs), students focus on the vowel and what follows (Ganske, 1994; Invernizzi, 1985, 1992; Viise, 1996). Short-vowel **rimes** are learned first with consonant blends in the context of simple word families or **phonograms** such as *h-at, ch-at,* or *fl-at.* These chunks come relatively easy probably as a result of their frequency in one-syllable words. Once the rime unit is solidified as a chunk, students appear to use but confuse the various long-vowel markers of English (Invernizzi, 1992). Other stage models of reading acquisition describe this chunking phenomenon as an *orthographic* stage in which readers use progressively higher-order units of word structures to read and spell (Chall, 1983; Frith, 1985; Gibson, 1965). Ehri & McCormick (1998) call this the *consolidated alphabetic phase* in which students' reading is supported by familiarity with frequently occurring letter pattern units.

From the beginning to the end of this stage, students move from needing support materials and techniques to being able to pick from various texts and reading them independently—from the Sunday comics to easy chapter books such as *Freckle Juice* (by Judith Blume), *Superfudge* (by Judith Blume), and *Ramona the Pest* (by Beverly Cleary). With easy, independent-level material, students stop fingerpointing and, for the first time, read silently (Bear, 1982; Henderson, 1990). Their reading moves from word-by-word to phrase-by-phrase reading with greater expression, and they can approach fluent reading at their instructional level (Zutell & Rasinski, 1989). During this stage, students integrate the knowledge and skills acquired in the previous two stages, so Chall (1983) described this stage as one of *confirmation and fluency.* Advances in word knowledge affect students' writing too. Their sizable sight word vocabulary allows them to write more quickly and with greater detail. Writing and reading speeds increase significantly between the letter name–alphabetic stage and the transitional within word pattern stage (Bear, 1992; Invernizzi, 1992).

Intermediate and Advanced Readers

Two additional stages of word knowledge characterize **intermediate** and **advanced readers:** syllables and affixes and derivational relations. As shown in Figure 1-7, these two periods of literacy development are generally accompanied by the ability to solve abstract problems and to reflect metacognitively on experience. Students operating within the meaning layer of English orthography have relatively automatic word recognition, and thus, their minds are free to think as rapidly as they can read. They can use reading as a vehicle for learning new information from texts, and thus, their vocabulary grows with their reading experience. Intermediate and advanced readers are also fluent writers. The content of their writing displays complex analysis and interpretation, and reflects a more sophisticated, content-oriented vocabulary.

Syllable and affix spellers read most texts with good accuracy and speed, both orally and silently. For these students, success in reading and understanding is related to familiarity and experience with the topic being discussed. Students in this intermediate

Reading and Writing Stages:

Emergent *Early Middle Late*	Beginning *Early Middle Late*	Transitional *Early Middle Late*	Intermediate *Early Middle Late*	Advanced *Early Middle Late*
Pretend read	Read aloud, word-by-word, fingerpoint reading	Approaching fluency, some expression in oral reading	Reads fluently with expression. Develops a variety of reading styles. Vocabulary grows with experience, reading, and writing.	
Pretend write	Word-by-word writing, may write a few words or lines	Approaching fluency, more organization, several paragraphs	Writes fluently with expression and voice. Experiences different writing styles and genres. Writing shows personal problem solving and reflection.	

Spelling Stages:

Emergent—> CHAPTER 4	Letter Name—Alphabetic—> CHAPTER 5	Within Word Pattern—> CHAPTER 6	Syllables and Affixes—> CHAPTER 7	Derivational Relations—> CHAPTER 8
Examples:				
bed	b bd bad	*bed*		
ship	s sp sep shep	*ship*		
float	f ft fot flot flott	flowt floaut flote *float*		
train	t trn jian tan chran tran	teran traen trane *train*		
cattle	c kd catl	catel catol	cattel *cattle*	
cellar	s slr salr	celr	saler celer seler celler seller *cellar*	
pleasure	p pjr plasr	plager	plejer pleser plesher	pleser plesher plesour plesure *pleasure*
confident			confedent	confident confednet confident confident *confident*
opposition				opasishan oppasishion oppasistian oposition oposistion *opposition*

FIGURE 1-7 The Synchrony of Literacy Development From *The Synchrony of Literacy Development: A Guide to Instruction* by D. Bear, 1998.

stage acquire, through plenty of practice, a repertoire of reading styles that reflects their experience with different genres. They may obsess on reading fantasy or historical fiction and voraciously consume all of the books in a series such as *Red Wall* (by Brian Jacques) or *His Dark Materials* (by Philip Pullman). The same is true for writing. Students who are in this stage of word knowledge delight in writing persuasive essays, editorials, poetry, or their own versions of fantasy or realistic fiction.

Derivational relations spellers have a broader experience base that allows them to choose among a variety of reading styles to suit the text and their purposes for reading. They read according to their own interests and professional needs and they seek to integrate their knowledge with the knowledge of others. The same picture is evidenced in their writing. With purpose and practice, derivational relations students develop and master a variety of writing styles and even write to create a new body of knowledge.

These two stages of word knowledge correspond roughly to Chall's (1983) *multiple viewpoints* and *construction and reconstruction* stages. Others refer to this period as one during which students learn to become strategic readers and ultimately become proficient adult readers (Spear-Swerling & Sternberg, 2000). Still others lump these two stages of reading together as the *automatic* stage (Gough & Hillinger, 1980), even though there is much that is still not automatic. Syllable and affix spellers will still struggle with such issues as how to pronounce the name of the main character in *Caddie Woodlawn* (sometimes calling her "Cadie") or when to double at the juncture of two syllables (Is it robbin or robin?). Derivational relations spellers may not be aware of the *confide* in *confident* and spell it CONFENDENT, as indicated in the bottom right corner of Figure 1-7.

Vocabulary and word use plays a central role in the connections that intermediate and advanced readers forge between reading and writing. From adolescence on, except perhaps for slang, most of the new vocabulary students learn comes from reading and reflects new domains of content-specific knowledge that students explore (Beck & McKeown, 1991). Studying spelling-meaning connections is central to maximizing this vocabulary growth (Templeton, 1976, 1992).

Understanding the harmonious development of reading, writing, and spelling development is crucial for effective literacy instruction. Figure 1-7 presents an integrated model of how reading, writing, and spelling progress, in synchrony. Teachers might refer to this figure when they discuss each student's development in parent-teacher conferences, or when they share a student's writing with parents or show a collection of books that illustrates the range of instructional reading levels that correspond to the **developmental levels** in the figure. Parents can better understand where their children are along the developmental continuum and across reading, writing, and spelling by looking at the described behaviors and the invented spelling samples.

Word study activities in this textbook are organized around this model. If you can identify your students by the stages of reading, writing, and spelling, then you will know which chapters contain the activities that are most relevant to your students' development, as shown in Figure 1-3 on page 9.

USING INVENTED SPELLING AS A GUIDE FOR INSTRUCTION

Developmental spelling theory suggests that invented spelling is a window into a child's knowledge of how written words work and can be used to guide instruction (Invernizzi et al., 1994). Specific kinds of spelling errors at particular levels of orthographic knowledge reflect a progressive differentiation of word elements that determine how quickly students can read words and how easily they can write them. Insight into students' conceptual understanding of these word elements helps teachers direct their efforts as students learn to read and spell.

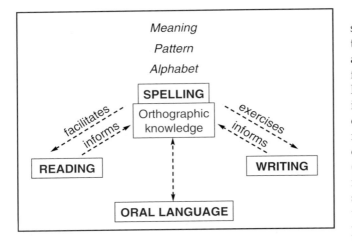

FIGURE 1-8   Word Study: Reading and Writing

There is considerable consistency between spelling achievement and reading achievement through the fifth grade (Zutell & Rasinski, 1989), and students' spelling attempts provide a powerful medium for establishing predictive validity. Morris and Perney (1984) found that first grader's invented spellings were a better predictor of end-of-grade reading than a standardized reading readiness test. Sawyer et al. (1997) reported that a child's score on a developmental spelling inventory (Ganske, 1999) was a powerful predictor of decoding. In the Sawyer et al. (1997) study, developmental spelling predicted word decoding better than curricular experience, phoneme segmentation, and phoneme manipulation. Moreover, the spelling inventory identified the exact word elements students had already mastered, and those currently under negotiation. Thus, establishing levels of development in spelling and reading has enormous potential for guiding instruction.

In this textbook we suggest that orthographic knowledge plays a central role in a comprehensive language arts program, linking reading and writing. Word knowledge accumulates as students develop orthographic understandings at the alphabetic level, the pattern level, and the meaning level in overarching layers of complexity. Our complete understanding of phonics, word recognition, spelling, vocabulary, and even word usage (syntax) is part of our word knowledge. Reading provides the corpus of words and defines the parameters of what may be studied. Through word study, students learn how the spelling system, or orthography, works to represent sound, pattern, and meaning. Writing then exercises that word knowledge. Figure 1-8 illustrates the theory of developmental word knowledge and shows how word study links reading and writing.

 Listen carefully to students' dialects for ways that their speech influences the way they spell. Students' apply the alphabetic principle with their own speech in mind.

WHERE DO I BEGIN?

Students acquire word knowledge through implicit learning that takes place as they read and write, and through explicit instruction orchestrated by the teacher. However, it is impossible to know exactly what to teach and when to teach it until we have a living child before us. An informed, developmental interpretation of students' efforts as they read and write shows us which words they can read and spell, and of those, which they might learn more about. There is more to pacing instruction than plugging students into a sequence of phonics or spelling features. Instructional pacing must be synonymous with instructional placing—fitting the features of words to be taught into the students' understanding of what is to be learned. How do we know where to begin word study? We find out the extent of students' word knowledge: how words sound, how words are spelled, what words mean, and how they are used. A good deal of what students know about the orthography is revealed in their invented spellings. Research on invented spelling has shown that students learn the features of English orthography in a common progression. According to Henderson (1990), teachers can use spelling assessments (see Chapter 2) to select the content of instruction in word recognition, alphabet study, phonics, vocabulary, and spelling.

WORDS THEIR WAY

When we say that we want to help students explore and learn about words their way, we mean that our instruction will be sensitive to two fundamental tenets:

1. Students' learning of spelling and vocabulary is based on their developmental or instructional level.
2. Students' learning is based on the way they are naturally inclined to learn, on their natural course of conceptual learning.

When we honor these two tenets we almost guarantee that our students will learn their way—building from what is known about words to what is new. Rather than a hodge-podge of rote memorization activities designed only to ensure repeated exposure, our teaching tasks encourage active exploration and examination of word features that are within a child's stage of literacy development. Word study is active, and by making judgments about words and sorting words according to similar features, students construct their own rules for how the features work. The simple act of making judgments about words this way helps students learn the relationships among alphabet, pattern, and meaning. Meaningful practice helps students internalize word features and become automatic in using what they have learned.

Guide to the Book

We conclude this first chapter by pointing out the organization of *Words Their Way*. The instructional match we make between the levels of information contained in the structure of words and the synchrony of reading, writing, and spelling development has been the topic of this chapter. In Chapter 2 we present an assessment process to gather and interpret students' spelling to ascertain what they know about written words and what they are trying to learn. In Chapter 3 we discuss classroom organization as well as principles and procedures for word study. Chapters 4 through 8 are the teaching/learning heart of the book. The type of instruction described herein is reflected in these chapters as they present appropriate word study for each of the stages of developmental word knowledge. Each chapter begins with a description of the stage and general teaching guidelines. The second part of each chapter then presents specific activities for that stage. Both parts are demonstrated in the accompanying *Words Their Way* video.

Now that we have looked at the makeup of words and the spelling system that represents them in print, it is time to examine the nature of these stages of developmental spelling knowledge and the type of reading and writing that is characteristic of each stage. Figure 1-9 details the characteristics of each stage of development to help you understand the reading and writing context for the word study instruction that is appropriate for each stage. After learning how to assess the developmental word knowledge of your students in Chapter 2, the remaining chapters will offer more detail about planning word study instruction for each stage of development.

I. Emergent Stage—Chapter 4

Characteristics
1. Scribbles letters and numbers
2. Lacks concept of word
3. Lacks letter-sound correspondence or represents most salient sound with single letters
4. Pretends to read and write

Reading and Writing Activities
1. Read to students and encourage oral language activities
2. Model writing using dictations and charts
3. Encourage pretend reading and writing

Word Study Focus
1. Develop concept sorts
2. Play with speech sounds to develop phonological awareness
3. Plan alphabet activities
4. Sort pictures by beginning sound
5. Encourage fingerpoint memory reading of rhymes, dictations, and simple pattern books
6. Encourage invented spelling

II. Letter Name–Alphabetic Stage—Chapter 5

Early Letter Name–Alphabetic
Characteristics
1. Represents beginning and ending sounds
2. Has rudimentary / functional concept of word
3. Reads word by word in beginning reading materials

Reading and Writing Activities
1. Read to students and encourage oral language activities
2. Secure concept of word by plenty of reading in patterned trade books, dictations, and simple rhymes
3. Record and reread individual dictations one paragraph long
4. Label pictures and write in journals regularly

Word Study Focus
1. Collect known words for word bank
2. Sort pictures and words by beginning sounds
3. Study word families that share a common vowel
4. Study beginning consonant blends and digraphs
5. Encourage invented spelling

Middle to Late Letter Name–Alphabetic Stage
Characteristics
1. Correctly spells initial and final consonants and some blends and digraphs
2. Uses letter names to spell vowel sounds
3. Spells phonetically representing all salient sounds in a one-to-one linear fashion
4. Omits most silent letters
5. Omits preconsonantal nasals in spelling (BOP or BUP for *bump*)
6. Fingerpoints and reads aloud
7. Reads slowly in a word-by-word manner

Reading and Writing Activities
1. Read to students
2. Encourage invented spellings in independent writing but hold students accountable for features and words they have studied
3. Collect two- to three-paragraph dictations which are reread regularly
4. Encourage more expansive writing and consider some simple editing such as punctuation and high frequency words

FIGURE 1-9 Sequence of Development and Instruction

Word Study Focus
1. Sort pictures and words by different short-vowel word families
2. Sort pictures and words by short-vowel sounds and CVC patterns
3. Continue to examine consonant blends and digraphs
4. Begin simple sound sorts comparing short- and long-vowel sounds
5. Collect known words for word bank (up to 200)

III. Within Word Pattern Stage—Chapter 6

Characteristics
1. Spells most single-syllable short-vowel words correctly
2. Spells most beginning consonant digraphs and two-letter consonant blends
3. Attempts to use silent long-vowel markers (NALE for *nail*)
4. Reads silently and with more fluency and expression
5. Writes more fluently and in extended fashion
6. Can revise and edit

Reading and Writing Activities
1. Continue to read aloud to students
2. Plan self-selected silent reading of simple chapter books
3. Write each day, writers' workshops, conferencing, and publication

Word Study Focus
1. Complete daily activities in word study notebook
2. Sort words by long- and short-vowel sounds and by common long-vowel patterns
3. Compare words with *r*-controlled vowels
4. After mastering common long vowels, explore less common vowels and diphthongs (*oi, ou, au, ow*)
5. Review blends and digraphs as needed and examine triple blends and complex consonant units such as *thr, str, dge, tch, ck*
6. Examine homographs and homophones

IV. Syllables and Affixes—Chapter 7

Characteristics
1. Spells most single-syllable words correctly
2. Makes errors at syllable juncture and in unaccented syllables
3. Reads with good fluency and expression
4. Reads faster silently than orally
5. Writes responses that are sophisticated and critical

Reading and Writing Activities
1. Plan read-alouds and literature discussions
2. Include self-selected or assigned silent reading of novels of different genres
3. Begin simple note taking and outlining skills, and work with adjusting reading rates for different purposes
4. Explore reading and writing styles and genres

Word Study Focus
1. Examine consonant doubling and inflected endings
2. Focus on unaccented syllables such as *er* and *le*
3. Join spelling and vocabulary studies; link meaning and spelling
4. Explore grammar through word study
5. Sort and study affixes (prefixes and suffixes)
6. Study stress or accent in two-syllable words

FIGURE 1-9 Continued

V. Derivational Relations—Chapter 8

Characteristics
1. Has mastered high frequency words
2. Makes errors on low frequency multisyllabic words derived from Latin and Greek combining forms
3. Reads with good fluency and expression
4. Reads faster silently than orally
5. Writes responses that are sophisticated and critical

Reading and Writing Activities
1. Include silent reading and writing, exploring various genres as interests arise
2. Develop study skills, including textbook reading, note taking, reading rates, test taking, report writing, and reference work
3. Focus on literary analysis

Word Study Focus
1. Focus on words that students bring to word study from their reading and writing
2. Join spelling and vocabulary studies; link meaning and spelling
3. Examine common and then less common roots, prefixes, and suffixes
4. Examine vowel alternations in derivationally related pairs
5. Explore etymology, especially in the content areas
6. Examine content-related foreign borrowings

FIGURE 1-9   Sequence of Development and Instruction—Concluded

Getting Started: The Assessment of Orthographic Development

2

Teaching is about understanding students and their learning. This chapter is about understanding students' orthographic knowledge through an informal assessment process that includes observations of student writing and informal tests or spelling inventories. These assessments will enable you to:

a. Find out what individual students know about words and what they need to learn.
b. Plan a program of word study that helps students learn at their instructional level.
c. Group students for instruction, and
d. Monitor students' growth in word knowledge over time.

The assessments described in this chapter will guide you to determine an instructional level for each student and particular orthographic features that should be studied during word study.

INFORMAL OBSERVATIONS TO ASSESS ORTHOGRAPHIC KNOWLEDGE

Observe Students' Writing

Teachers have daily opportunities to observe students as they write for a variety of purposes. These observations help to reveal what students understand about words. The following example demonstrates what you might learn about a kindergartner's literacy development. Sarah called this her "first restaurant review." Although it appears to be a menu, she posted it on the wall the way she had seen reviews posted in restaurants.

What Sarah wrote:	How she read what she wrote:
1 CRS KAM SAS	(First course, clam sauce)
2 CRS FESH	(Second course, fish)
3 CRS SAGATE	(Third course, spaghetti)
4 CRS POSH POPS	(Fourth course, Push Pops)

This writing tells a lot about Sarah: She sees a practical use for writing, she has written a long and complete message, and she enjoys writing and displaying her work. Sarah has a good grasp of how to compose a list and she is even beginning to understand menu planning!

Her spelling shows what she knows about the orthography. She represents many consonant sounds, but blends are incomplete (as in KAM for *clam*). Other than in the word *course,* she has placed a vowel in each syllable; however, she is *using but confusing* short vowels (Invernizzi, Abouzeid, & Gill, 1994). In spelling *fish* as FESH, Sarah uses a vowel but she confuses *e* and *i*. This substitution is entirely predictable given the research on spelling development (Bear & Templeton, 1998; Templeton, 2002; Templeton & Bear, 1992a; Templeton & Morris, 1999; Zutell, 1994). The deletion of the vowel in CRS is due to the *semivocalic* nature of the *r*. In this example, the letter *r* represents the /r/ and the vowel sound. According to the sequence of development presented in Chapter 1, Sarah is considered a letter name–alphabetic speller who would still benefit from activities described in Chapter 5.

In Figure 2-1 we see a writing sample from Jake, an older student. The writing is readable because many words are spelled correctly and the others are close approximations. Clearly Jake has mastered most consonant relationships—even the three-letter blend in *scraped*—but not the complex *tch* unit in *stitches*. Jake shows some experimentation with vowel patterns in CHIAN for *chin* and CREM for *cream,* when he inserts extra vowels where none are needed and omits some where they are needed. Most long and short vowels are correctly represented, however, as in *had, have, went, cone, home,* and *day.* Based on the vowel errors, Jake would probably be considered a middle to late within word pattern speller. He needs to review some common patterns before addressing the ambiguous vowels in such words as *bought* (BOUT) and *tired* (TIRD). We look at Jake's word knowledge when we look at his spelling on an inventory later in this chapter.

Student writings, especially unedited rough drafts, are a goldmine of information about their orthographic knowledge. Many teachers keep a variety of student writing samples to document students' needs and growth over time. The Qualitative Spelling Checklist discussed in this chapter and presented in the Appendix is a tool used to determine a student's developmental spelling stage from his or her writing.

Relying entirely upon writing samples has drawbacks, however. Some students will only use words they know how to spell. Others will use resources in the room, such as word walls, dictionaries, and the person sitting nearby, to write with few errors. Using these resources, students' writing may overestimate what they really know. However, when students concentrate on getting their ideas on paper, they may not pay attention to the spelling and thus make excessive errors. Some students are anxious about the accuracy of their spelling and others write freely with little concern about it. Knowing your

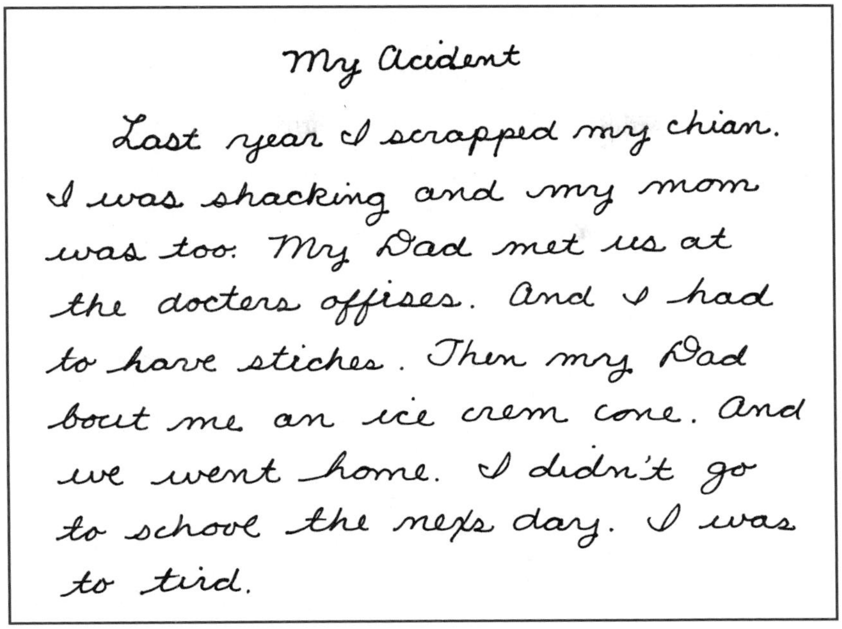

> My Accident
>
> Last year I scrapped my chian.
> I was shacking and my mom
> was too. My Dad met us at
> the docters offises. And I had
> to have stiches. Then my Dad
> bout me an ice crem cone. And
> we went home. I didn't go
> to school the nexs day. I was
> to tird.

FIGURE 2-1   Writing Sample with Examples of Using but Confusing

students through daily observations will help you to determine not only their orthographic knowledge but also their habits and dispositions.

Observe Students' Reading

Important insights into orthographic knowledge are also made when we observe students reading. According to Chapter 1, a close relationship exists between reading and spelling, described as the synchrony of development. Drawing from the same knowledge base, students' reading and spelling are related (Ehri, 1997; Henderson, 1990), but are not mirror images, because the processes differ slightly. In reading, words can be recognized with many types of textual supports and students can read more difficult words than they can spell.

In terms of the synchrony of literacy, the greater accuracy in reading compared with spelling is illustrated as a slant of development (Bear & Templeton, 2000). The ability to read words correctly lies a little ahead of students' spelling accuracy. For example, within word pattern spellers, who are also transitional readers, may read many two-syllable words correctly, but are still learning how to spell long-vowel patterns (*steep*) and complex short-vowel patterns (*fought*) in single-syllable words. They also have not learned to double the consonants in spelling words like *stepping* and *battle*. Spelling is a conservative measure of what students know about words in general. If students can spell a word, then we know they can read the word. When students consult reference materials such as a spell check or dictionary, the spelling task becomes a reading task; we all know the phenomenon of being able to recognize the correct spelling if we just see it.

As students read, we can listen for oral reading behaviors that are characteristic of the different reading levels described in Chapter 1. Figure 1-7 describes specific reading characteristics that we expect to hear among students in particular spelling stages; for example, it indicates that letter name–alphabetic spellers are usually beginning readers. Such readers are described as disfluent; they read without expression and relatively slowly (40 to 60 words per minute in instructional-level text).

We can expect to hear particular reading errors at different instructional levels. Like spelling errors, reading errors show us what students are using but confusing when they read. Teachers who understand students' developmental word knowledge will be in a

good position to interpret students' reading errors and to make decisions about the appropriate prompt to use. A student who substitutes *bunny* for *rabbit* in the sentence, "The farmer saw a rabbit," is a beginning reader and an early letter name–alphabetic speller. The student uses the picture to invent a logical response, not knowledge about sound-symbol correspondences. For students at this developmental stage, drawing attention to the first sound can help them use their consonant knowledge.

Further in development, assessments of oral reading substitutions take on a different meaning. A transitional reader who substitutes *growled* for *groaned* in the sentence, "Jason groaned when he missed the ball," is probably attending to several orthographic features of the word. It is unlikely that any picture could have been helpful in this case, but the student appears to use the initial blend *gr* and the *-ed* ending to come up with a word that fits the meaning of the sentence. Because this student shows vowel knowledge, a teacher might revisit this word at some point in a small group setting and direct students' attention to the *oa* pattern. Our response to reading errors and our expectations for correcting such errors or sounding out unknown words depend upon a number of factors, one of which is knowing where students are developmentally in terms of their orthographic and word knowledge.

Teachers' knowledge of students' orthographic knowledge suggests what words students can analyze in word study lessons or sound out successfully in oral reading. For example, it would be inappropriate to ask students in the early letter name–alphabetic stage to sound out the entire word *flat*, or even to look for a familiar part within the word in the hope that they might use their knowledge of *-at* words by analogy. Early letter name–alphabetic spellers can only deal with the beginnings of words in print. Emergent and early letter name–alphabetic spellers turn to context clues when their knowledge of letters and sounds is insufficient to read the words on the page (Biemiller, 1970). However, students in the latter part of the letter name–alphabetic stage could manipulate the sounds in *flat* easily. Having students read at their instructional levels means that when they encounter unfamiliar words in text, their orthographic knowledge can enable them to read the words accurately. To advance students' orthographic knowledge, keep instruction within their range, for it is orthographic information that enables students to identify words in any context and eventually make word recognition automatic.

Although observations made during writing and reading provide some insight into students' development, the best assessments include a combination of writing samples, observations during oral reading, and analysis of spelling errors as part of an informal qualitative spelling inventory. Together, reading, writing, and spelling samples obtained from inventories provide a rich collection of information to understand students' knowledge of the three layers of the orthography. Informal qualitative spelling inventories and methods of their analysis are described next.

QUALITATIVE SPELLING INVENTORIES

What Are Spelling Inventories?

Spelling inventories are words specially chosen to represent a variety of spelling features or patterns at increasing levels of difficulty. The words in spelling inventories are designed to show students' knowledge of key spelling features that relate to the different spelling stages. The lists are not exhaustive in that they do not test all spelling features; rather, they include orthographic features that are most helpful in understanding where to begin instruction. Students take an inventory as they would a spelling test. The results are then analyzed to obtain a general picture of their development. Spelling inventories are a powerful yet easy way to see what students understand about the orthography. For this reason we devote the remainder of this chapter to them.

The first inventories were developed under the leadership of Edmund Henderson at the University of Virginia. One of Henderson's best inventories is the McGuffey Inventory, a series of eight grade-level lists (Schlagal, 1992). The McGuffey Inventory is included in this chapter and represents a wide array of orthographic features across eight grade levels.

Many of Henderson's students developed shorter lists in research studies which focused on particular periods of spelling or specific languages (Bear & Templeton, 2000; Templeton, 2003). These lists strive to "catch" many of the same spelling errors, and each list has its own elegance that shows how students learn to read and spell.

One specialized list covers the range from emergent through within word pattern spelling by asking students to spell increasingly difficult words. Using a point system to score the presence of certain phonics features (e.g., initial consonant, initial and final consonant, short vowel), the spelling score predicts achievement at the end of first grade with greater power than a standardized reading measure (Morris, Nelson, & Perney, 1986). In studies of students across all grade levels, scores from the students' spelling on these inventories are consistently related and predict reading achievement at all age levels from kindergartners through adult learners.

Table 2-1 shows the collection of inventories that may be used with a broad range of students, including primary, intermediate, Spanish, and secondary inventories. (All inventories are in the Appendix of this textbook.) The Elementary Spelling Inventory covers the instructional range from emergent to derivational relations. Fewer words are used and a single list can help predict reading achievement throughout grades K to 12. Other lists that are more focused cover a narrower instructional range with more words to explore more features. For example, the Primary Spelling Inventory includes more short-vowel words. The Upper Level Spelling Inventory begins with words to assess within word pattern spellers and explores in depth the orthographic features negotiated during the last two stages.

The **feature guides** are an extenuation of research conducted at the McGuffey Reading Center at the University of Virginia. They are used to classify students' errors within a hierarchy of orthographic features. Like the inventories presented here, students from the McGuffey Reading Center have also developed scoring guides (Ganske, 1994; Invernizzi & Meier, 2002; Morris, 1999). After collecting and analyzing thousands of samples, researchers have developed **error guides** to match students to spelling levels from emergent to derivational relations (Bear, 1992; Bear, Templeton, & Warner, 1991; Edwards, 2002).

TABLE 2-1 *Words Their Way* Spelling Assessments

Spelling Assessment	Grade Range	Developmental Range
Qualitative Checklist (p. 296)	K – 8	All stages
Emergent Class Record (p. 297)	Pre-K – K	Emergent to letter name–alphabetic
Kindergarten Spelling Inventory (p. 298)	Pre-K – K	Emergent to middle of letter name–alphabetic
Primary Spelling Inventory (p. 300)	K–3	Emergent to early syllables and affixes
Elementary Spelling Inventory-1 (p. 304)	K–6	Late emergent to early derivational relations
Intermediate Spelling Inventory (p. 308)	3–8	Late letter name–alphabetic to middle derivational relations
Upper Level Spelling Inventory (p. 311)	5–12	Within word pattern to derivational relations
McGuffey Spelling Inventory (p. 317)	1–8	All stages
Spanish Spelling Inventory (p. 318)	1–6	Emergent to syllables and affixes

Additional Inventories on the *Words Their Way* Companion Website

Elementary Spelling Inventory-2	K–8	Late emergent to early derivational relations
Content Area Spelling Inventories in Biology, Geometry, & U.S. History	9–12	Within word pattern to derivational relations

An Overview: Three Steps to Assess Spelling

Spelling inventories are quick and easy to administer and score, and they are reliable and valid measures of what students know about words. The analyses of these inventories help us plan word study and spelling instruction.

Use of these spelling inventories requires three basic steps: (a) selecting and administering a spelling inventory, (b) analyzing students' spelling, and (c) monitoring growth and planning instruction.

First select a spelling inventory to use with students that suits your particular instructional purpose and then become familiar with the directions to administer it. Table 2-1 is a valuable resource to use when making your selection. Each of the inventories is also discussed at the end of this chapter.

Directions to administer the inventories are in the Appendix. Call the words aloud and encourage students to spell them the best they can. These inventories are not used for grading purposes and students should not study the words in advance. Students should not study the particular words either before or after the inventory is administered. The Qualitative Spelling Checklist and the Emergent Class Record are assessment guides for analyzing students' spelling, based on their independent, individual, uncorrected writing (both are in the Appendix).

You may be wondering how often to administer the inventories, and if the same inventory can be used repeatedly. Most teachers use the same list throughout the year; however, as students progress, a more advanced spelling inventory may be chosen to examine how students spell more challenging words. Some teachers begin with the same list for all students and after 10 or 20 words, shift to small group administration of segments from other lists. For example, a second-grade teacher may begin with the Primary Spelling Inventory, and decide to discontinue testing with all but a group of students who spelled most of the words correctly. This teacher may then move to the Intermediate Spelling Inventory with this group. A key point to keep in mind is that students must generate a number of errors for you to determine a spelling stage.

After selecting and administering the spelling inventory that best suits your instructional purpose, the next step is to analyze students' spelling using checklists, feature guides, and error guides. Because analysis is more than giving a point for a correctly spelled word and applying a percentage or raw score, we have developed these aids to provide *qualitative* information regarding what students know about specific spelling features and what they are ready to study next.

The final step, then, is to plan instruction to meet assessed needs. The results of the spelling analysis are entered onto the Classroom Organization and Composite forms also included in the Appendix. The classroom forms will provide an overview of the class that will aid in forming groups for instruction. Many teachers find these spelling inventories to be the most helpful and easily administered literacy assessment in their repertoire.

To summarize, the three steps used in the qualitative spelling inventories are as follows:

1. *Select and administer a spelling inventory.* Become familiar with the instructions to administer the inventory. Inventories discussed in this chapter are found on pages 300–316.
2. *Analyze students' spelling.* Use the feature and error guides.
3. *Monitor growth and plan instruction.* Create a classroom profile with the organization and composite charts presented on pages 322–327.

Box 2-1 presents five guidelines to conducting assessments. Consider these points to help anticipate what factors may inhibit students in their spelling. The guidelines urge you to work from the synchrony of literacy model presented in Figure 1-7, and to look for synchronous behaviors in reading and writing as you use informal spelling

BOX 2-1   *Five Guidelines for Assessment*

Consider the following guidelines when assessing and organizing instruction for word study in the classroom.

1. *Work from a developmental model.*

Use the developmental model in Figure 1-7 by reading from top to bottom across the literacy behaviors of reading, spelling, and writing. Look for corroborating evidence to place students' achievement somewhere along the developmental continuum. This model helps to generate expectations for student development using an integrated literacy approach. For example, a student's reading behaviors should be in synchrony with his or her range of writing behaviors.

2. *Use informal assessments as you teach.*

Informal assessments teach us how to observe students' literacy behaviors in daily teaching. After watching students participate in reading, writing, and word sorts, you can determine what students are learning about the orthography. By observing while teaching, you gather information and, based on the developmental model in Chapter 1, make sense of what students do in their spelling and word recognition.

Teachers observe a variety of behaviors. Consider these examples:

- Teachers learn about students through their oral reading fluency and expression.
- Teachers learn about students at the beginning of the year with learning and literacy interviews, writing samples, and reader response activities.
- Throughout the year, teachers learn about students by talking with them and by trying to solve problems together. These problems can be part of highly verbal situations such as Guided Reading-Thinking Activities (GR-TAs) (Bear & Barone, 1998; Templeton, 1997), or less verbal situations such as working puzzles or playing checkers.

3. *Welcome surprises for what they say about individual students.*

The expectations you develop by using the model illustrated in Figure 1-7 are not always visible in a student's performance. Expectations are one thing; what students can do and what they want to show may not match expectations based on the developmental model. The mismatches observed between reading, writing, and spelling development are most interesting and informative, and must be examined carefully (Bear & Templeton, 2000).

Some students are out of synchrony in their development. This is true for the student who is notoriously bad at spelling, but who is a capable reader. When the student is mismatched between reading and spelling, you can help improve the spelling and obtain a developmental synchrony by pinpointing the stage of spelling development and then providing developmentally rich instruction that addresses the student's needs. Using these assessments and the developmental model, you can develop individual educational plans for students and plan for small group instruction accordingly.

4. *Do not assess students at their frustration levels.*

The **frustration level** is the level at which students are far from being correct in their work—where even your assistance would not be sufficient for them to learn. Although at times you may dip into students' frustration level, this is no place to collect meaningful information about development. Avoid this mistake and take a commonsense approach: How well does anyone do when under extreme pressure to perform, and, in this case, when the speller knows that he or she is not doing well? How realistic a reflection of proficiency is this performance anyway? Part of the frustration a student experiences comes from not having the structural and cognitive background to support a reasonable guess. Students' frustration work can put you off the developmental track, because often work performed at the frustration level contains a fair amount of "spitting at the page," where students spell by plugging in letters.

5. *Start with what students can do and track progress over time.*

In the assessment process, focus on what students' errors tell us about what they know. For example, a student who spells *feet* as FETE has moved beyond the simple linear approach to spelling; otherwise the student would have spelled *feet* as FET.

The assessment must be conducted on a schedule that is helpful. Assess informally throughout the year to track progress and to help explain students' development to the next teacher. To most successfully assess your students' development and progress, conduct informal spelling assessments three times over a school year.

assessments. By analyzing what students use but confuse instead of what is absent, teachers can plan instruction that builds on what students *can* do and track progress over time.

HOW TO ADMINISTER SPELLING INVENTORIES

We have discussed ideas for selecting the inventories, and you will learn more about the inventories later in the chapter. Here we consider general guidelines for how the spelling inventories are to be administered. The spelling inventories should take only 15 to 20 minutes to administer, and can be discontinued after students miss several words, so kindergartners and first grades may only spell 5 to 10 words.

Create a Relaxed Atmosphere

Students must understand the season for taking the inventory. Because they may be particularly edgy about taking a test, be direct in your explanation:

> I am going to ask you to spell some words. You have not studied these words and will not be graded on them. Some of the words may be easy and others may be difficult. Do the best you can. Your work will help me understand how you are learning to read and write and how I can help you learn.

Teachers often tell students that as long as they try their best in spelling the words, they will earn an A for the assignment. Once these things are explained, most students are able to give the spelling a good effort.

You can conduct lessons like the one described in Box 2-2 to show students how to sound out words they are unsure of how to spell.

It is easier to create a relaxed environment working in small groups, especially with kindergarten and first-grade students. Children who are in second grade and older are usually comfortable with spelling and can take the inventory as a whole class. If one student appears upset trying to spell, you may assess that student at another time, individually, or use samples of the student's writing to determine an instructional level. With younger children you might ask them individually to spell words to you.

Copying can be a problem when you gather assessment information. Sometimes students copy because they are accustomed to helping each other with their writing or because they lack confidence in their own spelling. Students in the earlier stages of development enunciate the words orally or spell them aloud, which can give cues to those around them.

Seat students to minimize the risk of copying or give them cover sheets. Some teachers give students manila folders to set upright around their paper to create a personal work space. There will be many opportunities to collect corroborating information, so there is no reason to be upset if primary students copy. If it is clear that a student has copied, make a note to this effect after collecting the papers or administer the inventory individually at another time.

Call the Words Aloud

For younger children you may want to prepare papers in advance with one or two numbered columns. (Invariably, a few younger students write across the page from left to right.) Very young children will need an alphabet strip on their desks for reference in case they forget how to form a particular letter. Sentences are provided with the word lists in the Appendix. For most words, however, saying every word in a sentence is time consuming and may even be distracting. Say each word twice and use it in a sentence if the context will be helpful to the student in knowing what word is being called. For example, we use *cellar* in a sentence to differentiate it from *seller*. Pronounce the words naturally. Leave the task of elongating sounds and breaking words into syllables for the student.

BOX 2-2   *Spelling the Best We Can: A Lesson to Encourage Students to Spell*

If we want students to produce quality writing in the elementary grades, then they have to be comfortable attempting words they may not know how to spell. A hesitant writer who labors over spelling words will lose the reward of expressing new ideas. Students who are willing to risk being wrong by inventing their spelling have an easier time getting their ideas down.

To help students feel more comfortable writing, before the spelling assessments, conduct a few lessons either in small groups or with the whole class, using the theme, "How to spell the best we can." Lessons like the one to follow can be conducted over several days. Each aspect of the lesson should be repeated a few times.

Part I: A Discussion to Encourage Invented Spelling

"We're going to do a lot of writing this year. We will write nearly every day. Sometimes our writing will be drawings and pictures. We will also write stories and write about what we see and do. When we write, there are times when we do not know how to spell a word. This is part of learning: If we already knew how to spell all words, we wouldn't need to learn. When we want to write a word, and we don't know how to spell it, what might we do?"

Student responses usually include:

Ask the teacher.
Ask someone.
Look it up.
Skip it.

If no one suggests it you can tell your students, "Write down all the sounds you hear and feel when you say the word and then go on. We can work on the spelling together later, but for now, get your ideas down."

Part II: Spell a Few Words Together

"Who has a word they want to spell? What is a tough word you don't know how to spell?" Following a lesson on sea life, a student may offer, "Sea turtle."
"That's a great one. Can we keep to the second word, *turtle*?"

Assuming that they agree, ask students to say the word *turtle*.
"Turtle."
Begin then to examine the orthographic features: "What's the first letter at the beginning of *turtle*? Say the word again, and then tell me."
"Turtle. T."
Write down a *T.* Then ask a few students what the next sounds are that they "hear and feel."

After a few minutes, you may generate several spellings of turtle: TL, TRTL, TERDL, and TERTUL.

Finally, talk about what to do if the student can only figure out one or two sounds in a word. "Start with the sound at the beginning. Write the first letter and then draw a line." Here, you would write *T* with a line: T _____.

Occasionally, a student will be critical about another student's attempt: "That's not the right way to spell it!" You cannot allow someone being criticized for earnest effort. Be careful to handle this criticism firmly. You may say: "The important thing is that you have written your word down, and that you can reread what you have written." Then direct the group's attention back to the board: "On the board here, there are four spellings of *turtle*. We can read them all." Remind students that they are learning; there will be times when they do not know how to spell a word and it is okay to spell it the best they can. "We learn over the years, and you will see your writing improve the more you write. At the end of the year, you will be surprised by how much more you can write."

One lesson to discuss spelling will not suffice, so plan to conduct similar lessons over a 2-week period. Keep in mind the following three points:

- Model for students—show them how to stretch out the sounds and match sounds to letters.
- Conduct writing workshop lessons on what to do when an author does not know how to spell a word.
- Have students reread their writing to be sure that they can read what they have written.

Occasionally, after spelling an entire list, and if there is time, students are asked to circle the words they may not have spelled correctly, and to take a second try at spelling them. Through this reexamination, students show their willingness to reflect on their work. These notations and successive attempts are additional indicators of the depth of students' orthographic knowledge.

After collecting the papers, or while walking around the room, teachers should look for words they cannot read due to poor handwriting. Without making students feel that something is wrong, it is appropriate to ask them to read the letters in the words that cannot be deciphered. Students who write in cursive and whose writing is difficult to read can be asked to print. For some students, the meaning of the words is in question. Note when you observe this and then look at the spelling attempts.

Know When to Stop

Keep in mind that because you need a collection of spelling errors to establish a stage, some spellers may be asked to spell more words than other students and some may even need a different inventory (either easier or harder). As you walk around the room or work with a small group, scan students' papers after each set of five words to determine whether to continue.

We avoid overtesting, and yet, we want to see enough misspellings to assess students' orthographic knowledge. The assessment can stop as soon as you know the stage of each student. For example, you will know students are emergent spellers after they spell the first five words. Students working at a frustration level may "plug in" letters, a word, or a word ending (-ed) that they do know just to put something down on paper. The administration of the inventory can be spread over a few days; for those who need to continue, subsequent sets can be administered in groups on another day. The spelling sample in Figure 2-2 is the kind of raw data used to determine a spelling stage.

In the next section we walk through the steps of analyzing students' orthographic knowledge.

Jake		September 8	
1. bed		14. caryes	carries
2. ship		15. martched	marched
3. when		16. showers	shower
4. lump		17. botel	bottle
5. float		18. fayvor	favor
6. train		19. rippin	ripen
7. place		20. selar	cellar
8. drive		21. pleascher	pleasure
9. brite	bright	22. forchunate	fortunate
10. throte	throat	23. confdant	confident
11. spoyle	spoil	24. sivulise	civilize
12. serving		25. opozishun	opposition
13. chooed	chewed		

Middle to Late Within Word Pattern 9/25
Feature Score 35/53

FIGURE 2-2   Sample of Jake's Spelling Paper

HOW TO SCORE AND ANALYZE SPELLING INVENTORIES

Once you have administered the inventory, collect the papers and set aside time to score and analyze the results. In this section we explain the different options you have for this analysis and how you can create a classroom profile that helps you identify the range of development and possible grouping patterns in your classroom.

As you learn the types of spelling errors that are characteristic of each stage, you will be able to analyze students' development globally, as described in the next section. The feature and error guides in this chapter and in the Appendix help you to examine the features students know and to determine their instructional levels. Even with the help of these scoring guides, it is best to consult with a colleague about students' spelling and instructional groups. This dialogue will confirm each other's assessments. In many schools, literacy specialists meet with teachers in grade-level collegial meetings to review papers, discuss grouping, and explore activities by this grouping.

Global Analysis

A global analysis of students' orthographic knowledge will guide you quickly to instructional levels. Chapters 4 through 8 provide numerous activities for word study instruction. The key to a global analysis is to determine the student's stage, and then within the stage, to decide if the student is in the early, middle, or late part.

The two basic activities of global analysis are documentation and interpretation of students' spelling.

1. Documentation
   a. Date each paper and write the correct word beside each error as shown in Figure 2-2. This step allows time to look at each word. Scoring in this way makes it easier for other teachers and parents to review papers.
   b. Count the words spelled correctly. Record the number as a ratio of words spelled correctly to the total number of words spelled, for example, Jake spelled 9 out of 25 words for a ratio of 9/25.
2. Interpretation
   a. Determine each student's spelling level (see Figure 2-3).
   b. Look within the stage and decide if the student is in the early, middle, or late part of the stage. Jake's teacher noted that he is using but confusing long vowels and placed him in a group with students in the middle and late within word pattern stage.

The continuum in Figure 2-3 matches features with three gradations for each instructional level. A student who has learned to spell most of the features relevant to a stage is probably at the end of that stage (e.g., late letter name–alphabetic stage). Conversely, if a student is beginning to use the key elements of a stage, but still has some misspellings from the previous stage, the student is at an early point in that new stage (e.g., early letter name–alphabetic stage). For example, Jake spelled all of the short- and

SPELLING STAGES →	EMERGENT		LETTER NAME–ALPHABETIC		WITHIN WORD PATTERN			SYLLABLES & AFFIXES			DERIVATIONAL RELATIONS		
	LATE	EARLY	MIDDLE	LATE	EARLY	MIDDLE	LATE	EARLY	MIDDLE	LATE	EARLY	MIDDLE	LATE
Features →		Consonants Beginning Final	Short Vowels	Digraphs & Blends	Long-Vowel Patterns	Other Vowel Patterns	Complex Consonants	Syllable Junctures & Easy Prefixes & Suffixes	Harder Prefixes, Suffixes, & Unaccented Final Syllables		Reduced & Altered Vowels, Bases, Roots, & Derivatives		

FIGURE 2-3 Continuum of Features and Stages

many long-vowel features correctly, and it is clear by referring to the spelling stage row and the sequence of features in Figure 2-3 that Jake is at least in the middle of the within word pattern stage. Gradations within each stage make the assessment of orthographic knowledge more precise than simply an overall stage designation, which will be useful in designing a word study curriculum.

The stage and gradation within the stage may be recorded on the back of each spelling page to ensure independent ratings (e.g., the abbreviation LWWP stands for late within word pattern speller). We also record these ratings on the classroom composite chart (described later in the chapter).

When we work with colleagues we may not always agree on a student's stage. The gradations within each stage make it possible to resolve scoring differences between raters. For example, a teacher who may have noted that a student is in the late letter name–alphabetic stage is quite close to a teacher who has determined that the student is an early within word pattern stage speller.

You do not need to make the discrimination within stages too weighty a decision, because when it comes to planning instruction, many teachers take a step backwards to choose word study activities at a slightly easier level than the stage determination may indicate. It is important to take this step backwards, because students need to learn how to sort and the weekly word study activities and schedule clearly, it is easier to teach students how to sort when they can read the words easily. One of the fundamental principles of word study described in the next chapter is to take a step backwards when planning instruction, and so the determination of a stage for students is tempered by this practice.

Common Confusions in Scoring

Reversals present a small problem when scoring an inventory. Reversals should be noted, but in the qualitative analysis they should be seen as the letters they were meant to represent. For example, a static reversal such as the *b* written backwards in *bed* or the *p* written backwards in *ship*, should be counted as correct. These letter reversals occur with decreasing frequency through the letter name–alphabetic stage, but can be expected in young writers.

Confusions can also arise in counting letter correspondences when the letters are out of order. For example, beginning spellers sometimes spell the familiar consonant sounds and then tag on a vowel at the end (e.g., FNA for *fan*). This can be due to their extending the final consonant sound or to repeating each sound in the word *fan* and extracting the short *-a* after having already recorded the FN. Early beginning spellers

TABLE 2-2   Words Spelled Correctly/Total Feature Points + Words Spelled Correctly by Spelling Stages

Stages of Development→	Emergent			Letter Name–Alphabetic			
Inventories ↓	EARLY	MIDDLE	LATE	EARLY	MIDDLE	LATE	
Kindergarten 5/20	0/0	0/1	0/4	2/9	3/16	–	
Primary 26/82	0/0	0/2	0/6	2/16	3/26	7/36	
Elementary-1 25/78	0/0	0/3	0/3	0/7	2/13	3/18	
Intermediate 25/75	–	–	–	–	6/12	3/12	
Upper Level 40/120	–	–	–	–	1/5	2/12	
Spanish 25/77	0/0	0/3	0/5	2/11	5/21	9/32	

sometimes spell part of the word and then add random strings of letters to make it look longer (e.g., FNWZTY for *fan*). A rule of thumb is to give students credit when in doubt and to make a note of the strategy that a student might be using. Such errors offer interesting insights into their developing word knowledge.

Words Spelled Correctly and the Stages of Development

The correlations between the number of words spelled correctly and the scores from the feature and error guides are always quite high, as reflected in Table 2-2. In numerous studies from kindergarten through postsecondary levels, the total number of words spelled correctly is highly related to standardized reading and spelling measures, including the general analyses and feature score totals (Bear & Templeton, 2000; Invernizzi, 2002; Templeton, 2003). Table 2-2 outlines the relationship between the words spelled correctly on the inventories and the stages of spelling development. This table provides another way to check the accuracy of qualitative assessments.

Notice in Figure 2-2 that Jake's total score of nine words correct and a total feature score of 35 corresponds on the Elementary Spelling Inventory 1 to the scores between middle within word pattern (7/32) and late within word pattern (9/40).

Counting the number of words spelled correctly is an easy starting point, but there is more to analyzing students' spelling than marking words right or wrong. Qualitative information is also needed to determine a stage of spelling development or to plan word study activities. Therefore, teachers use the error and feature guides to help analyze students' orthographic knowledge.

Feature Guides

Perhaps the most popular and straightforward way to analyze students' spelling is to use a feature guide (Figure 2-4). Feature guides accompany each inventory included in the Appendix. The spelling features are presented in the second row of the feature guide and follow the developmental sequence observed in research. Every feature in every word is not scored, but the features sampled are key to knowing about the stages of spelling. As you check off what students spell correctly, there is a gradual increase in the number of spelling features misspelled or omitted. Check the features spelled correctly; add a point if the word is spelled correctly. At the bottom of each column, record the

Within Word Pattern			Syllables & Affixes			Derivational Relations		
EARLY	MIDDLE	LATE	EARLY	MIDDLE	LATE	EARLY	MIDDLE	LATE
-	-	-	-	-	-	-	-	-
8/49	11/61	17/76	23/94	-	-	-	-	-
	7/32	9/40	12/48	15/57	18/68	20/70	22/75	-
3/13	5/19	10/29	13/37	17/47	21/61	22/68	24/74	-
4/16	5/20	6/25	8/30	12/48	18/72	25/79	33/105	38/120
14/42	-	18/54	-	22/67	-	-	23/73	-

Directions: Check the features that are present in each student's spelling. In the bottom row, total features used correctly. Check the spelling stage that summarizes the student's development. Begin instruction at that stage with a focus on the types of features where the student missed two or more features in a column.

Student's Name __Jake Fisher__ Teacher __P. Atkinson__ Grade _____ Date _____

SPELLING STAGES →	LETTER NAME–ALPHABETIC Consonants Beginning (EMERGENT LATE)	LETTER NAME–ALPHABETIC Consonants Final (EARLY)	Short Vowels (MIDDLE / LATE)	Digraphs & Blends (LATE)	WITHIN WORD PATTERN Long-Vowel Patterns (EARLY MIDDLE LATE)	Other Vowel Patterns	SYLLABLES & AFFIXES Syllable Junctures & Easy Prefixes & Suffixes (EARLY MIDDLE LATE)	Harder Prefixes, Suffixes, & Unaccented Final Syllables (LATE)	DERIVATIONAL RELATIONS Reduced & Altered Vowels, Bases, Roots, & Derivatives (EARLY MIDDLE LATE)	Feature Points	Words Spelled Correctly
Late EMERGENT to LETTER NAME–ALPHABETIC											
1. bed	b ✓	d ✓	e ✓							3	1
2. ship		p ✓	i ✓	sh ✓						3	1
3. when		n ✓	e ✓	wh ✓						3	1
4. lump	l ✓		u ✓	mp ✓						3	1
WITHIN WORD PATTERN											
5. float				fl ✓	oa ✓					2	1
6. train		n ✓		tr ✓	ai ✓					3	1
7. place					a-e ✓					1	1
8. drive		v ✓		dr ✓	i-e ✓					3	1
9. bright					igh					0	0
10. throat					oa					0	0
11. spoil						oi				0	0
SYLLABLES & AFFIXES											
12. serving						er ✓	ing ✓			2	1
13. chewed				ch ✓		ew	ed ✓			2	0
14. carries							rr ies			0	0
15. marched				ch		ar ✓	ed ✓			2	0
16. shower						ow ✓	er ✓			2	0
17. bottle							tt	le		0	0
18. favor								or ✓		1	0
19. ripen							en			0	0
20. cellar							ll	ar ✓		1	0
Middle SYLLABLES & AFFIXES to Middle DERIVATIONAL RELATIONS											
21. pleasure								ure	pleas ✓	1	0
22. fortunate						or ✓		ate ✓	fortun	2	0
23. confident								ent	confid	0	0
24. civilize								ize	civil	0	0
25. opposition								op ✓	position	1	0
Totals →	2 (2)	5 (5)	4 (4)	7 (8)	4 (6)	4 (6)	4 (9)	4 (8)	1 (5)	35 (53)	9 (25)

SPELLING STAGES:

☐ EARLY ☐ MIDDLE ☑ LATE

☐ LETTER NAME–ALPHABETIC
☑ WITHIN WORD PATTERN
☐ SYLLABLES & AFFIXES
☐ DERIVATIONAL RELATIONS

Words Spelled Correctly: __9 / 25__
Feature Points: __35 / 53__
Total: __44 / 78__

FIGURE 2-4 Feature Guide for Elementary Spelling Inventory-1

44

number of features spelled correctly. Total the scores in each column and compare with the total possible number. A good rule of thumb is to begin instruction at the level where a student misses two or more features in a column.

Figure 2-4 shows how Jake, the student who wrote about his accident in Figure 2-1, scored on the feature guide for the Elementary Spelling Inventory-1. Following the last row across, note that Jake began to have difficulties with the long and complex vowels, and while he included other features in the next several columns, it will be best to begin word study instruction with long vowels. In actuality, a teacher may begin with basic contrasts between long- and short-vowel patterns and then move quickly to the study of long and complex vowel patterns. Referring back to Jake's writing in Figure 2-1, we see that he spelled most single-syllable words correctly, but spelled *cream* as CREM and *chin* as CHIAN. His experimentation with long-vowel patterns is what we would expect of a student in the within word pattern stage of spelling.

As you can see in the total scores in Table 2-2, there will be overlaps of features across columns. We can see this in Jake's misspelling when he spells a few long vowels and the correct spelling of several more advanced features. Most commonly, you will find that students who misspell a few long vowels may also misspell a few digraphs and blends. Likewise, some students miss just two features in both the long vowel and other vowel columns. Instructionally, there is good reason to explore both types of features in the word sorts.

Instructional levels can be determined by finding the stage that corresponds to the features. Refer to the bar across the top of the feature guide in Figure 2-4 and notice where Jake first begins to make more than one error on a feature under long vowels. He is clearly in the middle-to-late within word pattern stage, because he got four of the long-vowel features and four of the other vowel features in the words that fall under these designations. This can guide you to the appropriate chapter for teaching ideas. In Jake's case, we would refer to Chapter 6 for activities. Beyond the features, we also interpret what we learn about students' orthographic knowledge to think about their reading and the instructional practices to guide their learning to read, write, and spell.

Error Guides

Error guides contain samples of common spelling errors arranged along a developmental continuum, as shown in Figures 2-5 and 2-6. These can be found in the Appendix with corresponding inventories. For example, the growing sophistication in errors for *bright* can be seen from B, BT, BRT, BRIT, to BRITE. Score each word on the error guide by circling the error that is the same or write the student's spelling closest to the spelling error that is most similar. When a word is spelled correctly, circle the spelling at the end of the string of errors. After all words have been analyzed, determine where most circled words lie and look at the second row at the top of the table for the developmental spelling range for this student. Total the words spelled correctly and note the gradation within the stage the student is spelling.

The error guide in Figure 2-5 corroborates the other analyses that showed Jake to be a middle to late within word pattern stage speller. It is clear that Jake has learned to spell short and most long-vowel patterns. He used two vowels to mark the long and complex vowels as in the OY for the *oi* in *spoil*, the OO for the *ew* in *chewed* and the AY in *favor*. Jake has also learned to spell consonant digraphs and blends. The one consonant digraph that he did misspell was a final sound that is made more difficult by the /t/ sound for the -ed ending in *marched*. This will be a feature he will study later as his word study group examines two-syllable words later when they are in the syllables and affixes stage. For now, Ms. Atkinson will focus on studying long-vowel patterns of single-syllable words. Given Jake's strong knowledge of long-vowel patterns, he will be taught at a fast pace for the within word pattern word study in Chapter 6.

Directions: Check the features that are present in each student's spelling. In the bottom row, total features used correctly. Check the spelling stage that summarizes the student's development. Begin instruction at that stage with a focus on the types of features where the student missed two or more features in a column.

Student's Name *Jake Fisher* Teacher *P. Atkinson* Grade ______ Date ______

SPELLING STAGES→	EMERGENT: LATE	LETTER NAME–ALPHABETIC: EARLY, MIDDLE	LETTER NAME–ALPHABETIC: LATE; WITHIN WORD PATTERN: EARLY	WITHIN WORD PATTERN: MIDDLE	WITHIN WORD PATTERN: LATE; SYLLABLES & AFFIXES: EARLY	SYLLABLES & AFFIXES: MIDDLE	SYLLABLES & AFFIXES: LATE; DERIVATIONAL RELATIONS: EARLY	DERIVATIONAL RELATIONS: MIDDLE, LATE
Features→	Consonants Beginning Final	Short Vowels	Consonant Digraphs & Blends	Long-Vowel Patterns	Other Vowel Patterns	Syllable Junctures & Easy Prefixes & Suffixes	Harder Prefixes & Suffixes, & Unaccented Final Syllables	Reduced & Altered Vowels, Bases, Roots, & Derivatives

Word	Spellings
Late EMERGENT to LETTER NAME–ALPHABETIC	
1. bed	b bd bad bed
2. ship	s sp shp sep shep ship
3. when	w yn wn wan whan when
4. lump	l lp lmp lop lomp lump
WITHIN WORD PATTERN	
5. float	f ft vt flt fot flot flott flowt floaut flote float
6. train	j t trn jran chran tan tran teran traen trane train
7. place	p ps pls pas pas palac plas plac pase plais plase place
8. drive	d j jrv drf drv griv jriv driv jrive drieve draive drive
9. bright	b bt brt bit brit bite brite briete bright
10. throat	trot throt throte throate throat
11. spoil	spol sole sool spoyle spole spoal spoil
SYLLABLES & AFFIXES	
12. serving	sefng srvng srbving sering serfing surving serveing serving
13. chewed	cud chud cooed chood cuwed chüed chewd choud chewed
14. carries	keres cares carres carise carys cairries carrys carries
15. marched	much march marchet marchd marchted marched
16. shower	shewr showr shour shawer shoer shuor shouer showers
17. bottle	badl badol bắtel batle bottel bottle
18. favor	favr faver favir fayvor favor
19. ripen	ribn ripn ripun ripan ripon rippin ripen
20. cellar	salr selr celr salar selar seller sellar cellar cellar

SPELLING STAGES:

- ☐ EARLY ☑ MIDDLE ☑ LATE
- ☐ LETTER NAME–ALPHABETIC
- ☑ WITHIN WORD PATTERN
- ☐ SYLLABLES & AFFIXES
- ☐ DERIVATIONAL RELATIONS

Words Spelled Correctly: 9/20

FIGURE 2-5 Error Guide for Elementary Spelling Inventory-1

Directions: Check the features that are present in each student's spelling. In the bottom row, total features used correctly. Check the spelling stage that summarizes the student's development. Begin instruction at that stage with a focus on the types of features where the student missed two or more features in a column.

Student's Name: _Marshall_   Teacher _S. Gardner_   Grade _Sr._   Date _9/22_

SPELLING STAGES →	LETTER NAME–ALPHABETIC	WITHIN WORD PATTERN			SYLLABLES & AFFIXES			DERIVATIONAL RELATIONS		
	LATE	EARLY	MIDDLE	LATE	EARLY	MIDDLE	LATE	EARLY	MIDDLE	LATE
Features	Short Vowels	Consonant Digraphs & Blends	Long & Other Vowel Patterns	Complex Consonants	Syllable Junctures & Easy Prefixes & Suffixes	Harder Prefixes, Suffixes, & Unaccented Final Syllables		Reduced & Altered Vowels	Bases, Roots & Derivatives	Words Spelled Correctly

Late SYLLABLES & AFFIXES through EARLY DERIVATIONAL RELATIONS

16. resident — resatint reserdent reseadent resudint res(e)(d)ent residant **resident**
17. puncture — pucshr pungchr puncur puncker punksher punchure puncure punture puncsure (puncture)
18. confidence — confadents confidence confadence confidence confidince (confidence)
19. confusion — confushon confution confusion confussion (confusion)
20. fortunate — forhnat frehnit foohinit forchenut fochininte (fortunint) **fortunate**

Late SYLLABLES & AFFIXES & DERIVATIONAL RELATIONS

21. dominance — domanese domannce domenense (domeneance) dominince dominense **dominance**
22. prosperity — proparty proparity property prospearaty (prosparity) prosperaty prosperity **prosperity**
23. decorator — dector decrater decorator decarator decratore decorator (decorator)
24. opposition — opasion opasishan opozcison opasitian oppisition oppsision oposision oposition (opposition)
25. visible — visbel visabul visble visabal visible visabel visibal **(visible)**
26. correspond — corspond corispond (corespond) corrospond **correspond**
27. voluminous — vlumnus vulomus valomus voluminus voluminenis voluminus (vulominus) **voluminous**
28. succession — sucksession sucsession sucesion succession succession **succession**
29. emphasize — infaside infacize (ephacise) emphacise emfasize imfasize emphasize **emphasize**
30. category — cadagoure catagery cadigore catagore category catiguorie catigory catagory catagory **(category)**

DERIVATIONAL RELATIONS

31. hilarious — halaris halaryous halaries heleriaus halareous (halarius) hilerious hilarous **hilarious**
32. commotion — comoushown comoshion comosion camotion (cumotion) comocion comossion comotion **commotion**
33. inheritable — inharbul enherable inharitable (inhairetable) inharetable inhairtible inharitible **inharitable**
34. criticize — critise crisize critize critasise critasize critisise critisize criticise (criticize) critisize **criticize**
35. excerpt — exherpt exhert exherpt exsort exerp ecsert exserp exsort exsurpt exsrupt (excerpt)
36. reversible — reversbell reversabul reversobol reversabel (reverseable) reversabile reverscible reverisble reversabile reversible **reversible**
37. chlorophyll — clorafil cloarphil cloraful clorifil chlorafil (chlorafil) chloraphyl chlorophyl chloraphyll **chlorophyll**
38. adjourn — (ajurn) agern ajourn ajorne ajurne adgurn adjourn adjurn adjourne **adjourn**
39. camouflage — camaflag camaflosh comoflodge camapholauge camapholage (camophloage) camoflauge camofloge camaflauge camaflauge **camouflage**
40. indictment — enditmeant enditment inditmeant (inditement)endightment indighment indictment indictment **indictment**

SPELLING STAGES:

☐ EARLY ☐ MIDDLE ☑ LATE

☐ LETTER NAME–ALPHABETIC
☐ WITHIN WORD PATTERN
☑ SYLLABLES & AFFIXES
☐ DERIVATIONAL RELATIONS

Words Spelled Correctly: _20/40_

FIGURE 2-6 Error Guide for Upper Level Spelling Inventory

47

As an example of an upper level error guide, Figure 2-6 shows that Marshall is assessed to be in the later part of the syllables and affixes stage. His teacher has written in several of his spellings near a similar spelling (as in *fortunent*). Although Marshall's spelling errors cover the range of the last two spelling stages, a cluster of errors begins in the late part of the syllables and affixes stage. He has learned many of the more difficult affixes, and is learning when some words are spelled with double consonants. He spelled *opposition* correctly and omitted the double consonants when he spelled SUCESSION for *succession* and CORESPOND for *correspond*. The FORTUNET error that was not listed on this page was written beside the closest invented spelling. Activities in the later part of Chapter 7 would be in focus in this student's word study program.

WORD STUDY GROUPS

Your spelling analysis as discussed in the previous section will pinpoint students' instructional levels and the features that are ripe for instruction. After analyzing students individually, you can create a classroom profile by recording the individual assessments on a single chart. We present two ways to record information about the class: the **classroom composite** for the feature guides and the **spelling-by-stage classroom organization chart** to group students by instructional levels. These charts show you the instructional groups at a glance. Before we discuss them, however, let us consider the importance of grouping for instruction in word study.

Why Group?

Many teachers organize three and sometimes four small groups by instructional level for reading. Word study can be incorporated in these small group reading lessons, especially in the lower grades where students work with words under the teacher's supervision and then complete other activities at their desks or centers. In other classes, especially in the upper grades, word study occurs at a separate time of the day, but two to four groups are needed to meet students' needs. Word study instruction with the teacher is a special time for sorting words and discussion at a table or on the floor. The fundamental question of how to manage groups is explored in Chapter 3.

Recent trends in literacy instruction have discouraged some teachers from grouping for instruction. Indeed, there are many reasons to be suspicious of homogeneous or ability grouping, because often the lower ability groups receive inferior instruction (Stanovich, 1986), but clearly students benefit from developmentally appropriate instruction. Experience has shown that when students study a particular orthographic feature, it is best if they are in groups with students who are ready to benefit from the same word study. For example, it is difficult to study long-vowel patterns when some of the students in the group are in the middle of the letter name–alphabetic stage and still working on easy digraphs or blends and may not even be able to read the words.

Groups should be fluid, and if a student is challenged to frustration, or if a student is not challenged by the activities, then groups should be reorganized. There are many literacy activities in which students are not grouped by developmental level, as in partner reading, writing workshops, science, social studies, and the many small group projects related to units of study.

Classroom Composite Chart

After administering an inventory and completing a feature analysis form for each student, you can transfer the individual scores to a classroom composite chart (Figure 2-7) to get a sense of the group as a whole. Before you begin, sort student papers by the total

Directions: Record students' scores beginning with the student with the highest total feature points. Identify students who missed 2 or more of any of the features in a category. In the bottom row, total the number of students in each category who missed 2 or more features.

Teacher _Freedman_   School _Kridel Elementary_   Grade _5_   Date _September_

SPELLING STAGES →		EMERGENT LATE	LETTER NAME–ALPHABETIC EARLY	MIDDLE	LATE	WITHIN WORD PATTERN MIDDLE	LATE	SYLLABLES & AFFIXES EARLY	DERIVATIONAL RELATIONS LATE	MIDDLE
↓ Students' Names	Total Feature Points and Words	Consonants Beginning Final	Consonants Beginning Final	Short Vowels	Digraphs & Blends	Long-Vowel Patterns	Other Vowel Patterns	Syllable Junctures & Easy Prefixes & Suffixes	Harder Prefixes & Suffixes, & Unaccented Final Syllables	Reduced & Altered Vowels, Bases, Roots, & Derivatives
Possible points →	78	2	5	4	8	6	6	9	8	5
1. Stephanie Lovel	75	2	5	4	8	6	6	9	7	4
2. Andi Warren	70	2	5	3	8	6	6	8	6	5
3. Henry Washington	69	2	5	4	8	6	6	8	7	3
4. Molly Maltis	65	2	5	4	8	6	6	7	6	2
5. Jasmine Rogers	63	2	5	4	8	6	6	7	6	2
6. Maria Hernandez	62	2	5	4	8	6	6	6	5	2
7. Mike Melton	61	2	5	4	7	6	6	6	6	2
8. Lee Stephens	57	2	5	4	8	6	6	6	5	2
9. Beth Hall	56	2	5	4	8	6	5	5	5	3
10. Gabriel Sargent	56	2	5	4	8	6	6	5	4	2
11. Yamal Mitiv	55	2	5	4	8	6	5	6	4	2
12. John Mortensen	47	2	5	4	8	5	4	5	5	2
13. Elizabeth Stanton	46	2	5	4	8	5	5	4	4	1
14. Maria Herrera	45	2	5	4	7	4	5	5	5	1
15. Patty Lerker	44	2	5	4	8	5	6	4	4	0
16. Sarah Hamilton	42	2	5	4	7	6	4	4	3	0
17. Jared Wards	40	2	5	3	7	5	4	5	2	0
18. William Letis	39	2	5	4	8	5	2	3	3	0
19. Steve Willmes	38	2	5	3	7	4	4	4	2	0
20. Anna Lecheg	38	2	5	4	7	3	4	4	2	0
21. Nicole Wooster	35	1	4	4	7	2	3	3	2	2
22. Robert Herbert	32	1	4	3	7	3	3	3	2	0
23. Celia Chambers	32	2	5	3	6	2	3	4	1	0
24. Jim Shaw	32	2	5	4	7	3	2	2	1	0
25. Nicole Roberts	32	2	5	3	7	2	3	3	0	0
26. Mike Stevens	16	2	4	2	5	0	0	1	0	0
Number who missed two or more features ≥ 2 →				1	2	2	12	23	24	24

FIGURE 2-7 Example of Classroom Composite for Elementary Spelling Inventory-1 Feature Guide

number correct and record students' names from top to bottom on the composite form on the basis of this rank order. Then record the total number of words a student has spelled correctly under each feature. Once all the feature scores have been entered, highlight cells in which the students are making two or more errors on a particular feature. For example, a student who spells all but one of the short vowels correctly has a good understanding of short vowels and is considered to be at an independent level; however, students who spell correctly two or three of the short vowels need more work on that feature. Highlighted cells indicate a need for sustained instruction on a feature. Note, however, that if students are new to word study activities, then the independent level would be a good place to start instruction.

If you rank order your students before completing the composite chart, it is easy to see clusters of highlighted cells which can be used to assign students to developmental stages and word study groups. For example, the fifth-grade class composite in Figure 2-7 shows that most of the students are in the syllables and affixes stage of development. A smaller group of students fall in the middle-to-late within word pattern stage; thus, begin word study by looking at single-syllable word patterns for long vowels and less frequent short-vowel patterns. One student (Mike) needs individualized help, so begins with short-vowel as well as digraphs and blends.

Spelling-by-Stage Classroom Organization Chart

When you know students' spelling development, you can form groups using the spelling-by-stage classroom organization chart (Figure 2-8). Students' names are recorded underneath a gradation within a spelling stage on the classroom organization chart found on page 327 in the Appendix. Once the names are entered, begin to look for groups. In the examples in Figure 2-8, three or four groups have been circled.

You can see different ways to organize word study instruction in the three classroom profiles presented in Figure 2-8. The first profile is of a first-grade class with many emergent spellers. The four groups suggested for this class are also the teacher's reading groups.

In the third-grade and sixth-grade examples, teachers have drawn circles to create groups across spelling stages. You can see where teachers have reconsidered the group placement of a few students. The students may have scored slightly higher or lower than anticipated based on other observations of their writing or spelling. We use arrows to indicate students who we want to consider placing slightly higher or lower as the groups take shape. Some of the group placement decisions are based on social and psychological factors related to self-esteem, leadership, and behavior dynamics.

The teacher in the sixth-grade classroom could consider running two groups at the upper levels, and at times, combine them as one group. The three students in the letter name–alphabetic stage will need special attention because they are significantly behind for sixth graders. Ideally, these students will have additional instruction in a tutoring program to review and practice activities that are appropriate for the letter name–alphabetic spelling stage.

Organize Groups

The classroom composite chart and the spelling-by-stage classroom organization chart help to determine word study groups for instruction. Some groups are quite similar in development, and it is fine to conduct the same activity with two groups. Smaller groups of 8 to 10 students make it easier for students to listen to each other, and for you to observe how they sort. In many classrooms, there are also students at each end of the developmental continuum who, in terms of word study and orthographic development, are outliers. It can be helpful to include these students in the closest developmental group, and work with them on separate activities but within the group. For example, when the group is sorting, the teacher may ask these students to work with a different pack of words, or to

Directions: Write students' names underneath the gradation within the stage the students have scored. Use an arrow to the left (←) or right (→) to indicate students who could go up or down a gradation. Draw a circle around students' names to form word study groups. In most classrooms we try to form three groups.

First-Grade Spelling-by-Stage Classroom Organization Chart

SPELLING STAGES →	EMERGENT			LETTER NAME—ALPHABETIC			WITHIN WORD PATTERN			SYLLABLES & AFFIXES			DERIVATIONAL RELATIONS		
	EARLY	MIDDLE	LATE	EARLY	MIDDLE	LATE	EARLY	MIDDLE	LATE	EARLY	MIDDLE	LATE	EARLY	MIDDLE	LATE

Emergent Middle: Buck, Felicia 7, Brad
Emergent Late: Tammy, Kristy, Brandon, J.J.
Letter Name Early: Milo, Jennifer
Letter Name Middle: Brendon, Jennifer, Matthew, Jerrilynn 5
Dong, Danielle, Jon 5, Jennifer, Luis, Jona 6, Adam, Carisha, Reyba, Gerald, Shaun

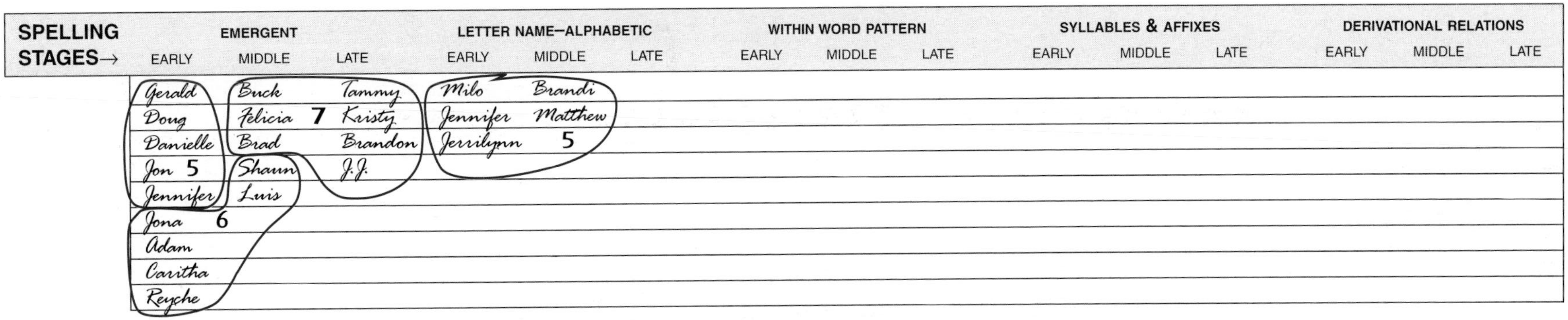

Third-Grade Spelling-by-Stage Classroom Chart

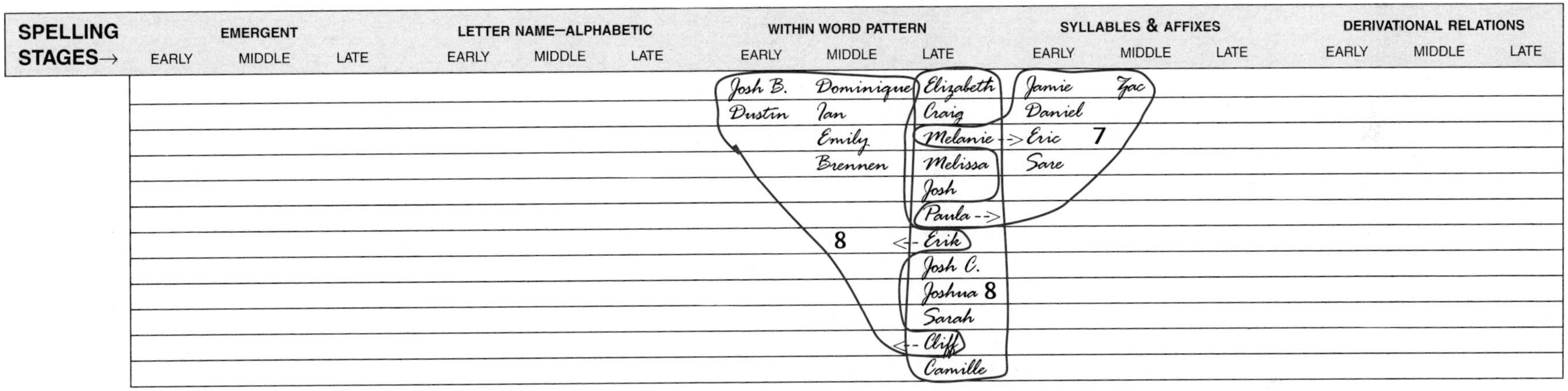

SPELLING STAGES →	EMERGENT			LETTER NAME—ALPHABETIC			WITHIN WORD PATTERN			SYLLABLES & AFFIXES			DERIVATIONAL RELATIONS		
	EARLY	MIDDLE	LATE	EARLY	MIDDLE	LATE	EARLY	MIDDLE	LATE	EARLY	MIDDLE	LATE	EARLY	MIDDLE	LATE

Within Word Early: Josh B., Dustin, Dominique, Ian, Emily, Brennen
Within Word Middle: Elizabeth, Craig, Melanie →Eric, Melissa, Josh, Paula →, ←Erik, Josh C., Joshua 8, Serah, ←Cliff, Camille
Syllables & Affixes Early: Jamie, Daniel, →Eric, Sara, Joe 7
8

Sixth-Grade Spelling-by-Stage Classroom Organization Chart

SPELLING STAGES →	EMERGENT			LETTER NAME—ALPHABETIC			WITHIN WORD PATTERN			SYLLABLES & AFFIXES			DERIVATIONAL RELATIONS		
	EARLY	MIDDLE	LATE	EARLY	MIDDLE	LATE	EARLY	MIDDLE	LATE	EARLY	MIDDLE	LATE	EARLY	MIDDLE	LATE

Letter Name Middle: Victoria, Juan 3, Mike
Within Word Late: Jon, Elizabeth →Nicole
Syllables & Affixes Early: ←Arcelia, 9
Syllables & Affixes Middle: Phong, Ray, Scott, Don
Syllables & Affixes Late: Sean, Maro, Christa, Jonna 6, Heather, Esther, ←Rashid
Derivational Early: Steve, Sheri, Eric, Mary 5
Derivational: Desiree, 11

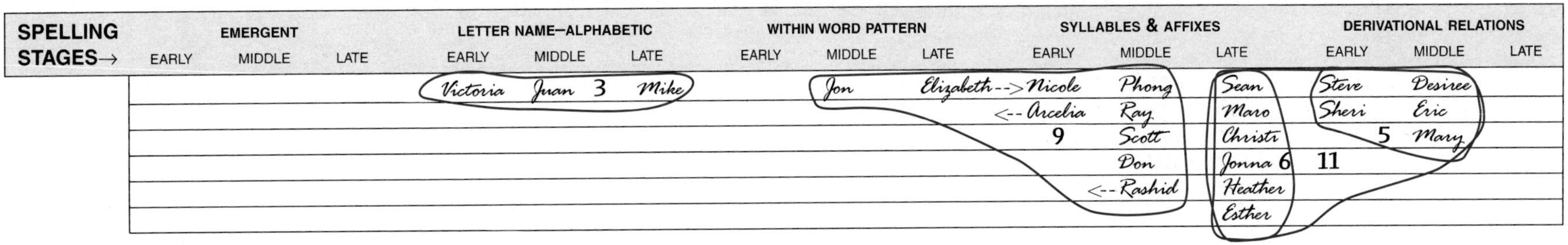

FIGURE 2-8 Examples of Spelling-by-Stage Classroom Organization Charts

work with a partner. In addition, the teacher should look for other ways to allow these students more practice through individual tutoring and work with a literacy specialist.

In addition to the homogeneous groups that work with the teacher in circle or small group sessions, and the word-sorting partners in word study centers, at times students will work together in word study workshops or whole-class word study sessions. While students work on different feature sorts and with different words, they can still work side by side during word study sessions. This is a good time for teachers to observe students sorting, and for students to show each other how they sort. Different schemes for managing class, group, and individual sorts are discussed in Chapter 3.

MORE INFORMATION ABOUT INVENTORIES

The basic steps for selecting, administering, and analyzing students' spelling have been discussed in the previous sections. This chapter and the Appendix pages 296–327 include a variety of spelling inventories from which to choose. It would be useful to know something more about each of these inventories so that you can choose the one that will work best for you.

Qualitative Spelling Checklist

When we look at students' writing in their journals or at the first drafts of their reports and stories, we use the Qualitative Spelling Checklist (see Appendix) to verify what types of orthographic features students have mastered and what types of features they misspell. This checklist on page 296 walks you through the types of spelling errors students make and matches these errors to stages of spelling. Through a series of 20 questions, you check off the student's progress through the stages. Consider what features are used consistently, often, or not at all. The examples of misspellings drawn from the Elementary Spelling Inventory Error Guide are a point of reference when the checklist is used to assess a sample from student writing. We compare the spelling of the inventories with the spelling in students' writing to see if they perform at similar levels.

Emergent Class Record

The Emergent Class Record (see Appendix page 297) is used to assess daily writing or the spelling of Pre-K or kindergartners (or other emergent spellers) on a primary or elementary spelling inventory. The Class Record presents the progression from emergent through letter name–alphabetic spelling. A space is provided on this record sheet for a whole class, and the detailed checklist for emergent spelling captures the prephonetic writing progression (from random marks to letters) that is missing on other qualitative guides.

Kindergarten Spelling Inventory

The Kindergarten Spelling Inventory has been used widely and is part of Virginia's Phonological Assessment and Literacy Screening (PALS) (Invernizzi & Meier, 2002). This statewide screening test is used throughout Virginia as part of its early intervention reading initiative. This inventory has been studied intensively with very large numbers of children. Five (three-phoneme) words have been carefully chosen after extensive research. Each of the five words is scored for the number of phonemes represented in the students' spelling. You will want to take a closer look at any kindergartners who after 6 weeks of school score below the benchmark score. This spelling task has consistently been a reliable discriminator of children in need of additional instruction in phonological awareness and early literacy skills in both kindergarten and first grade, and has proven to be a powerful predictor of success on the state literacy test at the end of third grade (Invernizzi & Meier, 2002).

 To find out more about Virginia's Phonological Assessment and Literacy Screening, link to its website from the Weblinks on our Companion Website at www.prenhall.com/bear

Primary Spelling Inventory

The Primary Spelling Inventory (see Appendix page 300) is recommended for kindergarten through third grade, because it assesses features found from the emergent stage to the syllables and affixes stage. This inventory has been popular, and used widely along with the accompanying feature guide.

For kindergarten or early first grade you may only need to call out the first five words. In a first-grade classroom, call out 15 words; and use the entire list of 25 words for second and third grades. If any students spell more than 20 words correctly, you may want to use the Elementary Spelling Inventory. Feature and error guides are available for this inventory, and the classroom composite chart on page 327 can be used for a classroom profile.

Elementary Spelling Inventory-1

The Elementary Spelling Inventory presented in the Appendix on page 304 taps a wide range of features throughout the elementary grades (K through 6). The inventory is divided into groups of five words, and you can consider discontinuing the spelling when students miss three or more of the words. Variations of this inventory have been used in a number of studies to show the relationship between spelling and reading levels. There is a strong relationship between the words spelled correctly, as well as the stage analysis, and standardized reading test scores.

Kindergartners can take the first five words of inventory, and by October, every first grader can attempt the first 10 words. By second grade, nearly all students can try to spell all 25 words. The same inventory can be used several times during the year as long as these words are not taught directly or assigned in spelling tests (Bear, Templeton, & Warner, 1991).

Intermediate Spelling Inventory

The Intermediate Spelling assesses features found from the late letter name–alphabetic to early derivational relations stage. The words are grouped by stage and most are rank ordered from easy to most difficult to spell. For example, the first word, *speck*, was spelled correctly by 86% of a large group of fourth graders; and the twentieth word, *sailor*, was spelled correctly by 30% of the students.

Upper Level Spelling Inventory

The Upper Level Spelling Inventory is used in upper elementary, middle, and high school, through postsecondary classrooms. The words in this list were chosen because they help identify, more specifically than the elementary inventory, what students in the syllables and affixes and derivational relations stages are doing in their spelling. These words are arranged in order of difficulty, and the directions presented with the inventory suggest that the teacher stop giving the inventory to students who have missed five of the first seven words—the words that assess for spelling in the letter name–alphabetic and the within word pattern stages. On a subsequent day, the teacher can pick up with the test in small groups. For the students who missed many of the first seven words, the teacher should move back to the elementary list.

Students' spelling on this upper level list shows how they make "the meaning connection" with the orthography (Templeton, 1983). Students in the derivational relations stage learn to preserve meaning in spite of changes in sound. For example, in pronunciation, the second vowel in *reside* changes from a long -*i* to a schwa sound in *resident*. In spite of this sound change, the spelling remains the same and is a cue to meaning.

The Upper Level Spelling Inventory has been used in studies to relate spelling development and reading development throughout the secondary grades (Bear, Templeton, & Warner, 1991). Students' feature scores relate to their standardized reading comprehension and spelling scores. This list has also been used to assess the orthographic knowledge of students at the university level who experience reading difficulties and to assess students' ability to read well enough to perform in general equivalency diploma (GED) programs.

The McGuffey Spelling Inventory

The McGuffey Qualitative Inventory of Word Knowledge (Schlagal, 1992) is useful for conducting individual testing and for obtaining grade-level information. The inventory spans grades 1 through 8 with from 20 to 30 list words in each level. Instructional spelling levels are found when a student scores above 50% on a graded list (Morris, Blanton, Blanton, & Perney, 1995; Morris, Nelson, & Perney, 1986). You may need to administer more than one list to determine a level. The McGuffey Inventory is especially useful when teachers want to use a longer and more detailed spelling list and when they want to report spelling achievement in terms of grade levels. The words in these lists present plenty of opportunities to observe a student's spelling across a variety of features. For example, a teacher may want to obtain a fuller assessment of prefixes, suffixes, and roots. Levels 5 and 6 would offer a large number of words to analyze. You can find the McGuffey Inventory on page 317 in the Appendix, along with more detailed information about using it.

Since a qualitative analysis guide has not been developed for the McGuffey Inventory, you must analyze errors yourself to determine what features and patterns students know and what they are using but confusing. You can refer to the sequence of development described at the end of Chapter 1 to see where the students are developmentally and the kinds of features to note. For example, students who show a high level of correctness in spelling the single-syllable words on the third-grade list may begin to show the edge of their learning in spelling the many two-syllable words on the fourth-grade list. Speaking developmentally, students in the syllables and affixes stage will make spelling errors that demonstrate their experimentation with how syllables combine (e.g., spelling *fossil* as FOSEL, and *striped* as STRIPPED). Use Figure 1-3 to correlate the instructional levels related to grade levels, as indicated by this inventory, to developmental spelling stages.

 ## Spanish Spelling Inventory

 To find more resources for using *Words Their Way* with students whose home language is Spanish, visit our Companion Website at www.prenhall.com/bear

Many students in the United States speak Spanish and may read in Spanish. Teachers want to know about students' spelling in Spanish to determine what level of literacy and level of orthographic knowledge they bring to learning to read and write in English. The Spanish Spelling Inventory and accompanying scoring guides were developed by Lori Helman, a leader in English language learning who brings considerable experience as a bilingual teacher. This 25-word inventory covers the range of instructional levels that we have observed in Spanish.

SPELLING AMONG STUDENTS WHO SPEAK OTHER LANGUAGES

To obtain a complete understanding of the word knowledge of students who are English Language Learners, we study what students know about literacy in their first language. A spelling inventory in students' spoken language can indicate what their literacy levels might be and, specifically, show what orthographic features they already understand.

Comparing students' spelling on an inventory in their first language with their spelling in English, the second language, will show the possible confusions students experience. In addition to the Spanish Spelling Inventory, other newly created spelling inventories in numerous languages take similar developmental approaches (Bear, Templeton, Helman, & Baren, 2003). Most comparisons are made across the sound systems, but others are made of the pattern and meaning layers of our students' languages and literacies. A number of these interactions are examined in the appropriate instructional chapters as we suggest ideas for instruction.

 For specific instructional tools for students who speak Spanish, or students learning Spanish, visit the Spanish Word Study section of the accompanying CD-ROM.

The Influence of Spanish on Spelling in English

Spanish is the first language of many students, and the considerations for Spanish that we discuss here are adaptable to other first languages that students may speak. For students who speak Spanish, it is useful to study how their pronunciation and knowledge of Spanish are used when they spell in English; we discuss this in more detail in Chapters 5 and 6. A variety of substitutions can be traced to the influence of Spanish on the students' spelling. Consider why a student who speaks Spanish would spell *th* as DA. There is no *th* in the Spanish language, so students who are more familiar with Spanish may spell *the* as DA. The same is true for the *sh* consonant digraph, and so the word *ship* may be spelled CHAP, because CH and A are as close as Spanish can offer to the *sh* and the short *-i* sound.

The silent *h* in Spanish can be spelled with a *J*, and so *hit* may be spelled JET. The contrasts in vowels are presented in Figures 2-9 and 2-10. Short *-i* is a bit confusing for Spanish-speaking students, and the short *-i* may be spelled with an *e*. The correspondence between the English short *-o* sound, as in *pop*, is represented with an *a*, which seems close to the strong *a* vowel in Spanish; *hot* could be spelled JAT.

The impact of a student's knowledge of spoken Spanish on English spelling can be seen in this spelling sample from Rosa, a second grader.

The WTW 3rd edition CD has a similar outline of development and instruction in Spanish. These activities are used in transition activities, and as a word study program to teach Spanish in foreign language instruction.

a	as in	man
e		pen
i		tip
u		cup
ou		could

FIGURE 2-10 English Vowel Sounds not Present in Spanish

English letter and word			Comparable Spanish letter and word (pronunciation / translation)					
a	as in	cake	e	as in	hecho	(āchō	/	make)
e		bean	i		ido	(ēdō	/	gone)
i		like	ai		aire	(ī ēr ĕ	/	air)
o		hope	o		ocho	(ōchō	/	eight)
o		top	a		ajo	(ăhō	/	garlic)
u		June	u		usted	(oostĕd	/	you)
oy		toy	oy		voy	(voi	/	I go)

FIGURE 2-9 Vowel Sounds in English and Comparable Sounds in Spanish

1. bed	BED	11. spoil	SPOYO
2. ship	SHEP	12. serving	SORVEN
3. when	WAN	13. chewed	SHOD
4. lump	LAMP	14. carries	CARES
5. float	FLOWT	15. marched	MARSH
6. train	TRAYN	16. shower	SHOWAR
7. place	PLEAYS	17. cattle	CADOTO
8. drive	TRAYV	18. favor	FAYVR
9. bright	BRAYT	19. ripen	RAYPN
10. shopping	SHAPEN	20. cellar	SALLAR

Several of Rosa's spellings follow the logical substitutions that are seen in English-speaking students in the letter name–alphabetic stage, that is, SHEP for *ship* and WAN for *when*. Many of Rosa's spelling errors make a good deal of sense in relation to her knowledge of Spanish. For example, given that there is no short -*u* in Spanish, her substitution of LAMP for *lump* makes sense given the way *a* is pronounced in Spanish, as in the /a/ in *father* and *gracias*. The AY in three of her spellings shows that Rosa is trying to find a spelling for the long -*i*. The long -*i* is really two vowels (a diphthong), and the Y, pronounced as a long -*e* in Spanish, is used to spell the second half of the long -*i*. In *spoil* as SPOYO, Rosa seems to be using the /y/ sound as in *yes* to help spell /oil/. We find the substitution of SH for the *ch* in *chewed* as further evidence that Rosa is learning English spelling. Because there is no /sh/ sound, it is very common for students to spell *shoes* as CHOES; the *ch* is close to the /sh/ in pronunciation. In this misspelling, Rosa may have overgeneralized what she knew about *sh* in English.

Word Study Teachers as Dialecticians

As Rosa's spelling illustrates, students' invented spellings in other languages are not wrong, but are logical and interestingly correct. You will find it easy to spot spelling errors that are derived from your students' first language or dialect. One teacher explored the oral language of her students from Russia and the influence it had on their spelling. Another teacher observed the influence of different Indian dialects, with confusions of /p/ sounds for words that began with an *f*, and students who substituted /sh/ sounds for words with *s*.

Through observing students' other languages, teachers understand their literacy development in English. Look in each of the instructional chapters for specific guidance on the interrelatedness of students' home languages and literacies and the English language and literacy skills they are learning in the classroom. For example, Chapter 4 includes a discussion of English Language Learning and concept sorts, and Chapter 6 discusses the way students' dialects are observed in their spelling.

SAMPLE PRACTICE

The spelling sample in Box 2-3 can be used to compare assessments of spelling development. With a pack of class papers and the feature and error guides, teachers can see the differences in development among students. The order that the chapters are presented in this book follows this developmental scheme. Until you get to be experienced in the use of these guides, it can be extremely helpful to review each other's assessments collaboratively.

BOX 2-3 *Assessment Check*

If you do not have a classroom of children, or if you want to see a broad spectrum of responses, review the spelling of the following five students.

Our spelling analyses are below the samples. Were you close to our assessments? Was there an agreement of stages? If you are off on more than one or two students, try again. One mental anchor is that within word pattern students have mastered simple short-vowel patterns, and they experiment with different long-vowel spellings. If you scored the spelling in terms of three gradations within a stage, you may find that though your assessment may differ by a stage name, it is possible that we differ by just one gradation. Chapters 4 through 8 include other spelling samples to consider.

Examples of Students' Spelling in September

	Greg	*Jean*	*Reba*	*Alan*	*Mitch*
Grade	1	1	2	3	3
bed	BD	bed	bed	bed	bed
ship	SP	SEP	ship	ship	ship
when	WN	WHAN	when	when	when
lump	L	LOP	lump	lump	lump
float	F	FLOT	FLOTE	FLOTE	float
train		TRAN	TRANE	train	train
place		PLAC	PLAIS	place	place
drive		DRIV	drive	drive	drive
bright		BRIT	BRITE	BRIGT	bright
shopping		SOPNG	SHOPEN	SHOPING	shopping
spoil			SPOAL	SPOALE	spoil
serving			serving	SERVEING	serving
chewed			CHUD	CHOUED	chewed
carries			CARES	CARRES	carries
marched			MARCD	marched	marched
shower				SHOUER	shower
cattle				CATTEL	cattle
favor				FAVIR	favor
ripen				ripen	ripen
cellar				SELLER	CELLER

Spelling-by-Stage Assessment
Greg—early letter name–alphabetic
Jean—middle letter name–alphabetic
Reba—middle within word pattern
Alan—late within word pattern
Mitch—At least in the middle of the syllables and affixes stage. Another five words would be helpful.

Spelling inventories guide teachers in determining students' developmental level.

The study of students' spelling is a powerful assessment of word recognition among all learners (McBride-Chang, 1999), and spelling is among the best predictors of word analysis and word synthesis (Torgesen & Davis, 1996). You may refer to the developmental sequence inside the front and back covers, as well as the detailed sequences of word study in Chapters 4 through 8, for the specific types of features to explore in word study activities for reading and spelling. Remember that the inventories only sample the most common features. At each stage there is a considerable body of knowledge that students should master before they move on to the next stage.

Organizing for Word Study: Principles and Practices

3

O nce you have ascertained the developmental level of each of your students as described in Chapter 2, you are ready to organize your classroom for word study. In this chapter we will describe for you the basic activities of word study, how to create and organize materials, and how to set up weekly routines that will facilitate effective and efficient word study. We will address related issues such as expectations for editing and grading, before ending with a review of guiding principles and an outline for matching activities to development. To illustrate the details that make up this chapter, let us first visit the classroom of Judy Zimmerman as she introduces a group of her students to *r*-influenced vowels.

Earlier in the year Judy assessed her third graders and divided them into three instructional groups for word study. On Mondays she meets with each group for about 15 to 20 minutes to go over the words, model the word sort for the week, and help her students make discoveries about the particular group of words she has chosen. After getting her students started on independent reading and journal writing, Judy calls her first group together on the carpet. She has a set of words written on cards that she lays out for everyone to see. She begins by saying, "Let's read over these words to be sure everyone knows how to read them and what they mean. After discussing *mare,* which Julio defines as a "mother horse," she picks up *bear* and *bare* and reads them both. "Who remembers what those words are called? That's right, they are **homophones.**" She holds up *bear* and asks who knows what it means.

"It's an animal and I saw one last summer when we went camping," offers Shannon. "What about this *bare*?" asks Judy, as she holds up the word. Rayshad explains that it means "having no hair, like being bald."

"Right," says Judy, "or you might go barefooted without shoes. There is another set of homophones here. Can anyone find them?" Mason finds *hair* and *hare* and again they talk about the meaning of each. They recall that they have heard the word *hare* in the story, *The Hare and the Tortoise,* which they read during a unit on fables.

Judy continues the lesson by saying, "We are going to begin today by thinking about the sound in these words. I am going to put *cart* here as one of our key words and *care* over here for the other. Listen to the middle sounds in each: *caaarrrt, caaarrrre.*" Then she picks up the word *farm.* "Does the middle sound like *cart* or *care*? Right, we will put it under *cart.* How about *chair*? Does the middle sound like *cart* or *care*?" After sorting several more words Judy hands out the rest of the word cards and calls on students to read and sort each word. After sorting all the words, the students read the words down each column to verify that they all have the same sound in the middle. The final sort by sound looks like Figure 3-1A.

Next, Judy directs her students' attention to the spelling patterns of the words. "How are all the words in the first column alike?" she asks. Lisa replies that they all have an *a* and *r* in them. "That's right," says Judy, "and what about the words under *care*?" William volunteers that they all have an *ar* also, but sometimes there is an *e* at the end or an *i* in the middle. "Can we put these words into two separate categories?" asks Judy. "What shall we use as headers?" The students agree to keep *care* as one header and to use *chair* for the other. Judy passes out the rest of the word cards and students take turns placing each word under *care* or *chair.*

"I have an **oddball!**" calls out Tan and she places the word *bear* off to the right. "I am glad you caught that," says Judy. "Why is it an oddball?" "It is the only one with an

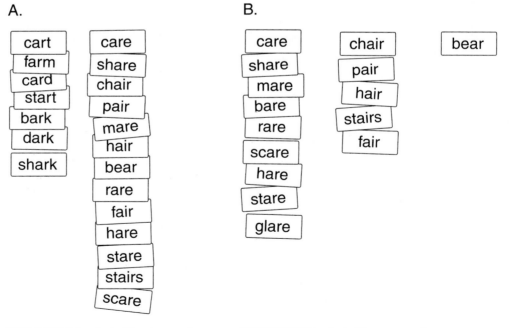

A.

cart	care
farm	share
card	chair
start	pair
bark	mare
dark	hair
shark	bear
	rare
	fair
	hare
	stare
	stairs
	scare

B.

care	chair	bear
share	pair	
mare	hair	
bare	stairs	
rare	fair	
scare		
hare		
stare		
glare		

FIGURE 3-1A Judy Zimmerman's Sound Sort

FIGURE 3-1B Judy Zimmerman's Pattern Sort

ea," explains Tan. After sorting all the words, as shown in Figure 3-1B, Judy asks her students to tell her how all the words are alike in each column and they read the words once more to verify that they all have the same sound as well as the same pattern. Judy then asks the students if the patterns remind them of other words they have studied. Brian points out that *ai* and *a* with an *e* on the end are patterns that go with long -*a*. "Are these long -*a* words?" probes Judy. "Listen: *caaaare, chaaair.*" The children agree that they can hear the sound of /a/ in those words. "What about the *a* in *cart*? Does that sound like an *a*?" asks Judy. This time there is some discussion as students come to the conclusion that they cannot even hear a vowel! Judy tells the students that over the next few weeks they will look at more words with an *r* after the vowel and they should keep these ideas in mind.

Before returning to their seats Judy gives each student a handout of word cards to cut apart for sorting independently at their seats. She reminds them to sort by sound and by pattern as they did in their final group sort. Two volunteers agree to illustrate the homophones for the class homophone dictionary. After Judy meets with her next word study group she quickly checks in with each student to look at their sorts. As she moves around the room she asks individual students to read a column of words and explain how they are alike. On Tuesday she will ask all her students to sort their words once more and then to write the words by categories in word study notebooks. On other days they will work with partners to sort and to find more words that fit the sound and/or pattern. On Friday, Judy assesses the three groups at once by calling out a word in turn for each group to spell.

THE ROLE OF WORD SORTING

Throughout this textbook you will see many examples of games and activities, but the simple process of sorting words into categories, like the word sort described in Judy Zimmerman's class, is the heart of word study. Categorizing is the fundamental way that humans make sense of the world. It allows us to find order and similarities among various objects, events, ideas, and words that we encounter. When students sort words they are engaged in the active process of searching, comparing, contrasting, and analyzing. Word sorts help students organize what they know about words and to form generalizations that they can then apply to new words they encounter in their reading (Gillet & Kita, 1978).

Because sorting is such a powerful way to help students make sense of words, we will take some time here to discuss it in depth. We recommend this same categorization routine for students in all stages who are studying a variety of word features. At first, emergent and beginning readers learn to pay attention to sounds at the beginning of words by sorting pictures. By the time they are transitional readers, reading their first *Frog and Toad* (by A. Lobel) books, students benefit from sorting written words by vowel patterns. Later, in middle school, students enhance their vocabulary by sorting words by syllables and affixes. In high school, students sort words by Greek and Latin stems and roots that share common meanings. As children progress in word knowledge, they learn how to look at words differently.

Word sorting offers the best of both constructivist learning and teacher-directed instruction. The teacher begins by "stacking the deck" with words that can be contrasted by sound, pattern, or meaning. In the process of sorting, students have an opportunity to make their own discoveries and form their own generalizations about how the English spelling system works. Notice that Judy avoids telling the students any rules or generalizations herself, but instead leads them to some tentative conclusions through careful questioning. Over the next few weeks they will continue to explore *r*-influenced vowels through a series of sorts and will discover that *r* often "robs" the vowel of the sounds we normally associate with it. Rather than simply memorizing 20 words each week for a spelling test, they have the opportunity to construct their own word knowledge that they can apply to both reading and writing.

Picture and word sorting differ from commercial phonics programs in some important ways. First, word sorts are interesting and fun for students because they are hands-on and manipulative. The process of sorting requires students to pay attention to words and to make logical decisions about their sound, pattern, and/or meaning as they place each one in a column. Consider the ancient proverb, "I hear and I forget, I see and I remember, I do and I understand." Word sorts help students learn by doing (Morris, 1982).

Second, students work with words or the names of pictures that they can already pronounce. In this way, sorting works from the known to the unknown and as children sort through a stack of cards, they concentrate on analyzing the sounds within each word. This is not possible if students cannot first name the words. Because learning to spell involves making associations between the spelling of words and their pronunciations, it is important that children know and can already pronounce most of the words to be sorted.

A third way in which sorting differs from packaged phonics programs is that sorting is **analytic,** whereas most phonics programs are **synthetic.** In synthetic programs students are first taught many letter-sound correspondences and are then expected to sound out unknown words, sometimes every word in a sentence! This makes reading tedious and can detract from meaning and engagement. Rather than building up from the phoneme to the word in a synthetic approach, sorting builds on known words and then examines their parts. In learning about vowel sounds, for example, the known word is first pronounced—"cat." Only then is the initial consonant (the **onset**) peeled off from the "at" to examine the medial vowel and final sound (the **rime**). Students learn phonic synthesis when they work with word families where they are first introduced to analogy as a decoding strategy. After analyzing the familiar word *cat,* the onset may be changed to *m* and the students may be challenged to blend the new onset with the familiar rime (*mat*). Analytic phonics supports the synthetic skill necessary to decode new words when reading.

A fourth way in which sorts differ from most phonics and spelling programs is that sorting does not rely on rote memorization, or the recitation of rules prior to an understanding of the underlying principles. During sorting, students determine similarities and differences among targeted features as they utilize higher level critical thinking skills to make categorical judgments. When students make decisions about whether the middle vowel sound in *cat* sounds more like the medial vowel sound in *map* or *top,* independent analysis and judgment are required. Memorization *is* necessary to master the English spelling system. One simply must remember that the animal is spelled *bear* and the adjective is spelled *bare,* but memorization is easier when served by knowledge and understanding of the principles of English spelling. Likewise, rules are a useful mnemonic for concepts already understood.

Efficiency is a fifth reason why sorts are effective and offer more concentrated practice than most commercial phonics programs. Sorting doubles or triples the number of examples children study, and they study them in a shorter amount of time. Phonics workbooks may have only three to five examples per page, and most of these exercises ask children to fill in the blank or color their choices from the answers provided. It takes an average first grader 10 to 20 minutes to complete such a workbook activity—time that could be better spent reading. In contrast, sorting a stack of 15 to 25 cards takes only a few minutes and the same stack can be used for a variety of sorting activities throughout the week. Compare the number of examples in Figure 3-2 to see the difference. The efficiency of sorting also makes it more cost effective. Picture and word cards can be reused indefinitely, and the low cost of preparing sorts for word study instruction leaves a larger chunk of the budget for children's books.

Finally, because of the simplicity of sorting routines, teachers find it easier to differentiate instruction among different groups of learners. Workbooks are not very flexible,

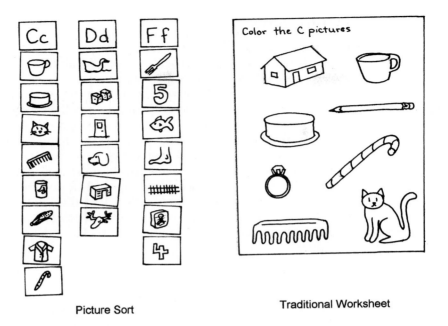

Picture Sort

Traditional Worksheet

FIGURE 3-2 Picture Sorting Offers More Practice Than Traditional Worksheets

and any given classroom would require several different levels to accommodate each student's instructional level, or zone of proximal development. In contrast, sorting is infinitely adaptable and the process involved in categorizing word features lends itself to cooperative learning.

One central goal of word study is to teach students how to spell and decode new words and to improve their word recognition speed in general. To accomplish this goal, we teach our students how to examine words to learn the regularities that exist in the spelling system. Word recognition and decoding; phonics and spelling are two sides of the same word knowledge coin. Picture sorts and word sorts are designed to help students learn how and where to look at words.

TYPES OF SORTS

There are three basic types of sorts that reflect the three layers of English orthography: sound, pattern, and meaning. In addition there are variations of these sorts that students can do under the teacher's direction, with a partner, or by themselves for additional practice. In this section we describe all of these.

Sound Sorts

Sound is the first layer of English orthography that students must negotiate to make sense of the alphabetic nature of English spelling. Pictures are naturally suited for sound sorts, because the picture begs to be named yet there is no printed form of the word for reference. As students pronounce the name of each picture, they pay attention to the speech sounds contained in the name and work to match certain sound segments to the letters that represent them. Printed words, too, can be sorted for sound as Judy did using the key words *cart* and *care.* Students may sort by rhyme, by the number of syllables, and even by syllable stress when they compare such words as *pro' duce* versus *pro duce'.* There are several basic sound sorts.

Picture Sorts

Picture sorting is particularly suited for students in the emergent, letter name–alphabetic, and early within word pattern stages of spelling development who do not have extensive reading vocabularies. Picture sorts can be used to develop **phonological awareness,** the ability to identify and categorize various speech sounds such as rhyme and alliteration. Picture sorts can also be used to teach **phonics,** the consistent relationship between letters and sounds. At different points in development, students sort pictures by initial sounds, consonant blends or digraphs, rhyming families, or vowel sounds.

 In picture sorts, English Language Learners sort pictures and attend to English sounds that may not exist in their mother tongue. Your guidance as you demonstrate sorts is important.

Teachers first model picture sorts, such as the one shown on page 63 in Figure 3-2, as they work with students who are learning initial consonant sounds. Working as a group, children are given a collection of picture cards to sort into contrasting sound categories. They say the names of the pictures as they place them under the letters they need to associate with the sound. At the end of this guided activity, students work independently to sort similar sets of pictures into the same categories. For variety, small objects can be used instead of pictures.

Words Sorts

Words sorts can also draw students' attention to sound, and because sound is the first aspect of a word a speller has for reference, these sound sorts are very important. For example, only after the long -*a* in *tape* is identified can the speller consider which of several spelling patterns might be used (*taip* or *tape*?). Judy began with a sound sort when she met with her group for the first time to introduce the weekly sort. This laid an important foundation for the pattern sort that followed. Not all word sorts involve a sound contrast, but many do.

No-Peeking Sorts

When students are asked to sort words by sound, the printed form of the word can sometimes "give away" the category (as when short -*a* words are compared with short -*u*). In a no-peeking sort, the printed word is unseen. A key word or picture for each sound is established; the teacher or a partner shuffles the word cards, and then calls the words aloud without showing them. The student indicates the correct category by pointing to or naming the key word that has the same sound. The response can be checked and corrected immediately when the printed word is revealed and put in place. A variation of the no-peeking sort is a **no-peeking writing sort,** where the students must write each word under the correct key word before seeing the word. In a no-peeking writing sort, students must rely on the sound they hear in the word, as well as their memory for the letters associated with it, cued by the key word at the top of the column. This is what spelling is all about. No-peeking writing sorts are an established weekly routine in many classrooms. Some teachers conduct them with a large group on the overhead projector, saying the word aloud and letting the students write it before they lay the word down to be checked. After a key word is laid down for each category, one partner calls out a word without showing it and the other points to the key word it would follow. This sort is important for students who could use some time attending less to the visual patterns and more to the sounds. No-peeking writing sorts can help identify what words need more attention and can serve as a pretest for the final assessment. No-peeking writing sorts, however, should only be used after plenty of word sorts, so students have an opportunity to see the printed form and examine the orthography first.

Parents, volunteers, assistants, and classroom peers can serve as buddies for no-peeking sorts. No-peeking sorts are a good way to increase the time students practice and also encourage cooperative learning. Students enjoy working with and learning from each other. The task is well defined and the time spent is productive when teachers have taken the time to teach children how to work together through modeling and role-play.

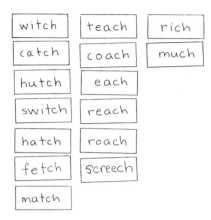

FIGURE 3-3 Word Sort by Final *ch* and *tch* Patterns

Pattern Sorts

When students use the printed form of the word they can sort by the visual patterns formed by groups of letters or letter sequences. Letter name–alphabetic spellers sort their words into groups that share the same **word families** or rime (*hat, rat, pat; ran, fan, tan*). Students in the within word pattern stage sort their words into groups by vowel patterns (*wait, train, mail, pain* versus *plate, take, blame*). Syllables and affixes spellers sort words into groups by the pattern of consonants and vowels at the syllable juncture (*button, pillow, ribbon* versus *window, public, basket*). Spellers who are learning derivational relations will sort word pairs by patterns of constancy and change across derivationally related words (e.g., *divine-divinity, mental-mentality*).

Sometimes a new feature is best introduced with a pattern sort, to reveal a related sound difference. Consider the words in Figure 3-3 that have been sorted by the final *ch* or *tch* pattern. The final sound in all the words is the same, so a sound sort would not help to differentiate their spelling. However, now that the words are sorted by the final consonant patterns, read down each column to see if you notice anything about the vowel sounds within each column. What did you discover? *Tch* is associated with the short-vowel sound and *ch* is associated with the long-vowel sound. Exceptions are *rich* and *such,* and they should be moved to a new column of oddballs or exceptions and remembered as such.

Pattern sorts often follow a sound sort as we saw in the lesson with Judy. The words under *care* were subdivided into two pattern sorts: words spelled with *air* and words spelled with *are*. One fundamental tenet for pattern sorts is to sort first by sound and then by pattern. Because certain patterns go with certain categories of sound, students must be taught to first listen for the sound and then to consider alternative ways to spell that sound. When students sort by sound and by pattern they discover those alternatives as well as the small number of words that do not fit the more common patterns.

 For samples of each kind of sort, visit the accompanying CD-ROM and look into the sorts available for each developmental stage.

Picture Sorts

Because pattern sorts depend on the visual array of letters within printed words, picture sorts are not appropriate. However, pictures can be placed at the top of the sorting columns in place of key words. Using key pictures to head a column forces students to think about sound while they are learning about patterns. For example, a student learning short- and long-vowel sounds might first categorize such words as *grass, plate, rain, tack, fast, rake,* and *drain* into two columns by sound headed by the key pictures *cat* and *cake*. After sorting the words by vowel sound, students would then sort the *cake* column into two subgroups by pattern: *ai* and *a*-consonant-*e*.

Although pictures cannot teach patterns, it is sometimes a good idea to mix a few pictures into a pattern word sort. Because it is easier to sort words by their visual pattern, students can lose sight of the fact that certain patterns go with certain sounds. By mixing a few pictures in with a stack of word cards, students are challenged to be flexible in their word analysis and capitalize on the pattern-to-sound regularities of English spelling.

 English Language Learners examine sounds that do not exist in their first languages in word sorts that you assign. Visual contrasts in spelling highlight what may be subtle differences in pronunciation that may go undetected; for example, students compare and contrast the spelling and pronunciation of *shape* and *shoe* with *ch*ase and *ch*urch and as they sort, they pronounce the different sounds at the beginning.

Word Sorts

Word sorts using printed word cards are the mainstay of pattern sorts and are useful for all students who have a functional sight word vocabulary. Key words containing the pattern under study are used to label each category and students sort word cards by matching the pattern in each word to the pattern in the key word at the top of the column. Judy led her students to sort words into two pattern groups, those spelled with *air* and those spelled with *are*. Recurring patterns are often represented as an abbreviated code that stands for the pattern of consonants and vowels in the feature of study. The letter C represents consonants; the letter *V* represents vowels. The abbreviation CVC may be used as a column header for recurring patterns of three-letter, short-vowel words such as *cat*, *tub*, *sun*, *net*, or *mop*. The abbreviation CVVC may be used as a column header for the recurring pattern in long-vowel words such as *rain, coat, suit,* or *green*.

Writing Sorts

Teachers who use word sorts to highlight the stability of the pattern-to-sound ordering principle of English orthography often have their students record their sorts into neatly labeled columns in a word study notebook such as the one shown in Figure 3-4. The columns in the notebook are headed by the same key picture, key word, or key pattern used in the pattern sorts. A question mark can be used for the oddball category. Students simply copy the words they sorted into their notebooks in the appropriate column. Secondary students might write the words listed at the bottom of a worksheet into the appropriate category.

Meaning Sorts

Students will learn that meaning also influences the spelling of words, and so sometimes the focus of a sort is upon meaning. In meaning sorts, either pictures, words, or phrases are grouped by their similarity in meaning or use. The two major types of meaning sorts are concept sorts and meaning sorts related to spelling. Meaning sorts related to spelling include (a) homophone and homograph sorts, and (b) roots, stems, and affix sorts. The earliest sorts by meaning are picture concept sorts that do not involve spelling.

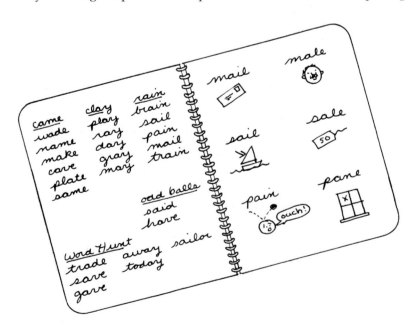

FIGURE 3-4   Word Study Notebook

Concept Sorts

Sorting pictures or words by concepts or meaning is a good way to link vocabulary instruction to what your students already know and to expand their conceptual understanding of essential reading vocabulary. **Concept sorts** are appropriate for all ages and stages of word knowledge and should be used regularly in the content areas. Mathematical terms, science concepts, and social studies vocabulary words all can be sorted into conceptual categories for greater understanding.

Concept sorts can be used for assessing and providing background knowledge before embarking on a new unit of study. A science unit on matter, for example, might begin by having children categorize the following words into groups that go together: *steam, wood, air, ice cube, rain, metal, glue, paint, plastic, smoke, milk,* and *fog.* A discussion of the reasons behind their conceptual groupings is most revealing! As the unit progresses, this sort can be revisited and used for teaching core concepts and terminology. Having students categorize examples under the key words *solid, liquid,* and *gas* will help them sort out the essential characteristics for each state of matter. Concept sorts are great for dealing with new terminology in novels, too. While reading *Stuart Little* (by E. B. White), a group of Mrs. Birckhead's third graders sorted some of the vocabulary they encountered as follows:

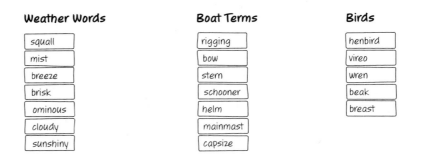

Weather Words	Boat Terms	Birds
squall	rigging	henbird
mist	bow	vireo
breeze	stern	wren
brisk	schooner	beak
ominous	helm	breast
cloudy	mainmast	
sunshiny	capsize	

The creative possibilities for concept sorts are endless. They can be used as advanced organizers for anticipating new reading, they can be revisited and refined after reading, and they can be used to organize ideas before writing. Concept sorts are even useful for teaching grammar. Words can be sorted by parts of speech.

Although picture sorts are used mainly for sound, pictures can also be used to teach word meanings. Concept picture sorts are particularly useful for English Language Learners as they work to develop more semantic variety within their vocabularies. Pictures of a dog, a cat, a duck, and so on can all be grouped to make an animal category. These can be contrasted with pictures of a flower, a tree, a cornfield, a pumpkin, and so on—all examples of plants. English vocabulary is expanded as students sort pictures into conceptual groupings and repeat the names of each picture and the category to which each belongs.

Meaning Sorts Related to Spelling

Students see that meaning influences the spelling of words when they first encounter sound-alike word pairs like *by* and *buy,* or *to* and *too.* Words that sound alike but are spelled differently are called homophones. Students enjoy homophones because they are interesting and it makes such sense that words with different meanings take a different spelling pattern. When teachers teach homophones through word sorting, students expand their vocabularies and learn about spelling patterns at the same time, as demonstrated by the discussion of *bare* in Judy's class. The study of homographs also provides a prime opportunity for vocabulary enrichment. **Homographs** are words that are spelled the same but are pronounced differently depending on their part of speech: We *record* our sorts so that we will have an ongoing *record* of them. By sorting homographs into grammatical categories by part of speech, students enrich their vocabulary while learning how to pay attention to syllable stress.

When students read and write many words of more than one syllable, they must learn a new ordering principle of English orthography: Words that are related in meaning often share similar spellings. This spelling-meaning connection in derivationally related words provides a rich arena for meaning sorts that build on Greek and Latin roots, stems, and affixes. Spellers who are learning derivational relations will sort words by similarities in roots and stems such as the *spect* in *spectator, spectacle, inspect,* and *spectacular* versus the *port* in *transport, import, portable,* and *port-o-john.*

Variations of Sorts

Variations of picture sorts and word sorts serve different instructional purposes. Direct instruction through explicit teaching, problem solving by hypothesis testing, connecting word study to reading and writing, building speed and automaticity all are important instructional goals, and for each, there is a sort. Closed sorts, open sorts, word hunts, no-peeking sorts, writing sorts, repeated sorts, and speed sorts will be described in relation to their instructional purpose. These sorts differ greatly from traditional spelling instruction. Sorting activities give students plenty of practice and experience manipulating and categorizing words until they can sort quickly and accurately.

1. Teacher-Directed Word Sorts

Most of the introductory word sort tasks described in this textbook are teacher-directed or **closed sorts.** In closed sorts, teachers define the categories and model the sorting procedure (Gillet & Kita, 1978). For example, in a beginning-sound phonics sort, the teacher isolates the beginning sound to be taught and explicitly connects it to the letter that represents it using a **key word** to designate the categories. The teacher models additional beginning sounds, then gradually releases the task to the students' control as they replicate the process. As they work, teachers and students discuss the characteristics of the words in each column. Students may then sort independently or collaboratively in no-peeking pairs under the teacher's guidance. This practice is carefully monitored and corrective feedback is provided.

2. Student-Centered Sorts

Student-centered or **open sorts** are particularly useful after students are already accustomed to sorting and are quite adept at finding commonalties among words. In open sorts, students create their own categories with the set of words. These sorts are more diagnostic in nature, because they reveal what students know about examining the orthography when they work independently. Open sorts provide an opportunity for students to test their own hypotheses and they often come up with unexpected ways to organize words. For example, when given the words shown in Figure 3-3, some students sort by the final patterns (*tch* or *ch*), others sort by the vowel sounds (long and short), and others sort by rhyming words. These open sorts are interesting for the teacher to observe and to discover what students already understand or misunderstand. Some of the most productive discussions about the orthography come when students explain *why* they sorted the way they did in an open sort. As students become sorting pros, they begin to anticipate the teacher-directed closed sorts. In many classrooms, students are given their words for the week on Monday morning, and they sort their words before school begins in anticipation of the categories they will be sorting later in groups.

3. Guess My Category

When children are comfortable with sorts, you can introduce any new area of study with a collection of objects, words, or pictures with an activity called Guess My Category. In this sort you do not label or describe the categories in advance. Rather, it will be the job of your students to decide how the things in each category are alike. You begin by sorting two or three pictures or words into each group. When you pick up the next picture or word, invite someone to guess where it will go. Continue doing this until all the pictures or words have been sorted. Try to keep the children who have caught on to the attributes of interest from telling the others until the end.

Guess My Category is particularly useful for exploring content-specific vocabulary and stimulates creative thinking. You could give small groups sets of words or pictures that might be grouped in a variety of ways. Ask each group to come up with their own categories working together. Allow them to have a miscellaneous group for those things that do not fit the categories they establish. After the groups are finished working, let them visit each other's sorts and try to guess the categories that were used. For example, pictures of animals might be sorted into groups according to body covering, habitat, or number of legs.

4. Writing Sorts

Writing words as a study technique for spelling is well established. Undoubtedly the motoric act reinforces the memory for associating letters and patterns with sounds and meanings. However, the practice of assigning students to write words five or more times is of questionable value, because it can become simply mindless copying. Where there is no thinking, there is no learning. Writing words into categories demands that students attend to the sound and/or the pattern of letters and to think about how those characteristics correspond with the established categories cued by the key word, picture, or pattern at the top of the column. Figure 3-4 shows a completed writing sort in a word study notebook. Writing sorts encourage the use of analogy as students use the key word as a clue for the spelling of words that have the same sound or pattern.

As described earlier, in a writing sort, key words label each category. The words are then written down in the appropriate categories. Students can do this individually by copying a sort they have done with word cards or by turning over one word at a time from their collection and writing each down. Even better is for someone to call the words aloud for the student to write and then to immediately show the word to check the spelling and placement in a no-peeking writing sort. Teachers can do this in a group, partners can do it with each other, and parents can do it at home. Writing sorts are also an instructionally sound way to construct spelling tests. Key words are written and then students sort and spell the words as they are called. They can get credit for putting the word in the right category as well as for spelling the word correctly.

5. Word Hunts

Students do not automatically make the connection between spelling words and reading words. Word hunts help students make this connection. In **word hunts,** students hunt through their reading and writing for words that are further examples of the sound, pattern, or meaning unit they are studying. They see, for example, the many short -*a* words or that -*le* is much more common at the end of words than -*el*. Some patterns are found in virtually every text again and again, whereas others are harder to find; thus, word hunts are more appropriate for some features than others.

Before students are expected to do word hunts, the teacher should model word hunting. This can be done with a portion of text copied onto chart pages, copies of text on overhead transparencies, a big book, or simply a book being used for instruction. Working line by line, teachers demonstrate how to locate words that fit the categories under study and how to record those words into categories. After the teacher demonstration, students return to texts they are reading and writing, and they hunt for other words that contain the same features. These words are then added to written sorts in the word study notebook under the corresponding key word. See Figure 3-4 for words added to the long -a categories at the bottom of the notebook page. It is important that students not confuse skimming for word patterns with reading for meaning. The teacher asks the students to use the trade books they have already read or the already-read portion of the book they are currently reading.

Word hunts can be conducted in small groups, with a partner, or individually for seatwork or homework. Figure 3-5 shows how students have gathered around a large sheet of paper on which key words have been written. Students skim and scan pages of books that they have already read, looking for words that match the key words according to the feature under study. Much discussion may ensue as to whether a word contains the spelling feature in question. Often students consult the dictionary, particularly to resolve questions of stress, syllabication, or meaning.

Figure 3-6 shows an example of a word hunt conducted on a charted story retelling by a small group of students in Mrs. Fitzgerald's third-grade class during a unit on folktales. After working with long -o and short -o in word study, students found and charted these lists on page 71 from *The Three Billy Goats Gruff* (by P. Galdone).

After this sound sort, students sorted these words by orthographic patterns and organized them in their word study notebooks.

Five words, including *gobble*, were added to the short -o column.

Groaned and *goat* were added to the *oa* column.
Home was added to the *o*-consonant-*e* column.
Troll was added to the *o*-consonant-consonant column.
Meadow was added to the *ow* column.
A new pattern of open, single, long -o spellings was discovered with *so, go,* and *over*.

This word hunt added more examples for the students to consider and created new categories. Word hunts connect word study to other literacy contexts and can also extend the reach to more difficult vocabulary such as *meadow* and *gobble*. With these words, students are able to generalize the pattern within one-syllable words to two-syllable words. Word hunts provide a step up in word power!

When conducting word hunts with emergent to beginning readers, teachers should have children scan texts that they have already read *and* that are guaranteed to contain the phonics features targeted in their search. Several companies publish books for emer-

FIGURE 3-5   Cooperative Group Word Hunt

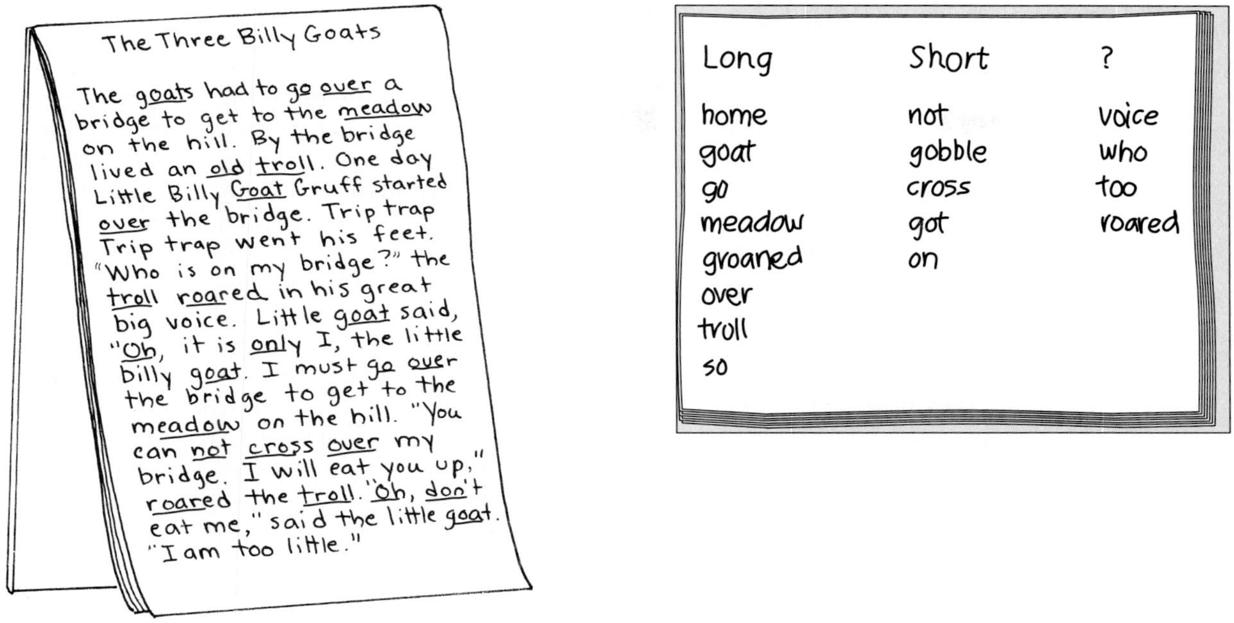

The Three Billy Goats

The goats had to go over a bridge to get to the meadow on the hill. By the bridge lived an old troll. One day Little Billy Goat Gruff started over the bridge. Trip trap Trip trap went his feet. "Who is on my bridge?" the troll roared in his great big voice. Little goat said, "Oh, it is only I, the little billy goat. I must go over the bridge to get to the meadow on the hill. "You can not cross over my bridge. I will eat you up," roared the troll. "Oh, don't eat me," said the little goat. "I am too little."

Long	Short	?
home	not	voice
goat	gobble	who
go	cross	too
meadow	got	roared
groaned	on	
over		
troll		
so		

FIGURE 3-6 Word Hunt with Story Retelling

gent readers that contain recurring phonics elements. *Ready Readers*® by Modern Curriculum Press and the **phonics readers** published by Creative Teaching Materials are two examples of simple books organized around specific phonics features that repeat in the text. Although such text may not be the heart of your reading program, they offer children a chance to put into practice what they are learning about words and to see many words at the same time that work the same way.

6. Brainstorming

While word hunts can extend the number of examples to consider, students can also supply additional examples through brainstorming. Brainstorming might be considered a word hunt through one's own memory. The teacher asks for more words that rhyme with *cat*, words that describe people ending in /er/, or words that have *spire* as a root. Word hunts through current reading materials are just not as productive when it comes to some features. It is unlikely, for example, that a word hunt would turn up many words with the Latin stem *spire*, but students may be able to brainstorm words they already know with *spire* in them, such as *inspire* or *perspire*. Words brainstormed by students can be added to established categories listed on the board, a chart, or a word study notebook.

Brainstorming can also be used to introduce a sort. The teacher may ask students for words that have particular sounds, patterns, or roots and write them on the board. The teacher might write words in categories as they are given as in a Guess My Category sort, or categories might be determined by discussion. These words might then be transferred to word study sheets for weekly word sorting routines. After one student raised a question about why the word *receive* had an *e* on the end when it already had the *ei*, Judy asked her students to think of other words that ended in either *ve* or *v*. After listing their brainstormed words on the board, students sorted them into two groups—those that had a long-vowel sound and needed the *e* to mark the vowel (*stove, alive, cave*) and those that did not (*give, love, achieve*). After a while, students realized that there were no words that ended in plain *v*. There was always an *e* after *v*, whether the vowel needed it or not. *Luv,* as in the diapers, became the only oddball.

7. Repeated Individual Sorts

To become fluent readers, students must achieve fast, accurate recognition of words in context. The words they encounter in context are made of the same sounds, patterns, and meaning units they examine out of context, in word study. One of the best ways to build accuracy and **automaticity** in word recognition is to build fast, accurate recognition of these spelling units. To meet that goal, it is necessary to have students do a given picture or word sort more than one time. Repeated individual sorts are designed for just that—repeated sorting. Just as repeated reading of familiar texts builds fluency, repeated individual sorts provide a student with the necessary practice to build automaticity. In Judy's class the students sort individually after the group lesson, again on Tuesday, and then with a partner on Wednesday. They are also expected to take their words home to sort several days a week. All this adds up to sorting the same words five to seven times throughout the week.

They may simply take turns sorting a collection of pictures or words and then talking to each other about what they discover. Another sort that is particularly useful to do with a partner is a **no-peeking sort.** The third way partners can work together is to complete no-peeking writing sorts. One partner calls the words while the other writes, and then the partners switch roles. No-peeking sorts are a good way to prepare for tests, especially the writing sort format.

8. Speed Sorts

Once students have become accurate with a particular sort, **speed sorts** are motivating and develop fluency. Speed sorting is no different than ordinary word or picture sorting except that students time themselves using a stopwatch. Students can be paired with other students to time each other and learn to chart their progress. We recommend not pitting students against each other in a competitive mode, however; instead, students should compare their speed with their own earlier speeds and work toward individual improvement.

Some teachers have found that students are highly motivated to practice their sorts in preparation for a **beat-the-teacher speed sort** which takes place later in the week. The teacher circulates from group to group and sorts the word cards while being timed. The group members then try to beat this time.

9. Draw and Label / Cut and Paste

Drawing is particularly useful for teaching emergent and letter name–alphabet spellers initial consonant sounds, as it encourages them to brainstorm other words that begin with the same sounds. Some teachers provide special drawing and labeling paper that has been divided into columns headed by a key letter (see Figure 3-7). Each column is divided into boxes so that students can see where to draw, how big to draw, and how many to draw. Students brainstorm other words that start with the same sound, illustrate the word in a box under the appropriate key letter and picture, and then label the picture with their best writing. Students are held accountable for spelling the word study feature correctly, but they are encouraged to invent the rest if they do not know how to spell the entire word. Drawing and labeling is also useful for within word pattern and syllables and affixes spellers who are studying homophones. Homophones can be illustrated and labeled, and sentences can be composed to highlight their meaning (see Figure 3-13 later in the chapter).

A variation of the draw and label activity is the cut and paste activity, which is like a word hunt using pictures instead of written words and is appropriate for emergent and letter

FIGURE 3-7   Draw and Label Activity

name–alphabetic spellers. Students hunt through old catalogs and magazines for pictures beginning with a certain sound and then cut out the pictures to paste them in the appropriate column. They then label the pictures as indicated. Pictures that have been used for sorting can also be pasted on a sheet of paper and labeled.

GUIDELINES FOR PREPARING AND INTRODUCING WORD SORTS

Now that we have described the rationale for sorting and a variety of ways to sort, we will focus on some guidelines for preparing and conducting a teacher-directed sort.

Introducing a Class to Sorting

Teachers may find the act of sorting to be a new instructional activity for some students. It may be difficult for students to handle the conceptual challenge of sorting words by spelling features while learning how to cut apart the words, set up categories, and manipulate the cards. For students who are not familiar with the process of sorting, a series of introductory lessons over a week or two might begin with concept sorts using objects, pictures, or words that they can readily identify. Kindergarten or first-grade students might begin by sorting objects such as buttons, pencils, or shoes. These may be sorted in various ways on different days, by color or size, for example. Next students sort pictures by shape or color; and then sort pictures by rhyme or the beginning sound. In elementary grades, students might do a concept sort with pictures (such as different means of transportation) followed by a concept sort with words, and then a spelling feature sort. At first, begin with whole-class sorts that will be relatively easy for everyone in the class, then model some of the routines you will want your students to use such as cutting, drawing, labeling, and pasting. You will need to demonstrate the process of sorting, writing sorts, and categorizing words from word hunts. Once routines are well established, you can begin to work with small groups of students as other students work independently or with partners using the now-familiar routines.

 A detailed, 2-week schedule for introducing sorts to both primary-level and intermediate-level students can be found on the *Words Their Way* Companion Website at www.prenhall.com/bear

Teacher-Created Sorts

After identifying proper spelling stages and grouping students for instruction, you must decide on what orthographic features to study and prepare collections of words for sorting. The particular feature you choose to study (initial consonant sounds, short-vowel sounds, consonant doubling, etc.) should be based on what you see students using but confusing in their writing and other diagnostic information such as a spelling inventory. The upcoming chapters in this book will provide information about orthographic features to study within each stage. No matter what the feature is, when preparing word lists for sorting, it is best to collect sets of words that offer a contrast between at least two sounds, patterns, or meaning categories. Compare *b* to *s*, compare short -*u* to short -*a*, compare words that double the final consonant before adding -*ing* with those that do not. By carefully setting up contrasts in a collection of words, you are stacking the deck for students' discoveries as they sort.

 Familiarize yourself with many different sorting options for each developmental level by spending some time on the accompanying CD-ROM, where you'll find prepared sorts for all your students' needs.

You can utilize several resources to help prepare sorts. Chapters 4 through 8 have suggestions for each stage; the Appendix provides pictures and word lists, examples of sorts, and there are numerous other *Words Their Way* products to help. We suggest these as a starting point for eventually creating your own sorts. Only you can be sure of what words your students can already read and thus use for sorting. It is unlikely any prepared collection of sorts or sequence of study will be just right for your students. For that reason, the following suggestions are a valuable resource.

ELL The ESL Teacher's Book of Lists is an excellent resource for word lists in other languages that students can compare to English words.

1. Prepared word lists: Valuable references include the *WTW* Appendix, *The Reading Teacher's Book of Lists* (Fry, Kress, & Fountoukidis, 1993), *The Spelling Teachers' Book of Lists* (Phenix, 1996), and *Word Journeys* (Ganske, 2000).

2. Finding words by feature: Special dictionaries such as the *Scholastic Rhyming Dictionary* (Young, 1994) lists words by rimes and vowel patterns. Regular dictionaries are good for finding words with such beginning features as blends, digraphs, and prefixes. Online dictionaries and those on CD-ROM can be used to search for internal spelling patterns such as vowel digraphs or root words. Some of these websites have excellent vocabulary enrichment activities such as a "word of the day" with information about the origins and use of the word. Take some time to explore them.

 Visit our Companion Website at www.prenhall.com/bear to link to some great online dictionaries.

3. Basal spelling series: The spelling features introduced across the grade levels in basal spellers generally follow the same progression of orthographic features that are outlined in Chapters 4 through 8 of this textbook. Words can be culled from basal spellers to create word sorts. Depending on your basal spelling series, you may have to pull words from more than one unit to achieve a categorical contrast.

 You can find a sample of prepared sorts at our companion website at www.prenhall.com/bear. In addition, the *Words Their Way* CD-ROM provides ready-to-print sorts.

Teacher-Directed Lesson Plan

The teacher-directed sort is the most commonly used sort when introducing a new feature and provides a model of direct instruction that is explicit and systematic, yet sensitive to individual variation. It is described in detail here, but it is only one model. You might also choose to begin with an open sort or with a Guess My Category sort. The teacher-directed sort follows a four-step process: (a) demonstrate, (b) sort and check, (c) reflect, and (d) extend (see Figure 3-8).

 Visit our Companion Website at www.prenhall.com/bear for a blackline master of this four-step lesson plan.

Demonstrate: Introduce the Sort Using Key Pictures or Words

1. Look over the words or pictures for ones that are potentially difficult to identify or that may be unfamiliar to the students. Pictures can be named ("This is a picture of a yard") and words can be pronounced, defined, and used in a sentence. ("Does anyone

Demonstrate	Introduce sort, use key words or pictures
Sort and check	Individually or with a partner
Reflect	Declare, compare, and contrast
Extend	Introduce and assign activities to complete at seats, in centers, or at home: sorts, games, cut and paste, add to word study notebook, make word charts

FIGURE 3-8 Word Study Lesson Plan Format

ELL These picture sorts may require you to preteach a few of the words or pictures to English Language Learners. Preteaching these words and pictures in concept sorts earlier in the year make sound and pattern sorts more accessible.

know what a hutch is? Pet rabbits often live in hutches.") Do not make reading words or naming the pictures into a guessing game. Tell your students the names of the pictures immediately.

2. Next establish the categories. An open-ended question such as, "What do you notice about these words" or "How might we sort these words" can be used to get students thinking about categories. If you have stacked the deck with words that share common patterns or sounds and if your students are familiar with categorizing, then they should notice common features fairly quickly. If they do not, then define the categories for them directly as Judy did with the two *r*-influenced vowel sounds in *cart* and *care*.

3. Use letter cards, key pictures, key words, or pattern cues such as CVC as column headers. If you are working with sounds, you can emphasize or elongate them by stretching them out. If you are working with patterns, you can think aloud as you point out the spelling pattern. If you are working with syllables, affixes, or derivational relations, you can explicitly point out the unit you are using to compare and contrast.

4. Shuffle the rest of the cards and say, for example, "We are going to listen for the sound in the middle of these words and decide if they sound like *map* or like *duck*. I'll do a few first. Here is a rug. Ruuuuug, uuuug, uuuuuuh. *Rug* has the /uh/ sound in the middle so I'll put it under *duck*, uuuuck, uuuuh. Here is a flag. Flaaaaag, aaaag, aaaah. I'll put *flag* under *maaaap*. *Flag* and *map* both have the /ă/ sound in the middle; the /ă/ sound is made by the vowel letter *a*."

5. After modeling several words, turn the task over to the students. Display the rest of the pictures or words, pass them out, or continue to hold them up one at a time. Students even enjoy the anticipation of turning over a word in the stack when it is their turn. Students should name or read the word aloud and then place it in the correct category. If students make a mistake at the very beginning, correct it immediately. Simply say: "*Sack* would go under *map*. Its middle sound is /ă/." Then model the phoneme segmentation process for isolating the medial vowel: /s/ /ă/ /k/.

Sort and Check: *Individually or with a Partner*

After the students have completed the first sort under your guidance, immediately ask them to shuffle and sort again, but this time cooperatively or independently. Unless your students are in the last two levels of word knowledge (syllables and affixes or derivational relations), ask them to name each word or picture aloud as they sort. If someone does not know what to call a picture, tell the student immediately. If someone cannot read a word, discard it or lay it aside to consider later. During the second, repeated sort, do not correct your students, but when they are through, have them name the words or pictures in each column to check themselves. If there are misplaced cards students fail to find, tell how many and in which column, and ask the students to find them.

Reflect: Declare, Compare, and Contrast

At the end of the sort, have students verbalize what the words or pictures in each column have in common. The best way to initiate such a discussion is to say, "What do you notice about the words in each column?" Guide them to consider sound, pattern, and meaning with open-ended questions such as, "How are the sounds in these words alike? What kind of pattern do you notice? Are any of these words similar in meaning?" Avoid telling rules, but help students shape their ideas into statements, such as, "All of these words have the letter *u* in the middle and have the /uh/ sound" or, "The words with an *e* on the end have the /ā/ sound in the middle." During the reflection part of the lesson, students are asked to declare their knowledge about sound, pattern, and meaning.

Extend: Activities to Complete at Seats, in Centers, or at Home

After the group demonstration, sorting, and reflection, students participate in a number of activities that reinforce and extend their understandings. They continue to sort a number of times individually and with partners. They hunt for similar words. They draw and label pictures, add to word charts, complete word study notebooks, and play games. Sometimes teachers extend the word sort into a phonemic awareness activity by having students divide some words in each column into individual phonemes and then blend them back together again. Through extensions, word sorts can be made more synthetic, or creative, depending on your instructional goal. Shortly we will talk about how to establish schedules and routines in your classroom to keep students organized and actively engaged in learning.

Making Sorts Harder or Easier

The difficulty of sorts can be adjusted in several ways:

1. Increasing the number of contrasts in the sort provides more challenge. If children are young or inexperienced, starting with two categories is a good idea. As they become adept at sorting into two groups, step up to three categories and then four. Even after working with four categories or more, however, you may want to go back to fewer categories when you introduce a new concept.

2. Another way to make sorts easier or harder is by the contrasts you choose. It is easier to compare the sounds for /b/ and /s/ than for /b/ and /p/, for example, because the letter names *b* and *s* are made in different parts of the mouth. Likewise, it is easier for students to learn the letter sound for /f/ when it is contrasted with the sound of /k/ or /d/ than with a /v/. The letters *f* and *v* are both produced in the same place in the mouth, so they are more difficult to tell apart. Start with obvious contrasts, then move to finer distinctions.

3. The difficulty of sorts can also be increased or decreased by the actual words you choose as examples within each category. For example, adding words with blends and digraphs (*black, chest, trunk*) to a short-vowel sort can make those words more challenging. Ideally, children should be able to read all of the words in a word sort. In reality, however, this may not always be the case. The more unfamiliar words in a given sort, the more difficult that sort will be. This caveat applies to both being able to read the word and knowing what the word means. A fifth grader studying derivational relations will need easier words to study than a tenth grader, simply because the fifth grader will have a more limited vocabulary. If there are unfamiliar words in a sort, try to place them toward the end of the deck so that known words are the first to be sorted. When new words come up, you can encourage your students to compare the new spelling with the known words already sorted in the columns to arrive at a pronunciation.

4. Finally, adding an oddball column and including "exception" words that do not fit the targeted letter-sound or pattern feature can increase the difficulty of a sort. Oddballs are discussed in more detail next.

Oddballs

Oddballs, words that are at odds with the consistencies within each category, will inevitably turn up in word hunts and should be deliberately included in teacher-developed sorts. The word *have,* for example, would be an oddball in a short -*a* versus long -*a* vowel sort. The vowel sound of the *a* in *have* is short, yet it appears to be spelled with a long-vowel pattern. Oddballs are often high frequency words such as *have, said, was,* and *again.* Such words become memorable from repeated usage, but are also memorable because they are odd. They stand out in the crowd. Such words should be included in the sorts you prepare, but not too many. One to three oddballs are plenty, so that they do not overwhelm the regularity you want students to discover.

The oddball category is also where students may place words if they are simply not sure about the sound they hear in the word. This often happens when students say words differently due to dialectical or regional pronunciations that vary from the "standard" pronunciation. For example, one student in Wise County, Virginia, pronounced the word *vein* as "vine" and was correct in placing *vein* in the oddball column as opposed to the long -*a* group. To this student, the word *vein* was a long -*i.* Sometimes students detect subtle variations that adults may miss. Students often put words like *mail* and *sail* in a different sound category than *maid, wait,* and *paid,* because the long -*a* sound is slightly different before liquid consonants like *r* and *l. Mail* may sound more like /may-ul/.

Dealing with Mistakes

Mistakes are part and parcel of learning, but not all mistakes are dealt with in the same way. As described in the preceding guidelines for sorting, mistakes made early on in a sort should probably be corrected immediately. Sometimes, however, it is useful to find out why a student sorted a picture or word in a particular way. Simply asking, "Why did you put that there?" can provide further insight into a student's word knowledge. If mistakes are made during the second sort, your students will learn more if you guide them to finding and correcting the mistake on their own. You might say, "I see one word in this column that doesn't fit. Start at the top of the column and see if you can figure out which one it is." If students are making a lot of mistakes it may indicate a need to take a step back or to make the sort easier.

Once you are familiar with the basic word study lesson plan, you are ready to organize your classroom for differentiating word study to meet the needs of all your students.

ORGANIZATION OF WORD STUDY INSTRUCTION

What does a word study classroom look like? What kinds of materials do you need? How much time does it take? What exactly do students do? These questions and more about organizing for word study are answered in the sections that follow.

Getting Materials Ready for Word Study Instruction

Word study does not require a great investment of money, because the basic materials are already available in most classrooms. Access to a copier and plenty of unlined paper will get you well on your way. Copies of word sheets or picture sheets like those in Figure 3-9 can easily be created by hand using the templates and pictures in this

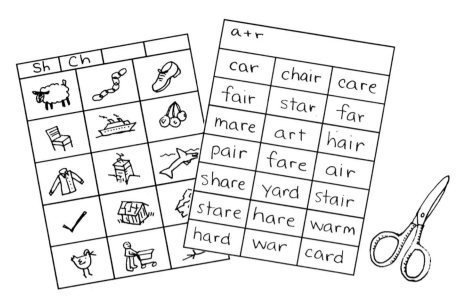

FIGURE 3-9   Sample Word Study Handouts

textbook or you can create them by computer (use the Tables format and set all margins at 0 inches). The copies are given to students to cut apart for sorting activities. Students quickly learn the routine of cutting words apart, sorting them into categories, and storing them in a notebook, library pocket, envelope, or plastic bag. Sturdy manila envelopes are recommended for each child because they can be reused for storing their sorts. Sometimes the cut-up words and pictures are kept and later combined with new words or pictures the following week; sometimes they are pasted into a notebook or onto paper, and sometimes they may be simply discarded. Creating these sheets of pictures or words is the first task teachers must tackle. Sample sorts and tips for the creation of sorts are given in the following chapters and in the Appendix.

> Remember to check out the ready-to-print sorts available for each developmental level on the accompanying CD-ROM.

Modeling the categorization procedure you want your students to use is important. In small groups, you may simply use the same cutout words your students will be using as you model on a table or on the floor. For larger groups you may want to model sorts on the chalkboard or whiteboard, overhead transparency using cut-up transparencies of the words, or with large word cards in a pocket chart. Large picture cards are available commercially or can be made by enlarging the pictures in this book and pasting them on cardstock. Some schools have chart-maker copiers that easily enlarge pictures. Magnetic tape can be attached to the back of pictures and word cards for sorting on a metal chalkboard.

You may also want to make your own special set of pictures for sorting by copying the pictures in this textbook onto cardstock and coloring them. Laminating the cardstock is optional as the material is quite durable. A set of these pictures can be stored by beginning sounds or by vowel sounds in library pockets or in envelopes. They can then be used for small group work or for individual sorting assignments. For example, you may find that you have one student who needs work on digraphs. You can pull out a set of *ch* and *sh* pictures, mix them together, and then challenge the student to sort them into columns using the pocket as a header. The **sound boards** in

FIGURE 3-10 Students Can Complete Sorts Independently Using Classification Folders

the Appendix can be copied, cut apart, and used to label the picture sets. It might be useful to have several of these picture sets, especially for resource teachers who work with individual children or small groups. Resource teachers may also want to create word card sets to be used repeatedly. Index cards can be cut apart or cards can be purchased to make word cards, but word sheets that are copied and cut apart by students may still be the easiest to manage. They can be stored in envelopes and reused from year to year to reduce paper consumption.

Many teachers use manila file folders to hold materials and to help students sort their words or pictures into categories as shown in Figure 3-10. Classification folders are divided into three to five columns with key words or pictures for headers glued in place. Words or pictures for sorting are stored in the folder and students sort directly in the columns. Laminating makes these sorting surfaces slippery, so you may not want to do that unless you anticipate heavy use. Once the folders have been developed, teachers can individualize word study fairly easily by pulling out the folders that target the exact needs of their students. When there is little room in a class for centers, teachers use these folders as a place to store the activities that students can take back to their desks.

Games are appealing for children and encourage them to practice in more depth and apply what they have learned in a new situation. This book contains many ideas for the creation of games, and you will want to begin making these to supplement the basic word or picture sorts as you have time. Look for generic games first, as many of them can be used with a variety of word features you will study across the year. For example, the follow-the-path game being played by the boys in Figure 3-11 can be laminated before labeling the spaces and then new letters substituted as they become the focus of study. Label the spaces with a washable overhead projector pen. Over time you can create more specific games.

Word study does not require dramatic changes to the physical setup of most classrooms. Storage space is needed for the word or picture sheets, large

FIGURE 3-11 Follow-the-Path Game for Initial Consonants

TABLE 3-1	Word Study Materials	
From the Supply Room	**From the Bookstore**	**From Printing Services**
copy paper for sorts	student dictionaries	photocopied picture cards
cardstock	rhyming dictionary	photocopied word cards
word study notebooks	etymological dictionary	student sound boards
manila folders	homophone books	poster sound boards
gameboard materials	alphabet books	
spinners and dice	phonics readers	
storage containers		
library pockets		
chart paper		

word cards, and games you create, but most of these can be stored in folders in a filing cabinet. Word study notebooks might be stored in a common area such as a plastic file box or tub to make it easy for the teacher to access them when checking student work.

Space is needed for group work, individual work, and partner work. Separate areas for word sorting and discussion are needed to convene a group on the floor or at tables in one part of the classroom while other children continue to work at their desks or in other areas of the room. Students' desks provide a surface for individual word sorting. In addition, centers or workstations can be set up where students work individually or with a partner to sort or play a game. A stopwatch is needed for speed sorts and can be placed in the word study center. Many teachers also post chart-size sound boards in this area. Table 3-1 summarizes what you might need, depending on the age and range of developmental word knowledge in your classroom.

Scheduling Issues

The second step to organize word study instruction is to set up a schedule and to develop weekly routines. There are many ways to organize word study. Some teachers conduct word study lessons as part of their reading groups. Other teachers work with two to three separate word study groups and may rotate their students from **circle time** with the teacher to individual **seat work** and **center times.** There may also be settings in which teachers conference individually with students in a largely independent workshop routine. In all settings, the focus of word study should be upon active inquiry and discovery, where students take much of the responsibility for their own learning. There are a number of things to consider when scheduling word study in your classroom.

1. *Develop a familiar weekly routine with daily activities.* Routines will save you planning time, ease transitions, and make the most of the time you devote to word study. Weekly schedules described in this chapter will give you ideas about how to create your own schedules. Include homework routines as well. When parents know what to expect every evening they are more likely to see that the work gets done.
2. *Schedule time for group work.* Students at the same developmental level should work with a teacher for directed word study. During this time, teachers model new sorts, guide practice sorts, and lead students in discussions that stimulate thinking and further their understanding. Chapter 2 offers suggestions for grouping students for instruction.
3. *Keep it short.* Word study should be a regular part of daily language arts, but it need not take up a great deal of time. Teacher-led introductory lessons may take 15 to 20 minutes, but subsequent activities should last only about 10 minutes a day and do not require a lot of supervision once students understand the routines. Word study

Whole Class Review of Schedule & Activities		9:00–9:25	9:25–9:30	9:30–9:55	9:55–10:00	10:00–10:25	
	Group 1	Circle	Evaluation and Break	Seat	Evaluation and Break	Center	Evaluation and Break
	Group 2	Center		Circle		Seat	Whole Class Activities
	Group 3	Seat		Center		Circle	

FIGURE 3-12   Circle-Seat-Center Morning Schedule

can fit easily into odd bits of time during the day. Children can play spelling games right before lunch or sort their words one more time before they pack up to go home.

4. *Plan time for students to sort independently and with partners.* Students need time to sort through words on their own. Teachers build this independent work into seat work, center activities, and group games. Word study lends itself nicely to many cooperative activities.

Figure 3-12 shows a 5-day schedule that accommodates a four-step word study lesson plan for three groups rotating through a circle-seat-center instructional plan. We will discuss the details later in the chapter.

Progressive Skill Development

An important decision that a teacher makes is how to schedule activities over the course of a week. Betty Lee, a renowned first-grade teacher of 30 years, developed a general progression in word study activities. In this progression, students recognize, recall, judge, and apply their growing word knowledge through the activities.

Recognize

With key pictures and key words, teachers guide the students as they compare words. For example, when students analyze initial consonants, they compare the picture of a man with the key picture of a mouse. They recognize that the words *man* and *mouse* begin with the same sound. To recognize is to be aware of a new orthographic feature.

Recall

In this second step in the progression, students recall examples of the features they have studied. A key word or key picture is provided to remind students of the types of words they are trying to recall as they endeavor to generate other examples. After sorting, young children may **draw and label** pictures of things that begin with *m* using the key word *mouse* to stimulate recall. If students' immediate recall stalls, they might be encouraged to look through alphabet books to trigger recall. Students in a later stage of orthographic development may generate rhyming words that follow a specific orthographic pattern. If

FIGURE 3-13   Class Homophone Book

the key word is *beat,* students might be shown how they can find other words by dropping the beginning consonant and adding another to obtain *seat, neat,* or *meat.* These words can then be recorded on a chart or in their word study notebooks.

Judge

In judgment activities, students hunt through word or picture books for words that match the features they are studying. In a word hunt, they make judgments as to which words fit in the categories. For example, students studying short -*a* will judge the sound of every *a* word they come to in scanning back through familiar texts. Children in the emergent stage may hunt through catalogs or magazines to cut out pictures of things that have a particular sound and paste these into sorts.

Apply

There are many application-type activities. Students apply what they have learned to create something new. Open sorts are application activities because students find and proclaim their own categories. For example, students who have studied the various patterns for long -*e* can apply the recurring pattern of consonants and vowels to sort long -*o* words. Another form of application involves guided proofreading. Many teachers have children return to their writing folders to look for words they may have written earlier that follow the sound or pattern they have just sorted. Board and card games that match and categorize word features also provide opportunities for application in an enjoyable context.

As students become wordsmiths, you will marvel at the lists of words they create. One class created an illustrated homophone dictionary in a "big book" format (see Figure 3-13). By the end of the year, students had collected 250 homophone pairs, illustrated them, and arranged them in alphabetical order. The children's spelling and vocabulary were enhanced by this cooperative project.

Word Study Schedules

Many teachers plan their weekly word study routine around these progressive skills. In the following examples, teachers begin with a directed word study session in which they introduce the categories. Betty Lee's plan works well for children who are in the emergent to early letter name–alphabetic stage, where sorting is done primarily with pictures and children cannot be expected to read or spell the printed words.

Betty Lee's Routine for Emergent to Early Letter Name–Alphabetic Spellers

In her first-grade class, Betty Lee organized her word study program around a circle-seat-center rotation format (see Figure 3-12). She introduced her spelling concepts with a picture sort at circle time, working with about a third of the class who were at the same developmental level. A second third of the class worked at their seats drawing and labeling pictures of words they recalled from a previous lesson. The remaining students were stationed at different centers where they worked at cutting and pasting, or playing word study games with a partner. These activities can be organized

Betty Lee's Schedule				
Monday	**Tuesday**	**Wednesday**	**Thursday**	**Friday**
Picture Sorting	Drawing and Labeling	Cutting and Pasting	Word Hunts Word Banks	Games

FIGURE 3-14 Betty Lee's Weekly Schedule of Word Study with Pictures

in a 5-day routine as summarized in Figure 3-14 and described in the following paragraphs, or this routine can be shortened into a 3-day plan for students who are reviewing and need to move more quickly. Figure 3-15 shows a student's pocket folder that can be used at this level to keep materials organized and guide students to the daily routines. Students can keep their cutout pictures in the envelope until they are pasted down or discarded. Each folder has a sound board (one of three sound charts that can be found in the Appendix) to use as a reference and a record of progress. Students can simply color the boxes lightly with crayon to indicate that they have worked with that sound.

Monday—Picture sort.   The teacher models the categorization routine using picture cards and helps students recognize the sounds and letters they are studying. Sound categories are established using a letter card and a key picture that is used repeatedly to help students develop a strong association between the beginning sound of the word and the letter that represents it. Each picture is named and compared with the key picture to listen for sounds that are the same. The sort might be repeated several times in the circle as a group or with partners. During their center or seat time, the children do the same picture sort again on their own or with a partner.

Tuesday—Draw and label.   Students recall the feature introduced on Monday in drawing and labeling activities. The examples in Figure 3-7 show a student's recall of initial consonants in a draw and label activity. Students are encouraged to write as much of the word as they can, using invented spelling to label their drawing. Teachers can use these spellings to judge student progress in hearing and representing sounds. Students may sort again at seats or centers.

Wednesday—Cut and paste.   Children make judgments and extend their understandings to other examples when they look through old catalogs and magazines for pictures that begin with a particular sound. These pictures are cut out, pasted into categories or into an alphabet book (see Chapter 4), and labeled. Children who have photocopies of picture sorts might paste these into categories and label them. This takes less time than looking through magazines but it is also less challenging. Large retail store catalogs are particularly useful because the index is arranged alphabetically. Teachers can tear out several pages and place them in a folder for students to look through as they search for pictures to cut and paste and then label.

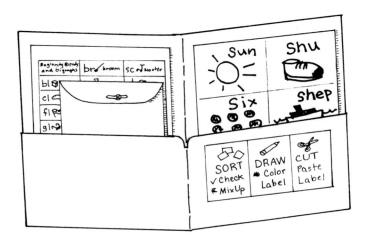

FIGURE 3-15 Pocket Folder for Organizing Materials

Thursday—Word and picture hunts.   Children apply what they have learned as they look for more words through word hunts, word bank activities, and other tasks. Children can reread nursery rhymes and jingles and they circle words that begin with the same sounds they have been categorizing all week. These words are added to their sorts. (Word bank activities are described in more detail in Chapter 5.)

Friday—Game day.   Children delight in the opportunity to play board or card games and other games in which the recognition, recall, and judgment of spelling features are applied. Assessment at this level is primarily informal as the teacher watches for automaticity and accuracy during sorting and how well students label pictures or use initial sounds in writing.

A Weekly Schedule for Students in the Primary and Elementary Grades

The next schedule works well for children who are readers and able to spell entire words. Sorting words in a variety of contexts and completing assignments in a word study notebook comprise most of the schedule summarized in Figure 3-16.

Word study notebooks provide a built-in, orderly record of activities and progress. Many teachers grade the notebooks as part of an overall spelling grade. Figure 3-17 is a list of the expectations and grading criteria used by Kathy Gankse when she taught her fourth-grade class. This chart can be reproduced and pasted inside the cover of the notebook. Composition books with stiff cardboard covers and sewn pages last all year. Below is a list of possible assignments to be completed in the notebook. You may want to make some "required" activities, such as writing the sort, and some "choice" activities, such as draw and label. There is no need to do all every week and some are more valuable at times than others.

1. *Writing word sorts.* Students write the words into the same categories developed during hands-on sorting. Key words are used as headers for each column.
2. *Selecting 10 words to draw and label.* Even older students enjoy the opportunity to illustrate words with simple drawings that reveal their meanings.
3. *Changing a letter (or letters) to make new words.* Initial letter(s) might be substituted to create lists of words that rhyme. For example, starting with the word *black,* a student might generate *stack, quack, track, shack,* and so on.
4. *Selecting 10 words to use in sentences.* This is important as children begin the study of homophones, inflected words (*ride, rides, riding*), and roots and suffixes where meaning is an issue.

Weekly Schedule for Students in the Primary and Elementary Grades				
Monday	**Tuesday**	**Wednesday**	**Thursday**	**Friday**
Introduce Sort in Group	Re-sort and Write Sort	Buddy Sort Writing Sort	Word Hunt	Testing and Games
Monday	**Tuesday**	**Wednesday**	**Thursday**	**Friday**
Introduce Sort in Group	Speed Sort with Partner	Word Hunts in Trade Books	Speed Sort with Teacher	Testing
Word Study Notebook Assignments Throughout the Week				

FIGURE 3-16   Two Schedules for Students Who Can Already Read

FIGURE 3-17   Expectations for Word Study Notebooks

5. *Recording words from word hunts in trade books and response journals.* Students add these words to the written sorts in their notebooks.

Monday—Introduce the sort.

Many teachers pass out the set of words for the week on Monday morning so the children can cut them apart in preparation for group work; other teachers pass out the handouts during group time for students to review (as shown in Figure 3-18). Some teachers may not hand them out until after the group sort. Each group in the class has different words, depending on the students' stage of development. Before cutting their words apart, students should draw three vertical lines down the backside of their paper using a crayon or colored marker. After the words are cut apart, this color stripe will distinguish their word cards from others as the children work together.

The teacher-directed introductory lesson should include demonstration, sorting, checking, and reflecting, as described on pages 74–76. These students are then sent back to their seat to repeat the sort and may be assigned the task of sorting again for homework. The teacher then repeats this procedure with the next group focusing on a different feature.

Tuesday—Practice the sort and write it.

On Tuesday, students sort again. This might be done at their seats as everyone sorts their own collection of words for 5 or 10 minutes as the teacher circulates and asks students to read the words and declare their categories. Or it might be done group by group as students bring their words to sort under the teacher's supervision in a brief session or as part of a guided reading group. Children are assigned a writing sort for seatwork or for homework. Speed sorts might also be planned for Tuesday. Students can be paired up for speed sorts, and follow a posted schedule of times and partners. Throughout the day, partners go back to the "sorting table" at 10-minute intervals to sort their word cards for accuracy and speed. One child times the other with a stopwatch kept at the table and then checks for correctness against an answer sheet. Partners work together to solve any discrepancies between their sort and the answer sheet. The partners return to their seats to complete work in word study notebooks and pick up where they left off with other assignments.

Wednesday—No-peeking sorts and writing sorts.

On Wednesday, students work in pairs to do no-peeking sorts as described earlier in this chapter. After each partner has led the sort, the pair might do a no-peeking writing sort in which the partners take turns calling words aloud for the other to write into categories. This can also be a homework assignment in which the parents call the words aloud.

Thursday—Word hunts.

Word hunts are conducted in groups, with partners, or individually. All the students in the class can be engaged in this at the

FIGURE 3-18   Students Gather with Weekly Word Lists for an Introductory Sort

same time by convening in their respective groups. The teacher circulates from group to group to comment and listen in on the students' discussion. The teacher asks group members to provide reasons for the agreed upon groupings. After this activity, the word hunt is recorded in each member's word study notebook. For homework that night, students find additional examples to add to their notebooks from the books they are reading at home.

Friday—Assessment and games.   A traditional spelling test format can be used for assessment. If you have two or three groups, simply call one word in turn for each group. This may sound confusing, but children will recognize the words they have studied over the week and rarely lose track. It is not necessary to call out every word studied during the week (10 words may be enough) and teachers may even call out some bonus or transfer words that were not among the original list to see if students can generalize the orthographic principles to new words. In this way, the discriminating orthographic feature is emphasized, as opposed to rote memorization of a given list of words. It is particularly effective to conduct the spelling test as a writing sort, having students write each word as it is called out into the category where it belongs. One point can be awarded for correct category placement, and one point for correct spelling. Spelling tests conducted as writing sorts reinforce the importance of categorization and press students to generalize from the specific word to the system as a whole. Although games can be played anytime, Fridays might be reserved for them.

Friday completes the cycle for the week. Results of the Friday test and observations made during the week influence the teacher's plans for the next week. The teacher may decide that students need to revisit a feature, compare it with another feature, or move on to new features. Group membership may also change depending on a given child's pace and progress.

Alternative Weekly Plan

If you do not want to take a large block of time on Monday to do all the introductions, you can spread them across the week by meeting with other groups on Tuesday and Wednesday while Monday's group works independently in an "offset" schedule (see Figure 3-19). In this schedule, students with the least ability get the most practice but everyone does similar activities by Thursday and Friday.

	Monday	**Tuesday**	**Wednesday**	**Thursday**	**Friday**
Lowest Group	*Meet with teacher* *Sort again at seats*	*Sort again and write sort for homework*	*Partner work*	*Word hunts* *No-peeking writing sort for homework*	*Assessment games*
Middle Group		*Meet with teacher* *Sort and write sort at home*	*Partner work*	*Word hunts* *No-peeking writing sort for homework*	*Assessment games*
Highest Group		*Sort words independently* *Write sort and reflect*	*Meet with teacher* *Partner work if time*	*Word hunts* *No-peeking writing sort for homework*	*Assessment games*

FIGURE 3-19   "Offset" Weekly Plan

Organizing Word Study in the Secondary Grades

Secondary students often change classes every 50 minutes, or if they have block scheduling, every 1 hour and 40 minutes. Either way, the constraints of periods or blocks limit the way word study is conducted. Because secondary English classes are not usually as heterogeneous as elementary classrooms, students are more likely to have similar word study needs. Still, the typical secondary English teacher plans instruction for students in at least two different stages of word knowledge. The range of word knowledge and the limited amounts of time make for a challenge.

One way to organize word study instruction in secondary classrooms is through the use of contracts or individualized assignment plans. In individual assignment plans, students agree to participate in a set number of word sorts, writing sorts, and word hunts each week. If students are in the late syllables and affixes stage or the derivational relations stage, it is less important for them to physically sort word cards. Instead, sorts can be conducted in writing, using a worksheet format. Here, students write the words listed at the bottom of the sheet into the appropriate category. All of the other word study activities may also be conducted as paper- and pencil-tasks and organized in a word study section of a three-ring binder.

Integrating Word Study into the Language Arts Curriculum

The weekly schedules described herein are one example of how to integrate spelling instruction into a process-oriented classroom. These routines are central to both reading and writing. Students return again and again to trade books they have already read to analyze the vocabulary. Word study is integrated into other studies as well. Poetry lessons begin with reference to a word study lesson on syllable stress. In a writing lesson, students discuss comparative adjectives from a previous word study lesson that focused on words ending in *-er*. During a lesson on parts of speech, the students are asked to sort their week's spelling words by nouns, verbs, and adjectives. Whatever routine you choose, your sequence of activities must fit comfortably within your reading/writing/language arts block of instruction.

Selecting Written Word Study Activities: A Caveat Regarding Tradition

There are many long-standing activities associated with spelling that teachers often assign their students such as writing words five times, writing them in alphabetical order, and copying definitions of words from the dictionary. Think critically about whether assignments like these fulfill the purpose of spelling instruction—which is not only to learn the spellings of particular words, but also to learn generalizations about the spelling system itself. Writing a word five times can be a rote meaningless activity, whereas writing words into categories requires the recognition of common spelling features and the use of judgment and critical thinking. Writing words in alphabetical order may teach alphabetization but it will not teach anything about spelling patterns. Alphabetizing words might be assigned occasionally as a separate dictionary skill, and children will be more successful at it when they can first sort their word cards into alphabetical order before writing them. Students do need to associate meanings with the words they are studying, particularly in upper-level word study when dealing with syllables and affixes and derivational relations. It is reasonable to ask students to look up the meanings of a few words they do not know, but asking students to write the definitions of long lists of words they already know is disheartening and not likely to encourage dictionary use.

Writing words in sentences can also be overdone. You might allow students to choose 10 words (out of 24) each week to write sentences in their word study notebooks. This is a more reasonable assignment than writing 24 isolated sentences with the weekly spelling list. Writing just a few sentences per day encourages the application of word use and meaning. Many teachers use sentence writing to work on handwriting, punctuation, and grammar (see expectations in Figure 3-17). Writing sentences is more useful at some levels of development than others. For example, sentences will help students show that they understand homophones or the tense of verb forms when studying inflected endings such as -ed and -ing.

Be wary of other traditional assignments that take up time and may even be fun, but have little value in teaching children about spelling. Activities such as hangman, word searches, and acrostics may keep students busy, but they impart little or no information about the English spelling system. Spelling bees reward those children who are already good spellers and eliminate early the children who need practice the most. Word study can be fun, but make good use of the time spent on it and do not overdo it. Remember that word study activities should be short in duration so that students can devote most of their attention and time to reading and writing for meaningful purposes.

Word Study Homework and Parental Expectations

Classrooms are busy places and many teachers find it difficult to devote a lot of time to word study. Homework can provide additional practice time, and parents are usually pleased to see that spelling is part of the curriculum. A letter sent home, such as the one shown in Figure 3-20, is a good way to encourage parents to become involved in their children's spelling homework. Parents are typically firm believers in the importance of

---

Dear Parents,

Your child will be bringing home a collection of spelling words weekly that have been introduced in class. Each night of the week your child is expected to do a different activity to ensure that these words and the spelling principles they represent are mastered. These activities have been modeled and practiced in school, so your child can teach you how to do them.

Monday   Remind your child to *sort the words* into categories like the ones we did in school. Your child should read each word aloud during this activity. Ask your child to explain to you why the words are sorted in a particular way—what does the sort reveal about spelling in general? Ask your child to sort them a second time as fast as possible.

Tuesday   Do a "*buddy sort*" with your child. Lay down a word from each category as a header and then read the rest of the words aloud. Your child must indicate where the word goes without seeing it. Lay it down and let your child move it if he or she is wrong. Repeat if your child makes more than one error.

Wednesday   Assist your child in doing a *word hunt*, looking for words in a familiar book that have the same sound, pattern, or both. Try to find two or three for each category.

Thursday   Do a *writing sort* to prepare for the Friday test. As you call out the words in a random order your child should write them in categories. Call out any words your child misspells a second or even third time.

Thank you for your support. Together we can help your child make valuable progress!

Sincerely,

Teacher Name

FIGURE 3-20   Parent Letter

spelling because it is such a visible sign of literacy, and many are even taking political action to see it reinstated. Unfortunately, invented spelling is often a scapegoat because parents, politicians, and even some teachers unfairly associate the acceptance of invented spelling with lack of instruction and an "anything goes" expectation regarding spelling accuracy in children's writing at all grade levels. Communicate clearly to parents that their children will be held accountable for what they have been taught. Homework assignments help them see what is being taught in phonics and spelling.

Expectations for Editing and Accuracy in Children's Written Work

Invented spellings free children to write even before they can read during the emergent stage, and children should be free to make spelling approximations when writing rough drafts at all levels. Invented spellings also offer teachers diagnostic information about what children know and what they need to learn. But that does not mean that teachers do not hold children accountable for accurate spelling. Knowing where children are in terms of levels of development and knowing what word features they have studied enable teachers to set reasonable expectations for accuracy and editing. Typical third graders in the within word pattern stage can be expected to spell words like *jet, flip,* and *must,* but it would be unreasonable to expect them to spell multisyllabic words like *leprechaun* or *celebration.* Just as students are gradually held more and more accountable for conventions of writing such as commas and semicolons, so too, they are gradually held more accountable for spelling accuracy. Understanding of how spelling develops over time enables teachers to have reasonable expectations for the class and for individuals within the class. Teachers also need to direct students to a range of spelling resources and help students learn to use them.

When teachers work with students in small groups, they often use chart paper to make lists of words that are then posted around the room. Words listed on the walls call attention to the richness and power of a versatile vocabulary. Sometimes these charts chronicle discussions of content studies, and sometimes they focus on the specific study of words: happy words, sad words, holiday or seasonal words, homophones, homographs, synonyms, and antonyms. They all provide a ready reference for writing.

Learning to use resources such as word walls (Cunningham, 1995), word banks, personal dictionaries, sound boards, and dictionaries should be a part of the word study curriculum. Even first graders can use simple dictionaries appropriate for their level to look up some special words, and they can be encouraged to refer to their own individual word banks for words. However, that does not mean you could expect them to look up all the words they need to use. A study by Clarke (1988) found that first graders who were encouraged to use invented spellings wrote more and could spell as well at the end of the year as first graders who had been told how to spell the words before writing. This indicates that children are not marred by their own invented spellings or perseverate with errors over time. However, unless teachers communicate that correct spelling is valued, students may develop careless habits.

Many teachers wonder when they should make the shift from allowing children to write in invented spelling to demanding correctness. The answer is from the start. Teachers must hold children accountable for what they have been taught. What they have not been taught can be politely ignored. For example, if a child has been taught the sound-to-letter correspondences for *b, m, r,* and *s,* the teacher would expect the child to spell these beginning sounds correctly; however, if the child has not yet been taught the short-vowel sounds, these should be allowed to stand as invented spellings. Because the sequence for phonics and spelling instruction is cumulative and progresses linearly from easier features such as individual letter sounds to harder features such as Latin-derived *-tion, -sion,* and *-cian* endings, there will always be some features that have not yet been taught. Thus, children (and adults!) will always invent a spelling for what they do not yet know.

TABLE 3-2	Grading Form for Word Study		
Name:	**Grading Period:**		
	Excellent Effort	**Good Effort**	**Needs Improvement**
Weekly Word Study			
Word sorts			
Word study notebook			
Partner work			
Final tests			
Editing Written Work			
Spells most words right			
Finds misspelled words to correct			
Assists others in editing work			
Uses a variety of resources to correct spelling			

A = Excellent work in most areas
B = Good work in most areas
C = Needs improvement in most areas

Recommended Grade _____

Comments:

Spelling Tests and Grades

Some teachers are expected to assign grades for spelling, or spelling may be part of an overall language arts or writing grade. Ideally such a grade should include more than an average of Friday test scores (which should all be high when children are working on words at their instructional level). Table 3-2 offers a more holistic assessment using a form that can be adapted for any grade level. Some teachers may wish to add a section for students to rate themselves. This one might be used with students in upper elementary who can be expected to spell most words correctly.

TEN PRINCIPLES OF WORD STUDY INSTRUCTION

A number of basic principles guide the kind of word study described in *Words Their Way*. These principles set word study apart from many other approaches to the teaching of phonics, spelling, or vocabulary. The 10 guiding principles are summarized in Figure 3-21 and discussed in detail in the following paragraphs.

1. *Look for what students use but confuse.* Students cannot learn things they do not already know something about. This is the underlying principle of Vygotsky's (1962) **zone of proximal development (ZPD)** and the motivating force behind the spelling-by-stage assessment described in Chapter 2. By classifying invented spellings developmentally, a zone of proximal development may be identified and instruction can be planned to address features the students are using but confusing, instead of those they totally neglect (Invernizzi, Abouzeid, & Gill, 1994). As was discussed in earlier chapters, using but confusing is a signal that students are trying to learn something

1. Look for what students use but confuse.

2. A step backward is a step forward.

3. Use words students can read.

4. Compare words "that do" with words "that don't."

5. Sort by sound and sight.

6. Begin with obvious contrasts.

7. Don't hide exceptions.

8. Avoid rules.

9. Work for automaticity.

10. Return to meaningful texts.

FIGURE 3-21 Principles of Word Study

new about the orthography. Take your cue from the students, not the curriculum. Teachers look to see what features are consistently present and correct to determine what aspects of English orthography the students already know. By looking for features that are used inconsistently, teachers determine those aspects of the orthography currently under negotiation. These are the features to target in word study instruction.

2. *A step backward is a step forward.* Once you have identified students' stages of developmental word knowledge and the orthographic features under negotiation, take a step backward and build a firm foundation. Then, in setting up your categories, contrast something new with something that is already known. If, for example, you are beginning to introduce a new sound or pattern, be sure to present it in contrast to a familiar sound or pattern. It is important to begin word study activities where the students will experience success. For example, students in the within word pattern stage who are ready to examine long-vowel patterns begin by sorting words by short-vowel sounds, which are familiar, and long-vowel sounds, which are being introduced for the first time. Then they move quickly to sorting by pattern. A step backward is the first step forward in word study instruction.

3. *Use words students can read.* Since learning to spell involves achieving a match between the spoken language and the orthography, your students should examine words that they can readily pronounce. Dialect does not alter the importance of this basic principle of word study. Whether one says "hog" or "hawg," it is still spelled *hog.* The consistency is in the orthography, and it is your job as the teacher to make those consistencies explicit. It is easier to look across words for consistency of pattern when the words are easy for students to pronounce. Known words come from any and all sources that the children can read: **language experience** stories, recent readings, poems, phonics readers, and even old spelling books collecting dust on the shelf. As much as possible, choose words to sort that students can read out of context.

4. *Compare words "that do" with words "that don't."* To learn what a Chesapeake Bay retriever looks like, you have to see a poodle or a bulldog, not another Chesapeake Bay retriever. What something *is* is also defined by what it is *not;* contrasts are essential to students building categories. Students' spelling errors suggest what contrasts will help them sort out their confusions. For example, a student who is spelling *stopping* as STOPING will benefit from a sort in which words with double consonants before adding *-ing* are contrasted with those that do not, as in Figure 3-22.

5. *Sort by sound and sight.* Students examine words by how they sound and how they are spelled. Both sound and visual pattern are integrated into students' orthographic knowledge. Too often, students focus on visual patterns at the expense of how words are alike in sound. The following sort illustrates the way students move from a **sound sort** to visual **pattern sort.** First, students sorted by the differences in sound between hard -*g* and soft -*g.* Then students subdivided the sound sort by orthographic patterns. See what you can discover from this sort.

hopping	raining
planning	cleaning
skipping	nailing
batting	reading
hugging	sleeping
	peeling
	feeling

FIGURE 3-22 Doubling Sort: Comparing Words "That Do" with Words "That Don't"

First Sort by Sound of *G*			Second Sort by Pattern		
Soft	*Hard*		*dge*	*ge*	*g*
edge	bag		edge	cage	bag
cage	twig		ridge	huge	twig
huge	slug		judge	stage	slug
judge	drug		badge	page	flag
stage	leg		lodge		drug
badge	flag				leg
page					
lodge					

6. *Begin with obvious contrasts.* When students begin the study of a new feature, teachers choose key words or pictures that are distinctive. For example, when students first examine initial consonants, teachers do not begin by contrasting *m* with *n*. They share too many features to be distinct to the novice: They are both nasals and visually similar. It is better to begin by contrasting *m* with something totally different at first—*s,* for example—then work toward finer distinctions as these categorizations become quite automatic. Move from general, gross discriminations to more specific ones.

Likewise, be wary of two-syllable words for beginners, even if only picture cards are used. *Banana* may start with a *b,* but the first /n/ sound is stressed or pronounced the loudest, and some beginners will be confused.

7. *Don't hide exceptions.* Exceptions arise when students make generalizations. Do not hide these exceptions. By placing so-called irregular words in a miscellaneous or oddball category, new categories of consistency frequently emerge. For example, in looking at long-vowel patterns, students find these exceptions: *give, have,* and *love;* yet it is no coincidence that they all have a *v.* They form a small but consistent pattern of their own. True exceptions do occasionally occur and become memorable by virtue of their rarity.

8. *Avoid rules.* Rules with many exceptions are disheartening and teach children nothing. They may have heard the long-vowel rule, "When two vowels go walking, the first one does the talking," but this rule is frequently violated in words like *head, boot,* or *soil.* Learning about English spelling requires students to consider sound and pattern simultaneously to discover consistencies in the orthography. This requires both reflection and continued practice. Students discover consistencies and make generalizations for themselves. The teacher's job is to stack the deck and structure categorization tasks to make these consistencies explicit and to instill in students the habit of looking at words, asking questions, and searching for order. Rules are useful mnemonics if you already understand the underlying concepts at work. They are the icing on the cake of knowledge. But memorizing rules is not the way children make sense of how words work. Rules are no substitute for experience.

9. *Work for automaticity.* Accuracy in sorting is not enough; accuracy *and* speed are the ultimate indicators of mastery. Acquiring automaticity in sorting and recognizing orthographic patterns leads to the fluency necessary for proficient reading and writing. Your students will move from hesitancy to fluency in their sorting. Keep sorting until they do.

10. *Return to meaningful texts.* After sorting, students need to return to meaningful texts to hunt for other examples to add to the sorts. These hunts extend their analysis to more words and more difficult vocabulary. For example, after sorting one-syllable words into categories labeled *cat, drain,* and *snake,* a student added *tadpole, complain,* and *relate.* Through a simple word hunt, this child extended the pattern-to-sound consistency in one-syllable words to stressed syllables in two-syllable words.

These 10 principles of word study boil down to one golden rule of word study instruction: *Teaching is not telling* (James, 1958). In word study, students examine, manipulate, and categorize words. Teachers stack the deck and create tasks that focus students' attention on critical contrasts. Stacking the deck for a discovery approach to word study is not the absence of direct instruction. To the contrary, a systematic program of word study, guided by an informed interpretation of spelling errors and other literacy behaviors, is a teacher-directed, child-centered approach to vocabulary growth and spelling development. The next five chapters will show you exactly how to provide effective word study instruction.

4

Word Study for Learners in the Emergent Stage

This chapter presents an overview of the literacy development that occurs during the emergent stage, a period in which young children imitate and experiment with the forms and functions of print. Emergent readers are busy orchestrating the many notes and movements essential to literacy: directionality, the distinctive features of print, the predictability of text, and how all of these correlate with oral language. The emergent stage lies at the beginning of a lifetime of learning about written language.

In Table 2-2 we saw that early emergent students score 0 on spelling inventories, because emergent children do not read or spell conventionally; they have very tenuous understandings of how units of speech and units of print are related. Nevertheless, children are developing remarkable insights into written language and with the help of caregivers and teachers they learn a great deal during what has sometimes been called the **preliterate stage** (Henderson, 1990). Before we go into a thorough description of the emergent stage, we will visit a classroom where 23 kindergartners explore literacy under the guidance of their teacher, Mrs. Collins.

During a unit on animals, Mrs. Collins shared the big book, *Oh, A-Hunting We Will Go,* by John Langstaff. This book is based on the traditional refrain, "Oh, a-hunting we will go, a-hunting we will go. We'll catch a fox and put him in a box and then we'll let him go." The pattern repeats with various animals and places substituting for *box* and *fox.* After reading several pages, Mrs. Collins began pausing to allow her students to guess the name of the place using their sense of rhyme and picture cues. When several students sang out that the *whale* would be put in a *bucket,* Mrs. Collins pointed to the word *pail* on the page and said, "Could that word be *bucket?* What does *bucket* start with? Listen. *[b]-bucket.* What does this word start with?"

In this fashion Mrs. Collins introduced a new book with her children as they enjoyed the silliness of the rhymes and pictures. In the process she drew her students' attention to letters and sounds and modeled directionality and fingerpointing as she read. After enjoying the big book version, she planned a number of follow-up activities to further develop emergent literacy skills.

Mrs. Collins created a chart with the first five lines of patterned text and posted it in the room for children to read from memory. She also wrote each of the first five lines on sentence strips and placed them in order in a pocket chart. After the children had read the lines several times chorally, Mrs. Collins passed out the strips. As a group they put the sentences back in order by comparing them to the chart. Another day, word cards for *fox, box, catch, go,* and *we* were held up one by one as volunteers came up to find the words on the chart or sentence strips. Mrs. Collins observed carefully to see which children were beginning to point accurately as they recited. She made sure the book, chart, and strips were left out where everyone could practice freely with them during the day.

Mrs. Collins had a group of children who were studying initial consonants. In previous lessons they had compared words that started with *s* and *m.* Now they looked for words that started with *b* and *f* on the five-line chart and found *fox* and *box.* Mrs. Collins wrote those words on cards as the key words for a picture sort. She brought out a collection of pictures that started with *b* and *f* and modeled how to sort several by beginning sound in the pocket chart. She then invited the children to take turns sorting the rest of the pictures that she placed in the pockets below. This sort was repeated by the group and on subsequent days all the children had a number of opportunities to sort on their own, to hunt for more pictures in alphabet books and magazines, and to draw and label pictures with those sounds. After the students compared the sounds for *b* and *f* in several ways, the pictures were combined with *m* and *s,* which had been studied previously, for a four-category sort. The students worked with all four letters and sounds for several days before moving on to a new contrast.

Mrs. Collins used a core book as the basis for teaching a variety of emergent literacy skills in a developmental and appropriate fashion. In Mrs. Collins's class, word study activities address issues critical to emergent literacy in the context of read-alouds and playful language lessons. We will discuss these critical issues and how teachers like Mrs. Collins promote literacy learning.

FROM SPEECH TO PRINT: THE SYNCHROMESH OF UNITS

Learning to read and spell is a process of matching oral and written language structures at three different levels: (a) the global level at which the text is organized into phrases and sentences, (b) the level of words within phrases, and (c) the level of sounds and letters within syllables. For someone learning to read, there is not always an obvious match between spoken and written language at any of these levels. Mismatches occur because of the inflexible nature of print and the flowing stream of speech it represents. Learning to make the match between speech and print is a gradual process, but essential. To learn to read and spell, children must explore the structures of both written and spoken language at these three levels.

The Phrase and Sentence Level

In oral language, the global level is characterized as **prosodic.** This is the "musical" level of language, usually consisting of phrases. Within these phrases, speakers produce and listeners hear intonation contours, expression, and tone of voice, all of which communicate ideas and emotions. For example, a rising note at the end of a statement indicates a question; precise, clipped words in a brusque tone may suggest anger or irritation. Oral language is a direct form of communication where there are partners who fill in the gaps in the incoming message and who indicate when communication breaks down. Written language is an indirect form of communication and must contain complete, freestanding messages in which meaning is clear. Punctuation and word choice are the reader's only cues to the emotions and intent of the writer. Written language tends to be more formal and carefully constructed, using recognizable structures and literacy devices such as "happily ever after" to cue the reader. When children learn to read, they must match the prosody of their oral language to these more formal structures of written language.

Words in Phrases

A second level of structures that students negotiate are the units of meaning called **words.** In speech, words are not distinct; there is not a clear, separable unit in speech that equates perfectly to individual words. For example, "once upon a time" represents a single idea composed of four words and five syllables. Because of this, when children try to match their speech to print, they often miss the mark. It takes practice and instruction to match words in speech to written words (Morris, 1980; Roberts, 1992).

This mismatch of meaning units between speech and print is most clearly illustrated through an instrument called a **spectrograph.** This acoustic representation of speech reveals a surprising thing: Humans do not speak in words! There are no demarcations for individual words when a person is talking. The only break in a spectrograph coincides with phrases and pauses for breathing. These breaks always occur between syllables. A word is a term specific to print, and according to Malinowski (1952), cultures that have no written language have no word for *word*. This remarkable state of affairs creates an enormous challenge for individuals learning to read.

Sounds in Syllables

Sounds and letters make up the third level of analysis. In learning to read, students must negotiate sounds within syllables. In speech, consonants and vowels are interconnected and cannot be easily separated (Liberman & Shankweiler, 1991). Yet the alphabet and letter sounds must be learned as discrete units. As children stabilize the match between print and speech at the phrase and sentence level, they come to discover the way the alphabet divides the sounds within syllables. Their first understanding develops through exploring the beginning sounds of words. Later, once they understand how the alphabet represents sounds, children begin to view the writing system—the **orthography**—as a series of patterns that are organized at the level of syllable.

CHARACTERISTICS OF THE EMERGENT STAGE OF READING AND SPELLING

Some emergent children may have well-developed language skills and know a great deal about stories and books; others may not. It is not necessary for children who have difficulty expressing themselves to learn to do that first before learning the alphabet or seeing printed words tracked in correspondence to speech. To withhold these essential components of the learning-to-read process would hold them in double jeopardy. Not only would they be behind in language and story development, but they also would be behind in acquiring the alphabetic principle. Of course all children need to be read to and immersed in the language and literature of their lives; but children can learn about stories *and* learn about words, sounds, and alphabet simultaneously as teachers model reading and writing and encourage children to imitate and experiment.

Emergent Reading

The reading of the emergent child is actually pretend reading, or reading from memory. Both are essential practices for movement into literacy. **Pretend reading** is basically a paraphrase or spontaneous retelling at the global level which children produce while turning the pages of a familiar book. In pretend reading, children pace their retelling to match the sequence of pictures and orchestrate many other concepts about books and print such as directionality, sequence, dialogue, and the voice and cadence of written language (Sulzby, 1986).

Memory reading is more exacting than pretend reading and involves an accurate recitation of the text accompanied by pointing to the print on the page in some fashion. Reading from memory helps children coordinate spoken language with print at the level of words, sounds, and letters. This phenomenon, called **concept of word,** is a watershed event that separates the emergent reader from the letter name–alphabetic beginning reader (Morris, 1981).

Emergent children's attempts to touch individual words while reading from memory are initially quite inconsistent and vague. Such children may realize that they should end up on the last word on the page, but the units that come in between are a blur. Their fingerpointing is likewise nebulous. This strategy for reading is mirrored in their writing, in which word boundaries and print distinctions are also obscured, even if some phoneme-grapheme correspondences have been made (see Figure 4-1).

Other children are aware that there are units to be reckoned with while reading, though they are not exactly sure what these units are. Such children may attempt to touch the print in correspondence to stressed beats in speech. Syllables may even be treated as separate words in print or articles (*the, a, an*) may be treated as part of the noun that follows it. Words gradually begin to evolve as distinct entities with their boundaries defined by beginning and ending sounds. Children's early letter name–alphabetic spelling also provides evidence of this understanding. Early letter name–alphabetic spelling is illustrated in Figure 4-2 and will be described in the next chapter.

IKSKP

"I like housekeeping"

FIGURE 4-1 Emergent Writing without Word Boundaries

i K hskpen

"I like housekeeping"

FIGURE 4-2 Early Letter Name–Alphabetic Spelling with Word Boundaries

Emergent Writing and Spelling

Like emergent reading, early emergent writing is largely pretend. Regardless of most children's culture or where they live, this pretend writing occurs spontaneously wherever writing is encouraged, modeled, and incorporated into play (Ferreiro & Teberosky, 1982). It begins with pictorial representations, and then advances to labeling of these pictures. Children first approximate the most global contours of the writing system: the top-to-bottom and linear arrangement. Later, smaller segments such as numbers, letters, and words are also imitated. Not until the end of this stage does writing achieve a direct relation to speech, and when it does, conventional literacy will soon follow.

The ability to write emerges in children in much the same way that it first emerged in humankind. Pictures, initially used for decorative purposes, came to be used intentionally as mnemonic devices. Later, a picture of a king and a picture of wood were combined to cue the name Kingwood. A rebus system of this sort led to the invention of the syllabary in which speech sounds were directly represented with hieroglyphs. This direct link to speech heralded the emergence of literacy everywhere. It was preceded, however, by a period of 40,000 years of prewriting with pictorial representations (Gelb, 1963).

Like the early humans, the child's first task is to discover that scribbling can represent something and, thereafter, to differentiate drawing from writing and representation from communication. The child must come to realize that a drawing of a flower does not actually say "flower." Writing is necessary to communicate the complete message. The top row of Figure 4-3 presents a progression of drawings and their accompanying utterances that show a clear differentiation between picture and writing.

There are many similarities between infant talk and emergent writing. When babies learn to talk, they do not begin by speaking in phonemes first, then syllables, words, and finally phrases. In fact, it is quite the opposite. They begin by cooing in phrasal contours, approximating the music of their mother tongue. Likewise, children begin to write by approximating the broader contours of the writing system; they begin with the linear arrangement of print. This kind of pretend writing has been called "mock linear" (Clay, 1975). Later, as some letters and numbers are learned, these are interchanged along with creative hieroglyphics or "symbol salad" as children experiment with the distinctive features of print. The bottom row of Figure 4-3 shows the movement from **mock linear** writing (bottom left) to real writing (bottom right).

When babies move into what is conventionally recognized as baby talk, they give up their melodious cooing to concentrate on smaller segments, usually stressed syllables. "Dat!" is hardly as fluid as cooing "Ah-ha-ah-ha," but these awkward exclamations will be smoothed out in time. Likewise, global knowledge of writing and letterforms is temporarily abandoned as children concentrate their attention on the specifics of letter formation and the representation of the most salient sounds of speech. Such attention sometimes leads children to spit out parts of words on paper, often using single consonants to stand for entire syllables. The message is often indecipherable, because children do not understand the purpose or need for spaces and they tend to run their syllables and words together on paper.

Here is where the similarity between spoken and written language breaks down. Humans do not actually talk in words, and there is no such thing as an isolated phoneme. Both words and phonemes are artifacts of print and do not naturally coincide with acoustic realities such as syllables. The concepts of word and phoneme must be taught; both will emerge as children gradually acquire the alphabetic principle and coordinate the units of speech with printed units on the page.

Emergence of Invented Spelling

By the end of the emergent stage, children are beginning to use letters to represent sounds in a systematic way, as shown in the last box in Figure 4-3. These partially phonetic in-

FIGURE 4-3 The Evolution of Emergent Writing

vented spellings represent a number of critical insights and skills. To invent a spelling, children must know some letters—not all, but enough to get started. Second, children must know how to form or write some of the letters they know. Third, children must know that letters represent sounds. Again, they do not have to know all of the letter sounds; indeed, if they know the names of the letters, they might use those as substitutes. Fourth, children must attend to the sounds within syllables and match those sound segments to letters. This ability to divide syllables into the smallest units of sound is called **phonemic awareness.** To invent a spelling, a child must have some degree of phonemic awareness and some knowledge of letter sounds. By the time children gain insight into all four of these aspects of sound and print, they are at the end of the emergent stage.

As emergent readers learn their letters and sounds, they use their alphabetic knowledge to represent the units of sound they perceive. If children are able to discern only the most **salient sound,** then they usually will put down only one letter: *s* for *mouse, n* for *and,* or *n* for *mitten,* for example. Until terms about language segments like "beginning sound" are sorted out, emergent children rely on the feel of their mouths as they analyze the speech stream. Say the phrase "once upon a time" aloud. Say it again while paying attention to what your tongue and lips are doing. The tongue touches another part of the mouth only for the /s/ sound of *once,* the /n/ sound of *upon,* and the /t/ sound of *time.* The lips touch each other twice: for the /p/ sound in the middle of *upon* and for the /m/ sound at the end of *time.* Middle to late emergent spellers pay attention to those tangible points of an utterance where one part of the mouth touches another, or to the most forcefully articulated sounds that make the most vibration or receive the most stress. To emergent spellers, this translates as "the loudest," and they choose the loudest, most prominent, or salient sound of stressed syllables to segment in their analysis of speech.

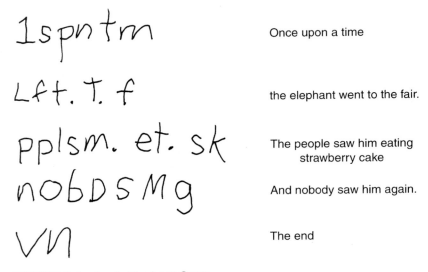

1spn tm	Once upon a time
Lft. T. f	the elephant went to the fair.
pplsm. et. sk	The people saw him eating strawberry cake
nobD S M g	And nobody saw him again.
VM	The end

FIGURE 4-4   Lee's Elephant Story

If some letters are known, they will be matched to these salient sounds accordingly. When literacy development has occurred in a balanced environment, phonemic awareness and the ability to invent a spelling go hand in hand.

Figure 4-4 illustrates Lee's phonemic analysis of words and phrases in her elephant story relative to her knowledge of the alphabet and letter sounds. As children begin to achieve a concept of word, they become more able to pay attention to sounds that correspond to the beginning and the end of word units. Such children will usually put down one or two letters, as in *f* for *fair* or *tm* for *time*. If children know how to write their letters, their invented spelling will reflect their degree of phonemic awareness. As the spellings in Lee's elephant story depict, the phonemes represented are always the most salient, but the most salient are not always at the beginning of a word; she spelled *went* as T and *him* as M. Notice her confusion with word boundaries and how she tries to help herself with periods. The goal of phonemic awareness instruction for emergent readers is to help them classify the sounds they know into categories that coincide with printed word boundaries—beginnings and ends. When letter names are coordinated with word boundaries in a consistent fashion, the student is no longer an emergent speller. Spelling that honors word boundaries consistently is early letter name–alphabetic.

Teaching students the names of the alphabet letters and the sounds they represent is absolutely essential during the emergent stage; but they do not have to get them all straight before they begin to read and write. As with oral language learning, written language learning involves forming and testing hypotheses as new bits of knowledge are perceived and internalized; and, like the incessant chatter of the growing child, it is the extensive practice in approximating the writing system that extends the child's reach. Pretend writing and pretend reading must come first, and as they evolve, real reading and real writing naturally follow (Chomsky, 1971).

Early Literacy Learning and Instruction

To move from emergent to beginning reading, students must have many opportunities to see and experiment with written language. They must see their own spoken language transcribed into print, and they must be supported in making the speech-to-print match by choral recitation and fingerpoint memory reading. They must be encouraged to write, even if this writing is little more than scribbles. The most important condition for emergent literacy to blossom is the opportunity to practice, no matter how closely the child may approximate the standard.

Emergent children will write, or pretend to write, well before they learn to read, provided they are encouraged to do so (Chomsky, 1971). The trick in developmental literacy instruction is how to give that encouragement. The mere act of leaving one's mark on paper (or walls and furniture!) has been called the "fundamental graphic act" (Gibson & Yonas, 1968)—an irresistible act of self-fulfillment. As the teacher, you have to do little more than provide immediate and ready access to implements of writing (markers, crayons, pencils, chalk) and provide a visible role model by drawing and writing yourself. Creating a conducive environment for writing also helps: a grocery store play area where grocery lists are drawn and labeled; a restaurant where menus are offered and orders are written; a writing center with a variety of paper, alphabet stamps, and markers. Outfitted and supported accordingly, writing will happen spontaneously without formal instruction and well before children can spell or properly compose (Strickland & Morrow, 1989). Emergent reading instruction consists of modeling the reading process as teachers read aloud from big books and charts. Early literacy instruction also consists of talk about where one begins to read and where one goes after that. Teachers demonstrate the left-to-right directionality and the return sweep at the end of each line. Of course, all the talk and demonstration in the world will not substitute for hands-on practice. Early literacy instruction includes lots of guided practice with fingerpointing to familiar texts in a left-to-right progression. In the process, pretend or memory reading gradually becomes real reading.

The reading materials best suited for emergent readers are simple predictable books, familiar nursery rhymes, poems, songs, jump rope jingles, and children's own talk written down. Familiarity with songs and rhymes helps bridge the gap between speech and print and cultivates the sense that what can be sung or recited can be written or read. Recording children's own language in the form of picture captions and dictated experience stories also nurtures the notion that print is talk written down. The ownership that comes with having one's own experiences recorded in print is a powerful incentive to explore the world of written language.

Useful techniques for fostering early literacy development include rebuilding familiar rhymes and jingles with sentence strips in pocket charts and matching word cards to individual words on the sentence strips as an explicit way to direct attention to words in print. Sorting objects, pictures, and words by beginning sounds draws attention to letter-sound correspondences. But, reading and rereading is the technique of choice. As is true with all of the stages of word knowledge described in this book, the best way to create a reader is to make reading happen, even if it is just pretend.

Through these activities, the word study instruction for the emergent reader must aim toward the development of five main components of the learning-to-read process:

1. Vocabulary growth and concept development
2. Phonological awareness
3. Alphabet knowledge
4. Letter-sound knowledge
5. Concept of word in print

These five components constitute a comprehensive diet for early literacy learning and instruction. If all five components are addressed on a daily basis, no matter how far along the emergent continuum a child may be, conventional reading and writing should inevitably follow.

COMPONENTS OF EARLY LITERACY LEARNING

This section examines the wondrous ways in which emergent spellers analyze speech and apply it to what they know about print. Bear in mind, however, that emergent understandings of how units of speech correspond to units of print operate within a larger context of concept, language, and vocabulary growth (Snow, 1983). For this reason, we will first look at emergent vocabulary growth and concept development. Then we will describe the other components of early literacy learning.

Vocabulary Growth and Concept Development

A flourishing child who is 4 or 5 years old has acquired a working oral vocabulary of over 5,000 words. The child has mastered the basic subject-verb-object word order of the English language, and may take great delight in the silliness of word sounds and meanings. Many children have learned to recite the days of the week, and some, the months of the year. But to assume that these children need no further experience with the vocabulary of time is to stunt their conceptual understanding of the larger framework of time—how days, weeks, months, and years relate to one another. Ask some precocious 5-year-olds to name the four seasons of the year, and 9 of 10 will recite the names of the months instead. Ask kindergartners to tell you what season of the year December falls in, and many will no doubt tell you "Christmas." These are the answers from children who know the names of the days, the months, and the seasons, but do not fully understand the relationships among them.

Young children use many words whose meanings they do not fully comprehend. Their knowledge of words is only partially formed by the information gleaned from their few years of life. To extend their partial understandings of words, and to acquire new word meanings, children must be given experiences that allow them to add new information to their existing store of word knowledge. Basic concept-development tasks are a surprisingly simple way to provide such experiences.

Concept Sorts

The human mind appears to work by using a compare-and-contrast categorization system to develop concepts and attributes. The sorting activities appropriate for emergent readers build on and reinforce this natural tendency. By stacking the deck with familiar objects, ideas, animals, and things, teachers can devise sorting tasks to help children differentiate and expand existing concepts and labels for those concepts. Fruits can be grouped separately from vegetables, and new vocabulary and interesting concepts are developed along the way.

 For ready-to-print examples of concept sorts appropriate for the Emergent learner, including material easily adaptable to the needs of the English Language Learners in this stage, visit the Emergent section on the accompanying CD-ROM.

One bright 5-year-old knew about tables, chairs, sofas, beds, ovens, refrigerators, microwaves, and blenders; but, in her mind these were all undifferentiated "things in a house." Simply by sorting these items into two different categories—tables, chairs, sofas, and beds; and refrigerators, ovens, microwaves, and blenders—she was able to differentiate the characteristics of *furniture* from those of *appliances*. In this way her concept of things in a house was refined to include these new concepts. The words followed shortly thereafter.

Read-alouds play a critical role in the development of vocabulary and concepts. Books provide background knowledge that some children may not have experienced. For example, books about seasons, weather, transportation, and how seeds grow provide basic vocabulary and information, both of which are essential to comprehending written texts. After listening to Ruth Heller's book, *Chickens Aren't the Only Ones*, children might be provided picture cards to sort into groups: birds, mammals, and reptiles. In this way children may build upon a simple conceptual understanding of where eggs come from to include other attributes of the animal kingdom. Concept sorts based on daily life experiences and information gleaned from books develop and expand chil-

FIGURE 4-5 Concept Sort with Farm Animals and Zoo Animals

ELL English Language Learners learn new vocabulary through concept sorts.

dren's understandings of their world and their language to talk about it. For example, during a unit on animals, a teacher could introduce children to a concept sort such as the one shown in Figure 4-5.

There are many things in daily life that, for the child, remain unclassified in a sea of unrelated variety. Because language is concept based, children of diverse cultures may have different conceptual foundations. Teachers must be particularly sensitive to ethnic and cultural diversity in the classroom. They cannot expect children to learn words that label notions unconnected to their experience. Teachers should provide opportunities for children to categorize familiar objects from their surroundings and from experiences in their daily lives at home and in the classroom according to similarity and difference. Read-alouds provide a common frame of reference to further concept development and vocabulary growth for everyone.

The concept sorts described in the activities section (starting on page 115) are all variations on the theme of categorization tasks. In addition to basic sorting, concept-development activities are generally followed by draw and label or cut and paste procedures. As always, we recommend having children write at every possible opportunity during or following the concept sorts. As a culminating activity for a unit on animals, one teacher helped her children create their own books in which they drew pictures of their favorite animals. Many of her children were able to label these pictures or write stories about the animals with either pretend writing or invented spelling. Her children's efforts ranged from scribbles and random letters to readable approximations such as I LIK THE LINS N TGRS.

Phonological Awareness

Phonological awareness refers to the ability to pay attention to, identify, and reflect on various sound segments of speech. It is the umbrella term for a range of understandings about speech sounds, including syllables, rhyme, and a sense of alliteration. Phonemic awareness is a subcategory of phonological awareness that is quite difficult to achieve. It refers to the ability to identify and reflect on the smallest units of speech sounds within syllables—speech sounds that roughly correspond to an alphabetic orthography. The ability to tell that the /s/ sound at the beginning of the word *sit* is the same sound as that at the end of the word *bus* is an example of phonemic awareness. Phonemic awareness develops gradually over time and has a reciprocal relationship to learning about print and the alphabetic code. Children who have phonemic awareness learn to read more easily than children who do not. At the same time, instruction in alphabet recognition, letter sounds, and concept of word increases a child's phonemic awareness.

Children can hear and use individual phonemes easily at a tacit level—they can talk and can understand when others talk to them. Bringing tacit, subconscious awareness of individual phonemes to the surface to be examined consciously and explicitly is a critical goal of emergent literacy instruction. Conscious awareness is necessary to learn an alphabetic writing system because letters represent individual sounds.

A certain amount of phonological awareness is critical to reading success, and participation in phonological awareness activities has a positive influence on beginning reading, especially when these activities coincide with word study instruction (Ball & Blachman, 1988). Newer research suggests that phonological awareness develops concurrently with students' growing understanding of how the spelling system works to represent sound (Stahl & McKenna, 2001). While children do need a certain amount of phonological awareness to grasp the alphabetic nature of English, awareness of beginning sounds will get them started. Thereafter, phonological awareness, word recognition, decoding, and spelling will continue to develop in a symbiotic fashion. Growth in one area stimulates growth in another (Perfetti, Beck, Bell, & Hughes, 1987).

Phonological awareness activities in the classroom can be fun oral and written language activities that benefit all students. Classroom teachers should include some of the instructional components that have been identified as successful and effective (Adams, Foorman, Lundberg, & Beeler, 1998, Blachman, 1994; Lundberg, Frost, & Peterson, 1988; Smith et al., 1995). Students should work with sound units that closely approximate their level of word knowledge and incorporate letters and print when working with sounds. Emergent readers participate in phonological awareness activities that focus attention on separating the initial consonant sound at the beginning of words from the rhyme chunk at the end. (Initial consonant sounds are called **onsets** and the rhyme chunk at the end is called **rime**. In the word *mat*, /m/ is the onset and *at* is the rime.) Onsets and rimes are more accessible to emergent readers than are individual phonemes within words. The ability to separate an onset from a rime and to match that onset to a letter of the alphabet enables emergent readers to locate words in context. You can see Ms. Purcell's kindergarten students do exactly this in the *Words Their Way* video. Being able to isolate the initial consonant sound is a prerequisite for children to use consonants in early word recognition and spelling (Ehri, 1998; Murray, 1998; Morris, Bloodgood, Lomax, & Perney, 2001).

ELL Combining phonological awareness activities with print concepts like beginning sounds helps English Language Learners whose native language may have a different phonological structure.

Rhymes and Jingles

Rhyme awareness activities are an easy, natural way for children to play with words and to begin to focus on speech sounds. Songs, jingles, nursery rhymes, and poems fill children's ears with the sounds of rhyme. Many children develop a sense of rhyme easily, whereas others need more structured activities that draw their attention specifically to rhyming words. The easiest activity involving rhyming books and poems is simply to pause and let the children supply the second rhyming word in a couplet. When picture books such as *Oh, A-Hunting We Will Go* are used, children have the support of the illustration to help them out. In the *Words Their Way* video, Ms. Purcell used *Pat the Puppet* to encourage the children to supply the second rhyming word. Other favorite rhyming books include *I Can't Said the Ant* (by Polly Cameron) and *Each Peach Pear Plum* (by Janet and Alan Ahlsberg). Many others are listed in the activities section at the end of this chapter.

Rhyming book read-alouds can be followed by picture sorts for rhymes. For example, Barbara Straus and Helen Friedland's *See You Later Alligator* features simple rhymes such as "See you eating honey, bunny." Laying out pictures of assorted animals and rhyming foods or objects can support children in creating their own "See you later" rhymes (see Figure 4-6). To make it easier for beginners, lay out just two pictures that rhyme and one that does not. This odd-one-out setup enables children to identify more readily the two rhyming pictures. They have only to pick up an animal and the rhyming object. As children grow in their ability to listen for rhymes, the number of possibilities can be increased from three to four sets of pictures at a time.

Songs are naturally full of rhythm and rhyme and hold great appeal for children. Several songs recorded by Raffi, a popular singer and songwriter for children, are particularly well suited for language play. Rhyme is featured prominently in the song "Willoughby Wallaby Woo" for example, from the taped collection *Singable Songs for the Very Young* (Raffi, 1976) .

The song features a rhyme starting with *W* for everyone's name. After hearing the song played several times, the children can begin to sing it using the names of their classmates around the circle, perhaps passing along a stuffed elephant to add to the fun. The song can be changed to focus on alliteration by holding up a particular

FIGURE 4-6 "See You Later Alligator" Odd-One-Out

 Rhyming book read-alouds and rhyming songs call attention to the natural division in all English words between the initial consonant element, or onset (if present), and the rime that follows.

letter to insert in front of every word. *B*, for example, would result in "Billaby Ballaby Boo," and *f* would produce "Fillaby Fallaby Foo."

As children become more adept at listening for rhymes, they can play a variety of categorization and matching games. Traditional games such as Bingo, Lotto, and Concentration are always winners in which picture cards are matched to other picture cards that rhyme. More ideas for rhyming games and activities can be found later in this chapter.

Look for more ideas for rhyming on activities pages of the Phonological Awareness Literacy Screening (PALS) website, available on the Weblinks on our Companion Website at www.prenhall.com/bear

Alliteration and Beginning Sounds

Alliteration refers to a series of two or more words that begin with the same sound. Activities that play with alliteration focus children's attention on beginning sounds that mark word boundaries in print and spoken language. This awareness of beginning sounds supports children as they learn to separate the speech stream into individual words. A number of activities help promote children's understanding of beginning sounds, starting with books such as *Dr. Seuss's ABC* which celebrates alliteration in the famous Seuss style.

Beginning-sound segmentation games can be played with puppets or stuffed animals that have a funny way of talking. The puppet teaches the children how to isolate the initial phoneme from the remaining portion of the word. The children are then asked to repeat what the puppet said. The children get to manipulate the puppet themselves as they segment words given to them by the teacher. For example, in the *Words Their Way* video, Pat the Puppet first says "f-in," and the students correct Pat by saying "fin." Later, Ms. Purcell says "fin" and asks the students to say the word like Pat the Puppet would say it in "puppet talk." The children respond with "f . . . in" (Treiman, 1985).

Riddles such as *I Spy* or *I'm Thinking of Something* can be used here, too. The hints given by the teacher should accentuate the initial sound. "This thing I'm thinking of begins with /mmmmm/. This thing is small and gray. It is an animal." As the children respond "mouse" or "mole," the teacher asks them to exaggerate the beginning sound. As children become proficient at playing this game, they create their own riddles. Always encourage students how to emphasize the beginning sounds of the words they guess as the answer to the riddles.

 Look for more ideas in the activities section of this chapter and on the PALS website, available on the Weblinks on our Companion Website at www.prenhall.com/bear

Children must become aware that speech can be divided into smaller segments of sound before they will advance in literacy and they must also learn some of the terminology used to talk about these sounds. Without this insight, instruction in phonics or letter-sound correspondences will have little success. Children have no trouble hearing sounds, but directions such as "Listen for the first sound" may mystify them. In response to the question "What sound does *cow* start with?" one puzzled child tentatively replied, "Moo?" Without a stable concept of word, "first" is a relative notion. Phonological awareness activities at the emergent level should help students attend to sounds and learn to label and categorize these sounds in various ways.

Alliteration or beginning-sound awareness is further developed as children sort pictures by beginning sound, an activity that will be described shortly. At this point, oral language activities (designed to teach phonological awareness) cross over into the learning of letter-sound correspondences (phonics). Children can learn these associations at the same time they are learning to reflect on their oral language. Phonological awareness does not have to precede or follow alphabet knowledge or other components of emergent literacy instruction. Awareness of sounds is heightened by print, and thus is a reciprocal, ongoing by-product of the learning-to-read process. Although phonological awareness is a key component of early reading acquisition, phonological awareness activities need not be conducted as isolated tasks, nor do they need to take up a lot of time. According to some estimates, an entire year of phonemic awareness instruction should not exceed 20 hours (Armbruster, Lehr, & Osborn, 2001, p. 9). As children develop phonological awareness, teachers should seek to make connections between sounds and letters in the context of daily reading and writing.

Alphabet Knowledge

Among the reading readiness skills that are traditionally studied, the one that appears to be the strongest predictor of later reading success on its own is letter naming (Snow, Burns, & Griffin, 1998). There is a great deal to learn about letters and it can take a long time. Letters have names and shapes, and they must be formed in particular ways. Unlike other aspects of life, directional orientation is vital. In the three-dimensional world, a chair is a chair whether you approach it from the front or from the back, whether you approach it from the left or from the right. Not so with letters: A *b* is a *b* and a *d* is a *d*. Print is one of the few things in life where direction makes a difference. Figure 4-3 shows emergent writing in the early stages of alphabet acquisition. Note the mixture of numbers and letters and backward formations in the child's efforts to spell *macaroni*.

Many letter names share similar sounds. The letter name *b* (bee), for example, shares the vowel sound of the letter name *e*, as do *p, d, t, c, g, v,* and *z*. There are visual similarities as well. There are verticals with circles in *p, q, d,* and *b*. Verticals and horizontals intersect in *T, L, H, F, E,* and *I*. Intersecting diagonals are shared by *K, A* (which also share parts of letter name sounds), *M, N, V, W, X,* and *Z*. Even movements overlap in the formation of letters: the up-down-up-down motion is basic to *M, N, W,* and *V;* a circular movement is required of *B, C, D, G, O, P, Q, R, U,* and *S;* and the direction of these movements hinges critically on where one begins on the page (see Clay [1975] for a detailed discussion of the acquisition of these distinctive features of letters).

Students in the emergent stage appear to practice these distinctive features on their own, provided they are given a model. First efforts at a global level mimic the kinds of letters children know best such as the letters in their own name (see Figure 4-7). Meanwhile, letters that share distinctive visual features will continue to be confused for some time; *B* may be mistaken for *D, N* for *U,* and so forth. Provided with the incentive to practice and the means to do so, emergent children will rehearse letter names, practice letter writing, and match uppercase to lowercase with delight.

Learning the names of the letters is an important first step toward learning the sounds associated with the letters. Most of the letters have names that include a sound commonly associated with it and can serve as a mnemonic device for remembering the sound. *B* (bee), *k* (kay),

Connie's "Writing"

Ellie's "Writing"

FIGURE 4-7   Connie's and Ellie's Emergent Writing

and *z* (zee) have their sounds at the beginnings of their names, and *f* (eff), *l* (ell), and *s* (es) have their sounds at the end. The names of the vowels are their long sounds. Only *h* (aich), *w* (doubleyou), and consonant *y* (wie) have no beginning-sound association and these letters are often the most difficult to learn. Letter names serve as the first reference point many children use when writing and explain some of the interesting invented spelling they create during the letter name–alphabetic stage discussed more in the next chapter.

Most mainstream, middle-class children take 5 years to acquire this alphabet knowledge at home and in preschool. Magnetic letters on the refrigerator door, alphabetic puzzles, and commercial alphabet games are staples in many middle-class homes (Adams, 1990). Truly advantaged youngsters also have attentive parents at the kitchen table modeling letter formation and speech segmentation as they encourage their child to write a grocery list or a note to Grandma using invented spelling. Yet many of these children also require the directed instruction provided by formal schooling to fully understand the complexity of the alphabet. The best way to share 5 years of accumulated alphabet knowledge with those who have not been privy to this information is to teach it directly, in as naturalistic, fun, and gamelike a manner as possible (Delpit, 1988). The word study activities described in the next section are designed to do just that.

Alphabet Games and Matching Activities

The alphabet is learned the same way that concepts and words for concepts are learned—through active exploration of the relationships between letter names, the sounds of the letter names, their visual characteristics, and the motor movement involved in their formation. By noting the salient, stable characteristics of *b* in many contexts and across many different fonts, sizes, shapes, and textures, a rudimentary concept of *b* is formed (see Figure 4-8). Every new encounter with *b* adds new attributes to the concept of the letter. Like concepts, the distinctive features entailed in a letter's name, look, feel, and formation must be actively manipulated to be identified and grouped.

Many alphabet activities begin with the child's name: Building it with letter tiles, cutting it out of play dough, or matching it letter for letter with a second set. Writing or copying their own name, and the names of other family members or friends, is alluring to emergent writers and is a great introduction to the alphabet as well as to writing. Letters take on personalities: *K* is Katie's letter and *T* is Tommy's letter. Familiar phrases like "I love you" and "Happy birthday" are frequently requested and demonstrate the compelling need for personalization, ownership, and purpose (Ashton-Warner, 1963).

The alphabet games and activities described at the end of this chapter build on the basic theme of compare-and-contrast categorization routines. Letters will be matched and sorted according to similarities and differences. The activities are designed to develop all aspects of alphabet knowledge including letter naming, letter recognition (both upper- and lowercase), letter writing, and letter sounds. To develop letter recognition skill, letters must be matched: uppercase to uppercase, lowercase to lowercase, and finally uppercase to lowercase. At the end of this chapter, you will see variations of many traditional games such as Bingo and Concentration. A writing component has been added to many of these games to incorporate letter formation, an important and often neglected component of early literacy instruction. Sorting tasks, matching games, picture labeling, and writing are as important to acquiring the alphabetic principle as seeing letters in meaningful print.

Toward the end of the emergent stage of word knowledge, children will have made the connection that letters can represent

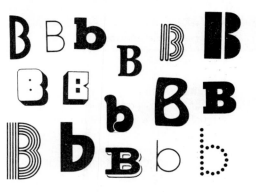

FIGURE 4-8 Different Print Styles

sound segments in speech. As this connection is developing, have your students sort picture cards into groups under letters that correspond to the beginning sound. It is important to have them do a lot of writing as well.

Letter-Sound Knowledge

During the emergent stage, children learn their letters, attend to speech sounds, and begin to make connections between letters and sounds. Toward the end of the emergent stage, many children will begin producing partial phonetic spellings that contain one or two letters for each syllable (see Figure 4-4). **Picture-sorting activities** by beginning sounds secures these tentative efforts and moves children along in acquiring more knowledge of letter-sound correspondences through a gamelike, manipulative phonics activity.

Some teachers choose *m* and *s* for students' first consonant contrast, because both letters have **continuant sounds** that can be isolated and elongated without undue distortion (*mmmmoon* and *ssssun*). The sounds also feel very different in the mouth in terms of how they are articulated, which makes it easier for children to judge the categories while sorting. However, the sound for /b/ cannot be elongated or isolated without adding a vowel to it (buh); but it is still fairly easy to learn, perhaps because it has a distinctive feel as the lips press together. However, to contrast *b* and *p* in an early sort would be confusing because they are both articulated the same way (Purcell, 2002). The only difference between them is that the sound for /b/ causes the vocal chords to vibrate and /p/ does not. Try placing two fingers on your larynx and feel the difference in **voiced** /b/ and **unvoiced** /p/. Other groups of letter sounds that share the same place of articulation in the mouth are shown in each row of Table 4-1. The letters in each row are best not contrasted in the very first letter-sound sorts. Remember the sixth principle of word study: Begin with obvious contrasts!

Understanding something about how sounds are produced may seem unnecessarily complicated, but it explains so many of the interesting things children do in their invented spellings during the emergent and letter name–alphabetic stages. Use the chart to see the logic in the invented spelling JP for *chip,* VN for *fan,* and PD for *pet.* Knowledge of articulation also helps teachers make decisions about setting up picture sorts.

 For printable samples of beginning sound picture sorts, visit the emergent section of the accompanying CD-ROM.

TABLE 4-1   Pronunciation Chart of Beginning Consonant Sounds

Unvoiced	Voiced	Nasals	Other	Place of Articulation
p	b	m		lips together
wh	w		qu	lips rounded
f	v			teeth and lips
th (the)	th (this)			tip of tongue and teeth
t	d	n	l	tip of tongue and roof of mouth
s	z			tongue and roof of mouth
sh			y	sides of tongue and teeth
ch	j			sides of tongue and roof of mouth
k	g	ng	x	back of tongue and throat
h				no articulation—breathy sound

Guidelines for Beginning Sound Picture Sorts

There are a number of other things to keep in mind when organizing sorts for beginning letter-sounds.

1. *Start with meaningful text.* Choose several sounds to contrast that represent key words from a familiar rhyme, patterned book, or dictation. One advantage of teacher-directed word study over published programs is that teachers can integrate phonics and the variety of print used in emergent classrooms.

2. *Make sorts easier or harder as needed.* Start with two obvious contrasts, then add one or two for up to four categories. Look for fast and accurate picture sorting before moving on. Be ready to drop back to fewer categories if a child has difficulty.

3. *Use a key word and a letter as headers.* Children should associate the letter and sound. The key words may be words selected from familiar text or they may be the same as the key words used on the sound boards in the Appendix. Whatever key word you use, be consistent and use the same one every time.

4. *Begin with directed sorts.* Discuss both the sound and the letter name, and model the placement of two or three words in each category. Be explicit about why you sort the way you do. Say, for example, "Foot, fffoot, ffffox. *Foot* and *fox* start with the same sound, *ffff*. I will put *foot* under the letter *f*." Over time, as children catch on to what it is they are to attend to, you can use fewer directives. Figure 4-9 shows how this sort would look after several pictures are sorted.

5. *Use sets of pictures that are easy to name and sort.* Introduce the pictures to be sure that children know what to call them. Use pictures that are easy to identify and do not start with consonant blends or digraphs. Single-syllable words are better than two-syllable words because they have fewer sounds that need attention.

6. *Correct mistakes on the first sort but allow errors to wait on subsequent sorts.* Show children how to check their sorts by naming the pictures down the columns, emphasizing the beginning sounds. Then ask if there are any pictures that need to be changed. Ask children to check their own work using the same process and praise them when they find their own errors. If they do not, prompt them by saying, "There is a picture in this row that needs to be changed. Can you find it?"

7. *Vary the group sorting.* Put out all the pictures face up and let children choose one that they feel confident in naming and sorting correctly. Ask them to name the picture and the letter by saying "__ begins with the __ sound and goes under the letter __." Another time pass out the pictures and call on children to come up and sort the card they were given. Then turn the pictures face down in a stack or spread them out on the floor and let children turn over the picture they will sort. Children enjoy the anticipation of not knowing which picture they will get. Include an "oddball" or "not sure" category headed by a question mark and add pictures to the sort that do not fit the established categories.

8. *Plan plenty of time for individual practice.* After group modeling and discussion, put sets of pictures in centers or create copies of picture sets for children to cut apart for more sorting. Sheets of pictures for sorting can be created by copying pictures from this book, cutting them apart, and pasting them in a mixed-up fashion on a template.

9. *Plan follow-up activities.* Cut and paste, draw and label, and word hunts through familiar chart stories, nursery rhymes, or little books are helpful follow-up activities. They require children to recognize, recall, judge, and apply (see Chapter 3).

10. *Encourage invented spelling.* In the process of inventing spellings, children exercise their developing letter-sound knowledge in a meaningful activity. To get students started,

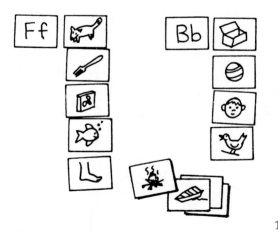

FIGURE 4-9 Sound Sort for Comparing *B* and *F*

demonstrate how to use letter names to represent the sounds in words. Using letter tiles or squares of paper with letters written on them, show students how they can write their aunt's name *Ellen* by saying the letter names for *l* and *n* while pushing letter tiles (*LN*) (Johnston, Invernizzi, & Juel, 1998).

Of course, all the phonological awareness, alphabet, and letter-sound knowledge in the world will not help children learn to read if they do not have a chance to apply this knowledge in context. Units of sound and the letters that represent them must be coordinated with printed word boundaries. This match must be synchronized with the flow of language over time and two-dimensional space. Beginning sounds depend upon a child's concept of word.

Concept of Word in Print

Emergent readers do not have a concept of word in print. What they point to as they recite may not coincide with printed word units at all. Like the babbling infant imitating the intonation contours of speech, the preliterate child points in a rhythmic approximation of the memorized text with little attention to word boundaries or even, perhaps, direction on the page. Prior to achieving a concept of word, emergent children, as well as emergent adults, have great difficulty identifying individual phonemes within words (Morais, Cary, Alegria, & Bertelson, 1979). There is an interaction between alphabetic knowledge, the ability to match speech to print, and phonemic awareness (Tunmer, 1991).

Through the teacher's demonstrations, children's fingerpointing behaviors change. Left-to-right movement becomes habitualized, though children may not routinely use letter or word units to guide their tracking. As white spaces are noted and much talk about words is introduced, children begin to track rhythmically across the text, pointing to words for each stressed beat in the recitation. As children become aware that print has something to do with sound, their fingerpointing becomes more precise and changes from a gross rhythm to a closer match with syllables. This works well for one-syllable words, but not so well for words of two or more syllables. This strategy is revealed in their fingerpoint reading as well as in their writing. For example, in the traditional ditty "Sam, Sam the Baker Man," children may pronounce "ker," the second syllable of *baker*, but point to the next word, *man*. Figure 4-10 illustrates the phenomenon of getting off track on two-syllable words.

FIGURE 4-10   Trying to Match Voice to Print

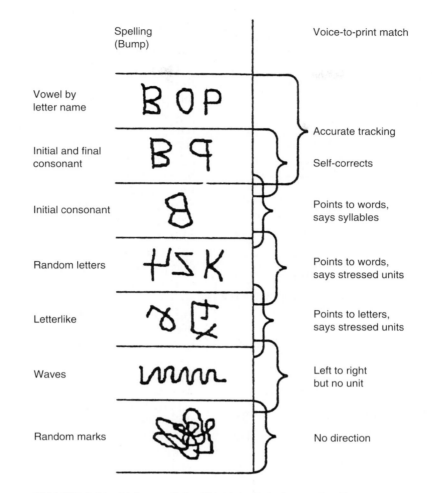

Spelling
(Bump)

Voice-to-print match

Vowel by
letter name

Initial and final
consonant

Accurate tracking

Self-corrects

Initial consonant

Points to words,
says syllables

Random letters

Points to words,
says stressed units

Letterlike

Points to letters,
says stressed units

Waves

Left to right
but no unit

Random marks

No direction

FIGURE 4-11   Voice-to-Print Match in Relation to Spelling
Development
Source: Focus on research: Development of word knowledge as it relates to
reading, spelling, and instruction. *Language Arts, 69,* 6, 444-453. Adapted with
permission from Gill (1992).

Later, as children learn the alphabet and the sounds associated with the letters, beginning sounds will anchor the children's fingerpointing more directly to the memorized recitation: They realize that when they say the word *man,* they need to have their
finger on a word beginning with an *m.* If they do not, then they must start again. These
self-corrections herald the onset of a concept of word in print. Figure 4-11 shows the progression of fingerpointing accuracy in relation to the orthographic development during
this emergent to early letter name–alphabetic stage of word knowledge.

Fingerpoint Reading and Tracking Words

The best way for children to achieve a concept of word is to have them point to the words
as they reread familiar text. These texts might be picture captions, dictated experience stories, poems, songs, simple patterned books, or excerpts from a favorite story printed on
sentence strips or chart paper. Once these texts become familiar, children can be encouraged to memory-read them, pointing to each word as it is spoken. We call this **fingerpoint
reading** or **tracking.**

Rhythmic texts are particularly appealing to young children and, like picture captions
and dictated accounts, are easily memorized. Eventually, knowledge of initial consonant

FIGURE 4-12   Drawing with Dictated Caption

FIGURE 4-13   Dictated Language Experience Chart

sounds will provide the necessary anchor to track accurately, even in the face of two-syllable words. At such times, though, rhythmic texts may throw children off in their tracking, and a move to less rhythmic, less predictable texts may be in order (Cathey, 1991). No matter what the source of text, the important thing from a word study point of view is to focus on individual words within the text. Fingerpointing, repeated reading, cut-up sentences, and word-card matching activities call attention to words and their letter-sound features.

One of the easiest ways to help children make connections between speech and print is to write captions beneath the pictures they draw. First have the children draw a picture of their favorite toy or Halloween costume and encourage them to include as much detail as possible. While they are finishing their drawings, walk around and ask each child to tell something about his or her picture. Choose a simple phrase or sentence that the child speaks, and write it verbatim beneath the picture (see Figure 4-12). Say each word as you write it, drawing attention to the sounds and letters. Read the caption by pointing to each word. Ask the child to read along with you and then to read it alone while pointing. Later, the child may attempt to reread the caption to a buddy.

Like picture captions, spoken or dictated accounts of children's experiences also help them link speech to print. This approach has traditionally been referred to as the **language experience approach,** or LEA (Hall, 1980; Nessel & Jones, 1981; Stauffer, 1980). Field trips, cooking activities, playground episodes, and class pets provide opportunities for shared experiences in which the children's own language abounds. Students' observations and comments can then be written next to each child's name. (Daniel says, "The pumpkins were rotten.") In this format, attention to words and to their boundaries will be highlighted in a meaningful context. For example, children may be asked to locate their own name in the dictated account or to find a word that starts with the same letter as their own name (see Figure 4-13). One teacher writes dictated accounts using carbon paper and then later has her children cut out individual words from the carbon copy to paste on top of the original. Other activities for focusing on words and word boundaries are described in the following activities section.

Word Study Routines and Management

The research in emergent literacy suggests that a comprehensive approach to instruction and early intervention is the most effective (Pressley, 1998). A comprehensive approach means that children engage in fingerprint reading and rereading familiar texts such as nursery rhymes, dictated experience stories, and simple pattern books right from the start. A comprehensive approach to emergent literacy instruction also means that we engage students in direct instruction in phonological awareness, the alphabet, and letter sounds. Finally, a comprehensive emergent literacy program provides students with ample opportunities to exercise what they know through learning to track new texts and through writing for sounds every day, and through talking about the books and experiences they have shared. An exemplary emergent literacy program can be thought of in terms of a comprehensive "diet"—first knowing what types of instructional activities are appropriate, then combining the activities into regular routines that meet the needs of all learners (Invernizzi, 2002).

Combining these activities into a cohesive routine is a challenging and rewarding part of teaching. It is important for activities to flow together in a logical way, and that the materials serve multiple purposes when possible. For example, materials used to develop the concept of word also contain examples of the alphabetic or phonological feature that students are studying. Repeated and explicit word work provides students with the judicious practice they need to develop as readers.

Emergent Lesson Plan

Terry Purcell follows a similar plan with small groups of kindergarten students. In Terry's school, kindergarten class sizes are reduced for reading and language arts instruction through parallel scheduling. Half of the kindergarten classes go to "specials," such as PE, Art, or Music, while the other half stays with Terry for direct instruction in reading and language arts. Scheduling in this way reduces the size of the kindergarten class by half and results in an uninterrupted block of reading and language arts instruction.

A key to classroom management for emergent learners is to establish a consistent routine within a predictable daily schedule (the previous chapter showed students ways to introduce these activities). The classroom management scheme Terry uses for her word study routine is a variation of Betty Lee's plan for emergent to early letter name-alphabetic spellers discussed in Chapter 3. The class begins and ends as a whole group, and in between, during 10–12 minute periods, students rotate through literacy centers in small groups or buddy pairs. This is also a lesson plan that is easily adaptable to early intervention programs in which tutors manage the centers with small, rotating groups of four students. See Figure 4-14.

Alphabet and Letter Sounds Center

In the Alphabet and Beginning Sound Center, students follow a set routine. They start by "tracking" the alphabet on the alphabet strip as they sing the ABC song. Then they play "I'm thinking of a letter that makes the same sound as _____." From your instruction during several reading group sessions, students learned to place a finger on the correct letter, identify its name, and then its sound. This is often followed by an upper- and lowercase matching activity using each student's name, or a beginning sound sort where students sort picture cards or objects into groups by beginning sounds. The groups of picture cards are labeled with the letters associated with each beginning sound. After they sort, check, and reflect, they cut and paste, or draw and label, additional words that start with the same sounds.

Word Awareness or Concept of Word Center

Another literacy center is the Word Awareness or Concept of Word Center, in which students reread familiar texts and work on word awareness for approximately 10 minutes a day. Students reread and track with their fingers previously "read" poems, songs, other patterned texts, and their individual sentences from group experience charts. These familiar, two-to-four-line rhymes are stored in students' own **personal readers,** discussed in more detail in the next chapter. They also work with partners to rebuild these familiar texts with sentence strips and word cards. After buddy reading and tracking the most recent entries in their personal readers, students locate specific words in context that match the word cards they have been given. This requires them to reread very carefully and to note the beginning letter of each word. They underline the word when they find a match.

Phonological Awareness or Language Play

A third literacy center is the phonological awareness or language play center where students focus on particular speech sounds for 10 minutes a day. They work with rhyme or alliteration and listen for beginning or ending sounds as they listen to a rhyming book, play Concentration, or work with one of the other phonological awareness games or activities described at the end of this chapter. Terry often incorporates print into these phonological awareness activities as she finds that children more easily attend to the sound when they have a concrete referent.

Concepts and Vocabulary as Whole Group Activities

An important part of Terry's word study routine and classroom management involves getting her students to talk, and to listen to others talk, so she encourages lots of oral language interaction. Terry involves her students in talk before, during, and after her whole group read alouds, and she plans interactive activities that extend their conceptual understanding of ideas and vocabulary. Before reading, Terry has students share their observations of the cover of a book and make predictions about what the book will be about. During the reading she pauses to engage them in evaluating their initial hypotheses and to explain what they think will happen next and why.

After reading to her students, she revisits the text to point out print concepts or to discuss the meaning of a particular word or phrase. Frequently, Terry engages the whole group in a Guess My Category activity based on the topic or theme of the book. Concept sorts, like those described in the activity section that follows, often conclude these daily sessions and stimulate meaningful conversation.

The word study activities described in the following section are designed to help you establish those routines and, in so doing, meet the literacy needs of your emergent learners. As you read through them, see which activities might fit in the lesson plan in Figure 4-14*.

Word Study Component	Time	Activity	Observations
Alphabet & Letter Sounds	10-12 min	**ABC Tracking:** **Letter Recognition & Letter Sounds:** **Writing for Sounds:**	❏ Track letters accurately? ❏ Identify letters? ❏ Identify sounds? ❏ Sort correctly? ❏ Sort automatically? ❏ Can write letter/sound?
Concept of Word (COW)	10 min	**Text title:** _____ **Book / Song / Rhyme / Poem** **COW activity:**	❏ Text was easy/ hard to track? # of times reread: _____ ❏ Describe fingerpointing:
Phonological Awareness (PA) & Language Play	10 min	**PA focus:** Syllables / Rhyme / Beginning Sounds / Ending Sound **Literacy term focus:** Word / Sentence / Beginning Sound/ Ending Sound **PA Activity:**	❏ PA task was easy/ hard/ just right? ❏ Record observations:
Concept & Vocabulary	15 min	**Book title:** _____ **Targeted Concepts or Semantic Category:** **Targeted Words:** **Activity:**	❏ Describe students' talk:

FIGURE 4-14   Word Study Lesson Plan for the Emergent Learner

*Thanks to Mary Fowler and Colleen Muldoon

Activities for Emergent Readers

This section provides specific activities arranged by these categories: concept sorts, phonological awareness, alphabet knowledge, letter-sound knowledge, and concept of word. Within each category the activities are roughly in order of increasing difficulty. However, as noted earlier in this chapter, it is not the case that concept sorts must precede sound awareness, which in turn must precede alphabet. In reality, these develop simultaneously during the emergent years and many activities cut across the categories. Many of the games are generic to all stages of developmental word knowledge as indicated by the adaptable symbol used throughout the book.

Adaptable for Other Stages

 For more activities appropriate for Emergent readers, visit the Emergent section of the accompanying CD-ROM.

CONCEPT SORTS

The activities for concept sorts are all variations on the theme of categorization tasks. In addition to the basic sorting tasks, activities are generally followed by draw and label, then cut and paste procedures as discussed in Chapter 3. As always, we recommend having children write at every possible opportunity during or following the concept sorts. Categories and examples can be labeled with invented spellings.

Beginning with Children's Books and Concept Sorts 4-1

Books make great beginnings for concept sorts. Here are just a few examples to get you started.

Materials

Gregory the Terrible Eater (by Marjorie Sharmat) tells the story of a young goat who wants to eat real food while his parents constantly urge him to eat "junk food." In this case, the goats' favorite foods really are junk from the local dump: tires, tin cans, old rags, and so on. Collect real objects or pictures of items suggested by the story, for example, fruits, vegetables, newspaper, shoe laces, spaghetti, and pieces of clothing.

Procedures

1. After enjoying this story together the children can be introduced to a concept sort categorized by real food and junk food. Gather the children on the rug, around a large table or pocket chart, and challenge them to group the items by the things Gregory liked and the things he disliked.
2. After deciding where everything should go, ask the students to describe how the things in that category are alike. Decide on a key word or descriptive phrase that will label each category. *Real food* and *junk food* are obvious choices, but your children

might be more inventive. As you print the selected key words on cards, model writing for the children. Say each word slowly and talk about the sounds you hear in the words and the letters you need to spell them. Each child in the group might also be given a card and asked to label one of the individual items using invented spelling.

3. Plan time for individual sorting. Keep the items and key word cards available so that children will be free to redo the sort on their own or with a partner at another time, perhaps during free time or center time.

4. Draw and label or cut and paste activities should follow the sorting. This may be done as a group activity, in which case a section of a bulletin board or a large sheet of paper is divided into two sections and labeled with the key words. If children do it individually, each child can be given a sheet of paper folded into two sections. The children might be asked to draw items or they might be given a collection of magazines or catalogs to search for pictures to cut out and paste into the correct category (seed catalogs are great for fruits and vegetables). Again, they can be encouraged to use invented spelling to label the pictures.

Variations

Other books will also serve as the starting point for concept sorts of many kinds. Here are just a few suggestions:

Noisy Nora by Rosemary Wells—sort pictures that suggest noisy activities or objects with pictures that suggest quiet activities.*

The Country Mouse and the City Mouse by Jan Brett and various authors—sort pictures of things you would see in the country and things you would see in the city.

Alexander and the Wind-Up Mouse by Leo Lionni—sort pictures of real animals and toy or imaginary animals.

Amos and Boris by William Steig—sort pictures of things that Amos would see on the land and things that Boris would see in the ocean.

Is It Red? Is It Yellow? Is It Blue? by Tana Hoban—one of many books that suggest sorting objects and pictures by color.

My Very First Book of Shapes by Eric Carle—one of many books that lead into a sorting activity based on shapes.

Adaptable for Other Stages

Paste the Pasta and Other Concrete Concept Sorts 4–2

Categorizing pasta by size, shape, and color is a good hands-on activity that introduces the idea of sorting to young children. Ann Fordham at the McGuffey Reading Center developed this sort. Many early childhood curricula include the study of pattern, but being able to categorize by particular attributes must come first. It is difficult for young children to stay focused on a single attribute of interest. They may begin sorting by color and then switch to shape in midstream. They will need many activities of this kind, sorting real, concrete objects that have different features.

Materials

You will need three to six types of pasta that vary in size and shape. You may find pasta of various colors or you can dye your own by shaking the pasta in a jar with a tablespoon of alcohol and a few drops of food coloring. Lay it out on newspaper to dry. If you dye your own, make sure that any one color has a variety of shapes and sizes. Two or three colors are enough. Children can sort onto paper divided into columns as shown in Figure 4-15 or simply into piles.

FIGURE 4-15   Paste the Pasta

*Thanks to Elizabeth Schuett for this idea.

Procedures

1. Prepare a mixture of the dried pasta and give each child a handful and a sorting paper.
2. Begin with an open sort in which you invite the students to come up with their own way of grouping. This will give you an opportunity to evaluate which of the children understand attribute sorting and who will need more guidance. Ask the children to share their ideas and show their groups. Discuss the different features or attributes by which they can sort.
3. Ask them to re-sort using a category different from their first one. You might end this activity by letting the students glue the pasta onto their paper by categories and labeling their chosen sorts.

Variations

There is no end to the concrete things you can sort with your students as you explore the different features that define your categories. Here are some suggestions:

Children—male/female, hair color, eye color, age, favorite color
Shoes—girls/boys, right/left, tie/Velcro/slip-on
Mittens and gloves—knit/woven, right/left
Coats—short/long, button/zip, hood/no hood
Buttons—two holes/four holes/no holes, shapes, colors, size
Bottle caps—size, color, plastic/metal, plain/printed, ribbed/smooth
Lunch containers—boxes/bags, plastic/metal/nylon
Legos—color, shape, number of pegs, length
Blocks—shape, color, size
Toys—size, color, purpose, hardness
Food—sweet/sour/bitter/salty

All My Friends Photograph Sort 4–3

Another example of an open-ended sort involves guessing each other's categories. Pat Love, from Hollymead Elementary School, Charlottesville, Virginia, developed this idea.

Materials

You can use photocopies of the children's school photographs made into a composite sheet or take digital pictures of your students and cut and paste them into sheets printed from a computer. The students will also need a sheet of construction paper to divide into columns for sorting.

Procedures

1. Brainstorm with the children some of the ways that the pictures might be grouped (by hair length, hair color, clothing, boys/girls, facial expressions).
2. Let them work in groups to sort by these or other categories they discover. After pasting their pictures into the columns on their paper, each group can hold up their effort and ask the others in the class to guess their categories. The category labels or key words should then be written on the papers.

Variations

Photographs from home may be sorted according to places (inside/outside, home/vacation, holidays, and so forth), number of people in the photograph (adults, sisters, brothers), number of animals in the photograph, seasons (by clothing, outside trees/plants), age, and so forth.

As children learn to recognize their classmates' names, have them match the names to the pictures. Later, these names may be sorted by beginning letter, and then placed under the corresponding letter of an ABC wall strip to form a graph.

THEMATIC UNITS AS A STARTING POINT FOR CONCEPT SORTS

Teachers of young children often organize their curriculum into thematic units of study. Such units frequently lend themselves to concept sorts, which will review and extend the understandings central to the goals of the unit. Here are some examples.

Food Group Unit 4–4

Gregory the Terrible Eater serves as an excellent introduction to the study of healthy eating. The same pictures the children have drawn or cut out can serve as the beginning pictures for categories such as meats, grains, fruits and vegetables, and dairy products. After categorizing the foods in a group sorting activity, the students should be asked to draw or cut out pictures of additional foods for a wall chart or individual sheet that is then labeled with invented spellings.

Animal Unit 4–5

The study of animals particularly lends itself to concept sorts and can be used as a way of introducing a unit. Lay out a collection of animal pictures and ask the students to think of ways that they can be grouped together. Such an open sort will result in many different categories based on attributes of color, number of legs, fur or feather coat, and so on. A lively discussion will arise as students discover that some animals will go in different categories.

The direction you eventually want this activity to go will depend on the goal of your unit. If you are studying animal habitats, then you will eventually guide the children to sorting the animals by the places they live. If you are studying classes of animals, then the students must eventually learn to sort them into mammals, fish, amphibians, and birds. If you are focusing on the food chain, your categories may be carnivores, herbivores, and omnivores.

Transportation Unit 4–6

Another open sort involves a unit on transportation. A collection of toy vehicles (planes, boats, cars, and trucks) can be laid on the floor or table and the children invited to think of which ones might go together. Encourage them to think up a variety of possibilities that will divide everything into only two or three categories. After each suggestion, sort the vehicles by the identified attributes, and write the key words on a chart or chalkboard. Some possibilities include plastic/metal, big/little, old/new, one color/many colors, windows/no windows, wheels/no wheels, and land/air/water.

After exploring this open sort thoroughly, have the children select the suggestion they liked the best. They can then be given construction paper to label their categories and draw or cut out pictures for each. As always, encourage them to label the pictures and the categories with invented spelling as shown in Figure 4-16.

Variations

Other concept sorts might be developed along the same lines. The following list of categories represents some that are frequently confused by preschool, kindergarten, and first-grade children.

real, imaginary
smooth, rough
kitchen tools, office tools, shop tools
plastic, wood, metal
hard, soft
holidays and seasons

FIGURE 4-16   Vehicle Draw and Label

PLAYING WITH SOUNDS TO DEVELOP PHONOLOGICAL AWARENESS

Phonological awareness consists of an array of understandings about sounds that include a sense of rhyme, alliteration, syllables, phonemic segmentation, and blending. Rhyme and alliteration are easier than others to develop and many activities for developing these are included here. There are also some activities in this section for syllable sense, segmenting, and blending, but they are also addressed as part of other activities such as The Morning Message (4-37) and One Child's Name (4-20).

Beginning with Rhyme in Children's Books 4-7

Filling children's heads with rhyme is one of the easiest and most natural ways to focus their attention on the sounds of the English language. Books written with rhyme provide one way to do this.

Materials

Many of the books enjoyed by children in the emergent stage feature rhymes. Here are just a few:

> Ahlsberg, J., & Ahlsberg, A. (1978). *Each peach pear plum: An "I spy" story.* New York: Scholastic.
>
> Cameron, P. (1961). *I can't said the ant.* New York: Putnam Publishing.
>
> Crews, D. (1986). *Ten black dots.* New York: Greenwillow.
>
> Degan, B. (1983). *Jamberry.* New York: Harper.
>
> Florian, D. (1987). *A winter day.* New York: Scholastic; (1990). *A beach day.* New York: Greenwillow.
>
> Guarina, D. (1989). *Is your mama a llama?* Illustrated by Steven Kellogg. New York: Scholastic.
>
> Hennessy, B. G. (1989). *The missing tarts.* Illustrated by T. C. Pearson. New York: Scholastic.
>
> Macmillan, B. (1990). *One sun.* New York: Holiday House; (1991). *Play day.* New York: Trumpet.
>
> Slate, J. (1996). *Mrs. Bindergarten gets ready for kindergarten.* New York: Scholastic.
>
> Strickland, P., & Strickland, H. (1994). *Dinosaur roar!* New York: Scholastic.
>
> Walton, R. (1998). *So many bunnies: A bedtime abc and counting book.* New York: Scholastic.

Procedures

1. As you read books with rhyme aloud, pause to allow the children to guess the rhyming word. The text in *Is Your Mama a Llama?* is set up to facilitate children's input as it poses a rhyming riddle and a page break before the animal's identity is revealed. *I Can't Said the Ant* is a favorite rhyming tale that invites student participation with each line cued by an illustration. You will find many books in which you can use this **cloze** procedure to let children supply the rhyming words.

2. Some rhyming books are so repetitive and simple that children can easily memorize them and read them on their own. *Play Day* and *One Sun,* by Bruce Macmillan, are some of the simplest rhyming books available. They feature "hinkpink" rhymes such as *white kite* or *bear chair* with a vivid photograph to cue the child's response. Douglas Florian has a series of books, including *A Beach Day* and *A Winter Day,* that feature only two or three words on a page. These books can also be used to introduce concept sorts in which summer/winter and city/country can be contrasted. After

hearing these books read aloud two or three times, young children may be able to recite the words or track the print successfully for themselves and will get great satisfaction from the feeling that they can read.

Matching and Sorting Rhyming Pictures 4–8

After reading rhyming books aloud, you can follow up with an activity that has the children sorting or matching rhyming pictures.

Materials

Rhyming pictures are available commercially or you can create your own. The Appendix of this book contains pictures grouped by initial sounds and by vowel sounds. These can be copied, colored lightly, and glued to cards to make sets for sorting. The following list is of pictures you can find in *Words Their Way* to make sets of at least four rhyming words. Most are in the vowel sets, but the consonant and blend pictures contain some as well. *Prepared sorts* may be found in the WTW supplements.

boat coat float goat	chop top mop hop shop	bell well shell smell yell
plane train chain cane rain	glue zoo shoe two	sleep jeep sheep sweep
nail whale pail snail sail mail	lip ship drip zip whip	spill grill hill mill
fan can pan man van	cat mat rat bat hat	wing ring swing king sting
drive hive five dive	bee tree pea key three	fly tie fry cry pie
shed bed sled bread	trap clap map cap snap	block clock rock lock
chick brick stick kick	nose rose hose toes	track quack crack sack jack pack

Procedures

1. After enjoying the story together several times, Mrs. Collins introduced her group to a collection of animal pictures from the story (fox, mouse, goat, whale) and pictures of the places they were put (box, house, boat, pail) for the children to match by rhyme. To make it easier for beginners, put out three pictures at a time: two pictures that rhyme and one that does not.
2. After sorting pictures as a group, put the book and the pictures in a center for children to reread on their own and play the matching game.

Variations

Simply set up two categories and lead the children in sorting pictures by rhyming sound. For example, lay down *cat* and *bee* as headers and sort other pictures in turn under the correct header. Add a third and fourth category when children are comfortable with two.

Inventing Rhymes 4–9

Nonsense rhymes and books with rhyme and word play are a delightful way to cultivate awareness of sounds. Word play directs children's attention to the sounds of the English language and can stimulate them to invent their own words. Jan Slepian and Ann Seidler's *The Hungry Thing* tells of a creature who comes to town begging for food but has trouble pronouncing what he wants: *Shmancakes* (pancakes), *feetloaf* (meatloaf), and *hookies* (cookies) are among his requests. It is only a small boy who figures out what he wants. After reading the book, children can act it out. As each takes the part of the Hungry Thing, they must come up with a rhyming word for the food they want: *blizza, band-wich, smello?*

Making up one's own rhymes is likely to come after the ability to identify rhymes. Thinking up rhyming words to make sense in a poem is quite an accomplishment, requiring a good sense of rhyme and an extensive vocabulary. Children need supported efforts to create rhymes, and a good place to start is pure nonsense. No one was a greater master of this than Dr. Seuss. *There's a Wocket in My Pocket* takes readers on a tour of a young boy's home in which all manners of odd creatures have taken up residence. There is a *woset* in his closet, a *zlock* behind the clock, and a *nink* in the sink. After reading this to a group, ask children to imagine what animal would live in their cubby, under the rug, or in the lunchroom. Their efforts should rhyme, to be sure, but anything will do: a *rubby, snubby,* or *frubby* might all live in a cubby.

Patterned text can be used to create rhymes. The rhyming pattern in *Ten Black Dots* can be extended to 11, 12, and so on: "Twelve dots can make ice cream cones or the buttons to dial a _____." In the supportive framework of a familiar patterned sentence, children are likely to be more successful at creating their own rhymes.

Using Songs to Develop a Sense of Rhyme and Alliteration 4–10

Earlier we mentioned how appropriate the singer/songwriter Raffi is for young children. Teaching these songs by Raffi can lead to inventive fun with rhymes and sounds, and some are available as books:

"Apples and Bananas" (from *One Light, One Sun*)
"Spider on the Floor" (from *Singable Songs for the Very Young*)
"Down by the Bay" (also available as a book, from *Singable Songs for the Very Young*)

Another song that features names, rhyme, and alliteration is "The Name Game," originally sung by Shirley Ellis. It has apparently passed into the oral tradition of neighborhood kids and may be known by some children in your class. Sing the song over and over, substituting the name of a different child on every round. It goes like this:

Sam Sam Bo Bam, Banana Fanna Bo Fam, Fee Fi Mo Mam, Sam!

Kaitlyn Kaitlyn Bo Baitlyn, Banana Fanna Bo Faitlyn, Fee Fi Mo Maitlyn, Kaitlyn!

Lend an ear to the playground songs and chants your children already know and encourage them to share them with you. Generations of children have made up variations of "Miss Mary Mack Mack Mack . . . " and a new generation with a taste for rap is creating a whole new repertoire. You can take an active role in teaching these jingles to your students—or letting them teach them to you! Write them down to become reading material. Here are some printed sources of traditional chants and jingles:

Cole, J. (1989). *101 jump-rope rhymes.* New York: Scholastic.
Cole, J., & Calmenson, S. (1990). *Miss Mary Mack and other children's street rhymes.* Illustrated by Alan Tiegreen. New York: Morrouno.
Schwartz, A. (1989). *I saw you in the bathtub.* New York: HarperCollins.
Withers, C. (1948). *Rocket in my pocket.* New York: Holt, Rinehart.
Yolan, J. (1992). *Street rhymes from around the world.* New York: Wordsong.

Rhyming Games

There are many commercially made games and computer software programs that feature rhyming words. The two games described here are easy to make and are based on familiar formats.

Adaptable for Other Stages

Rhyming Bingo 4–11

Materials

Prepare enough Bingo gameboards for the number of children who will participate (small groups of three to five children are probably ideal). An appropriate gameboard size for young children is a 9-by-9-inch board divided into nine 3-by-3-inch squares; for older students, the gameboard can be expanded to a 4-by-4-inch or 5-by-5-inch array. Copy sets of pictures from the Appendix and form rhyming groups such as those listed in activity 4-8. Randomly paste all but one of each rhyming group in the spaces on the gameboards, and then laminate them for durability. Each gameboard must be different.

Prepare a complementary set of cards on which you paste the remaining picture from each rhyming group. These will become the deck from which rhyming words are called aloud during the game. You will need some kind of marker to cover the squares on the gameboard. These may be as simple as 2-inch squares of construction paper, plastic chips, bottle caps, or pennies.

Procedures

1. Each child receives a gameboard and markers to cover spaces.
2. The teacher or a designated child is the caller who turns over cards from the deck and calls out the name of the picture.
3. Each player searches the gameboard for a picture that rhymes with the one that has been called out. Players can cover a match with a marker to claim the space.
4. The winner is the first player to cover a row in any direction, or the first player to fill his or her entire board.

Variations

When children are able to read, this game can be played with word cards instead of picture cards.

Rhyming Concentration 4–12

Materials

Adaptable for Other Stages

This game for two or three children is played like the traditional Concentration or the more current Memory game. Assemble a collection of 6 to 10 rhyming pairs from the pictures in the Appendix (listed in activity 4-8). Paste the pictures on cards and laminate for durability. Be sure the pictures do not show through from the backside.

Procedures

1. Shuffle the pictures and then lay them facedown in rows.
2. Players take turns flipping over two pictures at a time. If the two pictures rhyme, the player keeps the cards to hold to the end of the game. The player who makes a match gets another turn.
3. The winner is the child who has the most matches at the end of the game.

Variations

When children are able to read, this game can be played with word cards instead of picture cards.

Beginning-Middle-End: Finding Phonemes in Sound Boxes 4–13

Phonemic segmentation is best developed as teachers model writing and as children try to invent spellings, but at times you want to give some added emphasis to phonemic segmentation using sound boxes. Originally developed by Elkonin (1973), sound boxes serve as a concrete way to demonstrate how words are made of smaller pieces called sounds (or phonemes). Here is a variation developed by Erica Fulmer, a reading specialist, who has created a song she and her children sing as they try to find the location of each sound in the word.

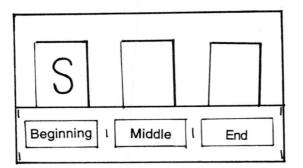

FIGURE 4-17   Sound Boxes

Materials

You will need large letter cards and a three-pocket holder such as the one shown in Figure 4-17.

Procedures

1. Place the letters needed to spell a three-letter word in the pocket backwards so the children cannot see the letters. Announce the word, such as *sun.* Choose words from a familiar book, poem, or dictation when possible. Words that start with continuant sounds such as |m|, |s|, or |f| work well because they can be said slowly.

2. Sing the song to the tune of "Are You Sleeping, Brother John?"

   Beginning, middle, end; beginning, middle, end
   Where is the sound? Where is the sound?
   Where's the ssss in sun? Where's the ssss in sun?
   Let's find out. Let's find out.

3. Children take turns coming forward to pick the position and check by turning the letter card.

Variations

Add a fourth box when children are able to do three sounds with ease. Draw sound boxes on the board anytime you want to model the segmentation process when writing a word. For example, as you take a group's dictation, the word *fast* might come up. Draw four boxes and invite the children to help you say the word slowly to figure out what letters need to go in each one.

It's in the Bag—A Phoneme Blending Game 4–14

Materials

You will need a paper bag (gift bags are attractive) and an assortment of small objects collected from around the classroom, from outside, or from home: chalk, pen, paper clip, tack, key, rock, stick, and so on. You might use a puppet to add interest.

Procedures

Lay out a dozen or so objects and name them with the children. Explain that you will use them to play a game. Introduce the puppet. The puppet will name an object in the bag, saying it very slowly, and the children will guess what it is saying.

Variations

Use objects or pictures related to a topic of study. For example, if you are teaching a unit on animals, you could put pictures of farm animals in the bag. You could also use plastic toy animals. This can be a sensory activity by letting children reach into the bag, figure out an object by touch, and then say it slowly for the other children to guess. Objects that begin with the same beginning sounds can also be put into the bag to sort.

Incorporating Phonological Skills into Daily Activities 4–15

Teachers of emergent children can incorporate sound play into many daily activities and routines.

1. *Lining up, taking attendance, or calling children to a group:* Call each child's name and then lead the class in clapping the syllables in the name. Announce that everyone whose name has two syllables can line up, then one syllable, three, and so on. Say each child's name slowly as it is called. Make up a rhyme for each child's name that starts with a sound of interest: Billy Willy, Mary Wary, Shanee Wanee, and so on. Substitute the first letter in everyone's name with the same letter: Will, Wary, Wanee, Wustin, and so on.

2. *During read-alouds:* Pause to let children fill in a rhyming word, especially on a second or third reading. If they have trouble, say the first sound for them with a clue: "It rhymes with *whale* and starts with /p/." Draw attention to a long word by repeating it and clapping the syllables: "That's a big word! Let's clap the syllables: hip-po-pot-a-mus, five syllables!" You might also pause while reading and say a key word very slowly before asking the children to repeat it fast: "The next day his dad picked him up in a red. . . jeeeep. What's that? A jeep, right." You might point to the letters as you do this.

There are many other published resources on the topic of phonological awareness and what teachers can do to facilitate it. The following are particularly worthwhile:

Adams, M. J., Foorman, B. A., Lundberg, I., & Beweler, T. (1998). *Phonemic awareness in young children.* Baltimore, MD: Paul H. Brookes Pub. Co.

Blevins, W. (1997). *Phonemic awareness activities for early reading success.* New York: Scholastic.

Ericson, L., & Juliebo, M. F. (1998). *The phonological awareness handbook for kindergarten and primary teachers.* Newark, DE: International Reading Association.

Fitzpatrick, J. (1998). *Phonemic awareness: Playing with sounds to strengthen beginning reading skills.* Cypress, CA: Creative Teaching Press.

Invernizzi, M., Meier, J., Swank, L., & Juel, C. (2002). *Phonological awareness literacy screening for kindergartners (PALS-K).* Charlottesville, VA: Univeristy Press.

Opitz, M. F. (2000). *Rhymes and reasons: Literature and language play for phonological awareness.* Portsmouth, NH: Heinemann.

Yopp, H. K., & Yopp, R. E. (2000). *Oo-pples and boo-noo-noos.* Portsmouth, NH: Heinemann.

ALPHABET ACTIVITIES AND GAMES

The following activities are designed to develop all aspects of alphabet knowledge, including letter recognition (both upper- and lowercase), letter naming, letter writing, and letter sounds. You may notice that these activities address more than one letter at a time: For children who have not cut their teeth on alphabet letters and picture books, one letter per week is not enough. We must deal with more than one letter at a time.

Beginning with Alphabet Books 4–16

Share alphabet books with a group as you would other good literature and plan follow-up activities when appropriate. Some books are suitable for toddlers and merely require the naming of the letter and a single accompanying picture, such as Dick Bruna's *B Is for Bear*. Others, such as Graeme Base's *Animalia*, will keep even upper elementary children engaged as they try to name all the things that are hidden in the illustrations. Look for alphabet books, such as the ones listed here, to draw children's attention to beginning sounds through alliteration.

Base, G. (1986). *Animalia.* New York: Harry Abrams.

Bayor, J. (1984). *A: My name is Alice.* Illustrated by Steven Kellogg. New York: Dial.

Berenstain, S., & Berenstain, J. (1971). *The Berenstain's B book.* New York: Random House.

Cole, J. (1993). *Six sick sheep: 101 tongue twisters.* New York: Morrow.

Obligado, L. (1987). *Faint frogs feeling feverish and other terrifically tantalizing tongue twisters.* New York: Viking Penguin.

Seuss, Dr. (1963). *Dr. Seuss's ABC.* New York: Random House.

Many ABC books can be incorporated into thematic units, such as Jerry Pallotta's many content alphabet books or Mary Azarian's *A Farmer's Alphabet*. Some alphabet books present special puzzles, such as Jan Garten's *The Alphabet Tale*. Children are invited to predict the upcoming animal by showing just the tip of its tail on the preceding page. Following is a list of some outstanding ABC books for school-age children.

Anglund, J. W. (1960). *In a pumpkin shell.* (Alphabet Mother Goose). San Diego, CA: Harcourt Brace, Jovanovich.

Anno, M. (1975). *Anno's alphabet.* New York: Crowell.

Aylesworth, J. (1992). *Old black fly.* Illustrated by Stephen Gammell. New York: Scholastic.

Azarian, M. (1981). *A farmer's alphabet.* Boston: David Godine.

Baskin, Leonard. (1972). *Hosie's alphabet.* New York: Viking Press.

Ernst, L. C. (1996). *The letters are lost.* New York: Scholastic.

Fain, K. (1993). *Handsigns: A sign language alphabet.* New York: Scholastic.

Falls, C. B. (1923). *ABC book.* New York: Doubleday.

Gág, W. (1933). *The ABC bunny.* Hand lettered by Howard Gág. New York: Coward-McCann.

Geisert, A. (1986). *Pigs from A to Z.* Boston: Houghton Mifflin.

Hague, K. (1984). *Alphabears: An ABC book.* Illustrated by Michael Hague. New York: Holt, Rinehart & Winston.

Horenstein, H. (1999) *Arf! Beg! Catch! Dogs from A to Z.* New York: Scholastic.

McPhail, D. (1989). *David McPhail's animals A to Z.* New York: Scholastic.

Musgrove, M. (1976). *Ashanti to Zulu: African traditions.* Illustrated by Leo and Diane Dillon. New York: Dial.

Owens, M. B. (1988). *A caribou alphabet.* Brunswick, ME: Dog Ear Press.

Pallotta, J. (1989). *The yucky reptile alphabet book;* (1991). *The dinosaur alphabet book.* Illustrated by Ralph Masiello. New York: Bantam Doubleday, Dell. (There are many more in this series.)

Shannon, G. (1996). *Tomarrow's alphabet.* Illustrated by Donald Crews. New York: Greenwillow.

Thornhill, J. (1988). *The wildlife A-B-C: A nature alphabet book.* New York: Simon & Schuster.

Tryon, L. (1991). *Albert's alphabet.* New York: MacMillan.

Alphabet Book Follow-Ups 4–17

Procedures

1. Discuss the pattern of the books, solve the puzzle, and talk about the words that begin with each letter as you go back through the books a second time.
2. Focus on alliteration by repeating tongue twisters and creating a list of words for a particular letter. Brainstorm other words that begin with that letter, and write them under the letter on chart paper.
3. Make individual or class alphabet books. You might decide on a theme or pattern for the book. Refer back to the alphabet books you have read for ideas. One idea might be a noun-verb format, for example, ants attack, bees buzz, cats cry, and dogs doze.
4. Look up a particular letter you are studying in several alphabet books or a picture dictionary to find other things that begin with that sound. This is an excellent introduction to using resource books.*

Chicka Chicka Boom Boom Sort 4–18

Martin and Archambault's *Chicka Chicka Boom Boom* is a great favorite and provides a wonderful way to move from children's books to alphabet recognition and letter-sound activities. After reading this delightful book with her children, Pat Love demonstrates how to match foam "Laurie Letters," one at a time, to the letters printed in the book. Pat's boom boards (see Figure 4-18) can be used for sorting letters and pictures by beginning sounds. Other teachers have created a large coconut tree on the side of their filing cabinet so that children can act out the story and match upper- and lower-case forms using magnetic letters.

Starting with Children's Names 4–19

Children are naturally interested in their own names and their friends' names. Names are an ideal point from which to begin the study of alphabet letters. We like the idea of a "name of the day"** so much better than a "letter of the week," because many more letters are covered in a much shorter time!

FIGURE 4-18   Chicka Chicka Boom Boom Board

---

*Thanks to Jennifer Sudduth for these activities.
**For more information on using names to develop alphabet knowledge, see *Phonics They Use: Words for Reading and Writing* by Pat Cunningham.

Materials

Prepare a card for each child on which his or her name is written in neatly executed block letters. Put all the names in a box or can. Have additional blank cards ready to be cut apart as described.

Procedures

1. Each day, with great fanfare, a name is drawn and becomes the name of the day. The teacher begins with a very open-ended question, "What do you notice about this name?" Children will respond in all sorts of ways depending upon what they know about letters: "It's a short name." "It has three letters." "It starts like Taneesh's name." "It has an *O* in the middle."

2. Next children chant or echo the letters in the name as the teacher points to each one. A cheer led by the teacher is lots of fun:

   Teacher: "Give me a *T*."   Children: "T"

   Teacher: "Give me an *O*."   Children: "O"

   Teacher: "Give me an *M*."   Children: "M"

   Teacher: "What have we got?"   Children: "Tom!"

3. On an additional card, the teacher writes the name of the child as the children recite the letters again. Then the teacher cuts the letters apart and hands out the letters to children in the group. The children are then challenged to put the letters back in order to spell the name correctly. This can be done in a pocket chart or on a chalkboard ledge and repeated many times. The cut-up letters are then put into an envelope with the child's name on the outside. The envelope is added to the name puzzle collection. Children love to pull out their friends' names to put together.

4. All the children in the group should attempt to spell the featured name. This might be done on individual chalkboards or on pieces of paper. This is an opportunity to offer some handwriting instruction as the teacher models for the children. Discuss the details of direction and movement of letter formation as the children imitate your motions.

5. Each day the featured name is added to a display of all the names that have come before. By displaying them in a pocket chart they can be compared to previous names and used for sorting activities:

   Sort the names by the number of letters.

   Sort the names by the number of syllables.

   Sort the names that share particular letters.

   Sort the names that belong to boys and girls.

   Sort the names by alphabetical order.

6. Create a permanent display of the names and encourage children to practice writing their own and their friends' names. If you have a writing center, you might put all the names on index cards in a box for reference. Children can be encouraged to reproduce names not only by copying the names with pencils, chalk, and markers, but also with rubber stamps, foam cutout letters, link letters, or letter tiles. The display of children's names becomes an important reference tool during writing time.

One Child's Name 4–20

Some children may need additional help learning the letters in their names. For them, the following activity is valuable.*

---

*Darrell Morris presents this activity in the context of a tutoring session for an Emergent reader in his excellent book *Case Studies in Teaching Beginning Reading: The Howard Street Tutoring Manual.*

FIGURE 4-19   Brandon's Name Puzzle

1. Spell out a child's name with letter cards, tiles, foam, or plastic letters using both upper- and lowercase.
2. Spell it with uppercase letters in the first row and ask the child to match lowercase letters in the row below, as shown in Figure 4-19.
3. Mix up the top row and have the child unscramble the letters to form the name once again. Have the child name the letters as this is done. Mix up the bottom row and repeat.
4. Rematch the upper- and lowercase tiles, letter for letter, naming each letter again as they are touched.
5. Next take blank cards and place one blank card beneath each letter. Write each letter on each blank card, discussing the details of direction and movement in letter formation as you do. Give the child a piece of paper to imitate your letter formations. Alternate this activity for upper- and lowercase.
6. Play Concentration with the set of upper- and lowercase letters needed to spell a child's name.

Alphabet Scrapbook 4-21

Materials

FIGURE 4-20   Alphabet Scrapbook

Prepare a blank dictionary for each child by stapling together sheets of paper. (Seven sheets of paper folded and stapled in the middle is enough for one letter per page.) Children can use this book in a variety of ways (see Figure 4-20).

1. Practice writing uppercase and lowercase forms of the letter on each page.
2. Cut out letters in different fonts or styles from magazines and newspapers and paste them into their scrapbooks.
3. Draw and label pictures and other things which begin with that letter sound.
4. Cut and paste magazine pictures onto the corresponding letter page. These pictures, too, can be labeled.
5. Add sight words as they become known to create a personal dictionary.

The Alphabet Song and Tracking Activities 4–22

Every early childhood classroom should have an alphabet strip or chart at eye level. Too often these strips are put up out of the children's reach. The best location for the strips is to be posted on desktops or tabletops for easy reference. Here are activities that make active use of these charts.

Materials

Commercial or teacher-made alphabet strips for both wall display and for individual children and individual letters.

Procedures

1. Learn the ABC song to the tune of "Twinkle Twinkle Little Star." Sing it many times!
2. Model pointing to each letter, as the song is sung or the letters are chanted. Then ask the children to fingerpoint to the letters as they sing or chant.

FIGURE 4-21   Alphabet Link Letters

3. When students know about half of the alphabet, they can work on putting a set of letter cards, tiles, or link letters in alphabetical order. Use upper-or lowercase letters, or match the two (see Figure 4-21). Keep an ABC strip or chart nearby as a ready reference.

Alphabet Eggs 4–23

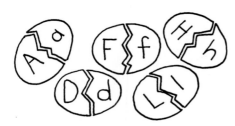

FIGURE 4-22   Alphabet Eggs

Materials

Create a simple set of puzzles designed to practice the pairing of upper-and lowercase letters. On poster board, draw and cut out enough 4-inch egg shapes for each letter in the alphabet. Write an uppercase letter on the left half and the matching lowercase letters on the right portion. Cut the eggs in half using a zigzag line (see Figure 4-22). Make each zigzag slightly different so the activity is self-checking. Students should say the letters to themselves and put the eggs back together by matching the upper- and lowercase form.*

Variations

Adaptable for Other Stages

There are many other shapes that can be cut in half for matching. In October, for example, pumpkin shapes can be cut into two and in February, heart shapes can be cut apart the same way. There is no end to the matching possibilities. Acorn caps can be matched to bottoms, balls to baseball gloves, frogs to lily pads, and so on. These matching sets can also be created to pair letters and a picture that starts with that letter, rhyming words, contractions, homophones, and so on.

Alphabet Concentration 4-24

Adaptable for Other Stages

This game works just like Concentration with rhyming words as described in activity 4-12. Create cards with upper- and lowercase forms of the letters written on one side. Be sure they cannot be seen from the backside. Use both familiar and not so familar letters. Do not try this with all 26 letters at once, or it may take a long time to complete; 8 to 10 pairs is probably enough.

Variations

To introduce this game or to make it easier, play it with the cards face up. As letter sounds are learned, matching consonant letters to pictures that begin with that letter sound can change the focus of this game.

_____

* Thanks to Elizabeth Schuett for this idea.

FIGURE 4-23   Letter Spin Game

Letter Spin 4-25

Materials

Adaptable for Other Stages

Make a spinner with six to eight spaces, and label each space with a capital letter. If you laminate the spinner before labeling, you can reuse it with other letters. Write the letters with a grease pencil or nonpermanent overhead transparency pen. Write the lowercase letters on small cards, creating five or six cards for each letter (see Figure 4-23).* See the Appendix for tips on making a spinner.

Procedures

1. Lay out all the lowercase cards faceup.
2. Each player in turn spins and lands on an uppercase letter. The player then picks up one card that has the corresponding lowercase form, orally identifying the letter.
3. Play continues until all the letter cards have been picked up.
4. The winner is the player with the most cards when the game ends.

Variations

Students can be asked to not only name but also write the upper- and lowercase forms of the letter after each turn. This game can be adapted to any feature that involves matching—letters to sounds, rhymes, vowel patterns, and so on.

Alphabet Cereal Sort 4-26

Materials

For this sorting activity, you will need a box of alphabet cereal—enough to give each child a handful. Prepare a sorting board for each child by dividing a paper into 26 squares. Label each square with an upper- or lowercase letter.

*Thanks to Alison Dwier-Seldon for this idea.

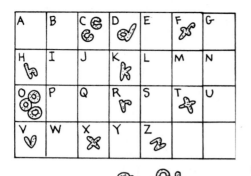

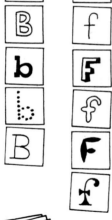

FIGURE 4-24 Cereal Sort

Procedures

1. Allow the children to work individually or in teams to sort their own cereal onto their papers (see Figure 4-24). Discard (or eat) broken or deformed letters.
2. After the children are finished they can count the number of letters in each category (e.g., A-8, B-4). This could become a graphing activity.
3. Eat the cereal! (Or glue it down.)*

Variations

Have the children spell their names or other words using the cereal.

Sorting Letters with Different Print Styles 4–27

Children need to see a variety of print styles before they will be readily able to identify their ABCs in different contexts. Draw children's attention to different letterforms wherever you encounter them. Environmental print is especially rich in creative lettering styles. Encourage the children to bring in samples from home—like the big letters on a bag of dog food or cereal—and create a display on a bulletin board or in a big book.

Materials

Get a collection of different print styles by cutting letters from newspapers, catalogs, magazines, and other print sources. You can also search your computer fonts and print out letters in the largest size possible. Cut the letters apart, mount them on small cards, and laminate for durability. Use both capitals and lowercase, but avoid cursive styles for now (see Figure 4-25).

Procedures

1. After modeling the sort with a group of children, place the materials in a center where the children can work independently.
2. Avoid putting out too many different letters at one time—four or five is probably enough, with 8 to 12 variations for each.

Variations

If you have created alphabet scrapbooks (activity 4-21), children can paste in samples of different lettering styles.

FIGURE 4-25 Sorting Letters with Different Print Styles

WORKING WITH BEGINNING SOUNDS

Specific guidelines for creating and using picture sorting for initial sounds were described earlier in this chapter and general guidelines were presented in Chapter 3. Picture and word sorts are at the heart of word study and the procedures will be revisited throughout this book. Games can be used to review beginning sounds after

---

*Thanks to Janet Brown Watts for this idea.

children have already practiced categorizing targeted sounds in basic picture-sorting activities.

Using Books to Enhance Beginning Sounds 4–28

Because alphabet books often include one or more examples of words that start with a targeted letter, they are a natural choice to use when teaching beginning sounds. Such books can be used to introduce an initial sound, or they can be used as a resource for a word hunt as children go searching for more words that start with targeted letters. Watch out for the choices authors and artists sometimes make, however. The C page may have words that start with the digraph *ch* (*chair*), hard *c* (*cat*), and soft *c* (*cymbals*). Children will eventually need to sort out these confusions, but not at this time.

Soundline 4-29

Adaptable for Other Stages

This classic activity can be used to focus on letter matching or letter-sound correspondences.

Materials

You will need rope, clothespins, markers, tagboard, glue, pictures, scissors, and laminating film.

Procedures

1. Write upper- and lowercase letters on the top of the clothespins.
2. Glue a picture beginning with each letter on a square of tagboard and laminate.
3. Students can match the picture card to the clothespin and hang it on the rope (see Figure 4-26).*

FIGURE 4-26   Soundline

Letter Spin for Sounds 4–30

Adaptable for Other Stages

This is a good game to review up to eight beginning sounds at a time. It is a variation of the letter spin described in activity 4–25.

Materials

You will need a spinner divided into four to eight sections and labeled with beginning letters to review. You will also need a collection of picture cards that correspond with the letters, with at least four pictures for each letter.

Procedures

1. Lay out all the pictures on a table or on the floor faceup.
2. Two to four players take turns spinning. The player can select one picture that begins with the sound indicated by the spinner. The next player spins and selects one picture. If there are no more pictures for a sound, the player must pass.
3. Play continues until all the pictures are gone. The winner is the one with the most pictures at the end.

*Leslie Robertson contributed this activity.

Variations

A large cube could be used like a die instead of a spinner.

Adaptable for Other Stages

Object Sorting by Sounds 4-31

Rule off a large sheet of poster board into squares and label each one according to the initial sounds you want to review. Collect miniature toys and animals or small objects (a button, bell, box, rock, ring, ribbon, etc.) that begin with the sounds of interest. Children are asked to sort the objects into the spaces on the board.

Adaptable for Other Stages

Initial Consonant Follow-the-Path Game 4-32

This game is simple enough that even preschoolers can learn the rules and it can be used throughout the primary grades to practice a variety of features. You will see this game adapted in many ways in Chapters 5 and 6.

Materials

You will need to copy the two halves of a follow-the-path gameboard found in the Appendix. To make the game in a folder that can be easily stored, paste each half on the inside of a manila folder (colored ones are nice) leaving a slight gap between the two sides in the middle (so the folder can still fold). Add some color and interest with stickers or cutout pictures to create a theme such as "Trip to the Pizza Parlor" or "Adventures in Space." Label each space on the path with one of the letters you want to review, using both upper- and lowercase forms (see Figure 4-27). Sets of four letter sounds at a time work best. Reproduce a set of picture cards that correspond to the letters. Copy them on cardstock or glue cutout pictures to cards. You will need two to four game pieces to move around the board. Flat ones like bottle caps or plastic disks store well. You might want to put the pictures and playing pieces in a labeled plastic zip-top bag inside the folder.

Procedures

1. Turn the picture cards facedown in a stack. Players go in alphabetical order.
2. Each player draws a picture in turn and moves the playing piece to the next space on the path that is marked by the corresponding beginning consonant.
3. The winner is the first to arrive at the destination.

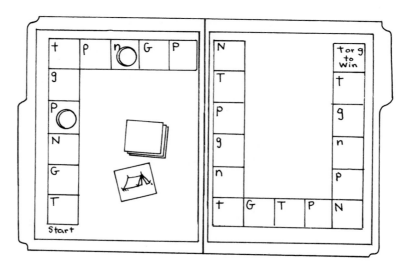

FIGURE 4-27 Follow-the-Path Game

Variations

This game can be adapted for alphabet, blends and digraphs, short vowels, and vowel patterns.

HELPING CHILDREN ACQUIRE A CONCEPT OF WORD

When children are learning about letters and sounds at the same time they are fingerpoint reading from memory, there is a complementary process at work. Learning one will give logic and purpose to learning the other. Fingerpoint reading to familiar rhymes and pattern books is the best way to achieve a concept of word. Emergent readers need much support in learning how to track print in correspondence with their speech. The following activities provide a few ways to go about getting kids connected to the words on the page.

Rhymes for Reading 4–33

After playing with the sounds in rhyming songs and jump rope jingles, an important further step is to let the children see and interact with the printed form. From such experiences children will begin to develop the concept of a printed word. Here is an example making use of a classic fingerplay which children will quickly be able to read from memory.

Materials

Record the words to a well-known jingle such as "I had a little turtle" on a sheet of 24-inch-wide chart paper—big enough for all to see (see Figure 4-28). Some teachers have special pointers (imaginative variations include the rib bone of a cow and the beam of a flashlight), but a finger will do fine when the chart is at eye level.

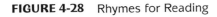

FIGURE 4-28   Rhymes for Reading

Procedures

1. Teach the children the words to the song and show them how to do the fingerplay if you know it. Sing it repeatedly until everyone knows it well.
2. Display the words to the song and model for the children how to point to the words as they are said. Invite children to take their own turn at tracking the words as they or their classmates chant the words. From repeated opportunities, teachers can easily monitor the children's developing concept of word, from vague left-to-right sweeps, to self-corrected, careful matching of speech to print.
3. Make smaller copies of the text and photocopy them so that every child can get their own finger on the print. Modeling with a large chart for a group is only a starting point. Nothing beats individual practice. Copies of familiar songs and poems can be left posted in the room and small copies can be put into personal readers (described in Chapter 5).

Cut-Up Sentences 4–34

Write sentences or phrases from a familiar piece of text on a sentence strip. Sentences might come from a book or a poem the group has read together such as the turtle rhyme in the previous activity. The sentences can then be used in the group to rebuild the text in order using a pocket chart. Individual copies of text can be cut apart so that each child gets to practice.

A further step is to ask the students to cut apart the words in the sentence and then challenge them to reconstruct the sentence. Hand out scissors and call out each word as

FIGURE 4-29 Cut-Up Sentences

the children cut it off. The spaces between words are not obvious to emergent children so be prepared to model for them. Demonstrate how to find the words in order to rebuild the sentence: "What letter would you expect to see at the beginning of *swam?*" Leave the word cards and model sentence strips with a pocket chart in a center for children to practice in their spare time. Put individual words into an envelope with the sentence written on the outside (see Figure 4-29). These can be sent home with the children to reassemble with their parents.

Be the Sentence 4–35

Children can also rebuild familiar sentences by pretending to be the words themselves. Write a familiar sentence on a chart or on the board. Start with short sentences such as "Today is Monday" or "I love you." Then write each word from the sentence on a large card. Give each word to a child, naming it for them. "Stephanie, you are the word *Monday;* Lorenzo, you are the word *is.*" Ask the children to work together to arrange themselves into the sentence. Have another child read the sentence to check the direction and order. Try this again with another group of children and then leave the words out for children to work with on their own.

Pulling It All Together as You Share the Pen 4–36

The act of writing for children offers teachers the opportunity to model the use of the alphabet, phonemic segmentation, letter-sound matching, concept of word, and conventions such as capitalization and punctuation all in the context of a meaningful group activity. As the teacher writes on the chalkboard, chart paper, or an overhead projector, children see their own ideas expressed in oral language transformed into print. What began as a key feature of the language experience approach to reading has undergone a recent transformation in the form of "shared writing" (McKenzie, 1985) or "interactive writing" (Button, Johnson, & Furgerson, 1996).

During interactive writing, children share the pen and are invited to come forward to add a letter, a word, or a period. Such writing can take place any time of the day and for any reason—for example, to list class rules, to make a shopping list, to record observations from a field trip, to create a new version of a familiar text, or to list questions for a classroom visitor. The following activity is a favorite form of group writing in which the teacher and children compose sentences that report on daily home and school events which are of importance to the class.

The Morning Message 4–37

Adaptable for Other Stages

Each morning the teacher talks with the entire group to discover bits of news, which can be part of the morning message. In preschool or early kindergarten, this may be only one sentence, but over time, it can grow to be as long as the teacher and children desire.

Materials

You will need a large chart paper or chalkboard with markers or chalk, and white tape for covering mistakes.

Procedures

1. Chat with children informally, sharing news from home or the classroom. Select a piece of news to record in the form of a single sentence.
2. Recite the sentence together with the children to decide how many words it contains, holding up a finger for each word. Then draw a line for each word on the board or chart (see Figure 4-30).
3. Repeat each word, emphasizing the sounds as they are written and invite the group to make suggestions about what letters are needed: "The first word we need to write is *we*. Wwwwwweeeeee. What letter do we need for the first sound in *wwweee*?" A child might suggest the letter *Y*. "The name of the letter *Y* does start with that sound. Does anyone have another idea?" Every letter in every word need not be discussed at length. Focus on what is appropriate for the developmental level of your students.
4. You can do the writing in the beginning, but as children learn to write their letters you can share the pen. White tape is used to cover any mistakes. Let children take turns writing, usually just one child per word at this level.
5. Model and talk about concepts of print such as left to right, return sweep, capitalization, punctuation, and letter formation. Clap the syllables in longer words, spelling one syllable at a time.

FIGURE 4-30 Morning Message

6. After each sentence is completed, read it aloud to the group, touching each word. If your sentence contains a two- or three-syllable word, touch it for every syllable, helping children see how it works. Invite children to fingerpoint as they read.

7. The morning message should be left up all day. Some children may want to copy it or you might want to use it for the cut-up sentence or be-the-sentence activities described earlier.

8. A collection of all the morning messages for a week can be sent home on Friday as a summary of class news that children will have a good chance of proudly reading to their parents.

Variations

Give each child a lap-sized white board, chalkboard, or clip board so everyone can participate in listening for sounds, handwriting, and use of punctuation.

The word study activities for the emergent stage promote concept and vocabulary development, awareness of sounds, concept of word, and the alphabetic principle. These activities spring from and return to children's books and are extended through writing. Once children achieve a concept of word in print and can segment speech and represent beginning and ending consonant sounds in their spelling, they are no longer emergent, but beginning readers. This is also when they move into the next stage of spelling, the letter name–alphabetic stage. Word study for the letter name–alphabetic speller/beginning reader is described in Chapter 5.

Emergent Readers

5 Word Study for Beginners in the Letter Name–Alphabetic Stage

The letter name–alphabetic stage of literacy development is a period of beginnings. Students begin to read and write in a conventional way. That is, they begin to learn words and actually read text, and their writing becomes more readable to themselves and others. However, this period of literacy development needs careful scaffolding, because students know how to read and write only a small number of words. The chosen reading materials and activities should provide rich contextual support. In word study, the earliest sorts are pictures; later, students work with words in families or words known by sight. In the following discussion of reading and writing development and instruction, we look closely at the support teachers provide and the way word knowledge develops during this stage. We suggest instructional practices that help teachers plan word study programs for beginners. Word study for letter name–alphabetic spellers helps beginners (a) acquire a sight vocabulary through reading and **word banks,** (b) construct phonics generalizations through picture and word sorts, and (c) create ever more sophisticated, if not completely accurate, spellings as they write. Before we examine this stage of word knowledge and provide guidelines for word study instruction, let us visit the first-grade classroom of Mr. Richard Perez.

TABLE 5-1	Invented Spellings of Three First Graders		
Word	Cynthia	Tony	Maria
fan	VN	FAN	FAN
pet	PD	PAT	PET
dig	DK	DKG	DEG
wait	YT	WAT	WAT
chunk	JK	HOK	CHOK
stick	CK	SEK	STEK

During the first weeks of school, Richard observed his first graders as they participated in reading and writing activities and he used an inventory described in Chapter 2 to collect samples of their spelling for analysis. Like most first-grade teachers, Richard has a range of ability in his classroom, so he manages three instructional groups for reading and word study and uses students' spellings as a guide to appropriate phonics instruction. Richard meets with each group daily for guided reading. Some days he uses part of that group time for teacher-directed word study.

Cynthia is a typical student of the early letter name–alphabetic group who writes slowly, often needing help sounding out a word and confusing consonants such as *v* and *f* and *s* and *c*. The results of their writing efforts are limited primarily to consonants with very few vowels, as shown by Cynthia's spellings in Table 5-1. Cynthia has memorized the words to jingles such as "Five Little Monkeys Jumping on the Bed," but frequently gets off track when she tries to point to the words as she reads. Richard decides to take a step back with this group and plans a review of beginning sounds. Each Monday he introduces a set of four initial consonants such as *b,m,r,* and *s*. After modeling the sort and practicing it in the group, he gives each student a handout of pictures to be cut apart for individual sorting practice, as shown in Figure 5-1A. The next day the students sort the pictures again and Richard observes how quickly and accurately they work. On subsequent days of the week during seat work time or center time, the students draw and label pictures beginning with those sounds, cut and paste pictures, and do word hunts (follow-up routines described in Chapter 3).

A. Beginning Consonant Sort

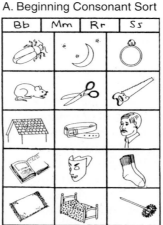

B. Word Family Sort

cat	man	can
rat	fan	hat
pan	sat	pat
that	tan	bat
van	mat	than
fat	ran	

C. Short-Vowel Sort

cap	pig	hot
sit	hat	shop
ship	stop	fast
camp	fish	lock
mad	job	will
him	trap	not
got	that	pin

FIGURE 5-1 Word Study Handouts for Letter Name–Alphabetic Spellers in Three Different Instructional Groups

Each day when Richard meets with Cynthia's group, they read chart stories, jingles, and big books with predictable texts. To help the students in this group develop a sight vocabulary, Richard started a word bank for each child. He wrote words the students could quickly identify on small cards for their collection. The students add a few new words several times a week and review their words on their own or with classroom volunteers.

Tony is part of a large group in the middle letter name–alphabetic stage who has beginning and ending consonants under control, but shows little accuracy when spelling digraphs and blends or short vowels. Tony points to the words as he reads "Five Little Monkeys" and self-corrects if he gets off track on words with more than one syllable such as *jumping* and *mama.* Richard decides to introduce the digraphs *sh, ch, th,* and *wh* using picture sorts, and then begins the study of word families such as *at* and *an* using word cards. He knows that Tony and the other students in that group can read words such as *cat, can,* and *man,* and that these words serve as the basis for the study of other words in the same family. Richard spends 10 minutes in group word study several times a week introducing new word families, modeling how to sort them into categories, and leading discussions which help the students focus on the features common to the words in each column. The children then receive their own set of words (Figure 5-1B) to cut apart for sorting, and work alone and with partners to practice the sort, write and illustrate the words, and play follow-up games.

Maria represents a third group of students in the late letter name–alphabet stage who use single consonants accurately, as well as many digraphs and blends, as shown in Table 5-1. This group uses vowels in most words, but the short vowels are often incorrect. Maria can read some books independently and is quickly accumulating a large sight vocabulary simply from doing lots of reading. Mr. Perez works with word families for several weeks, making an effort to include words with digraphs and blends, but he soon discovers that word families are too easy and thus decides to move to the study of short vowels in nonrhyming words. Each Monday he introduces a collection of words that can be sorted by short vowels into three or four groups. This group also receives a list of words, as shown in Figure 5–1C, to cut apart and use for sorting. They learn to work in pairs for buddy sorts, writing sorts, word hunts, and games on other days of the week.

LITERACY DEVELOPMENT OF LETTER NAME–ALPHABETIC STUDENTS

Letters have both names and sounds. Students typically learn the names of the letters first and then use them to spell. This phenomenon accounts for the name of the letter name–alphabetic stage. Spellers in this group operate in the first layer of English—the alphabetic layer. They understand that words can be segmented into sounds and that letters of the alphabet must be matched to these sounds in a systematic fashion. At first these matches may be limited to the most salient or prominent sounds in words, usually the beginning and ending consonants. By the middle of this stage, students include a vowel in each stressed syllable and they spell short vowels by matching the way they articulate the letter names of the vowels. By the end of the letter name–alphabetic stage, students have learned how to spell words with short vowels and they can read most single-syllable words in their reading.

Letter name–alphabetic spelling develops in synchrony with the beginning stages of reading and writing. As shown in Figure 2-1, spelling development matches reading and writing behaviors. The next section describes how students read and write during this stage.

READING AND WRITING IN THE LETTER NAME–ALPHABETIC STAGE

Students who are in the letter name–alphabetic stage of spelling have recently acquired a **concept of word**—the ability to track or fingerpoint read a memorized text. Students who have a concept of words can read familiar rhymes and pattern books and their own dictations. Beginning readers read slowly, except when they read well-memorized texts, and are often described as word-by-word readers (Bear, 1991b). Students' fluency is constrained by their lack of word knowledge. They do not remember enough words, nor do they know enough about the orthography to read words quickly enough to permit fluent reading or writing. Often beginning readers' reading rates are painfully slow. For example, a beginning reader may reread a familiar text, either a dictation or a pattern book, at fewer than 50 words per minute compared with mature readers who average 250 words per minute.

Most beginning readers fingerpoint the words when they read, and they read aloud when reading to themselves. This helps them to keep their place and to buy processing time. While they hold the words they have just read in memory, they read the next word, giving them time to try to fit the words together into a phrase. Silent reading is rarely evidenced. If you visit a first-grade classroom during "sustained silent reading" (SSR) or during "drop everything and read" (DEAR), you are likely to hear a steady hum of voices. Disfluency, fingerpointing, and reading aloud to oneself are natural reading behaviors to look for in beginning readers. There is a similar pattern of disfluency in beginning writing, because students usually write slowly, and they often work through spelling words sound by sound (Bear, 1991a). As in reading, orthographic knowledge makes writing easier and more fluent. The more students know about how words are spelled, the more easily and fluently they can write. Consequently, they can give more time to working with and expressing ideas.

In the previous, emergent stage of development, writers are often unable to read what they have written because they lack or have limited letter-to-sound correspondences. Students in the letter name–alphabetic stage can usually read what they write depending on how completely they spell, and their writing is generally readable to anyone who has worked with students in this stage and understands the logic of their letter-to-sound matches.

SUPPORTING BEGINNING LITERACY LEARNING

Letter name–alphabetic spellers are beginning readers who need support to make reading happen. Support can come from two sources: the text and the teacher. Support from the text comes from its degree of predictability and familiarity. Predictability means a student can predict what is coming up next because of certain recurring elements. A rhyming pattern may repeat: "Five little monkeys jumping on the bed, one fell off and bumped his head." A refrain may reoccur: "Have you seen my cat?" (Carle, 1987). A cumulative sequence may reoccur: "This is the cat that caught the rat that ate the malt that lay in the house that Jack built." Or specific words and spelling patterns may reoccur: "The cat sat on the mat. The dog sat on the mat. The goat sat on the mat" (Wildsmith, 1982).

Familiarity makes the text predictable as well. Familiarity with the subject, the language, and the words supports students as they read. Text becomes familiar when students have heard it many times before, or because they have read it many times. Texts also become familiar when the words are about an event experienced firsthand by the students, as in dictated stories.

Support from the teacher comes from the many ways a teacher may scaffold the reading experience. For example, the teacher may provide an oral book introduction (Clay, 1991) before the reading. Book introductions use the language of the text and anticipate difficult words and concepts. A teacher may also scaffold the reading experience by modeling the reading process and by encouraging students to reread the same text many times. Asking students to read in unison (**choral reading**) or immediately after the teacher reads (**echo reading**) are additional methods of scaffolding. The teacher can also provide support by recording a student's experiences in print (language-experience stories).

A tension lies between these two forms of support. The more predictable a text is, the less support is needed from the teacher. Conversely, the less support provided from recurring elements of text, the more scaffolding is needed from the teacher. Because early letter name–alphabetic spellers require support to make reading happen, we often call these beginners *"support readers."* As students develop as readers, they need less support from either teacher or text and they benefit from reading text that is not so predictable.

Support readers do not recognize many words by sight, and their letter-sound knowledge is not enough to sound out words. Word recognition must be supported by offering students text that is predictable and memorable. As students read and reread these beginning texts, they gradually remember words out of context as **sight words.** Rhyming books, nursery rhymes, simple decodable texts, group experience stories, and individual dictations support beginning readers as they rely on their memory and their limited knowledge of letter sounds to track their way through text. The redundancy provided by recurring letter sounds, rhymes, or refrains helps beginners feel successful. Textual support of this nature is necessary until students acquire a corpus of words they recognize automatically at first sight. For example, in the familiar rhyming book *Five Little Monkeys Jumping on the Bed* by Eileen Christelow (1989), beginning readers can point to the words using their memory for the rhyming pattern and their knowledge of beginning sounds /f/, /l/, /m/, /j/, and /b/. The words *fell* and *bed* might even be recognized out of context by virtue of their beginning and ending sounds alone. In another context, however, partial phonetic cues alone will not suffice. *Fell* might be confused with *fall* or *fill,* and *bed* might be confused with *bead* or *bad.* Partial information about the alphabetic code is not enough to support unerring word recognition.

Support reading must be accompanied by word study—the systematic categorization of known words by letter-sound correspondences. Students in the letter name–alphabetic stage learn about letter-sound correspondences needed for reading and spelling by working first with picture cards and then with words they know. We emphasize the use of known words, because it is difficult for students to study the orthography when they have to work hard at simply reading the word. Learning to read and spell is the process of matching the mother tongue to the spelling patterns that represent it. To facilitate that process, it helps to be able to pronounce the words under study. This chapter provides detailed instructions on how to use support reading materials to create word banks, a collection of known words that form the corpus of words to be studied. Students who do a lot of reading and writing and who examine words carefully in word study will gradually acquire the orthographic knowledge to remember words out of context, to recognize words fully, and to read and spell them quickly and automatically.

CHARACTERISTICS OF ORTHOGRAPHIC DEVELOPMENT

Students in the letter name–alphabetic stage provide a wonderful example of how learners construct knowledge in an attempt to make sense of the world of print. Without a mature knowledge of orthography, students carefully analyze the sound system more vigorously than do adults, and they make surprisingly fine distinctions about the way sounds and words are formed in the mouth. They match segmented sounds to the letter names of the alphabet in ways that may seem curious and random to the uninformed adult.

The letter name–alphabetic stage describes students who use their knowledge of the actual names of the letters of the alphabet to spell phonetically or alphabetically. For example, to spell the word *jeep,* students are likely to select *g* as the first letter because

TABLE 5-2		Names of the Letters of the Alphabet					
A	a	H	aich	O	oh	V	vee
B	bee	I	eye	P	pee	W	double you
C	see	J	jay	Q	kue	X	ecks
D	dee	K	kay	R	are	Y	wie
E	ee	L	ell	S	es	Z	zee
F	ef	M	em	T	tee		
G	gee	N	en	U	you		

of its name (gee) and *p* for the final letter because its letter name (pee) offers a clear clue to the sound it represents. GP for *jeep* is a typical spelling of the early letter name–alphabetic stage. According to letter name logic, there is no need to add the vowel because it is already part of the letter name for *g*. Sometimes early letter name–alphabetic spellers include vowels, especially when they spell long vowels that "say their name." For example, students might spell *jeep* as GEP. Using a strategy of letter names, students can luck out and include the correct long vowel, but early letter name–alphabetic spelling is largely consonantal. During the middle part of this stage, students' spellings gradually include more vowels.

Some letter names do not cue students to the sounds they represent. For example, the letter name for *w* is "double u," which offers no clue to its /wuh/ sound. Consequently, early letter name–alphabetic spellers may spell *when* as YN. Why do students use a *y*? When you say the letter name for *y*, you can feel your lips moving to make the shape of the /wuh/ sound. *Y* is the letter whose pronounced name is closest to the sound at the beginning of *when*. Table 5-2 shows what the letter names offer students in terms of sound matches.

HOW CONSONANT SOUNDS ARE ARTICULATED IN THE MOUTH

Letter name–alphabetic students rely not only on what they hear in the letter names, but also on how the letters are **articulated,** or formed in the mouth, when they spell. For example, consider how students spell the blend *dr* in *drive*. Students are misled in their spelling by the similarity between *dr* and *jr,* and they may spell *drive* as JRV. Test this yourself. Say *drive,* and then say *jrive*. Do they sound and feel alike? Linguists call these sounds **affricates,** made by forcing air through a small closure at the roof of the mouth to create a feeling of friction (*friction,* af*fric*atives—see the meaning connection?). English has several other letters and letter combinations that create the affricate sound and these are often substituted for each other: *j, g* (as in *gym*), *ch* (as in *chip*), *dr* (as in *drive*), *tr* (as in *trap*), and the letter name for *h* (aich). In their writing, students use the consonant digraphs and blends they know best. For example, students who are familiar with words that begin with *ch* may spell *train* as CHRAN.

There are several other ways in which students relate sounds to the ways the sounds are made. Basing a decision on the way a sound feels, students may spell *brave* as BRAF, or *oven* as OFN. What is the difference between the consonant sound spelled by *v* and that spelled by *f*? Both sounds feel exactly the same, but one is voiced and the other is unvoiced. When voiced phonemes are created, the vocal chords vibrate. You can feel this if you place your fingers on your larynx as you say them. Compare the way *v* and *f* feel in the words *van* and *fan*. There are similar voiced and unvoiced pairs listed in the pronunciation chart in Table 4-1 on page 108. One implication for instruction is that students in the letter name–alphabetic stage benefit from saying the words they are sorting so that they can feel the shape of their mouth as they say the words and can compare sound differences and the vibration in their vocal cords.

THE ISSUE OF VOWELS IN THE LETTER NAME–ALPHABETIC STAGE

Vowels pose special problems for letter name–alphabetic spellers who rely on the name of letters and how a sound feels in the mouth. Try saying the word *lip*. You can feel the initial consonant as your tongue curls up toward your palate and you can feel the final consonant as it explodes past your lips, but did you feel the vowel? Unlike the consonants—articulated by tongue, teeth, lips, and palate—the vowels are determined by more subtle variations: the shape of the mouth and jaw, the opening of the vocal tract, the force of air from the lungs, and the vibration of the vocal cords.

Vowels are elusive but central to every syllable humans speak. When consonants are electronically separated from vowels, they sound like noise, a click, or a snap of the fingers, and nothing like speech. Try to say a consonant such as *b*. What vowels did you attach to the *b*? If you said the letter name (bee), then you would have said the long *-e* vowel. Now say the sound associated with *b*: /buh/ or /ə/. The vowel this time is the **schwa,** a vowel made in the middle of the mouth. Now try to say a /b/ sound without a vowel. Try to whisper *b* and cut your breath short in a whisper. The whisper is as close as you come to separating a vowel from a consonant.

Studies in acoustical phonetics have demonstrated that vowels are like musical tones, and without the music of the vowel, the consonants become just noise. Because vowels are so closely wedded to the consonants around them, spellers in the early letter name–alphabetic stage have difficulty separating vowels from consonants in order to analyze them and make letter matches. It is as if the consonant were the proverbial squeaky wheel; at first, the consonants seem to demand more attention than the vowel and are more easily examined.

Talking About Vowels

Linguists refer to the distinctive sound within a given vowel according to its tenseness or laxness. The vocal cords are tense when producing the long *-a* sound in the middle of the word *shake*. Conversely, the vocal cords relax a bit in producing the short *-a* sound in the middle of *shack*. The difference in the medial vowel sounds in the words *shake* and *shack* can be described linguistically as **tense** and **lax.**

In phonics instruction, teachers have traditionally taught students the differences between long vowels (which say their name) and short vowels. This distinction between five long and five short vowels may be derived from the 10 central long and short vowels of classical Latin (*a, e, i, o,* and *u*). Supposedly, long-vowel sounds are longer in duration than short-vowel sounds, but this is not always the case. Even short-vowel sounds vary in duration. For example, the vowel in *bad* is different than the vowel sound in *bat*. In the first case, did you notice that the short *-a* in *bad* was longer than the short *-a* in *bat*? As a matter of fact, in many dictionaries you can find *bad* written as *ba:d,* meaning that the *a* has a longer duration than expected.

Although **long vowels** and **short vowels** may not be the most accurate terms linguistically, they are more common than *tense* and *lax* and teachers understand each other when these terms are used. The simplest way to talk about vowels is probably the best. For example, teachers can talk about the beginning and middle sounds in words: "Find a picture of a word that sounds like *ball* at the beginning" or "*Bet* and *best*—Do they sound alike in the middle?" Descriptions like "in the middle" may suffice to draw students' attention to the vowels at first, but students have no trouble learning such terms as **vowel** and **consonant.** Teachers need to establish a common language in word study discussions and such terms make it easier.

Students may be taught to use terms to describe sounds, but the important thing is their ability to read and write words quickly and easily enough to create meaning in the process. What students can do with words is certainly more important than mastering terms about words. Orthographic knowledge should come forward easily and tacitly. Experience has shown that the long–short distinction provides an adequate description for initial discussions with students about vowels.

How Vowels Are Articulated in the Mouth

Over the course of the letter name–alphabetic stage, students become adept at segmenting words into phonemes, even the vowel, and they use the alphabetic principle to represent each sound with a letter. Long-vowel sounds are easiest to distinguish because they say their name and the choices are obvious. Students spell *line* as LIN, *rain* as RAN, and *boat* as BOT. Perhaps what is most interesting about the invented spelling in the letter name–alphabetic stage is the way students spell the short vowels. They turn to the names of the letters but find no clear letter-sound matches for the short-vowel sounds. For example, there is no letter name that says the short *-i* sound in *bit* or the /uh/ sound in *cup*. They might use *f* (ef) or *s* (es) for short *-e*, but they seldom do. How do students choose a letter name for a short vowel? They use their knowledge of the alphabet to find the letter name closest to the place of articulation of the short-vowel sound they are trying to write.

Because you have probably never analyzed sounds at this level, take a moment to consider the vowels and where they are made in the vocal tract. The position of the words in Figure 5-2 illustrates some of the basic contrasts among vowels in English. The vowels are drawn in this space to mimic the general area where speakers can feel the articulation of the vowel. To talk about articulation is to describe the shape of the mouth, the openness of the jaw, and the position of the tongue while the word is being said. Compare the vowels in this figure by feeling the air pass through the oral cavity and the position of the mouth as the following words are said in a sequence from *beet* to *boot*:

beet bit bait bet bat bite but bah ball boat book boot

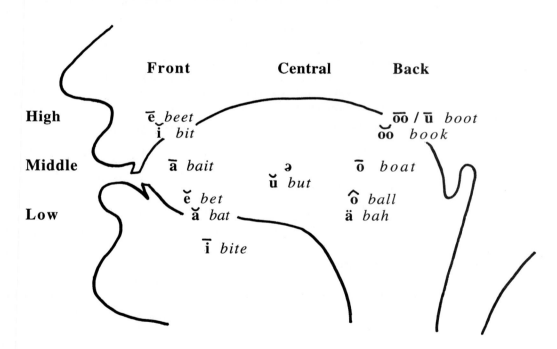

FIGURE 5-2 Vowels in the Mouth

Try saying this string several times, saying only the vowel sounds in each word. Feel how the production of the vowels moves from high in the front of the oral cavity (*beet*) to low in the oral cavity (*bite*) to the back of the oral cavity (*boat*), down the front, back, and up (*boot*). As you read the words *boot, foot,* and *boat,* do you feel how the vowels are rounded? Feel how the tongue is raised in the back and how the lips are pursed as the words are pronounced. Contrast the rounded vowel in *boot* with the way your lips feel when you say the high front vowel sounds in *beet* or *bit*.

The way a word is pronounced may vary by dialect. For example, many people say *caught* and *cot* the same way. Some native speakers of English pronounce *bought, bore, roof,* and *stalk* with different vowels. Teachers must be aware of dialectical differences when students sort and talk about words. These differences do not interfere with word study and learning to spell, but an awareness of these differences enhances word study. Everyone speaks a dialect.

A Letter Name Strategy to Spell Short Vowels

How do students choose a letter name to represent a short vowel? Without being consciously aware that they are doing this, letter name–alphabetic spellers spell short vowels with the letter name closest in articulation to that short vowel. There are five letter names from which to choose: *a, e, i, o,* and *u.* How would an alphabetic speller spell the word *bed?* What letter name is closest to the short *-e* sound in *bet?* Try saying *bed-beet* and *bed-bait* to compare how the short-vowel sounds and the long-vowel or letter names feel in your mouth. Repeat the pairs several times and pay attention to how the mouth is shaped. The long *-a* or letter name for *a* is closer in place of articulation to the short *-e* sound than to the letter names for *e, i, o,* or *u.*

Students in the letter name–alphabetic stage use their knowledge of letter names and the feel of the vowels as they are produced in the vocal tract to spell *bet* as BAT. What letter name is closest to the short *-i* sound in *ship?* Compare the vowel sound in the middle of *ship* with the letter names for *i* and *e.* Students often spell *ship* as SHEP, because the letter name for *e* is closer in place of articulation to the short *-i* sound than the letter name for *i.* The wondrous aspect of these letter name substitutions for short vowels is that they are so predictable. Read (1975) found that nearly all students go through a period of time when they substitute the short vowels in this way. Note that short *-a* poses little problem for spellers, because the short *-a* sound and the letter name for *a* are already close in place of articulation. Say *bat* and *bait* as an example. The following chart will help you remember how the letter names of vowels are substituted for the short-vowel sounds beginning readers try to spell.

Invented Spelling	Logical Vowel Substitution	
BAT for *bat*	None, short *-a* is closest to *a*	
BAT for *bet*	*a* for	short *-e*
BET for *bit*	*e* for	short *-i*
PIT for *pot*	*i* for	short *-o*
POT for *put*	*o* for	short *-u*

Through word study in the letter name–alphabetic stage, students learn to spell short-vowel words correctly and they see that short vowels follow a specific pattern, a **consonant-vowel-consonant (CVC)** pattern. This CVC pattern stretches across all short vowels from the short *-a* in *pat* to the short *-u* in *stuck.* In their study of short vowels, students notice that, regardless of how many consonant letters are on either side of the single vowel, one vowel letter in the pattern signals the short-vowel sound. Students' sight words—their known words—provide a base for studying the CVC pattern. In reading and directed word study, these known words provide the tension between what is and what they think about the orthography. The CVC pattern provides a basis for learning about vowel patterns.

As they mature and learn more sight words, students face the ambiguities of the **homographs,** words that are spelled the same but pronounced differently. For example, students in the letter name–alphabetic stage may spell *bent, bet, bat,* and *bait* the same way: BAT. The burden of so many homographs is a catalyst for change, which is a good problem. Letter name–alphabetic spellers are also readers, and when they reread their own spelling of *bait* as BAT, a word that they know spells something else, they experience disequilibrium. This forces them to find other ways to spell a word like *bait.* When students are able to spell these basic short-vowel patterns, and they begin to experiment with long-vowel patterns, they have entered the next spelling stage, within word pattern.

OTHER ORTHOGRAPHIC FEATURES

In addition to vowels, students work through four other features during this stage:

1. Consonant digraphs
2. Consonant blends
3. Influences on the vowel from certain consonants
4. Preconsonantal nasals

Although these features are usually studied toward the middle and end of this stage, they can be studied whenever students have enough known sight words in their word bank. For example, the influence of the letter *r* on the short-vowel sounds is profound and may become a topic of study when students realize that a word like *car* does not fit with other short a sounds even though it follows the CVC pattern.

Consonant Digraphs and Blends

Letter name–alphabetic spellers take some time to learn consonant digraphs and blends. A **digraph** is two letters that make a new sound or a single sound. The word *digraph* ends with a digraph, the *ph* that stands for the single sound of /f/. Digraphs are easier than blends and can be taught right along with other beginning consonants because they represent a simple phoneme. The most commonly recognized digraphs have an *h* as the second letter of the pair. Digraphs include the bold letters:

thin, fi**sh**, ea**ch**, **wh**en, **ph**one

A **consonant blend** is slightly different. A blend is a spelling unit (sometimes called a consonant cluster) of two or three consonants that retain their identity when pronounced. The word *blend* contains two blends: *bl* and *nd*. Each of the sounds in a blend can still be heard, but they are tightly bound and not easily segmented into individual phonemes, which makes blends difficult for students to spell accurately. The *st* blend in *stick* may be spelled simply as SEK or SEC. Blends can occur at the beginning or end of words and are represented by the bold letters in the following words.

Beginning Blends

black, **cl**ap, **fl**ash, **gl**ad, **pl**ug, **sl**ip, **pl**us (*l* blends), **br**ag, **cr**ash, **dr**eam, **fr**og, **gr**eat, **pr**ize, **tr**ee (*r* blends), **sc**out, **sk**ip, **sm**all, **sn**eeze, **sp**ell, **st**em, **sw**eet, **spl**ash, **str**eet, **squ**are (*s* blends), **tw**ice, **qu**ick

(*Note:* In the *qu* blend, the *u* represents the consonant sound of *w*.)

Ending Blends

ju**st**, li**sp**, ma**sk**, gi**ft**, swe**pt**, me**lt**, she**lf**, he**lp**

(*Note: mp, nt, nd, nk*, and so forth, are special ending blends we will consider under preconsonantal nasals.)

Throughout the letter name–alphabetic stage, students become more consistent in their spelling of consonant digraphs and blends. In their reading, they recognize words with consonant digraphs and blends with greater accuracy and fluency (Bear, 1992). Students' tacit understanding of consonant blends and digraphs grows with their sight vocabularies and their understanding of the basic CVC patterns that contain consonant digraphs and blends.

Influences on the Vowel

The letters *r, w,* and *l* influence the vowel sounds they follow. For example, the vowel sounds in words like *bar, ball,* and *saw* are not the same as the short-vowel sounds in *bat* and *fast.* They cannot be called short -*a*, yet all of these words have the CVC pattern. The consonant sounds /r/ and /l/ are known in linguistics as **liquids.** Both can change the pronunciation of the vowel they follow. These spellings are often known as *r* influenced or *r* controlled and *l* influenced or *l* controlled.

R-influenced vowels can be difficult to spell by sound alone. For example, *fur, her,* and *sir* have the same vowel sound yet are spelled three different ways. R-influenced vowels that follow a CVC pattern are examined during the late letter name–alphabetic stage and can be compared with short vowels in word sorts. Students might also contrast consonant **blends** with an *r* (*fr, tr, gr*) and *r*-influenced vowels (e.g., *from-farm, grill-girl, tarp-trap*) as a way to compare exactly where the *r* falls.

Preconsonantal Nasals

Some blends are more subtle than others. Nasal sounds, associated with *m, n,* and *ng,* are made by air passing through the nasal cavity in the mouth. The **preconsonantal nasals** are nasal sounds that come right before a final consonant such as the *m* in *jump* or the *n* in *pink.* In the pronunciation of preconsonantal nasals, it is as if the second consonant dominates and absorbs the nasal. Try saying *ban* and then *band.* You can not feel both the *n* and the *d* in *band.* Preconsonantal nasals are often omitted during the letter name–alphabetic stage (*bump* may be spelled BOP and *pink* may be spelled PEK). When students begin to spell words with preconsonantal nasals correctly, they are usually at the end of the letter name–alphabetic stage.

WORD STUDY INSTRUCTION FOR THE LETTER NAME–ALPHABETIC STAGE

The focus for word study in the letter name–alphabetic stage begins with initial consonants and continues through consonant digraphs, blends, and the study of short vowels. Word study during this stage makes use of pictures and known words from students' reading and word banks. This section discusses the sequence of word study throughout the letter name–alphabetic stage, presents ways to use word banks, and offers some tips for how to lead group sorting activities.

Sequence of Word Study

The sequence of word study is based on the alphabet, pattern, and meaning principles that have been observed in students' spelling. During this stage of development, students focus primarily on the alphabetic principle of matching sounds to letters. Consider the invented spellings in Table 5-1 and what they reveal about how students experiment with the orthography. Teachers can take the lead from their students' invented spellings in designing word study instruction. The sequence of word study instruction is designed to complement the natural course of learning.

Initially, students use beginning consonants in their writing, so this is the place to begin word study. After students have learned to use most of the consonants, they add vowels in each stressed syllable. When they start placing a vowel in each syllable, it is time to study short vowels. When students begin to use long-vowel patterns in their spelling, they are ready to examine long-vowel word patterns and move on to the next stage. Table 5-3 summarizes how students' spellings should be used to make instructional decisions.

Although there is a predictable pattern of development, the exact sequence and pace will not be precisely the same for every student. There are three factors that impact the sequence and the pace of the word study:

TABLE 5-3	Using Spelling Errors to Plan Word Study in the Letter Name–Alphabetic Stage	
Spelling Samples	**Characteristics of Spellings**	**Appropriate Word Study**
fan = F pet = PSLD dig = DK wait = YT junk = GK	Some consonant sounds are represented but incomplete or confused.	Picture sorts of beginning sounds.
fan = FN pet = PT dig = DG rope = ROP shine = CIN sled = SD	Single beginning and final consonants correct for the most part. Blends and digraphs not correct. Few, if any, vowels in middle.	1. Picture sorts of digraphs and blends. 2. Compare word families with the same vowel using words and pictures.
dig = DEG pet = PAT junk = JOK sled = SLAD dream = JREM shine = CHIN	Single beginning and final consonants correct. Blends and digraphs may still be confused. Short vowels are used but confused. Long-vowel markers are absent or rare. Missing preconsonantal nasals.	1. Compare word families with mixed vowels using word sorts. 2. Compare short vowels. 3. Include words with blends, digraphs, and preconsonantal nasals in word sorts.

From *Bookbuddies: Guidelines for Volunteer Tutors of Emergent and Beginning Readers* by F. R. Johnston, M. Invernizzi, & C. Juel, 1998, New York: Guilford Press. Reprinted by permission.

1. *Utmost is the students' development.* Although the general sequence will be the same, the pace varies and teachers need to vary the length of time they spend on word study activities with different students. For this reason, membership in word study groups must be fluid.

2. Because word study always works with known words, *word study during this stage is constrained by students' sight vocabularies.* Students at this level seldom have enough sight words for the study of initial consonants, digraphs, or blends so picture sorts are most effective.

3. The third factor is the *curriculum.* Some school districts and schools specify through their curriculum guides what orthographic features should be studied. The developmental outline presented in this book provides clear guidelines for what features to study in what order. Teachers can use the following sequence and still cover the features specified in most curricula.

   a. Review beginning sounds with picture sorts.
   b. Introduce consonant digraphs and blends with pictures.
   c. Introduce short vowels in word families.
   d. Continue to study consonant digraphs and blends in word families.
   e. Study short vowels as CVC patterns outside of rhyming families.
   f. Integrate the study of digraphs, blends, and preconsonantal nasals with short vowels.

 For a sequence of printable picture sorts appropriate for Letter-Name Alphabetic Spellers, visit the Letter Name–Alphabetic section on the accompanying CD-ROM.

The following discussion focuses on each of these areas of word study instruction.

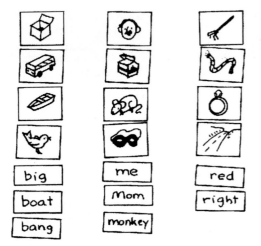

FIGURE 5-3 Initial Consonant Picture and Word Sort

The Study of Beginning Sounds

Word study starts with the study of initial sounds for students in the early letter name–alphabetic stage. Simple picture sorts give students an opportunity to compare pictures based on how they "sound at the beginning." Pictures are sorted and contrasted, starting with frequently occurring initial consonants where the contrasts or differences are clear both visually and by sound. Figure 5-3 is an example of a sort that started with pictures and then included sight words from the students' word banks.

Richard, whom we met at the beginning of this chapter, was wise in deciding to take a step back to firm up Cynthia's understandings of consonants. Many students benefit from a fast-paced review of consonants at the beginning of first grade to clear up lingering confusions or to secure tentative letter-sound matches. There is no particular order to the sequence of sounds, but starting with frequently occurring initial consonants where the contrasts or differences are clear both visually and by sound is recommended. Many teachers have found the following sequence to be effective. Chapter 4 offers suggestions for how to plan and carry out picture sorts for initial consonants.

B	M	R	S
T	G	N	P
C	H	F	D
L	K	J	W
Y	Z	V	

Modify this sequence if there are connections you can make to reading materials or classroom themes of study. In October you might want to focus on *h, j, p,* and *g* to tie in with words like *Halloween, jack-o-lanterns, pumpkins,* and *ghosts.* Picture sorts with initially occurring short vowels can also be included here as a way to introduce those letter-sound correspondences. Pictures for these beginning short vowels can be found in the Appendix, after the beginning consonant pictures.

A few final consonants might be introduced and studied, but once students have learned the frequently occurring initial consonants and phonemic segmentation, most of them can easily use their knowledge of letter-sound matches to spell final consonants. When students consistently omit final consonants in their writing, you can draw their attention to them through word study activities that are similar to the initial consonant sorts. For example, your students could hunt for words and pictures of words that end like *bat.* However, the study of final consonants is covered when the students examine word families, which is probably enough for most students.

Some students may have a few lingering confusions even when they are in control of most consonant matches. Do not hesitate to move on to other features since consonants will be reviewed again in word family comparisons. However, you may want to address occasional confusions in sorts that contrast what students are using with what they are confusing. If a student spells *fan* as VN, you may want to pull out pictures of words that start with *v* and *f* to help work out the correct associations. Such close comparisons should not, however, be the student's first introduction to those letter sounds.

 **Students who speak Spanish may spend more time examining final consonants.**

Word banks.   Word banks play a special role for beginning readers, helping them learn specific words as well as how words work in general. What students know about particular words during this time may only be partial. For example, as they read, they may substitute *leopard* for *lion* in a story of big cats at the zoo. From such errors, it appears that they are attending to the beginning letters for cues. This is also evident in the way they spell during this time. *Lion* is often spelled as LN. Ehri (1997) has described these readers as "partial alphabetic," because they use partial letter-sound cues— usually consonant cues—to identify and spell words. Students will acquire sight words, or words they know out of context, slowly during the early letter name–alphabetic period and they will need frequent exposure to those words. Examining words out of context makes a difference in how well they learn those words (Ehri & Wilce, 1980) and how many words they learn over time (Johnston, 1998).

Acquiring a sight vocabulary is critical for progress in reading. Automatic word recognition makes it possible to read fluently and to devote attention to comprehension rather than to figuring out words. A sight vocabulary also provides a corpus of known words from which students begin to discover generalizations about how words work.

A word bank is a collection of words chosen by the students (not the teacher) that they remember well enough to identify in isolation (Stauffer, 1980). The words are written on small cards and collected over time. They are reviewed regularly and words that have been forgotten are discarded. Sometimes we are asked why students need to review words they already know. The answer is, they do not know them the same way more mature readers do; they know them only partially and tentatively. Students reviewing their word bank may confuse *ran* and *run, stop* and *ship, lost* and *little*. They may get *gingerbread* every time because it is the only long word they have that starts with *g*, but when you ask them to spell it (GNRBRD) you get a better idea of what they really know about that word. Regular review of word bank words encourages students to look more thoroughly at words and to note individual letter-sound correspondences.

For students in the early letter name–alphabetic stage, word banks support their growing knowledge of sight words and letter-sound correspondences. As they study initial sounds, students can be asked to find words in their word bank that have those same sounds. This will help them make connections between the pictures they sort and the words they read. Later in the letter name–alphabetic stage, the word bank becomes a source of known words to be used in word sorts. It is crucial that students work with known words because it is easier to look across words for similarities and differences in sounds and letters than to figure out unknown words. There is an added burden in word study if students must labor to pronounce words before analyzing their features and relationships to other words.

Developing and using word banks and personal readers.   The words in a word bank come from many sources: dictations, small group experience charts, rhymes, poems, and the simple books and preprimers that they read. Words can come from students' names and from labels (like Wendy's, or BUM Equipment), but it is best if the words in the word banks can be traced back to meaningful and familiar text. By using words that come from familiar readings and by numbering the stories and rhymes and the word cards, students can be encouraged to return to the primary source to find a forgotten word and to match the word bank card to its counterpart in print.

Personal readers, as shown in Figure 5-4, are individual student copies of group experience charts, rhymes and jingles, individual dictations, and selected passages from simple books that students can read independently or with some support from a teacher or partner. Students are enormously proud of their personal readers and they reread them many times before taking them home to read some more. Except for the individual dictations, many of the selections in personal readers are the same among many students. The stories in the personal readers are numbered, and the date they are introduced is recorded. Personal readers are an ideal place for students to collect words from their word banks. They can simply underline the words they know best and these words can then be transferred to small cards. A number can be written on each word card that matches the numbered stories.

FIGURE 5-4   Personal Reader with Word Bank

In Figure 5-4, the student's word bank is a plastic bag that can be stored in the personal reader. You can also see that simple pattern books can fit inside the front pocket. The personal reader also contains a page that lists the words in the student's word bank. A reduced sound board of consonant sounds is included for a student reference in word study and writing.

Word banks increase slowly and steadily. At first, students do not have enough words in their banks to use them much for sorting. Gradually, word banks increase to 50 words, and then there are plenty of words for many sorts. Once the word banks grow to between 150 to 250 words, they become clumsy to manage. It takes students too long to hunt through their banks for examples of a particular short vowel. The three signs to indicate when it is time to discontinue word banks are as follows:

1. The student is at the end of the letter name–alphabetic stage of spelling.
2. The word bank contains at least 200 words.
3. It is possible to create word sorts in which students recognize nearly all of the words easily.

Word banks take extra work but are well worth the effort, particularly for students in the beginning of this stage. Word banks support students' sight word development and growing word knowledge. They are also motivating for students because they offer tangible evidence of their word learning and literacy growth (Johnston, 1998). Guidelines for making and using word banks, individual dictations, and group experience charts can be found in the first part of the activities section of this chapter.

The Study of Digraphs and Blends

After students study beginning consonants, they are ready to learn about initial consonant digraphs and blends.

The goal of word study of consonant digraphs and blends is to not only master letter-sound correspondences but also to help students see these two-letter combinations as single units in CVC patterns.

Beginning digraphs.
The first digraphs to be studied are *ch, sh, th,* and *wh.* Sorts for digraphs compare words "that do" with words "that don't." What contrasts are best? The answer lies in students' invented spellings. Some students substitute *j* for *ch* as they spell words like *chin* as JN or they may confuse the letter name of *h* (aich) with *ch* and spell *chin* as HN. These confusions suggest that a good sort to study *ch* would include words that start with *ch, h,* or even *c* and *j*. *Th* might be compared to single *t; sh* to single *s,* and *ch* to single *c*. Note, however, that it would be difficult to sort pictures by *w* and *wh,* because many words beginning with *wh* do not have a distinctive sound. (Which witch is which?) You might compare *wh* to *th, sh,* and *ch* in a culminating digraph sort. Possible contrasts for digraphs include:

1. *c / ch / h*
2. *s / sh / h*
3. *t / th / h*
4. *ch / sh / th*
5. *j / ch*
6. *wh / sh / th / ch*

Beginning blends. Beginning consonant blends come in three major groups: the *s* blends (*sn, sm, st, sk*), the *r* blends (*br, cr, dr, fr, gr, pr, tr*), and the *l* blends (*bl, cl, fl, gl, pl, sl*). The easiest group of blends is the *s* blends, because *s* is a continuant (the /s/ sound continues), and because with the exception of *sl*, the *s* blends do not contain the "slippery" *l* or *r*.

The study of beginning consonant blends starts with the easiest contrasts of single initial consonants with a blend. For example, pictures that begin with *st* may be contrasted with pictures that begin with *s* for spellers such as Tony who spell *stick* as SEK. After studying several blends in this fashion, it is best to pick up the pace and introduce other blends in groups. Some suggested contrasts are listed as follows, but as always, modify these in accordance with the kinds of words students are encountering in their reading. Once students catch on to how blends work and learn to segment the sounds in blends, they may move quickly through a sequence of study or skip some contrasts altogether. Possible contrasts for beginning blends include:

1. *s / st / t*
2. *sp / s / p*
3. *st / sp / sk / sm*
4. *sl / sn / sc / sw*
5. *bl / b / l*
6. *gl / pl / bl / cl*
7. *t / tr / r*
8. *d / dr / r*
9. *gr / tr / dr / pr*
10. *bl / br / gl / gr*
11. *cl / cr / fl / fr*
12. *k / qu / tw*

The procedures and routines for the study of digraphs and blends are the same as for other beginning sound sorts described in Chapter 4. Composite sheets of pictures can be created for individual practice at desks or students can work in centers with pictures for additional practice. Pictures needed for the study of digraphs and blends can be found in the Appendix. Chapter 3 describes follow-up activities such as cut and paste and draw and label, which are appropriate for digraphs and blends. Many of the games described for beginning consonants in Chapter 4 and in this chapter can be easily adapted to review digraphs and blends.

Unlike initial consonants, students in the early part of the letter name–alphabetic stage are not expected to acquire great fluency or accuracy in spelling and sorting consonant blends and digraphs, because they will be revisited throughout the stage. The study of blends can be alternated with the study of word families. Final blends are not studied with pictures due to the lack of examples, but should be included with beginning blends and digraphs in the study of word families and short vowels when words are used. Knowledge of blends and digraphs will help students understand the CVC as the basic short-vowel pattern. Even a word like *flash* is a CVC word in which *fl* is the first unit, *a* is the medial vowel, and *sh* is the final unit. Students also work through sorts in which they consider features such as the double *l* in *ball* and the *nd* in *blend* or *stand*.

 For more materials on digraphs and blends, as well as sorts for studying short vowels, visit the Letter Name–Alphabetic section on the accompanying CD-ROM

The Study of Word Families to Introduce Short Vowels

Once letter name–alphabetic spellers have a firm, if not complete, mastery of beginning and ending consonant sounds, and a stable concept of word, they are ready to examine the medial vowel. The study of vowels begins with word families or **phonograms** when vowels are still missing or used only occasionally in students' invented spellings. Once students are using short vowels consistently, they can be asked to compare short vowels in word sorts that examine the CVC pattern across a variety of vowels. This will happen toward the end of the stage. Refer again to Table 5-3 to see how to use student's spellings for planning instruction during this stage.

Word families offer an easy and appealing way to introduce the issue of vowels. Students are supported in their first efforts to analyze the vowel, because the vowel and the ending letter(s) are presented as a chunk or pattern. In linguistic terms, the **rime** consists of the vowel and what follows (Henderson, 1990). What comes before the vowel is the **onset.** Examples of onset-rime breaks are *m-an, bl-and, m-at,* and *th-at.* Dividing words into onsets and rimes is easier and more natural for students than dividing them into individual phonemes (Treiman, 1985).

The study of word families makes sense for several other reasons. First, 37 rimes can be used to generate 500 different words which students encounter in primary reading materials (Wylie & Durrell, 1970). In addition, these same rimes will be familiar chunks in thousands of multisyllabic words; the *an* chunk can be found in *canyon, incandescent,* and *fantastic.* Second, vowel sounds are more stable within families than across families (Adams, 1990; Wylie & Durrell, 1970). For example, the word *dog* is often presented as a short *-o* word in phonics programs; but in some regions of the United States, it is pronounced more like *dawg.* If you say it that way, then you probably pronounce *fog* as *fawg, frog* as *frawg,* and *log* as *lawg.* In the study of word families, the actual pronunciation of the short vowel does not matter; it is the *-og* chunk that is examined and compared.

There is no particular order to the study of word families, but starting with short *-a* families (*at, an, ad, ap, ack*) seems to be a good choice, because these words abound in early reading materials, and students are likely to already know several words from these families by sight. In addition, short *-a* is the least likely short vowel to be confused when students try to make matches based on letter names and place of articulation. Knowing that students initially have trouble isolating and attending to the medial vowel, it is a good idea to compare word families that share the same vowel before contrasting different vowels. This supports students' first efforts to read and spell those words. What they really must attend to are the beginning and ending consonants in order to sort and spell the words. The study of same-vowel word families serves to review those features. In sorting words like *mat* and *man,* for example, students must attend to the final consonant more than any place else. Move quickly, however, to comparing words that have different vowels. The difference between *mitt, met,* and *mat* lies in the medial vowel and it is through such contrasts that students are forced to attend to the vowel sound itself.

Table 5-4 offers a suggested sequence for the study of word families, but it is offered only as a model from which to plan your own course of study. Each of the words listed is intended to be an example of a particular word family and you would need to collect additional words to create the sorts. You will find lists of words for each family in the Appendix. As always, consider the words that your students have in their word banks and the kinds of words they encounter in their reading.

Word Sorting to Compare Two or More Word Families

In the following procedure for sorting two or more word families, the phonograms for *ig, ag,* and *og* are used as examples.

1. Make a collection of word cards to model the sort on a tabletop, pocket chart, or overhead projector. Students should be able to read two or more words in each family.
2. Begin by laying down a known word as a header for each family. Choose words you are sure the students can read such as *big, dog,* and *bag.* Explain that the rest of the words are to be sorted under one of the headers.
3. Pick up another word such as *frog* and say, "I am going to put this word under *dog.* Listen: *dog, frog.*" Continue to model one or two words in each category, always sorting first and then reading down, starting with the header.
4. Invite students to try sorting the next word. They should sort first and then read from the top of each column. They are not expected to sound it out first and then

TABLE 5-4   Possible Pace and Sequence of Word Family Study

Introductions	Moderate Pace	Fast Pace / Review
Use single initial consonants and some digraphs in words chosen.*	Use some blends and digraphs in words chosen for sorts.	Use plenty of blends and digraphs in words chosen for sorts.
Same-Vowel Word Families		
at family with pictures and words *an* and *ad* with pictures and words *ap* and *ag* with pictures and words *ot* and *og* with pictures and words *ip, ig, ill* with pictures and words *ug, ub, ut* *ed, et, eg, ell*	*at* and *an* *ag, ad, ap* *ip, ig, in, ill* *ot, og, ock* *ug, ub, uck, unk*	*at, an, ad, ap* *in, ip, ick, ing* *ub, ug, ush, unk*
Mixed-Vowel Word Families		
at, ot, it *ag, og, ap, op* *ill, ell, all* *ap, ip, op, up* *an, un, en* *all, ell, ill* *ag, eg, ig, og, ug* *ack, ock, ick, uck* *ish, ash, ush*	*at, ot, ag, og* *an, en, un* *ip, ap, op, up* *ack, ock, ick, uck* *ing, ish, ang, ash* *ang, ing, ung, ong* *ink, ank, unk*	*an, in, et, ot* *ag, ig, eg, ug, og* *ink, ank, unk* *all, ell, ill* *ack, ock, ick, uck, eck*

*Add blends and digraphs to sorts as they are studied, especially to later sorts.

sort. Instead, their sense of rhyme will support them as they read the new word by simply changing the first sound of a word they already know. The final sort might look like this:

big	dog	bag
dig	frog	wag
pig	hog	flag
wig	bog	rag
	fog	tag
	log	

5. After all the words have been sorted, lead a discussion to focus your students' attention on the common features in each word: "How are the words in each column alike?"
6. Reread the words in each column and then lead the students in sorting a second time. Any mistakes should be left until the end and checked by reading down the columns.
7. Students should be given their own set of words to sort (see Figure 5-1B). Appropriate follow-up routines include buddy sorting, writing sorts, and word hunts. These are described in Chapter 4 in the primary schedule.

Word family sorts can be made easier or harder in a number of ways. The study of word families can begin with the matching of words to pictures. Some of the short-vowel pictures in the Appendix may be useful, although pictures are not really necessary; you can create sheets of word cards or sorting folders. Sample word family sorts are presented in the Appendix. During the study of word families, it is appropriate to modify 1 of the 10 principles of word study described in Chapter 3—*use words students can read*. Since the words are in rhyming families, students are supported in their reading of the words, as long as the guide word and the first few words are familiar. Students will read unknown words by blending different onsets with the familiar rime. Be sure to include words with digraphs and blends as a review of those features and a chance to see them in another context. The *ack* family can grow to be quite large when you include *black, track, shack, quack, stack, snack,* and *crack.*

With the publication of research on onsets and rimes and renewed interest in word families, there has been a recent flood of reading materials designed around phono-grams. Little phonics readers have been created that feature a particular family or short vowel. Some of these little books are engaging and well written, offering students sup-port in the form of patterned or rhyming text. Such books can be used as a starting point or as a follow-up for word study, and students can use them to go on word hunts for ad-ditional words that follow the same phonics feature. However, choose these books care-fully. Stories featuring sentences such as, "The tan man ran the van," change reading from the making of meaning into exercises in word calling. Some phonics readers are better done than others and should never constitute the sole reading materials used at this level.

There are lots of activities and games to use in connection with the study of word families. Board games designed to study beginning sounds can be adapted to word fam-ilies. Sound wheels, flip charts, and the Show Me game are favorites and are included in the activities to follow. From this point on, students are expected to spell the words they sort in their entirety. Word study notebooks can be used to record writing sorts and the results of word hunts or brainstorming sessions.

The study of word families can take a long time if you feel compelled to study every one in a thorough fashion, but this should not be the case. Some students quickly pick up the notion that words that sound alike probably share similar rimes and are spelled alike. They will also be able to use this knowledge to figure out new words by analogy; noting the *and* in *stand,* they quickly decode it. However, these students may still make errors in spelling short vowels.

The Study of Short Vowels

 Students who learn English as another language may not pronounce English conso-nants and vowels in the same way that you do and they may omit sounds that do not fit the syllable structure of their first language. Word study helps students to focus on pronunciations and syllable structures that are unfamiliar. Refer to the next section for a discussion of specific differences and teaching strategies during the letter name-alphabetic stage.

Once students are using but confusing short vowels on a regular basis in their invented spelling and working with word families easily and accurately, they are ready for the study of short vowels in nonrhyming words outside of word families. This study will ask them to look at words in a new way, not as two units with various rimes (*m-ad, fl-ag, tr-ack*), but as three units with the same CVC pattern (*m-a-d, fl-a-g, tr-a-ck*) and the same short-vowel sound. This ability to see words as patterns is the key feature of the next stage, within word pattern. Over the course of studying the short vowels, students come to see that CVC is the basic pattern for all short vowels.

When beginning the study of short vowels, plan contrasts that are fairly distinct from each other. We recommend that students compare short -*a* to short -*i* or short -*o*. Do not try to move directly from a short -*a* to a short -*e* or from a short -*e* to a short -*i*, be-cause those are the very sounds students are most likely to confuse. Pictures for sorting can be found in the Appendix.

During the study of short vowels is a good time to establish the **oddball** or miscella-neous category, to accommodate variations in dialect and spelling. Some students may hear a short -*o* in *frost,* but others will hear a sound closer to /aw/. Some students hear a differ-ent vowel in *pin* and *pen,* but others consider them homophones. Rather than forcing stu-dents to doubt their own ear, the oddball category offers an alternative and acknowledges that people do not all speak quite the same way nor does spelling always match pronunci-ation. Some words, which initially go in the oddball category, will become regular categories of their own after enough words are accumulated. Good words to include are high fre-quency words students may already know as sight words such as *was, said, for, from,* and *put.*

Be prepared to spend some time on short vowels as they pose special problems for young spellers and persist as problems beyond first grade. However, short vowels will be reviewed when they are compared to long vowels in the next stage, so do not expect 100% accuracy.

Word Sorting to Compare Two or More Short Vowels

Most sorting for short vowels will be done with words. Consider what words your students already know from familiar texts and word banks. Lists of CVC and CVCC words spelled with short vowels can be found in the word lists in the Appendix. These lists can be used to create handouts similar to those used by Mr. Perez in Figure 5-1C. Additional short-vowel words can be selected from the word family lists. Following is the basic procedure for sorting words by short vowels.

1. Make a collection of word cards to model the sort on a tabletop, pocket chart, or overhead projector.
2. Model the sort with a group of students. Begin by laying down a well-known word as a header for each vowel. Read each word and isolate the vowel by saying, "Here is the word *cap*. Listen: *cap, ap, a*. We will listen for other words that have the same vowel sound in the middle." Repeat for each category.
3. Pick up a new word such as *fast* and say, "I am going to put this word under *cap*. Listen: *cap, fast*." Continue to model one or two words in each category, reading each new word and comparing it to the header. Hold up an oddball like *for* or *was*. Ask students if they have the same vowel sound in the middle. Model how to place it in the oddball category because it does not have the same vowel sound.
4. Invite students to try sorting next. Correct any errors made during the first sort. The final sort might look something like this:

cap	pig	hot	oddball
fast	ship	stop	for
camp	fish	lock	ball
hat	sit	shop	
mad	hill	job	
trap	him	not	

5. After all the words have been sorted, discuss the common features in each word: "How are the words in each column alike? How are the oddballs different?"
6. Reread the words in each column and then lead the students in sorting a second time. Any mistakes should be left until the end and checked by reading down the columns.
7. Students should be given their own set of words to sort at their seats, with partners, or for homework.
8. Appropriate follow-up routines include buddy sorting, writing sorts, word hunts, and games. Because it is easy to sort the words visually by attending to the vowel letters, the buddy sort described in Chapter 4 is particularly important as a follow-up activity. Model this sound sort first in the group and then let partners work together. One partner reads each word aloud while the other partner indicates where it goes without seeing the word.

If students are still making errors in the spelling of digraphs and blends, which is likely, include words that have those features in the short-vowel sorts. At this time, they have many more sight words that contain beginning and ending consonant digraphs and blends. Preconsonantal nasals can also be included in this study. You might even plan a two-way sort—first by vowel sounds and second by digraphs or blends:

First Sort by Vowel			Second Sort by Blends		
trap	trick	drug	trap	drag	crack
crack	trip	crumb	track	drip	crash
drag	trim	truck	trick	drum	crumb
crash	drip	drum	trim	drill	crab
track	crib	crush	truck		crib
crab	drill				crush

Sorts such as the preceding one help students see that the CVC pattern encompasses two-letter consonant units that work the same way as single consonants. Lead discussions that help students see that these words have a similar pattern—a single vowel surrounded by one or more consonants. This pattern will be more fully understood as students begin to contrast it with long-vowel patterns in the next stage. Following is a sort that focuses on the expanded idea of the CVC pattern across these consonant units.

Single Consonant	Double Final
hot	lost
job	pond
rob	sock
top	

	Double Initial and Final
Double Initial	block
shop	clock
stop	stomp
chop	soft

FURTHER STUDY OF VOWELS AT THE END OF THE LETTER NAME–ALPHABETIC STAGE

Words like *car* and *ball* look as though they follow the CVC pattern, but they do not have the short -*a* sound. Because words spelled with *ar* and *all* are common in beginning reading materials, it is worthwhile to spend some time with them. *R*-controlled vowels form a major subcategory of vowels that will need to be examined closely during the next stage. For now these words can be treated as word families and added to short-vowel sorts as oddballs that challenge students to listen carefully for the sounds and not just attend to the letters they see. Following is a special sort that might examine words with a single *a* in the middle.

Short -*a*	ar	all	Oddballs
clap	car	ball	saw
jam	star	hall	was
black	park	fall	
sand	yard	stall	
camp	jar	call	

FIGURE 5-5 Picture Sort by Short -*a* and Short -*i*

This chapter has presented many examples of teacher-directed sorts or **closed sorts.** The teacher selects the words and leads a group sorting activity accompanied by a discussion of the features of interest. Student-centered sorts or **open sorts,** as described in Chapter 3, allow students to establish their own categories and offer the teacher diagnostic information which will help to determine how much students understand about the orthography.

Figure 5-5 is an open sort by a student in the late letter name–alphabetic stage. Jeff was asked to go through his word bank, find the word cards that had an *a* in them, and sort them into categories. His first sort resulted in three categories: short -*a*, long -*a*, and a large pile of miscellaneous words. He was then challenged to take the miscellaneous words and sort them into a number of piles. His new categories include short -*a*, *l* controlled, broad -*a*, *r* controlled, schwa, and long -*a*. Figure 5-6 shows that Jeff has developed quite a good ear for vowel sounds and understands that *a* is used to represent a variety of sounds.

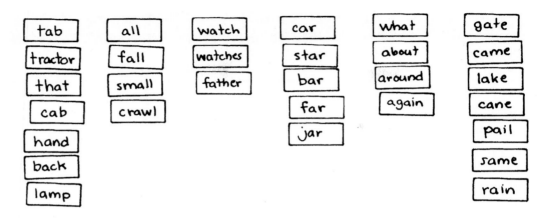

FIGURE 5-6   Jeff's Open Sort

WORD STUDY AND ENGLISH LANGUAGE LEARNING IN THE LETTER NAME–ALPHABETIC STAGE

In Chapter 2, we began the discussion of the influences students' primary languages and dialects have on their spelling. The spelling inventories in English can be examined for particular features. For example, we discussed the logical substitutions students make when their first language is Spanish.

 Visit the *Words Their Way* Companion Website at www.prenhall.com/bear to find a variety of spelling substitutions of English Language Learners.

For students who are literate in their first language, we recommend looking at their writing in that language, and then considering how this may show up in the English spelling. The Spanish spelling inventory in Chapter 2 and the Appendix can be used for elementary levels of literacy.

The two important areas of study to consider in the letter name–alphabetic stage when you work with English Language Learners are the comparisons of consonants and vowels. The difficult consonant sounds in English for Spanish speakers are presented in Table 5-5. Here you can see the sounds that students may mispronounce, and upon mispronouncing them, they may misspell the feature with a substitution or an omission. For example, it is common for students to omit the ending consonant sounds in words like *hard* that may be spelled HAR, or *test*, which may be spelled TES.

Spanish-speaking students may confuse words that begin with *d* and *th*, but at what level? For easy sight words, like the word *dog*, students know the beginning letter of *dog*, but in pronunciation they may pronounce *dog* with a *th* sound, more like *thog*. In sorting, students will begin to see the differences between these sounds when they have ample sight words that begin with *d* and *th*. In instruction this means that it will be worthwhile to include sorts that make these comparisons once the primary features are established. For Spanish speakers, you can use Table 5-5 and choose the features that are within students' grasps and sight vocabularies. Picture and word sorts that contrast *j* and *ch* can be undertaken once the students can read at least five or six words and pictures and words that begin with these sounds. Working on ending blend omissions is worthwhile when students in the middle of the letter name–alphabetic stage have enough sight words to match the pattern and to make the contrasts.

TABLE 5-5   Difficult Consonant Sounds in English for Spanish Speakers

Difficult Consonant Sounds for Spanish Speakers Learning English:	May Be Pronounced:
d as in *dog*	thog
j as in *jump*	chump
r as in *race*	(rolled *r*) race
v as in *very*	bery
z as in *zoo*	soo
sh as in *shine*	chine
th as in *think*	tink
zh as in *measure*	meachure
Beginning *s* blends *st-, sp-, sc-, sk-, sm-, sn-, scr-, squ-, str-, spr-, spl-*	espace, esquirt, esplash
Ending blends with *r*: *-rd, -rt, -rl, -rs*	har (hard), cur (curl), tar (tarp)
-ng as in *sing*	sin (g)
Ending blends with *s*: *-sp, -st, -sk*	was (wasp), pos (post), as (ask)

From the *Words Their Way CD*, Spanish Word Study, Emergent Stage, Beginning Consonants, p. 2.

 Spanish spelling influences the way students spell short vowels.

The vowels in English and Spanish differ in several ways. Spanish does not have vowels for short *-a, -e, -i,* or *-u*. The short *-o* in *pot* in English is spelled often with the letter *a*. When students sort their words they will see that words like *cab, mad,* and *ham* have the letter *a* in the middle. When students read the words, they may read them with the vowel sound that they would use in reading Spanish words spelled with an *a*, for example, *ajo*. It may sound to you that they are saying a short *-o* when they are checking their sort. While we read the words with students so that they can hear the differences, we do not turn this lesson into a speech lesson. Students focus on the CVC pattern. Over time, and by the time students are solidly in the next stage of spelling, they see that the short *-o* in English is pronounced one way (*hot, clot, stop*) and that there are a variety of ways to pronounce the short *-a* sounds; there are several different short *-a* sounds students will learn during this stage, such as *fat, far, father,* and *fall*.

WORD STUDY ROUTINES AND MANAGEMENT

Word study during the letter name–alphabetic stage begins with picture sorts for initial sounds and ends with word sorts for short vowels. During this transition there are a variety of routines and generic activities to help students explore features of study in depth (see Chapter 3). Betty Lee's schedule is particularly appropriate for students who are doing picture sorts, but once students are sorting words rather than pictures, other routines that involve word study notebooks can begin with activities like writing sorts.

In the letter name–alphabetic stage there is much to cover, so you might want to create 2- or 3-day cycles. For example, you might introduce two word families on Monday, another two on Wednesday, and then combine them both for several days. Pacing is an important issue. There are many blends and many word families and if every one were studied for a week, it could take many months. Be ready to pick up the pace by combining a number of blends or families into one sort (up to four or five) or by omitting some features. Only your own observations can dictate the particular pace appropriate for your students.

The letter name–alphabetic stage easily spans kindergarten through second grade as students master the reading and spelling of beginning sounds, blends and digraphs, and short vowels. While most achieving students will be through the stage by at least the middle of second grade, a handful of students in third grade and even a few students in fourth through sixth grade will still need to work on the features that characterize this stage. It may be tempting to rush through this stage, but word study in the letter name–alphabetic stage helps to build a solid foundation for the study of long vowels and other vowel patterns in the next stage.

Word study schedules at the group and classroom levels were discussed in Chapter 3. Figure 3-16 shows two schedules, the one that Betty Lee developed for first graders and another to use throughout the elementary grades. A routine to use throughout the letter name stage would follow these 5 days of activities:

Day 1: Group sort. This time is part of the regular reading group that you conduct daily with students. Take students through the four steps of a word study lesson plan as discussed in Chapter 3: demonstrate, sort and check, reflect, and extend. The extending step is an overview of the activities and the schedule for word study for the coming days.

Day 2: Buddy sort. Students use the same sorts, and with a photocopy of the correct sort, they check their work.

Day 3: Draw and label or word hunt. For early letter name–alphabetic spellers, use draw and label-type activities. Once students' sight vocabulary allows (when they study short-vowel patterns), turn to word hunts. Use the materials in personal readers for hunting for words.

Day 4: Games and activities. Choose from the plethora of activities in this chapter and in *Book Buddies* (Johnston et al., 1998). The Concentration, Bingo, Follow the Path, and Go Fish games presented in this chapter are adaptable and enjoyable throughout this stage of development.

Day 5: Repeated sorts and writing sorts. These activities help to cement the knowledge students have acquired. When they can sort fluently and correctly, we know that students' knowledge has begun to crystallize. The writing sorts are the beginnings of the word study notebooks, as discussed in Chapter 3.

We have been able to share many activities with parents on our websites and in handouts that go home to families. Link to these activities from our Companion Website at www.prenhall.com/bear

Activities for Beginning Readers in the Letter Name–Alphabetic Stage

In this section specific activities for students in the letter name–alphabetic stage have been organized into the following categories.

1. Development and use of personal readers and word banks
2. Review of initial sounds including digraphs and blends
3. Study of word families
4. Study of short vowels

These categories begin with ideas for supporting beginning readers and continue with word study games and activities that correspond to the hierarchy of features students study through picture and word sorts. Some of the games and activities are adaptable to a variety of features at different stages. These are indicated by the adaptable symbol.

Adaptable for Other Stages

For many more activities appropriate for Letter Name–Alphabetic readers, visit the accompanying CD-ROM.

DEVELOPMENT AND USE OF PERSONAL READERS AND WORD BANKS

Harvesting Words for Word Banks 5-1

Students need to have a stock of sight words that they can read with ease. The following activities help students develop and maintain a word bank. Through the use of familiar rhymes and small group and individual dictations, students begin to harvest sight words.

Materials

1. You will need copies of personal readers, dictations, familiar books, and so on.
2. Gather blank word cards. Tagboard and index cards can be cut to a size that is large enough to hold easily, yet small enough so that students can work with them on a desktop when sorting (1¼ by 3 inches is about right). Teachers can also create a sheet of words for a particular story or poem read by a group of students. These sheets can be reproduced and cut apart. And the words can then be quickly handed out as students identify them.
3. Each student will need to store his or her words. The word bank can be kept in a manila envelope, box, small margarine container, can, or fast-food container. Plastic and metal index card file boxes also work well, if available. When file boxes are at a premium, you can start with margarine containers for the first 50 words and then move to a box.

Procedures

Following are ways to harvest words for the word bank.

1. *From personal readers.* If students have an individual copy of dictations, jingles, parts of stories, and so on, they can simply be asked to underline the words they know. Many students will be tempted to underline every word, but over time they will begin to understand the procedure and realize they need to be selective and underline only words they really know. Suggesting that they scan through the text backwards can help some students find known words more accurately.

   A teacher, assistant, or classroom volunteer points to the underlined words in a random fashion to check if the student can indeed name the word quickly. Known words are then written on word cards. Having an adult write the word will ensure that it is neat and accurate. The student can be asked to spell it aloud as the adult writes. On each card write the number of the page in the personal reader. This will make it possible for the students to go back and use context clues to name the word if they forget it. The students can be asked to write their initials on the back of each card in case words get mixed up during word bank activities.

2. *From familiar books.* Students can also collect sight words independently from books they have read. Some of the words from the book are put on word cards that are stored in a library pocket in the back of the book. After reading the text, students are taught to read through the words in the pocket to see which ones they know at sight. Students write the words they know onto their own cards and place them in their word banks. Unknown words are matched back to their counterpart in the text.

3. *From any text.* The easiest procedure for harvesting words is to simply ask the students to point to words in a book or from a chart that they would like to put in their word bank. After several words have been written on cards, the teacher or helper can hold them up to check for recognition.

Variations

To ensure that unknown words do not enter students' word banks, a **short-term word bank** can be developed as a holding spot for words students want to harvest into their permanent or long-term word banks. A short-term word bank can be made from a 6-by-8-inch envelope or small plastic bag stored inside students' personal readers (see Figure 5-4). These envelopes are for words that students recognize from the latest stories and dictations. Periodically, sometimes once a week or when new materials are added to students' personal readers, teachers work with students in small groups to have them read through the words in their short-term word banks. Words they know from memory go into the permanent word bank.

Collecting Individual Dictations and Group Experience Stories 5-2

Recording students' individual or group dictations as they talk about personal or group experiences is a key feature of the language experience approach, or LEA (Stauffer, 1980). The text created makes especially good reading material for beginning readers because it is inherently familiar and easy to remember. When dictations are collected in groups, up to 10 students contribute one or two sentences, but dictations need to be kept to a reasonable length to be sure beginning readers will be able to read them back. This activity is divided into a 4-day sequence, but it can be accomplished in fewer days with smaller groups.

Materials

You will need chart paper, an overhead projector, a computer, or another way to record dictation so that students can observe as the teacher writes.

Procedures

Day 1: Share an experience and collect dictations.

Find a stimulus (a box turtle, fall leaves, parts of a flashlight) or experience (a trip to the bakery, a classroom visitor, the first snowfall) to share with students. It should be an interesting and memorable experience that encourages students to talk. For some individual dictations, students can be prompted to tell a personal experience without a prop or special event.

After a discussion that stimulates ideas and vocabulary, ask each student to tell you something to write down. Say each word as you write it and invite the group to help decide some of the letters or spellings you need. Talk about conventions such as capitals and punctuation. Reread each sentence and make any changes the speaker requests. Decide on a title at the end as a kind of summary of the ideas. Then reread the entire dictation. Reread it again as the students read along with you in a choral reading fashion. Then have them repeat after you, sentence by sentence in the manner of echo reading, as you point to each word.

Before day 2, make a copy of the dictation for each student in the group. Computers make it easy to create these copies. Select a font that has the type of letters easily recognized by young readers and enlarge it as much as possible. Without a computer it is still easy to make copies by writing neatly in your best manuscript handwriting. These copies will go into each student's personal reader and should be numbered.

Day 2: Reread dictations and underline known words.

Choral read the dictation again and encourage the students to follow along on their own copies, pointing to words as they read. Individual students can be called on to read a sentence. Once students can read the dictation successfully, they are invited to underline known words for their word bank. You can point to the underlined words randomly to make sure they know the words they underline. Students might also make an illustration to go with the dictation.

Day 3: Choral read and make word cards of known words.

Students can work together or individually to read the dictation again. Make word cards for underlined words that are recognized accurately and quickly.

Day 4 and on: Choral read and review new word cards.

Students continue to reread their dictations, review the words in their word banks, and complete their pictures. A new dictation or story cycle is begun when students can read their new readings with good accuracy and modest fluency.

In our Reading Buddies tutoring programs, students have personal readers that they take with them back and forth from the tutoring sessions to their classrooms. Students also take the personal readers home, where they reread the stories, review their word banks, and sort words and pictures. (Caserta-Henry, Bear, & Del Porto, 1997). In *Bookbuddies*, tutors store the personal readers in their tutoring boxes (Johnston et al., 1998).

Bilingual entries in the personal readers are particularly useful during the early part of the letter name–alphabetic stage (Bear & Barone, 1998). These billingual stories are written in both the first and second languages. Often these dictations are based on language experience activities conducted in class. These dictations are usually just one or two sentences long. A school aide or parent can help with the translations.

Support Reading with Rhymes and Pattern Stories 5–3

Rhymes and jingles and predictable patterned texts make good reading materials because they provide support for beginning readers and can then be used to harvest known words for word banks.

Materials

Find a rhyme, jingle, or predictable story that students will find memorable and readable. You can focus on one major pattern or verse. Find a big book or make a chart or overhead of the text for group work, and make copies of the rhymes and patterns for students' personal readers.

Procedures

Day 1: Introduce and read the text.

Talk about the title and cover and look at the pictures (if applicable) with the students for information about the rhyme or pattern story. Read the rhyme or story to students while fingerpointing the text. Read fluently and with expression but not too fast. Stop periodically to discuss and enjoy the story. Lead students to reflect on the story by asking general questions, such as "What do you think of the story? What is your favorite part?" Ask students to help you return to a few favorite pages. Reread these parts of the text and point to a few words to see if some students are able to recognize words at sight. Invite students to choral or echo read the entire text if it is short or read parts of the text. Decide which parts of the text will be compiled for personal readers. Type the text onto a single page or two that can be duplicated for each student. Number and date this entry.

Days 2, 3, and 4: Reread the rhyme or story and harvest words for word bank.

The same procedures described in activity 5-2 for dictations can be done as follow-ups for rhymes and predictable text. Sentences from the text can also be written on sentence strips, and the students can work to rebuild the text in a pocket chart.

In Figure 5-7 you see a sample of a rhyme taken from the story *Caps for Sale*. In this figure, Kari has made a tick mark each time she reread the rhyme. It is interesting to see that she has used a base-4 marking system. Kari has underlined a number of words that she harvested into her word bank for her personal reader.

The Grand Sort with Word Bank Words 5–4

This is an important sort in which students review their individual word banks. In this sort, students simply go through their word cards, saying the words they know, putting them in one pile, and placing the unknown words to the side. The student tries to move quickly through the pile. The words that students put in the "I know" pile can be used in subsequent sorts.

The unknown words can be discarded, but this can be a touchy point for some students who are hesitant to throw away words. There is no harm in letting a few temporarily unknown words remain, but the big mistake is when a student proceeds to another word study activity with a number of unknown words. Working with so many unknown words makes students' work hesitant, prone to errors, and frustrating. Students in the early letter name–alphabetic stage do not have the word knowledge they need to sound out unknown words, so the teacher should show them how to figure out an unknown word by using context. Referring to the number on the back of the card, the students return to their personal reader and find the word. Their familiarity with the story and the context usually ensures that they can figure out the unknown word. Because this procedure can be time consuming, it is important that only a small percent of words in a word bank are unknown.

Caps for sale
Caps for sale
Red and white and blue and green
The finest caps you have ever seen.

Caps for sale
Caps for sale
Red and white and blue and green
The finest caps you have ever seen.

FIGURE 5-7 Caps for Sale
Source: Caps for Sale, by Esphyr Slobodkina © 1940 and 1947, © renewed 1968 by Esphyr Slobodkina. Used by permission of HarperCollins Publishers.

Variations

Students can do this sort under the teacher's supervision, with a partner or classroom volunteer, or independently. This is a good opportunity for heterogeneous groups.

Reviewing Word Bank Words 5–5

There are other ways to review and work with words in the word bank.

1. *The pickup game.* Lay out a collection of 5 to 10 words faceup. Those words that the student does not know or frequently confuses are good candidates. A teacher, assistant, classroom volunteer, or another student calls out the words randomly for the student to find and pick up.
2. The *"I am thinking of"* game. This activity is similar to the pickup game, but the student is given clues instead of words: "I am thinking of a word that rhymes with *pet*" or "I am thinking of a word that starts like *play.*"
3. *Concentration.* Make a second set of words and play this classic game as described in activity 4-24.
4. *Word hunts.* Students look through their word banks for words that have a particular feature, for example, words that start with *t*, words that end in *m*, or words that have an *o* in them.
5. *Concept sorts.* Students look through their word banks for words that fit given semantic categories, for example, words that are animals, words that are people, color words, or things in a house.

   Note: You might want to keep a supply of low-tension rubber bands or library card envelopes to wrap or store selected words. In this way, word sorts can be started on one day and continued on the following day.

Alphabetizing Word Banks 5–6

Materials

Make and laminate a large alphabet strip up to 6 feet long.

Procedures

Ask a student to lay out the alphabet strip and, using his or her word bank words, place the words under the beginning letter. Pictures can be sorted by beginning sounds as well.

REVIEW OF BEGINNING SOUNDS INCLUDING DIGRAPHS AND BLENDS

 Spanish speakers use the Spanish picture and word sorts on the CD to have enough examples to make generalizations about beginning sounds.

A number of activities or games in Chapter 4 are appropriate for students in the letter name–alphabetic stage who are working to master single consonants, digraphs, and blends: Soundline (4-29), Letter Spin for Sounds (4-30), Object Sorting by Sounds (4-31), and Follow-the-Path Games (4-32). Concentration is another adaptable game. Any two pictures that begin with the same sound(s) make a match that can be claimed.

Sound Boards 5–7

Sound boards are references for letter-sound features (beginning consonants, digraphs and blends) and can be found in the Appendix. They provide a key word and picture for each letter-sound match, helping students internalize the associations.

Procedures

1. Place a copy of the sound boards at the front of students' writing folders. These boards make it easy for students to find letters to stand for the sounds they want to use. Reduced copies of relevant sound boards can be taped to students' desks.

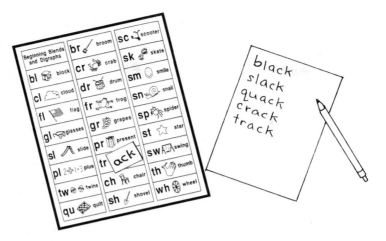

FIGURE 5-8   Expanding a Word Family Using a Sound Board

2. Teachers often post charts of various letter-sound features. Recently, the new technology of chart printers has made it possible to take the individual sound boards and enlarge them to poster size. The sound board posters can be displayed in a prominent place in primary classrooms. This gives beginning writers the opportunity to refer to the enlarged sound boards for the letters of a word they want to write.

3. A sound board can serve as a word study record. In Figure 5-8, a sound board is part of a student's word study folder. Students can indicate which features they have studied by coloring the boxes lightly.

4. Sound boards can be used to generate more words to add to a word family. The rime of the family is written on a small card and slid down beside the beginning sounds. In Figure 5-8 the word family *ack* has been expanded by adding many different blends and digraphs.

**Adaptable
for Other
Stages**

Word Hunts 5–9

Word hunts are conducted several different ways and at different times in the letter name–alphabetic stage.

Procedures

1. In the early letter name–alphabetic stage, students hunt for words that begin with the particular initial consonants, blends, or digraphs they are studying. They should look for words they know in familiar reading materials such as their personal reader or by going through their own word banks. Word hunts can be done independently, with a partner, or in small groups.

2. Students can also hunt for pictures that correspond to beginning sounds. Pictures can be cut from magazines or catalogs and pasted onto individual papers, group charts, or into alphabet books. When hunting for pictures, it helps if the teacher, aide, or student helper rips out pages on which there are pictures that contain the feature being hunted. Students can be asked to label the pictures they find by spelling as best they can.

3. Students can also hunt for words or pictures that sound like the short vowel they are studying. For example, a student could be asked to find words that sound like *red* in the middle.

4. Word hunts can be made into a game when teams of two or three students hunt for words in a given time period. Students read the words to the teacher or group.

5. One to three students can roam the room hunting for words they know. Students write down the words they find that are in their word banks.

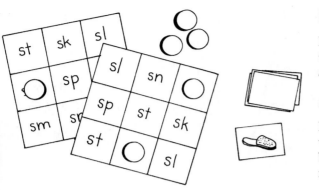

FIGURE 5-9   Blend Bingo Boards

Adaptable
for Other
Stages

Initial Sound Bingo 5-10

In this version of Bingo, students discriminate among the initial sounds. This is another activity that can be adapted to consonant blends, digraphs, and vowels.

Materials

Make Bingo cards with 9 or 16 squares. In each square, write a letter(s) that features the sounds students have been studying in sorts (Figure 5-9). You also need Bingo markers and picture cards to match sounds.

Procedures

Work in a center or with small groups of two to four students. Each student gets a Bingo card and markers. Students take turns drawing a card from the stack and calling out the picture name. Students place a marker on the corresponding square. Play continues until someone gets Bingo.

Gruff Drops Troll at Bridge 5-11

This activity is a special version of the basic follow-the-path game that reinforces *r* blends.* It was developed after reading Paul Galdone's *The Three Billy Goats Gruff*, which was part of a class study of books about monsters. Many of the books yielded a great crop of consonant-plus-*r* words such as *growl, groan,* and *fright.* These were sorted into categories by beginning blends.

Materials

Provide manila folders with a game path filled in with consonant-plus-*r* blend letters (as shown in Figure 5-10), four button markers, and picture cards of the features being stud-

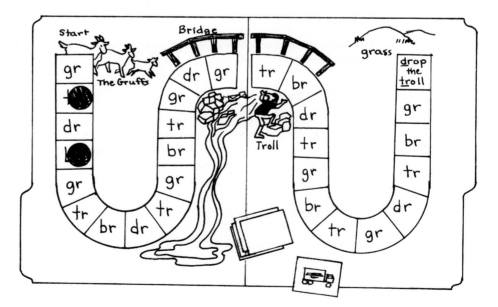

FIGURE 5-10   Gameboard for Gruff Drops Troll at Bridge

*Esther Heatley developed this board game as a literature extension.

ied. Follow-the-path templates and directions for preparing the boards can be found in the Appendix.

Procedures

1. Each player selects a button for a marker. Students turn over picture cards containing the consonant-plus-*r* blend pictures. Players take turns moving the marker to the correct space.

2. The winner drops the troll from the bridge by drawing a picture that begins with *dr* (for *drop*) or *tr* (for *troll*) for the last space.

Sea World Diorama 5–12

Students create a sea world diorama while they study the *sh* digraph.

Materials

You will need pictures and items that begin with *s* and *sh*. To make a diorama, students will need a shoe box, construction paper, colorful tissue paper, glue, scissors, markers, sand, and tiny shells or cut-up natural sponges.

Procedures

1. After sorting pictures that begin with *s* and *sh,* have students think of animals and things in the sea that begin with those sounds and make a list of them (e.g., starfish, seals, sea horses, sunfish, swordfish, scuba divers, sunken ships, sea snakes, sharks, sea anemone, seaweed, sponges, shrimp, and shells).*

2. Introduce students to how a diorama is constructed.

3. Students find or draw and cut out pictures of things that belong in the sea beginning with *s* and *sh*. Students might work in groups to glue, tape, or hang these items in their shoe boxes. Small shells or some natural sponges add decoration. Cover the bottom of the "sea" with sand.

Variations

Expand the sea diorama with sea blends (e.g., *st, sc, sw*) or create other types of dioramas. Similar books can be used. Elizabeth Schuett recommends *Sheep on a Ship* (by N. Shaw).

Match! 5–13

In this game, similar to the card game War, students look for matches of the beginning sounds they have recently studied.

Materials

Create a set of cards that feature pictures with four to eight different beginning sounds. Include at least four pictures for each sound. Pictures can be copied from the Appendix, glued on cardstock, and laminated.

Procedures

Each student has half the deck of pictures. Students turn a picture card faceup from their deck at the same time. If the pictures begin with the same sound, the first person to recognize and say "Match!" gets the pair. If the pictures do not match, another set is turned over until a match occurs. There can be penalties for calling out "Match" carelessly.

---

*Cindy Booth developed this activity.

Variations

This game can be played with word families, short vowels, and long vowels.

Beginning and End Dominoes 5–14

This activity is a picture sort to match initial and final consonants (e.g., *lamp* matches *pig*).

Materials

Pictures for these matches can be found in the Appendix. Wendy Brown put together a list of pictured words. Divide a 2-by-4-inch card in half and paste a picture from each of the following pairs on each side.

ghost-tub	book-leg	gate-pin	nurse-goat	ten-log
dishes-map	pencil-bed	desk-mop	pig-nut	tent-bed
rain-dog	goat-zip	pin-sit	tie-mad	door-pear
two-hat	toes-road	doll-sick	key-lips	seal-boat
pen-bug	gas-sun	net-belt	tail-sink	kite-jeep

Procedures

Students are given a set of five pairs mixed up and challenged to match the pairs as in the traditional game of dominoes.

Variations

Students compete to make the longest string they can with a collection of pictures (e.g., tub/book-kite/toad-doll/lip-pig/game-mad/door-rope/pen).

THE STUDY OF WORD FAMILIES

Once students begin the study of word families, they are expected to read and spell the words they sort. Many word games can be adapted as follow-up activities for word sorting. Some activities are especially designed to enhance students' understandings of how families work.

Building, Blending, and Extending 5-15

This series of teacher-led activities is designed to reinforce phoneme segmentation, phoneme blending, and the use of analogy as a spelling strategy (if I can spell *cat*, then I can spell *fat*,) as students work with onsets and rimes. This should follow sorting lessons in which students have worked with a collection of word families.

Materials

Prepare a set of cards to be used in a pocket chart. Write the targeted onsets and rimes on these cards, keeping the letters of the rime together. For the *at* family you would have cards with *at, b, c, f, h, m, p, r,* and *s.* As students study digraphs and blends those can be added as well, such as *th, ch,* and *fl.*

Procedures

1. *Building.* This procedure reinforces the spelling of word families. The teacher should model how to make the words in the family by putting up two cards such as *m* and *at.* Then the students are asked what letter would be needed to make the word *sat.* The teacher would model how to replace the *m* in *mat* with the *s* to make the new word.

Students could then be invited to make additional words in the family by substituting beginning letters.

2. *Blending.* This activity reinforces the reading of word families. It is similar to building except that the teacher starts with a word the students all know, such as *cat,* and then substitutes a different beginning letter. The teacher models how to blend the new onset with the familiar rime to read the word: "*Mmmmmm, aaaaaaat, mat.* The new word is *mat.*" Students are then asked to use the two parts of the onset and rime to sound out the word just as the teacher has modeled.

3. *Extending.* During the extending part of this activity, the teacher selects words that are not included in the sort to demonstrate to students that they can read and spell many more words once they know how to spell several words in a family. This is a time when you might demonstrate using unusual words like *vat* or challenging words with digraphs and blends such as *chat, flat,* or *scat.*

Variations

Students can work with small cards at their seats as the teacher leads the activity.

Add more digraphs and blends as they are studied. There will be many words you can make with families such as *ack* and *ick.*

For the study of short vowels and the CVC pattern the vowel is separated from the rime (*at* is cut apart into *a* and *t*).

After working with the cards, students can be asked to write the words on paper, small white boards, or chalk boards.

Word Family Wheels and Flip Charts 5–16

Wheels and flip charts, as shown in Figure 5-11, are fun for students to play with independently or with partners. The wheels and flip charts are used to reinforce the patterns. Prior to using the wheels and charts, students have worked in small groups to sort words from the various families.

Materials

To make word family wheels, follow these three steps:

1. Cut two 6-inch circles from tagboard. Cut a wedge from one circle and write the vowel and ending consonants or rime to the right of it. Make a round hole in the center.
2. On the second tagboard circle, write beginning sounds that form words with that family. For example, the *op* family can be formed with *b, c, h, l, m, p, s, t, ch, sh, cl,* and *st.* Space the letters evenly around the outside edge so that only one at a time will show through the "window" wedge.
3. Cut a slit in the middle of the circle. Put the circle with the wedge on top of the other circle. Push a brass fastener through the round hole and the slit. Flatten the fastener, making sure the top circle can turn.

To make flip charts, the steps are as follows:

1. Use a piece of tagboard or lightweight cardboard for the base of the flip book. Write the family or rime on the right half of the base.
2. Cut pages that are half the length of the base piece and staple to the left side of the base. Write beginning sounds or onsets on each one.

Variations

Students can draw a picture to accompany each word.

FIGURE 5-11 Word Family Wheel and Flip Chart

Show Me 5-17

This activity is a favorite with teachers who are teaching word families and short vowels.*

Materials

FIGURE 5-12
Show Me Game

Make each student an individual pocket to hold letter cards. To make a pocket, cut paper into rectangles about 7 × 5 inches. Fold up 1 inch along the 7-inch side, then fold the whole thing into overlapping thirds. Staple at the edges to make three pockets (see Figure 5-12). Cut additional paper into cards 1.5 × 4 inches to make 14 for each student. Print letters on the top half of each card, making sure the entire letter is visible when inserted in the pocket. A useful assortment of letters for this activity includes the five short vowels and *b, d, f, g, m, n, p, r,* and *t.* Too many consonants can be hard to manage.

Procedures

Each student gets a pocket and an assortment of letter cards. When the teacher or designated caller names a word, the students put the necessary letters in the spaces and fold up their pockets. When "show me" is announced, everyone opens their pocket at once for the teacher to see. The emphasis is on practice, not competition, but points for accuracy could be kept if desired.

Start with words having the same families such as *bad, sad,* or *mad,* where the students focus primarily on changing the initial consonants. Move on to a different family and different vowels. For example, you could follow this sequence: *mad, mat, hat, hot, pot, pet.*

Variations

1. The Show Me pockets are used for beginning sounds and/or ending sounds. Put digraphs or blends on cards to spell words such as sh-i-p or f-a-st.
2. Long-vowel patterns are spelled using a four-pocket folder.

Word Maker with Beginning Consonants, Digraphs, and Blends 5-18

Students match blends and digraphs with word families to make words.**

Materials

Create a collection of cards that have onsets on half (single consonants, blends, and digraphs) and common short-vowel rimes on the other. For students in the later letter name–alphabetic stage, include rimes with ending blends, digraphs, and preconsonantal nasals such as *ish, ash, ush, ing, ang, ast, ust, ank, ink, ump, amp, ack, ell,* and *all.*

Procedures

1. Each student begins by drawing five cards from the deck. With the five cards faceup, each student tries to create words as shown in Figure 5-13.
2. Once the students have made one or two words from their first five cards they begin taking turns drawing cards from the deck. Every time they make a word they can draw two more cards. If they cannot make a word they draw one card.
3. Play continues until all the letter cards are used up. The player with the most words is the winner.

---

*This excellent activity is attributed to Margery Beatty who taught in the Waynesboro, Virginia, Public Schools many years ago.
**Katherine Preston contributed to this activity.

FIGURE 5-13 Word Maker Cards

Variations

Students can work independently with the word maker cards to generate and record as many words as possible.

Read It, Find It 5-19*

This simple but fun game for two players reinforces the identification of words students have been studying in word family sorts.

Materials

You will need 30 pennies. Prepare a game board by writing words from familiar word families onto a 5 × 6 grid or a path. Prepare a set of word cards that have the same words as those on the board and place these facedown. Words can be duplicated, so it is okay if there are two or three of the same word on the board. Be sure that there are the same number of word cards as words on the board.

Procedures

1. One player flips a penny for heads or tails position. Each player chooses 15 pennies. One student will be heads and turn all his or her pennies to the heads side. The other will be tails and turn the pennies to the tails side.
2. The player who did not flip will begin by taking a card from the pile and reading it. The player then finds the word on the board and covers it with a penny. If the player cannot read the word or reads it incorrectly, he or she cannot cover the word.
3. The next player repeats, each player drawing one card per turn.
4. The first player to cover 15 words, using up all the pennies, is the winner.

Variations

This game can be adapted for short-vowel words and word families.

Roll the Dice 5-20

This game is for two to four players. It reinforces word families and builds automaticity.

Materials

You need a cube on which to write four contrasting word families, (e.g., *an, ap, ag,* and *at*). A blank side is labeled "Lose a Turn," and another is labeled "Roll Again" (see Figure 5-14). You will also need a blackboard or paper for recording words.

FIGURE 5-14 Cube for Roll the Dice Game

*This game was created by Liana Acevedo of Greensboro, North Carolina.

Procedures

Students roll the die. If it lands on a word family space, the student must come up with a word for that family and record it on the chalkboard or paper. Students keep their own lists and can use a word only once, although someone else may have used it. If a player is stumped or lands on Lose a Turn, the die is passed to the next person. If the student lands on Roll Again, he or she takes another turn. The person who records the most words at the end of the allotted time wins.

Variations

1. Play with two dice and have two teams for a relay. Each team has a recorder. The first person of each team rolls the dice and quickly calls out an appropriate word. The recorder writes the word on the board. The player hands the dice to the next player and play goes quickly to the end of the line. With this variation you would not need to lose a turn or roll again.
2. This game can also be used with vowel patterns, beginning consonants, or blends.

Rhyming Families 5–22

Materials

Prepare a follow-the-path gameboard as shown in Figure 5-15. You will also need a single die or a spinner, pieces to move around the board, pencils, and paper for each player. Directions for making gameboards and spinners as well as gameboard templates are in the Appendix. Write a word from each word family you have been studying in each space on the board. You can also write in special directions such again Roll Again, Free Space, Go Back 2 Spaces, and Write Two Words.

Adaptable for Other Stages

Procedures

The object is to make new words to rhyme with words on the gameboard that do not match the other players' words.

1. Spin to determine who goes first. Play proceeds clockwise.
2. The first player spins and moves the number of places indicated on the spinner.

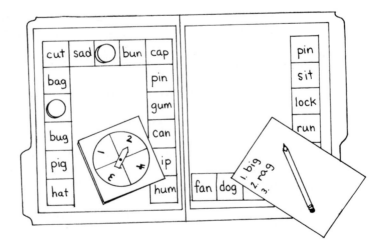

FIGURE 5-15   Gameboard for Word Families

3. The player reads the word in the space where he or she lands. All players write a rhyming word by changing initial letter(s). Players number their words as they go. Play continues until someone reaches the end of the path.

4. Beginning with the player who reaches the end first, each player reads the first word on his or her list. Players who have a word that does not match the other players' words get to circle that word. For example, if players have *cat, bat, cat,* and *splat,* only the players having *bat* and *splat* would circle their words. Continue until all words have been compared.

5. Each circle is worth one point, plus the player who reaches the end first receives two extra points. The student with the most points wins the game.

Variations

Label each space on the gameboard with the rime of a family you have studied (*at, an, ad, ack*). Use no more than five different rimes and repeat them around the path. Prepare a set of cards that have short-vowel pictures that correspond to the families. Students move around the board by selecting a picture and moving to the space it matches. For example, a student who has a picture of a hat would move to the next space with *at* written on it.

Go Fish 5–23

This classic game has been adapted to word study and can be played by two to four players. This version can be used as a review of word families.

Materials

Create decks of blank cards with four words from different word families written on them. (e.g., *that, bat, fat,* and *hat* are written on four cards). Write each word at the top of the card so that the words are visible when held in the hand, as shown in Figure 5-16.

Procedures

1. Five cards are dealt to each player and the remainder are placed in the middle as a draw pile. The first player asks any other player for a match to a card in his or her hand: "Give me all your words that rhyme with *hat*." If the player receives a matching card, he or she may put the pair down and ask for another card. If the other player does not have the card requested, that player tells the first player to "Go fish," which means that the first player must draw a card from the "fish pond." The first player's turn is over when he or she can no longer make a match.

2. Play continues around the circle until one player runs out of cards. Points can be awarded to the first person to go out and to the person who has the most matching cards.

FIGURE 5-16 Playing Cards for Go Fish

Variations

Go Fish can be adapted for beginning sounds and blends using pictures, or it can be used with vowel patterns.*

---

*Janet Bloodgood adapted this word study game from the familiar game of Go Fish.

STUDY OF SHORT VOWELS

Once students are automatic with word families, it is time to study short vowels in non-rhyming CVC words. After this feature has been explored through word sorts and weekly routines, games can provide additional practice.

Hopping Frog Game 5–24

This game for two to four players reviews the five short vowels.*

Materials

1. Use a gameboard or make your own course with a manila folder. Cut green circle lily pads for each space and write CVC words students have used in word sorts on each one (e.g., *pin, get, hot, bad, leg, run, bug, wish*).
2. You will need four frog markers. The spinner is marked into five sections, with a vowel and illustrating picture in each (*a*, apple; *e*, ten; *i*, fish; *o*, frog; *u*, sun). See the Appendix for directions on how to make a spinner. Figure 5-17 shows a sample board for the game.

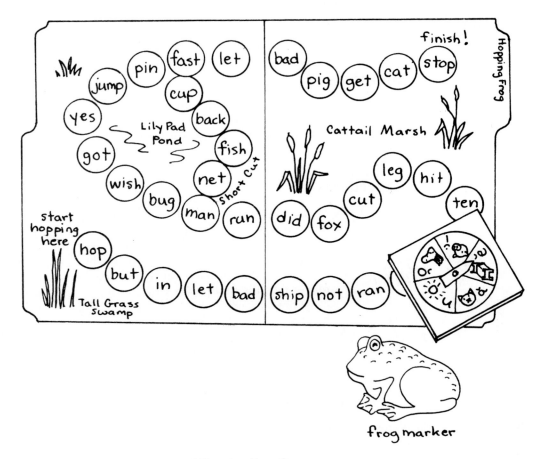

FIGURE 5-17   Frog Marker and Hopping Frog Game

---

*This game was developed by Janet Bloodgood and has become a favorite.

Procedures

Each student selects a frog marker. Players take turns spinning and moving their markers to the first word that matches the vowel sound on which they land (e.g., *e*, *get*). They then pronounce this word and must say another word with the same vowel sound to stay on that space. The next player then spins and plays. The first player who can finish the course and hop a frog off the board wins.

Variations

1. Students can write the words they land on and organize them in columns by short vowel.
2. The same game plan could be used for long-vowel patterns and inflected endings.

Making-Words-with-Cubes Game 5–25

Short-vowel words are built with letter cubes in this game. It can be used for other vowels as well.

Materials

Letter cubes that can be found in many games (Boggle and Perquackery) are needed. Playing pieces can also be made from blank wooden cubes. Write all the vowels on one cube to be sure that a vowel always lands faceup. Put a variety of consonants on five or six other cubes. (Pairs like *qu* and *ck* might be written together.) The students need a sand clock or timer, paper and pencil, and a record sheet such as the one shown in Figure 5-18.

Procedures

1. In pairs, students take turns being the player and the recorder. The recorder writes the words made by the player.
2. A player shakes the letters and spills them out onto the table, and then starts the timer.
3. The word maker moves the cubes about to create words and spells them to the scribe. The letters can be moved around to make more words. Errors should be ignored at this point. Write the words in columns by the number of letters in the words.

4. When the time ends, the students review the words and check for accuracy. Words are then scored. Count the total number of letters used. Students soon realize that the bigger the words they make, the greater their score.

Variations

Students in the within word pattern stage should work with two vowel cubes. On a second cube, write vowel markers such as *e* (put two or three), *a*, *i*, and *o*. By this time, students may be able to use multiplication to total the letters (e.g., four 3-letter words is 12).

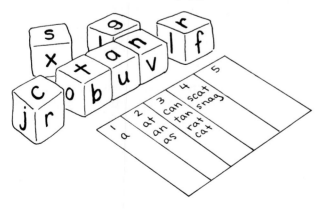

FIGURE 5-18   Making-Words-with-Cubes Game

The Bug Race 5–26

This is a variation of the basic follow-the-path game and reviews combinations of short vowels. This example uses a bug theme, but it can be adapted to many other themes such as the zoo, space travel, comic characters, or vehicles. Use stickers and cutouts to add interest to the basic path templates found in the Appendix.

Materials

Use one of the follow-the-path gameboards and label the spaces with *a, e, i, o,* or *u.* Add pictures of leaves, grass, and so on, to make it resemble a bug's world. Make copies of short-vowel pictures on tagboard and cut them apart or paste paper copies of the pictures onto cards. It is important that the pictures do not show through the card. On several additional cards write commands such as Skip a Turn, Go Back 2 Spaces, and Move Ahead 3 Spaces. Make buglike playing pieces from bottle caps by drawing in eyes, antennae, and spots with a permanent fine-tip marker.

Procedures

1. Shuffle the picture and command cards and turn them facedown in a pile. The players move around the board by turning over a picture and moving their playing piece to the next free space on the board that has the corresponding short vowel.
2. The student who reaches the end first is the winner.

Variations

Long-vowel pictures can be used for students in the within word pattern stage.

Follow the Pictures 5–27

This variation of the basic follow-the-path game works as a follow-up to word sorts for short-vowel words.

Materials

Use one of the follow-the-path templates in the Appendix. Make reduced copies of short-vowel pictures (about half size or 50% should work). Cut the pictures out and paste them in the spaces on the game path. Use two, three, four, or five short vowels. You will also need playing pieces to move along the path and a spinner or single die. In some spaces you can write Roll Again, Go Back 2 Spaces, and other directives. Include a card on which all the words are written in the same order they are pasted to settle any arguments about spelling.

Procedures

1. Students take turns spinning for a number. Before they can move to the space indicated by the spinner, they must correctly spell the word pictured. If they cannot spell the word, they must stay where they are for that turn.
2. The student who reaches the end first is the winner.

Variations

Any pictures can be pasted on the gameboard. Long-vowel pictures can be used for students in the within word pattern stage.

Slide-a-Word 5–28

Students can be asked to list and then read all the CVC words they are able to generate using the slider created by Jeradi Cohen (Figure 5-19). As different short vowels are studied, the central vowel letter can be changed.

Materials

Supplies include tagboard or posterboard, ruler, marker, single-edge razor blade, and scissors.

Procedures

1. Cut a piece of tagboard or posterboard into strips 8.5 by 2.5 inches. Using the razor, cut a pair of horizontal slits on each end 1.5 inches apart. Write a vowel in the center.
2. Cut two 12-by-1.5-inch strips for each slider. Thread them through the slits at each end and print a variety of consonants, blends, or digraphs in the spaces as they appear through the slits. Turn the strips over and print additional beginning and ending sounds on the back.

FIGURE 5-19 Slider for Slide-a-Word

Put in an M or N 5-29

Materials

Create word pairs on word cards for sorting:

rag	rang	rig	ring	sag	sang	tag	tang
cap	camp	rap	ramp	trap	tramp	bag	bang
dig	ding	pup	pump	hag	hang	lip	limp
rug	rung	gag	gang	bet	bent	wig	wing
sprig	spring	pin	ping	hug	hung	lap	lamp
swig	swing						

Procedures

Three or four students can play. Students read the words, shuffle the deck, and deal all of the cards out to players. Students dealt pairs throw them down and replace the pair before the first round of play. Students take turns putting down a word from their hand. The student who has the match to the pair takes the card and throws down one of the cards from his or her hand. The student with the most cards is the winner.

Variations

Nonsense words can be inserted to see if students lose a turn for putting in a nonword such as thim, stanp, or ramg.

6

Word Study for Transitional Learners in the Within Word Pattern Stage

Orthographic development and word study instruction during the within word pattern spelling stage is the subject of this chapter. We open with a discussion of the reading, writing, and spelling behaviors that are characteristic of transitional learners. Then we discuss the whys and hows to planning word study instruction. The activities at the end of the chapter are arranged in order along the developmental continuum for the within word pattern stage of spelling. Before we discuss development, let us visit the classroom of Mrs. Lynn Holmes, a second-grade teacher who has worked with a group of eight students in the early part of this stage of development.

It is Monday, and Lynn begins the small group reading with a comprehension lesson in which students share entries from their dual entry diaries (Barone, 1989) in response to what they read in *Fantastic Mr. Fox* (by R. Dahl, 1988).

Next, Lynn moves to the word study part of her lesson. Lynn has prepared word study sheets like the one in Figure 6-1A as well as a collection of the words written on index cards that she will use to model the sort in a pocket chart. The goals for word study instruction today are to show students a new sort, observe how well they can read the words, have them try the sort, and then store the words away to sort tomorrow. The students have studied long -*a* thoroughly, and some of the spelling patterns, such as common CVV and CVVC patterns (e.g., *say* and *nail*).

"Let's begin by reading these words together." As each of the words is read, Lynn places it randomly at the bottom of her pocket chart. There is some discussion of *read* when Jason points out that it can be read two ways. They agree for now to pronounce it as "reed."

Lynn introduces the sort by saying, "What do you notice about these words?" "They all have -*es* in them," explains Troy.

"Do they all have the same sound in the middle?" asks Lynn. She puts up pictures of a web and a queen as keys to the sounds they are to listen for: "We'll sort these words by how they sound in the middle. Place all the words that sound like *web* in the middle here, under this picture of a web. Put words that sound like *queen* here, under this picture of a queen. Place words that do not fit either under the odd-ball column." She places a blank word card on the right side of the pocket chart to make a third column. "Let's try a few. Jean, show us how you would figure out where to put this word."

Jean places the word *bed* underneath the picture of the web while she says, "Web. Bed."

"Fine, Jean. Why did you put *bed* under the web?" "Because they sound alike in the middle. They both say 'eh' in the middle."

"Yes. David, where would this word go?" Lynn hands David the word *team*. "Say the word and name the pictures and decide which two sound alike in the middle."

David takes the word card and checks out the fit as he talks himself through this sort: "Team, web. Team, queen. . . . Team, queen." He places the word *team* underneath the picture of the queen.

Further in to the sort, students decide that *been* does not fit under either picture and should go in the oddball column. After all the words have been sorted, Lynn and the students check each category by reading the words from top to bottom. Then Lynn poses the next important question, "How are the words in each column alike?"

David notes that the words under the web all have one *e*. Jean points out that the words in the second column all have two vowels. This leads to the next question: "Do you see some words in the second column that look alike or are spelled alike?" Lynn invites Jason to come up, and he quickly pulls out all the words spelled with *ee* and puts them in a new column leaving the words spelled with *ea*. Once more Lynn asks the students how the words in each column are alike. Then she removes all the cards from the pocket chart leaving only one word in each of the three categories as a key word. She mixes up the words and passes them out to the students. They then take turns coming up to sort their own three words. The final sort looks like the one in Figure 6-1B.

Lynn ends this lesson by giving each student a copy of the word study sheet in Figure 6-1A. The students return to their seats, cut apart the words, and sort them independently while Lynn checks in with another reading group.

When she returns, Lynn moves among the students and asks them, "Why did you put these words together?" This prompt gets students to explain their sorts to Lynn.

To close this word study activity, students store their word cards in plastic bags. The next day they will sort again when they convene in their group, and Lynn will watch to see how accurately and easily they sort this second day. Later either in a group or individually, they will write the sort in their word study notebooks.

 Among Spanish-speaking students, the short -*i* may be pronounced as it is in Spanish, as a long -*e* sound.

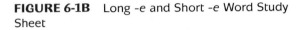

		Long E Short E Sort 1
web	queen	team
seat	bed	seen
yes	jeep	read
meal	tree	leg
treat	bell	sheep
jet	cream	seed
eat	been	feel

web	queen	team	been
bed	seen	seat	
yes	jeep	treat	
jet	feel	read	
leg	sheep	eat	
bell	tree	meal	
	seed	cream	

FIGURE 6-1A   Pattern Sort for Long -e and Short -e

FIGURE 6-1B   Long -e and Short -e Word Study Sheet

LITERACY DEVELOPMENT AND INSTRUCTION FOR STUDENTS IN THE WITHIN WORD PATTERN STAGE

The within word pattern stage is a period of development between the beginning stage when students' reading and writing are quite labored, and the intermediate stage when students can read nearly all texts that they encounter, including newspapers and magazines. Teachers find students' orthographic development during this period to be fresh and interesting because students make rapid progress in their understanding of single-syllable orthographic patterns. During this stage of development, students learn to spell long-vowel patterns, and they read most single-syllable words accurately and with increasing fluency. Transitional readers also can read many two- and three-syllable words when there is enough contextual support.

Reading and Writing

As noted in Figure 1-1, transitional readers can be found in grades 1 through 4. Students in this stage read and write with increasing fluency and expression compared with the disfluent reading of beginning readers. This stage begins when students stop reading in the word-by-word and inexpressive fashion apparent in the beginning stage of literacy. Transitional readers begin to read in phrases, pausing at the end of sentences, and they read with greater expression. Teachers observe that most of the fingerpointing characteristics of the beginning stage drop away, and transitional readers approach rates of 100 words per minute (Bear, 1992; Bear & Cathey, 1989). Transitional readers also begin to read silently during sustained silent reading (SSR) or drop everything and read (DEAR). We think of transitional readers as the Wright brothers of reading: They have limited elevation in their reading, and it does not take much to bring them down to frustration level, or to cause them to be less fluent in their reading.

Writing also becomes more fluent during this period of development and there is greater sophistication in the way transitional writers express their ideas. The physical act of writing is performed with greater speed and less conscious focus on the explicit act of writing (Bear, 1991a). This added fluency gives transitional writers more time to concentrate on ideas, which may account for the greater depth and complexity in their expression. Cognitively they compose with a better sense of the reader's background knowledge and with a greater complexity in the story line.

Literacy Learning and Instruction

Materials for transitional readers cover a wide range of levels, from the second-through some fourth-grade materials. To promote fluency and expression at the beginning of this stage, transitional readers read and reread familiar text from several sources: school readers, longer patterned or predictable books, favorite poems, three-paragraph-long individual dictations, and readers' theater selections. By the early part of this stage, there are many books that students can read at an independent level, such as the *Frog and Toad* books (by A. Lobel) and Henry and Mudge (by C. Rylant). By the end of this stage, students' reading includes easy chapter books such as *The Time Warp Trio* (by J. Scieska), *Encyclopedia Brown* (by D. Sobol), or the *Boxcar Children* series (by G. Warner). Transitional readers also explore different genres, and informational text becomes more accessible. For example, they read informational books from the *Let's Find Out* series and easy informational magazines such as *Ranger Rick.*

Students in the transitional stage meet in small groups for reading and writing workshops, where they discuss what they read and write in greater depth than they did as beginning readers, partly because what they read and write is longer and more complex. Students discuss the stories they have read, and when they discuss what they read, they look through their reading materials to share specific sentences and quotes that they found interesting. Independently and with partners, they read books without a teacher's support. This independence makes it possible to use reading group time to conference, share, and discuss in more detail.

Excerpts of Katrina's two-and-a-half-page, single-spaced story about a squirrel named Nuts (see Figure 6-2) shows how much students know about written language and spelling in the later part of the within word pattern stage. Katrina, a second grader, has a rich vocabulary and a rich language base. She writes with a strong voice and she uses dialogue effectively. She begins to use quotation marks by the end of her story.

In terms of orthographic knowledge, Katrina spells most long-vowel patterns and *r*-influenced words correctly (*woke, search*). But this knowledge is not stable as seen in

---

Twelve year old Chistine was glad it was
Fially Satarday alltow she loved school
Epspshelly math she loved taking her pet
Squrrle Nuts to the park even more.

(Nuts runs away and)

Christine orginizes a search. She
looked evrywhere. Christine climbd
a tree Nuts wasn't there.

(Nuts returns and the next day)

Christine and Nuts woke up
they went down stairs and there
breakfeast was ready it was
all difrent kinds of pancake
animals.

(Later)

Christine thought
Nuts ran away but he
didn't because Nuts went
taw a difrent park. Christine
serches the howl park.

(The story ends with Christine)

niting a sweter for Nuts
the colors where red, white
and blue.

FIGURE 6-2 Katrina's Story

her later spelling of *searches* as SERCHES, and her overgeneralizing patterns (BREAK-FEAST for *breakfast* and HOWL for *whole*). Later in the story Katrina spelled *thought as* TOOUGHT, and then went back and wrote in an h. She also confuses homophones (*two/too, there/their*). In the classroom, we observed that Katrina was in a word study group in which students were studying long vowels, dipthongs, and ambiguous vowels.

Teachers may find transitional stage students in the middle part of first grade, but transitional students are found mostly in the second, third, and beginning fourth-grade classrooms. You will also certainly find corrective and remedial readers in the middle and high schools who are in this stage of orthographic development.

Perhaps 25% of the adult population in the United States is stunted at this point of literacy proficiency. Many students who progress no further than the transitional stage revert to beginning behaviors as their knowledge atrophies. Even community college and university students who are poor spellers would benefit from the study of vowel patterns. These are the adults who can read at sight many of the words they see regularly, but they may have difficulty reading polysyllabic words like *repetition*. It is important to take a step back and conduct word study activities that help them cement their knowledge of vowel patterns in single-syllable words to get a running start as they study two-syllable words.

Lots of experience in reading and writing is crucial during this stage. Students must read for at least 25 to 30 minutes each day in instructional- and independent-level materials. They need this practice to propel them into the next stage; otherwise, they will stagnate as readers and writers. This puts word study into perspective. If students are not doing plenty of reading, all of the word study in the world will not help.

CHARACTERISTICS OF ORTHOGRAPHIC DEVELOPMENT DURING THE WITHIN WORD PATTERN STAGE

Students in the within word pattern or transitional stage use but confuse vowel patterns (Invernizzi, Abouzeid, & Gill, 1994). The examples discussed in Chapter 1 will show you the common vowel confusions students make during this stage. In Eduardo's writing in Figure 6-3, we can see that in the early part of this stage he has learned a good deal about short-vowel patterns, spelling *with, pick, on, it,* and *up* correctly and *blanket* quite predictably as BLANCKET. Eduardo is also experimenting with long-vowel patterns, as in PLAED for *played* and TOOTHE for an ambiguous vowel in *tooth*.

Like Eduardo, students in this stage no longer spell *boat* sound by sound to produce BOT, but as BOTE, BOWT, BOOT, or even BOAT as they experiment with possible patterns for the long -*o* sound. When spellers begin including silent letters, they are ripe for instruction in long-vowel patterns.

The Complexities of English Vowels

My toothe came
Owt beckus I plaed tugwoure
with a blancket with botes on it
and the tooth fairy
came tw pick it up.

FIGURE 6-3   Eduardo's Tooth

Vowels are certainly one of the most challenging aspects of learning to read and spell in English. The study of vowel patterns characterizes much of the word study during the within word pattern stage and accounts for the name selected to label it. Short vowels pose a problem because they do not match to a letter name, but once students have learned to associate the five common short-vowel sounds with *a, e, i, o,* and *u*, the relationship is usually one letter to one sound. In contrast, students in the within word pattern employ a higher degree of abstract thinking, because students face two tasks at once.

They must (a) segment words into phonemes to determine the sounds they hear and need to represent, and (b) choose from a variety of patterns that involve silent letters (*cute, boot, suit*) or special consonant patterns (*cold, itch*).

Mastery of vowels is complicated by the following factors.

1. There are many more vowel sounds than there are letters to represent them. Each designated vowel, and *y,* is pressed into service to represent more than one sound. Listen to the sound of *a* in these words: *hat, car, war, saw, father, play.* To spell the variety of sounds, vowels are often paired (e.g., the *oa* as a long -*o* in *boat* or *ou* for the diphthong in *shout*); or a second vowel or consonant is used to mark or signal a particular sound. The silent -*e* in *ride,* the *y* in *play,* and the *w* in *snow* are examples of silent **vowel markers.**

2. Not only are there more vowel sounds than vowels, many of those sounds are spelled a number of different ways. Some of these long-vowel patterns are more frequent or common than others, as indicated in Table 6-1.

3. In addition to short and long vowels, there are many more vowel sounds, all of which are spelled with a variety of patterns. These include *r-*influenced vowels (*car, sir, earn*), **diphthongs** (*brown, cloud, boil, toy*), and other ambiguous vowels that are neither long nor short (*caught, chalk, good, straw, thought*). These vowel patterns involve either a second vowel or the vowel is influenced by a letter that has some vowel-like qualities. The /l/ and /w/ sounds are examples of consonants that influence the sound of the vowel (*bulk, crowd*). These additional vowel patterns are also shown in Table 6-1.

4. The history of the English language explains why there are so many patterns. English has been enriched with the addition of vocabulary from many different languages,

TABLE 6-1   Vowel Patterns

Long–Vowel Patterns

Common long -*a* patterns:	*a-e* (*cave*), *ai* (*rain*), *ay* (*play*)
Less common:	*ei* (*eight*), *ey* (*prey*)
Common long -*e* patterns:	*ee* (*green*), *ea* (*team*), *e* (*me*)
Less common:	*ie* (*chief*)
Common long -*i* patterns:	*i-e* (*tribe*), *igh* (*sight*), *y* (*fly*)
Less common:	*i* followed by *nd* or *ld* (*mind, child*)
Common long -*o* patterns:	*o-e* (*home*), *oa* (*float*), *ow* (*grow*)
Less common:	*o* followed by two consonants (*cold, most, jolt*)
Common long -*u* patterns:	*u-e* (*flute*), *oo* (*moon*), *ew* (*blew*)
Less common:	*ue* (*blue*), *ui* (*suit*)

Consonant-Influenced Vowels

*R-*influenced vowels

a with *r:*	*ar* (*car*), *are* (*care*), *air* (*fair*)
o with *r:*	*or* (*for*), *ore* (*store*), *our* (*pour*), *oar* (*board*)
e with *r:*	*er* (*her*), *eer* (*deer*), *ear* (*dear*), *ear* (*learn*)
i with *r:*	*ir* (*shirt*), *ire* (*fire*)
u with *r:*	*ur* (*burn*), *ure* (*cure*)

Note: *er* (*her*), *ir* (*shirt*), and *ur* (*curl*) often spell the same sound.
W influences vowels that follow *wa* (*wash warn*), *wo* (*won word*).
L influences the *a* as heard in *all*, *al* (*talk*), and *aul* (*haul*).

Diphthongs and Ambiguous Vowels

oo (*moon*) and *oo* (*book*)
oy (*boy*), *oi* (*boil*)
ow (*brown*), *ou* (*cloud*)
aw (*crawl*) *au* (*caught*) *al* (*tall*)

but it has imported diverse spelling patterns as well. In addition, certain patterns represent sounds that have changed over the centuries. For example, *igh* was once a guttural sound different from long *-i*, but over time pronunciation tends toward simplification while spelling tends to stay the same. Therefore, one long-vowel sound is spelled many different ways (Vallins, 1954).

5. English is a language of infinite dialects, and the difference between dialects is most noticeable in the pronunciation of vowels. In some regions of the United States, the long *-i* sound in a word like *pie* is really more of a vowel glide or diphthong as in "pi-e." *House* may be pronounced more like "hoo-se" in some areas and *roof* may sound more like "ruff" than "rue-f." Sometimes the final *rs* in *r*-controlled vowels are dropped, as in Boston where you "pahk the cah" (park the car). In other regions a final *r* is added to words as in the "hollers" (hollows) of southwest Virginia. Such regional dialects add color and interest to the language, but complicate the teaching of vowels. Teachers may be worried about how speakers of such dialects will learn to spell if they cannot pronounce words correctly. Rest assured that these students will learn to associate certain letter patterns with their own pronunciations (Cantrell, 2001). The value of word sorting over inflexible phonics programs is that students can sort according to their own pronunciations, and a miscellaneous or oddball column can be used for variant pronunciations.

6. Many words in English do not match even one of the patterns listed in Table 6-1. These words have sometimes been called exceptions or rule breakers. We prefer to put them in the miscellaneous or oddball category. During word study in the within word pattern stage, the oddball category will get a lot of use. Sometimes these words are true exceptions as with *was, build,* and *been,* but other times they are not exceptions but part of a little known category. An example of these words are *dance, prince,* and *fence* which may look like they should have long-vowel patterns, but in these words the *e* is there to mark the /c/ sound "soft" (consider the alternative: *danc, princ,* and *fenc*). Such exceptions should not be ignored and in fact a few such words should be deliberately included in the sorts you plan. They become memorable because they deviate from the common patterns.

Despite the complexity of vowels, by the end of the within word pattern stage, students have a good understanding of vowel spelling patterns. This knowledge is prerequisite to the examination of the way syllables are joined during the next stage of development, the syllables and affixes stage. For example, when students have immediate recognition of words like *bet* and *beat*, they soon begin to see that *betting* has two *t*s and *beating* has one *t*.

Recall the three layers of the orthography. In this stage, students continue to rely on sound and are learning vowel patterns, but meaning also matters. The meaning connection is emphasized in the study of homophones (*meat* and *meet*) and homographs (*tear*: I *tear* the sheet into rags. You have a *tear* in your eye).

The Influence of Consonants on Vowels

In English, vowel patterns often consist of two vowels, one of which marks or signals a particular sound for the other vowel. Common examples are the silent *-e* in words such as *bake* and *green;* but consonants are also vowel markers, such as the *gh* in *night* and *sigh,* which signals the long *-i* sound. Students who have come to associate the CVC pattern with short vowels may be puzzled when presented with *car, joy, hall,* or *saw. R* retains its identity as a consonant in *car,* but the preceding vowel has a sound quite different from short *-a.* In *boy, ball,* and *saw, y, l,* and *w* are no longer acting as consonants but are taking on vowel-like qualities. These words may look like they are exceptions to the CVC rule, but are in fact simply additional patterns that are very regular. This is why it is so important to learn patterns at this stage rather than rules. The influence of *r* is particularly common and deserves further discussion.

R-influenced vowels.

As our friend Neva Viise says, "*R* is a robber!" The presence of an *r* following a vowel robs the sound from the vowel before it. This causes some words with different short vowels to become homophones (*fir/fur*) and makes vowel sounds spelled with *er, ir,* and *ur* indistinguishable in many cases (*herd, bird, curd*). Even long-vowel sounds before the robber *r* are not as clear as the same vowels preceding other consonants (*pair* versus *pain*).

The *r*-influenced vowel sorts draw students' attention to the location of the *r* and to the subtle difference in sound which location creates. Word study of *r*-influenced words can begin with activities that contrast initial consonant *r* blends (*grill*), with *r*-influenced vowels (*girl*).

Consonant Patterns and Another Look at Digraphs and Blends

Within word pattern spellers spell CVC words correctly and easily, and by this time, they know many beginning and ending consonant blends and digraphs (*frost, smash*). However lingering confusions can exist in three-letter digraphs and blends: *spr* (*spring*), *thr* (*throw*), *squ* (*square*), *scr* (*scream*), *shr* (*shred*), *sch* (*school*), *spl* (*splash*), and *str* (*string*). Words can be sorted by these combinations or included in other sorts over time. The hard and soft sounds of *g* and *c* can also be explored.

Continued study of digraphs and blends at this time is quite successful, because students have many sight words on which to draw when they sort words. As you may recall, letter name–alphabetic spellers have this problem when they examine consonant digraphs and blends.

What is of special interest in this stage are other characteristics of consonants. Based on Venesky's (1970) work, Henderson (1990) called these **complex consonant patterns.** For example, students in the within word pattern stage can examine words that end in *ck* (*kick*), *tch* (*catch*), and *edge* (*ledge*). You might ask: "What do you notice about the vowel sounds and patterns in these word sorts?"

tack	take	fetch	peach	fudge	huge
lick	like	notch	roach	badge	cage
rack	rake	patch	poach	ledge	siege
smock	smoke	sketch	reach	ridge	page

Contrasting these pairs will enable students to make interesting discoveries. Students see that *ck* (*tack*), *tch* (*fetch*), and *dge* (*fudge*) patterns are associated with short vowels, whereas *ke* (*take*), *ch* (*peach*), and *ge* (*huge*) are associated with long-vowel patterns.

 The Take a Card game is ideal for Within Word Pattern learners dealing with complex consonant patterns. Access this game through the Within Word Pattern Section on the accompanying CD-ROM.

Homophones and Homographs

Homophones will inevitably turn up in the study of vowel patterns and can be included in the word sorts you plan even at the beginning of this stage, but an intensive look at homophones at the end of this stage is also recommended. At this point, students know most of the vowel patterns and are ready to focus on the meaning of the words. Students enjoy creating lists of homophones (*bear/bare, Mary/marry/merry*) and homographs (*wind* up string/listen to the *wind*). In exploring the complexities of vowels, we learn the historical reasons why words that sound alike are spelled differently. The different spelling of homophones may even make reading easier and meaning clearer (cf., Taft, 1991; Templeton, 1992). You can see the need to spell words differently in a sentence in which homophones are substituted for one another:

> The weigh Peat cot the bare was knot fare.
> (The way Pete caught the bear was not fair.)

Often, when students hunt for words that are alike, they find there are not so many inconsistencies as they once thought, and as their vocabularies expand, they find patterns among words though there may not be many examples. A group of third graders observed that *weight* and *height* had two things in common: They were both spelled with *ei*, and they both made a sound that was unexpected.

The meaning layer of English orthography arises in discussions of homophones and homographs. Pairs of homographs and homophones differ grammatically as well as semantically. For example, when discussing the homophones *read* and *red*, it makes sense to talk about the past tense of the verb *to read* and the color word *red*. Students are beginning to scratch the meaning layer of the orthography. The study of contractions and possessives also presents a new series of patterns to examine that are rooted in the pattern and meaning layers of the orthography.

This new emphasis on meaning is a time to build vocabulary knowledge. Students refer to dictionaries to see what the three words *vein/vane/vain* mean. Also during the within word pattern stage, students create semantic sorts that are collections of words on a particular topic (e.g., baseball words, words related to outer space, government words, and key vocabulary words from their other content area texts and studies). This focus on meaning and spelling prepares students for the next stage of spelling when the meaning of syllables is examined, the syllables and affixes stage.

WORD STUDY INSTRUCTION FOR THE WITHIN WORD PATTERN STAGE

Word sorts and word study notebooks are the most common and crucial activities to use during this stage. Three brief reminders are constructive at this point: (a) Students must be able to read the words before sorting. (b) Choose sorts that match their development and represent what they use but confuse. (c) Avoid rules. Instead, have students find reliable patterns. Although it is common to teach students rules about silent -*e* and "when two vowels go walking," often these rules are less reliable than the categories of patterns themselves. For example, the rule about two vowels works for *oa* and *ai* in *boat* and *rain* but not for *oy* or *oi* in *boy* or *join*; yet *oy* and *oi* are very regular spelling patterns (Johnston, 2001). The time to teach a rule is when students have already observed and then understand the pattern that underlies the rule.

Two principles of word study listed in Chapter 3 have particular importance in this stage.

• *Sort by sight and sound.* Plan sorts that first ask students to contrast vowels by how they *sound*. Long vowels should be introduced by comparing them to their corresponding short vowels as Lynn did in the vignette at the beginning of this chapter. *R*-influenced vowels (such as the *ar* in *car*) can be compared with the short CVC patterns (such as short -*a* in *cash* or *trap*). Sound sorts are important, because sound is the first clue that spellers use. Long- and short-vowel pictures can be used for sound sorts, but most of these sound sorts are done with words at this stage. After sorting by sound, sort by sight—look for the different orthographic spelling patterns used to spell long-vowel sounds as well as other vowels in English.

• *Don't hide exceptions.* Include two or three oddball words or pictures when appropriate. For example, a long -*o* sort could include *love* and *some* which look as though they fit the CVCe but whose vowel sounds are not long. However, don't over-do it. Too many oddballs placed in a sort can make it difficult for students to find the pattern.

Sequence of Word Study

The sequence of word study in the within word pattern–transitional stage begins by taking a step back with a review of short vowels as they are compared with long vowels. Then the focus shifts to common long-vowel patterns and *r*-influenced vowel patterns. Less common patterns, complex patterns, and ambiguous patterns are studied after the students have learned the common patterns.

A suggested sequence is summarized in Table 6-2 where one word is used as an exemplar for the categories you would set up. Remember to use students' spellings to determine where in this sequence to start. Observations of students' writings and the inventories described in Chapter 2 help to pinpoint the features students have learned and those that pose problems. The vowels you choose to study first should be ones you see students using but confusing.

You may spend as much as a month on the first long vowel. It takes time to introduce the long-vowel patterns, to contrast the long-vowel patterns with the CVC short-vowel pattern, and to set up word study notebooks to incorporate these new patterns. The extensive repertoire of vowel patterns for each long-vowel sound requires equally extensive instruction. Low frequency patterns are explored toward the end of study for each vowel (e.g., *height* as a long -*i* word). Subsequent long vowels can be covered more quickly. Pacing can be adjusted by adding more categories to a single sort (up to four or five) or dropping back to fewer categories when students exhibit confusion. A sense of the pacing of word study during this time can be seen in the three pacing sequences in Table 6-2. Late first graders would probably need a slow introduction to only common long-vowel patterns, whereas achieving fourth graders might benefit from a fast-paced review with more challenging words. Because there is a lot to cover in this stage, 2 years is not too long to address the range of features.

Let us pause to summarize the sequence of word study instruction during this stage.

1. Focus first on sound by sorting pictures of words by long- and short-vowel sounds. The pictures, sorts, and word lists in the Appendix and on the *Words Their Way* CD are good sources for sorts.

2. Study one vowel by comparing the long and short sounds (the CVC pattern in *ran* compared with the CVCe pattern in *came*), and then by exploring common patterns for that long-vowel sound (long -*a*: CVCe in *cake*, CVVC in *rain*, and CVV in *say*).

3. Study each long vowel in the same fashion. As you study additional vowels, help students to see the similarities in patterns among vowels (e.g., *bay* and *key* are CVV words, and *nail* and *feet* are CVVC patterns).

4. Study less common patterns and vowel sounds that are neither long nor short. These include ambiguous vowel digraphs such as *mouth* and *taught*, diphthongs such as *boil* and *loud*, and *r*-influenced vowels and *l*-influenced vowels like *car* and *chalk*. Contrast these less common patterns to the familiar long- and short-vowel patterns. For example, *dart* and *share* can be contrasted to *trap* and *face*.

5. Examine the way that certain consonant sounds and vowels interact. The consonants *c* and *g* change their sounds (hard or soft) according to the vowels that follow them, and certain complex consonant spellings are determined by the vowels that precede them (*ch/tch, ge/dge*).

TABLE 6-2 Possible Sequence for the Study of Single-Syllable Vowel Patterns

Introductory Pace	Moderate Pace	Advanced Pace/Review
Focus on most common patterns and use easy words. Less common patterns may be oddballs.	Use oddballs and some words with blends and digraphs.	Use more words spelled with blends and digraphs, oddballs, and less common patterns.

Long Vowels (and some vowels that are neither long nor short)

Introductory Pace	Moderate Pace	Advanced Pace/Review
hat face	hat face pay	chat place stray train
hat face paid	hat face paid pay	train sleigh great
face paid pay		
pet feet	nest sleet cream	nest bread sleet cream
pet feet seat	nest bread cream	chief sleigh pie
pet feet seat me		
sit like	ship prize slight	chick prize slight fly
sit like light	ship prize lie fly	chick child find
sit like fly	sick sight wild find	
like light fly lie		
pot nose	sock stove toast	stock stove groan grow
pot nose road	sock stove toast grow	stock sold ghost
pot nose road grow	sock sold post	grow plow cloud
pot road grow go	grow plow	cloud boil
	loud boy boil	
rug cute	drum flute glue suit	drum flute glue flew
rug cute new	flute shoot group	shoot group brook could
cute boot book	drum rough group	
rug book boot flew		

R-Controlled Vowels

Introductory Pace	Moderate Pace	Advanced Pace/Review
hat car	hat car face fare	shark stare chair warm
hat car face fare	car fare fair war	
pet her	pet her screen cheer	clerk learn clear cheer
feet deer seat fear	feet cheer cream fear	
her deer fear learn	her fear cheer learn	
pot for	for more	short store pour word
nose more	for more pour poor	
for more your		
sit girl	girl her fur learn	swirl burn fern learn
like fire		
girl fur her		

Complex Consonant Clusters

Introductory Pace	Moderate Pace	Advanced Pace/Review
shr thr sh th	shr thr spr str	include words with these clusters in all sorts
scr squ str spl	scr spl squ	
spr thr shr str	kn wr gn	
kn wr gn		

Diphthongs and Other Vowels

Introductory Pace	Moderate Pace	Advanced Pace/Review
cot boy boil	float boy boil	boil brown cloud
hat ball saw	boil brown loud	salt hawk fault cough
	hat ball saw fault	
	grow grew saw	

TABLE 6-2 continued

Introductory Pace	Moderate Pace	Advanced Pace/Review
Focus on most common patterns and use easy words. Less common patterns may be oddballs.	Use oddballs and some words with blends and digraphs.	Use more words spelled with blends and digraphs, oddballs, and less common patterns.

Syllable Patterns Across Vowels Use a variety of vowels and sort by the pattern rather than by the vowel sound. For example, game, like, cute, and cone all go under CVCe.		
CVC CVCe CVC CVCC CVVC	CVC CVCe CVVC CVCe CVVC CVC CVCC	CVC CVCC CVCe CVVC

Complex Consonants and Vowel Patterns		
hard/soft c (cent, cut) hard/soft g (gym, goat) ck (luck), k (leak), ke (like)	hard/soft g (gym, goat) hard/soft c (cent, cut) ck (luck), k (leak), ke (like) g (log), ge (age), dge (edge) ce (once), ve (glove), ge (age), dge (edge) ch (each), tch (itch)	hard/soft g (gym, goat) hard/soft c (cent, cut) g (log), ge (age), dge (edge) ce (once), ve (glove), ge (age) ch (each), tch (itch), k (leak), ck (luck)

As you begin creating word sorts for your Within Word Pattern learners, visit the accompanying CD-ROM for numerous printable samples.

WORD STUDY AND ENGLISH LANGUAGE LEARNING IN THE WITHIN WORD PATTERN STAGE

 The vowels in English and Spanish differ in the ways shown in Table 6-3. In this stage, when there is a focus on long vowels, English vowels will sound like other vowels in Spanish. These differences in sound-spelling correspondences may explain some students' misspellings. For example, the word *reach* may be spelled RICH, because the letter *i* in Spanish has a long -*e* sound.

TABLE 6-3   Vowel Sounds in English and Spanish

English Letter and Word		Spanish Letter and Word	
a as in	cake	e as in	hecho
e	bean	i	ido
i	like	ai	aire
o	hope	o	ocho
o	top	a	ajo
u	June	u	usted
oy	toy	oy	voy

From Bear, D. R., Templeton, S., Helman L. A., and Baren, T. (2003). Orthographic development and learning to read in different languages. In G. G. Garcia, *English learners: Reaching the highest levels of English literacy.* Newark, DE: International Reading Association. Copyright by the International Reading Association.

Word and orthographic knowledge of English gained during the within word pattern stage contributes to slight changes in students' dialect and pronunciation. Studies of within word pattern learners provide insight into the shifts in pronunciation of some long vowels (e.g., Cantrell, 2001). Eventually, literate students from other dialects and first languages acquire a literate flavor to their speech that reflects their expanded knowledge of two or more languages.

Some able English Language Learners with strong sight vocabularies may appear more advanced than they are in both their vocabulary knowledge and pronunciation. Students may have learned to spell many words correctly, but their strategies for spelling unknown words indicate that their orthographic knowledge could be deeper. For example, a student memorized the spelling of *rain,* but continued to spell unknown, long -*a* words with an *e,* using the Spanish spelling of the long -*a* sound as in Table 6-3, with an *e* as in *hecho.* When it seems that specific word knowledge is ahead of students' more conceptually based orthographic knowledge, use a moderate or introductory pace when following the sequence of word study in Table 6-2.

During this stage, when pattern is the focus, at times a word study lesson that was meant to focus on a particular spelling pattern becomes unexpectedly focused on pronunciation and meaning. Consider priorities and plan for many additional language experiences to cement the meaning and sound layers. English Language Learners who have strong sight vocabularies and do not know the meaning of words benefit from being involved in the semantic sorts and activities described at the end of this chapter.

WORD STUDY ROUTINES AND MANAGEMENT

Word study notebooks are an important tool as students record their sorts and create written reflections to accompany some sorts. In this section, we discuss classroom routines that incorporate the word study notebooks, and we show how to organize word sorts during this stage. High frequency words come into focus during this period and we present some suggestions to study these words. During this stage, students explore orthographic patterns for long vowels and other vowels with a confidence that makes it easy for them to work independently and in small groups.

The Word Study Lesson Plan in the Within Word Pattern Stage

In small group, teacher-guided activities, students are shown the fundamental ways to examine the vowel patterns. Chapter 3 has guidelines for sorting to review. Steps for sorting are described briefly here to discuss relevant experiences in word study lessons during this stage.

1. Demonstrate the Sort

There are many ways to introduce sorts. You may direct the sort or ask students to look for their own categories in an open sort. A teacher-directed sort is helpful when students are new to word sorts or when they start the study of a new feature. In a teacher-directed sort, introduce the **key words** to be used at the top of the columns, and then say, "Find all the words you can that sound like *fish* in the middle and words that sound like *kite* in the middle." After sorting, lead a discussion to focus students' attention on the distinguishing features: "How are the words in this column alike?"

Probably the first thing you will do, perhaps even the first step of the demonstration, is read the words with students to be sure they are able to read them, and talk briefly about

 English Language Learners may not know several words, so introduce some of the words, but move on after a few minutes of such work.

the meaning of unfamiliar words. If there are more than a few words students do not know, and this may be so for English Language Learners, note that meaning is not there, but that the primary goal of the sort would be to introduce the pattern. Because the focus of the sort may only be to identify the vowel pattern, plan for long-term vocabulary development in meaningful contexts. Concept sorts with pictures and words enhance vocabulary development when students sort and then talk about how they sorted for meaning. This can be a very rich form of vocabulary instruction with English Language Learners.

2. Sort and Check

Students work independently or with a partner and use sets of words or word sheets prepared by the teacher, or classification folders like those discussed in Chapter 3. These manila folders have the key words or pictures at the top, and the words to sort are in a plastic bag attached to the folder. Figure 6-4 shows the student isolating the long -e sound in *leaf* before placing it in the column with the picture of the *feet* at the top. Saying the words aloud and comparing them in this way is a necessary strategy when students begin a sort.

3. Reflect: Declare, Compare, and Contrast

"Why did you sort the way you did?" is the question that often starts the reflection part of a lesson. From your demonstrations, students know that they will need to be able to explain why they sorted the way they did. Practice with partners is a good next step for students as they learn to talk about what they learned.

These reflections lead to discussions, and the reflections can be written as described later in this chapter. A sort is successful when students sort accurately and fluently, and can discuss why they sorted the way they did. If students seem just to mimic other students, you can ask them to say it another way, or ask the student, "What else did you notice about the words we sorted?"

FIGURE 6-4 Long-Vowel Sorts: Student Sorts by Sound

4. *Extend:* Students Work Independently Across the Week

Word study is extended beyond the small group sessions. These extensions include activities students complete at their seats, at a word study center, or at home.

As was discussed in Chapter 4, weekly routines incorporate spelling activities and word study games as a regular part of the word study program. No-peeking sorts, which involve students sorting words by sound as a partner reads them aloud, are particularly recommended because students must not only distinguish the sound of the vowel but associate it with a particular orthographic pattern. Games give enjoyable practice in reading the words and thinking about their patterns. Many games are described in the activities section at the end of this chapter.

The word study notebook is used across the week for a number of activities. Students record their sorts as well as the results of word hunts. Word study notebooks are used to document activities, and they serve as handy references that preserve continuity from one small group word study session to another. More ideas for the use of word study notebooks are described later.

Guidelines for Creating Word Sorts

In this section, you will learn more about creating word sorts for students in the within word pattern stage of development.

• *Select the features.* Sorts that contrast sounds and patterns are the key to effective word study. To create these sorts you need to decide what kind of words or features you will contrast. There are a number of resources to help you. The sequence presented in Table 6-2 shows the basic contrast at three paces.

• *Select the words.* Once you have decided upon the features or patterns you are going to contrast, you will need words for each category. Begin with the word lists and suggested sorts in the Appendix and on the *Words Their Way* CD.

Look to students' writing and reading materials for words to include in sorts. You can also ask students to brainstorm words that follow sound or spelling patterns. Students see the way words they can read are pronounced, and they see how words they can say are spelled. The words students can already read and spell are still useful when they are looking for patterns and generalizations. There should be at least some words in sorts that are familiar; remember one of our principles is to compare the known with the unknown.

Many teachers use their school district's adopted spelling program to look for features to study and to find words in weekly lists. Often these published programs are set at a fast pace and they cover several patterns at one time. You can adjust these lists by choosing clusters of words and adding other words for students who need a slower pace, and postponing the study of some patterns.

You can write the words for sorts on the blank word study sheets found in the Appendix or enter them on a word processor by creating your own word study template. Set your margins at zero and create three columns and six to seven rows. Choose a clear font such as Comic Sans MS, and size to fit your cells. For closed sorts, key words for sorting can be posted at the top of the word sort page, and the key words can be highlighted with underlining, bolding, or with a star in the corner. Other teachers like the key words to be established as part of the group discussion and students can then underline them.

Dialects and Sorting

The pronunciation of vowel sounds in words varies because of individual and regional dialectical differences. Teachers need to accept differences in pronunciation. This means that some students will sort words a little differently than the teacher or other classmates, but there is no harm in this. Let students sort in ways that make sense to them, and observe what students do differently but consistently. The goal is for students to associate patterns with their own pronunciations.

Occasionally, disputes arise among the students about whether words are oddballs. Some students say *again* with a long *-a*, whereas others say it with a short *-i*. *Poem* has a long *-o* to some students and an /oi/ sound to others. Some people pronounce *bear* and *bar* as homophones. Students find these dialectical contrasts interesting and teachers should treat them as variations, not as issues of right or wrong. You will find that the fourth-grade social studies curriculum in many parts of the United States is a great place to discuss dialects as students study the diverse groups that have settled the state in which they live.

Word Study Notebooks in the Within Word Pattern Stage

Word study notebooks may begin at the end of the previous letter name–alphabetic spelling stage. Now, word study notebooks become a primary form of working with sorts independently, and particularly in extending the word study beyond the small group session. You may tell a group of students in the morning orientation period: "Please bring your word study notebook to the reading group later today."

As you learned in Chapter 3, word study notebooks serve as a record of some of the routine word study activities and as such they provide documentation of student work for assessment and grading. After sorting in a group students return to their seats, record the sort in columns in their word study notebooks, and either that day or for homework add words to each of the categories.

Written Reflections

At times, you may have students write about why they sorted the way they did. As fairly fluent writers, within word pattern stage spellers can spend just a few minutes at the end of a sort to summarize discoveries. Such is the case in Figure 6-5, which shows what Graciela has learned about long vowels. It is clear that she is aware of the various patterns for long *-i*. Her written reflection shows that she has made a generalization about the *imb* and *ind* words: "*Climb* is the same as *bind*, *wind*, and *hind*." These written reflections help teachers assess students' progress. They also give students a starting place at the beginning of small group word study lessons; when we ask: "Read one reason why you sorted the way you did."

Sections in Word Study Notebooks

The word study notebook can also serve as an organized collection of words students examine for different purposes. Word study notebooks have a long instructional life in learning and students should have ready access to their notebooks throughout the day. Students become accustomed to bringing them to small group sessions, along with reading materials and response journals or logs.

The notebooks can be divided into separate sections, and for word study during this stage, each vowel comprises a small section. Post-it notes make it easy to refer to specific sections of the notebook. For example, in the study of long *-o,* there may be two pages of words that all have the short *-o* sound, followed by separate pages for the various long *-o* patterns—a page of CVVC *coat* words and CVCe *joke* words. Students are challenged to be on the lookout for new words all the time. In this way the sounds and patterns are constantly revisited.

Other sections you might see as you thumb through word study notebooks include pages dedicated to content areas and concept sorts. Content-oriented word lists encourage students to think relationally about their content vocabulary which ushers in the study of spelling and meaning in subsequent spelling stages. As examples, you might

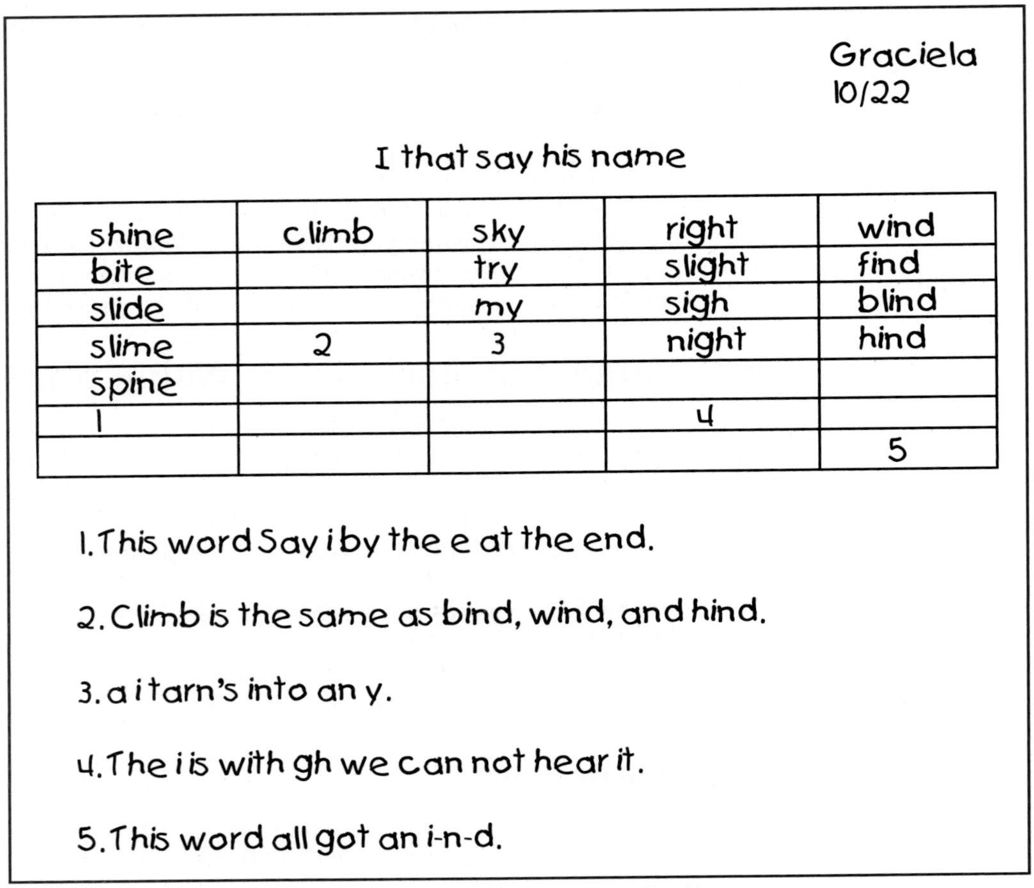

Graciela
10/22

I that say his name

shine	climb	sky	right	wind
bite		try	slight	find
slide		my	sigh	blind
slime	2	3	night	hind
spine				
1			4	
				5

1. This word Say i by the e at the end.

2. Climb is the same as bind, wind, and hind.

3. a i tarn's into an y.

4. The i is with gh we can not hear it.

5. This word all got an i-n-d.

FIGURE 6-5   A Page from Graciela's Word Study Notebook

see a science web on pandas, a list of concepts related to immigration to summarize a discussion in social studies, and a page comparing soccer terms to football terms. A complete word study program addresses the spelling, phonics, *and* vocabulary curricula.

What about High Frequency Words?

Currently there are a number of commercial spelling programs that feature high frequency or high utility words. The authors of these programs argue that spelling instruction should focus on a small core of words students need the most, words such as *said, because, there, they're, friend,* and *again.* Unfortunately, this narrow view of word study reduces spelling to a matter of brute memorization and offers students no opportunity to form generalizations, which can extend to the spelling of thousands of unstudied words.

Many of these high frequency words do not follow common spelling patterns, but can be included in word sorts as oddballs. For example, the word *said* is usually examined with other words that have the *ai* pattern such as *paid, faint,* and *wait.* It becomes memorable because it stands alone in contrast to the many words that work as the pattern would suggest. It is also likely to be spelled correctly by most students because they have seen it so often when they read. Some words in English, however, persist as problems for young writers. There are also some words students need to write frequently in the lower grades that are not included in the weekly lessons designed to meet their developmental needs. An example of this is the word *because,* which occurs often in the writings of first graders. Many teachers will accept students' inventions for such words (BECUZ, BECALZ, BECAWS), but some teachers grow tired and concerned about such errors, especially beyond the primary grades. Although we feel confident that such errors will be worked out over time, some teachers may wish to consider these guidelines when they study high frequency words.

We offer this way of studying words with some caution. Studying high frequency words should not replace the developmental study of words by features, but can supplement such study. *The words chosen should be highly functional words seen in your own students' writing and should be kept small in number.* The words should also not be too far in advance of your students' developmental levels. Interesting content or theme words which students need for short periods of time such as *Thanksgiving, leprechaun,* and *tyrannosaurus* can simply be posted for easy reference.

Guidelines to Study High Frequency Words

1. Select 6 to 10 words for 1 week of each 9-week period for a total of 24 to 40 words a year. (Short weeks of 2 to 3 days might be good for these.) A list developed in a second-grade class might include *know, friend, again, our, went, would,* and *once.* Students can take part in this selection by choosing words they have difficulty spelling and by choosing words from the teacher's master list. A cumulative list of these words in alphabetical order is posted in the room for reference with the understanding that students are expected to spell those words correctly in all their written work once they have been studied (Cunningham, 1995). Individual student copies of these words in alphabetical order can also be distributed. Students may place the individual lists in their writing workshop folders, in the back of their journals, or in a section of their word study notebooks.

2. Develop routines to help students examine and study the words carefully. Here are some suggestions:

- *Introduction and discussion.* As the teacher writes the words on the board, the students copy them on their own paper in a column. (Be sure that everyone copies correctly!) The teacher should then lead a discussion about each word. "What part of this word might be hard to remember and why?" (For the word *friend,* the discussion would focus on the fact that it has a silent -*i.*) "What might help you remember how to spell this word?" (Students might note that it ends with *end.*)
- *Self-corrected test method.* After each word has been written and discussed, students should fold their paper over so that the list is covered. The teacher calls the words aloud while the students write them again. The students then check their own work by unfolding the paper to compare what they copied to what they spelled. Any words spelled incorrectly should be rewritten again. This method has been well researched (Horn, 1954).
- *Self-study method.* The self-study method is another long-standing activity that appears in most published spelling books. This process can be used independently, but students need to be taught to follow these steps: (a) Look at the word and say it; (b) cover the word; (c) write the word; (d) check the word; and (e) write the word again if it was spelled wrong.
- *Practice test.* The words are called aloud. Students spell the word and then immediately check it by looking at the chart posted in the room. Students become familiar with using the chart as a reference, and can call the words to each other in pairs or small groups, or the teacher may lead the practice test.
- *Final test.* The chart is covered and students spell the words as they are called aloud. Because the number of words is kept small, the chance of 100% success is high. Once students have been tested they are responsible for those words from then on. The teacher will undoubtedly need to remind students often to reread a piece of written work to check for the posted words in the editing stage. Any word that continues to be a problem can reappear on the next list, but students will have about 8 weeks to work at getting it under control.

Activities for Students in the Within Word Pattern Stage

This section begins with three model word sorts and several routines to summarize the basic approach to word study at this time, and to highlight the importance of categorization and discovery in the study of words. Games are offered as follow-ups designed to extend and reinforce students' understandings, not to substitute for instruction. In addition, many games from the previous chapter—particularly the ones marked with the adaptable logo—can be utilized with different words. The activities for students are grouped according to difficulty, with common long-vowel games coming before less common vowel sounds and patterns.

For printable resources appropriate for the Within Word Pattern learner, visit the accompanying CD-ROM.

Picture Sorts to Contrast Long and Short Vowels 6-1

This excellent bridge activity is for students in the early part of the within word pattern stage. Students work individually and in small groups to examine the basic sound differences among short- and long-vowel patterns. This sort will help to identify students who are having problems recognizing the differences in the vowel sounds.

Materials

Focus on one vowel and choose 10-14 short-vowel pictures and 10-14 long-vowel pictures. Use pictures in the Appendix and in graphics programs.

Procedures

1. The teacher holds up the pictures for the students to name and supplies any words that are unknown.
2. The teacher places a picture at the top of the first two columns to fit the categories the students are to use in their sorting. An oddball column is established for words that for various reasons do not fit.
3. Students sort the pictures underneath the key pictures placed at the tops of the columns.
4. Students read their completed sorts by column, at which time they make any changes they wish. At the end of reading each column, students declare the reason why they sorted as they did.

Teacher-Directed Word Sorts for Long Vowels 6-2

This basic procedure involves setting up and carrying out a sort that begins with sound and moves to pattern.

Materials

Using the word lists in the Appendix or other resources, select about 20 short -*a* words and long -*a* words that are spelled with the CVVC pattern (*rain, pail*) and the CVCe pattern (*cake, tape*). A picture card of a short -*a* and long -*a* picture may be used. Select words that your students will already know how to read. You may also include one or two oddballs that do not fit the expected sound or pattern (*was* or *have,* for example). Prepare word cards or write the words randomly on a word study handout template for students to cut apart for independent sorting.

Procedures

1. Introduce the sort by reading the words together and talking about any whose meaning may be unclear. Invite students to make observations about the words: "What do you notice?"
2. Sort the words first by the sound of the vowel in the middle. You can use the short -*a* and long -*a* pictures as the key pictures in this sort.
3. After discussing the rationale for the sort, ask students to look for patterns in the long -*a* column and separate them into two categories.
4. Again talk about how the words in each column are alike.
5. Scramble the words and re-sort a second time under designated headers or key words. The categories will look something like the following sort.
6. Ask students to sort independently. After the sort, students shuffle the words and store them for activities on subsequent days.

Short -*a*	Long -*a*		Oddballs
cap	cape	chain	have
gas	came	rain	was
back	name	pail	
fan	lake	pain	
has	gate	paint	
	fast	safe	
	rake		

Variations

Study sounds and patterns for *e, i, o,* and *u* in the same manner.

Open Sort Using R-Influenced Vowels 6-3

Many vowels which are neither long nor short should be examined as well. After students are familiar with listening and looking for the vowel patterns, they can be very successful at open-ended sorts such as the one described here.

Materials

Using the word lists in the Appendix or other resources, select about 20 words that are spelled with *ar* (*bark*), *are* (*bare*), or *air* (*chair*). Select words that your students should already know how to read. You may also include one or two oddballs that have the same sound but not the same spelling pattern (*pear* and *bear,* for example). Write the words randomly on a word study handout template for students to cut apart for independent sorting.

Procedures

1. Introduce the sort by reading the words together and talking about any whose meaning may be unclear. Invite students to make observations about the words: "What do you notice?"

2. Ask students to sort the words into categories of their own choosing. Call on different students to describe the rationale for their sorts. Accept all reasonable categories.
3. Designate key words or headers and ask all the students to sort the same way. The categories will look something like the following sort. Discuss the categories and oddballs.
4. Ask the students to scramble their words and re-sort a second time.
5. Ask students to identify the homophones (*fare/fair, bare/bear, hare/hair*) and define them or use them in sentences.
6. Shuffle and store the words for sorting activities on subsequent days.

bark	bare	air	war	pear
chart	share	chair	warm	bear
yarn	stare	pair	warn	
large	scare	hair		
sharp	square	fair		
	hare			
	fare			

Variations

Any number of sounds and patterns can be explored in a similar fashion.

Word Hunts 6-4

Word hunts are excellent seat work activities. Students can work independently or with a partner. They enjoy going back into familiar texts to look for words that fit a particular pattern. Word hunts will usually turn up many miscellaneous words or oddballs, and interesting discussions arise as students work together to decide where certain words should be categorized.

Procedures

1. Ask students to go through what they have recently read to find words that fit a particular sound or pattern: "Find all the words you can that sound like *cake* in the middle."
2. Words that fit the desired patterns are written down in notebooks.
3. Students meet in small groups and read their words aloud. The students or the teacher may record the words on chart paper for display.
4. Students are asked what words could be grouped together.
5. Students check to see what words they can add to their word study notebooks.

Variations

1. Students can hunt for sight words, similar vowel patterns, words to which inflected endings or plural forms may be added, or compound words.
2. Use a newspaper for the hunt. Teams are sent in search of various long-vowel patterns (an *ai* team, an *ay* team, a CVCe team, etc.). Words fitting the desired patterns are circled in crayon or highlighted, written down, and shared in small group instruction.

Train Station Game 6-5

This easy board game for up to four people is used to emphasize automaticity with common long vowels.*

Materials

Use a basic pathway board found in the Appendix and decorated like the one shown in Figure 6-6. Write in words that have been studied in word sorts, or use some of the many words listed in the Appendix. Incorporate four special squares into the gameboard:

---

*Thanks to Janet Bloodgood for this activity.

Adaptable for Other Stages

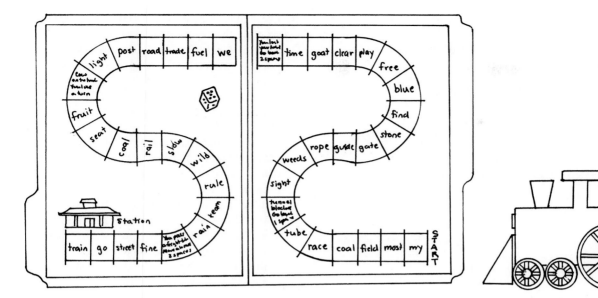

FIGURE 6-6 Train Station Game: Long-Vowel Patterns

1. Cow on the track. Lose 1 turn.
2. You pass a freight train. Move ahead 2 spaces.
3. Tunnel blocked. Go back 1 space.
4. You lost your ticket. Go back 2 spaces.

Procedures

Each child selects a game piece. The first child then spins or rolls the die and places the game piece on the appropriate space. The child pronounces the word and identifies the vowel. In addition, the child must say another word containing the same vowel sound to stay on that space. Play continues in this fashion until someone finishes the course.

If students have studied the long-vowel patterns within each long vowel, they can be asked to say what the pattern is, for example, "*Nail* is a long *-a* with a CVVC pattern."

Variations

Divide a spinner into five sections and label each with a vowel. Students move to the next word with the vowel sound they spin.

Turkey Feathers 6-6

In this game, two players compare visual patterns across a single long vowel.*

Materials

You will need two paper or cardboard turkeys without tail feathers, such as the one in Figure 6-7; 10 construction paper feathers; and word cards representing the long vowel studied, for example, for long *-a*, CVCe, *ai*, and *ay*.

Procedures

1. One player shuffles and deals five cards and five feathers to each player.
2. Remaining cards are placed facedown for the draw pile.

*Marilyn Edwards developed this easy game.

FIGURE 6-7   Turkey Feathers: Comparing Vowel Patterns

3. Each player puts down pairs that match by pattern. For example, *cake/lane* would be a pair, but *pain/lane* would not. Each time a pair is laid down, the player puts one feather on his or her turkey.
4. The dealer goes first, says a word from his or her hand, and asks if the second player has a card that has the same pattern.
5. If player 2 has a card that matches the pattern, player 1 gets a feather; if not, player 1 must draw a card. If the player draws a card that matches any word in his or her hand, the pair can be discarded, and a feather is earned. Player 2 proceeds in the same manner.
6. The player using all five feathers first wins. If a player uses all the cards before earning five feathers, the player must draw a card before the other player's turn.

Adaptable for Other Stages

Variations

Upon using all five feathers, a player must correctly pronounce words. If a word is mispronounced, the player loses a feather and the game continues.

The Racetrack Game 6-7

Players move around a track and match words in their hand with words on the track. This is a great way to examine long-vowel patterns. A racetrack template can be found in the Appendix. A sample game board appears in Figure 6-8.*

Procedures

This game for two to four players is played on an oval track divided into 20 to 30 spaces. Different words following particular patterns are written into each space, and a star is drawn in two spaces. For example, *night, light, tie, kite, like, my, fly, wish,* and *dig* could be used on a game designed to practice patterns for long and short *-i*. A collection of 40 to 50 cards is prepared with words that share the same patterns. A number spinner or a single die is used to move players around the track.

1. Shuffle the word cards and deal six to each player. Turn the rest facedown to become the deck.
2. Playing pieces are placed anywhere on the board and moved according to the number spinner or die.
3. When players land on a space, they read the word and then look for words in their hand that have the same pattern. For example, a player who lands on *night* may pull *sign* and *right* to put in the winning pile. If they move to a space with a star, they dispose of any oddballs they might have (such as *give*) or choose a pattern.
4. The cards placed in the winning pile are replaced by drawing the same number from the deck before play passes to the next player.
5. A player who has no match for the pattern must draw a card anyway.
6. The game is over when there are no more cards to play. The winner is the player with the most word cards in the winning pile.

---

*Darrell Morris developed this game and has written extensively on word sorting (Morris, 1982, 1992).

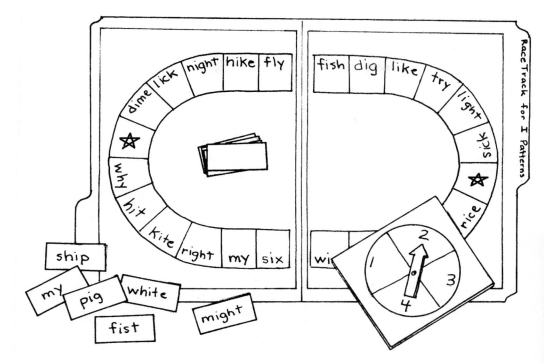

FIGURE 6-8   Racetrack Games Are Popular, Easy to Make, and Simple to Play

Variations

This game can be used for any vowel patterns and serves as a good review of the many patterns for the different vowels. Generally limit your categories to five or six.

Adaptable for Other Stages

The Spelling Game 6-8

This game for two to four players can be used for any feature and is easily changed from week to week.

Materials

Use a follow-the-path gameboard, but leave the spaces blank except for several spaces where you may write directions such as Go Back 3 Spaces, Lose a Turn, and Go Ahead 2 Spaces. Add playing pieces and a spinner or die. Students use their own collection of words for the week.

1. Students roll or spin. Whoever has the highest number will start and play proceeds clockwise.
2. The second player draws a card from the stack of words placed facedown. The player reads the word aloud to the first player who must spell the word aloud. If players spell correctly, they can spin or roll to move around the path. If they misspell the word they cannot move.
3. The winner is the first one to get to the end of the path.

Variations

This game can be used with word families, short vowels, and multisyllabic words as well as the many one-syllable words explored in the within word pattern stage.

Within Word Pattern Stage

The Classic Card Game 6-9

This card game is a favorite for two to five players; three is optimal. The many variations show the game's versatility.*

Materials

Use known words representing the vowel patterns you wish to review. For card games, write the words at the top of the word card so students can easily see them in their hand. If students have trouble holding the cards in one hand as a fan, the players usually agree to lay them out and not to look at each other's words. You may actually prefer that students play in this way so that they get more practice with the words.

Procedures

1. Each player gets seven cards.
2. Roll the dice to see who goes first.
3. The first player places a card down, reads the word, and designates the vowel pattern to be followed, for example, *rain, ai.*
4. The next player places a card down with the *ai* pattern and reads it aloud.
5. The play continues around the circle until all of the players are out of *ai* pattern word cards.
6. Players pass if they do not have a word card to match the category.
7. Players forfeit a turn if they do not read their contribution correctly.
8. The player who last played the pattern card begins the new round. This player chooses a different card from his or her hand, places it in the middle, and declares what vowel pattern is to be followed.
9. The object of the game is to be the first player to play all your cards.

Variations

1. Students who do not have a match must draw from the remaining cards until a match is found.
2. Wild cards can be added so players can change categories in midstream.
3. Write words arranged by pattern in the word study notebooks.
4. The rules of the game can be expanded to include parts of speech (e.g., nouns, adjectives, verbs).

Computer Sorts, Materials, and Games 6-10

The amount of phonics materials and games on the market offers a wide range of materials, from stand-alone electronic games to free software found on the World Wide Web. A search engine will yield many word study resources (search "word study," "phonics," or the actual feature you want to study).

Word sorts on computer.   Computer word sorts is an exciting area of growth. A fair amount of free software is available. For example, the BBC has made game-oriented software available. Another site is maintained by Sadlier-Oxford. The difficult part is to choose the contrasts you want. To sort for *oa* contrasted to *oo* is a great activity if the student is toward the end of this stage and has studied these patterns already.

---

*This game is a McGuffey Reading Center classic that has been recorded by Cindy Aldrete-Frazer.

Link to the BBC and Sadlier-Oxford site from the Weblinks on our Companion Website at www.prenhall.com/bear

Students in the within word pattern stage sort words on the computer with a software program called Word Sort. This software was developed by Ed Henderson, his son, and several students. It is suitable for students in the within word pattern stage because the 215 sorts focus on long-vowel patterns. The teacher's guide and disk contain a management system. A student report form is included as well as ways for teachers to compile ongoing class profiles. Teachers also can check students' accuracy and fluency in sorting. Analyses of students' sorts and printouts of class profiles are possible. Students enjoy this independent activity, especially the timed version. Mac and PC versions are available.

 For information on obtaining the Word Sort software (a limited number of sorts are free), link to their website from the Weblinks on our Companion Website at www.prenhall.com/bear

Word sort materials.   A search on the World Wide Web provides a variety of materials that teachers post for free and to purchase.

The *Words Their Way* CD contains numerous sorts and word study games arranged by stage of development and the chapters in this book. For example, Turkey Feathers is one game that you can print out from this CD. There are picture and word sorts for each long vowel, the complex consonant clusters, dipthongs, and other vowels, as well as a series of word sorts in Spanish.

Computer word games.   There are many computer word games that can be useful. Word Muncher (MECC) is especially good and asks students to listen for sounds and patterns. In choosing software, be sure the games use words that students can read, patterns that they need to study, and that allow a fast enough pace. Look for software in which students match words by sound and spelling patterns. In the classroom be sure that the word study games do not take away time students need for writing and reading. Davidson, Hartley, and Heartsoft are active in the production of word study software. Most basal reading and spelling companies offer similar software with their programs.

The ways students use software can be adapted so that they examine spelling and sounds. Many games ask students to recognize whether two words rhyme. In such games, students can write the words and arrange them by columns in word study notebooks according to orthographic patterns, for example, CVVC, CVV, and CV.

Letter Spin 6-11

Players spin for a feature and remove pictures or words from their gameboards that match the feature. For pictures, the features are sounds (long -*o*, short -*o*, long -*i*). For words, the features are patterns (*o, oa, o-e, ow*).

Materials

You will need the following items.

1. A spinner divided into three to six sections and labeled with the patterns to be practiced (see directions for making the spinner in the Appendix).
2. A collection of picture or word cards turned facedown in a deck.
3. Playing boards divided like a Tic-Tac-Toe board. Use a 9-by-9-inch board for 3-by-3-inch pictures (see Figure 6-9). The game can be played without the board by simply laying out the word cards in a 3-by-3 array.

Adaptable for Other Stages

Within Word Pattern Stage

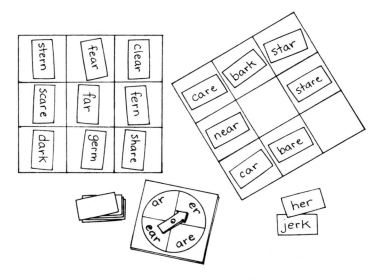

FIGURE 6-9   Letter Spin Game: Finding Words to Match the Spinner

Procedures

1. Players draw nine cards and turn them faceup on their boards or in a 3-by-3 array.
2. The first player spins and removes the picture or word cards that fit the sound or pattern indicated by the spinner. The cards go into the player's "point pile." That same player draws enough cards from the pile to replace the gaps in the playing board before play moves to the next player.
3. Play continues until a player has removed all cards and there are no more to be drawn as replacements. The player who has the most cards in their point pile wins.

Variations

1. Following is a Tic-Tac-Toe version: Players prepare boards as described, but when they spin they can turn facedown one picture that has that feature. The winner is the one who turns down three in a row. Blackout is a longer version of Tic-Tac-Toe. Players turn over their cards. The player who turns over all of the words on the board wins.
2. This game can be used to study initial sounds and blends. The spinner and the pictures change accordingly.
3. A large cube (1-inch square) is used like a die instead of a spinner. Use sticky dots to label the sides with the different features.

Board Game with Sheep in a Jeep 6-12

This activity features *Sheep in a Jeep* (by N. Shaw, illustrated by M. Apple). In this game, two people examine two CVVC patterns (e.g., *ee* and *ea*).*

Materials

1. Prepare a gameboard using a follow-the-path template as shown in Figure 6-10. Write words from the book as well as other words with the same patterns in each space.
2. You will need a spinner with numbers 1 through 4 (see directions for spinners in the Appendix), playing pieces to move around the board, and a pencil and small piece of paper for each player.

---

*Alison Dwier-Seldon developed this game.

FIGURE 6-10 Board Game for *Sheep in a Jeep*

Procedures

1. After reading *Sheep in a Jeep* and sorting words with the *ee* and *ea* patterns, players move to the board game and place game markers at the start position.
2. One player spins and moves that number of spaces on the board.
3. The player reads the word on the space. A player moves back a space if he or she reads the word incorrectly. Students "add a sheep to the jeep" by saying or writing a word that rhymes with their word from the gameboard.
4. Players alternate turns. The first player to the finish wins.

Variations

1. Players can move two or three times around the board.
2. Students hunt for these words or words that follow the same patterns in other texts.

Jeopardy Game 6-13

In this game, four or five students recall and spell words that follow a particular pattern, for example, the final *ch* pattern. A poster board is divided into 5-by-5-inch sections such as the one shown in Figure 6-11, and clue cards are placed in each space.* One side of each card holds a clue about a word in that category; the other side shows an amount (100 to 500).

Procedures

1. One player is the moderator or game host. The others roll the dice to determine who goes first.
2. The game begins when the first player picks a category and an amount for the moderator to read, for example, "I'll take short vowels for 100." The moderator reads the

---

*This game was contributed by Charlotte Tucker.

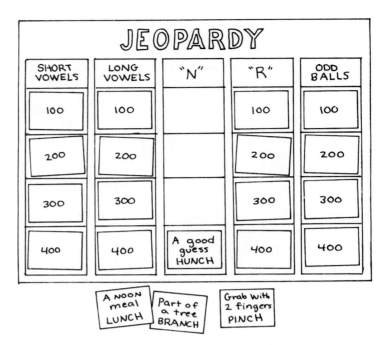

FIGURE 6-11   Word Jeopardy Game: "I'll Take Long Vowels for 100"

clue and the player must respond by phrasing a question and spelling the word. For example:

Moderator: "When struck it produces fire."

Player: "What is a match? m-a-t-c-h."

3. The player receives the card if the answer is correct. This player chooses another clue. (A player can only have two consecutive turns.) If the player misses, the player to the left may answer.

4. The game continues until all the clue cards are read and won or left unanswered. Players add their points, and the one with the highest amount wins.

Word lists.   Here are a few words that would be used to study words ending in *ch* and *tch*. A more complete list of words can be found in the Appendix.

R	N	Short Vowels	Long Vowels	Oddballs
march	bench	stitch	beach	much
perch	lunch	watch	teach	such
porch	branch	sketch	roach	rich
torch	pinch	witch	coach	

Word Study Scattergories 6-14

This is an independent activity for three to five students for review of patterns. Students make a list of words that follow a pattern (*at*/*flat*). Students read their answers and earn a point when their word is different than the other players' words.*

Materials

Prepare gamecards as shown in Figure 6-12. These can be used for five games. The answer sheet shown in the figure can be used for three games.

---

*Brenda Reibel adapted Scattergories by Milton Bradley Company for this fast moving word study game.

```
GAMECARD

ONE          TWO          THREE        FOUR         FIVE
 1. at        1. et        1. ig        1. og        1. ug
 2. ad        2. en        2. in        2. ot        2. ut
 3. an        3. est       3. it        3. op        3. us
 4. al        4. el        4. ing       4. ope       4. ute
 5. ame       5. ea        5. ice       5. or        5. ew
 6. ai        6. ear       6. ite       6. oo        6. ur
 7. ay        7. ee        7. ile       7. oi        7. ue
 8. ar        8. ie        8. igh       8. ow        8. ui
 9. aw        9. ew        9. ir        9. ou        9. un
10. atch     10. er       10. y        10. oy       10. ush

ANSWER SHEET

   ONE                TWO                  THREE
 1.(flat)          1. hat              1. chat
 2.(glad)          2. had              2. mad
 3. man            3.(plan)            3. tan
 4. walk           4. chalk            4.(final)
 5. game           5. blame            5. same
 6.(pain)          6. wait             6. straight
 7. pay            7. play             7. today
 8. car            8. star             8. farther
 9.(claw)          9. saw              9. straw
10. match         10. catch           10. hatch
TOTAL  4            3                    4
```

FIGURE 6-12 Word Study Scattergories Gamecard and the Answer Sheet

Procedures

The game is played in three rounds.

1. Each player has a Scattergories word study game card and an answer sheet.
2. The timer is set for 2 minutes.
3. All players quickly fill in the first column of their answer sheet using the patterns in the first column of the game card. Answers must fit the category and must use the vowel pattern given.
4. Scoring a round: Players take turns reading their answers aloud for each number. Players score their own answer sheets by circling an acceptable answer that does *not* match any other player's answer. Continue reading answers until all 10 categories have been scored. Score one point for each circled answer. Record the score at the bottom of the column of the answer sheet.
5. Starting a new round: Set the timer again; continue playing using the *same* category list as in the previous round. Fill in the next column with new answers.
6. Winning the game: After three rounds, players total the three scores on their answer sheets. The player with the highest score is the winner.
7. Rules for acceptable answers: The same answer *cannot* be given twice in one round. A player cannot answer *push* for both *us* and *ush*.
8. Challenging answers: While answers are being read, other players may challenge their acceptability. When an answer is challenged, all players vote on whether it is acceptable. Players who accept the answer give a thumbs-up sign. Players who do not accept the answer give a thumbs-down sign. Majority rules. In the case of a tie, the challenged player's vote does not count.

Variations

Create additional cards to use to play Word Study Scattergories.

Building Word Categories 6-15

Word cards are the playing cards in this matching game. Up to four students practice grouping short- and long-vowel words by pattern (sight, sound, and meaning). Older students like this game because of the poker terms.*

Materials

A deck of 45 cards is needed. The patterns can vary. A good starting combination is a blend of five cards of each short vowel (CVC) and five cards of each long vowel except for *e* in the CVCe pattern because there are so few words in that category (e.g., *Pete*).

Procedures

1. Five cards are dealt to each player. Players look in their hands for patterns.
2. Unwanted cards are discarded, and new cards are drawn to keep a hand of five cards. For example, *bone, rope, rat, pet, rake* could be one player's hand. This player may want to discard *rat, pet,* and *rake,* and draw three other cards to possibly create a better hand.
3. Each player has a chance to draw up to four cards from the deck one time to create a better hand.
4. The possible combinations are a pair (*hat, rat*); two pairs (*hat, rat, bone, tone*); three of a kind (*bone, phone, tone*); four of a kind (*phone, bone, tone, cone*); three of a kind plus a pair (*bone, phone, tone, rope, mope*); or five of a kind (*phone, bone, tone, cone, drone*). In poker, three of a kind plus a pair combination is a full house, and five of a kind is a flush.
5. Determining winners: Five of a kind beats three of a kind with a pair, four of a kind, three of a kind, two pairs, and a pair. Four of a kind beats everything except five of a kind. Two pairs beats three of a kind and a pair. Three of a kind beats two pairs, and a pair wins if it is the highest matching family. In case of ties, players can draw from the deck until one player comes up with a card that will break the tie.

Variations

1. Using guide words, students sort the words in their hands.
2. Pictures can be sorted with the words.
3. Wild cards can be included.

Declare Your Category! 6-16

One player finds a way to match a guide word and the other players have to guess how the words are categorized. This game is for two to five players (three is optimal) to study long-vowel patterns.

Materials

Combine long-vowel words from the word lists in the Appendix. You will need 45 word cards from the vowels students have studied.

---

*Fran de Maio recorded the directions to this traditional game.

Procedures

This is similar to the Classic Card Game in activity 6-9, but a little more complex. It works best with students who have had some experience playing games. In this game, players guess the first player's category.

1. Seven cards are dealt to each player and the remainder are placed facedown as a draw pile. Players lay out their seven cards. Players should always have seven cards.

2. The first player turns up a card (*home*) from the draw pile in the middle and looks for a word in his or her hand to match (*bone*). If the player can match the guide word in some way, he or she puts the card underneath the guide word. This player becomes the judge for the other players as they try to match the guide word and the way this first player matched the words. The player who started the category keeps the sorting strategy a secret, and waits until the last player puts a card down to declare the category. To keep the starter from changing categories, he or she can write down the reason for the match: "*Home* and *bone* are both long -*o* words and have the same pattern, the CVCe."

3. The next player places a card down underneath the guide word and reads the new word aloud. (*Tone* would be acceptable because they are both long -*o* and CVCe words. *Gone* would be unacceptable because it only looks like *home*, but does not have the long -*o* sound.) What happens if the person who set up the category does not think the next player put down an acceptable card? The person who established the category is the judge and can send a card back and give that player another chance. Mistakes by the judge are discussed at the end of the game.

4. The play continues around the circle until players stop putting words down to fit the pattern. Players can pass when they wish.

5. The player who plays the last card reads the list and then has to declare the category. If the last player has correctly guessed the category established by the first player, then the last player to lay down a card keeps the words. If the last player's guess is wrong, the previous player gets a chance to declare the category.

6. At the end of each round, students are dealt enough cards to get them back to seven. The player to the left of the winner of the round turns up a card from the pile, and is the person who makes up the category.

7. The player with the most cards wins.

Variations

1. Add wild cards to the pile to change categories in midstream. The person who establishes a new category must guess the original category correctly. This player becomes the new judge: "Your sort was by words that sound like *bone* and look like *bone*. I am putting down my wild card, and laying down *loan*. Guess my category."

2. The rules of the game can be expanded to include semantic (e.g., types of birds) and grammatical (e.g., nouns) categories.

Home Sorts 6-17

In Chapter 3 there is a letter for parents describing homework routines for each day of the week. These routines are especially appropriate for within word pattern spellers and homework will provide much needed extra practice. A checklist such as the one in Figure 6-13 can be used to monitor homework.

Materials

Copy an extra word study sheet for each student, and provide a baggy for the home sort. Insert the handout in the baggies.

Name _____

Word Work at Home—Check off those you do and return this to your teacher

_____ Sort the words again in the same categories you did in school.

_____ Write the words in categories as you copy the words.

_____ Do a no-peeking sort with someone at home.

_____ Write the words into categories as someone calls them aloud.

_____ Find more words in your reading that have the same sound and/or pattern.
      Write them here:

Signature of Parent _____

FIGURE 6-13   Homework Checklist

Procedures

Send home an extra work study sheet and checklist. Students complete each activity, check it off and return the checklist on Friday signed by a parent. Students might be allowed to choose 2 or 3 activities and more options can be added to the checklist occasionally, such as using a small number of words in sentences.

Word Study Trivial Pursuit 6-18

This game is designed for up to four players and one referee. After initial introduction by the teacher, students can play the game independently. This game works particularly well when two or more long vowels are part of the list and has students focus on sound and patterns.*

Materials

You will need poster board, $1\frac{1}{2}$-inch squares of construction paper in four different colors, word cards for the spelling concept being studied, envelopes made from the four colors of construction paper (or plastic bags), die or spinner, and game piece markers.

Procedures

1. To construct the gameboard, glue squares of colored construction paper onto the poster board, alternating colors and making a trail from start to finish covering the entire board.
2. Make four envelopes to hold four different packets of word cards out of construction paper corresponding to the four colors on the game board (red squares and red envelope, orange squares and orange envelope, brown squares and brown envelope, green squares and green envelope). You can also use color swatches or colored stickers on plastic bags.

To Play

1. Players pick order by spinning or tossing the die. The winner chooses a color; each player in turn selects a color.

---

*This version of Trivial Pursuit was developed by Rita Loyacono.

2. Players take the packet of word cards corresponding to their color and call these words out when another player lands on their respective color. If players land on their own color, they may take another turn. When a student lands on a space where there is already another card, the player sorts by pattern as well, placing a word that sounds alike and looks alike on top of the word or to the side if it sounds alike but does not look the same.

   For example, suppose Adam spins a five and lands on a green square. If he is not holding the green packet, the person with the green packet calls out a word. Adam spells the word correctly, and the card is placed faceup next to the caller. Bonnie takes a turn and also lands on a green square. After successfully spelling her word, she must decide if it is to be placed on top of the first word (follows the same pattern) or beside it (is a different pattern). The players continue, starting a new pile when necessary. In this way, they spell the words as well as sort them by pattern.

   Whichever color the player lands on is the packet from which the word is chosen for the player to spell and sort, unless it is the player's own color.

3. Players who misspell the word must go back one square and try a word from that color providing it is not their own color (in which case they move back two squares). If players are unable to spell that word, they remain where they are and lose one turn. If players are unable to sort the word properly, they must move back one space (again providing it is not their color, if so, two spaces), but do not lose a turn. The first player to get to the finish square is the winner and will be referee the next time. Since the students have been previously exposed to the pattern in the pockets and are approaching automaticity, there should be few spelling or sorting mistakes.

Variations

1. This game is *only* for word sorting (without the spelling practice). In this variation, players present the word instead of calling it out for another player, and the player reads the word and sorts it.
2. The game is played with four different categories of words, one for each envelope, or with three categories and the fourth color being the free space, or with two patterns divided up between the four envelopes.
3. Since neither the gameboard nor the envelopes would be marked, the board can be used for any word patterns that are being studied. Having several sets of the game allows different groups of five students to play the same game while practicing different patterns. Refer to the word sorting lists to develop sets.

Word Study UNO 6-19

This game uses word cards, and students group patterns together. This game is for three to four players.*

Materials

Make six Wild cards, six Skip cards, six Draw 2 cards, and 27 word cards. Use the word lists in the Appendix. For example, if students are studying long -*o* patterns, create two of each of the following cards:

Skip	*o-e*	Draw 2	*o-e*
Skip	*ow*	Draw 2	*ow*
Skip	*oa*	Draw 2	*oa*

---

*Rita Loyacono developed this word study version of the UNO game.

Procedures

1. Model this game in a small group. Cards are shuffled and the dealer deals five cards to each player. The remaining cards are placed facedown and the top card is turned faceup.
2. Players alternate and discard a card that changes only one letter at a time, or by playing one of the special cards (Skip, Draw 2, Wild). Here is a good example: If the beginning card was *boat*, the player could discard *soap, road,* or *goat*. A player who did not have one of those cards, or chose not to use one of those, could discard a Skip or Draw 2 card. The Skip card indicates that the next player cannot discard. The Draw 2 card forces the next player to pick two cards from the pile, and no cards may be discarded.
3. Skip, Draw 2, and Wild cards may be used successively to move from one pattern to another. A player who cannot discard must draw from the pile. Unless it is a Draw 2 situation, the player may discard if the card drawn follows the pattern.
4. As players alternate turns, they are attempting to discard all their cards. A player who has only one card remaining must say, "UNO." If the player forgets, another player can tell the player with one card to draw another card.
5. The first player to run out of cards wins the game.

Homophone Win, Lose, or Draw 6-20

Four or more students work in teams to draw and guess each others' words in a game that resembles charades.* A list of homophones can be found in the Appendix.

Procedures

1. Write homophone pairs on cards and shuffle.
2. Students divide the group into two equal teams, and one player from each team is selected as the artist for that round. The artist must draw a picture representing the given homophone which will elicit the homophone itself, the spelling, and the meaning.
3. A card is pulled from the deck and shown simultaneously to the artists for both teams. As the artists draw, their teammates call out possible answers. When the correct word is offered, the artist calls on someone to spell both words in a pair.
4. A point is awarded to the team that provides the correct information first. Play proceeds in the same fashion.

Adaptable for Other Stages

Homophone Rummy 6-21

This activity is suitable for two to six students. The object of the game is to discard all of the cards in one hand as well as to get the most number of homophone pairs or points (Figure 6-14).

Materials

Prepare several decks of homophone pairs (52 cards, 26 pairs). A list of homophones can be found in the Appendix. Select words your students know.

FIGURE 6-14   Homophone Rummy

---

*Barry Mahanes based this on the television show.

Procedures

1. Each player is dealt 10 cards (two players); 7 cards (three to four players); 6 cards (five to six players).
2. Players check their hands for already existing pairs. Once a pair is discovered, the meaning for each word is given in order to receive points. In giving definitions, the players may use the actual word in a sentence to show the meaning until they become well versed in homophone definitions; then, they must give a definition of the word separate from its use in a sentence or a synonym for the word. Each pair receives one point; any additional homophone for the pair receives an extra point.
3. The remainder of the deck is placed in a central location as the drawing pile in which the first card is turned up.
4. The person on the left of the dealer goes first. Each player draws from the deck or the discard pile. The player lays down any pairs as described in step 2. The player must then discard one card to end the turn.
   Note: If a card is taken from the discard line, all cards appearing below the card wanted also have to be taken. Also, the top card must be used.
5. The game is over when one player has no cards left. That person yells "Rummy!" Then the pairs are counted up.

Variations

1. Rather than having a random mix of homophone pairs, the decks can be divided into homophones by sound or syllable accent. This creates an opportunity to examine homophones by both sound and spelling patterns as well as syllable and accent patterns. Each deck of cards can consist of two to four contrasting sound patterns or syllable/accent patterns which the students must sort.
2. A player can be challenged by someone else disagreeing with the definitions. The person who challenges looks up the words in the dictionary. Whoever is right gets to keep the pair.
3. Each player can play off of other players' cards, receiving additional points for each homophone found.
4. If a player has a card that can be added to a set or sequence but does not realize it and discards it, another player detecting what happened can pick up the card discarded, and add it to a sequence. That player then gets to discard one card.
5. Homophone synonyms can be used in this game. For each homophone, a child has to come up with at least one synonym. For example, if the pair was *through* and *threw*, synonyms corresponding to this pair might be *finished* and *pitched*.

FIGURE 6-15 Terse Verse: Create a Clever Rhyme

Terse Verse Rhyme 6-22

In small groups, students think of rhyming pairs that describe an object, for example, *pink/sink, bear/lair, sled/bed.**

Procedures

Read *One Sun* (by B. McMillan, 1990) to the group. Discuss the structure of the language and the book. Students will see how the author uses photographs to illustrate the "terse verse."

Work with students to create a terse verse. First, think of an object (e.g., sink, bear, bed). Then ask the group to think of rhyming words that correspond with the object (see Figure 6-15). Accept all

*Carolyn Melchiorre developed this literature extension.

responses and write them on a chart. Continue this process with the group until they are confident they understand the task.

Students can create their own terse verse to challenge the group. They might opt to omit one word in the sequence:

> There's a _____ in the pail. (whale)
> The _____ is sad. (Dad)

Rhyming pairs collected from terse verse may be sorted by sound and pattern and may serve as the basis for other games.

Variations

1. Challenge students to draw a picture card and exchange with a friend who must figure out the terse verse.
2. For a real challenge, students use multisyllabic words.

Homophone Decks 6-23

A variety of games can be played with decks of homophone cards. The Homophone Deck is a series of decks arranged by difficulty. Developed by Marilyn Pryle and Jeff Cantrell, these decks are used by students to play games in which they match the words by patterns including Homophone Rummy, Homophone Go-Fish, and Homophone Memory.

 Decks are available from Dr. Jeffrey Cantrell, who can be contacted via the Weblinks at our Companion Website at www.prenhall.com/bear

Semantic Brainstorms 6-24

This small group activity focuses on the meaning of the words and serves as a great activity for content studies.

Procedures

1. Choose a topic for students to study. Topics can be chosen by students and can be related to content studies. Start with easy, familiar topics such as sports and locations (as well as countries, animal life, clothes, furniture, modes of transportation).
2. Students brainstorm related words and then record them. Look for fluency of the brainstorming to assess success. Using chart paper is a good way to record these sorts.
3. Students share their findings and see if they can come up with subcategories from their brainstorming. Categories can be circled by color or written over into columns.

Variations

1. Look in magazines, newspapers, and catalogs. Circle words that express feelings, color words, people's names, or parts of speech.
2. Organizing software (e.g., Inspiration) can be used to record these brainstorms in a chart form. Additional software, such as VISIO software for drawing graphics, can be used in the same way. You can record student responses within circles and rectangles using the drawing toolbar in PowerPoint software.

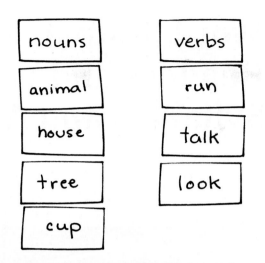

FIGURE 6-16 Grammatical Relations Can
Be Examined in Semantic Sorts

Semantic Sorts 6-25

Students work with content-related words to compare and contrast.

Procedures

1. Look through a chapter or unit in a textbook and make a list of the key terms. Often they are listed at the end of a unit. Make word cards for the words.
2. Students sort the words in an open sort, establishing their own categories. Start with easy and familiar topics.
3. The sorts are copied into word study notebooks in a separate section for that content area.

Variations

Grammatical Sorts is a variation in which students sort by parts of speech (see Figure 6-16). For example, students can collect nouns and then divide them into different types (e.g., things that move/animate versus stationary/ inanimate nouns).

cow	rock
boat	uranium
cats	plants

When students look for differences in the concepts, they begin to debate. In this easy example, one could even argue that there is something quite active about both uranium and plants.

7

Word Study for Intermediate Readers and Writers: The Syllables and Affixes Stage

As you learned in Chapter 1, the stages of word knowledge through which most students will move during the intermediate and middle grade years are termed *syllables and affixes* and *derivational relations*. Beginning in second and third grade for some students, and in fourth grade for most, cognitive and language potential allows children to make new and richer connections among the words they know and the words they will learn. In this chapter addressing syllables and affixes, and the next chapter addressing derivational relations, you will learn how teachers can establish a firm foundation in spelling and in vocabulary development as they facilitate students' move into understanding the role of structure and meaning in the spelling system.

As you teach students at these levels, you will find the whole enterprise of learning about words to be fascinating as well as never ending. This awareness can sustain your own interest and delight in words and in what your students will be learning about words. As at earlier stages, you will facilitate students' word explorations to help them discover the patterns of sound, spelling, and meaning that link thousands of words. This knowledge will help them read, write, and spell much more effectively.

Before we talk in detail about the features of study in this stage, let us visit Sharon Lee's fourth-grade classroom in midyear. Sharon has a range of abilities in her classroom that are evident in both reading levels and spelling inventory results. She has a large group of 14 students who fall into the syllables and affixes stage, 4 students who remain in the within word pattern stage, and 5 students who are in derivational relations. She makes time to meet with the within word pattern group several times a week for systematic word study, whereas the derivational relations group works independently in their word study a good amount of time. Sharon tries to meet with the derivational relations group at least twice a week. In the following vignette, Sharon calls for the attention of the larger syllables and affixes group at the front of the room for a 20-minute lesson while the rest of the students find comfortable places to read and discuss in the "Book Club" format (Raphael, Highfield, & McMahon, 1997). The syllables and affixes students are studying final *ar/er/or* syllable spelling. This final unaccented syllable poses a challenge for spellers because it is pronounced the same, /ə + r/, across different spellings. Notice how Sharon models for students where to focus their attention in examining two-syllable words:

In preparation for a directed spelling thinking activity (Zutell, 1996), Sharon begins her word study unit for this week by asking her students to spell three words: *dollar, faster,* and *actor.* She then calls on several students to tell how they spelled each word as she writes their answers on the overhead transparency, encouraging a variety of answers. The results include DOLLER, DOLLOR, DOLLAR, FASTER, ACTER, ACTOR. Sharon then "thinks aloud": "Hmmm . . . . This is very interesting. We agree on how to spell the first syllable of each word, but we don't agree about how to spell the final syllable. What makes this part hard?" Jason volunteers that the words sound the same at the end. "Do the rest of you agree?" Sharon asks. "Let's say each word and listen carefully. Do they sound alike? Let's find out if this is true for other words as well."

Sharon has made a transparency of the weekly word sort and cut it apart to sort on the overhead projector.

She discusses *blister* and *mayor* with the students to make sure they are clear on the words' meaning, and reviews the meaning of *lunar* and *solar,* words used in their recent study of space travel. Then she asks, "How might we sort these words?" Sara suggests that they sort by the last two letters. "Let's do that," Sharon responds, "and as we sort them, let's say them aloud and listen for the sound in the last syllable." Sharon removes all the words except *dollar, faster,* and *actor,* which she uses as key words for the sort. She then places each word in turn on the overhead and calls on a student to read it and tell her where to put it. The final sort resembles the one shown in Figure 7-1. Sharon asks the students, "What have we found out about these words?" Several students offer ideas, and Sharon summarizes by saying, "When we hear /ə + r/, the sound will not help us spell it, so we will have to concentrate on remembering whether it is spelled -ER, -OR, or -AR."

Sharon hands out the word sort for these words and goes over the students' word study assignments for the week. Students are expected to cut apart and sort the words independently and then write the word sort in their word study notebooks. While they do that, Sharon will meet with another group for word study. On other days they will work independently by sorting again with a buddy, sorting at home, and hunting for additional words in trade books to add to their lists. On Friday, Sharon will test them on these words but she will also call the group together to compile a large class list of the words they were able to find in their word hunts. This will be used to introduce the following week's lesson where students will be helped to discover that ER is the most common way to spell the final sound, that it is always used to spell comparative adjectives (*faster, smaller, longer*), and

 This is an excellent opportunity for clarifying meaning as well as spelling features. You may need to spend more time exploring these sounds and features, use fewer words, and look for opportunities to point out cognates (*lunar, solar*).

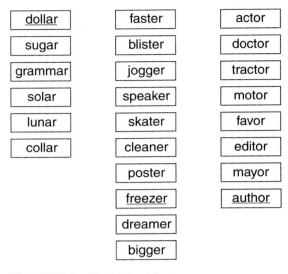

FIGURE 7-1   Final Word Sort

that ER and OR are often used to spell agents or people who do things (*teacher, worker, author, sailor*).

Sharon's lesson promotes two key ideas of this stage: (a) It demonstrates to students how much they already know about spelling a particular word—spelling is not an all-or-none affair where they "get a word wrong." Usually they will get most of the word correct, and teachers need to remind and reassure students about this. (b) It demonstrates to students what they need to focus on when they look at a word. Because they already know most of the word, they need to attend to the part that is still challenging.

LITERACY DEVELOPMENT AND INSTRUCTION FOR STUDENTS IN SYLLABLES AND AFFIXES STAGE

The intermediate stage is a time of expanding reading interests and fine-tuning reading strategies. In previous developmental stages, the challenges posed by reading stem more from children's ability to identify words than from their background knowledge about the topic or genre. At the intermediate and advanced levels, however, the challenges they encounter will come more from the conceptual load in whatever they are trying to read. Developing word knowledge allows them to read more fluently, which in turn allows them to exercise and expand their increasing level of cognitive and language sophistication.

When possible, word study should relate to the reading and writing that students are doing. Word study should emphasize how the structure or spelling of words is a direct clue to learning and remembering the meaning of words. The intermediate and middle grades are a critical time for consolidating knowledge about the spelling of words with knowledge about how this spelling represents meaning. Word study at the intermediate level should demonstrate to students how their word knowledge can be applied to advance their *spelling knowledge,* their *vocabulary,* and their *strategies* for figuring out unknown words. At the intermediate and middle grades, the following principles should guide instruction:

- Students should be *actively involved* in the exploration of words; they are then more likely to develop a positive attitude toward word learning and a curiosity about words.
- Students' *prior knowledge* should be engaged; this is especially important if they are learning the specialized vocabulary in different disciplines or content areas.
- Students should have *many exposures to words in meaningful contexts,* both in and out of connected text.
- Students should receive a sequence of teaching about structural elements and how these elements combine; elements include syllables, affixes, and the effects of affixes on the base words to which they are attached.

In previous chapters, the recommended spelling study has been limited to single-syllable words, even though students have been reading, and even writing, polysyllabic words for some time. Knowledge of vowel and consonant patterns within single-syllable words builds a foundation for the polysyllabic words of intermediate word study in much the same way that basic math facts build a foundation for long division. Once students have this foundation, they are ready to begin the study of polysyllabic words: syllables, affixes, base words, and how they combine. Major features of study at the syllables and affixes stage include the following:

1. How consonant and vowel patterns are represented in polysyllabic words
2. What occurs when syllables join together (syllable juncture)
3. How stress or lack of stress determines the clarity of the sounds in syllables
4. How simple affixes (prefixes and suffixes) change the usage, meaning, and spelling of words

When students attend to these types of features as they examine polysyllabic words, they are building their spelling efficiency. They are also developing more efficient word identification strategies as they become better at perceiving syllabic units and **meaning** or **morphemic** units—prefixes, suffixes, and base words—within polysyllabic words. One of your most important responsibilities for word study instruction at this stage is to engage students in examining how important word elements—prefixes, suffixes, and base words—combine; this understanding is a powerful tool for vocabulary development, spelling, and figuring out unfamiliar words during reading. You can directly show students how to apply this knowledge by modeling the following strategy for analyzing unfamiliar words in their reading that they cannot identify after attempting to sound them out:

1. Examine the word for meaningful parts—base word, prefixes, or suffixes.
   - If there is a prefix, take it off first.
   - If there is a suffix, take it off second.
   - Look at the base to see if you know it or if you can think of a related word (a word that has the same base).
   - Reassemble the word, thinking about the meaning contributed by the base, the suffix, and then the prefix. This should give you a more specific idea of what the word is.
2. Try out the meaning in the sentence; check if it makes sense in the context of the sentence and the larger context of the text that is being read.
3. If the word still does not make sense and is critical to the meaning of the overall passage, look it up in the dictionary.
4. Record the new word in your word study notebook.

Let us take a look at how Sharon Lee models this process for students, beginning with a familiar word, and then extending the lesson to an unfamiliar word:

"I've underlined one of the words in this sentence: They had to redo the pro-grams after they were printed with a spelling error. What does redo mean? Yes, Adrienne?"

"When you have to do something over again?"

"Okay! So you already had done something once, right? Now, let's cover up this first part of the word [covers re]. What word do we have? Right—do. Now, let's look at these words."

Sharon writes the words join, tell, and organize on the board, then the prefix re- in front of each base word as she pronounces the new word. "When we join the prefix re- to each of them, what happens? Right! We are going to be doing these things again—we can rejoin a group, retell a story, reorganize our classroom." She then asks the students what they think the prefix re- means. After a brief discussion, she asks a student to look up the prefix in the dictionary to check their definitions.

Sharon's next step is to model this strategy with a word she is fairly certain the students do not yet know. She shows the following sentence on the overhead:

As they got closer to the front of the line, her friends had to reassure Tanya that the Big Thunder roller coaster ride was safe.

"Okay," Sharon proceeds, "I've underlined this word [pointing to reassure]. Any ideas what this word is?" Most students shake their heads; Kaitlin squinches up her face as she slowly pronounces "REE - sure." "Good try, Kaitlin," Sharon responds. "You're trying to pronounce it, but it doesn't sound like a word we've heard before. What about the beginning of the word, though? Could that be the prefix we've just been thinking about?"

This prompt works for the students and they start trying to pronounce the base, assure, without the prefix re-. "Right," Sharon encourages. "You've taken off the pre-fix, re-, and are trying to figure out the base word. Any ideas?" Though a couple of students are pronouncing assure correctly, they are uncertain about its meaning.

Sharon continues: "Well, we know that, whatever assure means, the prefix re- means it's being done again! Let's look back at the sentence. Do you think Tanya can't wait to go on the roller coaster—or is she beginning to be worried?" After some discussion with the students, Sharon talks about the base word, assure, and explains that Tanya's friends had probably already talked with her about how safe the roller coaster was, that there had never been any accidents, had helped Tanya to feel more confident about going on the ride—assured her—that Big Thunder was safe. [Most students are nodding their heads now, saying things such as "Oh, yeah, I've heard that word before."] As Tanya and her friends got closer to actually go-ing on the roller coaster, however, they had to assure her again—reassure her.

Sharon summarizes: "Most of the time, by looking carefully at a word you don't know—looking for any prefixes, suffixes, and thinking about the base—you can get pretty close to the actual meaning of the word. Then ask yourself if this meaning makes sense in the sentence and text that you're reading."

It is critical to model and reinforce this strategic approach to analyzing unfamiliar words in text, and students need plenty of opportunities to try it out under your guid-ance. Encourage them to talk about their ideas as they apply the process so that you can encourage, facilitate, and redirect as necessary. In addition to helping students read through texts with more ease, this strategy will become one of the most effective means of developing and extending their vocabulary knowledge. It is also important, however, to model what to do when the process does not yield an appropriate mean-ing for the unfamiliar word—analyzing repel into re + pel will not be of much help to intermediate students—and when the dictionary needs to be consulted.

The dictionary offers opportunities for determining the precise meaning of a word students need to know in their reading as well as for understanding a word deeply.

For example, based on Robyn Montana Turner's biography of Faith Ringgold, Sharon Lee focuses on the word *enhancing* in the sentence, "Faith Ringgold decided to use cloth frames as a way of enhancing her art." Pronouncing the word does not seem to help, because it is not in the students' speaking/listening vocabularies. Sharon talks about the context in which the word occurs; it may narrow the possibilities somewhat, but possible meanings suggested by the context might include, for example, "protecting" or "showing." This is definitely a situation in which the dictionary will be of use.

> Sharon underlines the word *enhancing* and explains that, to check the meaning of this word in the dictionary, they would need to look up the base word, *enhance*. Reminding the students that they may need to watch out for changes in spelling when they are trying to figure out the base word for an unfamiliar word, she notes that the *e* is dropped when the *-ing* is added. Looking up a base word also helps to highlight the spelling of other forms of the word.
>
> The dictionary definition for *enhance* is "to make greater, as in value, beauty, or reputation." Sharon has the students return to the sentence in the text and discuss which of these features they believe Faith Ringgold had in mind when she decided to use cloth frames. The students agree that, in the context of the sentence and the overall text, Faith Ringgold probably wanted to make her quilts more "beautiful."

Dictionaries can also provide helpful information about the history of a word and make explicit the interrelationships among words in the same meaning "families." For example, a discussion of run-on entries illustrates how one word's entry can include information about words related in spelling and meaning—the entry for *entrap*, for example, also includes *entraps* and *entrapment*. Boxes labeled "Usage Notes," "Synonyms," and "Word History" provide important information about the appropriateness of particular words, subtle but important differences among the meanings of words, and stories that explain spellings and extend *deep* understanding of important terms.

You will notice that authors of many textbooks try to provide a rich context to support new vocabulary as well as highlighting important new terms for the reader. Although students need to learn about these features, they also need to learn the strategy discussed here so that they can grow confidently and competently into independent word learners. This strategy depends critically on the students' knowledge of word structure. Adams (1990) best emphasized this importance:

> Learning from context is a very, very important component of vocabulary acquisition. But this means of learning is available only to the extent that children . . . bother to process the spelling—the orthographic structure—of the unknown words they encounter. Where they skip over an unknown word without attending to it, and often readers do, no learning can occur. (p. 150)

CHARACTERISTICS OF ORTHOGRAPHIC DEVELOPMENT DURING THE SYLLABLES AND AFFIXES STAGE

In Chapter 1 we described some of the characteristic errors made by students in this stage and the spelling issues they will need to explore (see Table 1-4). Table 7-1 provides a more fine-grained analysis of some representative errors by students in the early and middle/late syllables and affixes stage. In the spelling of CROLL or CRAUL for *crawl* and ERLY or EIRLY for *early*, we can see lingering confusions with less common or ambiguous vowel patterns. The spellings of HOPING for *hopping*, SKIPING for *skipping*, and PERRADDING for *parading* reveal that the student knows how to

TABLE 7-1	Examples of Spelling at the Syllables and Affixes Stage		
Early		**Middle/Late**	
hopping	HOPING	barber	BARBAR
crawl	CROLL, CRAUL	helmet	HELMIT, HELMENT
dollar	DOLER	skipping	SKIPING
useful	USFUL, USFULL	ugly	UGLEY
circle	CIRCEL, CIRCILE	hurry	HEARY, HURREY
early	ERLY, EIRLY	traced	TRAISSED
keeper	KEPER, KEPPER	parading	PERADDING, PARRADING
		damage	DAMIGE, DAMADGE

spell the *ing* suffix but lacks knowledge about the doubling rule where syllables join. Other syllable juncture problems can be seen in the using but confusing of doubled letters in KEPPER for *keeper* and DOLER for *dollar*. Problems with unaccented final syllables are evident in BARBAR for *barber*, CIRCEL for *circle*, HELMIT for *helmet*, and DAMIGE for *damage*. In TRAISSED for *traced* and KEPER for *keeper*, the student may have relied upon sound rather than prior knowledge of the meaning and spelling of the base word.

Students should learn several important concepts during this stage. We explore these concepts here in a way that will also give you ideas about how to introduce the concepts to your students. A sequence of word study during this stage is presented in Table 7-2. This sequence touches on the important patterns and features to consider, and is based on what students do developmentally.

Compound Words

When students explore compound words, they can develop several types of understandings. First, they learn how words can combine in different ways to form new words (*sunlight, lightweight*). This is an introduction to the combinatorial features of English words. Second, they lay the foundation for explicit attention to syllables, because so often compound words comprise two smaller words, each of which is a single syllable. Third, students reinforce their knowledge of the spelling of many high frequency, high utility words in English, because these words include so many compound words. Look in the activities section for specific ideas related to the study of compound words.

Base Words and Inflectional Endings/Suffixes

Inflectional endings or suffixes include *-s, -ed,* and *-ing.* These suffixes change the number and tense of the base word, but do not change the meaning or part of speech. To help students learn about syllable juncture and about base words, begin with **inflectional endings.** The basic rule for adding inflectional suffixes is: *When a suffix beginning with a vowel is added to a base word containing a short vowel followed by a single consonant, double the final consonant.*

The doubling rule has few exceptions and is worth learning. It does takes time, however, for students to develop a firm understanding of it. Rather than teaching rules, we suggest a series of word sorts that will allow children to discover the many principles at

TABLE 7-2   Sequence of Word Study: Syllables and Affixes

Early

Plural endings -s and -es	*books/dishes*
Compound Words	*pancake, sidewalk*
Inflectional Endings	
Sort by sound of -*ed* suffix	*walked* /t/, *wagged* /d/, *shouted* /ed/
Doubling	*stopping, stopped* (CVC)
E drop	*skating, skated* (CVCe)
No change	*walking, walked* (CVCC) and *nailing, nailed* (CVVC)
Change final *y* to *i* and add -*ed* or -*s*	*cried* (*y* after a consonant), *plays* (*y* after a vowel)
Ambiguous Vowels in One-Syllable Words—Diphthongs	
/ô/	**haul, straw, thought**
/oi/	en**joy, embroi**der
/ou/	m**ou**ntain, ch**ow**der

Middle

Open and Closed Syllables	
VCCV doublet at juncture	*button, happy*
VCCV different consonants at juncture	*window, sister*
V/CV open with long vowel	*bacon, lazy*
VC/V closed with short vowel	*river, camel*
VCCCV blend or digraph at juncture	*pilgrim, tangle*
Vowel Patterns in Accented Syllables	
Familiar vowel patterns in accented syllable	*beyond, lonely, toaster, owner*
Less familiar and ambiguous vowels in accented syllables	*fountain, powder, laundry, awful, marble, prepare, repair, narrow*
Final Unaccented Syllables	
ə + *r*	*beggar/barber/actor*
ə + *n*	*captain/human/frighten/basin/apron*
ə + *l*	*angel/able/central/civil/fertile*
/cher/	*culture, measure, teacher*
Spelling /j/	*badger/major/village*
Two-syllable homophones	*pedal, petal, peddle*
Two-syllable homographs	**reb**el/re**bel**
Plurals that involve changing *y* to *i*	*babies, monkeys*
Unusual Plurals	*goose/geese, fish, knife/knives*

Late

Simple Prefixes and Base Words	*un* (not—*unlock*), *re* (again—*remake*), *dis* (opposite—*dismiss*), *in* (not—*indecent*),* *non* (not—*nonfiction*), *mis* (wrong—*misfire*), *pre* (before—*preview*), *uni* (one—*unicycle*), *bi* (two—*bicycle*), *tri* (three—*tricycle*)
Simple Suffixes	-*y* (adjective—like, tending toward: *jumpy*), -*ly* (adverb—like: *gladly*), -*er*, -*est* (comparatives), -*ful* (full of, like: *graceful*), -*less* (without: *penniless*), -*ness* (condition—*happiness*)
Spelling-Meaning Connection	

*There are other meanings for *in*, but this is the most frequent and occurs more often in words at this level of reading.

work. In Figure 7-2, the students first sort the words by those that double and those that do not and are asked to underline the base word.

Sort 1		Sort 2		
		CVVC	CVCC	CVC
resting	jogging	reading	resting	jogging
reading	running	feeding	walking	running
feeding	shopping	sleeping	jumping	shopping
walking	winning	waiting	smelling	winning
sleeping	planning	raining	dressing	planning
jumping	skipping			skipping
waiting	sobbing			sobbing
smelling	hugging			snapping
dressing	snapping			

FIGURE 7-2   Adding Inflectional Ending to Base Words

Visit our Companion Website at www.prenhall.com/bear for a sort to address doubling.

In sort 2, sorting by the vowel pattern in the base word helps students discover that there are two conditions when the ending is simply added. This will help clear up the confusion of *smelling* and *dressing,* words that students may initially place in the doubled column. Table 7-3 summarizes the conditions that govern the addition of inflectional endings. The rules can get quite complicated, but when planning instruction, begin with the easiest in the early syllables and affixes stage (Numbers 1-4) and expect to reinforce these throughout elementary school and even beyond in the case of two- and three-syllable words (where the accent can vary between the last syllable and the next to last syllable). Remember, it will take time for children to master these generalizations and they should know the spelling of the base words before they are asked to think about how to add suffixes.

One of the earliest suffixes students learn to use is the plural, adding -*s* even when the sound it represents varies, as in *cats* and *bags.* However, plurals deserve to be addressed throughout this stage to cover additional issues.

1. Add -*es* when words end in *ch, sh, ss, s,* and *x.* When -*es* is added to a word, students can usually "hear" the difference because it adds another syllable to the word (*dish* becomes *dishes,* unlike *spoons*).
2. Change the *y* at the end of a word to *i* before adding -*es* when the word ends in a consonant + *y* (*baby* to *babies*), but not when it ends in a vowel + *y* (*monkeys*).
3. Some words change a final *f* or *fe* to *v* and add the suffix -*es* (*wife* to *wives, wolf* to *wolves*).
4. Some words change their internal spelling and pronunciation for the plural form, as in *goose* to *geese* and *mouse* to *mice,* and some words remain the same (*fish, sheep*).

(See sorts 63 and 64 for examples of word sorts with plurals.)

TABLE 7-3	Changes to Base Words When Adding Inflectional Endings or Other Suffixes That Start with a Vowel		
Base Words	+ ing	+ ed (or er)	+ s
1. CVVC Ex: *look*	No change Ex: *looking*	No change Ex: *looked*	No change Ex: *looks*
2. CVCC Ex: *walk*	No change Ex: *walking*	No change Ex: *walked*	No change Ex: *walks*
3. CVC Ex: *bat*	Double final letter Ex: *batting*	Double final letter Ex: *batted, batter*	No change Ex: *bats*
4. CVCe Ex: *rake*	Drop final -*e* Ex: *raking*	Drop final -*e* Ex: *raked*	No change Ex: *rakes*
5. Words that end in a consonant + *y* Ex: *cry*	No change Ex: *crying*	Change *y* to *i* Ex: *cried, crier*	Change *y* to *i* Ex: *cries*
6. Words that end in a vowel + *y* Ex: *play*	No change Ex: *playing*	No change Ex: *played*	No change Ex: *plays*
7. Two-syllable words accented on second syllable Ex: *admit, invite, apply, enjoy*	Follow rules for 1–6 Ex: *admitting, inviting, applying, enjoying*	Follow rules for 1–6 Ex: *admitted, invited, applied, enjoyed*	Follow rules for 1–6 Ex: *admits, invites, applies, enjoys*
8. Words that end in a *c* Ex: *panic*	Add a *k* Ex: *panicked*	Add a *k* Ex: *panicking*	No change Ex: *panics*

Note: Words ending in *x* do not double (e.g., *boxed, boxing*). Words that end in *ck* avoid having to double a final *k* (*blocked, blocking* versus *blokking*). Words that end in *ve* avoid having to double a final *v* (*loved, loving*).

 The Syllables and Affixes section of the accompanying CD-ROM contains numerous sorts appropriate for studying inflectional endings.

Open/Closed Syllables and Syllable Patterns

Why is Tigger, the tiger from *Winnie the Pooh*, spelled with two *g*s? How do you pronounce Caddie Woodlawn? Answering these questions depends on whether you are dealing with an open or a closed syllable. **Open syllables** end with a long-vowel sound: *tiger, Katy, reason.* **Closed syllables** contain a short-vowel sound that is usually "closed" by two consonants: *Tigger, Caddie, rabbit, racket.*

Most students in second and third grade learn the basics of open and closed syllables when they examine what happens when -*ed* and -*ing* are added to short- and long-vowel pattern words. Consider these examples:

hop + *ing* = **hop**p*ing*   *hope* + *ing* = **hop***ing*
strip + *ing* = **strip**p*ing*   *stripe* + *ing* = **strip***ing*

As Henderson (1985) explained, "The core principle of **syllable juncture** (bold added) is that of doubling consonants to mark the short English vowel" (p. 65). Students learn that when you are uncertain about whether to double the consonants at the juncture of

TABLE 7-4   Syllable Patterns

Label	Type	Examples
VCCV	Closed	*skipping, button, rubber* (doublets) *chapter, window, garden* (two different consonants)
V/CV	Open	*lazy, coma, beacon, bacon*
VC/V	Closed	*river, robin, cover, planet*
VCCCV	Closed	*laughter, pilgrim, instant, complain*
VV	Open	*create, riot, liar*

syllables, you should say the word and listen to the vowel sounds. If you hear a long sound, the syllable is open and will be followed by a single consonant. If you hear a short-vowel sound, the odds are likely that the syllable will need to be closed by two consonants. For example, if you are writing about how a rabbit moves along the ground (*hopping*) and do not double the *p,* you will wind up with an entirely different meaning (*hoping*). This knowledge about whether to double, developed first through examining base words plus inflectional suffixes, is later applied *within* base words: Because the vowel in the first syllable of *simmer* is short, the *m* is doubled; because the vowel in the first syllable of *hotel* is long, the *t* is not doubled.

Another way of describing what goes on at the juncture of syllables is through syllable **patterns.** For example *hopping, Tigger,* and *simmer* illustrate the VCCV syllable pattern; *hoping, tiger,* and *hotel* illustrate the VCV syllable pattern. Table 7-4 lists the common syllable patterns. The first two syllable patterns, the open V/CV pattern and the closed VCCV pattern, are the most frequent. The third pattern, the closed VC/V pattern, occurs less frequently than the others. The fourth pattern, the closed VCCCV pattern, is quite frequent. Words that follow this pattern include a consonant digraph or blend at the syllable juncture. If a blend occurs at the juncture, the word is divided before the blend (*pilgrim*); if a digraph is at the juncture, the word is divided after the digraph (*laugh-ter*). The VV pattern has each vowel contributing a sound; the word is usually divided after the long-vowel sound (*ri-ot, du-el*).

Figure 7-3 shows a sort that can be used to introduce syllable juncture patterns. You might start by sorting three to four words into each column in a Guess My Category activity. Begin asking students to help you sort the rest of the words. After sorting, ask the students how the words in column 1 are alike. Probe by asking them if anyone noticed the vowel sounds and where the words were "divided" when you pronounced them. Then go to column 2 and guide the students' examination in the same fashion.

After completing this first sort, the words in the second column could be sorted further by those that have different consonants at the juncture and those that have the same, as shown in Figure 7-4.

CV/C

baby
human
basic
bacon
music
silent

VCCV

contest
dinner
basket
summer
dentist
winter
kitten

FIGURE 7-3   Introducing Syllable Juncture Patterns

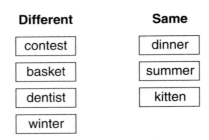

FIGURE 7-4   Different vs. Same Consonants at Syllable Junctures

The accompanying CD-ROM contains many activities you can use to reinforce your study of open and closed syllables.

maintain	dismay	debate
raisin	crayon	bracelet
dainty	decay	parade
trainer	layer	mistake
sailor	today	escape

FIGURE 7-5 Common Long -a Spellings in Two-Syllable Words

Vowel Patterns

All vowel patterns can be reexamined in two-syllable words as a way to review those patterns and extend students' understanding of how those patterns work in multisyllabic words. For example, look at the familiar long -*a* patterns in the sort in Figure 7-5.

There are a number of vowel patterns within single-syllable and polysyllabic words that are not sorted out until the upper elementary years—particularly those that spell diphthongs (see Table 7-2). These are often called **ambiguous vowels,** because they represent a range of sounds and spellings. For example, the /ô/ sound is the same in *cause, lawn,* and *false,* but is spelled three different ways. In contrast, the *ou* has four different sounds in *shout, touch, your,* and *thought.* These patterns are often cited as examples of the irregularity of English spelling, but word sorting allows students to see that they nevertheless represent categories like other vowel patterns (Johnston, 2001). As we saw in Chapter 6, by paying attention to the position of many ambiguous vowels, students can often determine which spelling pattern occurs most often. For example, *aw* and *oy* usually occur at the end of words or syllables (*straw, boycott*), whereas *au* and *oi* are found within syllables (*fault, voice*). If these patterns persist as problems into the syllables and affixes stage, then it is appropriate to take a step back and spend a little more time with one-syllable words. They also can be examined, with other vowel patterns, in two-syllable words.

Accent or Stress

In most words of two or more syllables, one syllable is emphasized, stressed, or accented more than the others. Dictionaries use bold apostrophes to show which syllables are stressed. Intermediate dictionaries often boldface the stressed syllable, for example, rabbit /**răb'** ĭt/ or deposit /dĭ **pŏz'** ĭt/. As with open and closed syllables, however, accent is first thought of in terms of sound rather than print. Start with your first name (if it contains two or more syllables) or the name of a friend. When you pronounce it, where are you putting most emphasis? Which syllable seems to sound louder than the others? If your name is Molly, you pronounce it /**moll** ee/, not /mo **lee**/. If your name is Jennifer, you pronounce it /**jen** ifer/, not /je **ni** fer/ or /jenni **fer**/. One way you can test for accent is to hold your hand lightly under your chin as you say a two-syllable word such as *a-round.* Your jaw probably drops more for the accented syllable.

 English Language Lessons

Now try this with certain **homographs**—words that are spelled alike but whose meaning and part of speech changes with a shift in accent:

You give someone a **pres**ent, not a pre**sent.**
You re**cord** a message, you don't **rec**ord it.
You are con**tent** when you are with someone you care deeply about, not **con**tent.

Thinking about accent as it works with names and then with certain homographs should help solidify this concept for you. This is also the sequence you should follow with your students, beginning in the upper elementary grades.

When examining words of more than one syllable, knowing about accent helps students identify what they know about the spelling of a polysyllabic word and what they do not know, that is, what they will need to pay particular attention to. For example, when students pronounce the word *market*, they realize they know the spelling of the accented syllable (*mar*) yet may be uncertain about the vowel spelling in the final **unaccented** syllable. When students grasp the concept of an accented syllable, therefore, they also learn about the other side of this concept, the unaccented syllable. The unaccented syllable is the one in which the spelling of the vowel is not clearly long or short, so students will need to pay close attention to it. The sound in this syllable is often represented by the **schwa** sound—the upside down *e* you see in dictionaries. By the middle of the syllables and affixes stage, word study can focus on these unaccented final syllables.

ə*r* as in *super, actor,* and *sugar*
ə*l* as in *angle, angel, metal, civil,* and *fertile*
ə*n* as in *sudden, human, basin, apron,* and *captain*
Chə*r* as in *lecture, pitcher,* and *treasure*
/j/ as in *village, bridge,* and *damage*

When sorting these words you will find there is no tidy generalization that governs the spelling, but that some spellings are much more common than others. For example, there are over 1,000 words than end in -*le*, but only about 200 that end in -*el*, and -*er* is by far more common than -*or* or -*ar*. An excellent follow-up to sorting these words is creating class lists that will give students insight into their frequencies. Then they might use a "best guess" strategy when spelling an unfamiliar word.

Identifying the vowel in unaccented syllables is one of the biggest challenges we all face as spellers. As our colleague Tom Gill explains to students, "When the sound goes down you can't trust the sound." However, as we shall see in the next chapter, the spelling of the schwa in the unaccented syllable can sometimes be explained in terms of meaning.

Base Words and Derivational Affixes

While students are spending time examining and consolidating their word knowledge at the level of the syllable, part of their focus will naturally include attention to **base words** and simple **derivational affixes** (both **prefixes** and **suffixes**). Unlike inflectional suffixes that do not significantly affect the bases to which they are attached, derivational affixes affect their bases—their meaning and often their grammatical function in a sentence. Students' word learning strategies benefit tremendously by examining the processes according to which these important word parts combine to form words and their meaning. It is important that students encounter and learn to read numerous words that are constructed from these meaning or morphemic elements.

The terms *base word* and *root word* are often used interchangeably. We prefer to use base word when referring to words that stand on their own after all prefixes and suffixes have been removed (*govern* in *government; agree* in *disagreement*). We want to avoid confusion with the term to be explored in Chapter 8, **word root**, which refers to the part of a word that remains after all prefixes and suffixes have been removed, but is *not* a word that can stand by itself (*vis* in *visible* and *spec* in *spectator*); these word roots usually come from Greek or Latin.

Research in vocabulary instruction has underscored the critical importance of students' understanding how prefixes and suffixes combine with base words and word roots to create new words. This understanding can help students analyze un-

unfair	retell	disagree
unable	replay	disorder
uncover	research	disobey
unplug	reuse	disarm
undress	retrain	disown
unkind	return	disappear

FIGURE 7-6 Simple Prefix Sort

known words they encounter in their reading and leads to a rich expansion and elaboration of their vocabularies. Attention to the spelling and the meaning of these word parts reinforces this understanding. Teachers begin to facilitate students' examination of these features when students are farther along in the syllables and affixes stage. The groundwork for this examination is laid when students begin to investigate the addition of plural and inflectional endings to base words. They will then examine the meaning and spelling effects of combining simple prefixes, suffixes, and base words. For example, Figure 7-6 shows three prefixes that are attached to base words which students are likely to understand and already are able to spell.

 For a word sort for prefixes appropriate for the Syllables and Affixes stage, visit the Resources on the Companion Website at www.prenhall.com/bear

ELL This sort might be introduced by inviting the students to do an open sort. Many students will probably sort by the prefix and this term can be introduced when you ask how all the words in a column are alike. Do not begin this sort by telling the students what the prefixes mean; the meanings will evolve as students talk about the meaning of the base word and how it changes with the addition of the prefix. Students might be encouraged to use the words in sentences, such as "I must *obey* my parents because if I *disobey* I can get in trouble." The generative aspect of combining prefixes and bases can be explored by constructing different words through combining and recombining prefix and base word cards or tiles in various ways: *dis, re, un* can be combined with *able* and *order* to produce *disable, disorder, reorder, unable.*

Suffixes can also be introduced through sorts in which students make discoveries about how the suffixes change the meanings of known words as well as parts of speech. For example, adding *y* to the noun *guilt* produces the adjective *guilty*; adding *-ly* produces the adverb *guiltily.* Some suffixes to study in this stage include:

> *-er* as in *quicker* and *-est* in *quickest* (denotes a comparison of some type)
> *-er* as in *baker* and *farmer* and *-or* as in *professor* (both denote "agents or someone or something who does something"; words of Latin origin use the *-or* spelling)
> *-y, -ly, -ful -less,* and *-ness* (these generally change the meaning and part of speech)

This type of study will extend to more complex prefixes, suffixes, and Greek and Latin word roots in the derivational relations stage discussed in Chapter 8. Students will need to revisit the rules that govern *e-* drop and doubling as they add suffixes that begin with vowels to base words. *Brave* becomes *bravely* with no change; but in *flatter,* the doubling rule applies. In addition, *y* must be changed to *i* before adding suffixes (*silly* to *sillier, silliest, silliness*).

Spelling-Meaning Connection

In the mid to late syllables and affixes stage, as students explore how morphemes combine—prefixes, suffixes, and base words—they are developing the foundation for understanding the **spelling-meaning connection:** Words that are related in meaning are often related in spelling as well, despite changes in sound (Templeton, 1983, 1992). According to Chapter 1, the meaning layer of the spelling system ensures that word parts that have similar meanings tend to be spelled similarly. This foundation develops as students learn that the spelling of base words usually does not change a lot when prefixes and suffixes are added; the spelling of most if not all of a morpheme stays the same: *dis + like = dislike; like + able = likable.* For literally thousands of words in English, however, the pronunciation changes depending on which morphemes comprise them. For example, compare the pronunciation *sign* with *signal:* Not only does the pronunciation of the letter *i* change from long to short, but the *g* that is silent in *sign* becomes pronounced in *signal.* The common spelling SIGN visually preserves the meaning similarity shared by these two words, despite quite a variation in sound.

When we first direct students' attention to this spelling-meaning aspect, we begin with words they know: We talk about a stop *sign* and a stop *signal* and write the words in a column so that their common spelling clearly lines up. We write the word *crumb* on the board and ask, "Why do you suppose there's a *b* at the end?" We then write the word *crumble* directly underneath *crumb* and ask the students if these two words are similar in meaning: If you *crumble* a cookie you have a lot of *crumbs,* and isn't it interesting, we ask, that we don't hear the *b* in *crumb* but we do hear it in *crumble*? We write *wise* and underneath it, *wisdom.* We talk about how they are related in meaning; when we add *-dom* to *wise,* we drop the *e,* but the letters *wis* stay the same, even though the pronunciation of the *i* changes. There are many such examples of words that students already know but have yet to think about in this way—indeed, most adults are not aware of the relationship between spelling and meaning. When you help students discover this relationship you are helping them "break through the sound barrier" of spelling and attend to the ways in which *meaning* is consistently spelled (Templeton & Morris, 2000). This is a powerful awareness that will continue to guide students' spelling knowledge, but even more important, their vocabulary knowledge throughout their lives. In Chapter 8 we will explore in more depth the types of spelling-meaning relationships to which skilled, proficient readers may attend.

WORD STUDY ROUTINES AND MANAGEMENT

At the intermediate and middle grade levels, word study should take place in two important ways: (a) It should continue to be systematic as teachers identify stages of development and features students need to study, and (b) it should also be serendipitous, taking place whenever the teacher sees an opportunity to draw students' attention to interesting facts about words that arise in reading, writing, and content areas. Word study instruction takes place all day long in incidental discussions with small groups and large groups, but most students will need in-depth systematic attention to features at their developmental level as well. Organizing instructional-level groups is a challenge but will best serve the needs of students, especially those who might be below grade level. How do you find time to meet with small groups? The key is establishing routines. When students learn weekly word study routines, they become responsible for completing much of their work independently which leaves teachers free to work with small groups.

Word Study Notebooks

Sorting the weekly words, not once but four times or more, is the most valuable routine for students and should be at the heart of systematic, developmental word study. Even high school students enjoy the opportunity to move words around to discover categories! It is very important to model and talk about the sorts with your students as Ms. Lee did at the beginning of this chapter. However, students in this stage of development are usually ready for a fair amount of independent work as well. Consider the classroom organization discussed in Chapter 3 as you aim for self-direction in student work.

The use of word study notebooks (see Chapter 3) in this stage continues to be an easy way to help students and teachers manage the routines and organization of word study. Notebooks can be divided into various sections. Tamara Baren has her students divide their word study notebooks into two sections. The first section is titled "Word Study" and contains the assigned sorts. This section includes weekly records of sorts, word hunts, lists generated in small groups, written reflections of sorts, and sorts assigned for homework. The second section is called "Looking into Language" and contains lists of words related to themes and units, words categorized by parts of speech, and student-generated semantic webs of content area studies. Other teachers add a section called a "personal dictionary" where students record words they frequently need to use in writing. Since these notebooks will be used constantly, we recommend stiff-backed stitched composition books that often come with marbleized covers.

In addition to the basic word sorting routines you may want to develop a list of additional word study notebook activities from which students select when they work independently or for homework. Some of these may be more appropriate at times than others and some can be done to review previous lessons.

ELL

1. Find words that have base words and underline the base word.
2. Make appropriate words on your lists plural or add -*ing* or -*ed.*
3. Circle any prefixes or suffixes you find in the words on your list.
4. Add a prefix and/or suffix, when possible, to words on your list.
5. Select several words and use them in sentences.
6. Choose several words on your list. Change at least one letter to create a new word.
7. Sort your words by parts of speech or subject areas and record your sort.
8. Sort your word cards in alphabetical order and then record them.
9. Go for speed. Sort your words three times and record your times.

Games and other activities are another way to engage students in further exploration and review of the features they are leaning in their sorts. In the following section of this chapter, you will find additional ideas to help your students examine syllable patterns and affixes in both small groups and with partners.

Activities for Students in the Syllables and Affixes Stage

This section outlines activities and games for students in the syllables and affixes stage. The activities and games are designed to reinforce word study introduced first in word sorting activities. Most of the activities are tied to particular sorts offered in the Appendix.

 For many more activities appropriate for the Syllables and Affixes learner, visit the accompanying CD-ROM.

Compound Word Activities 7-1

When examining compound words, consider the difficulty of the base words that make them up. *Cupcake* and *outfit* are made up of two words that have common one-syllable patterns mastered in the within word pattern stage, but *cheeseburger* and *grandparent* are made up of two-syllable words that students may find challenging (*burger* and *parent*). Following are ways you can explore these words.

1. Share some common compound words with the students (e.g., *cookbook* and *bedroom*). Discuss their meaning, pointing out how each word in the compound contributes to the meaning of the whole word. You might ask students to draw pictures to illustrate these. For example, a student might draw a horse and a shoe and then a horseshoe.
2. Prepare word sorts with the words presented in the Appendix that can be sorted in a variety of ways. The sort can focus on shared words (*headlight, headband, headache, headphone* versus *football, foothill, footprint, footstep*). You might also conduct concept sorts, for example, words that have to do with people (*anyone, someone, somebody, nobody, anybody*) or things we find outdoors (*sunshine, airplane, campfire, airport*).
3. Have students cut a set of compound words apart. Then challenge them to create as many new compound words as they can. Some words will be legitimate words (*mailbox*); others will be words that do not yet exist, but they could (*bookbox*). Share and discuss their words. Students may then write sentences using these pseudo words, and draw a picture that illustrates the meaning of each.
4. Students can be given such words as *fire, book,* or *rain* and challenged to see how many related compound words they can brainstorm (*fireplace, firefighter, cookbook, bookmark, rainbow, raincoat*).
5. Create a yearlong class collection of compound words. This collection can include hyphenated words as well (*good-bye, show-off, push-up,* etc.).

VCCV and Doublets Word Sort 7-2

This activity is suitable for small groups, and its purpose is to look at patterns in words when students are deciding how to divide words into syllables. This sort compares VCCV words (*ten-der*) and doublets that also follow this pattern (*kit-ten*).

Materials

Use the syllable patterns sorts in the Appendix, for example, sort 72.

Procedures

1. Explain to your students that you are going to place each word card under the pattern that it matches. Ask the students to attend to patterns as you say each word, and tell them that the patterns they are looking at will help them better remember the spelling of these words.
2. Next, shuffle the word cards and say each word as you place it in the appropriate column (e.g., *lum-ber, mar-ket, dol-lar, din-ner*). Sort three to four words into each column. After you have sorted the words, ask the students how the words in column 1 are alike. Encourage the students to look at patterns in column 1, and then ask them if anyone noticed where the words were "divided" when you pronounced them. Then go to column 2 and guide the students' examination in the same fashion.
3. On their own, students can sort these words until they are comfortable with the pattern.
4. On another occasion, you could call out the words and the students would write them in the appropriate column in their word study notebook.

Variations

1. Use the VCCV pattern words and, together with the following V/CV pattern words, sort according to V/CV or VC/CV pattern (exemplars, for example, may be *canvas* and *basic*).

   baby hoping writer before begin beside
   basic even waving bacon chosen moment
   raking human pilot silent season navy
   music female stolen robot prefer

      Guide the students through these questions: In which pattern is the first vowel usually short? Why? In which pattern is the first vowel usually long? Why?
2. Sort the preceding V/CV words with the following VC/V words:
   cabin planet finish robin magic limit cousin prison
   habit punish cover manage medal promise closet camel

Spelling -*ed* and -*t* Endings 7-3

In these three sorts, students look at past tense spelling patterns.* (See sorts 62 and 68 in the Appendix.)

Procedures

1. Establish the three sound categories for words that end in -*ed:* /t/ *stopped,* /ed/ *traded,* and /d/ *mailed.* Students try to find common features with each list. Notice that most -*ed* words which sound like /t/ have a base word that ends in *k, p, s,* or *x.* In contrast, the base words in the next category combine with the ending to form two syllables. These words can be easily recognized by the /d/ or /t/ ending on the base word. The last category includes base words with a variety of endings. The base word combines with the -*ed* ending to form a single-syllable word with a distinctive /d/ sound at the end.
2. In this sort, students sort for word endings.

-*t*	-*ed*
knelt	*chased*

3. Ask the students to name the present tense verb for each past tense verb. Place word cards by each column so that the students can make comparisons. If the student is having difficulty producing the present tense verb, use sentences as models (e.g.,

Mary swept the house yesterday, but today Mary needs to sweep the house again). The cards should look like this:

knelt (kneel)   chased (chase)

4. Compare the lists. Most students will easily see that the first column with -t endings contains verbs where the past tense verb is a completely different word from the present tense verb. In the second column, the students might notice that the -ed ending is added to the present tense to form the past tense verb, and that you can always find the complete present tense verb in a past tense verb.

5. Ask students to circle the present tense within each of the past tense words in the second column.

6. Ask students to search for the one exception to this pattern in the sort. Most students will discover the present tense verb deal in dealt, but usually students can remember this exception by the change in vowel sound.

Double Scoop 7-4

This board game will help children review and master inflectional endings. It is appropriate for small groups of two to four students.*

Materials

Prepare a gameboard as shown in Figure 7-7 and write each of the sentences below on a card. You will also need playing pieces, a spinner or die, and a board for writing answers with the categories of e drop, double, and no change.

FIGURE 7-7 Double Scoop Gameboard

---

*Marilyn Edwards developed this game.

The bunny was *hopping* down the road.
The cat is *sunning* herself on the chair.
Brittany *shopped* at her favorite store.
We go *swimming* in the summer.
Danny *flopped* down on his bed.
The child was *running* through the store.
I don't like people who go around *bragging*.
I *slipped* on the ice.
Jerry was so tired he felt like *quitting*.
The kite string became *knotted*.
He *pushed* the cart.
Why are they *jumping* around?
Stop *kicking* me!
She *pumped* her arms up and down.
My dog is good at *finding* his way home.
The frogs *croaked* loudly.
I felt like I was *floating* on the wind.
My brother is *sleeping* in today.
I *peeled* the banana.
The bucket *leaked*.

I enjoy *trading* baseball cards.
He is *diving* into the pool.
She *glided* across the ice.
I like *riding* bikes.
I *hoped* you would come.
I like *sliding* down water slides.
We went *skating* across the ice.
He *wasted* his time at the movie.
Will you please stop your *whining*.
The paint was *flaking* off.

Procedures

1. Players put their pieces on the sun to start.
2. Player 1 reads a sentence card and repeats the underlined word.
3. Player 2 then writes the word under the correct heading on the board.
4. The caller then checks the opponent's answer by comparing it with the sentence card. If it is correct, the writer spins and moves that number of spaces on the playing board.
5. The players then switch roles—one becomes the reader and the other becomes the writer.
6. The first player to reach the double scoop of ice cream wins.

Freddy, the Hopping, Diving, Jumping Frog 7-5

In this board game for two to four players, students sort words that end in *-ing* according to three categories.

Materials

Create a game board using one of the follow-the-path templates in the Appendix or by arranging green circles in a path to represent lily pads. Prepare a board like the one used in double scoop (Figure 7-7). Prepare playing cards by writing *-ing* words with doubling, *e* drop, or no change (i.e., *hopping, diving, jumping*). Use words that students have been sorting and add more words from the word list in the Appendix. You can also add penalty or bonus cards such as:

You have the strongest legs. Jump ahead to the next lily pad.
You are the fastest swimmer. Skip 2 spaces.
Your croaking made me lose sleep. Move back 2 spaces.
You ate too many flies. Move back 2 spaces.

Procedures

1. Place playing cards facedown.
2. Player 1 draws one card, reads the card aloud, and moves to the closest space that matches the features of the word. For example, if the card says *hopping,* the player moves to the nearest space that says double.
3. A player who draws a penalty or advancement card must follow the directions on the card.
4. Upon reaching the home lily pad, a player must correctly read the words on the board in order to win. A player who misreads a word must move back five spaces, and play continues.

Variations

1. Players draw for each other, read the word aloud, and the player whose turn it is must spell the word correctly before moving to the appropriate space.
2. Write uninflected forms on cards (*hop, jump, dive*), and have players write how the word should be spelled before moving to the appropriate place. Include an answer sheet with words in alphabetical order to check if there is a disagreement.

Slap Jack 7-6

This card game may be used to contrast open- and closed-syllable words as represented by any of the syllable spelling patterns (V/CV with VCCV; V/CV with VC/V). It is played by two students. The object of the game is for one player to win all 52 cards.

Materials

On 52 small cards, write the words that you want to be contrasted. For example, 26 words would follow the open-syllable VCV pattern (*pilot, human*) and 26 would follow the closed-syllable VCCV pattern (*funny, basket*). See lists in the Appendix for a VCV versus VCCV deck. Additional decks may be made from the other lists in the Appendix. Students must be able to pronounce the words.

Directions

1. The cards are dealt one at a time until the deck is gone. Players keep their cards facedown in a pile in front of them.
2. Each player turns a card faceup in a common pile at the same time. When two words with either open syllables or closed syllables are turned up together, the first player to slap the pile takes all the cards in the common pile and adds them at the bottom of his or her pile.
3. Turning cards and slapping must be done with the same hand.
4. A player who slaps the common pile when there are not two open- or closed-syllable words must give both cards to the other player.
5. Play continues until one player has all the cards. If time runs out, the winner is the player with the most cards.

Variations

1. Once students are comfortable contrasting two-syllable patterns, an additional pattern may be added to the deck, for example, closed-syllable VCV (*cabin, water*).
2. Word cards could be prepared for any feature that has two or three categories; for example, inflected forms with -*ed* could be used and players would slap when the words both represented *e* drop, double, or no change.

Double Crazy Eights 7-7

This activity is designed to review teacher-directed instruction on consonant doubling and *e* drop, and at the same time to reexamine the various spellings of /k/ in two-syllable words. On the basis of the traditional card game "Crazy Eights," students can play in groups of two or three. The object of the game is to get rid of all the cards in your hand. This is a good follow-up to sort 70 in the Appendix.

Materials

Prepare 52 word cards comprising four suits: (1) V-ck pattern (*tacking*), (2) V-k-e pattern (*baking*), (3) VV-k pattern (*looking, speaking*), (4) VC-k pattern (*asking*). Use 13 words per suit. Four Crazy Eight cards are designated by the words *eight, ate,* or the numeral *8*. See sort 70 in the Appendix for sample words.

Directions

1. Dealer gives each player eight cards. The remaining cards become the draw pile. The dealer turns the top card of the draw pile over and places it beside the deck. This card becomes the starter card and is the first card in the discard pile.
2. The player to the left of the dealer begins by placing a card that matches the starter card onto the discard pile. Matches may be made in three ways:
   a. By sound—long, short, or neither
   b. By pattern—V-ck (*lick*), V-k-e (*like*), VV-k (*leak*) , or VC-k (*drank*)
   c. By rule—whether the consonant *s* doubled, the *e* dropped, or no change made
3. With a Crazy Eight card, the player can change its suit to anything the player chooses.
4. If the player does not have a match, he or she must draw from the draw pile until one is found.
5. If all the cards in the draw pile are used up, reserve the top card from the discard pile, shuffle the rest of the cards, and place them facedown on the table as the new draw pile.
6. Play continues until one player has discarded all cards.

Variations

This game can be adapted simply by making up a new deck using words that focus on another spelling feature. Remember that the deck must have four suits and allow for matching by at least two different elements. For example, long-vowel patterns in two-syllable words could be matched by pattern (*debate* and *bracelet*), by sound (long *u* in both *include* and *human*), or by stress (*explain* and *include*).

Base Word/Suffix Sorts: Changing y to i 7-8

The purpose of this sort is to look at patterns in words when students are deciding when *y* changes to *i* and when it remains the same. It works well with small groups.

Materials

You will need a file folder and word cards; label the inside of the file folder with *carry* and *carried* as column heads. See sort 64 in the Appendix.

Directions

1. Explain to your students that you are going to place each word card under either the base word or the related word. After you have sorted the words, ask the students why they think the spelling of the base word changed when *-ed* or *-es* was added.

2. On their own, students can sort these words until they are comfortable with the pattern. You could then lead a closed sort and have the students write the words down on a paper they have labeled with two columns, *penny* and *pennies*.
3. On another occasion, you could call out the words and the students would write them in the appropriate column in their word study notebook.

Variations

1. Now explore single-syllable base words that end in *y: dry, dried; cry, cries; try, tried; fly, flies.*
2. Add the following base and related words to words from the previous sorts; why does the *y* not change to *i? turkey, turkeys; donkey, donkeys; chimney, chimneys.*
3. Sort base words and related words to which the suffixes *-er* and *-est* have been added: *tiny, tinier, tiniest; pretty, prettier, prettiest; crazy, crazier, craziest; early, earlier, earliest; happy, happier, happiest.*
4. In some words, such as *tiny* and *baby*, the spelling of *y* does not change when suffixes beginning with *i* are added. Present the following words, ask the students why they think the spelling does not change, then go on a word hunt to find other examples: *baby, babyish; copy, copyist.*

You're Up 7-9

The purpose of the game, which should be played with five students, is to contrast the spellings for the /ure/ sound: *ure* as in picture and *cher* as in preacher, as well as other incidents of the suffix *ure.**

Materials

You will need a scoring pad and pencil; stopwatch; window cards such as the one in Figure 7-8.

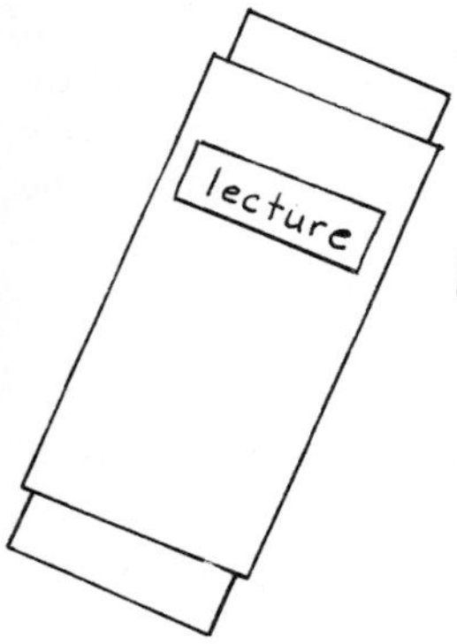

Procedures

1. One student is designated as the recorder, while the other four pair up into two teams of two players. Each team decides who is player A and player B. The recorder flips a coin to see which team will go first.
2. Both players are given the window card with the first word to be played showing through the window. (Both teams are given the same word.) See Figure 7-8.
3. Player A from the team that won the coin toss begins by giving player B (on the same team) a one-word clue as to the word on the card. This clue may not be any part of the word to be guessed, or contain the word in any form. For example, if the word is *pasture*, the clue might be *meadow* or *field*. If player B does not guess the correct word on the first attempt, the other team has a chance.
4. Play moves back and forth between teams until one team guesses the word. If both teams have given five clues and the word is still not guessed, the referee throws the word out. Player B's are given the second word, and the second team's player B leads off with a one-word clue to his or her partner.
5. Each time a team successfully guesses a word, they receive one point. If the same player that guessed the word can also spell the word, the team receives another point (total of two). If the player cannot spell the word, the opposing team has a chance to do so with whichever player was guessing the clues. The team with the most points wins.

FIGURE 7-8
Password Cover for
You're Up

*This game is courtesy of Charlotte Tucker.

6. For the teacher to assess students' knowledge of the targeted feature, and in the interest of fairness, the recorder is to write down the given clues on a sheet provided with the words played. The recorder also acts as referee and timekeeper, making sure only one-word clues are given and that those clues are in keeping with the rule. Keeping time involves allowing each team 15 seconds total for giving clues and guessing the word during each round, as well as a 15-second limit to spell the word.

Variations

1. Have students create their own window cards with this feature, or another, for their fellow students to use.
2. This game could also be played with *ant*/*ent* words, providing an engaging way to practice spelling these words as well as sharpen vocabulary (see Chapter 8).

The Apple and the Bushel 7-10

The purpose of this board game is to help students differentiate between -*le* and -*el* endings. A prerequisite skill is the ability to sort rapidly words with -*le* and -*el* endings.*

Materials

Prepare the Apple and Bushel gameboard (see Figure 7-9) and word cards with words that end in -*el* and -*le* (*bushel, angel, apple, angle*). See Appendix for more words.

Procedures

1. Players draw for each other and read the word aloud.
2. Players take turns moving the marker to the nearest -*le* or -*el* ending that spells the word.

FIGURE 7-9 Apple and Bushel Gameboard

---

*This game is courtesy of Charlotte Tucker.

Syllables and Affixes Stage

3. The game continues until one player reaches the bushel. (*Note:* To get in the bushel, an *-le* word must be drawn. A player who draws an *-el* word must move backwards and continue playing from that space.)

Variations

Students may sort word cards as they draw them from the pile to reinforce the spelling patterns. You can use *apple* and *bushel* as the guide words for sorting. Add words that end with *-il* (*pencil*) and *-al* (*pedal*).

Homograph Concentration 7-11

This game follows the Concentration format and may be played by two to four students. The object of the game is to collect the most pairs of sentence cards with matching homograph pronunciations.*

Materials

Prepare a sentence card for each of the following sentences. There are four sentences for each homograph—two each for the different meanings and pronunciations.

There was a tear in her jeans.	A tear ran down his cheek.
Be careful not to tear the paper.	The end of the movie brought a tear to my eye.
Will you read the newspaper tomorrow?	I like to read mysteries.
The teacher read to us after lunch.	I read a lot of books last year.
I saw a live performance by that band.	I used to live in a small town.
We are going to need live bait for fishing.	I live close to my best friend.
We plan to sow many new seeds in our garden this spring.	That is the largest sow I've ever seen at a livestock show.
An old saying goes, "You reap what you sow."	The sow and her piglets played in the mud.
Wind the scarf around your neck.	The wind is really cold at this time of year.
I think this road will wind around the mountain.	The wind blew over the trash cans.
My dad does a good job of cooking.	The does brought their fawns down to the stream.
She does not have my favorite sweater.	Does are not as large as bucks.
The dove is often a symbol for peace.	Jerry quickly dove into the river.
My favorite birdcall is that of the dove.	I was so hungry I dove into the spaghetti.
The wind will definitely buffet that small boat.	We ate at a terrific seafood buffet.
I'm afraid that hard winds will really buffet that small tent.	My grandma stores her good dishes in a large buffet.
The distant object appeared to be approaching quickly.	I object to the way you're talking about my best friend.
I don't understand the object of this game.	I object to your tone of voice.
She set the record for the fastest time in the race.	I don't like to record my own voice.

*Credit goes to Elizabeth Harrison, Teliz Blackard, and Lisbeth Kling.

There is no record of her living in this town.

I can't wait until they record their new CD.

Math is my favorite subject.

I hope they won't subject us to a lot of noise.

That's a subject we don't talk about very often.

I don't want to subject you to any more discomfort.

I can't wait to find out what my birthday present will be.

We would like to present you with this award.

She was present for every meeting.

The drama club is going to present their first play.

Our group project was a success.

I try to project a confident image.

The new building project cost millions of dollars.

You will have to project your voice better so we can hear you.

Wait just one more minute.

There was a minute speck of dust on the lens.

I don't have a minute to spare.

Our problems seem minute compared to theirs.

The band just signed a recording contract.

I hope I don't contract a serious illness.

The actor was offered her first movie contract.

My muscles contract when I get cold.

Directions

1. Select five to eight homographs for each game (32 to 40 sentences). *Important:* Students should know at least one of the two pronunciations for each homograph.
2. Shuffle the sentence cards. Place the cards facedown on the tabletop.
3. Players alternate turning over two sentence cards in hopes of locating homographs with matching pronunciations. Players must read aloud the sentence cards they turn over or they do not get to keep the pair if they do match.
4. A player may keep the two sentence cards if (a) the two sentence cards have matching homographs that also have the same pronunciation, and (b) the player pronounces the homographs correctly when reading the sentences. The player then gets another turn. The player may not keep the sentence cards if (a) they do not have matching homographs underlined or (b) they have matching homographs but their pronunciations are different. In both of these cases the cards are turned facedown again and the next player takes a turn.
5. The player with the most pairs is the winner.

Variations

Other features can be reviewed in a Concentration card game. For example, sets of cards can feature words that share the same prefixes (create a deck with *un-, re-, dis-, in-, pre-, non-,* and *mis-*) or suffixes (*-ful, -ly, -less, -ness, -ion,* and *-tion*).

Prefix Spin 7-12

This game for two to four players reinforces the idea that prefixes and base words can be combined in different ways. Let students play this after they have sorted words with the featured prefixes.

Materials

Make a spinner using the directions on page 417. Divide the spinner into six sections and write each of these prefixes in a section: *mis, pre, un, dis,* and *re* (use *re* twice because it can be used in twice as many words as the others). Prepare a deck of 24 cards with the following base words written on them: *count, judge, match, take, use, set, test, view, charge, pay, able, like, form, place, wrap, order, cover,* and *pack* (you can duplicate the last five to enlarge the deck; they each can combine with three of the prefixes, for example, *misplace, replace,* and *displace*). Include paper and pencil for each player to record their matches. You may also want to include a list of allowable words to solve disputes. Matches include:

miscount, misjudge, mismatch, misplace, mistake, misuse, prejudge, preset, pretest, preview, preorder, prepay, recount, rematch, replace, retake, reuse, reset, retest, review, recharge, reform, reorder, repay, recover, repack, rewrap, unable, uncover, unlike, unpack, unwrap, discount, displace, discharge, disorder, disable, discover, dislike

Procedures

1. Turn the base word cards facedown in a deck in the center of the playing area. Turn one card up at a time.
2. The first player spins for a prefix (such as *un*). If the prefix can be added to the base word to form a real word (such as *unwrap*), the player takes the card and records the whole word on paper.
3. If the first player spins a prefix that cannot be added (such as *mis*), the next player spins and hopes to land on a prefix that will work with the base word. This continues until someone can form a word.
4. A new base word is turned up for the next player and the game continues.
5. The winner is the player who has the most base word cards at the end of the game.

Variation

Two spinners could be used with suffixes written on the second one, such as *-s, -ed, -ing,* and *-able*. A bonus point could be assigned when a player can use both the prefix and suffix with a base word, as in *replaceable* or *discovering*.

Oygo 7-13

Oygo is intended for three to four students. It reinforces the spelling patterns *oi* and *oy* for the /oy/ sound. There are different groups of words that may be used in each game.* See sort 92 in the Appendix for a sample sort.

Materials

Prepare a set of word cards spelled with *oi* and *oy* such as those in sort 92 and related word lists. Also prepare a set of number cards (1 to 12, five cards for each number) and feature cards (*oi* or *oy* spelling). Number the pouches in an egg carton from 1 to 12 and place the number cards into the correct pouch.

Directions

1. Number carton, word cards, and feature cards are placed in the center of the table.
2. The caller shuffles the deck of cards and then deals out four cards to each player.
3. The players place the cards faceup in front of them.
4. The caller turns up the rest of the cards one at a time, calling out the word and the number of the card. The caller should make sure the cards are in order by placing a number card on top of each called word card.

---

*Credit to Geraldine Robinson; adapted from the game "Bango," by Robert Harbin in *Family Card Games.*

5. A player who has a card of the same feature turns it facedown. The player then takes a number card of the called word from the number carton and places it on top of the facedown card. Numbers are used to check the winner's cards.
6. The first player to have turned down all cards shouts "Oygo!"
7. The winner's facedown cards can be checked by comparing them to the called words.
8. The players place the number cards back into the carton.
9. The winner becomes the next caller.
10. The game starts over using the same feature or another feature, or a combination of features.
11. The caller can use the word list to choose a different group of word cards illustrating a different feature or a combination of features.

Variations

The game can be changed to Owgo, using words in sort 93. The game will reinforce the two common spellings for the /ow/ sound—*ou* and *ow*.

Pulling Two-Syllable Words Together 7-14

A word sort that pulls together much of the exploration you have been doing with two-syllable words is this three-step sort. In this type of sort, a group of words is sorted according to three different criteria: accent, sound, and pattern.

1. Locate accent. Sort the words according to which syllable is accented:

First Syllable	Second Syllable
ze / bra	a / *way*
fe / ver	to / *day*

2. Sort by sound. Sort according to the sound you hear in the accented syllable. For example, long vowel versus short vowel:

Long Vowel	Short Vowel
lazy	ladder
climate	better

3. Identify pattern. Sort the sounds according to the pattern in the accented syllable. For example, final long-vowel pattern versus medial long vowel:

Final Long Vowel	Medial Long Vowel
today	remain
reply	impeach

Spelling-Meaning Word Sort 7-15

1. Have students sort the following words into two categories: base words and derived (suffixed) words.

sign	please	soft	bomb	muscle
signal	pleasant	soften	bombard	muscular
signature	pleasure	softly		

2. Match each base word with its derivative(s).
3. Discuss how the words are related in meaning. Discuss how the sound changes when a suffix is added.
4. Ask students if they can think of additional words that are part of each spelling-meaning "family." These may be added to the sort and/or to the vocabulary notebook.

Homophone Solitaire 7-16

Building on the traditional game Solitaire, this simple card game requires flexible thinking and versatile attention to words. Word cards are matched by homophone, syllable pattern, or whether the homophonic spelling change is in the stressed or unstressed syllable. The object of the game is to end up with all the words in one pile. Refer to sort 97 and the list of homophones in the Appendix.

Materials

You will need 52 word cards using two-syllable homophones. The cards comprise two suits: (a) homophones in the stressed syllable and (b) homophones in the unstressed syllable. There are 13 pairs of matching homophones from each suit. (See the homophone list in the Appendix.)

Directions

1. Shuffle the deck; then turn one card over at a time. Say the word, observe the pattern, and place the card down, faceup.
2. Turn over the next card. Place it on top of the previously placed card if it matches by any of the following three features:
   a. Exact homophone (e.g., *alter–altar*).
   b. Syllable pattern: VCCV doublet (e.g., *mussel* could be placed on *lesson*); VCCV different (e.g., *canvas* could be placed on *incite*); open VCV (e.g., *miner* could be placed on *rumor*); closed VCV (e.g., *baron* could be placed on *profit*).
   c. Spelling change in the stressed or unstressed syllable. For example, suppose *sender* was the last card played; the homophone for *sender* is *cinder*—the spelling change in the *sender/cinder* homophone pair occurs in the stressed syllable. If a student is holding the card *morning,* she could place it on *sender,* because the homophone for *morning* is *mourning* which also has the spelling change in the stressed syllable. Alternately, if the student is holding the card *presents,* he could play it on *miner,* because the homophone for *presents* is *presence* and the homophone for *miner* is *minor*—the spelling change occurs in the *un*stressed syllables.
3. If there is no match, place the card to the right of the last card played.
4. Continue play in this way, placing cards with no matches to the right of the last card played. Stacks may be picked up and consolidated at any time. The top card played on a stack determines the movement.
5. You may move back no more than four stacks for play.
6. Play continues until the entire deck is played. Then shuffle and play again!

Stressbusters 7-17

The purpose of this board game is to determine the correct placement of accent or stress in a given word. Students can play the game in pairs after they have conducted their initial sorting of the words by accented pattern under the teacher's guidance.* Refer to sorts 84 to 88 for sample words.

Materials

Create a Stressbusters gameboard using a template from the Appendix or using circles as shown in Figure 7-10. Prepare game cards made from the word lists in the Appendix. You will also need pennies for playing pieces and a dictionary (to check placement of stress or accent).

---

*This activity comes to us courtesy of Brenda Reibel.

FIGURE 7-10 Stressbusters Gameboard

Procedures

1. As students identify the placement of stress, they will do the following: If the accent falls in the beginning syllable and is correctly identified, the player moves the penny one space; if the accent falls in the second syllable and is correctly identified, the player moves the penny two spaces; if the accent is on the third syllable, then the player moves the penny three spaces.

2. Player 1 takes a card from the word stack and identifies if the accent falls on the first, second, or third syllable. If unchallenged, player 1 moves the correct number of spaces depending on where the accent falls. If there is more than one accented syllable and the player realizes this (as in **con**sti**tu**tion), the player may choose which syllable to "count"; the player may decide that *constitution* should count for three spaces.

3. Player 2 then takes a card from the game card stack, identifies the accent, and moves the correct number of spaces depending on where the accent falls.

4. The game continues until one player reaches the finish circle.

5. Challenging answers: Game players may challenge acceptability of accent answers. When an answer is challenged, the challenger looks the words up in the dictionary to determine the accented syllable. If correct, the challenger gets to move the gamepiece forward one, two, or three places, depending on where the accent falls. If the player is correct, and the challenger is wrong, the challenger must move back one space.

Words that are accented on the third syllable are also accented on the first syllable. These words may be challenged. If a player moves one space for the word *constitution,* for example, not realizing it is also accented on the third syllable, then the other player could challenge. An incorrect challenge, however, costs the challenger the corresponding number of spaces. If the challenger thinks the word is accented on the second syllable and is incorrect, he or she must move back two spaces; if the challenger thinks the accent is on the third syllable and is incorrect, he or she moves back three spaces.

Semantic Chart Sorts 7-18

You can use a bulletin board to create an interactive word wall related to content studies. Like the semantic sorts in Chapter 6, students arrange words conceptually. As an ongoing activity, students look for words that are tied to their content studies.

1. Students collect words from a unit of study on a bulletin board. Words selected for the board are defined and reviewed as an ongoing class activity.
2. These words are given to groups to sort into meaning- or association-based groups. Students write the groups on chart paper with an explanation for each grouping.

Vocabulary Jeopardy 7-19

Students enjoy the familiar Jeopardy game after brainstorming terms related to a unit of study.

1. Students generate vocabulary cards from a unit of study. Tamara Baren starts with the vocabulary students generate on their own, followed by a scan through texts and materials.
2. With these cards, students make a Jeopardy game. A sample of a gameboard can be found in activity 6-13. Students write questions on cards that relate to facts and concepts studied. Answers are written on the back upside down. The cards are sorted into categories.
3. Teams of students play the game as a whole-class vocabulary review of the unit.

Word Study for Advanced Readers and Writers: The Derivational Relations Stage

We use the term **derivational relations** to describe the type of word knowledge that more advanced readers and writers possess. The term emphasizes how spelling and vocabulary knowledge at this stage grow primarily through processes of *derivation*—from a single base word or word root, a number of related words are *derived* through the addition of prefixes and suffixes. Students begin to explore these processes at the syllables and affixes stage, but their understanding expands and becomes much more elaborated at the derivational relations stage. In contrast to the syllables and affixes stage, exploration of words at the derivational relations stage draws upon more extensive experience in reading and writing: There is reciprocity between growth in vocabulary and spelling knowledge and the amount of reading and writing in which students are engaged (e.g., Carlisle, 2000; Mahony, Singson, & Mann, 2000; Smith, 1998). Effective word study at this level builds and extends this reciprocity by engaging students in significant and productive patterns in spelling and meaning that we select; we then show students how to apply their knowledge of these patterns in their independent exploration of words.

LITERACY DEVELOPMENT AND INSTRUCTION FOR STUDENTS IN THE DERIVATIONAL RELATIONS STAGE

The type of word knowledge that underlies advanced reading and writing includes an ever-expanding conceptual foundation and the addition of words that represent this foundation. Advanced readers are able to explore the Greek and Latin word elements that are the important morphemes out of which thousands of words are constructed. In most instances, these words are derived from a single base or root morpheme through the addition of affixes—prefixes and suffixes. During the reading process, this additional layer of word knowledge makes it possible to add a morphological layer to the perception of polysyllabic words: While the intermediate reader (syllables and affixes) picks up syllabic chunks in such words, the advanced reader (derivational relations) picks up morphemic chunks as well (Taft, 1991; Templeton, 1992). For example, an intermediate reader attempting to read the word *morphology* would most likely analyze it syllable by syllable, picking up the letter sequences *mor-pho-lo-gy.* The advanced reader would most likely pick up the letter sequences *morph-ology,* which cross syllable boundaries.

CHARACTERISTICS OF ORTHOGRAPHIC DEVELOPMENT DURING THE DERIVATIONAL RELATIONS STAGE

As noted in Chapter 7, most students beginning in the intermediate school years are capable of understanding that the way words are spelled can provide clues to their meanings. The principles for instruction listed for intermediate readers and writers (page 220) also guide our instruction at the advanced level. As at the intermediate level, word study for advanced readers emphasizes active exploration of words and the application of word knowledge to spelling, vocabulary development, and the analysis of unknown words encountered in reading.

The Spelling-Meaning Connection

We begin to explore spelling-meaning relationships, helping students become explicitly aware of the spelling-meaning principle as it applies in English: *Words that are related in meaning are often related in spelling as well, despite changes in sound* (Chomsky, 1970; Templeton, 1983). Because of this similarity in meaning in similarly spelled words, intermediate students can learn the following strategy: *If you are unsure how to spell a word, try to think of a word that is similar in spelling and meaning* and which you **do** know how to spell. In the following teaching/learning example, Jorge Ramirez illustrates how a teacher can guide students to an awareness of the spelling-meaning connection.

> Writing the misspelled word *compisition* on the board, Jorge begins:
> "I'd like to point something out to you: Words that are related in meaning are often related in spelling as well. For example [pointing to *compisition*], everything is correct in this word except for the letter *i* in the second syllable. However, there's a word that is related in spelling *and* meaning that actually provides a clue to the correct spelling. Any ideas what this word might be? [No one responds; Jorge continues.] Well, let's look at this word [writes *compose* directly above *compisition*]. Are *compose* and *composition* related in meaning? Yes, they are! Can you hear the long *-o* sound in *compose*? You know how to spell this sound, and because *compose* and *composition* are related in meaning, the *o* in *compose* is the clue to the spelling of what we call the schwa sound in *composition.*

"Keeping this fact in mind can help you spell a word you may not be sure of, like *composition*. Why? Because schwas don't give you any clue to the spelling—they can be spelled with any of the vowel letters. You've got a powerful strategy you can use, though: By thinking of a related word, like *compose*, you can get a clue.

"Let's try another one. Here's a misspelling I've seen a lot [writes *oppisition* on the board]. Is there a word that is related in meaning *and* spelling that can give you a clue about how to spell the schwa sound [pointing to the *i* in the second syllable of *oppisition*]? [There are a few seconds of silence, then a student tentatively responds, "*oppose*?"] Could be! Let's check it out [writes *oppose* directly above *oppisition*]. We can clearly hear the sound that *o* in the second syllable of *oppose* stands for, and sure enough, *opposition* comes from *oppose*—they're similar in meaning—so Darci is right! *Oppose* gives us the clue for remembering the spelling of *opposition*. Remember, *words that are related in meaning are often related in spelling as well*. So, by thinking of a word that is related to one you're trying to spell, you will often discover a helpful clue to the spelling."

The spelling-meaning connection is another way of referring to the significant role that *morphology* plays in the spelling system: Morphemes with similar meanings tend to be spelled similarly. This consistency applies to the majority of words in English and, as we will explore in this chapter, presents an excellent opportunity to integrate spelling and vocabulary instruction.

Students will encounter more and more of these words in their reading, In fact, *reading* is the primary means by which students gain access to these words; they simply do not occur with nearly as great a frequency in oral language. As teachers, we can initiate students' examination of these spelling-meaning patterns by observing, "You know, when you first learned to read you had to learn how spelling stands for sounds. Now you're going to be learning how spelling stands for *meaning*."

Table 8-1 presents examples of misspellings from derivational relations spellers.

 To aid in your study of the spelling/meaning connection, utilize the many appropriate word sorts and activities in the Derivational Relations section of the accompanying CD-ROM.

Recognizing Advanced Patterns in Spelling-Meaning Word Features

At first glance, misspellings at the derivational relations stage appear similar in type to those at the syllables and affixes stage: Errors occur at the juncture of syllables and with the vowel in unaccented syllables. Earlier, at the syllables and affixes stage, students' exploration of words established a secure foundation for exploring and understanding morphemic analysis and more abstract morphemes at the derivational relations stage. Understanding the more advanced patterns that underlie the correct spelling of words illustrated in Table 8-1, however, requires additional extensive experience with reading and writing that provides the words and the knowledge to support learning about their spelling and meaning features. Students will explore how these morphemic elements combine—Greek and Latin bases, roots, and affixes—and they will see how this knowledge can be applied flexibly across reading and writing tasks.

In examining the types of spelling errors in Table 8-1, notice how in CONFESION and PROSPARITY an understanding that the spelling of the base word (*confess* or *prosper*) must remain constant with the addition of suffixes might have helped this speller. In RESADENT, CONFADENCE, OPPISITION, and PROHABITION, the speller is making errors in the second unaccented syllable in which the vowel sound is reduced to a schwa. Again, understanding that derived spellings need to keep the base word or

TABLE 8-1   Examples of Spelling at the Derivational Relations Stage

Early Derivational Relations

enclosed	INCLOSED
confession	CONFESION
resident	RESADENT
confidence	CONFADENCE
opposition	OPPISITION

Mid Derivational Relations

prosperity	PROSPARITY
emphasize	EMFASIZE
benefit	BENAFIT
criticize	CRITISIZE
prohibition	PROHABITION
indictment	INDITEMENT

Late Derivational Relations

accommodate	ACCOMODATE
appearance	APPEERENCE
irrelevant	IRELEVANT
alleged	ALLEDGED

root spelling constant is an important insight such spellers need. Misspellings such as INDITEMENT, ALLEDGED, IRELEVANT, and ACCOMODATE are common in highly skilled and accomplished readers and writers (indeed, the persistence of such misspellings leads many adults to lament that, though they are good readers, they are "terrible" spellers!). Exploring the logic underlying the correct spellings of these words not only helps individuals learn and remember their correct spelling but, more important, leads to a deeper understanding and appreciation of how words work. This understanding and appreciation leads in turn to the growth and differentiation of concepts—to vocabulary development.

Literacy Development for Spelling-Meaning Connections

Spelling provides a direct *visual* link to the "core" meaning shared by related words. Because of this, you can help students learn a strategy for examining words that are related in spelling and meaning as well as help them become aware of the several different spelling-meaning patterns that characterize so many words in English. Beginning with known words and then expanding to include unknown words, having awareness of the spelling-meaning connection will not only help students fine-tune their spelling ability, but also help expand their vocabulary. This is because students develop the awareness that there are logical spelling-meaning patterns that apply to most words in the English language, and this awareness and expectation of logical pattern results in far more productive and reassuring word learning than the traditional one-word-at-a-time approach.

For example, in the intermediate grades students will first learn about relationships primarily in known words (*sign–signal, muscle–muscular*), but their awareness will grow to include unknown words that are related to known words: *paradigmatic* will be better learned, understood, and retained when related to *paradigm,* as well as providing a helpful clue to remembering the silent *-g* in *paradigm; mnemonic* will be related to *amnesia* and *amnesty* (and also yield a surprising connection with Greek mythology, as we will explore later in the context of Greek word roots).

Though a number of sound changes may occur in a group of related words while the spelling remains the same, we guide students first to notice particular changes that represent an increasing order of difficulty and abstractness. Templeton (1976, 1979, 1983, 1989, 1992) and Templeton and Scarborough-Franks (1985) originally identified this order of difficulty and abstractness; recent work by Leong (2000) further substantiates this sequence. Let us examine each in turn.

Consonant Alternation

Consonant alternation patterns are those in which the spelling of consonants remains the same in related words despite an alternation or change in the sound represented by the spelling (see Table 8-2). For example, note the *g* in *sign* and *signal*, the *t* in *connect* and *connection*, the *c* in *music* and *musician*. We begin the examination of consonant alternation with the *silent/sounded* pattern, illustrated by the following introductory sort.

Silent	Sounded
crumb	*crumble*
sign	*signal*
bomb	*bombard*
muscle	*muscular*
hasten	*haste*
column	*columnist*
soften	*soft*

Consonants that are silent in one word are "sounded" in a related word, as in the words *sign* and *signal*. Rather than trying simply to remember the spelling of one silent consonant in one word, students learn the following strategy: *To remember the spelling of a word with a silent consonant, try to think of a word related in spelling and meaning—you may get a clue from the consonant that is sounded.* As students move through the grades, they will encounter a large number of words that follow this pattern and will help expand their vocabulary: *solemn/solemnity, assign/assignation, diagnose/diagnosis.*

The next consonant alternation patterns to be studied involve alternations in which the sound represented by a consistent spelling alternates with a different sound. For example, the following sort includes two patterns, /k/-/sh/ and /k/-/s/; you will find that for most students the order of presentation is not significant.

/k/	/sh/	/k/	/s/
clinic	*clinician*	*critic*	*criticize*
politic	*politician*	*political*	*politicize*
cosmetic	*cosmetician*	*ethics*	*ethicist*
technical	*technician*	*italics*	*italicize*
diagnostic	*diagnostician*	*public*	*publicize*
pediatrics	*pediatrician*	*physics*	*physicist*

Vowel Alternation

Vowel alternation patterns are those in which the spelling of the vowels remains the same in related words despite an alternation or change in the sound represented by the spelling (see Table 8-2). Students benefit most from their study of the spelling-meaning connection as reflected in vowel alternation patterns when these patterns are presented

TABLE 8-2   Sequence of Word Study in the Derivational Relations Stage

The Spelling-Meaning Connection:
Words that are related in meaning are often related in spelling as well, despite changes in sound.

1. Consonant Alternations
   a. silent/sounded
   b. /t/ to /sh/

   c. /k/ to /sh/
   d. /k/ to /s/
   e. /s/ to /sh/

   sign/signal, condemn/condemnation, soften/soft
   connect/connection, select/selection, attract/attraction
   music/musician, magic/magician
   critic/criticize, politic (political)/politicize
   prejudice/prejudicial, office/official, artifice/artificial, malice/malicious

2. Vowel Alternations
   a. Long to short

   b. Long to schwa

   c. Short to schwa

   crime/criminal, ignite/ignition, humane/humanity, suffice/sufficient
   compete/competition, define/definition, reside/resident, gene/genetic, impose/imposition, confide/confidence
   locality/local, legality/legal, relativity/relative, metallic/metal, adapt/adaptation

Greek and Latin Word Elements

1. Start with Greek number prefixes *mono-* (one), *bi-* (two), *tri-* (three), and move to the Greek roots *-tele* (far, distant), *-therm-* (heat), *-photo-* (light), and *astr-* (star). (See lists on page 274.)
2. Move to frequent Latin roots with the aim of gaining a working understanding of a few frequently occurring roots with relatively concrete and constant meanings: *-tract-* (draw, pull), *-spect-* (look), *-port-* (carry), *-dict-* (to say), *-rupt-* (to break), and *scrib* (to write). (See lists on page 272.)
3. Explore additional Latin and Greek prefixes, building on those already taught at the syllables and affixes stage.

Prefix	*Meaning*
inter-	between
intra-	within
super	over; greater
counter-	opposing
ex-	out
fore-	before
post-	after
pro-	in front of, forward
co-/com-/con-	together, with
sub-	under
pre-	before
anti-	against
demi-	half
semi-	half
quadr-	four
pent-	five

TABLE 8-2   continued

4. Explore common Greek suffixes that students will frequently encounter:

Suffix	Meaning
-crat/-cracy	rule (*democracy*—rule by the *demos,* people)
-emia	condition of the blood (*leukemia*—the blood has too many white [*leuk*] blood cells)
-ician	specialist in (*dietician*)
-ine	chemical substance (*chlorine, Benzedrine*)
-ism/-ist	belief in, one who believes (*communism/communist, capitalism/capitalist*)
-logy/-logist	science of, scientist (*geology*—science of the earth, studying the earth; *geologist*—one who studies the earth)
-pathy/-path	disease, one who suffers from a disease (*osteopathy*—disease of the bones; *osteopath,* one who suffers from such a disease)
-phobia	abnormal fear (*claustrophobia*—fear of being closed in or shut in [*claus*])

The Spelling-Meaning Connection: Predictable Spelling Changes in Consonants and Vowels

1. /t/ to /sh/	*permit/permission, transmit/transmission*
2. /t/ to /s/	*silent/silence*
3. /d/ to /zh/	*explode/explosion, erode/erosion, decide/decision, divide/division*
4. /sh/ to /s/	*ferocious/ferocity, precocious/precocity*
5. Long to short	*vain/vanity, consume/consumption, receive/reception, retain/retention, detain/detention*
6. Long to schwa	*explain/explanation, exclaim/exclamation*

Advanced Suffix Study

1. -able/-ible	*respectable, favorable* versus *visible, audible*
2. -ant /-ance	*fragrant/fragrance, dominant/dominance*
-ent/-ence	*dependent/dependence, florescent/florescence*
3. Consonant doubling and accent	*occurred, permitted* versus *traveled, benefited*

Absorbed Prefixes

a. Prefix + base word	*in + mobile = immobile; ad + count = account*
b. Prefix + word root	*ad + cept = accept, in + mune = immune*

in a logical sequence: Related words that illustrate vowel alternation begin with simple long-to-short vowel changes such as *revise/revision,* in which the long *-i* in the base word *revise* changes to a short *-i* in the derived word *revision.*

Long	Short
nature	*natural*
sane	*sanity*
nation	*national*
sign	*signal*
divine	*divinity*
atrocious	*atrocity*
Iranian	*Iran*
Palestine	*Palestinian*

After several long-to-short patterns are examined, students may explore in depth the spelling of the schwa, or least-accented vowel sound in the second syllable of words such as *resident, confidence, opposition,* and *prohibition*. This spelling becomes obvious when paired with related words in which the corresponding vowel sound is clearly heard, as follows:

resident	*confidence*	*opposition*	*prohibition*
reside	*confide*	*oppose*	*prohibit*

Again, the strategy is reinforced: *To remember the spelling of the schwa in an unaccented syllable, think of a related word in which that syllable is accented.* Exploration of the schwa begins with this long-to-schwa pattern, as follows:

Long	**Schwa**
compose	*composition*
invite	*invitation*
define	*definition*
recite	*recitation*
inspire	*inspiration*
preside	*president*

In many words, the schwa occurs in the base word and alternates with the long vowel in the derived word, as follows:

Schwa	**Long**
Canada	*Canadian*
comedy	*comedian*
tutor	*tutorial*
custody	*custodian*
Amazon	*Amazonian*
labor	*laborious*
janitor	*janitorial*

The short-to-schwa vowel alternation pattern is illustrated in the following sort.

rigid	*rigidity*
rhapsody	*rhapsodic*
reciprocate	*reciprocity*
polar	*polarity*
allege	*allegation*

Predictable Spelling Changes in Vowels and Consonants

After students have begun their systematic exploration of word roots, they examine related words in which both the sound *and* the spelling changes, but this change is predictable. For example, although the spelling of the long *-a* in *explain* changes from *ai* to simply *a* in the derived word *explanation,* these are not the only words in which this change occurs; this predictable pattern also occurs in many other related words such as *exclaim/exclamation* and *proclaim/proclamation*. Students learn that, if the base word has the *ai* spelling, the derived word's spelling of the schwa is *a*. Students are ready to examine these words because they understand the spelling-meaning patterns presented earlier. The following sort illustrates this feature.

receive/reception	*exclaim/exclamation*	*detain/detention*
conceive/conception	*proclaim/proclamation*	*retain/retention*
deceive/deception	*reclaim/reclamation*	
perceive/perception	*acclaim/acclamation*	

Students first do a closed sort in which each base word is paired with its derivative (*receive/reception; retain/retention*), and then sort the word pairs according to the specific spelling change that occurs: *deceive/deception; conceive/conception; reclaim/reclamation; proclaim/proclamation; detain/detention; retain/retention.*

In the following sort, predictable consonant alternation patterns are highlighted. Students first sort the words by pairing the base word with its derivative, sorting similar patterns, and then examining each pattern to determine the type of alternation that has occurred.

divide	*division*	*brilliant*	*brilliance*
delude	*delusion*	*prominent*	*prominence*
deride	*derision*	*reverent*	*reverence*
allude	*allusion*	*fragrant*	*fragrance*
protrude	*protrusion*	*equivalent*	*equivalence*
intrude	*intrusion*	*confident*	*confidence*

Students learn that, if the derived word contains a sound they are unsure how to spell, attending to the spelling of a related word often provides a clue. For example, if students are unsure whether *confidence* ends in *-se* or *-ce*, they can think of *confident*; it ends with a *t*, so the spelling of the /s/ sound is *-ce* (other words that illustrate this particular predictable pattern are *incident/incidence; diffident/diffidence; attendant/attendance*).

As pointed out, we are suggesting a general sequence according to which spelling-meaning patterns are explored. Your students will probably notice, however, that very often *multiple* alternations are occurring in a group of related words. This insight leads to an investigation of how many vowel and consonant alternations students can find within a group of words, as follows:

ferocious	*ferocity*
diplomatic	*diplomacy*
specific	*specificity*
perspicacious	*perspicacity*
pugnacious	*pugnacity*

In *ferocious* and *ferocity*, for example, there is a long-to-short *o* vowel alternation and a /sh/-/s/ consonant alternation.

In summary, the *spelling-meaning connection* plays a very important role in fine-tuning spelling knowledge and in expanding students' vocabularies. Once students understand how the principle operates in known words, we show them how it applies in unknown words. For example, let us say a student has used the word *solemn* in his writing—he knows the meaning of the word and understands it when he runs across it in his reading, but he misspells it as SOLEM. You would then show him the related word *solemnity*. In so doing, you have the opportunity to address two important objectives: First, the reason for the so-called silent *-n* in *solemn* becomes clear—the word is related to *solemnity* in which the *n* is pronounced. Second, because students already know the meaning of *solemn*, they are able to understand the meaning of the new but related word *solemnity*. You have just used the spelling system, in other words, to expand this student's vocabulary!

 Exploring spelling-meaning similarities across languages is exciting. ELL students will take time in noticing the differences in placement of stress, however, in the pronunciation of the cognates in English.

Greek and Latin Elements

After exploring a number of spelling-meaning relationships and examining the meaning changes accompanying the addition and deletion of affixes to known base words, students may be ready to explore the incredibly rich terrain of **word roots**—those elements from Greek and Latin that remain at the root or the core of the word after all prefixes and suffixes have been removed but which usually do not stand alone like base words; for example, *chron* ("time") in *chronology* and *struc* ("build") in *restructure*.

In the following lesson, Jorge Ramirez shows his students how Latin *word roots* function within words. He begins with a discussion briefly reviewing how *base words* and affixes combine to create a family of related words, using examples such as **payment/repay** and **governing/government**. He then goes on to say: "In thousands of words, there is a word part that is like a base word in that prefixes and suffixes attach to it. Unlike base words, however, this word part usually cannot stand by itself as a word. Still, it is the most important part of the word in which it occurs. We call it a *word root*. Let me show you one that's in a couple of words you know quite well."

Jorge then writes *fracture* and *fraction* on the board: "We know what these two words are and what they mean. What happens when you *fracture* your arm? [You break it.] What do you do when you divide something into *fractions?* [Jorge elicits from the students that you break whole numbers down into fractions.] Good! Now, both of the words *fracture* and *fraction* have the word root *fract* in them. Is *fract* a word? [No.] It's a very important part of the words *fracture* and *fraction*, however. We call *fract* a word root. It comes from a word in Latin that means 'to break.' Remember our discussion about the history of English and how so many words and word parts in English come from the Greek and Latin languages? So, *fract* is a Latin word root and it lives on in the words *fracture* and *fraction*.

"Word roots are everywhere! Let's look at these words. [Jorge writes *construct, construction*, and *structure* in a column on the board.] What's the same in these three words? [Students point out *struct*.] Good! You've found the word root! Now, let's think about what this word root might mean—think about what happens when construction workers construct a building or structure. [Students engage in a brief discussion in which the meaning "to build" emerges.] Right! *Construct* means 'to build something,' and *structure* is another term we often use to refer to a building or something that has been built."

Next, Jorge adds the word *instruct* to the list and asks the students how the meaning of "build" might apply to the word. Through discussion, students come to the realization that *instruct* refers to how learning or knowledge is "built."

Jorge assigns his students the task over the next few days of finding more words with the -*fract*- and -*struct*- roots. Students brainstorm, use the class dictionary, and consult an online dictionary to develop a long list of words including **frac**tious, **fract**als, in**frac**tion, re**frac**tion, super**struct**ure, con**struct**ion, un**struct**ured, de**struct**ion, inde**struct**ible, ob**struct**ion, recon**struct**ion, and in**struct**ional. Students will record the words they find in the vocabulary section of their word study notebooks and come together to compare their findings.

Word roots nestle within a word and are the meaningful anchor to which prefixes and suffixes may attach. These roots also follow the basic spelling-meaning premise that words with similar meanings are usually spelled similarly, and it is important to point out to students that spelling still *visually* represents the meaning of these elements and preserves the meaning relationships among words that at first may appear quite different. Notice, for example, the consistent spelling -*jud*- in the words **jud**ge, pre**jud**ice, and ad**jud**icate.

Because roots are usually not base words or affixes, they are at first more challenging to locate. Their consistent spelling, however, is the best clue to identifying them and examining how they function within words. Usually their spelling remains the same (in**spect**, **spect**ator; pre**dict**, in**dict**). When the spelling does change, however, it also does so predictably (re**ceive**/re**cep**tion; con**ceive**/con**cep**tion). Students may already have noted these predictable changes in their exploration of spelling-meaning relationships, as for example thinking about how *receive* and *reception* are related in meaning; they can now examine them while attending to the meaning of the root within the related words (*ceiv* and *cep* both mean "take").

At the derivational relations stage, exploration of Greek and Latin word roots begins with (a) those that occur with greatest frequency in the language, and (b) how these elements combine within words. These Greek and Latin word roots should be sequenced according to the abstractness of their meaning, from concrete to more abstract. For example, the Greek roots *phon* (sound), *auto* (self), and *graph* (writing) and the Latin roots *spect* (to look), *rupt* (to break, burst), and *dic* (to speak, say) are introduced and explored early in the sequence; more abstract roots such as the Latin *fer* (to carry) and *spir* (to breathe) are explored later. In this chapter we present the roots that occur most frequently in the reading material that intermediate and middle grade students encounter. Because of this frequency of occurrence, these roots warrant students' direct attention and exploration. Table 8-3 presents resources for Greek and Latin word studies; Tables 8-6 and 8-7 later in the chapter present Greek and Latin word roots. We extend examination of word roots to those encountered at the secondary level.

 Many activities appropriate for your study of Greek and Latin elements are available in the Derivational Relations section of the accompanying CD-ROM.

Following is an example of a word sort focused on word roots that may be conducted after you have discussed word roots with your students, talked about how they function within words, and given some examples. Ask the students to sort the words

TABLE 8-3 Resources for Word Study

Greek and Latin Elements
For students and teachers:
Crutchfield, R. (1997). *English vocabulary quick reference: A comprehensive dictionary arranged by word roots.* Leesburg, VA: LexaDyne Publishing, Inc.
Kennedy, J. (1996). *Word stems: A dictionary.* New York: Soho Press.
Moore, B., & Moore, M. (1997). *NTC's dictionary of Latin and Greek origins: A comprehensive guide to the classical origins of English words.* Chicago: NTC Publishing Group.
For teachers:
Ayers, D. M. (1986). *English words from Latin and Greek elements* (2nd ed., revised by Thomas Worthen). Tucson: The University of Arizona Press.
Schleifer, R. (1995). *Grow your own vocabulary.* New York: Random House.
For secondary students and teachers:
Danner, H., & Noel, R. (1996). *Discover it! A better vocabulary the better way.* Occoquan, VA: Imprimis Books.

Word Origins
For students and teachers:
Ayto, J. *Dictionary of word origins.* New York: Arcade.
Merriam Webster new book of word histories. (1991). Springfield, MA: Merriam-Webster Inc.
For teachers:
Shipley, J. (1984). *The origins of English words.* Baltimore: Johns Hopkins University Press. (For truly dedicated wordsmiths, Shipley's book is the ultimate source. A delightful read!)

Books for Students and Teachers
Asimov, I. (1961). *Words from the myths.* Boston: Houghton Mifflin (The most readable and most interesting resource of this kind).
D'Aulaire, I., & D'Aulaire, E. (1980). *D'Aulaires' book of Greek myths.* New York: Doubleday (Of interest to third graders and up; upper intermediate reading level).
Fisher, L. (1984). *The Olympians: Great gods and goddesses of ancient Greece.* Holiday (Of interest to third graders and up; third-grade reading level).
Gates, D. (1974). *Two queens of heaven: Aphrodite and Demeter.* Viking [Of interest to fourth graders and up; upper intermediate reading level).
Kingsley, C. (1980). *The heroes.* Mayflower (Of interest to third graders and up; intermediate reading level). The stories behind many present-day words that come from myths and legends help students remember the meanings of the terms and their spellings.

by their word roots; then have them discuss the possible meanings of the roots *-tract-* and *-spect-*:

tractor	inspect
contract	inspection
subtract	spectacle
distraction	spectator

Following is a sort focused on word roots that would be appropriate later in word study; students could offer hypotheses about the meaning of each root (given here in parentheses) and then check in an unabridged dictionary.

-greg- (flock)	**-carn-** (flesh)	**-gress-** (move)
congregate	carnation	digress
aggregate	carnivore	aggressive
segregate	reincarnation	egress
gregarious	carnage	congress

-hum- (lowly; literally, "from the ground")	**-fac-** ("to make, to do")
human	factory
humble	manufacture
humility	artifact
posthumous	benefactor
exhume	facsimile

 The Companion Website www.prenhall.com/bear has a word sort on the meanings found in *millennium* and related words, as well as a sort that compares words that end in *-ium* and *-um*.

Word roots also offer a very rich terrain for exploring **cognates** in other languages: *nocturno* and *extensor* in Spanish have very similar meanings to *nocturnal* and *extensive* in English. Consider the following sort:

producir	producto	
filosofía	filosofo	filosófico
ideología	ideologico	

 Native Spanish speakers will notice English cognates, and native English speakers will notice the Spanish cognates.

Advanced Suffix Study

A handful of suffixes present occasional challenges even for advanced readers and writers. Following are examples of how word study at this level can reduce students' uncertainty about persistent spelling errors in these suffixes at this level.

The adjective-forming suffix *-able/-ible* seems to be a classic for misspelling. There is a generalization that usually helps determine whether this suffix is spelled *-able* or *-ible*. Consider this sort:

dependable	credible
profitable	audible
agreeable	edible
predictable	visible
acceptable	feasible
profitable	terrible
punishable	indelible

A fairly powerful generalization emerges: If the suffix is attached to a base word it is usually spelled *-able*; if it is attached to a word root it is usually spelled *-ible*.

The distinction between the pairs of suffixes *-ant/-ance* and *-ent/-ence* can be explained etymologically, but you would have to be an historical linguist to understand when to use which spelling consistently, and even then there is variability. The best strategy is the following: If you know the spelling of a word that ends in one of these suffixes, that word is a clue to the spelling of the suffix in the related word (Templeton, 1980). For example, quite often individuals who spell *independence* correctly will also use the spelling *independant*. Similarly, the misspelling of *confidant* can be fixed by thinking of *confidence*. At this level, most individuals know how to spell one of the words in such pairs correctly; making this relationship explicit is extremely helpful for the learner.

The relationship between consonant doubling and accent, illustrated by words such as *committed* and *benefited*, can be explored through the type of activity modeled once again by Jorge Ramirez:

"Okay, we've got a few words here to sort. Notice that all of them end with *-ed*. But when we look at the base word, we see that in some cases the final consonant has been doubled before adding *-ed*, and in others it has stayed the same. Sort the words into two columns—those that are doubled and those that are not—and let's see if we can figure out what's going on here."

occurred	benefited
submitted	orbited
referred	conquered

Jorge asks the students to work in pairs to talk about what they see and hear when they contrast the words in both columns. If no one brings up "accent" as a possible explanation he directs their attention to it: "In the words in which the final consonant is doubled before adding *-ed*, does the *-ed* follow a syllable that is stressed? [Yes.] How about the words in which the final consonant is *not* doubled? Does the *-ed* follow a syllable that is stressed? [No.] Would someone like to have a go at stating a rule for when we double and when we don't?"

The generalization toward which Jorge is working with the students is this: If the last syllable of the base word is accented, double the final consonant before adding -ed (and -ing as well). If the last syllable is not accented, then do not double the final consonant.

Jorge follows up the sort by pointing out the following bit of history:

"Remember when Daire brought in the British copy of *Harry Potter and the Goblet of Fire* that her grandma bought for her in England and we noticed how the spelling of some of the words was different than in American English? For example, there were a lot of doubled consonants that we don't have—*benefited* had two *t*s at the end. Actually, in just about every situation where we in America do not double the final consonant, people in other English-speaking countries do. Do you know who we can blame for making it so that Americans have to think about whether or not to double . . . ? Would you believe it was Noah Webster? Yes! The man who brought us our dictionary!

"Actually, what Webster wanted to do was make English spoken and written in America different in many ways from English spoken in Britain. When he did this, America wasn't getting along too well with Britain—after all, we had fought a war to become independent not long before! So, in his dictionary of American English—the first of its kind—Webster decided to change many spellings. One of the most obvious was to take out the *u* in words such as *honour* and *behaviour* [Jorge writes these on the board]. He also switched the *re* in words such as *theatre* and *centre* [he writes these on the board]."

When students notice exceptions to this principle—when they see the spelling *traveled* or *benefitted*, for example—ask them to check the dictionary: Though they will see the correct spelling they will also see the so-called incorrect spelling listed. In other words, over time, if enough people misspell a word, the misspelling will work its way into the dictionary as an accepted if not the preferred spelling.

Absorbed Prefixes

Jorge Ramirez first explores the concept of **absorbed prefixes** with his students (a fairly advanced understanding) in this type of lesson:

> "Jared, you checked the prefix *in-* in the dictionary yesterday and were a little perplexed! You discovered that this prefix is also spelled *il-*, *im-*, and *ir-*. It seems a little peculiar, doesn't it? Well, let's look at why this is so.
>
> "Let's take the word *immobile*. What does it mean. . . ? Right! Something is 'not moving.' The word is constructed from the prefix *in-*, meaning 'not,' and the base word *mobile*, which means 'capable of moving.' When we put *in-* and *mobile* together, two things happen. First, the word parts combine to mean 'not mobile, not capable of moving.' Second, notice that the spelling of the prefix *in-* has changed to *im*. Let's think about why this happened.
>
> "A long time ago, someone realized that instead of always saying something was 'not mobile' they could simply combine the prefix *in-* with the word *mobile* to create a new word that meant 'not mobile.' Now, try pronouncing the word like it was pronounced when it first came into existence: *in*mobile. Does that feel kind of weird? Does your tongue kind of get stuck on the beginning of 'mobile'? Mine sure does! Well, the same thing happened to speakers a long time ago—it became easier for people to leave out the n sound when pronouncing the word. The sound of the n became 'absorbed' into the m sound at the beginning of the base word *mobile*. Before long, the spelling of the *n* changed to indicate this change in pronunciation—but it's important to remember that this letter didn't disappear. They knew it was necessary to keep the two letters in the prefix to indicate that it was still a prefix. If the last letter of the prefix had been dropped, then the meaning of the prefix would have been lost.
>
> "Here are some other words that have absorbed the *in-* prefix into the base word [writes the words *immeasureable*, *immodest*, and *immortal* on the board]. These started out as *inmeasureable*, *inmodest*, and *inmortal*."

The next step in this lesson or on the following day is to show how *in-* changes to *ir-* when combined with a base that begins with *r* (*irresponsible*) and how it changes to *il-* when combined with a base that begins with *l* (*illiterate*). Other absorbed prefixes may be studied as they arise. Students will come to realize that absorbed prefixes are widespread in the language.

Also referred to as **assimilated prefixes,** these prefixes are primarily Latin in origin. They are addressed later in the instructional sequence because they depend on considerable prior knowledge about other basic spelling-meaning patterns, processes of adding prefixes to base words, and simple Greek and Latin stems. Here is how they work: In the word *attract* the *at-* is an absorbed prefix. A long time ago the word began as *adtract*. It was created by combining the prefix *ad-*, meaning "to, toward," with the word root *tract*, meaning "to draw, pull." Because of the difficulty in pronouncing *adtract* and keeping the /d/ and the /t/ sounds separate, over a period of time the /d/ sound became absorbed into the /t/ sound, in effect disappearing altogether. The spelling of *adtract* also changed. Absorbed prefixes should first be presented in the context of base words: *con + respond = correspond, in + mobilize = immobilize*. Once understood in these types of words, they may be taught in the context of word roots: *ad + tain = attain, con + rode = corrode*. Table 8-7 on page 286 presents the important and most frequently occurring absorbed prefixes.

Below is a sort that might be used by a middle or high school English teacher to explore the idea of absorbed prefixes. The words are first presented in a random list and the students are asked to discuss their meanings. The students are likely to conclude that they all seem to mean "not" or "the opposite of." When asked how they might sort the words, the following categories emerge:

ineffective	illiterate	immature	irregular	impossible
inorganic	illegal	immobile	irrational	impatient
inactive	illogical	immortal	irresponsible	improper
infinite		immodest	irrelevant	

The students might then be asked what they notice about the base words in each column. The particular spelling of the prefix *in-* depends on the first letter of the base word, taking on the same spelling except in the case of words beginning with *p*.

Word Origins

Exploring the origins of words and the processes of word creation provides a powerful knowledge base for learning spelling and vocabulary, as well as for facilitating more effective reading and writing. **Etymology,** the study of word origins (from the Greek *etumon,* meaning "true sense of a word"), may develop into a lifelong fascination for many students. As you engage students in examining word roots and their combinations with affixes and other roots you are laying the groundwork for more focused exploration in etymology, because students are developing a real sense of how words work at this level and a general sense of how words can move through history.

Many times the spelling of a word may appear odd, but an understanding of its origin provides the most powerful key to remembering the spelling. Knowing that so many words have come from mythology, literature, and historical events and figures provides important background knowledge for students' reading in the various content areas. Sensitivity to and interest in word origins, in other words, will provide invaluable insight into the concepts and content of much of our students' continuing education.

In addition to the historical origin of words, a significant number of words that have recently come into American English arrive from other contemporary languages: primarily Spanish, but some French (e.g., *bistro, a la carte*). A popular classroom activity is to post a large world map on the wall and post words according to country of origin.

WORD STUDY ROUTINES AND MANAGEMENT

Table 8-2 presents the derivational relationships we have discussed, and instruction may follow the general sequence presented therein. The sequence for derivational relations begins with a straightforward exploration of the spelling-meaning connection, then moves to Greek and Latin word roots and affixes, to predictable spelling changes in related words, and then on to another look at prefixes. Study of Greek and Latin word roots begins with those that occur with the greatest frequency in the reading in which students are engaged. Importantly, you will emphasize *how these elements combine within words*—this knowledge provides a powerful foundation and productive strategy for continuing vocabulary and spelling growth. It extends the basic understandings developed during the syllables and affixes stage when students examined how simpler prefixes, suffixes, and base words combined. This more advanced word knowledge will help tremendously when students realize how many of these elements occur in the vocabulary terms that represent core concepts in science, social studies, and math.

There are three basic points to keep in mind regarding students' word study at this level (Templeton, 1989, 1992):

1. Words and word elements selected for study should be *generative,* which means that, when possible, we teach about words in meaning "families." This highlights the awareness that particular patterns of relationships can be extended or generalized to other words. For example, an awareness of the long-to-short vowel alternation pattern that was introduced during the syllables and affixes with words such as **please** and **pleas***ant* can generalize to words such as **compet***e*/**compet***itive*.

2. The words that we initially select for exploration by our students should be selected based on how obvious their relationship is. For example, we will teach clearly related words such as *represent/misrepresent* before teaching about words that are less clearly related, such as *expose/exposition*.

3. There should be a balance of teacher-directed instruction with students' explorations and discussions.

Teacher Directed Word Study Instruction

 ELL students have the potential to be *more* sensitive to words than monolingual speakers, simply because they must be more analytical–of their home language as well as of English–in order to negotiate the nature of spelling/sound/meaning relationships.

As in other stages, students in the derivational relations stage still need in-depth systematic attention to features at their developmental level. We emphasize the importance of word study at this developmental level for middle and secondary students, especially if these students have not experienced this type of systematic word study in school prior to this time.

Teachers who use the upper-level spelling inventory described in Chapter 2 will be able to identify what features to address in instruction. Typically there is a plateau effect with upper-level assessments which suggests that students in homogeneous classes may all benefit from similar instruction and small-group organization is less important. This may be reassuring for secondary teachers who only have their students for short periods of time each day. Chapter 3 describes a variety of routines and word study notebook activities that can be adapted for word study at this level and there are some specific suggestions for word study notebooks to follow. The categorization of words through sorting is still a powerful learning activity; however, most teachers rely more upon writing words into categories than upon cutting out words and sorting them physically.

There are a number of word sorts and activities in the Appendix and on the accompanying *Words Their Way* CD that are appropriate for more advanced derivational relations students. Middle school and secondary English/language arts teachers should find this section to be helpful, as it extends the types of word knowledge that are possible to develop at this level. In particular, it presents avenues of word study that will be engaging and quite rewarding for students who are verbally advanced. Look for examples of these sorts in the activity section that follows.

This type of exploration and curiosity about words will unavoidably become part of students' learning repertoires. Indeed, it is more a mindset than a strategy per se. Such students become lifelong wordsmiths and almost automatically wonder about the relationships among words in general and about a particular word specifically; for example, does the similarity in spelling between *applaud/plaudit* and *mordant/morsel* capture underlying meaning relationships? (Yes) This type of awareness leads to the continual nourishment and growth of underlying conceptual networks. Table 8-4 expands on this aspect of word awareness.

In the derivational relations stage, the meaning connections are especially important and dictionaries will get a lot of use. The following materials should always be readily available to students.

- Intermediate and collegiate dictionaries, enough copies for six to eight students to work in a small group
- Thesaurus collection, enough for six to eight students in small group work
- Several word history (etymological) dictionaries and root books (see Table 8-3 on page 259 for an annotated list)

TABLE 8-4 Growing Students' Sensitivity to Words

Writers who use words effectively usually have a solid awareness and knowledge of the sound, structure, and meaning of words. This is why they can select and link those words that work most effectively in a particular context. Similarly, readers who read most effectively have a solid awareness of sound, structure, and meaning. Our ultimate goal is of course to grow *wordsmiths*—students who know how words are put into play (e.g., how writers use them to craft images, to engage feelings, and to prompt action). Here we are moving into areas beyond the scope of this book, but we cannot leave our exploration of the sound, structure, and meaning of words without at least mentioning how writers put words to use, and the vocabulary we can use to describe this use of words. We should help students see how this is done, identify instances of effective word use, and learn the terms that help us talk about this usage (e.g., **denotation/connotation, simile,** and **metaphor**). There are more, but these are the most common and most important for intermediate and middle level students to know.

Words have **denotative** meanings (e.g., what they literally mean or refer to). They also have **connotative** meanings (e.g., what they suggest to us, how they make us feel, the associations we bring to them beyond their literal meanings). For example, it makes a difference if we refer to a person as "old" or as "elderly"; elderly has a kinder, more respectful association than if we were to refer to someone simply as "old." Both words literally refer to or denote an older person, but we select one over the other in most contexts because of its more effective and appropriate connotative meaning.

Simile and metaphor are much more common than we realize in our language. Students can learn the straightforward definitions: Simile expresses a comparison using the terms *like* or *as.* In *Timothy of the Cay,* Theodore Taylor writes in the first person of how young Phillip was rescued from the cay on which he had been stranded, and how "I'd been brought aboard from the rescue boat, naked as a plucked pigeon. . ." (p. 2). Taylor has used a simile to describe Phillip's condition. Metaphor also expresses a comparison, but without the words *like* or *as.* In *On My Honor* (1986), Marion Dane Bauer offers the following description as young Joel finally staggers onto the riverbank after nearly drowning: "When the river bottom came up to meet his feet, he stood. The sky was an inverted china bowl above his head" (p. 33). Of course, the sky is not literally an inverted china bowl; through the use of metaphor, Bauer has helped us construct a vivid mental image. The starkness of this image—a white glare after he had been struggling underwater—also captures Joel's sense of being caught in a nightmare from which he cannot escape: He has just realized that his friend Tony, who has also been swimming in the river, has probably drowned. Scott O'Dell, in *Black Star, Bright Dawn* (1989), describes Bright Dawn's realization that she is caught in a whiteout while on the grueling Alaskan Iditarod: "There was nothing to see except swirling curtains of white cotton. There was no sky above me, no ice beneath my feet" (p. 83). O'Dell does not have to say "The snow was like 'swirling curtains of white cotton'." We know he is talking about the snow, and his description is the more effective because he states it directly.

We should let students know that our purpose for exploring simile and metaphor is to identify instances when words have been used to express something in a fresh, new way. We then help them apply this awareness in their writing and in their appreciation of what they read (see also Beck, McKeown, & Kucan, 2002).

Activities for Students in the Derivational Relations Stage

Derivational Relations Stage

Here we present illustrative activities, word sorts, and games for students in the derivational relations stage.

 For many more activities appropriate for the Derivational Relations learner, visit the accompanying CD-ROM.

 The Vocabulary Notebook becomes an especially important learning tool for ELL students. They will better be able to learn and remember more fine-tuned distinctions in meaning and appropriate usage of new terms.

Vocabulary Notebooks 8-1

Vocabulary notebooks are an integral part of students' word learning at the derivational relations phase (Gill & Bear, 1989). They can also be used with many activities, for example, to record word sorts and add words to the sorts after going on word hunts. To begin, divide the notebooks into two sections:

Word Study: A weekly record of sorts, explanations of sorts, and homework
Looking into Language: Records of whole group word study of related words, semantic sorts, interesting word collections, investigations, and theme study words

Following is a description of how to facilitate older students' collections of "interesting" words:

1. While reading, place a question mark above words you find difficult, and place a question mark in the margin for easy reference. When you are through reading or studying, go back to your question marks. Read around the word, and think about its possible meaning.
2. Write the word, followed by the sentence in which it was used, the page number, and an abbreviation for the title of the book. (At times the sentence will be too long. Write enough of it to give a clue to meaning.) Think about the word's meaning.
3. Look at the different parts of the word—prefixes, suffixes, and base word or root word. Think about the meaning of the affixes and base or root.
4. Think of other words that are like this word, and write them underneath the part of the word that is similar.
5. Look the word up in the dictionary, read the various definitions, and in a few words record the meaning (the one that applies to the word in the book you are reading) in your notebook or on a card. Look for similar words (both in form and meaning) above and below the target word, and add them to the list you started in step 4.
6. Look at the origin of the word, and add it to your entry if it is interesting.

A realistic goal is to collect 10 words a week. These words may be brought up in class and shared. In addition, record words that consistently present spelling challenges in the notebook or on the cards. For each word, think of words that are related to this particular word again, as in step 4.

Let us summarize the process:

1. Collect the word.
2. Record the word and sentence.
3. Look at word parts and think about their meaning.
4. Record related words.
5. Study the word in the dictionary, and record interesting information.
6. Review the words.

Here is an example:

1. [Word] ORTHOGRAPHY
2. [Sentence] "English orthography is not crazy, and it carries the history of the word with it." p. 22, *Sounds of Language*
3. [Look at word parts] ortho graph ("may have something to do with writing")
4. [Think of possible related words]

ortho	graphy
orthodontist	graphic
orthodox	
orthographer	[*Note:* These are added from step 5.]
orthographist	
orthomolecular	
orthodox	

5. [Definition] "a method of representing the sounds of a language by letters; spelling" *Note:* The third definition fits most nearly the meaning of orthography as it was used in the sentence. The first two meanings are "1. the art or study of standard spelling; 2. the aspect of language study concerned with letters and spelling" (*The American Heritage College Dictionary* (1993), p. 965).
6. [Origins] ortho: correct graph: something written*

ELL Spelling-Meaning Word Sort: The Long, the Short, and the Schwa 8-2

This sort helps students focus attention on the major types of vowel alternation patterns.

Materials

Word lists with paired examples of each of the three predominant alternation patterns: (a) long to short (*divine/divinity*); (b) long to schwa (*compose/composition*); (c) short to schwa (*similar/similarity*).

Procedures

1. Before introducing the categories long to short, long to schwa, or short to schwa, lead students through an examination of each of the word pairs provided. Ask the students how the sound of the highlighted vowel changes in each word pair: For example, "What happens to this vowel sound [pointing to the *i* in *divine*] when we put the suffix *-ity* onto it?" Ask students if they can think of any other words that follow this same type of pattern in which the long vowel changes to the short vowel.

---

*Thanks to Tamara Baren for suggestions and examples.

2. Walk through this discussion for each of the alternation patterns.
3. Provide a copy of the following form for each student (or have students write these categories in their vocabulary notebooks):

Long to Short   **Long to Schwa**   **Short to Schwa**
divine/divinity   compose/composition   similar/similarity

Select a number of word pairs from word sorts 109 through 113 in the Appendix and randomly arrange them on a handout for the students.

4. Working independently or in pairs, students will decide which alternation pattern each word pair illustrates and write it in the appropriate column. Students will later compare their categorizations.

(Thanks to Lisbeth Kling for her assistance.)

 Additional spelling-meaning sorts are available in the Derivational Relations Section of the accompanying CD-ROM.

Spelling/Meaning Word Sort: Is it -*sion* or -*tion*? 8-3

This activity will involve students in small groups or two teams of two each, examining words to determine clues for spelling the -*tion* or -*sion* suffixes.

Materials

Each team or group needs a sheet divided into two columns. The left column is labeled "We Think" and the right column is labeled "Because."

Procedures

1. Each team gets a stack of cards to sort. The same words are in each stack; to keep word cards for each team separate, one stack is printed in black letters and the other in red.
2. Each team then sorts the words into two categories: base words and derived words.
3. After looking closely at the words sorted, each team individually fills out their "We Think" sheets with generalities that they notice about when words took the -*tion* or the -*sion* ending.
4. After the teams have filled out their "We Think" sheets and supported their generalized rules under the "Because" section, the teams have a meeting of the minds to compare findings.

Variations

1. Students look for other words with -*tion* or -*sion* endings, determine the base or root, and then determine whether it fits the spelling generalization developed by the team. This gives students the opportunity to keep a running record in their vocabulary notebook and to monitor their generalization to see if it continues to work for new words that are encountered.
2. This activity will work with other base words, word roots, and derivatives.

Word List

separate	separation	convulse	convulsion	act	action
fascinate	fascination	express	expression	extinct	extinction
educate	education	profess	profession	contract	contraction
complicate	complication	confess	confession	conduct	conduction
generate	generation			affect	affection
navigate	navigation				
vegetate	vegetation				

Words that Grow from Base Words and Word Roots 8-4

In this whole class or small group activity, students see directly how words "grow" from base words and word roots. It builds on and extends the understanding, begun during the syllables and affixes stage, of how word elements combine.

Materials

You will need a poster board of a tree (see Figure 8-1).

Procedures

1. Decide on a base word or a word root to highlight (word roots may be selected from Tables 8-5 and 8-6). When roots are used, begin with more frequently occurring ones; over time, move to less frequently occurring roots.
2. Write the base word or word root at the bottom of the tree, and think of as many forms as possible.
3. Write the different forms on individual branches.
4. Display the word tree in the classroom for several days and encourage students to think of, find, and record more derived words. At the end of the week wipe them off and begin again with the introduction of a new base or word root.

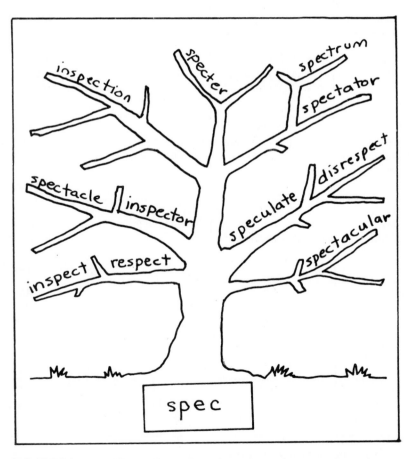

FIGURE 8-1 Word Tree: Words That Grow From Base and Root Words

Variations

After making the words, students may use them individually in sentences and/or discuss their meanings. Confirm with the dictionary.

ELL Spelling-meaning relationships allow most ELL learners to explore cognates and morphological similarities between English and their home language.

Game: Greek and Latin Jeopardy 8-5

A total of six students are involved in this game. Three students are the contestants: one student is in charge of the answers and questions, one student is the scorekeeper, and one person can be the judge in case of the need to question a decision.

Materials

Enlarge the Latin Root Jeopardy and Double Latin Root Jeopardy boards shown in Figures 8-2 and 8-3, or make an overhead transparency and project it on a screen. Cover the clues with squares of paper or sticky notes on the overhead. On a chalk board use tape to fix squares of paper in the correct order. Write the amount on one side and the answer on the other. Turn over the square that is requested during the playing of the game so the answer can be read.

Derivational Relations Stage

LATIN ROOT JEOPARDY				
SPECT (to look)	FORM (shape)	PORT (to carry)	TRACT (draw or pull)	DICT (to say, speak)
100 One who watches; an onlooker	100 One "form" or style of clothing such as is worn by nurses	100 Goods brought into a country from another country to be sold	100 Adjective: having power to attract; alluring; inviting	100 A book containing the words of a language explained
200 The prospect of good to come; anticipation	200 One who does not conform	200 One who carries burdens for hire	200 A powerful motor vehicle for pulling farm machinery, heavy loads, etc.	200 A speaking against, a denial
300 To regard with suspicion and mistrust	300 To form or make anew; to reclaim	300 To remove from one place to another	300 The power to grip or hold to a surface while moving, without slipping	300 A blessing often at the end of a worship service
400 Verb: to esteem Noun: regard, deference Literally: to look again	400 To change into another substance, change of form	400 To give an account of	400 An agreement: literally, to draw together	400 An order proclaimed by an authority
500 Looking around, watchful, prudent	500 Disfigurement, spoiling the shape	500 A case for carrying loose papers	500 To take apart from the rest, to deduct	500 To charge with a crime

FIGURE 8-2 Latin Root Jeopardy Board

Procedures

The teacher should go over the rules of the game first. The game consists of three rounds: Jeopardy, Double Jeopardy, and Final Jeopardy.

1. The game is modeled after the *Jeopardy* television game. The answer will appear when it is uncovered in this version. The players must phrase their answers in the form of a question:

> Answer: Coming from the Latin root meaning "to draw or pull," its definition means "a machine for pulling heavy loads."
> Question: What is *tractor*?

2. Determine who will go first. The player will select the first category and point value. The leader uncovers the clue and reads it aloud.
3. The first player responding correctly adds the point amount of the question to his or her total and chooses the next category and point amount. An incorrect answer means that the points are subtracted.

DOUBLE LATIN ROOT JEOPARDY				
CRED (to believe)	DUCT (to lead)	FER (to bear, carry)	PRESS (to press)	SPIR (to breathe)
200 A system of doing business by trusting that a person will pay at a later date for goods or services	200 A person who directs the performance of a choir or an orchestra	200 (Plants) able to bear fruit; (Animals) able or likely to conceive young	200 A printing machine	200 An immaterial intelligent being
400 A set of beliefs or principles	400 To train the mind and abilities of	400 To carry again; to submit to another for opinion	400 Verb: to utter; Noun: any fast conveyance	400 To breathe out: to die
600 Unbelievable	600 To enroll as a member of a military service	600 To convey to another place, passed from one place to another	600 To press against, to burden, to overpower	600 To breathe through; to emit through the pores of the skin
800 Verb, prefix meaning "not"; word means to damage the good reputation of	800 The formal presentation of one person to another	800 Endurance of pain; distress	800 State of being "pressed down" or saddened	800 To breathe into; to instruct by divine influence
1000 An adjective, prefix *ac*, word means officially recognized	1000 An artificial channel carrying water across country	1000 Cone bearing, as the fir tree	1000 To put down, to prevent circulation	1000 To plot; to band together for an evil purpose

FIGURE 8-3   Double Latin Root Jeopardy Board

Derivational Relations Stage

4. When it is time for the Final Jeopardy question, players see the category, but not the answer. They then decide how many of their points they will risk. When they see the answer, they have 30 seconds to write the question. If they are correct, they add the number of points they risked to their total; if incorrect, that number of points is subtracted from their total.

Word list.   In the word lists, we have used modern English spellings of roots and their contemporary meanings, rather than tracing the evolution of each root from its original spelling and literal meaning in Latin (see Table 8-5).

Questions for Latin Root Jeopardy

	100	200	300	400	500
spect	spectator	expectation	suspect	respect	circumspect
form	uniform	nonconformist	reform	transform	deformity
port	import	porter	transport	report	portfolio
tract	attractive	tractor	traction	contract	subtract
dict	dictionary	contradiction	benediction	edict	indict

TABLE 8-5   Latin Roots

aud: to hear—audible, inaudible, audience, auditory, audio, audition, auditorium
bene: well, good—benefit, beneficial, benevolent, benefactor, benediction
cred: to believe, to trust—credit, credible, credence, discredit, credulous, incredible
dict: to say—dictate, diction, dictator, dictionary, contradict, predict, edict, jurisdiction, contradiction, indict, benediction
duc(t): to lead—conducive, deduce, deduct, educate, induce, introduce, produce, reduce, aquaduct
fac: to do, to make—fact, factual, factory, facilitate, manufacture, benefactor
flec/flex: to bend—reflection, deflect, flexible, inflection, reflect
form: shape—formation, formative, deform, formula
fract: to break—fracture, refract, fraction
ject: throw—reject, projectile, eject, inject, interject, object
jud: judge—judgment, prejudice, adjudicate, judiciary
junct: to join—juncture, junction, conjunction
port: to carry—import, export, transport, portable, portfolio, report
rupt: to break—abrupt, corrupt, disrupt, eruption, interrupt, bankrupt, rupture
scrib/script: to write—inscribe, transcribe, transcript, manuscript, prescription, describe
sect/sec: cut—dissect, intersect, insect, bisect, midsection
spect: to look—spectator, inspect, prospect, suspect, spectacle, respect
spir: to breathe—respiration, inspire, conspirators, dispirited, perspire
st/sta/stat/stit: to stand—stable, station, constant, establish, statue, arrest, constitute, institute, obstacle
struct: to build—construct, instruct, destruct, structure
tang/tact: to touch—tangible/intangible, tangent, contact, tactile
trac/tract: to drag, pull—tractable, tractor, detract, extract, distract
vert/vers: to turn—revert, inversion, vertical, convert
vid/vis: to see—video, invisible, television, revise, advise, vista, visit, supervise
voc: voice, to call—vocal, advocate, vociferous, vocabulary, convocation

Questions for Double Latin Root Jeopardy

	200	400	600	800	1000
cred	credit	creed	incredible	discredit	accredited
duct	conductor	educate	induct	introduction	aqueduct
fer	fertile	refer	transfer	suffering	coniferous
press	press	express	oppress	depression	suppress
spir	spirit	expire	perspire	inspire	conspire

See Figure 8-4 for alternate suggestions for Latin Root Jeopardy.

VAL (to be strong, worth)
100 The worth of thing in money or goods (noun)   100 What is *value?*
200 Courage or bravery (noun)   200 What is *valor?*
300 To value at less than the real worth (verb)   300 What is *undervalue?*
400 Brave, full of courage (adjective)   400 What is *valiant?*
500 Priceless, precious (adjective)   500 What is *invaluable?*

SIGN (to sign, seal)
100 To write one's name on (verb)   100 What is *sign?*
200 A person's name written by oneself (noun)   200 What is *signature?*
300 A thing or happening that shows, warns, or   300 What is *signal?*
    points out (noun)
400 To be a sign of, to mean (verb)   400 What is *signify?*
500 A seal or other mark stamped on a paper   500 What is *signet?*
    to make it official (noun)

NOM (name)
100 To name as a candidate for election (verb)   100 What is *nominate?*
200 A person who is nominated (noun)   200 What is *nominee?*
300 In name only (adjective)   300 What is *nominal?*
400 A system of names, as those used in   400 What is *nomenclature?*
    studying a certain science (noun)
500 Showing the subject of a verb, or the words   500 What is *nominative?*
    that agree with the subject (noun)

RUPT (to break)
100 To burst forth, as lava from a volcano (verb)   100 What is *erupt?*
200 To break in between, as in conversation (verb)   200 What is *interrupt?*
300 To part violently (verb); a hernia (noun)   300 What is *rupture?*
400 A rending asunder, something you do not   400 What is *disruption?*
    want in the classroom (noun)
500 To defile, taint (verb)   500 What is *corrupt?*

STRUC(T) (to build)
100 A building (noun)   100 What is *structure?*
200 "Good" criticism (adjective)   200 What is *constructive?*
300 Ruin (noun)   300 What is *destruction?*
400 To teach or train (verb)   400 What is *instruct?*
500 That part of the building above the   500 What is *superstructure?*
    foundation (noun)

Derivational Relations Stage

FIGURE 8-4   Alternate Items for Latin Root Jeopardy

Variations

1. The gameboard may be copied and given to players who work alone. A sketch of the gameboard may be drawn on the chalk board with the point amount in the square. Mark off the square chosen before the answer is read by the leader. Daily Doubles may be included, if desired (the number of points for an answer is doubled, and if correct, added to the player's score; if incorrect, the doubled number of points is subtracted from the player's score).
2. Develop a Vocabulary Jeopardy to accompany a unit of study.
   - Students generate vocabulary cards from a unit of study.
   - Students write questions on cards that relate to facts and concepts studied. Answers are written on the back upside down. The cards are sorted into categories.
   - Teams of students play the game as a whole class vocabulary review of unit.

Hidden Greek Roots 8-6

This word sort is a more advanced activity with Greek roots for one to three students.

Materials

You will need the Greek root reference sheet, Greek root word cards, definition cards, and a dictionary. See Table 8-6.

TABLE 8-6   Greek Word Roots

aer: air—aerial, aerate, aerobics, aerosol, aerospace
agog: leader—demagogue, pedagogue, synagogue
angel: messenger—evangelist, angelic
aster/astr: star—asteroid, astronomer, astronomy, astrology, asterisk
auto: self—autograph, autobiography
bio: life—biology, biome, biotic, antibiotic, biopsy
chron: time—chronic, chonicle, chronology, synchrony
derm: skin—epidermis, dermatology, taxidermist, hypodermic, pachyderm
gram: thing written—diagram, monogram, telegram, grammar, program
graph: writing—autograph, biography, photography, telegraph, graphic, calligraphy, polygraph, digraph
hydr: water—hydrant, hydrology, hydroplane, hydraulic
logo: word, reason—logic, analogy, catalogue, prologue, epilogue, monologue
meter/metr: measure—metric, barometer, diameter, geometry, perimeter, symmetry
micro: small—microscope, micrometer, microfilm, microwave
mono: one, single—monotone, monotonous, monastery, monk
od/hod: road, way—episode, method, methodical, exodus
phe/phem: to speak—blaspheme, emphasis, emphatic, euphemism
phil: love—philanthropy, Philadelphia, philosophy, philharmonic
phon: sound—telephone, phonics, symphonic, euphony, homophone
photo/phos: light—photograph, telephoto, phosphorescent
pol/polis: city, state—police, metropolis, politics, cosmopolitan
scope: instrument for viewing—microscope, telescope, kaleidoscope, periscope
techn: art, skill, craft—technical, technology, polytechnic
therm: heat—thermometer, thermostat, thermal, exothermic
zoo: animal—zoo, zoology

Procedures

1. The teacher initiates discussion and background material for this Greek word root activity.
2. Student(s) sort word cards by Greek word families and match word cards to root definition cards. Through discussion and use of dictionaries, students may discover related word families.

It's All Greek to Us 8-7

In this card game, the deck is composed of Greek word cards. Two to four players may participate, one of whom will serve as game master and hold and read definition cards.

Procedures

1. Prepare definition card and word cards from the Definitions and Words List below.
2. The game master shuffles word cards, deals 10 cards per player, and places the remaining word cards facedown in front of the players.
3. The game master reads a definition card. A player who is holding a card to match the definition places it below the corresponding Greek root. Upon discarding, players must draw one word card from the remaining deck. If no player can respond to the definition, the game master places the definition card on the bottom of his or her cards for rereading later in the game. If a player successfully responds and matches a word card and definition, the game master places that definition card to the side.
4. When the word card deck is depleted, the player who discards all word cards first is the winner.

Variations

Students may create additional deck(s) by composing definitions for the additional example words in the Greek roots list in Table 8-6.

Definitions and Words List

Adj.	1. Of long duration, continuing, constant 2. Prolonged *chronic*
Adj.	Arranged in order of time of occurrence *chronological*
N.	The medical study of the physiology and pathology of the skin *dermatology*
N.	The outer, protective, nonvascular layer of the skin *epidermis*
N.	A design composed of one or more letters, usually the initials of a name *monogram*
Adj.	Without variation or variety; repetitiously dull *monotonous*
Adj.	1. Bold and definite in expression or action 2. Accentuated; definite *emphatic*
V.	To speak of God (or something sacred) in an irreverent or impious manner *blaspheme*
N.	The substitution of an inoffensive term for one considered offensively explicit *euphemism*
Adj.	Devoted to or appreciative of music *philharmonic*
N.	A listing of the order of events and other pertinent information for some public presentation *chronicle*
Adj.	1. Of or pertaining to written or pictorial representation 2. Described in vivid detail *graphic*
N.	The process of rendering optical images on photosensitive surfaces *photography*
N.	A movement away; a departure, usually of a large number *exodus*

Derivational Relations Stage

N.   A means or manner of procedure; especially a regular and systematic way of accomplishing anything *methodical*

N.   An outlet from a water main consisting of an upright pipe with one or more nozzles or spouts *hydrant*

Adj.   1. Showing consistency of reasoning
2. Able to reason clearly *logic*

N.   A short addition or concluding section at the end of any literary work or play *epilogue*

N.   An instrument for measuring atmospheric pressure, used in weather forecasting and in determining elevation *barometer*

N.   1. Mathematics—the distance around an enclosed area
2. Military—a fortified strip or boundary protecting a position *perimeter*

N.   A long speech or talk made by one person *monologue*

N.   A succession of sounds or words uttered in a single tone of voice *monotone*

N.   Public park or institution in which living animals are kept and exhibited to the public *zoo*

N.   The biological science of animals *zoology*

N.   Science that deals with microorganisms, especially their effects on other forms of life *microbiology*

N.   A tiny, representative world *microscopic*

N.   A film upon which documents or photographs are greatly reduced in size *microfilm*

N.   The scientific study of celestial bodies and phenomena *astronomy*

Adj.   1. Of or pertaining to astronomy
2. Inconceivably large; immense *astronomical*

N.   A self-told story of one's life; memoirs *autobiography*

N.   A person's own signature or handwriting *autograph*

V.   To expose to the circulation of air for purification *aerate*

Adj.   1. Of, in, or caused by the air
2. Reaching high into the air; lofty *aerial*

N.   A leader who obtains power by means of impassioned appeals to the emotions and prejudices of the populace *demagogue*

N.   Schoolteacher; educator *pedagogue*

N.   The suffering of intense physical or mental pain *chronic*

Adj.   Of, or pertaining to, consisting of, or belonging to angels *angelic*

N.   A star-shaped figure (*) used in print to indicate an omission or a reference to a footnote *asterisk*

N.   1. City of Brotherly Love
2. Large metropolitan city in Pennsylvania *Philadelphia*

N.   The effort or inclination to increase the well-being of humankind, as by charitable aid or donations *philanthropy*

Adj.   Occurring at the same time *synchronous*

N.   The study of the position and aspects of heavenly bodies with a view to predicting their influence on the course of human affairs *astrology*

Adj.   1. Too small to be seen by the unaided eye
2. Exceedingly small, minute *microscopic*

N.   A small tube in which patterns of colors are optically produced and viewed for amusement *kaleidoscope*

Adj.   Pertaining to or dealing with many arts and sciences *polytechnic*

N.   Beautiful handwriting *calligraphy*

Adj.   Of or pertaining to, or having the nature of sound, especially speech sounds

Adj.   1. Common to the whole world
2. At home in all parts of the earth, or in many spheres of interest *cosmopolitan*

N.   1. A major city
2. A large urban center of culture, trade, or other activity *Philadelphia*

Joined at the Roots 8-8

This word sort is an effective extension of students' exploration of Latin and Greek word roots. It is appropriate for individuals, partners, or small groups.

Materials

You will need a word sort board, word cards, and word study notebook.

Procedures

1. The teacher begins by modeling how to place words with appropriate roots under a particular category, for example, "speaking and writing," "building/construction," "thinking and feeling," and "movement." The teacher then involves the students in the categorization.
2. Once students have grasped how this categorization scheme works, they can work in small groups or in pairs: Each group or pair will take a different category and sort words whose roots justify their membership in that category.
3. Lists can be written in word study notebooks and brought back to the larger group to share and discuss. (*Note:* Several of the words to be sorted may be placed under different categories.) Following are some examples of categories and a few illustrative words.

 Visit the Word Study Section for Derivational Relations to find a sort for science-related prefixes.

Word List

Building/Construction	Thinking and Feeling	Movement	Travel
technology	philanthropy	synchrony	astronaut
construct	philosophy	fracture	exodus
tractor	attraction		

Government	Speaking and Writing
economy	autobiography
demagogue	photograph
politics	catalogue
	emphasis

Variations

Group Root Study

1. Choose a set of common roots, such as *photo-*, *geo-*, *aqua-*, *astro-*.
2. While the teacher models on an overhead, in their word study notebooks students create their own webs of words in which the root can be found (see Figure 8-5).
3. Brainstorm related words. Figure out root meaning.
4. Students use dictionaries to locate root, verify meaning, find origin, and search for related words.
5. Eliminate words that do not fit meaning of root. Honor all suggestions. Lead students to examine parts and meaning.

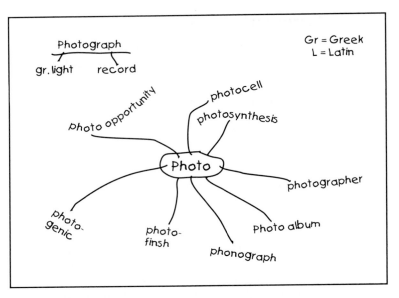

FIGURE 8-5   "Root Web" in Student's Vocabulary Notebook

Identifying the Meaning of Word Roots 8-9

Given a series of words that share the same root, students analyze the words to determine the meaning of the root. Each group of three words can be finished with one of the words provided:

introspection interrupt distract

1. spectator, inspect, prospector, _____
   The root *spect* means _____. (look, count, divide)

2. corrupt, disrupt, eruption, _____
   The root *rupt* means _____. (speak, break, fall)

3. tractor, attract, extract, _____
   The root *tract* means _____. (place, look, pull)

refract contradict audience

1. audible, auditory, audio, _____
   The root *aud* means _____. (throw, hear, touch)
2. fraction, fracture, infraction, _____
   The root *fract* means _____. (stretch, eat, break)

3. dictate, diction, predict, _____
   The root *dict* means _____. (say, touch, fight)

dermatologist nominative invaluable

1. nominate, nominal, nominee, _____
   The root *nom* means _____. (write, figure, name)

2. value, valor, devalue, _____
   The root *val* means _____. (money, to be strong/to be worth, truth)

3. hypodermic, epidermis, dermatology, _____
   The root *derm* means _____. (skin, medicine, platform)

Variations

Following this format, groups of students can construct their own exercises and then swap with other groups. Table 8-5 and 8-6 can be used for additional roots and ideas.

Combining Roots and Affixes 8-10

In the following chart, students indicate with an *x* words that are made by combining the prefix and the root. Then they write the words below. An engaging variation is to indicate with a "?" words that do not exist in English, but could! Students may write these words in a special section of their vocabulary notebooks, create a definition for each, and use each in a sentence. When students are uncertain about whether a word is an actual word in English, they may check it in the dictionary.

	duce/duc/duct	port	spect	dict	tract
in/im		x			
trans					
ex					
pre					
		import			

Set up three columns: prefixes, roots, and suffixes. As with the chart activity, students see how many real words they can construct—and how many "possible words" they can create. Again, follow up with the vocabulary notebooks. Given the number of possibilities, this activity can occur over several days.

re-	tract	-able/-ible
in-/im-	dict	-ion/-ation
ex-	cred	-ic
pre-	gress	-ibility/-ability
trans-	port	

From Spanish to English—A Dictionary Word Hunt 8-11

Purpose

Expand vocabularies through finding relations among languages.

Procedures

1. With a Spanish-English dictionary, find words in Spanish that remind you of words in English. Briefly note the definition or synonym.
2. With an English dictionary, find words that share the same root or affix. Write these related words into your word study notebooks.
3. Use a Spanish dictionary to find related words with the same meaning: night–noche.

Following are sample entries on a class chart of related words that students collected in this activity.

Spanish	(Translation)	English Relations	Spanish Relations
presumir	(*boast*)	presume, presumption, presumptuous	presumido, presunción
extenso	(*extensive*)	extend, extension	extensivo, extender
nocturno	(*nightly*)	nocturnal, nocturne	noche, noctámbulo
polvo	(*powder*)	pulverize (from Latin, *pulvis*, dust)	polvillo, polvorear

The Synonym/Antonym Continuum 8-12

Provide students with a list of words or use prepared word cards. Have students arrange the words along a continuum: At the ends of the continuum will be the antonyms (words that are most opposite in meaning). Next to each of these words students will decide where to place synonyms (words that are closest to the meaning of the opposite words) and so on until all words have been used.

For example, the words *balmy, frigid, chilly, boiling, frozen, tepid, hot, cool,* and *warm* could be arranged this way:

frigid frozen chilly cool tepid balmy warm hot

First, the students work individually. Then they compare their continua with one another. They should discuss differences and provide rationale for why they arranged particular words the way they did. The dictionary will be the final judge of any disagreements.

Semantic Webs 8-13

Adaptable for Other Stages

Semantic webs are graphic aids that may be used to (a) fine-tune students' understanding of words/concepts in the same semantic "family," and (b) expand students' vocabulary by presenting new terms. The example in Figure 8-6 elaborates and expands the concepts associated with "trip." All the words except *excursion* are familiar to the students.

Procedures

1. When first introducing semantic webs, present a completed web. Later, students will help you create them.

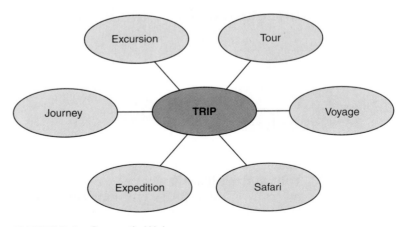

FIGURE 8-6   Semantic Web

Derivational Relations Stage

2. Have students discuss their understandings of the familiar words (as with the synonym/antonym activity, this discussion requires them to make finer distinctions among the concepts). As they discuss meanings, encourage them to use the words in sentences. As always, the dictionary can resolve uncertainties.
3. Ask students if they have heard or seen the unfamiliar word (*excursion*) before. Discuss its possible meanings. Check the dictionary.
4. Ask students if they can think of any other words that could be added to the web.

Variations

When students are used to this format, involve them in generating a web. Present your "core" word/concept, and then have the students brainstorm other words that occur to them. You may then add one or two of your own words that will extend the students' vocabulary.

Semantic Feature Analysis 8-14

Adaptable for Other Stages

This analysis (Anders & Bos, 1986) engages students in the examination of words/ definitions in relation to each other.

Following is a description of how the semantic feature analysis is constructed and taught.

- Write the words to be examined down the left margin. (In this example the words are *prefix, base word, affix, suffix,* and *word root*.) Then write the features of these words across the top. When you first introduce this activity to students, we list these features ourselves. Later, after students understand how the analysis works, they can be involved in suggesting the features that will be listed.
- Discuss the matrix with the whole class or in small groups. The students will mark each cell with one of the following symbols: a plus sign (+) indicates a definite relationship between the word and a feature; a minus sign (−) indicates the word does not have that feature; and a question mark (?) indicates that the students feel they need more information before responding.
- After students complete the matrix, point out (1) they now *really* know how much they know about each word; and (2) they also know what they still need to find out (Templeton, 1997).

Figure 8-7 illustrates a semantic feature analysis completed by a group of sixth-grade students under the teacher's guidance to clarify the meanings of word study terms.

	Cannot Stand Alone	Comes Before a Base Word or Root Word	Usually Comes from Greek or Latin	Can Stand Alone	Comes After Base Word or Word Root
Prefix	+	+	+	-	-
Base word	-	-	?	+	-
Affix	+	?	+	-	?
Suffix	+	-	+	-	+
Word root	+	-	+	-	-

FIGURE 8-7   Semantic Feature Analysis

Derivational Relations Stage

Is it -*able* or -*ible*? 8-15

This word sort may be done as a class activity from the board or in a small group.

Procedures

The features to be examined must be controlled. Students in the middle derivational stage need only examine the first three or four concepts. Students in the late derivational stage may explore the less frequent patterns.

1. Sort words that end in -*able* into one group and those that end in -*ible* into the other group.

dependable	credible
expendable	audible
passable	edible
profitable	plausible
breakable	visible
agreeable	feasible
predictable	compatible
perishable	terrible
acceptable	horrible
remarkable	possible
readable	indelible
laughable	legible
profitable	
punishable	

   Do you see a generalization that tells you when you spell the suffix -*able* and when you spell it -*ible*? (If the suffix is attached to a base word it is spelled -*able*; if it is attached to a word root it is spelled -*ible*.)

2. Sort the words that drop the *e* before adding -*able* into one group. Sort those that keep the *e* when -*able* is added into the other group.

presumable	noticeable
pleasurable	peaceable
desirable	marriageable
dispensable	bridgeable
blamable	manageable
usable	changeable
excusable	serviceable
lovable	
deplorable	
comparable	

   Can you come up with a generalization that tells you when to drop the *e* and when to keep it? If a word ends with a soft /g/ or /c/ sound, as in *gem* or *cite*, it cannot precede an *a*. So, to keep the soft sound, words ending in *ce* or *ge* keep the *e* before adding -*able*.

3. Sort the words into two categories: those that end with -*ible* or with -*able*.

negligible	applicable
invincible	navigable
eligible	amicable
intelligible	despicable
legible	impeccable
crucible	
tangible	

Is there a generalization for spelling the words in the first column with *-ible*? Soft *c* or *g* endings without silent *e* must, for the same reason as in sort 2, go to *-ible*. Is there a generalization for spelling the words in the second column with *-able*? The suffix follows a hard /g/ or /c/ sound and must therefore take *-able*.

4. Sort the words according to the suffix *-ible* or *-able*.

convincible	applicable
inducible	navigable
reducible	amicable
forcible	despicable
producible	impeccable

Is there a generalization? A few words ending in silent *e* do not retain the *e*, and therefore they also must go to *-ible* to maintain the soft c sound.

Because *-able*/*-ible* is a complex issue, it is possible to find exceptions or low frequency patterns. It is interesting to compare and contrast these words and discover or hypothesize reasons for these findings. Because few students (or adults) will ever totally conquer the mysteries of *-ible*/*-able*, it is useful to point out that, if you have tried the different generalizations for adding the suffix and are still not sure how to spell it, go with *-able*, because there are more words that end in *-able* than there are that end in *-ible*.

5. Related words: Many base words that are verbs become nouns by adding some form of *-ion*. If the *-ion* form of the word ends in *-ation*, the suffix will be *-able*. This is a helpful rule because *-ation* endings include the long /a/ sound.

irritate	irritation	irritable
demonstrate	demonstration	demonstrable
estimate	estimation	estimable
tolerate	toleration	tolerable
separate	separation	separable
commend	commendation	commendable
inflame	inflammation	inflammable
vegetate	vegetation	vegetable
educate	education	educable
navigate	navigation	navigable
admire	admiration	admirable
observe	observation	observable
reclaim	reclamation	reclaimable
apply	application	applicable

6. In the same way, if the *-ion* form derived from the verb root does not include *-ation*, the *-ble* form will be *-ible*.

collect	collection	collectible
access	accession	accessible
contract	contraction	contractible
suppress	suppression	suppressible
repress	repression	repressible
exhaust	exhaustion	exhaustible
reduce	reduction	reducible
produce	production	producible
express	expression	expressible

This strong rule overrides the simpler idea that base words go to *-able*. Exceptions that apply to this rule involve base words that end in *ct* (*correct* to *correctable*, *detect* to *detectable*, *predict* to *predictable*). The *ct* endings must therefore be noted and memorized.

7. When a root ends in *ss* or *ns,* the ending is *-ible.* Often the root actually ends in *t* (*permit*) or *d* (*comprehend*) and follows the same pattern as the movement to the *-ion* or *-ive* endings.

permit	permission	permissible
admit	admission	admissible
dismiss	dismissal	dismissible
transmit	transmission	transmissible
comprehend	comprehension	comprehensible

Which Suffix? 8-16

This activity is an excellent follow-up to previous work with base words, word roots, and suffixes. It is appropriate for individuals, buddies, or small groups. The suffixes included are: *-ible/-able* (use words in previous activity), *-tion/-sion* (use words from lists on page 268), *-ence/-ance, -ary/-ery* (see lists in the Appendix).

Materials

You will need a word sort board, word cards, and word study notebook.

Procedures

1. The teacher chooses how many suffixes to place at the top of the word sort board. (Note that several of the words to be sorted may be placed under different suffixes, for example, *permit: permissible, permission.*) Each card has the base word written on one side and the same word with allowable suffixes on the other side.
2. The teacher mixes up the word cards and places the deck with base words faceup. The students in turn choose the top card and decide in which suffix category it belongs.
3. After all the cards are placed, the students record in their word study notebooks what they think is the correct spelling of the word.
4. After recording all the words, students turn the cards over to self-check the correct spelling.

Variations

Students can work as buddies to explore a particular suffix "team" (e.g., *-tion* and *-sion*) to see what generalization(s) may underlie the use of a suffix.

Defiance or Patience? 8-17

The game Defiance (if using the *ant/ance/ancy* family) or Patience (if using the *ent/ence/ency* family) is simply a version of Go Fish for three to five players. The object of the game is to make as many groups of two, three, or four cards of the same derivation and to be the first to run out of cards.

Materials

You will need two decks of 52 blank cards, as close to regular card size as possible. Use words from the lists in the Appendix, as well as word roots when applicable. To prepare for the game, select words from the list of your choice in groups of two, three, and four until you have a total of 52 words. Do not split any groupings, as this may be misleading. Write each word across the top of a card, and your deck is prepared.

Pregame warmup. Before playing Defiance and/or Patience, students should engage in a word study activity that addresses both categories of *ant/ance/ancy* and *ent/ence/ency* words. A suggested order follows:

> Sort 1: *ent* versus *ant*.
>
> Sort 2: Add the related *-ence* and *-ance* words. Sort *ent/ence* versus *ant/ance*. Then match *ent/ence* pairs and *ant/ance* pairs.
>
> Sort 3: Add the related *-ency* and *-ancy* words. Sort *ent/ence/ency* versus *ant/ance/ancy*. Then sort *ent/ence/ency* triples, followed by *ant/ance/ancy* triples.
>
> Sort 4: Add those words that do not come in triples, but simply in pairs for both word families.
>
> Sort 5: Add roots to any of the pairs or triplets, sorting first by the *-ant* or *-ent* category, then by groups of two, three, or four in the same derivational family.

Procedures

1. Each player is dealt five cards from the deck. The player to the left of the dealer begins the game. The player may first lay down any existing groups of two, three, or four held in hand. This player then may ask any other player for a card of a certain derivation in his or her own hand: "Matthew, give me all of your *resistance.*" (This could result in gaining *resistance, resistant, resistancy,* or *resist.*)

2. If a player does not have cards with the feature being sought, he or she responds, "Be Defiant" or "Be Patient" depending on which game is being played.

3. At this, the asking player must draw another card from the deck. If the card is of the same family being sought, the player may lay down the match and continue asking other players for cards. If the card is not of the correct derivational group, play passes to the person on the left and continues around the circle in the same manner. If the drawn card makes a match in the asking player's hand, but was not that which was being sought, he or she must hold the pair in hand until his turn comes up again. Of course this means there is a risk of another player taking the pair before the next turn.

4. Play ends when one of the students runs out of cards. The player with the most points wins.

5. Players may play on other people's card groups, laying related cards down in front of themselves, not in front of the player who made the original match.

6. Scoring is as follows:

Singles played on other people's matches	1 point
Pairs	2 points
Triples	6 points
Groups of four	10 points
First player to run out of cards	10 points

Variations

1. The game Defy My Patience could be the version that mixes sets of words from both lists to create an *ent/ant* deck.

2. Challenge My Patience or Defy My Challenge: In this version, during scoring before everyone throws down their hand, students should secretly write additional words for groups they have laid down, which have not been played. Before hands are revealed, these lists should be shared, and an additional point added to every player's score for each related word they wrote. If other players doubt the authenticity of a word claimed by an opponent, someone may challenge the word. The

challenger loses a point if the word is valid, or gains a point if it is not. The player, likewise, counts the word if it is valid, or loses a point if the challenger proves him or her wrong.

3. Students should be encouraged to develop their own derivational families to be added to this game or another feature to be substituted for the *ant/ent* contrast.

Exploring Absorbed (Assimilated) Prefixes: *ad-*, *com-*, and *in-* 8-18

Materials

1. You will need a chalk board, word cards, and word study notebook. Use the list in Table 8-7 to prepare word cards and prefix cards such as the ones in Figure 8-8.
2. Obtain word cards for individual sorting activity (see list in Table 8-7).
3. Obtain sorting folders with given exemplars for sort.

TABLE 8-7   Absorbed Prefixes

ad- (to, toward)
ac- accompany, account, accustom, accommodate
af- affect, affirm, affix, affront, affluent
ag- aggression, aggrieve, aggravate
al- allay, allocate, allot, alleviate
an- announce, annotate
ar- arrange, arrest, array, arrive
as- assign, assort, assure, assimilate, assemble
at- attend, attention, attune, attract

sub- (under)
suc- succeed, success, succumb
suf- suffix, suffuse, suffocate, suffer
sup- support, supplant, suppress

in- (not, into)
il- illiterate, illegal, illuminate, illegitimate, illogical
im- immature, immigrant, immobile, immortal, immediate
ir- irresponsible, irradiate, irregular, irreligious, irrational

ex- (out)
ef- efface, effect, efferent

com- (with)
col- collaborate, colleague, collide, collocate, collect
con- connect, connote
cor- correspond, correct

ob- (against, toward)
oc- occur, occult, occupation, occlude
of- offend
op- oppose, oppress, opposite

dis- (opposite)
dif- diffuse, different, diffident

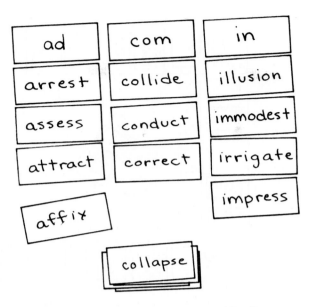

FIGURE 8-8 Exploration of Absorbed Prefixes

Procedures

1. Introduce the three prefixes as headers for each category of the sort. Place the exemplars on the board in three columns.
2. Students read each card and place the card in the appropriate column (see Figure 8-8).
3. Discuss any word meanings, if necessary, and how the prefix changes the meaning of the base word. Ask the class if they can think of why the prefix spelling changes in certain words.
4. The students write the words in their word study notebooks under the appropriate exemplar.
5. After all example words have been studied, mix the cards, and have students sort as a small group or individually.
6. Have students go on a word hunt for words with these assimilated prefixes, and add to the word study notebook.

Assimile 8-19

This game can be played by two to six players.*

Materials

Gameboard modeled after Monopoly (see Figure 8-9); dice; game playing pieces; chance cards (colored word cards with base words written on each); deck of absorbed/assimilated prefix base words (only readily apparent base words such as *accompany* or *immortal*; see list in Table 8-7); sheet of paper and pencil or pen for each player (to use in spelling words).

Procedures

This game is modeled after Monopoly.

---

*Telia Blackard contributed this activity.

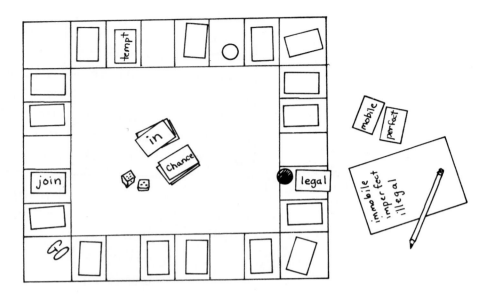

FIGURE 8-9   Assimile Gameboard

Derivational Relations Stage

1. Place base words *company* and *mortal* facedown around the board. A particular prefix is chosen as the focus, and placed faceup in the center of the board. Chance cards are also placed in the middle. Chance cards provide players a chance to think of one's own assimilated prefix word using the base word on the card and any assimilated prefix. Chance cards are picked up every time a player passes Go.
2. Players roll the dice to see who goes first. The player with the highest number rolls again and moves the number of spaces on the board.
3. Upon landing on a particular space, the player turns up a word card and must determine whether this word can be assimilated to the prefix in the center of the board. If the card can be made into a word, the player attempts to both say the word and correctly spell it. A player who is able to correctly spell the word receives one point and is also allowed another turn. (The word card is actually removed and retained by the player.) If the word cannot be assimilated, it is kept on the board faceup (this word will not be played again). However, if the word can be assimilated, but the player misspells the word, the card is turned back over to be played later in the game.
4. A player who is unable to come up with a word (for whatever reason) forfeits a turn, and play moves to the next player.
5. The game is over when all cards that can be played are played, and the winner is the one with the most correctly spelled words.

Variations

A separate set of Community Chest cards using all of the original assimilated prefixes can be placed in the middle of the board, from which players can draw after each round of turns. This ensures that all prefixes are studied. (Community Chest cards will have the prefixes *ad-*, *in-*, *com-*, *ob-*, *sub-*, *ex-*, *per-*, and *dis-*.) With this method, the word cards that cannot be played with one particular prefix are turned back over until they are able to be played.

Rolling Prefixes 8-20

Materials

Create a deck of 32 word cards of assimilated prefixes (eight sets of four). Each group of four should consist of a mixed sort from each of the seven sets of assimilated prefixes: *ad-*, *in-*, *com-*, *ob-*, *sub-*, *ex-*, and *dis-*. One set will have to be a "wild set" (words with the aforementioned prefixes).*

Procedures

1. After the initial sorting of assimilated prefixes, each player is dealt eight cards—three cards to each player on the first round, two cards to each player the second round, and three cards to each player the third round.
2. The player on the dealer's left starts the game by putting a card faceup in the center of the table. It does not matter what the card is, but the player must read the word and state the prefix.
3. The next player to the left and the others that follow attempt to play a card of the same suit as the first one put on the table ("suit" meaning having the same prefix). Players must read their word and state the prefix.
4. If everybody follows suit, the cards in the center of the table are picked up after all the players have added their cards, and are put to the side. No one scores.
5. The game continues in the same fashion until someone is unable to follow suit. When this occurs, the player can look through his or her hand for a "wild card" and play it, changing the suit for the following players.
6. A player may change suit in this manner at any point in the game if he or she so chooses. For example, a player may play the word *collide* (prefix *com-*), and the next player may either play a *com-* prefix word (such as *concoct*) or a word with *com-* elsewhere in the word, such as *accommodate*. If the player chooses *accommodate*, the prefix the following player must concentrate on is *ad-* or a form of *ad-*. Players must be familiar with all types of assimilated prefixes.
7. A player who is unable to follow suit must pick up the center deck of cards. The player who picks up the cards begins the next round. The game continues this way until someone runs out of cards.

Variations

1. At first, players may not wish to state the original prefix of the words.
2. Multiple decks of assimilated prefixes can be made, allowing for variation.
3. Instead of ending the game after one person runs out of cards, the game can continue by the winner of the first round receiving one point for each card that the other players hold in their hands at the end of the game.

Words from Greek and Roman Myths and Legends 8-21

Similar to the Jeopardy format but involving more students, this game is intended for advanced students in the intermediate grades and many others in the middle and secondary grades. It is appropriate to use after a number of myths and legends have been read and discussed. The object of the game is to gain the most number of points by correctly answering the questions.

*This was adapted from the game Rolling Stone from *Games and Fun with Playing Cards* by J. Leeming. Thanks also to Telia Blackard for her contributions.

Derivational Relations Stage

Materials

Using Table 8-8 as a reference, you will need at least 20 word cards with questions representing four categories (see also Table 8-9). In the following example game, the categories are Science, Arts, Timely Events, and Everyday Words. Write the questions on one side of a word card and the assigned points on the other side. As in Jeopardy, the questions progress in difficulty for each category, from 10 to 50. Make a heading card with the name of each category and then attach these heading cards and word cards, with points facing out, into columns of notches made on poster board.

TABLE 8-8   Words from Greek and Roman Myths and Legends

Greek

Chaos: The raw material of the universe—a great, dark, confused mass in which air, earth, and water were all mixed together. *chaos, chaotic, chasm, gas*

Cosmos: The opposite of chaos—things with form and shape; in order, good arrangement. *cosmic, cosmopolitan, cosmetic*

Gaea (JEEuh or GAYuh): Goddess of earth; Greek word for earth. *geography, geology, geometry, geode*

Uranus: God of sky, heaven. *uranium, Uranus* (the planet)

Gigantes: Children of Uranus and Gaea, ferocious beings of tremendous size and power. *giants, gigantic*

Cyclops: Children of Uranus and Gaea; from a Greek word meaning "round-eyed"—monstrous giants with one eye in the forehead. *cyclone*

Titans/Titanesses: Offspring of Uranus and Gaea; these were a race of giants who ruled the world before the Greek gods and goddesses took over. They warred with the gods and lost; their fate was eternal punishment of some sort or another. *Titanic, titanium*

Cronus: Most powerful of Titans; because of the similarity to the Greek word *chronos*, he is often mistakenly referred to as the god of time. *chronological, synchrony, synchronous*

Oceanus (ohSEEuhnus): Oldest of Titans; symbolized water that encircled the land of the world. *ocean, oceanic*

Atlas: One of the Titans, his punishment was to support the world on his shoulders. A picture of this was often included in the early books of maps, so over time such a book came to be called an atlas. *atlas, Atlas Mountains* (the god Atlas turned to stone), *Atlantic, Atlanta*

Luna: Goddess of the moon. At one time people believed the moon had the power to drive some people out of their minds. *lunar, lunacy, lunatic*

Clotho: Controlled the course of the universe; pictured as spinning all the threads that represent life. *cloth, clothes*

Hypnos: Greek god of sleep. *hypnosis, hypnotic, hypnotism*

Mt. Olympus: Where the Greek gods and goddesses lived. *Olympian*

Nox: From Chaos, goddess of darkness of night. *nocturnal, nocturne*

Lethe: Means "forgetfulness." The river in Hades where the spirits of the dead drink and then forget their former life and become listless ghosts. *lethargic, lethal*

Europa: She lived on the Asiatic coast of the Mediterranean and was the first person on the continent of Europe. Zeus turned himself into a white bull and Europa jumped on his back. She rode him to the continent of present-day Europe. *Europe, European*

Athena: Goddess of knowledge, arts, war, and peace; daughter of Zeus. *Athens, Athenian*

Phobos: Son of Ares, the Greek god of war. His name means "fear." *phobia, phobic*

Eros: Greek god of young love. *erotic*

Pan: God of fields, forests, wild animals. Part man/part goat, he often caused serious trouble. The belief that he was nearby caused people to run in terror. *panic, pandemonium*

Iris: Meaning "rainbow," she was a messenger of the gods. *iris* (flower, part of the eye), *iridescence*

TABLE 8-8 continued

Muses: Zeus's nine daughters. *music, museum*
   1. Calliope: Muse of eloquence *calliope*
   2. Polyhymnia: Muse of religious music *hymn, hymnal*
   3. Orpheus: Poet-musician with magic musical powers o*rpheus, orphic*
Mnemosyne: Mother of muses, goddess of memory. *mnemonic, amnesia, amnesty*
Gratiae: The Graces, three sisters who were goddesses of all that is charming in women. *grace, graceful, gracious*
Hygeia: Greek goddess of health. *hygiene, hygienic*
Nemesis: God of retribution, justice, or vengeance.
Tantalus: Human son of Zeus. He boasted of his friendship with the gods, so Nemesis followed him and had him punished by a lifetime of standing in water up to his neck with grapes not quite within reach; when he bent to drink the water receded. *tantalize*
Ambrosia: The food of the gods.
Nectar: The drink of the gods. *nectar, nectarine*
Echo: A mountain nymph, she offended Zeus's wife, Hera, because she talked so much. Hera condemned Echo to haunt the mountainsides, being able only to repeat the last few words of the person speaking. Echo was in love with Narcissus; after he died, she wasted away until nothing was left but her voice.
Narcissus: A young man who fell in love with his own reflection in a pool of water. *narcissism*
Psyche: A maiden who fell in love with Eros. Her name means "soul." *psychology, psychiatrist*
Marathon: A plain located 22 miles from Athens on which a battle was fought between the Greeks and the Persians. A greek courier ran to Athens to tell the city of the Greek victory and then died. *marathon*
Heracles: The strongest of the Greek heroes, through his Roman bane "Hercules" he gave us our word *herculean,* meaning "very powerful." We often speak of "herculean" tasks, which means they are very difficult and trying. Heracles had to perform several seemingly impossible tasks (e.g., the slaying of a nine-headed monster, the Hydra; when one of its heads was severed, two grew in its place). *herculean*
Hydra: A water serpent that was slain by Heracles. *hydraulics, hydrophobia, hydrant*
Laconia: A part of Greece where the Spartans lived. The Spartans were warlike but not given to boasting. They spoke few words and in few sentences. *laconic*
Odysseus (Roman Ulysses): The Greek king whose voyages took him away from home. *Odyssey*
Helios: God of the sun. *helium, heliocentric*

Roman
Jupiter or *Jove:* Chief of the Roman gods. *jovial*
Terra: Roman goddess of the earth. *territory, terrain, terrestrial, terrace, terrarium*
Vulcan: Roman god of fire. *volcano, volcanic, vulcanize*
Sol: Roman god of sun. *solar, solar system, solarium, parasol*
Morta: Roman sister of Fate. *mortal, immortal, mortician*
Somnus: Roman god of sleep. *insomnia, somnabulate* (sleepwalk)
Furies: Three sisters who punished those guilty of particularly horrible crimes. *fury, furious*
Ceres: Goddess of grain and the harvest. *cereal*
Venus: The Roman goddess of beauty and love. Her symbol, a looking glass, became the symbol for female Venus, the planet. *venusian, venerate, venerable*
Mars: The Roman god of war. His symbols, the shield and the spear, became the universal symbol for "male"; also means "bloody." *March, Mars* (the red planet), *martial*
Cupid: Roman god of young love.
Faunus: Roman god of animal life. *fauna*
Salus: Roman god of health. *salute, salutation, salutory, salubrious*
Janus: Roman god of doors—entrance and exit. He had two faces. *January, janitor*
Romulus and Remus: Twin brothers who were raised by a she-wolf. *Rome, Roman, Romanic, romance*

Derivational Relations Stage

291

TABLE 8-9 Greek Mythology: A Very Brief Primer

This "Very Brief Primer" can give a "home" to the words in Table 8-8. It can also pique students' interest in the role of Greek and Latin in English. While there are many different versions and interpretations of the myths, we draw primarily on Isaac Asimov's *Words from the Myths* (1961).

At first, there was *chaos*, no form or order. The Greeks believed that *Gaea* (earth) and *Uranus* (sky) came out of chaos. They had many children: Their first were the *Titans*. *Oceanus*, the ocean, was the oldest Titan. Another Titan, *Cronus*, eventually led the other Titans in overthrowing *Uranus*. Interestingly, his mother, Gaea, helped him in this effort by giving him a sickle-shaped sword to use. When Uranus's blood hit the ground, it gave birth to the *Erinyes*, known by their more common Roman name, the *Furies*.

The Titans then ruled the world. The children of Uranus and his wife, *Rhea*, would also rise up against their parents. The children lived on Mt. Olympus, and were led in their revolt by *Zeus*. After the children were victorious, one of the Titans, *Atlas*, was condemned to hold up the earth on his shoulders for eternity.

Zeus becomes the most important god, but shared rule of the cosmos with his brothers *Poseidon*, who ruled the sea, and *Hades*, who ruled the underworld—the world of the dead. The gods were not all-powerful, however. The Fates, who may also be the offspring of Uranus, play an important role in ruling the universe—the gods could not affect an individual's fate. There were three fates: *Clotho*, who spun the thread of life; *Lachesis*, who determined the length of the thread, and *Atropos*, who cut the thread.

Zeus and his wife, *Hera*, had many children, including *Hephaestus*, the god of the forge (Roman equivalent *Vulcan*) and *Ares*, the god of war (who in turn had two sons, *Phobus*, meaning "fear," from which we get *phobia*, and *Deimus*, meaning "terror"). Zeus had children by mortals as well: *Dionysus*, the god of agriculture, who is most notable for his responsibility for the grape harvest. Also known as *Bacchus*, from which we get *bacchanalia* (extremely festive celebrations), his followers were known as *Maenads*. They would fly into extreme reveries, and the word *mania* comes from them.

Two other "lesser" deities in the Greek pantheon were *Iris* and *Pan*. *Iris*, a winged messenger from the gods, was the goddess of the rainbow. She probably slid down the rainbow to deliver her messages to mortals. (The *iris* in the eye can be many different colors; *iridescent* refers to "many colors.") *Pan* was the god of woodlands and the patron of shepherds and their flocks. He often attended the revels held by Dionysus, and was unpredictable—he could inspire fear or "panic" among groups of people or animals.

Procedures

1. Assign students to three teams of four each. Flip a coin to determine who goes first.
2. Select a student to act as emcee, who reads question cards from the chart.

   All questions begin: "Relating to the category you've selected, what is a word that comes from _____?" For example, "Relating to the category you've selected, what is a word that comes from the Cyclops, a monstrous giant with an eye in his forehead?"
3. Players take turns responding, but can be helped by any of their co-players for the answer. Out of turn responses result in no points, even if the answer given is correct.
4. Team A's player 1 selects a category and question card (may be any level of points). The student emcee reads the card aloud.
5. Player 1 can answer immediately or discuss with teammates and then answer. Points are awarded if the answer is correct, deducted if the answer is incorrect. (Yes, a team may wind up getting negative scores!)
6. The procedure continues until one team wins.

Other words from the list in Table 8-8 can be used in these categories as well. You may select other categories and words, and students may also be involved in suggesting categories and in preparing games for classmates. Use this game format for vocabulary words in other content areas such as math and social studies.

This game format may also be used for eponyms (see Table 8-10).

TABLE 8-10 Eponyms: Places, Things, Actions

Eponyms are words that refer to places, things, and actions that have been named after an individual (from Greek *epi-*, after, + *noma*, name). Students' interest in word origins is often sparked by finding out where such words originate.
Following is a sampler of common eponyms.

bloomers	Amelia Bloomer, an American feminist in the late 19th century
boycott	Charles Boycott, whose servants and staff refused to work for him because he would not lower rents
diesel	Rudolph Diesel, a German engineer who invented an alternative engine to the slow-moving steam engine
ferris wheel	G. W. C. Ferris, designer of this exciting new ride for the 1893 World's Fair
guillotine	Joseph Guillotin, a French physician and the inventor of the device
leotard	Jules Leotard, a French circus performer who designed his own trapeze costume
magnolia	Pierre Magnol, French botanist
pasteurize	Louis Pasteur, who developed the process whereby bacteria are killed in food and drink
sandwich	John Montagu, the Earl of Sandwich, who requested a new type of meal
sax	Antoine Joseph Sax, Belgian instrument maker, designer and builder of the first *saxophone*

The following resources include lists and information about eponyms.

Dale, D., O'Rourke, J., & Bamman, H. (1971). *Techniques of teaching vocabulary.* Palo Alto, Calif.: Field Educational Enterprises.

Fry, E., Kress, J., Fountoukidis, D., & Fry, E. (2000). *The reading teachers book of lists* (4th ed.). San Francisco: Jossey-Bass.

Terban, Marvin. *Guppies in tuxedos: Funny eponyms.* New York: Clarion.

Sample Game: Categories and Questions

Science

		Arts
hygiene	Saturn	music
iris	Neptune	calliope
cosmos	cyclone	hymn
Pluto	aurora	museum
Jupiter	lunar	Orpheum
Uranus	solar	
Mars	hydraulics	
Venus		
Mercury		
Earth		

Timely Events

	Everyday Words	
Easter	giant	mnemonic
dawn	cosmetics	panacea
January	ocean	salute
March	chaos	tantalize
chronological	atlas	nectarine
The Olympics	furious	ambrosia
nocturnal	clothes	echo
June	cereal	narcissism
Valentine's Day	lethargic	clue
	panic	labyrinth
	pomegranate	

Derivational Relations Stage

Answers	Questions
Science	
cyclone	Cyclops, a monstrous giant with an eye in his forehead?
solar	Sol, the Roman god of the sun?
hydraulics	Hydra, the nine-headed water serpent slain by Heracles?
iris	Iris, the messenger of the gods who used the rainbow as her stairway to Earth?
hygiene	Hygeia, the goddess of health?
Arts	
music	The Muses, Zeus' nine daughters?
calliope	Calliope, the muse of eloquence?
hymn	Polyhymnia, the muse of religious music?
mnemonic	Mnemosyne, the mother of the muses?
Timely Events	
January	Janus, the two-faced god of doors?
nocturnal	Nox, the goddess of darkness or night?
Easter	Eos, the goddess of dawn?
chronological	Chronos, the god of time?
June	Juno, the goddess of love?
Everyday Words	
giant	Gigantes, ferocious beings of tremendous size and power?
ocean	Oceanus, who symbolized the water that encircled the land of the world?
atlas	Atlas, a Titan god who supported the heavens on his shoulders?
clothes	Clotho, who was pictured as spinning all the threads that represent life?

Derivational Relations Stage

Appendix

This Appendix contains eight sections. The first section contains the materials you will need for assessments. Most of the Appendix consists of pictures, sorts, lists, and materials that you can use to create your own sets of picture and word cards for the basic sorting activities described throughout the book.

ASSESSMENT MATERIALS FOR CHAPTER 2

QUALITATIVE SPELLING CHECKLIST

Student _____ Observer _____

Use this checklist to analyze students' uncorrected writing and to locate their appropriate stages of spelling development. There are three gradations within each stage—early, middle, and late. Examples in parentheses are from the Elementary Spelling Inventory 1 and the Intermediate list.

The spaces for dates at the top of the checklist are used to follow students' progress. Check when certain features are observed in students' spelling. When a feature is always present check "Yes." The last place where you check "Often" corresponds to the student's stage of spelling development.

Dates: _____ _____ _____

Emergent Stage

Early
- Does the child scribble on the page? Yes _____ Often _____ No _____
- Do the scribbles follow the conventional direction? (left to right in English) Yes _____ Often _____ No _____

Middle
- Are there random letters and numbers used in pretend writing? (4BT for *ship*) Yes _____ Often _____ No _____

Late
- Are key sounds used in syllabic writing? (/s/ or /p/ for *ship*) Yes _____ Often _____ No _____

Letter Name–Alphabetic

Early
- Are beginning consonants included? (*b* for *bed*, *s* for *ship*) Yes _____ Often _____ No _____
- Is there a vowel in each word? Yes _____ Often _____ No _____

Middle
- Are some consonant digraphs and blends spelled correctly? (**sh**ip, **wh**en, **fl**oat) Yes _____ Often _____ No _____
- Are there logical vowel substitutions with a letter name strategy? (FLOT for *float*, BAD for *bed*) Yes _____ Often _____ No _____

Late
- Are short vowels spelled correctly? (b**e**d, sh**i**p, wh**e**n, l**u**mp) Yes _____ Often _____ No _____
- Is the *m* or *n* included in front of other consonants? (lu**m**p, sta**n**d) Yes _____ Often _____ No _____

Within Word Pattern

Early
- Are long vowels in single-syllable words used but confused? (FLOTE for *float*, TRANE for *train*) Yes _____ Often _____ No _____

Middle
- Are most long vowel words spelled correctly, but some long vowel spelling and other vowel patterns used but confused? (DRIEV for *drive*) Yes _____ Often _____ No _____
- Are the most common consonant digraphs and blends spelled correctly (**sl**ed, **dr**eam, **fr**igh**t**) Yes _____ Often _____ No _____

Late
- Are the harder consonant digraphs and blends spelled correctly? (spe**ck**, s**w**i**tch**, s**m**u**dge**) Yes _____ Often _____ No _____
- Are most other vowel patterns spelled correctly? (sp**oi**l, ch**ew**ed, s**er**ving) Yes _____ Often _____ No _____

Syllables & Affixes

Early
- Are inflectional endings added correctly to base vowel patterns with short-vowel patterns? (shopp**ing**, march**ed**) Yes _____ Often _____ No _____
- Are junctures between syllables spelled correctly? (ca**ttle**, ce**llar**, ca**rries**, bo**ttle**) Yes _____ Often _____ No _____

Middle
- Are inflectional endings added correctly to base words? (chew**ed**, march**ed**, show**er**) Yes _____ Often _____ No _____

Late
- Are unaccented final syllables spelled correctly? (bo**ttle**, fortun**ate**, civil**ize**) Yes _____ Often _____ No _____
- Are less frequent prefixes and suffixes spelled correctly? (**con**fident, favor, rip**en**, cellar, plea**sure**) Yes _____ Often _____ No _____

Derivational Relations

Early
- Are most polysyllabic words spelled correctly? (*fortunate, confident*) Yes _____ Often _____ No _____

Middle
- Are unaccented vowels in derived words spelled correctly? (conf**i**dent, civ**i**lize, cat**e**gory) Yes _____ Often _____ No _____

Late
- Are words from derived forms spelled correctly? (**pleas**ure, **oppos**ition, **crit**icize) Yes _____ Often _____ No _____

EMERGENT CLASS RECORD

Class Record to Assess Emergent and Letter Name – Alphabetic Stage Spelling, Pre-Kindergarten – Kindergarten

Directions: Check boxes or date entries over several observations. A check minus (✓–) indicates features used occasionally. A check plus (✓+) indicates consistent use.

Teacher _____   Class _____   Grade _____   Date(s) _____

SPELLING STAGES→	EMERGENT STAGE						LETTER NAME–ALPHABETIC STAGE				
	EARLY		MIDDLE		LATE	EARLY			MIDDLE		LATE
↓ Name of Student / Spelling Features →	Random Marks	Linear Scribbles	Letterlike Writing	Random Letters	Beginning Consonants	Final Consonants	Logical Vowel Substitutions*	Consonant Digraphs	Consonant Blends	Correct Short Vowels

*Logical vowel substitutions show how a student would use a letter name strategy to spell long vowels (as in HOP for *hope*) or short vowels (PAT for *pet* or DEG for *dig*).

Directions

From the Phonological Awareness Literacy Screening (PALS), Fall 2002 (Invernizzi & Meier).

Instructions

1. Tell the student that you want him or her to spell some words. First, demonstrate the procedure by "spelling" a word aloud, on a blackboard, or on chart paper. Say, **"We're going to spell some words. I'll go first. The word I want to spell is** *mat.* **I am going to begin by saying the word slowly. MMM-AAA-TTT. Now I'm going to think about each sound I hear. Listen. MMM. I hear a /m/ sound so I will write down the letter** *m.* **MMM-AAA. After the /m/, I hear an /a/ sound so I will write down the letter** *a.* **MMM-AAA-TTT. At the end of the word, I hear a /t/ sound, so I will write down the letter** *t.*

2. Say, **"Now I want you to spell some words. Put down a letter for each sound you hear. You can use the alphabet strip at the top of your sheet if you forget how to make a letter. Ready?"** (*Note:* Children should not have studied these before tests and they should not be posted in the room.)

3. Ask the student to spell the following words in this order: If it helps your students, use the word in a simple sentence (i.e., I ran to the *top* of the hill). Do not demonstrate the sounding and process except for the example word *mat.* You may prompt the student by saying "What else do you hear?"

4. Look over the students' writing as they work to be sure you can determine what letters they are using. Probe letter formation by asking each student what letter he or she intended to use by naming it or pointing to it on an alphabet strip.

   1. **top**
   2. **lid**
   3. **wag**
   4. **bet**
   5. **run**

Scoring

Please note that spelling is scored based on phonetically acceptable letter-sound matches. Therefore, you may see more than one possible phonetic representation for each sound.

1. Compare students' spelling to the boxes on the Student Summary Sheet.
2. Reading the grid for each word vertically, column by column, left to right, place one check per column in the box that matches the student's spelling. Each check is worth one point. **Only one check per column is possible.**
3. Leave each box blank if there are no matches and proceed to the next column.
4. Count the number of boxes checked and record on the line marked "# Checked."
5. One bonus point per word is awarded for perfect spelling. If the word is spelled correctly, record a 1 on the line marked "Bonus Point."
6. Add all points (# Checked and Bonus Points). Record this total on the line marked "Score."

Scoring Notes

- Static reversals, where the student writes a mirror image of a single letter (e.g., Я for R) and self-corrections are **not** counted as errors. Spellings that contain static reversals are still eligible for the bonus point.
- Kinetic reversals are errors of order, as in writing *net* for *ten.* These may be scored for the presence or absence of phonemic letter-sound matches by reading and scoring the sample from right to left. Spellings that contain kinetic reversals are **not** eligible for the bonus point.
- *Note:* Scoring examples may be found on the following page. You can find more scoring samples on the PALS website at http://curry.edschool.virginia.edu/centers/pals/home.html

Spelling

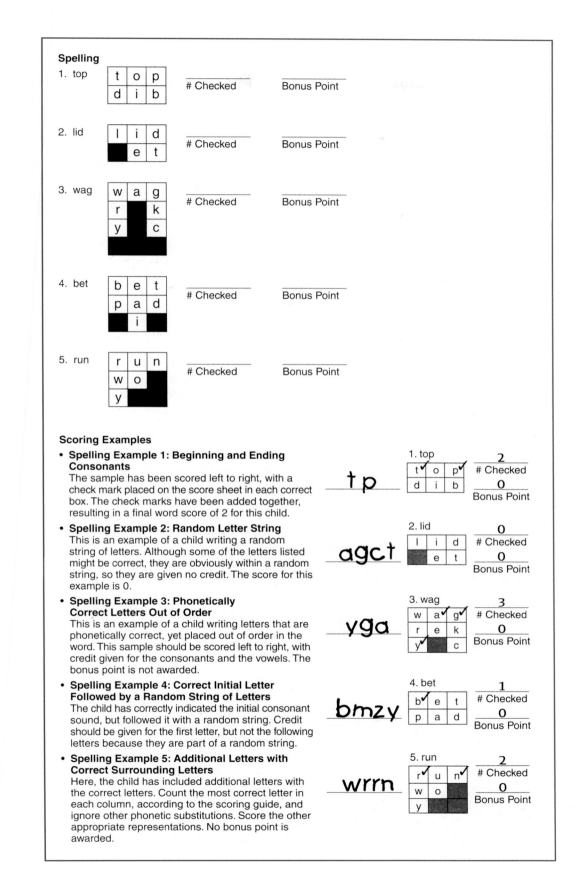

1. top

t	o	p
d	i	b

_____ # Checked   _____ Bonus Point

2. lid

l	i	d
■	e	t

_____ # Checked   _____ Bonus Point

3. wag

w	a	g
r	■	k
y	■	c
■	■	

_____ # Checked   _____ Bonus Point

4. bet

b	e	t
p	a	d
■	i	■

_____ # Checked   _____ Bonus Point

5. run

r	u	n
w	o	■
y	■	

_____ # Checked   _____ Bonus Point

Scoring Examples

- **Spelling Example 1: Beginning and Ending Consonants**
  The sample has been scored left to right, with a check mark placed on the score sheet in each correct box. The check marks have been added together, resulting in a final word score of 2 for this child.

- **Spelling Example 2: Random Letter String**
  This is an example of a child writing a random string of letters. Although some of the letters listed might be correct, they are obviously within a random string, so they are given no credit. The score for this example is 0.

- **Spelling Example 3: Phonetically Correct Letters Out of Order**
  This is an example of a child writing letters that are phonetically correct, yet placed out of order in the word. This sample should be scored left to right, with credit given for the consonants and the vowels. The bonus point is not awarded.

- **Spelling Example 4: Correct Initial Letter Followed by a Random String of Letters**
  The child has correctly indicated the initial consonant sound, but followed it with a random string. Credit should be given for the first letter, but not the following letters because they are part of a random string.

- **Spelling Example 5: Additional Letters with Correct Surrounding Letters**
  Here, the child has included additional letters with the correct letters. Count the most correct letter in each column, according to the scoring guide, and ignore other phonetic substitutions. Score the other appropriate representations. No bonus point is awarded.

1. top   t p

t✓	o	p✓
d	i	b

2 # Checked   0 Bonus Point

2. lid   agct

l	i	d
▓	e	t

0 # Checked   0 Bonus Point

3. wag   yga

w	a✓	g✓
r	e	k
y✓	▓	c

3 # Checked   0 Bonus Point

4. bet   bmzy

b✓	e	t
p	a	d

1 # Checked   0 Bonus Point

5. run   wrrn

r✓	u	n✓
w	o	▓
y	▓	▓

2 # Checked   0 Bonus Point

PRIMARY SPELLING INVENTORY

This inventory is designed to assess the word knowledge students bring to their reading and spelling. Students are not to study these words because that would invalidate the purpose of the inventory, which is to find out what they truly know. You can administer this same list of words three times (September, January, and May) to measure students' progress.

The words are ordered by their difficulty for grade levels K through 3 and sample the features students are to master during these years. Have students spell enough words to give a sense of the range of ability in your class. For kindergarten, students spell the first 5 to 8 words. First graders spell at least 15 words and second and third graders spell all of the words on this list. Students who spell nearly all of the words correctly can be asked to spell words from the Elementary Spelling Inventory.

Instructions

Administer the spelling inventory the same way you would a spelling test, but assure the students that this is not for a grade but to help you plan for their needs. Call the word aloud and use it in a sentence to be sure students know the exact word. Copy a Feature or Error Guide for each student and staple it to the student's paper.

Directions for Using the Feature Guide. For each word, check the features spelled correctly that are noted in the columns at the top of the Feature Guide on page 302. Add an additional point in the "correct" column if the word is spelled correctly. Do not count reversed letters as errors but note them in the boxes. If unnecessary letters are added, give them credit for what is correct but do not give them credit for a correct spelling (e.g., If *fan* is spelled FANE, the student still gets credit for representing the short vowel).

Total the number of points under each feature and across each word, allowing you to double-check your numbers. The total score can be compared over time, but the most useful information will be the feature analysis. Look down each feature column to determine the needs of individual students. For example, a student who spells 6 of 7 short vowels correctly on the primary inventory is knowledgeable about short vowels although some review work might be in order. A student who spells only 2 or 3 of the 7 short vowels needs to be involved in word study around this feature. If a student did not get any points for a feature, then earlier features need to be studied first. To determine a stage of development note where errors fall under the stages listed at the top of the Feature Guide.

Arrange students' papers in order from highest total points to lowest total points before transferring the numbers across the bottom row of each student's Feature Guide to the Classroom Composite on page 322. For a sense of your groups' needs and to form groups for instruction, *highlight* students who make *two or more errors* on a particular feature. If you call out less than the total list, *adjust the totals* on the Classroom Composite.

Directions for Using the Error Guide. Using the Error Guide on page 303, circle each error or write in the student's spelling by the error that is most similar. When a word is spelled correctly, circle the spelling at the end of the string of errors. After all words have been scored, determine where most circled words lie and look at the top row of the table for the developmental spelling level for this student. Total the words spelled correctly and note where the student is within the stage: *early* in the stage, in the *middle*, or *late* in the stage. Use the Spelling-by-Stage Classroom Organization Chart on page 327 to organize word study groups and to find the developmental levels, the types of features, and the chapter in *Words Their Way* to turn to for activities.

Sentences to Use with the Primary Spelling Inventory

Set One	
1. fan	I could use a fan on a hot day. *fan*
2. pet	I have a pet cat who likes to play. *pet*
3. dig	He will dig a hole in the sand. *dig*
4. rob	A raccoon will rob a bird's nest for eggs. *rob*
5. hope	I hope you will do well on this test. *hope*
6. wait	You will need to wait for the letter. *wait*
7. gum	I stepped on some bubble gum. *gum*
8. sled	The dog sled was pulled by huskies. *sled*
(You may stop here for kindergarten unless a child has spelled 5 correctly.)	
Set Two	
9. stick	I used a stick to poke in the hole. *stick*
10. shine	He rubbed the coin to make it shine. *shine*
11. dream	I had a funny dream last night. *dream*
12. blade	The blade of the knife was very sharp. *blade*
13. coach	The coach called the team off the field. *coach*
14. fright	She was a fright in her Halloween costume. *fright*
15. chewing	Don't talk until you finish chewing your food. *chewing*
(You may stop here for first grade unless a child has spelled 10 correct.)	
Set Three	
16. crawl	You will get dirty if you crawl under the bed. *crawl*
17. wishes	In fairy tales wishes often come true. *wishes*
18. thorn	The thorn from the rose bush stuck me. *thorn*
19. shouted	They shouted at the barking dog. *shouted*
20. spoil	The food will spoil if it sits out too long. *spoil*
21. growl	The dog will growl if you bother him. *growl*
22. third	I was the third person in line. *third*
23. camped	We camped down by the river last weekend. *camped*
24. tries	He tries hard every day to finish his work. *tries*
25. clapping	The audience was clapping after the program. *clapping*
26. riding	They are riding their bikes to the park today. *riding*

Feature Guide for Primary Spelling Inventory

Directions: Check the features that are present in each student's spelling. In the bottom row, total features used correctly. Check the spelling stage that summarizes the student's development. Begin instruction at that stage with a focus on the types of features where the student missed two or more features in a column.

Student's Name _____   Teacher _____   Grade _____   Date _____

SPELLING STAGES:
- ☐ EMERGENT ☐ LATE
- ☐ LETTER NAME–ALPHABETIC
- ☐ WITHIN WORD PATTERN
- ☐ SYLLABLES & AFFIXES
- ☐ DERIVATIONAL RELATIONS

Words Spelled Correctly: /26
Feature Points: /56
Total /82

Features →	Beginning Consonants (EMERGENT/LATE)	Final Consonants (EARLY)	Short Vowels (MIDDLE)	Consonant Digraphs (LATE)	Consonant Blends (EARLY)	Long Vowel Patterns (MIDDLE)	Other Vowel Patterns	Inflected Endings (LATE)	Feature Points	Words Spelled Correctly (MIDDLE)
1. fan	f	n	a							
2. pet	p	t	e							
3. dig	d	g	i							
4. rob	r	b	o							
5. hope	h	p				o-e				
6. wait	w	t				ai				
7. gum	g	m	u							
8. sled			e		sl					
9. stick			i		st					
10. shine				sh		i-e				
11. dream					dr	ea				
12. blade					bl	a-e				
13. coach				ch		oa				
14. fright					fr	igh				
15. chewing				ch			ew	ing		
16. crawl					cr		aw			
17. wishes				sh				es		
18. thorn				th			or			
19. shouted				sh			ou	ed		
20. spoil					sp		oi			
21. growl							ow			
22. third				th			ir			
23. camped								ed		
24. tries								ies		
25. clapping								pping		
26. riding								ding		
Cells with 2 or more errors	(7)	(7)	(7)	(7)	(7)	(7)	(7)	(7)	(56)	(26)

SPELLING STAGES → EMERGENT LATE / LETTER NAME–ALPHABETIC / WITHIN WORD PATTERN / SYLLABLES & AFFIXES

Words Their Way Appendix © 2004 by Prentice-Hall, Inc.

Error Guide for Primary Spelling Inventory

Directions: Circle student's spelling attempts below. If a spelling is not listed, write it in where it belongs on the developmental continuum. Determine a spelling stage that summarizes the student's development. Begin instruction at that level with a focus on features characteristic of that stage.

Student's Name _____ Teacher _____ Grade _____ Date _____

SPELLING STAGES →	EMERGENT LATE	LETTER NAME–ALPHABETIC EARLY / MIDDLE	LETTER NAME–ALPHABETIC LATE	WITHIN WORD PATTERN EARLY / MIDDLE	WITHIN WORD PATTERN LATE	SYLLABLES & AFFIXES EARLY / MIDDLE
Features ↓	Consonants Beginning Final	Short Vowels	Consonant Digraphs & Blends	Long Vowel Patterns	Other Vowel Patterns	Inflected Endings
1. fan	v f fn	f(o,i,e)n *fan*				
2. pet	p pt	pa(o,i)t *pet*				
3. dig	d dk dg	deg *dig*				
4. rob	w r rb	rib rub *rob*				
5. hope	h hp	hop	*hope*			
6. wait	y w yt wt	wat	wate wei(ie)ght *wait*			
7. gum	k g km gm	gom *gum*				
8. sled	s sd	sad slad	*sled*			
9. stick	s sk	stek stik	*stick*			
10. shine	s sn	sin shin	shai(y)ne shien *shine*			
11. dream	j g grm jrm	g(j)rem drem	dreme *dream*			
12. blade	b bd	bad blad	blaid *blade*			
13. coach	ch kh	coc koch coch	coche *coach*			
14. fright		fit frit	frite	friet friht *fright*		
15. chewing		chon chun	chuing	chooing *chewing*		
16. crawl	kl krl	crol crall	crool crall *crawl*			
17. wishes	wechz weshs	wishis wishs	wishis *wishes*			
18. thorn	trn thrn	thurn thorne *thorn*				
19. shouted	st cht sht	shotd	showted shauted *shouted*			
20. spoil	spl	spol	spole spollo spoyl *spoil*			
21. growl	gral	grall	grille groul *growl*			
22. third	thrd	therd thurd	thurd *third*			
23. camped	capt camt	campt campted *camped*				
24. tries	chrs	chris tris trys	tris trise tryse *tries*			
25. clapping	clapn	cklaping	claping *clapping*			
26. riding	redn ridn	wriding	rideing rideing *riding*			

SPELLING STAGES:

☐ EARLY ☐ MIDDLE ☐ LATE
☐ LETTER NAME–ALPHABETIC
☐ WITHIN WORD PATTERN
☐ SYLLABLES & AFFIXES
☐ DERIVATIONAL RELATIONS

Words Spelled Correctly: ____ /26

Words Their Way Appendix © 2004 by Prentice-Hall, Inc.

ELEMENTARY SPELLING INVENTORY-1

This short spelling inventory will assess the word knowledge students bring to their reading and spelling. You can administer this same list of words three times (September, January, and May) to measure students' progress.

Instructions

Let students know that you are administering this inventory to learn about how they spell. Let them know that this is not a test, but that they can help you plan your teaching if they do their best. Students are not to study these words beforehand.

Possible script: "I am going to ask you to spell some words. Spell them the best you can. Some of the words will be easy to spell; some may be difficult. When you do not know how to spell a word, spell it the best you can; write down all the sounds you feel and hear."

Say the word once, read the sentence if the meaning is unclear, and then say the word again. Work with groups of 5 words. You may want to stop testing when students miss 3 of 5 words. Have students check their papers for their name and the date. See Chapter 2 for further instructions on administration and interpretation. Copy a Feature or Error Guide for each student, and staple it to the student's paper.

Directions for Using the Feature Guide. For each word, check the features that are noted in the columns at the top of the Feature Guide on page 306. Add an additional point in the "correct" column if the word is spelled correctly. Do not count reversed letters as errors but note them in the boxes.

Total the number of points under each feature and across each word; this is a way to check your addition. The total score can be compared over time but the most useful information will be the feature analysis. Look down each feature column to determine the needs of individual students. For example, a student who spells 5 of 6 long vowels correctly is knowledgeable about long vowels although some review work might be in order. A student who spells only 2 or 3 of the 6 long vowels needs to be involved in word study around this feature. If a student did not get any points for a feature, then the feature is beyond the student's instructional range and earlier features need to be studied first. You can determine a student's stage of development by noting where errors fall under the stages listed at the top of the Feature Guide.

Arrange students' papers in order from highest total points to lowest total points before transferring the numbers across the bottom row of each student's Feature Guide to the Classroom Composite on page 323. For a sense of your groups' needs and to form groups for instruction, *highlight* students who make 2 *or more errors* on a particular feature. If you call out less than the total list *adjust the totals* on the Classroom Composite.

Directions for Using the Error Guide. Using the Error Guide on page 307, circle each error or write in the student's spelling by the error that is most similar. When a word is spelled correctly, circle the spelling at the end of the string of errors. After all words have been scored, determine where most circled words lie and look at the top row of the table for the developmental spelling level for this student. Total the words spelled correctly and note where the student is within the stage: *early* in the stage, in the *middle*, or *late* in the stage. Use the Spelling-by-Stage Classroom Organization Chart on page 327 to organize word study groups and to find the developmental levels, the types of features, and the chapter in *Words Their Way* to turn to for activities.

Set One	
1. bed	I hopped out of bed this morning. *bed*
2. ship	The ship sailed around the island. *ship*
3. when	When will you come back? *when*
4. lump	He had a lump on his head after he fell. *lump*
5. float	I can float on the water with my new raft. *float*
Set Two	
6. train	I rode the train to the next town. *train*
7. place	I found a new place to put my books. *place*
8. drive	I learned to drive a car. *drive*
9. bright	The light is very bright. *bright*
10. throat	She had a sore throat. *throat*
Set Three	
11. spoil	The food will spoil if it is not kept cool. *spoil*
12. serving	The restaurant is serving dinner tonight. *serving*
13. chewed	The dog chewed up my favorite sweater yesterday. *chewed*
14. carries	She carries apples in her basket. *carries*
15. marched	We marched in the parade. *marched*
Set Four	
16. shower	The shower in the bathroom was very hot. *shower*
17. bottle	The cowboy fed the calf through a bottle. *bottle*
18. favor	He did his brother a favor by taking out the trash. *favor*
19. ripen	The fruit will ripen over the next few days. *ripen*
20. cellar	I went down to the cellar for the can of paint. *cellar*
Set Five	
21. pleasure	It was a pleasure to listen to the choir sing. *pleasure*
22. fortunate	It was fortunate that the driver had snow tires during the snowstorm. *fortunate*
23. confident	I am confident that we can win the game. *confident*
24. civilize	They had the idea that they could civilize the forest people. *civilize*
25. opposition	The coach said the opposition would give us a tough game. *opposition*

Feature Guide for Elementary Spelling Inventory-1

Directions: Check the features that are present in each student's spelling. In the bottom row, total features used correctly. Check the spelling stage that summarizes the student's development. Begin instruction at that stage with a focus on the types of features where the student missed two or more features in a column.

Student's Name _____ Teacher _____ Grade _____ Date _____

SPELLING STAGES → Features ↓	EMERGENT / LETTER NAME Consonants Beginning	Consonants Final	Short Vowels	Digraphs & Blends	Long-Vowel Patterns	Other Vowel Patterns	Syllable Junctures & Easy Prefixes & Suffixes	Harder Prefixes, Suffixes, & Unaccented Final Syllables	Reduced & Altered Vowels, Bases, Roots, & Derivatives	Feature Points	Words Spelled Correctly
Late EMERGENT to LETTER NAME–ALPHABETIC											
1. bed	b	d	e								
2. ship		p	i	sh							
3. when		n	e	wh							
4. lump	l		u	mp							
WITHIN WORD PATTERN											
5. float				fl	oa						
6. train		n		tr	ai						
7. place					a-e						
8. drive		v		dr	i-e						
9. bright					igh						
10. throat					oa						
11. spoil						oi					
SYLLABLES & AFFIXES											
12. serving						er	ing				
13. chewed				ch		ew	ed				
14. carries							rr ies				
15. marched				ch		ar	ed				
16. shower						ow	er				
17. bottle							tt	le			
18. favor						or		or			
19. ripen							en				
20. cellar							ll	ar			
Middle SYLLABLES & AFFIXES to Middle DERIVATIONAL RELATIONS											
21. pleasure								ure	pleas		
22. fortunate						or		ate	fortun		
23. confident								ent	confid		
24. civilize								ize	civil		
25. opposition								op	position		
Totals →	(2)	(5)	(4)	(8)	(6)	(6)	(9)	(8)	(5)	(53)	(25)

SPELLING STAGES:

☐ EARLY ☐ MIDDLE ☐ LATE
☐ LETTER NAME–ALPHABETIC
☐ WITHIN WORD PATTERN
☐ SYLLABLES & AFFIXES
☐ DERIVATIONAL RELATIONS

Words Spelled Correctly: /25
Feature Points: /53
Total: /78

Error Guide for Elementary Spelling Inventory-1

Student's Name _____   Teacher _____   Grade _____   Date _____

SPELLING STAGES →	EMERGENT	LETTER NAME–ALPHABETIC		WITHIN WORD PATTERN		SYLLABLES & AFFIXES		DERIVATIONAL RELATIONS
	LATE	EARLY MIDDLE	LATE	EARLY MIDDLE	LATE	EARLY MIDDLE	LATE	MIDDLE LATE
Features →	Consonants Beginning Final	Short Vowels	Consonant Digraphs & Blends	Long-Vowel Patterns	Other Vowel Patterns	Syllable Junctures & Easy Prefixes & Suffixes	Harder Prefixes & Suffixes & Unaccented Final Syllables	Reduced & Altered Vowels, Bases, Roots, & Derivatives

Late EMERGENT – LETTER NAME–ALPHABETIC

Feature	Spellings (early → correct)
1. bed	b bd bad *bed*
2. ship	s sp shp sep shep *ship*
3. when	w yn wn wan whan *when*
4. lump	l lp lmp lop lomp *lump*

WITHIN WORD PATTERN

Feature	Spellings
5. float	f ft vt flt fot flot flott flowt floaut flote *float*
6. train	j t trn jran chran tan tran teran traen trane *train*
7. place	p ps pls pas palac plas plac pase plais plase *place*
8. drive	d j jrv drf drv griv jriv driv jrive drieve draive *drive*
9. bright	b bt brt bit brit bite brite briete *bright*
10. throat	trot throt throte throate *throat*
11. spoil	spol sole sool spoyle spole spoal *spoil*

SYLLABLES & AFFIXES

Feature	Spellings
12. serving	sefng srvng sefing sering serving serveing *serving*
13. chewed	cud chud cooed chood cuwed c(h)ued chewd choud *chewed*
14. carries	keres cares carres carise carys cairries carrys *carries*
15. marched	much march marchet marchd marched marchted *marched*
16. shower	shewr showr shour shawer shoer shouer shower *shower*
17. bottle	badl badol bâtel batle bottel *bottle*
18. favor	favr faver favir *favor*
19. ripen	ribn ripn ripun ripan ripon *ripen*
20. cellar	salr selr celr salar selar seller sellar cellar *cellar*

Late SYLLABLES & AFFIXES–Middle DERIVATIONAL RELATIONS

Feature	Spellings
21. pleasure	plasr plager pleser plejer plesher plesour pleser *pleasure*
22. fortunate	forhnat frehnit foohinit forchenut fochininte fortunet *fortunate*
23. confident	confa(e)de(i)nt confia(e)dent confa(e)dent confodent *confident*
24. civilize	sivils sevelies sivilicse cifillazas sivelize civa(i)liz(s)e *civilize*
25. opposition	opasishan opasion opozcison opasitian opasition oppisition oppsition oposit(s)ion *opposition*

SPELLING STAGES:

☐ EARLY ☐ MIDDLE ☐ LATE
☐ LETTER NAME–ALPHABETIC
☐ WITHIN WORD PATTERN
☐ SYLLABLES & AFFIXES
☐ DERIVATIONAL RELATIONS

Words Spelled Correctly: _____ /25

Words Their Way Appendix © 2004 by Prentice-Hall, Inc.

INTERMEDIATE SPELLING INVENTORY

This inventory will help you assess the orthographic knowledge elementary students bring to reading and spelling. This inventory begins with the middle of the letter name–alphabetic stage and continues to the middle of the derivational relations stage of spelling. The results of the spelling inventories will have implications for reading, writing, vocabulary, and spelling instruction.

Instructions

Let students know that you are administering this inventory to learn about how they spell. Let them know that this is not a test, but that they will be helping you to teach by doing their best. Students are not to study this inventory beforehand.

Possible script: "I am going to ask you to spell some words. Spell them the best you can. Some of the words will be easy to spell; some will be more difficult. When you do not know how to spell a word, spell it the best you can."

Say the word once, read the sentence if the meaning is unclear, and then say the word again. Work with groups of words. Have students check their papers for their name and the date. You may want to stop administering the inventory when students miss most of the words and you can clearly determine a spelling stage. Consider using the Upper Level Spelling Inventory if students spell most of these words correctly.

Use either the Feature Guide on page 309 or the Error Guide on page 310. See Chapter 2 for further instructions on administration and interpretation.

Letter Name–Alphabetic and Within Word Pattern	
1. speck	The well-dressed man brushed away a **speck** of lint from his jacket. *speck*
2. charge	She bought new clothes with a **charge** card. *charge*
3. switch	The sick boy could **switch** television channels from his bed. *switch*
4. scrape	The fall caused her to **scrape** her knee. *scrape*
5. nurse	The **nurse** checked her blood pressure. *nurse*
6. flown	It was the first time he'd **flown** in a helicopter. *flown*
7. squirt	She squeezed the bottle to **squirt** ketchup on her hamburger. *squirt*
8. pounce	The cat was ready to **pounce** on the mouse. *pounce*
9. throat	The doctor gave him medicine for his sore **throat**. *throat*
10. smudge	The big **smudge** on the mirror made it difficult to see. *smudge*
Syllables & Affixes	
11. shaving	The teenager looked forward to **shaving**. *shaving*
12. chewed	They **chewed** slowly as they listened to the dinner speaker. *chewed*
13. pennies	The children threw **pennies** in the fountain. *pennies*
14. fraction	The team was disappointed to get only a **fraction** of the credit for the job. *fraction*
15. bottle	The **bottle** of shampoo fell from his slippery hands. *bottle*
16. discovery	The **discovery** of the gold made many people rich. *discovery*
17. lesson	She arrived at the **lesson** with a notebook and pencil. *lesson*
18. distance	The boys measured the **distance** between their houses. *distance*
19. trapped	The new graduate felt **trapped** by a low-paying job. *trapped*
20. sailor	He wanted to go to sea as a **sailor**. *sailor*
Early–Middle Derivational Relations	
21. resident	Mr. Squires has been a **resident** of this town for over 40 years. *resident*
22. confusion	There was **confusion** when there was a power failure. *confusion*
23. visible	The singer was **visible** to everyone in the room. *visible*
24. category	I will put the bottles in one **category** and the cans in another. *category*
25. criticize	The boss will **criticize** you for your work. *criticize*

Feature Guide for Intermediate Spelling Inventory

Directions: Check the features that are present in each student's spelling. In the bottom row, total features used correctly. Check the spelling stage that summarizes the student's development. Begin instruction at that stage with a focus on the types of features where the student missed two or more features in a column.

Student's Name _____ Class _____ Grade _____ Date _____

SPELLING STAGES:

- ☐ EARLY ☐ MIDDLE ☐ LATE
- ☐ LETTER NAME–ALPHABETIC
- ☐ WITHIN WORD PATTERN
- ☐ SYLLABLES & AFFIXES
- ☐ DERIVATIONAL RELATIONS

Words Spelled Correctly: ___ /25
Feature Points: ___ /50
Total: ___ /75

SPELLING STAGES → / Features ↓	LETTER NAME–ALPHABETIC — Short Vowels (MIDDLE)	LETTER NAME–ALPHABETIC — Consonant Digraphs & Blends (LATE)	WITHIN WORD PATTERN — Long Vowel Patterns (EARLY)	WITHIN WORD PATTERN — Other Vowel Patterns (MIDDLE)	WITHIN WORD PATTERN — Complex Consonants (LATE / EARLY)	SYLLABLES & AFFIXES — Syllable Junctures & Easy Prefixes & Suffixes (EARLY / MIDDLE / LATE)	DERIVATIONAL RELATIONS — Harder Prefixes, Suffixes, & Unaccented Final Syllables (EARLY)	DERIVATIONAL RELATIONS — Reduced Vowels, Bases & Roots (MIDDLE / LATE)	Feature Points	Words Spelled Correctly
LETTER NAME–ALPHABETIC & WITHIN WORD PATTERNS										
1. speck	e				ck					
2. charge		ch		ar						
3. switch	i	sw			tch					
4. scrape		scr	a-e							
5. nurse				ur						
6. flown			ow							
7. squirt				ir	squ					
8. pounce				ou						
9. throat		thr	oa							
10. smudge	u				dge					
SYLLABLES & AFFIXES										
11. shaving						e-drop ing				
12. chewed				ew		ed				
13. pennies						nn ies				
14. fraction							tion	fra		
15. bottle	o					tt	le			
16. discovery							dis y	cover		
17. lesson						ss	on			
18. distance							ance	dis		
19. trapped						pp dd				
20. sailor			ai				or			
Early–Middle DERIVATIONAL RELATIONS										
21. resident							ent	i		
22. confusion							con sion	fus		
23. visible							ible	vis		
24. category								e		
25. criticize							ize	critic		
Highlight cells with 2 or more errors	(4)	(4)	(4)	(5)	(4)	(9)	(12)	(8)	(50)	(25)

Error Guide for Intermediate Spelling Inventory

Directions: Circle student's spelling attempts below. If a spelling is not listed, write it in where it belongs on the developmental continuum. Determine a spelling stage that summarizes the student's development. Begin instruction at that level with a focus on features characteristic of that stage.

Student's Name _____   Teacher _____   Grade _____   Date _____

SPELLING STAGES:
- ☐ EARLY ☐ MIDDLE ☐ LATE
- ☐ LETTER NAME–ALPHABETIC
- ☐ WITHIN WORD PATTERN
- ☐ SYLLABLES & AFFIXES
- ☐ DERIVATIONAL RELATIONS

Words Spelled Correctly: ____ /25

SPELLING STAGES→	LETTER NAME–ALPHABETIC		WITHIN WORD PATTERN			SYLLABLES AND AFFIXES		DERIVATIONAL RELATIONS	
	MIDDLE	LATE	EARLY	MIDDLE	LATE	EARLY	MIDDLE / LATE	EARLY / MIDDLE	
Features→	Short Vowels	Consonant Digraphs & Blends	Long Vowel Patterns	Other Vowel Patterns	Complex Consonants	Syllable Junctures & Easy Prefixes & Suffixes	Harder Prefixes & Suffixes, & Unaccented Final Syllables	Reduced Vowels Bases & Roots	Words Spelled Correctly
LETTER NAME–ALPHABETIC & WITHIN WORD PATTERN									
1. speck	spak	spic spak spick	**speck**						
2. charge	carg	chorg chorch charge	**charge**						
3. switch	swet	swech swaitch	switch	**switch**					
4. scrape	srap skraap	skrap	scrap	**scrape**					
5. nurse	ners neras nurs			nerce nerse nurce	**nurse**				
6. flown	flon		flone floan		**flown**				
7. squirt	skurt skort skwert skwirt			squart squrt squirt	**squirt**				
8. pounce	pos pons ponc			pouns pounse	pounce **pounce**				
9. throat	trot	throt		throte throate	**throat**				
10. smudge	smug smuch smach	smud		smuge	**smudge**				
SYLLABLES & AFFIXES									
11. shaving		safng	shavin	saving	saveing	**shaving**			
12. chewed		cud chud	cooed	chood cuwed c(h)ued	chewd choud	**chewed**			
13. pennies				panes	penes	pennes penies pennys	**pennies**		
14. fraction					facshun	frackshun	fraksion frackshun **fraction**		
15. bottle		badl	badol		batel	batle battel	**bottle**		
16. discovery					discofry	di(e)scovry	disco(a)vary descovry **discovery**		
17. lesson					lasun	lesen	lessen leson **lesson**		
18. distance				destns	destase destns	destense	distense **distance**		
19. trapped		chrapt	trapt chraped			teraped trappt traped	**trapped**		
20. sailor				selar saler saleor	sialer saler	sailor	**sailor**		
Early–Middle DERIVATIONAL RELATIONS									
21. resident						resatint	reserdent reseadent resudint	res(e)(a)dent resdent resident **resident**	
22. confusion						confushon	confution confusion confussion	confution confusion **confusion**	
23. visible						visbel	visbal visabul visible visabal	visable visibel visbel visabel visibel visible **visible**	
24. category						cadagoure	catagery cadigore catagore	category catiguorie catigory catagory category **category**	
25. criticize							critise crisize	critize crisize critase critasize crisise criticize critisize criticise **criticize**	

UPPER LEVEL SPELLING INVENTORY

This inventory will help you assess the orthographic knowledge students bring to reading and spelling. The inventory begins with single-syllable word knowledge and stretches to students' knowledge of roots.

Instructions

Let students know that you are administering this inventory to learn about how they spell. Let them know that this is not a test, but that they will be helping you by doing their best.

Possible script: "I am going to ask you to spell some words. Try to spell them the best you can. Some of the words will be easy to spell; some will be more difficult. When you do not know how to spell a word, spell it the best you can; write down all the sounds you feel and hear."

Say the word once, use the word in a sentence, and then say the word a second time.

Consider students' spelling of the first 7 words before continuing. Students who miss 2 or more of these words could be given either the elementary or upper elementary inventory. You may want to stop testing when students miss 5 of 8 words. Use either the Feature Guide on page 313 or the Error Guide on page 315. See Chapter 2 for further instructions on administration and interpretation. Have students check their papers for their name and the date.

Within Word Patterns

1. speck	The well-dressed man brushed away a **speck** of lint from his jacket. *speck*
2. switch	The sick boy could **switch** television channels from his bed. *switch*
3. smudge	The big **smudge** on the mirror made it difficult to see. *smudge*
4. scrape	The fall caused her to **scrape** her knee. *scrape*
5. flown	It was the first time he'd **flown** in a helicopter. *flown*
6. nurse	The **nurse** checked her blood pressure. *nurse*
7. throat	The doctor gave him medicine for his sore **throat**. *throat*

Syllables & Affixes

8. powerful	He was a **powerful** force on the team. *powerful*
9. shaving	The teenager looked forward to **shaving**. *shaving*
10. bottle	The **bottle** of shampoo fell from his slippery hands. *bottle*
11. discovery	The **discovery** of the gold made many people rich. *discovery*
12. lesson	She arrived at the **lesson** with a notebook and pencil. *lesson*
13. fever	The boy was sick in bed with a high **fever**. *fever*
14. trapped	The new graduate felt **trapped** by a low-paying job. *trapped*
15. sailor	He wanted to go to sea as a **sailor**. *sailor*

Derivational Relations

16. resident	Mr. Squires has been a **resident** of this town for over 40 years. *resident*
17. puncture	Joan saw the **puncture** in her bicycle tire. *puncture*
18. confidence	Her **confidence** grew with her success. *confidence*
19. confusion	There was **confusion** when there was a power failure. *confusion*
20. fortunate	It was **fortunate** that the driver had snow tires in the snowstorm. *fortunate*
21. dominance	**Dominance** was established by the stronger lion. *dominance*
22. prosperity	During this period of **prosperity**, our income increased dramatically. *prosperity*
23. decorator	She hired a **decorator** to design the living room. *decorator*
24. opposition	The coach said the **opposition** would give us a tough game. *opposition*
25. visible	The singer was **visible** to everyone in the room. *visible*
26. correspond	The student decided to **correspond** with the instructor. *correspond*
27. voluminous	The volunteers counted the **voluminous** votes on Tuesday. *voluminous*
28. succession	He fired several shots in rapid **succession**. *succession*
29. emphasize	In conclusion, I want to **emphasize** the most important points. *emphasize*
30. category	I will put the bottles in one **category** and the cans in another. *category*
31. hilarious	John thought the comedian was absolutely **hilarious**. *hilarious*
32. commotion	The audience heard the **commotion** backstage. *commotion*
33. inheritable	She had an **inheritable** disease that was passed from one generation to another. *inheritable*
34. criticize	The boss will **criticize** you for your work. *criticize*
35. excerpt	I am going to read one **excerpt** from this chapter. *excerpt*
36. reversible	Terry wears a **reversible** coat in the winter. *reversible*
37. chlorophyll	**Chlorophyll** is a green pigment essential to photosynthesis. *chlorophyll*
38. adjourn	The meeting will **adjourn** at five o'clock. *adjourn*
39. camouflage	The soldier wore **camouflage** to avoid detection. *camouflage*
40. indictment	The **indictment** from the grand jury was delivered to the suspect. *indictment*

Words Their Way Appendix © 2004 by Prentice-Hall, Inc.

Feature Guide for Upper Level Spelling Inventory

Directions: Check the features that are present in each student's spelling. In the bottom rows, total features used correctly in each category. Check the stage that summarizes the student's development. Begin instruction at that stage with a focus on the types of features where the student began to miss two or more features in a column.

Student's Name _____   Teacher _____   Grade _____   Date _____

| SPELLING STAGES → | LETTER NAME–ALPHABETIC | | WITHIN WORD PATTERN | | SYLLABLES & AFFIXES | | DERIVATIONAL RELATIONS | | Feature Points | Words Spelled Correctly |
| | | LATE | EARLY | MIDDLE   LATE | EARLY | MIDDLE   LATE | EARLY | MIDDLE   LATE | | |
Features →	Short Vowels	Consonant Digraphs & Blends	Long & Other Vowel Patterns	Complex Consonants	Syllable Junctures & Easy Prefixes & Suffixes	Harder Prefixes, Suffixes, & Unaccented Final Syllables	Reduced & Altered Vowels	Bases, Roots & Derivatives	Feature Points	Words Spelled Correctly
LETTER NAME–ALPHABETIC & WITHIN WORD PATTERN										
1. speck	e	sp ck								
2. switch	i	sw		tch						
3. smudge	u	sm		dge						
4. scrape		scr	a-e	scr						
5. flown		fl	ow							
6. nurse			ur							
7. throat			oa	thr						
SYLLABLES & AFFIXES										
8. powerful					ful					
9. shaving		sh			(e-drop) ing					
10. bottle					tt	le				
11. discovery					dis y					
12. lesson					ss	on				
13. fever						er				
14. trapped		tr			pp ed					
15. sailor			ai		or					
Late SYLLABLES & AFFIXES through EARLY DERIVATIONAL RELATIONS										
16. resident						ent	i			
17. puncture						ure		punct		
18. confidence					con	ence	i			
19. confusion						sion		fus		
20. fortunate						ate		fortun		
Subtotals	(3)	(8)	(6)	(4)	(11)	(8)	(2)	(3)	(45)	(20)

SPELLING STAGES:

☐ EARLY ☐ MIDDLE ☐ LATE
☐ LETTER NAME–ALPHABETIC
☐ WITHIN WORD PATTERN
☐ SYLLABLES & AFFIXES
☐ DERIVATIONAL RELATIONS

Words Spelled Correctly: /40
Feature Points: /86
Total: /126

Feature Guide for Upper Level Spelling Inventory—Continued

Student's Name _____   Teacher _____   Grade _____   Date _____

SPELLING STAGES→	LETTER NAME–ALPHABETIC		WITHIN WORD PATTERN		SYLLABLES & AFFIXES		DERIVATIONAL RELATIONS			
	LATE	LATE	EARLY	MIDDLE	LATE / EARLY	MIDDLE / LATE	EARLY / MIDDLE	LATE		
Features→	Short Vowels	Consonant Digraphs & Blends	Long & Other Vowel Patterns	Complex Consonants	Syllable Junctures & Easy Prefixes & Suffixes	Harder Prefixes, Suffixes, & Unaccented Final Syllables	Reduced & Altered Vowels	Bases, Roots, & Derivatives	Feature Points	Words Spelled Correctly
Late SYLLABLES & AFFIXES & DERIVATIONAL RELATIONS										
21. dominance						ance	i			
22. prosperity					ity		er			
23. decorator					(e-drop) or			decor		
24. opposition						op		position		
25. visible							i(ble)	vis		
26. correspond						cor	e			
27. voluminous						ous	i	volum		
28. succession								success		
29. emphasize					ize	em		phas		
30. category							e			
DERIVATIONAL RELATIONS										
31. hilarious						ious		hilar		
32. commotion					com	tion		motion		
33. inheritable						able		inherit		
34. criticize						ize	i			
35. excerpt						ex		cerpt		
36. reversible						ible				
37. chlorophyll							o	chlor phyll		
38. adjourn						ad		journ		
39. camouflage						age		camoufl		
40. indictment								indict		
Subtotals →					(5)	(13)	(8)	(15)	(41)	(20)
Totals →	(3)	(8)	(6)	(4)	(16)	(21)	(10)	(18)	(86)	(40)

Words Their Way Appendix © 2004 by Prentice-Hall, Inc.

Error Guide for Upper Level Spelling Inventory

Directions: Circle student's spelling attempts below. If a spelling is not listed, write it in where it belongs on the developmental continuum. Determine a spelling stage that summarizes the student's development. Begin instruction at that level with a focus on features characteristic of that stage.

Student's Name _____ Teacher _____ Grade _____ Date _____

SPELLING STAGES →

Stage groupings across the feature columns:
- **LETTER NAME–ALPHABETIC** (LATE): Short Vowels; Consonant Digraphs & Blends
- **WITHIN WORD PATTERN** (EARLY / MIDDLE / LATE): Long & Other Vowel Patterns; Complex Consonants
- **SYLLABLES & AFFIXES** (EARLY / MIDDLE / LATE): Syllable Junctures & Easy Prefixes & Suffixes; Harder Prefixes, Suffixes, & Unaccented Final Syllables
- **DERIVATIONAL RELATIONS** (EARLY / MIDDLE / LATE): Reduced & Altered Vowels; Bases, Roots, & Derivatives
- Words Spelled Correctly

Features →	Short Vowels	Consonant Digraphs & Blends	Long & Other Vowel Patterns	Complex Consonants	Syllable Junctures & Easy Prefixes & Suffixes	Harder Prefixes, Suffixes, & Unaccented Final Syllables	Reduced & Altered Vowels	Bases, Roots, & Derivatives	Words Spelled Correctly
LETTER NAME–ALPHABETIC AND WITHIN WORD PATTERN									
1. speck	spic spek spak spick	**speck**							
2. switch	swet	swech swaitch **switch**							
3. smudge	smud	smuch	smuge	smuge **smudge**					
4. scrape	srap skraap	skrap scrap	scrap **scrape**						
5. flown		flon	flone floan **flown**						
6. nurse	ners	neras nurs	nerce nerse nurce	**nurse**					
7. throat	trot	throt	throte throte throat **throat**						
Early to MIDDLE SYLLABLES & AFFIXES									
8. powerful				powrful	porful pauerful pauerful **powerful**				
9. shaving				safng	shavin saveing shaveing **shaving**				
10. bottle				badl	badol batel batle bottel **bottle**				
11. discovery					discofry di(e)scovry disco(a)vary	descovery **discovery**			
12. lesson					lasun lesen lasen	lessen leson **lesson**			
13. fever					fevr fevir feafer	feaver feevor **fever**			
14. trapped				trapt	chrapt chraped teraped trappt traped **trapped**				
15. sailor					selar saler saleor saler	sialer sailer sailer **sailor**			
Late SYLLABLES & AFFIXES through EARLY DERIVATIONAL RELATIONS									
16. resident						resatint reserdent reseadent resudint	res(e)(a)dent residant	**resident**	
17. puncture						pucshr pungchr puncur puncker	punksher punchure puncure punsure	**puncture**	
18. confidence						confadents	confadence confedense confidence	**confidence**	
19. confusion							confushon confution confustion confushon confusion confussion	**confusion**	
20. fortunate						forhnat frehnit foohinit	forchenut fochinite fortunet	**fortunate**	

SPELLING STAGES:
- ☐ EARLY ☐ MIDDLE ☐ LATE
- ☐ LETTER NAME–ALPHABETIC
- ☐ WITHIN WORD PATTERN
- ☐ SYLLABLES & AFFIXES
- ☐ DERIVATIONAL RELATIONS

Words Spelled Correctly: _____ /40

Words Their Way Appendix © 2004 by Prentice-Hall, Inc.

Error Guide for Upper Level Spelling Inventory–Continued

Student's Name _____   Teacher _____   Grade _____   Date _____

SPELLING STAGES→	LETTER NAME–ALPHABETIC		WITHIN WORD PATTERN			SYLLABLES & AFFIXES		DERIVATIONAL RELATIONS		
		LATE	EARLY	MIDDLE	LATE	MIDDLE		EARLY	MIDDLE	
Features→	Short Vowels	Consonant Digraphs & Blends	Long & Other Vowel Patterns	Complex Consonants	Syllable Junctures & Easy Prefixes & Suffixes	Harder Prefixes, Suffixes, & Unaccented Final Syllables		Reduced & Altered Vowels	Bases, Roots & Derivatives	Words Spelled Correctly
Late SYLLABLES AND AFFIXES & DERIVATIONAL RELATIONS										
21. dominance					domfanese domance domenense domenence	dominince dominense		**dominance**		
22. prosperity					proparty propraty property	prospearaty prosperaty prosperity		**prosperity**		
23. decorator					dector decrater decorater	decorater decorator decorater decorator		**decorator**		
24. opposition				opasion	opasishan opozcison opasitian opasition	oppisition oposision oposition		**opposition**		
25. visible					visbel visabul visble visabal	visibel visibal **visible**				
26. correspond					corspond corispond correspond corrospond	**correspond**				
27. voluminous				vlumnus vulomus valomus	vlominus vulomanus volumanus	voluminus voluminis volumenis		**voluminous**		
28. succession				sucksession	sucesion succession sucsession	succesion succession succestion		**succession**		
29. emphasize					infaside infacize ephacise empasize	emfasize imfasize emphasize		**emphasize**		
30. category				cadagoure	cadagore catagery cadigore	catagore category catiguorie		catigory category	**category**	
DERIVATIONAL RELATIONS										
31. hilarious					halaris halaryous halaries heleriaus halareous	halarious helarious hileriuse		helarious hilerious	**hilarious**	
32. commotion				comoushown	comoshion comotion cumotion	comosion camotion comocion comosion comotion **commotion**				
33. inheritable					inharbul enherable inhairtable inharetable	inhairtable inharitible inhairtible		**inheritable**		
34. criticize					critise crisize critize	critisaise critisise critasize critiicise		criticize critiicise criticise	**criticize**	
35. excerpt					exherpt exhert exsort exerp	exsort exerp ecsert exsert		excert exsurpt exserpt	**excerpt**	
36. reversible					reversbell reversabul reversobol	reverseable reversabile revercible		reverseable reversabile reversible	**reversible**	
37. chlorophyll				clorafil cloarphil cloraful clorifil	chlorafil	chloraphyl chloraphyl chloraphyll		**chlorophyll**		
38. adjourn				ajurn agern	ajoum ajorne	ajurne adjurn		adjorn adjourne	**adjourn**	
39. camouflage				camaflag camoflosh	comoflodge camaphlauge	camaflag camoflage camaflouge		camaflaug camoflauge	**camouflage**	
40. indictment					enditment inditmeant	indictmeant inditement endightment enditment		indictment indightment indicment	**indictment**	

Words Their Way Appendix © 2004 by Prentice-Hall, Inc.

MCGUFFEY QUALITATIVE SPELLING INVENTORY

The words on these lists have been selected as representative of the words students are expected to master at different grade levels. The features are consistent with the developmental progression established for word knowledge.

Directions

Step 1. Establish a starting point. Begin with the spelling list that matches the grade level. First grade and kindergarten teachers begin with level I.

Step 2. Call the words, use them in a sentence, and then repeat the word. Students write the words in a horizontal column. Kindergartners and first graders might be given paper with boxes for writing or blank paper rather than lined paper.

Step 3. Collect the papers and check them. Determine a percentage score for each child. Words spelled with reversals are accepted as correct. Make a list of students who scored above 50% and those who scored below 50%.

Step 4. Test again on the next day. Students who scored above 50% should be given the next higher level. Students who scored below 50% should be given the next lower level. In working with intermediate grade students, you may find it useful to call out only half the words on a list. When students score greater than 80%, you may want to move to a more advanced list.

Step 5. Again check the papers. Continue to test until every child has scored above or below 50% so that you can establish an instructional level for everyone. The last level at which a student scores between 50% and 90% is his or her instructional level. For example, if Mary scores 30% on level III but 65% on level II, then she is clearly instructional at level II.

Step 6. Create a class roster by listing scores achieved by each student at all levels. Circle the instructional level scores. This will allow you to form groups for instruction.

Step 7. Examine the spelling errors of students in the groups you form. Errors will give you ideas about the features that students are ready to study.

McGuffey Qualitative Inventory of Word Knowledge

Level I	Level II	Level III	Level IV	Level V	Level VI	Level VII	Level VIII
bump	batted	find	square	enclosed	absence	illiteracy	meddle
net	such	paint	hockey	piece	civilize	communicate	posture
with	once	crawl	helmet	novel	accomplish	irresponsible	knuckle
trap	chop	dollar	allow	lecture	prohibition	succeed	succumb
chin	milk	knife	skipping	pillar	pledge	patience	newsstand
bell	funny	mouth	ugly	confession	sensibility	confident	permissible
shade	start	fought	hurry	aware	official	analyze	transparent
pig	glasses	comb	bounce	loneliest	inspire	tomatoes	assumption
drum	hugging	useful	lodge	service	permission	necessary	impurities
hid	named	circle	fossil	loyal	irrelevant	beret	pennant
father	pool	early	traced	expansion	conclusion	unbearable	boutique
track	stick	letter	lumber	production	invisible	hasten	wooden
pink	when	weigh	middle	deposited	democratic	aluminum	warrant
drip	easy	real	striped	revenge	responsible	miserable	probable
brave	make	tight	bacon	awaiting	accidental	subscription	respiration
job	went	sock	capture	unskilled	composition	exhibition	reverse
sister	shell	voice	damage	installment	relying	device	Olympic
slide	pinned	campfire	nickel	horrible	changeable	regretted	gaseous
box	class	keeper	barber	relate	amusement	arisen	subtle
white	boat	throat	curve	earl	conference	miniature	bookkeeping
	story	waving	statement	uniform	advertise	monopoly	fictional
	plain	carried	collar	rifle	opposition	dissolve	overrate
	smoke	scratch	parading	correction	community	equipped	granular
	size	tripping	sailor	discovering	advantage	solemn	endorse
	sleep	nurse	wrinkle	retirement	cooperation	correspond	insistent
			dinner	salute	spacious	emphasize	snorkel
			medal	treasure	carriage	scoundrel	personality
			tanner	homemade	presumption	cubic	prosperous
			dimmed	conviction	appearance	flexible	
			careful	creature	description	arctic	

INVENTARIO ORTOGRÁFICO EN ESPAÑOL
SPANISH SPELLING INVENTORY

Developed by Lori Helman

This is a short spelling inventory to help you learn about students' orthographic knowledge. The results of the spelling inventories have implications for reading, writing, vocabulary, and spelling instruction.

Instructions*

Let students know that you are administering this inventory to learn about how they spell. Let them know that this is not a test, but that they will be helping you teach them by doing their best. Students should not study this inventory beforehand.

Possible script: "I am going to ask you to spell some words. Spell them the best you can. Some of the words will be easy to spell; some will be more difficult. When you do not know how to spell a word, spell it the best you can; write down all the sounds you feel and hear."

Say the word once, read the sentence if the meaning is unclear, and then say the word again. Work with groups of 5 words. You may want to stop testing when students miss 3 of 5 words. Have students check their papers for their name and the date. See Chapter 2 for further instructions on administration and interpretation.

Analyze Students' Papers

Copy a Feature or Error Guide for each student. Do not count reversed letters as errors. Staple the student's paper to the Feature or Error Guide.

Directions for Using the Feature Guide. For each word, check the features that are noted in the columns at the bottom of the Feature Guide on page 320. Add an additional point in the "correct" column if the word is spelled correctly. Note that not all orthographic features are scored for all words, and the number of feature points varies.

Total the number of points under each feature and across each word; this is a way to check your addition. The total score can be compared over time but the most useful information will be the feature analysis. Look down each feature column to determine the needs of individual students. For example, a student who spells 9 of the 10 representación de sonidos correctly is knowledgeable about these features although some review work might be in order. A student who spells 7 or 8 of the 10 representación de sonidos needs to be involved in word study around this feature. If a student did not get any points for a feature, then the feature is beyond the student's instructional range and earlier features need to be studied first.

Arrange students' papers in order from highest total points to lowest total points before transferring the numbers across the bottom row of each student's Feature Guide to the Classroom Composite on page 326. For a sense of your groups' needs and to form groups for instruction, *highlight* students who make *2 or more errors* on a particular feature. If you call out less than the total list *adjust the totals* on the Classroom Composite.

Directions for Using the Error Guide. Using the Error Guide on page 321, circle each error or write in the student's spelling by the error that is most similar. When a word is spelled correctly, circle the spelling at the end of the string of errors. After all words have been scored, determine where most circled words lie and look at the top row of the table for the developmental spelling level for this student. Total the words spelled correctly and note where the student is within the stage: *early* in the stage, in the *middle*, or *late* in the stage. Use the Spelling-by-Stage Classroom Organization Chart on page 327 to organize word study groups and to find the developmental levels, the types of features, and the chapter in *Words Their Way* to turn to for activities.

---

*Instructions in Spanish are found on the *Words Their Way* website.

Grupo Uno

1.	el	Me gusta el café. *el*
2.	suma	Ella hace la suma bien. *suma*
3.	pan	Quiero queso con mi pan. *pan*
4.	red	Uso una red para pescar. *red*

Grupo Dos

5.	campos	Los campos están listos para plantar. *campos*
6.	plancha	Ten cuidado con la plancha. *plancha*
7.	brincar	¿ Quieres brincar a la soga? *brincar*
8.	fresa	La fresa es roja y dulce. *fresa*
9.	aprieto	Yo aprieto la mano de mi hermanito. *aprieto*
10.	guisante	El guisante crece bien en el jardín. *guisante*

Grupo Tres

11.	quisiera	Yo quisiera viajar a la luna algún día. *quisiera*
12.	gigante	Había un gigante feroz en el cuento. *gigante*
13.	actrices	La película tenía buenas actrices. *actrices*
14.	voy	Ya me voy a la casa. *voy*
15.	hierro	Es fuerte porque es hecho de hierro. *hierro*

Grupo Cuatro

16.	bilingüe	Cuando sabes dos idiomas eres bilingüe. *bilingüe*
17.	lápices	Todos mis lápices están rotos. *lápices*
18.	extraño	Es muy extraño que ho han llegado. *extraño*
19.	autobús	El autobús nos lleva al parque. *autobús*
20.	hoya	Hice una hoya en el suelo para plantar mi árbol. *hoya*

Grupo Cinco

21.	geometría	La geometría es parte de las matemáticas. *geometría*
22.	caimán	El caimán tiene muchos dientes. *caimán*
23.	intangible	No puedes conseguir lo que es intangible. *intangible*
24.	herbívoro	El toro no come carne, es herbívoro. *herbívoro*
25.	psicólogo	El psicólogo viene a la clase a ayudarnos. *psicólogo*

Feature Guide for Spanish Spelling Inventory

Directions: Check the features that are present in each student's spelling. In the bottom row, total features used correctly. Check the spelling stage that summarizes the student's development. Begin instruction at that stage with a focus on the types of features where the student missed two or more features in a column.

Student's Name _____ Teacher _____ Grade _____ Date _____

ETAPAS DE DELETREADO →	EMERGENTE TARDE		ALFABÉTICA TEMPRANO/MEDIANO		TARDE	PATRONES TEMPRANO	TARDE	ACENTOS Y AFIJOS	DERIVACIONES Y SUS RELACIONES		
Características →	Vocal Prominente	Consonante Prominente	Vocales/Consonants	Represtación de Sonidos	Dígrafos, Sílabas Cerradas	Contrastes, Letras Mudas	Diptongos Homófonos	Tildes, Plurales, Afijos	Raíces	Puntos	Palabra
1. el	e	l									
2. suma	u	s									
3. pan	a	p									
4. red			re	d							
5. campos				os	mp						
6. plancha				pl	ch						
7. brincar			c (k)	ar	n						
8. fresa			sa	fr							
9. aprieto			o	ie							
10. guisante				ante		gui					
11. quisiera				iera		qui					
12. gigante			ga		nt	gi					
13. actrices			tr		ac			ces			
14. voy						v	oy				
15. hierro						h	ie				
16. bilingüe						b	üe				
17. lápices						c		á			
18. extraño				ñ				ex			
19. autobús								ú	auto		
20. hoya							h-y				
21. geometría								ía	metr		
22. caimán							ai	án			
23. intangible								ible	tang		
24. herbívoro								í	herb		
25. psicólogo								có	psi		
Totales	(3)	(3)	(5)	(10)	(5)	(7)	(5)	(9)	(5)	(52)	(25)

SPELLING STAGES:

□ TEMPRANO □ MEDIANO □ TARDE

□ TEMPRANO
□ EMERGENTE
□ ALFABÉTICA
□ PATRONES
□ ACENTOS Y AFIJOS
□ DERIVACIONES Y SUS RELACIONES

Words Spelled Correctly: ___/25
Feature Points: ___/52
Total ___/77

Error Guide to the Spanish Spelling Inventory

Directions: Circle students' spelling attempts below. If a spelling is not listed, write it in where it belongs on the developmental continuum. Determine a spelling stage that summarizes the student's development. Begin instruction at that level with a focus on features characteristic of that stage.

Student's Name _____ Teacher _____ Grade _____ Date _____

Stage groupings (ETAPAS DE DELETREADO →):
- **EMERGENTE (TARDE):** Vocal Prominente, Consonante Prominente
- **ALFABÉTICA:** Vocales Consonants (TEMPRANO), Digrafos Representación de Sonidos (MEDIANO), Contrastes, Silabas Cerradas (TARDE)
- **PATRONES:** Letras Mudas (TEMPRANO), Tildes, Diptongos Homófonos (TARDE)
- **ACENTOS Y AFIJOS:** Plurales, Afijos
- **DERIVACIONES Y SUS RELACIONS:** Raíces

Características →	Vocal Prominente	Consonante Prominente	Vocales Consonants	Digrafos Representación de Sonidos	Contrastes, Silabas Cerradas	Letras Mudas	Tildes, Diptongos Homófonos	Plurales, Afijos	Raíces
1. el	e	l	**el**						
2. suma	u	s	ua sua **suma**						
3. pan	a	p	pa **pan**						
4. red	e	r	re **red**						
5. campos	a	c/k	ca cao capo	capos	**campos**				
6. plancha	a	p	pa paa paha	plaha placha	**plancha**				
7. brincar	i	b/v	bi bia bica	brica bricar	**brincar**				
8. fresa	e	f	ea fea fesa	**fresa**					
9. aprieto	a	p	ao apo apito	apieto	**aprieto**				
10. guisante	i	g/c/k	ia gia gisae	gisate	**guisante**				
11. quisiera			kia kisia kicia	kisiera	cisiera qisuera	**quisiera**			
12. gigante			jia jiae jiate jigate	jigante	**gigante**				
13. actrices			aise atises atrises	atrises actrises	**actrices**				
14. voy			bo vo boi	voi			**voy**		
15. hierro			iro yro yero	iero yero	ierro yerro	**hierro**			
16. bilingüe			bilige/vilige	bilingwe bilingue	bilingue		**bilingüe**		
17. lápices			laises	lapices	lapices		**lápices**		
18. extraño			esrano	estraño estr(dr)año	ecstraño		**extraño**		
19. autobús			otob(v)us aotob(v)us		autobus			**autobús**	
20. hoya			oia oya	olla	holla		**hoya**		
21. geometría			gamea gemeia	gemeya geomeya	geomet(ch)ia			**geometría**	**geometría**
22. caimán			kayma	k(c)ayman			caiman	**caimán**	
23. intangible			itajibe itajibe	itanjible itanjible	itani(g)ible				**intangible**
24. herbívoro			eb(v)ib(v)oro	erbiboro		herb(v)iboro			**herbívoro**
25. psicólogo			s(c)ikogo	sikologo	sicologo		sicólogo		**psicólogo**

SPELLING STAGES:

☐ TEMPRANO   ☐ MEDIANO   ☐ TARDE

☐ EMERGENTE
☐ ALFABÉTICA
☐ PATRONES
☐ ACENTOS Y AFIJOS
☐ DERIVACIONES Y SUS RELACIONES

Words Spelled Correctly: _____ /25

Classroom Composite to Feature Guide for Primary Spelling Inventory

Directions: Record students' scores beginning with the student with the highest total feature points. Identify students who missed 2 or more of any of the features in a category. In the bottom row, total the number of students in each category who missed 2 or more features.

Teacher _____   School _____   Grade _____   Date _____

SPELLING STAGES→	Total Feature Points and Words	EMERGENT LATE / EARLY — Beginning Consonants	LETTER NAME–ALPHABETIC MIDDLE — Final Consonants	LATE — Short Vowels	EARLY — Consonant Digraphs	WITHIN WORD PATTERN MIDDLE — Consonant & Blends	LATE — Long-Vowel Patterns	SYLLABLES & AFFIXES EARLY — Other Vowel Patterns	MIDDLE — Inflected Endings
↓ Students' Names Possible points→	82	7 7	7	7	7	7	7	7	7
1.									
2.									
3.									
4.									
5.									
6.									
7.									
8.									
9.									
10.									
11.									
12.									
13.									
14.									
15.									
16.									
17.									
18.									
19.									
20.									
21.									
22.									
23.									
24.									
25.									
26.									
Number who missed two or more features ≥ 2 →									

Words Their Way Appendix © 2004 by Prentice-Hall, Inc.

Classroom Composite to Feature Guide for Elementary Spelling Inventory-1

Directions: Record students' scores beginning with the student with the highest total feature points. Identify students who missed 2 or more of any of the features in a category. In the bottom row, total the number of students in each category who missed 2 or more features.

Teacher _____ School _____ Grade _____ Date _____

SPELLING STAGES→		EMERGENT		LETTER NAME–ALPHABETIC			WITHIN WORD PATTERN			SYLLABLES & AFFIXES		DERIVATIONAL RELATIONS	
			LATE	EARLY	MIDDLE	LATE	EARLY	MIDDLE	LATE	EARLY	MIDDLE	LATE	EARLY	MIDDLE
↓ Students' Names	Total Feature Points and Words	Consonants Beginning Final		Short Vowels	Digraphs & Blends	Long-Vowel Patterns	Other Vowel Patterns	Syllable Junctures & Easy Prefixes & Suffixes	Harder Prefixes & Suffixes, & Unaccented Final Syllables	Reduced & Altered Vowels, Bases, Roots, & Derivatives
Possible points→	78	2	5	4	8	6	6	9	8	5
1.										
2.										
3.										
4.										
5.										
6.										
7.										
8.										
9.										
10.										
11.										
12.										
13.										
14.										
15.										
16.										
17.										
18.										
19.										
20.										
21.										
22.										
23.										
24.										
25.										
26.										
Number who missed two or more features ≥ 2 →										

Classroom Composite to Feature Guide for Intermediate Spelling Inventory-1

Directions: Record students' scores beginning with the student with the highest total feature points. Identify students who missed 2 or more of any of the features in a category. In the bottom row, total the number of students in each category who missed 2 or more features.

Teacher _____   School _____   Grade _____   Date _____

SPELLING STAGES→		EMERGENT	LETTER NAME–ALPHABETIC			WITHIN WORD PATTERN			SYLLABLES & AFFIXES		DERIVATIONAL RELATIONS	
		LATE	EARLY	MIDDLE	LATE	EARLY	MIDDLE	LATE	EARLY	MIDDLE	LATE	EARLY	MIDDLE
↓ Students' Names	Total Feature Points and Words	Short Vowels	Easy Digraphs & Blends	Long Vowels	Other Vowels	Complex Digraphs & Blends	Syllable Junctures & Easy Prefixes & Suffixes	Harder Prefixes, Suffixes, & Unaccented Final Syllables	Reduced Vowels, Bases & Roots
Possible points→	75	4	4	4	5	4	9	12	8
1.									
2.									
3.									
4.									
5.									
6.									
7.									
8.									
9.									
10.									
11.									
12.									
13.									
14.									
15.									
16.									
17.									
18.									
19.									
20.									
21.									
22.									
23.									
24.									
25.									
26.									
Number who missed two or more features ≥ 2 →									

Words Their Way Appendix © 2004 by Prentice-Hall, Inc.

Classroom Composite for Upper Level Spelling Inventory

Directions: Record students' scores beginning with the student with the highest total feature points. Identify students who missed 2 or more of any of the features in a category. In the bottom row, total the number of students in each category who missed 2 or more features.

Teacher _____ School _____ Grade _____ Date _____

SPELLING STAGES→		LETTER NAME–ALPHABETIC		WITHIN WORD PATTERN			SYLLABLES & AFFIXES		DERIVATIONAL RELATIONS	
		MIDDLE	LATE	EARLY	MIDDLE	LATE	EARLY	MIDDLE	EARLY	MIDDLE LATE
↓ Students' Names	Total Features and Words	Short Vowels	Easy Digraphs & Blends	Long Vowels & Other Vowels	Complex Digraphs & Blends	Syllable Junctures & Easy Prefixes & Suffixes	Harder Prefixes, Suffixes, & Unaccented Final Syllables	Reduced and Altered Vowels	Bases Roots & Derivatives	
Possible points→	120	3	8	6	4	16	21	10	18	
1.										
2.										
3.										
4.										
5.										
6.										
7.										
8.										
9.										
10.										
11.										
12.										
13.										
14.										
15.										
16.										
17.										
18.										
19.										
20.										
21.										
22.										
23.										
24.										
25.										
26.										
Number who missed two or more features ≥ 2 →										

Words Their Way Appendix © 2004 by Prentice-Hall, Inc.

Classroom Composite to Feature Guide for Spanish Spelling Inventory

Directions: Record students' scores beginning with the student with the highest total feature points. Identify students who missed 2 or more of any of the features in a category. In the bottom row, total the number of students in each category who missed 2 or more features.

Teacher _____ School _____ Grade _____ Date _____

SPELLING STAGES →	Total Features Points & Words	EMERGENTE		ALFABÉTICA		PATRONES		ACENTOS Y AFIJOS	DERIVACIONES Y SUS RELACIONS
		TARDE		TEMPRANO	MEDIANO	TARDE	TEMPRANO	TARDE	
↓ Students' Names		Vocal Prominente	Consonante Prominente	Vocales/ Consonantes	Representacion de Sonidos	Digrafos Silabas Cerradas	Contrastes Letras Mudas	Diptongos Homofonos	Tildes, Plurales Afijoss	Raices
Possible points →	77	3	3	5	10	5	7	5	9	5
1.										
2.										
3.										
4.										
5.										
6.										
7.										
8.										
9.										
10.										
11.										
12.										
13.										
14.										
15.										
16.										
17.										
18.										
19.										
20.										
21.										
22.										
23.										
24.										
25.										
26.										
Number who missed two or more features ≥ 2 →										

Words Their Way Appendix © 2004 by Prentice-Hall, Inc.

SPELLING-BY-STAGE CLASSROOM ORGANIZATION CHART

Directions: Write students' names underneath the gradation within the stage the students have scored. Use an arrow to the left (←) or right (→) to indicate students who could go up or down a gradation. Draw a circle around students' names to form word study groups. In most classrooms we try to form three groups.

SPELLING STAGES→	EMERGENT			LETTER NAME—ALPHABETIC			WITHIN WORD PATTERN			SYLLABLES & AFFIXES			DERIVATIONAL RELATIONS		
	EARLY	MIDDLE	LATE	EARLY	MIDDLE	LATE	EARLY	MIDDLE	LATE	EARLY	MIDDLE	LATE	EARLY	MIDDLE	LATE

CHAPTERS IN *WORDS THEIR WAY*	CHAPTER 4	CHAPTER 5	CHAPTER 6	CHAPTER 7	CHAPTER 8

SOUND BOARDS
SOUND BOARD FOR BEGINNING CONSONANT AND DIGRAPHS

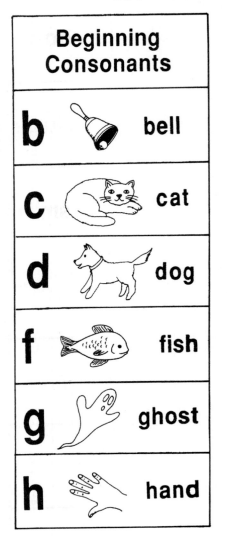

Beginning Consonants

b bell

c cat

d dog

f fish

g ghost

h hand

j jug

k key

l lamp

m mouse

n net

p pig

r ring

s sun

t tent

y yarn

w watch

v van

z zip

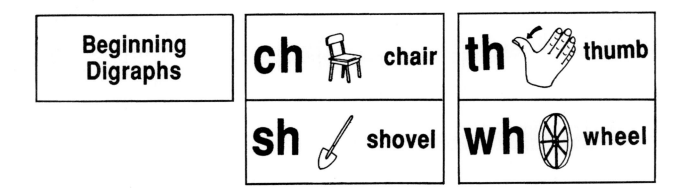

Beginning Digraphs

ch chair

sh shovel

th thumb

wh wheel

Words Their Way Appendix © 2004 by Prentice-Hall, Inc.

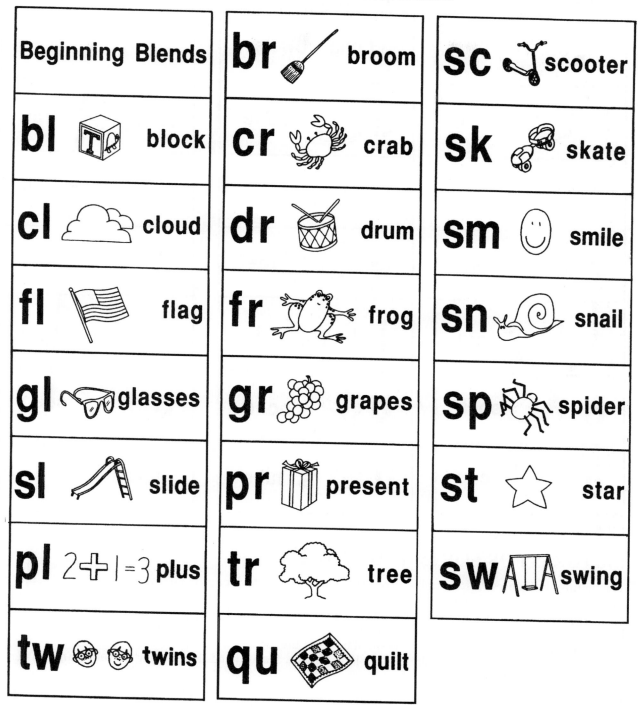

Beginning Blends	br broom	sc scooter
bl block	cr crab	sk skate
cl cloud	dr drum	sm smile
fl flag	fr frog	sn snail
gl glasses	gr grapes	sp spider
sl slide	pr present	st star
pl 2+1=3 plus	tr tree	sw swing
tw twins	qu quilt	

SOUND BOARD FOR LONG AND SHORT VOWELS

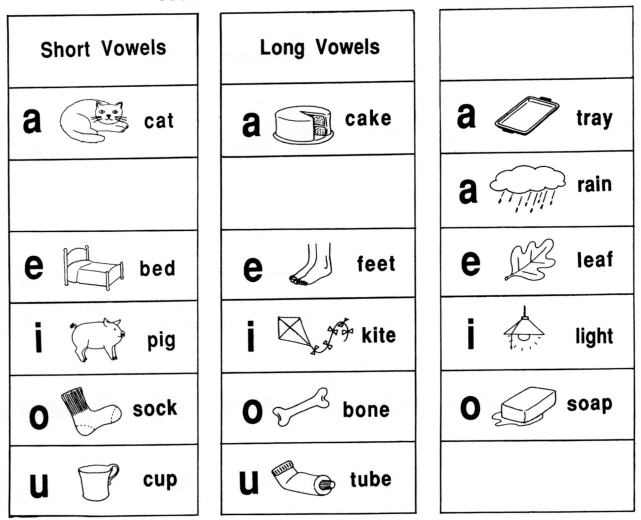

Short Vowels		Long Vowels			
a	cat	**a**	cake	**a**	tray
				a	rain
e	bed	**e**	feet	**e**	leaf
i	pig	**i**	kite	**i**	light
o	sock	**o**	bone	**o**	soap
u	cup	**u**	tube		

PICTURES FOR SORTS AND GAMES

The pictures in Figures A-1 through A-6 can be copied on cardstock or glued to cardstock to create a set of pictures to use for sorting activities. Many teachers find it easiest to create a sheet of pictures which can be cut apart by the students for sorting by using the pictures like clip art. Make copies of the pictures you need (combining two, three, or four sounds) and glue them randomly onto a template such as the one on page 405. Write the letters you will use as headers in the small boxes at the top.

The pictures in Figure A-6 are labeled for long vowels. There are additional long vowel pictures in Figures A-1 through A-3.

Long-a:	gate	game	nail	paint	rake	vase	shave	chair	blade	plane
	plate	scale	skate	train	grapes					
Long-e:	deer	jeep	key	leaf	seal	sheep	dream			
	wheel	sleeve	sleep	sweep	queen	tree				
Long-i:	nine	dice	smile	prize	drive	fire	tie			
	tire	price	cry	fly						
Long-o:	boat	goat	rope	hose	nose	comb	ghost			
	toes	float	globe	yo-yo	snow					

Words Their Way Appendix © 2004 by Prentice-Hall, Inc.

FIGURE A-1 Picture Cards for Beginning Consonants

FIGURE A-1 Picture Cards for Beginning Consonants *(continued)*

Words Their Way Appendix © 2004 by Prentice-Hall, Inc.

Words Their Way Appendix © 2004 by Prentice-Hall, Inc.

FIGURE A-1 Picture Cards for Beginning Consonants *(continued)*

Words Their Way Appendix © 2004 by Prentice-Hall, Inc.

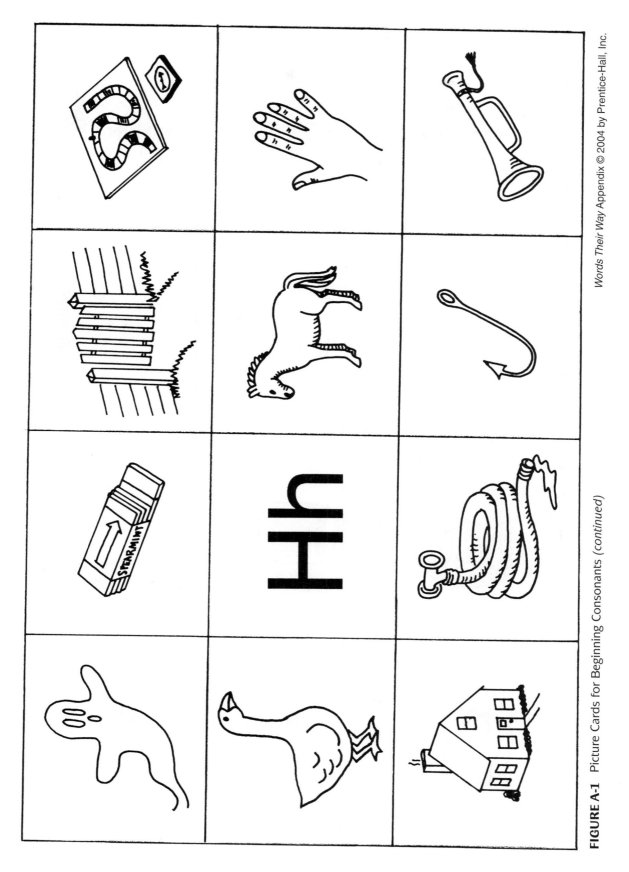

FIGURE A-1 Picture Cards for Beginning Consonants *(continued)*

Words Their Way Appendix © 2004 by Prentice-Hall, Inc.

FIGURE A-1 Picture Cards for Beginning Consonants (*continued*)

Words Their Way Appendix © 2004 by Prentice-Hall, Inc.

Words Their Way Appendix © 2004 by Prentice-Hall, Inc.

FIGURE A-1 Picture Cards for Beginning Consonants (*continued*)

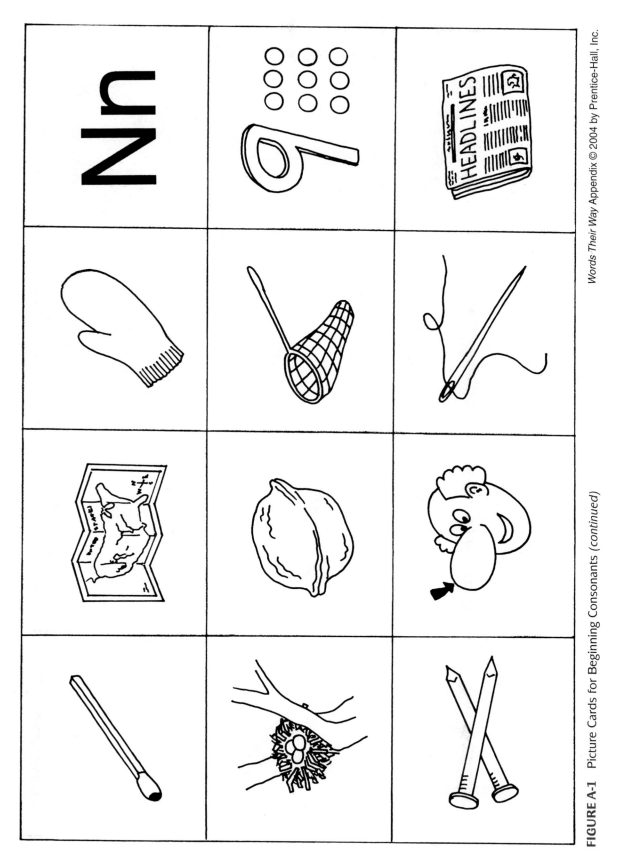

FIGURE A-1 Picture Cards for Beginning Consonants (*continued*)

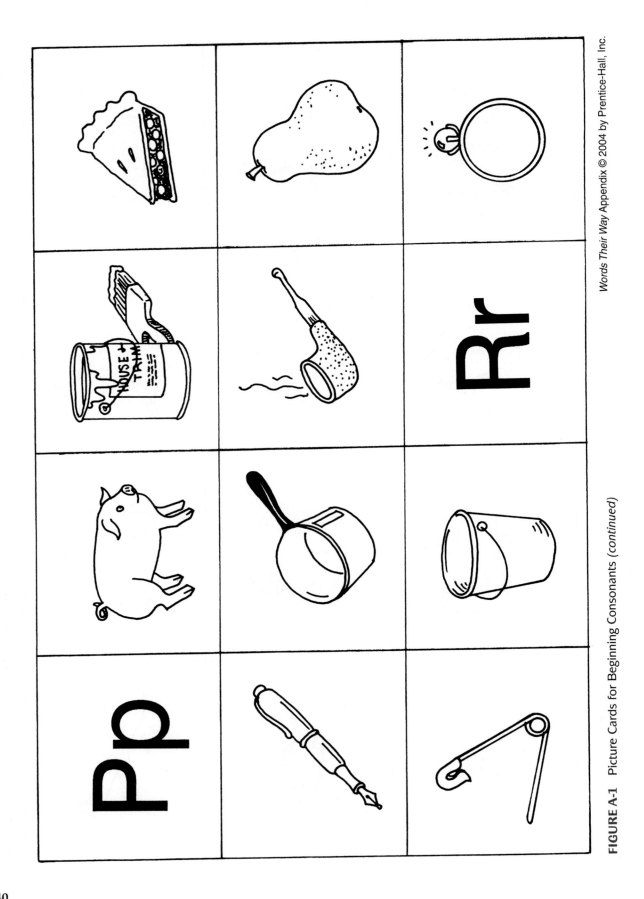

FIGURE A-1 Picture Cards for Beginning Consonants (*continued*)

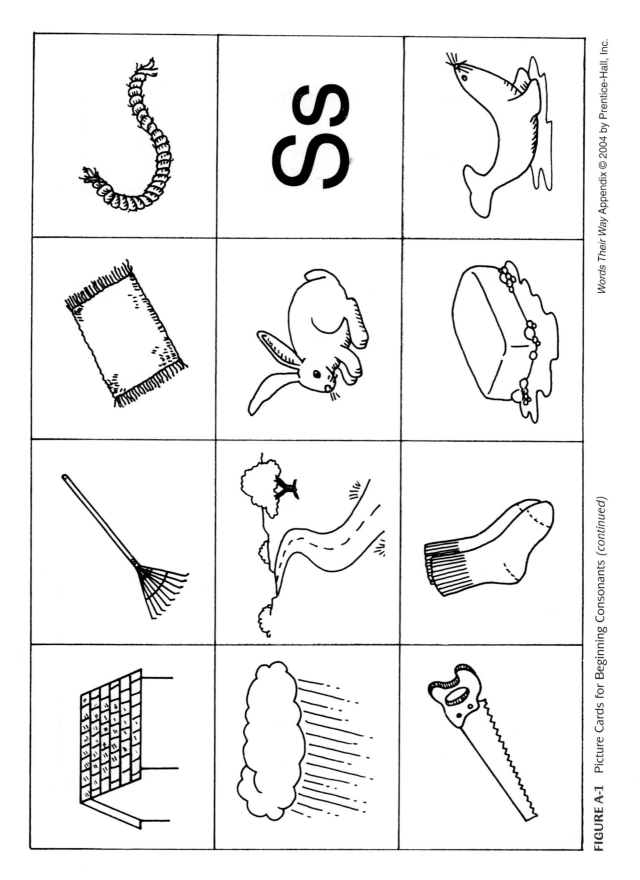

FIGURE A-1 Picture Cards for Beginning Consonants *(continued)*

FIGURE A-1 Picture Cards for Beginning Consonants (*continued*)

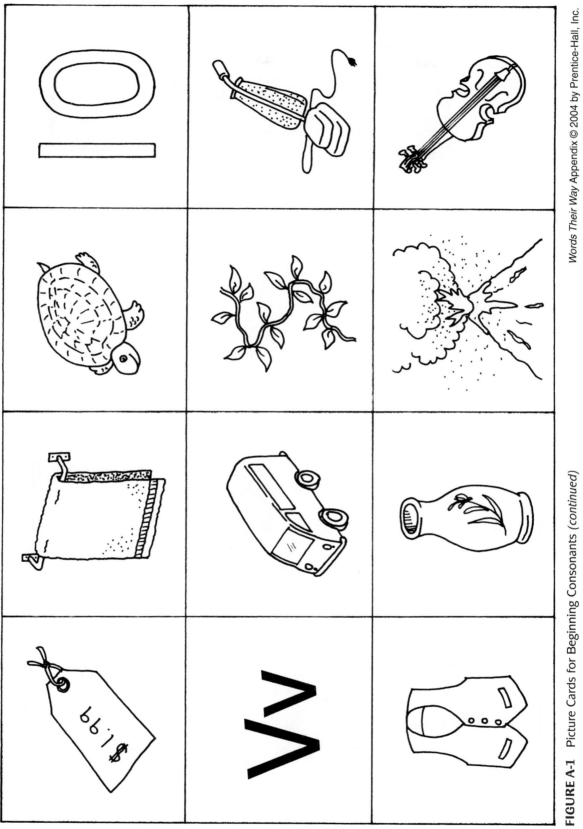

FIGURE A-1 Picture Cards for Beginning Consonants (continued)

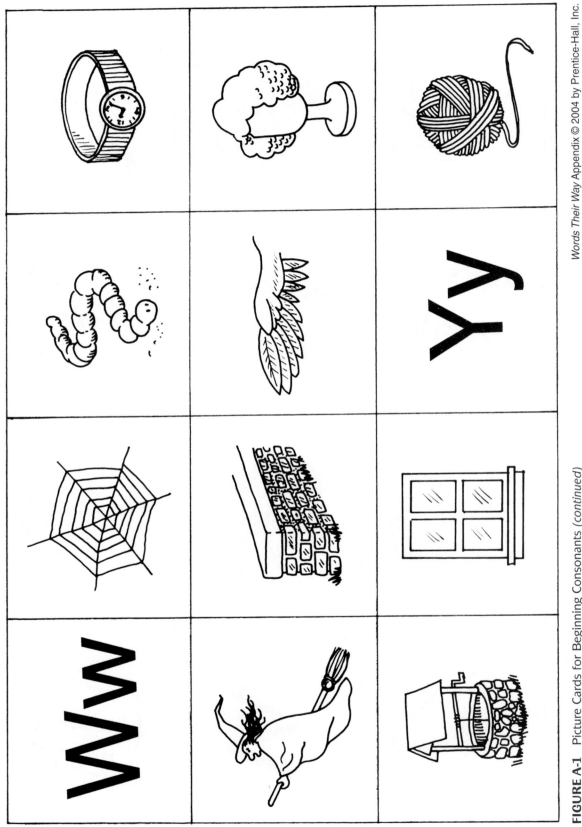

FIGURE A-1 Picture Cards for Beginning Consonants *(continued)*

Words Their Way Appendix © 2004 by Prentice-Hall, Inc.

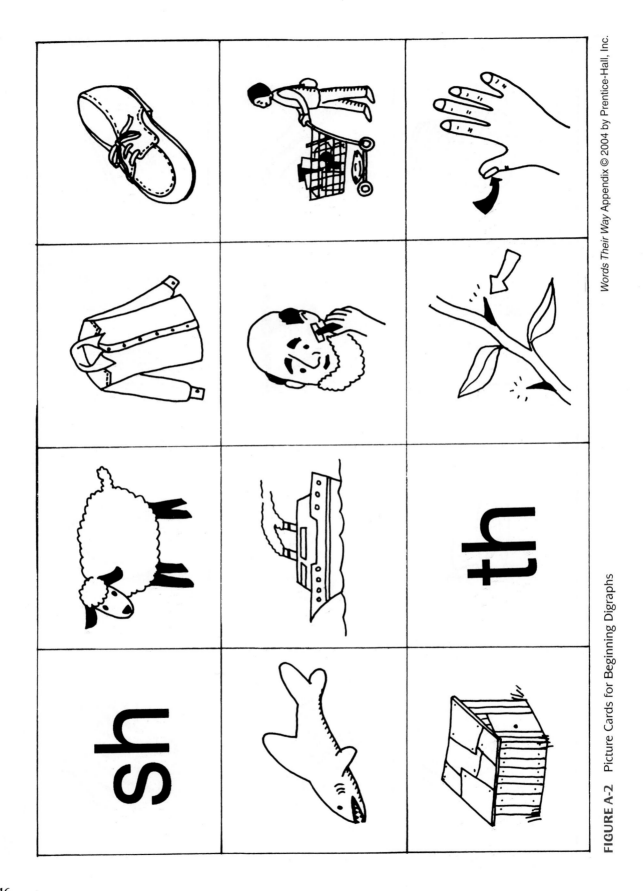

FIGURE A-2 Picture Cards for Beginning Digraphs

346

FIGURE A-2 Picture Cards for Beginning Digraphs *(continued)*

FIGURE A-2 Picture Cards for Beginning Digraphs *(continued)*

FIGURE A-3 Picture Cards for Beginning Blends

FIGURE A-3 Picture Cards for Beginning Blends (*continued*)

Words Their Way Appendix © 2004 by Prentice-Hall, Inc.

FIGURE A-3 Picture Cards for Beginning Blends (continued)

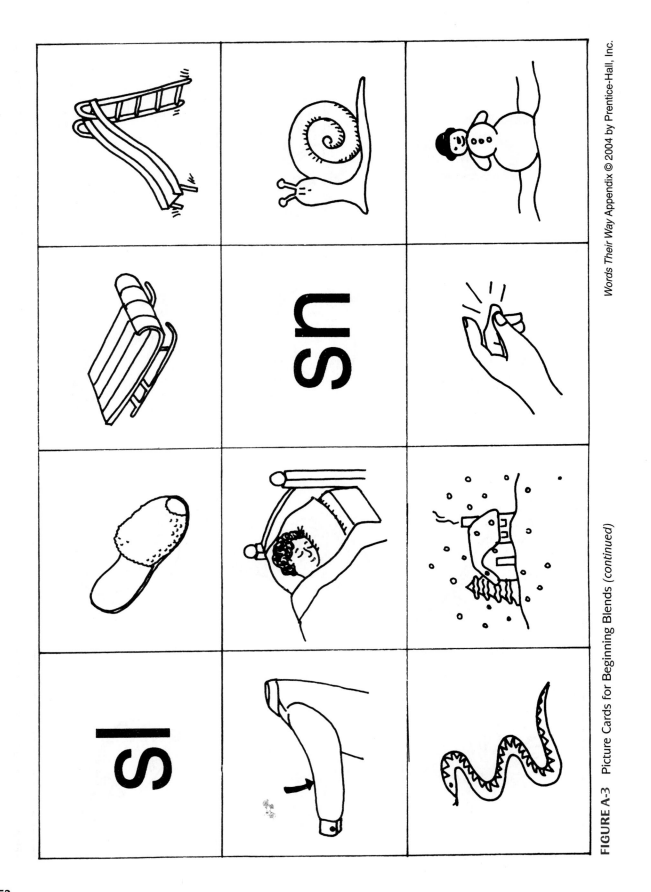

FIGURE A-3 Picture Cards for Beginning Blends (*continued*)

Words Their Way Appendix © 2004 by Prentice-Hall, Inc.

FIGURE A-3 Picture Cards for Beginning Blends (continued)

Words Their Way Appendix © 2004 by Prentice-Hall, Inc.

FIGURE A-3 Picture Cards for Beginning Blends *(continued)*

Words Their Way Appendix © 2004 by Prentice-Hall, Inc.

FIGURE A-3 Picture Cards for Beginning Blends (continued)

FIGURE A-3 Picture Cards for Beginning Blends (*continued*)

Words Their Way Appendix © 2004 by Prentice-Hall, Inc.

Words Their Way Appendix © 2004 by Prentice-Hall, Inc.

357

Words Their Way Appendix © 2004 by Prentice-Hall, Inc.

FIGURE A-3 Picture Cards for Beginning Blends (continued)

FIGURE A-3 Picture Cards for Beginning Blends (continued)

FIGURE A-3 Picture Cards for Beginning Blends *(continued)*

Words Their Way Appendix © 2004 by Prentice-Hall, Inc.

FIGURE A-4 Picture Cards for Beginning Short Vowels

Pictures include: astronaut, ant, ax, alligator, apple, add, egg, Eskimo, etch-a-sketch®, and Ed.

Words Their Way Appendix © 2004 by Prentice-Hall, Inc.

FIGURE A-4 Picture Cards for Beginning Short Vowels (*continued*)
Pictures include: itch, ick, igloo, ill, in, ostrich, olive, otter, octopus, and ox.

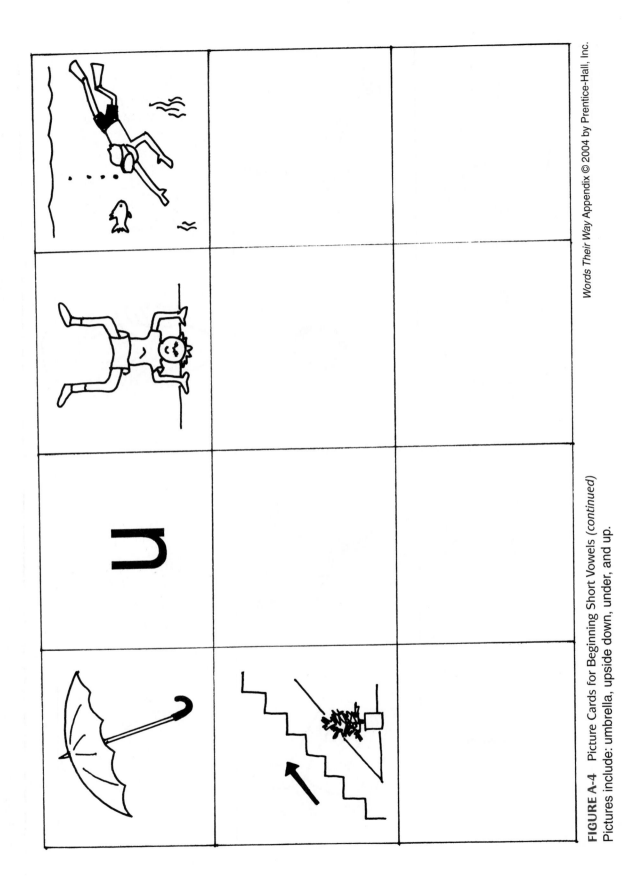

FIGURE A-4 Picture Cards for Beginning Short Vowels (*continued*)
Pictures include: umbrella, upside down, under, and up.

Words Their Way Appendix © 2004 by Prentice-Hall, Inc.

Words Their Way Appendix © 2004 by Prentice-Hall, Inc.

FIGURE A-5 Picture Cards for Medial Short Vowels

Words Their Way Appendix © 2004 by Prentice-Hall, Inc.

FIGURE A-5 Picture Cards for Medial Short Vowels *(continued)*

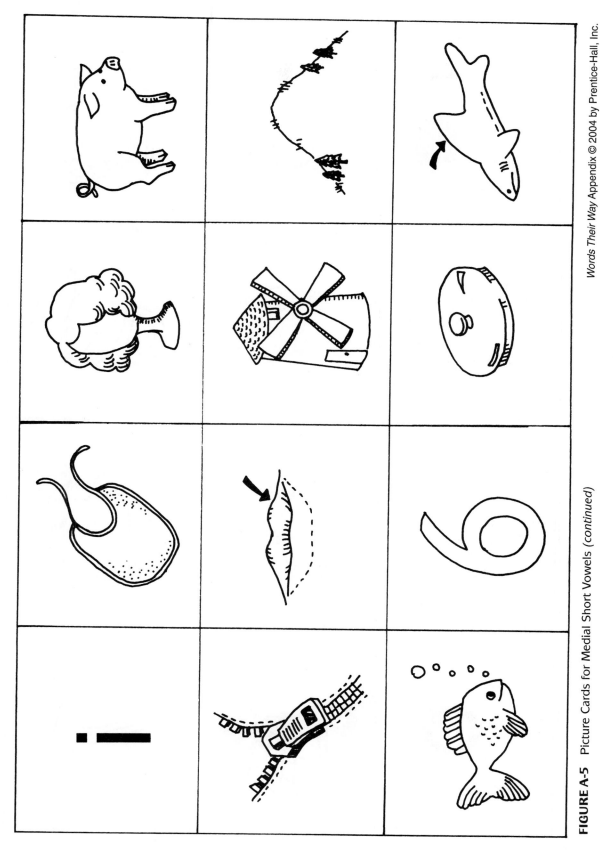

FIGURE A-5 Picture Cards for Medial Short Vowels (*continued*)

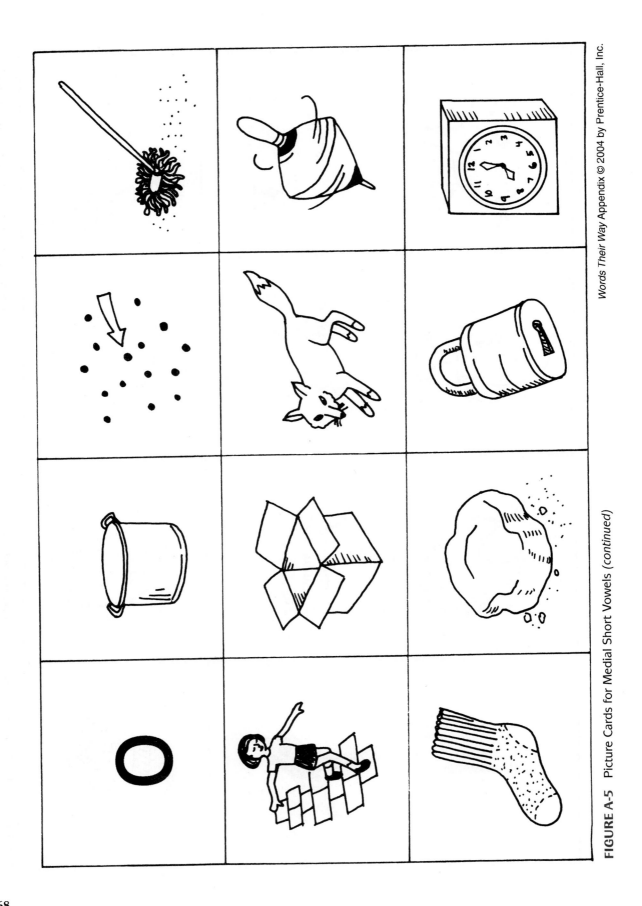

Words Their Way Appendix © 2004 by Prentice-Hall, Inc.

FIGURE A-5 Picture Cards for Medial Short Vowels *(continued)*

FIGURE A-5 Picture Cards for Medial Short Vowels (continued)

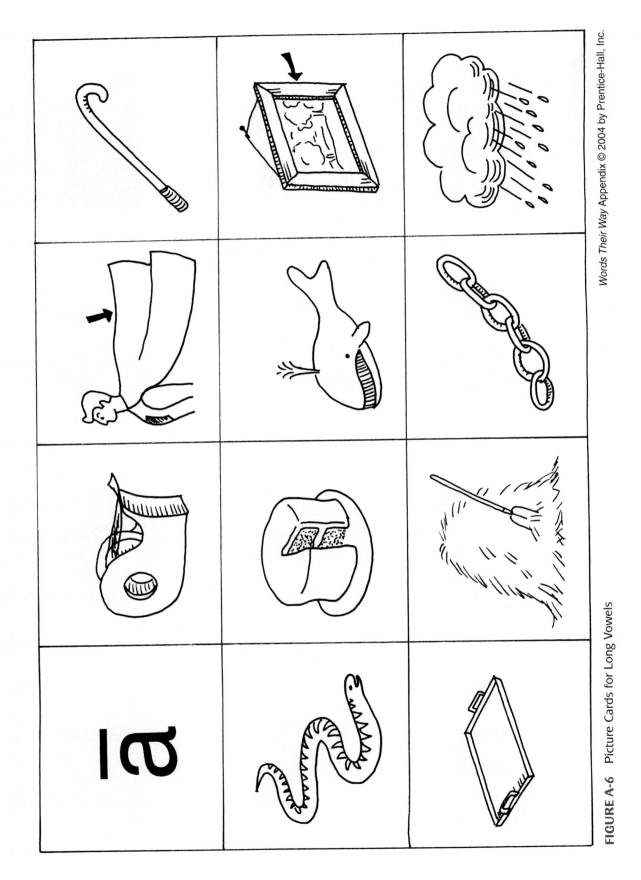

FIGURE A-6 Picture Cards for Long Vowels

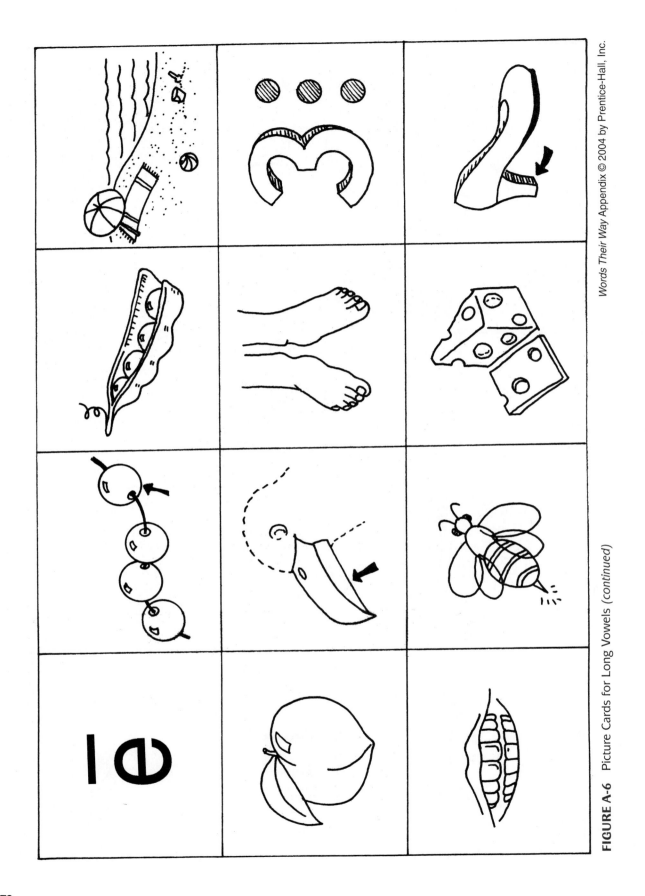

FIGURE A-6 Picture Cards for Long Vowels *(continued)*

Words Their Way Appendix © 2004 by Prentice-Hall, Inc.

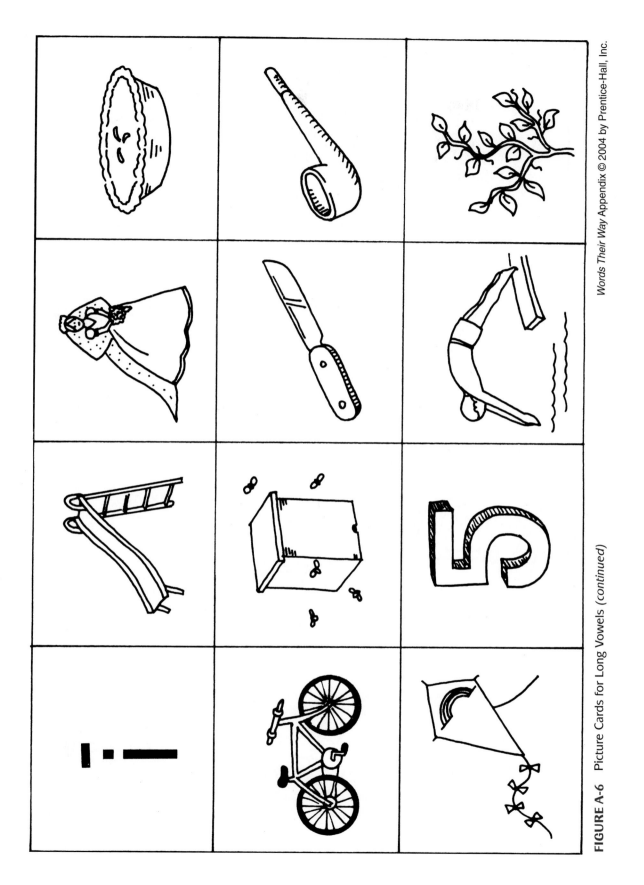

FIGURE A-6 Picture Cards for Long Vowels (*continued*)

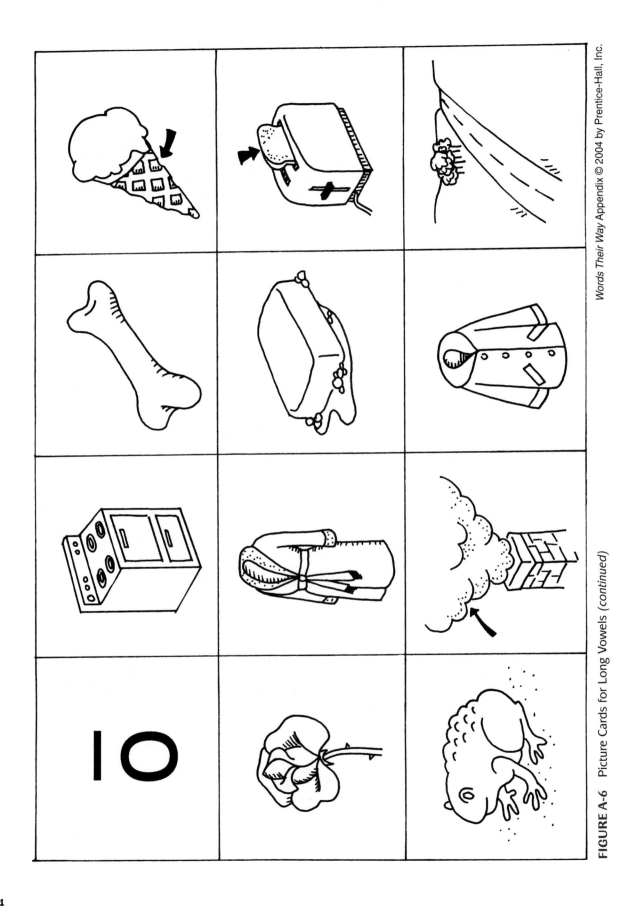

FIGURE A-6 Picture Cards for Long Vowels (continued)

SAMPLE WORD SORTS BY SPELLING STAGE

The sample word sorts on the following pages are arranged by spelling stage and can be used with many of the activities described in the instructional chapters. Prepare word sorts to use with your own students by copying the words on cards or on a template such as the one on page 406. Be sure to write the words in randomly so students can make their own discoveries as they sort. Several points need to be made considering the use of these sorts.

1. These sorts are not intended to be a sequence for all students. Chapter 2 will help you match your students to the stages of spelling. There are further suggestions in each instructional chapter about the pacing and sequencing of word study for each stage. Choose appropriate sorts from among those presented here.

2. This is not an exhaustive list of sorts, but it does give you a starting point for creating your own. You can adapt these sorts by adding, subtracting, or substituting words that are more appropriate for your students. Words in a sort can be made easier or harder in a number of ways:
   - Common words like *hat* or *store* are easier than uncommon words like *vat* or *boar*. Use words students know from their own reading in the early stages to make sorts easier. This is less important when you get to syllables and affixes and derivational relations where extending a student's vocabulary is important.
   - Add words with blends, digraphs, and complex consonant units like *ce, dge,* or *tch* to make words harder. *Bat* and *blast* are both CVC words but *blast* is harder to spell.
   - Adding more oddballs to a sort makes it harder. Oddballs should never, however, constitute more than about 20% of the words in a sort or students might fail to see the generalizations that govern the majority of words. Don't use oddballs children are not likely to know (like *plaid* in a long-a sort for students early in the within word pattern stage).

3. Due to regional dialects you and your students may pronounce words differently and need to categorize words differently from those indicated in the sorts. These pronunciations should be honored. Substitute words or change categories as needed.

4. Words that look or sound as though they should match the features of a sort, but do not, are included in many of the sorts under an asterisk (*) to mark the oddball category.

LETTER NAME–ALPHABETIC SORTS

Same Short-Vowel Families, CVC

Words from sorts 1 to 20 can be used in connection with games and activities in Chapter 5.

1. Short-a

cat	*man*
bat	can
sat	pan
fat	ran
mat	fan
rat	van
hat	tan

2. More Short-a's

sad	*cap*	*bag*
mad	tap	rag
dad	map	wag
had	nap	tag
pad	lap	flag
	rap	

3. Short-i

sit	*big*
bit	wig
hit	pig
fit	dig
kit	fig
quit	

4. More Short-i's

pin	*pill*	*rip*	*sick*
win	will	lip	pick
fin	fill	hip	lick
thin	hill	zip	kick
	mill	dip	tick
	bill		
	kill		

5. Short-o

not	*hop*
got	pop
hot	mop
lot	cop
pot	stop
dot	shop
shot	

6. More Short-o's

job	*lock*	*dog*
rob	rock	log
cob	sock	frog
mob	dock	fog
blob	clock	jog
sob	block	

7. Short-e

pet	*ten*	*bed*	*bell*
net	hen	red	tell
met	pen	fed	well
set	men	led	fell
jet	then	sled	shell
bet	when		
get			

8. Short-u

cut	*tub*	*bug*	*fun*	*duck*
nut	rub	rug	bun	luck
hut	cub	dug	run	suck
but	club	jug	sun	truck
shut		hug	gun	tuck
			tug	

Mixed Short-Vowel Families, CVC

9. Short-a, i, u

man	pin	fun
can	win	run
fan	fin	sun
ran	thin	bun
than	grin	gun
plan	chin	

10. Short-a, i, o, u

cat	sit	not	cut
mat	fit	hot	shut
hat	hit	got	nut
that	quit	pot	but
rat	bit	rot	hut

11. Short-a, i, e

bag	big	pill	bell
rag	wig	will	sell
wag	pig	hill	tell
flag	jig	fill	well
tag		bill	shell

12. Families with *ck*

back	sick	lock	duck
sack	lick	rock	suck
tack	pick	sock	tuck
jack	tick	dock	truck
pack		clock	

13. Preconsonantal Nasals

camp	jump	band	sink
lamp	dump	hand	pink
ramp	hump	sand	think
stamp	stump	land	wink
damp	lump	stand	drink

14. Families Ending in *sh*

mash	fish	mush
cash	dish	hush
trash	wish	rush
rash		gush

Short Vowels, CVC

15. Short-a and Short-o

cat	not
bag	job
mad	stop
pan	fox
pat	lock
tack	got
lamp	top

16. Short-e and Short-u

pet	nut
bell	sun
red	cup
yes	mud
help	jump
test	hug
beg	duck

17. Short-a, Short-i, and Short-o

hat	dig	pop
fast	lick	rock
sand	lip	spot
tax	did	mom
bath	dish	stop
sack	nip	not

18. All Short Vowels

can	let	hit	rock	hug
that	best	fish	mop	luck
lap	met	fill	dot	run
last	web	six	box	bus
back	nest	this	rob	much
	wet	rich		just

19. Short Vowels with Blends

brat	grab	trip	crab
brick	grin	trap	crib
brag	grass	trot	crash
bring	grand	trick	cram
	grip	truck	
		track	

20. Two-Step Sort

a. Initial consonant and blends

rack	tack	dug	trick	drum
rag	tag	dip	track	drill
rash	tap	duck	trash	drag
rug			trap	drug
rip			trip	drip
			truck	

b. Short-vowel sort

tack	tick	truck
tap	trip	drum
trash	drill	dug
drag	dip	rug
rack	rip	duck
rag	trick	drug
rash	drip	
trap		

WITHIN WORD PATTERN SORTS

Words from sorts 21 to 61 can be used in connection with games and activities in Chapter 6.

Vowel Sorts: Words That Compare Short and Long Vowels, Explore Long-Vowel Patterns (CVCe, CVVC, CVV, CV), and R-influenced Words

21. Short/Long-a

hat	name	*
jack	date	was
ask	race	
slap	plane	
fast	cape	
lap	page	
flag	same	
pass	safe	
path	gave	
glad	gate	

22. Short/Long-a

cap	lake	rain
last	wave	wait
plan	late	nail
sat	tape	gain
flat	bake	fail
tax	base	pail
	shade	plain
	made	sail
	maze	
	sale	

23. Long-a Patterns

same	mail	day	*
whale	pain	say	said
flake	train	play	have
grape	paid	may	
stage	brain	pay	
grade	snail	stay	
chase	chain	clay	
shave	tail		
tale	waist		
waste			

24. Less Common Long-a

hay	prey	eight	break
tray	they	weigh	great
stray	obey	vein	steak
pray	hey	veil	
sway		freight	
play		sleigh	
		neigh	

 Words Their Way Appendix © 2004 by Prentice-Hall, Inc.

25. R-influenced *a*

car	care	chair	*
star	share	pair	bear
bark	bare	hair	
card	mare	air	
far	rare		
dark	scare		
arm			
start			

26. Short/Long-*e*

well	week	she
step	peel	he
west	weed	we
men	peek	me
bed	speed	
help	keep	
	peep	

27. Short/Long-*e*

best	green	mean	*
left	wheel	team	been
neck	sheet	deal	head
bell	street	reach	
bled	bleed	beach	
yet	teeth	steam	
	creep	clean	
	speed	bean	

28. Short/Long-*e*

mess	head	neat
rest	dead	meal
bell	deaf	speak
kept	breath	meat
nest	death	treat
shell	dread	sneak
vest		heat

29. Less Common Long-*e*

greed	chief	these	*
speech	field	scene	vein
greet	brief	theme	friend
creek	grief	eve	seize
fleet	shriek		
geese	piece		
cheese	thief		
	niece		

30. R-influenced *e*

her	near	cheer	bear	*
fern	clear	deer	pear	heart
germ	dear	sneer	wear	
jerk	year	queer	swear	
herb	spear	peer		
herd	beard			
perch				

31. Short/Long-*i*

dish	hike	*
chip	ride	give
king	ripe	live
whip	nice	
twin	white	
miss	dime	
pink	fine	
rich	life	

32. Short/Long-*i*

clip	mine	try	*
win	price	fly	eye
trick	spine	shy	buy
gift	lime	why	bye
list	wife	sky	
mitt	vine	dry	
thick	five		
swim			

33. Long-*i* Patterns

kite	might	mind
bride	night	wild
write	right	kind
spice	bright	blind
hide	light	find
wipe	tight	child
mice	sight	mild
		grind

34. R-blends/R-influenced *i*

grin	third	hire
bring	shirt	tire
drip	dirt	fire
grill	bird	wire
trick	skirt	tired
drink	girl	
brick		
crib		

35. Short/Long-*o*

lock	home	*
doll	slope	love
crop	note	gone
shot	hose	
clock	vote	
shock	joke	
knob	smoke	
slot	hope	
	choke	

36. Long-*o* Patterns

rope	road	blow	*
woke	boat	grow	now
close	soap	know	cow
stone	soak	slow	
bone	moan	throw	
phone	loaf	snow	
broke	coach		
hole	load		
	toast		

37. Short/Long-*o*

mock	roll	ghost	*
dock	cold	most	lost
soft	stroll	host	cost
cross	mold	post	
cloth	scold		
lost	fold		
frost	told		
odd	folk		

38. R-influenced *o*

for	more	door	*
born	store	poor	your
short	chore	floor	
porch	tore		
storm	shore		
north	score		
fort	wore		
torch	swore		

39. Short/Long-*u*

bun	June	blue	*
fuss	cute	glue	truth
luck	rule	clue	
lump	tube	due	
trust	tune	true	
plum	huge		
crust	cube		

40. Long-*u* Patterns

rude	fruit	new	*
crude	suit	chew	fuel
flute	juice	drew	build
mule	bruise	knew	
fume		stew	
chute		few	
		threw	
		screw	

41. Other Long-*u*

gloom	dew	who
bloom	grew	to
roost	crew	too
smooth	flew	two
scoop	blew	
school		
mood		
pool		

42. R-influenced *u*

hurt	cure	heard
turn	pure	learn
church	sure	earn
burst	lure	pearl
curl		yearn
purr		earth
purse		search

43. R-blends/Vowels

grill	girl
trap	tarp
crush	curl
fry	first
price	purse
track	dark
brag	bark
drip	dirt
frog	fort

44. R-influenced Vowels

car	her	for
shark	first	short
farm	bird	corn
hard	burn	horn
card	word	scorn
yard	worm	torn
scar	world	
march	dirt	
	jerk	

45. CVCe Sorts Across Vowels

cave	drive	drove	huge
crane	while	those	fume
change	smile	throne	prune
stage	twice	phone	chute
range	crime	wrote	flute
waste	guide	quote	

46. Sorts Across Long Vowels

day	team	fine	rope	rule
gate	seat	light	post	fruit
mail	free	pie	gold	blue
trade	field	wild	coal	tube
stay	street	time	stone	
eight	she	shy	throw	

47. CVVC Across Vowels

road	team	rain	*
boast	stream	strain	board
coach	sweet	claim	great
groan	queen	waist	
throat	peach	faith	
toast	thief	praise	
roast	peace	strain	
		trail	

Diphthongs and Complex Consonants

48. Diphthongs

toy	*coin*	*town*	*sound*
boy	foil	clown	mouth
joy	boil	brown	scout
	spoil	crown	round
	noise	frown	couch
	point	howl	loud

49. More Diphthongs

salt	*hawk*	*fault*	*
bald	draw	caught	fought
chalk	lawn	cause	ought
stall	raw	taught	
false	crawl	sauce	
small	claw	haul	
	paw		

50. Words Spelled With *w*

watch	*war*	*wrap*
swamp	warn	wreak
swan	warm	write
wand	dwarf	wrist
swat	swarm	wren
wash	wart	wrong

51. Complex Consonants

scram	*straight*	*shrank*	*square*
scrape	strange	shrink	squawk
scratch	stretch	shred	squint
screech	strict	shrunk	squash
screw	string		
	strong		

52. *ck, k, ke*

lick	*leak*	*like*
lack	seek	lake
tack	soak	take
snack	sleek	snake
stuck	weak	stake
stick	week	strike
whack	croak	wake

53. *ch* and *tch*

catch	*reach*	*
witch	coach	rich
patch	peach	such
fetch	roach	
hutch	screech	
itch	beach	
switch	pouch	

54. *ge* and *dge*

badge	*page*
ridge	stage
edge	huge
fudge	rage
bridge	cage
judge	
hedge	

55. Hard and Soft *c* and *g* Across Vowels

cave	*coat*	*cute*	*cent*	*cyst*
camp	coast	cup	cell	gym
cast	cost	cue	cease	
gave	gold	gum	gem	
gain	golf	gush	germ	
gasp	goof			

56. *ce, ge, ve, se*

dance	*charge*	*glove*	*cheese*
chance	large	give	please
prince	wedge	curve	tease
fence	dodge	shove	loose
since	ridge	live	choose
voice	edge	above	
juice	change	have	

Concept Sorts

57. What Lives in Water?

Yes	*No*
frog	toad
fish	lizard
whale	zebra
sea turtle	tortoise
clam	elephant
crab	horse

58. Edible Plants

Grain	*Fruit*	*Vegetable*
wheat	apples	carrots
oats	peaches	beans
rice	berries	lettuce
rye	pears	cucumber
barley	bananas	cabbage
	oranges	beets

59. Animal Attributes

Fish	*Bird*	*Mammal*
scale	feather	hair
eggs	eggs	born alive
gills	lungs	lungs
heart	heart	heart
no legs	two legs	legs
fins	wings	

60. States

East	*West*	*North*	*South*
Virginia	California	Maine	Florida
North Carolina	Nevada	Vermont	Mississippi
Maryland	Utah	New York	Texas
Delaware	Arizona		Alabama

61. Geometry Terms

Shapes	*Lines*	*Measurements*
triangle	ray	perimeter
rhombus	angle	degrees
square	line	diameter
rectangle	right angle	circumference
parallelogram	obtuse angle	area
isosceles triangle		radius

SYLLABLES AND AFFIXES SORTS

Words from sorts 62 to 99 can be used in connection with games and activities in Chapter 7.

Inflected Endings (ed and ing), Consonant Doubling, and Plurals

62. Sort for Sound of *ed*

trapped	*waited*	*played*
mixed	dotted	mailed
stopped	patted	boiled
chased	treated	raised
cracked	traded	tried
walked	ended	filled
asked	handed	seemed
jumped	needed	yelled

63. Plural Words (*s*, and *es*)

cows	*boxes*	*buses*	*dishes*
chicks	mixes	glasses	benches
farms	axes	dresses	watches
fences		passes	lashes
gates		gases	churches
			dishes
			brushes

parties

64. Plurals with *y*

babies	*plays*
carries	monkeys
ponies	boys
bodies	trays
pennies	donkeys
worries	enjoys
daddies	turkeys
berries	

65. Base Words + *ed* and *ing*

jump	*jumped*	*jumping*
reach	reached	reaching
dress	dressed	dressing
wait	waited	waiting
crack	cracked	cracking
pass	passed	passing

66. Adding *ing*

batting	*baking*
shopping	skating
bragging	biting
hopping	hoping
stopping	sliding
begging	waving
skipping	moving
swimming	caring

67. Adding *ing*

trimming	*diving*	*pushing*	*floating*	*
running	riding	jumping	raining	mixing
popping	sliding	finding	sleeping	taxing
dragging	driving	kicking	boating	
wagging	wasting	wanting	waiting	
quitting	whining	munching	cheering	

68. Past Tense Verbs

kneel	*knelt*	*chase*	*chased*
teach	taught	mix	mixed
bring	brought	walk	walked
deal	dealt	bake	baked
sweep	swept	shop	shopped
send	sent		
think	thought		
lend	lent		
drink	drank		

69. Adding *ed* (Double, Nothing)

slipped	*picked*	*traded*
grabbed	called	baked
stopped	tracked	wasted
wagged	peeled	liked
tripped	watched	stared
knotted	cheered	waved
rubbed	talked	skated
whizzed	dreamed	tasted

70. Adding *ing* to *k* words (*ck*, e-drop, CVVC, VCk)

tacking	*baking*	*leaking*	*asking*
sticking	flaking	speaking	spending
tracking	shaking	croaking	shrinking
plucking	smoking	squeaking	drinking
wrecking	stroking	hooking	marking
clucking	making	looking	working
quacking	raking	cooking	frisking

Use with Double Crazy Eights Game.

Syllable Juncture Sorts, Open and Closed Syllables (VCCV, VCV)

71. Compound Words

someone	*downtown*	*backyard*
something	downstairs	backbone
somehow	lowdown	backpack
someday	downcast	backward
somewhere	downfall	bareback
sometime	downpour	flashback
	breakdown	piggyback
	countdown	paperback

72. VCCV at Juncture (same/different)

button	*market*
sunny	garden
yellow	signal
happy	member
happen	basket
sitting	center
fellow	plastic
matter	tablet

73. Syllable Juncture (VCCV, VCV)

tablet	*baby*
napkin	human
happen	music
winter	fever
foggy	silent
tennis	duty
sudden	writer
fossil	rival

74. VCV Open and Closed

meter	*petal*
human	rapid
secret	punish
paper	magic
lazy	shiver
even	comet
major	river
climate	clever
crater	proper
clover	liquid
bacon	

Use with Slap Jack Activity.

75. Closed VCCV/Open VCV

funny	*picture*	*pilot*
happen	expert	navy
pretty	until	nature
dollar	forget	music
goggles	napkin	spoken
gossip	canyon	frozen
letter	sister	spider
mattress	army	student

76. Closed/Open With Endings

sadden	*dusting*	*sliding*
chipped	rented	shining
matted	helping	named
scarred	sifted	scaring
winner	faster	rider
biggest	longest	tamest
running	walker	moping

Unaccented Final Syllable Sorts

77. *le* and *el*

fable	*camel*
angle	angel
little	model
rattle	gravel
settle	motel
cattle	bushel
nibble	level
turtle	pretzel
table	travel
	smaller

78. *er, ar, or*

bigger	*burglar*	*doctor*
freezer	grammar	favor
dreamer	collar	author
faster	dollar	editor
blister	lunar	tractor
jogger	solar	motor
speaker		mayor
skater		

79. *er, ar, or*

comparatives	*agents*	*things*
sweeter	worker	cellar
thinner	teacher	meter
smarter	waiter	river
slower	voter	pillar
younger	actor	anchor
gentler	beggar	vapor
steeper	director	trailer
cheaper	barber	

80. /j/ Sound

carriage	*budget*	*magic*
voyage	agent	engine
message	angel	region
postage	gorgeous	fragile
village	danger	margin
storage	legend	logic
sausage	pigeon	
savage	dungeon	
courage	gadget	

81. Changing *y* to *i*

cry	*cries*	*cried*
hurry	hurries	hurried
party	parties	partied
empty	empties	emptied
baby	babies	babied
reply	replies	replied
supply	supplies	supplied
carry	carries	carried
fry	fries	fried

82. *y* Words by Part of Speech

Long-*i* *verb*	*noun*	Long-*e* *adjective*	*adverb*
try	celery	happy	happily
certify	candy	pretty	correctly
apply	gypsy	guilty	clearly
occupy	quarry	angry	safely
rely	country	silly	horribly
	cemetery		hourly
	category		certainly
	copy		sensibly

Sorts to Explore Stress

83. Stress in Homographs

re'cord n.	*re cord' v.*
protest n.	protest v.
conduct n.	conduct v.
subject n.	subject v.
extract n.	extract v.
permit n.	permit v.
insert n.	insert v.
desert n.	desert v.
rebel n.	rebel v.
combat n.	combat v.
conflict n.	conflict v.

84. Stress in VCV Words

me'ter	*be cause'*
pilot	away
omen	around
never	below
picture	regard
famous	awake
wagon	again
diner	reward
habit	become
open	delay
vivid	defend

85. Two-Step First-Syllable Stress

a. Sort by closed/open

closed		**b.** Pattern *open*	
VCV	VCCV	VCCV	VCV
radish	*dentist*	*diaper*	*bison*
decade	nostril	foggy	major
novel	children	spatter	pirate
atom	chapter	sudden	climate
lizard	picnic	cottage	agent

86. Stress in VCCV Words

per' son	*at tend'*
welcome	perform
offer	support
expert	survive
harvest	escape
fellow	allow
barber	disturb
tender	suppose
common	hello
urgent	raccoon

87. Stress in Three Syllables

cam' er a	*to ge' ther*
yesterday	deliver
victory	important
animal	hamburger
library	department
enemy	tomorrow
carpenter	another
several	however
article	edition
alphabet	remember

88. Long-*u* in Stressed Syllable

bu' gle	*a muse'*
future	compute
ruby	confuse
rumor	reduce
tulip	perfume
tuna	pollute
tutor	salute
super	excuse
pupil	abuse
ruler	include

Revisiting Patterns in Longer Words

89. Short / Long-a

canvas	*agent*
lantern	basic
package	cradle
tragic	fatal
attic	labor
bandage	vapor
tablet	sacred
cannon	April

90. Patterns for Long-a

debate	*explain*	*layer*
mistake	dainty	dismay
grapefruit	trainer	payment
parade	complain	crayons
engage	acquaint	hooray
bracelet	raisin	decay
estate	refrain	betray

91. Sort by Number of Syllables

hazard	*banana*	*motorcycle*	*hippopotamus*
number	alphabet	unusual	inspirational
helmet	hospital	supermarket	refrigerator
lumber	decimal	intersection	
machine	important	information	
sister	yesterday	transportation	

92. Diphthongs in Two Syllables

coin	*moisture*	*joyful*
spoil	appoint	boycott
broil	poison	royal
void	turquoise	soybean
coil	moisten	oyster
poise	pointless	voyage
noise	broiler	annoy
join	embroider	enjoy
point	rejoice	destroy
moist		employ

Use for Oygo.

93. More Dipthongs in Two Syllables

county	*flower*
council	allow
lousy	brownie
fountain	vowel
mountain	shower
scoundrel	towel
counter	tower
around	chowder
bounty	coward
foundry	drowsy
mouthful	powder
rowdy	prowler
	power

94. *or, ar, er,* and Parts of Speech

noun	*adjective*	*comparative adjective*
doctor	circular	thinner
conductor	rectangular	cleaner
agitator	lunar	smarter
inspector	solar	happier
refrigerator	similar	sorrier
instigator	particular	dirtier
incubator	spectacular	sleepier
employer	peculiar	slower

95. Spelling the /er/ Sound in Stressed and Unstressed Syllables

cer' tain	*re verse'*	*sur prise'*	*lan'tern*
person	observe	perhaps	concert
thirsty	alert	survive	modern
service	prefer	surround	western
hurry	emerge		govern
turkey			

96. Words With *ure* and *er* (ture, sure, cher)

capture	*measure*	*archer*	*
creature	treasure	butcher	injure
fracture	pleasure	preacher	failure
mixture	closure	stretcher	manicure
pasture	leisure	teacher	procedure
texture		rancher	
future			
nature			

97. Advanced Homophones

Stressed Syllable		*Unstressed Syllable*	
aloud	*allowed*	*patience*	*patients*
cinder	sender	accept	except
morning	mourning	alter	altar
berry	bury	miner	minor
roomer	rumor	council	counsel
kernel	colonel	hanger	hangar
holy	wholly	profit	prophet
oral	aural	mussel	muscle
vary	very	lesson	lessen
censor	sensor	presence	presents
awful	offal	canvas	canvass
incite	insight	baron	barren

98. Prefixes

unfair	*retell*	*disagree*
unable	replay	disappear
uncover	retrain	disgrace
unkind	return	disarm
undress	reuse	disorder
unplug	research	disobey
		disable

99. More Prefixes

preschool	*explode*	*triangle*	*subway*
preview	exceed	tricycle	submarine
prevent	expose	triad	subsoil
preheat	explore	tripod	subtract
prefix	exile	trio	subset
prepare			
predict			

DERIVATIONAL RELATIONS SORTS

Words from sorts 100 to 117 can be used in connection with games and activities in Chapter 8.

Adding Suffixes

100. Adding *ion*

ct + ion		*ss + ion*	
affect	affection	express	expression
distinct	distinction	impress	impression
select	selection	process	procession
extinct	extinction	depress	depression
predict	prediction	success	succession
subtract	subtraction	profess	profession
contract	contraction	discuss	discussion

101. E-drop + *ion*

te + ion		*ce + ion*		*se + ion*	
educate	education	induce	induction	expulse	expulsion
congratulate	congratulation	introduce	introduction	convulse	convulsion
create	creation	produce	production	repulse	repulsion
decorate	decoration	deduce	deduction		
generate	generation	reproduce	reproduction		
imitate	imitation	reduce	reduction		

102. *sion* and Spelling Changes

t to s + *sion*

commit	commission
transmit	transmission
permit	permission
emit	emission
omit	omission
regret	regression
remit	remission

E-drop, then d to s, + ion

explode	explosion
collide	collision
conclude	conclusion
persuade	persuasion
erode	erosion
delude	delusion
include	inclusion

103. E-drop + *ation* or *ition*

E-drop + *ation*

admire	admiration
determine	determination
explore	exploration
combine	combination
declare	declaration
inspire	inspiration
organize	organization
examine	examination
perspire	perspiration

E-drop + *ition*

compose	composition
define	definition
dispose	disposition
oppose	opposition
expose	exposition
decompose	decomposition

104. *ible* and *able*

base + *able*

dependable
expendable
breakable
agreeable
predictable
remarkable
readable
profitable
perishable
punishable
laughable

root + *ible*

audible
edible
visible
feasible
terrible
possible
legible
plausible
horrible
tangible

105. *ible* and *able* after *e*

e-drop

presumable
desirable
usable
lovable
deplorable
comparable
excusable
eligible
intelligible
legible

soft ce/ge

changeable
manageable
peaceable
serviceable
noticeable

hard c/g

navigable
amicable
despicable
impeccable
applicable

106. Related Words + *able* and *ible*

ation to able

toleration	tolerable
separation	separable
education	educable
vegetation	vegetable
application	applicable
observation	observable
navigation	navigable

sion or tion to ible

collection	collectible
contraction	contractible
reduction	reducible
exhaustion	exhaustible
repression	repressible
expression	expressible
production	producible

107. *tion*, from Verbs to Nouns

Use this sort with "Is it sion or tion?" Making the Spelling-Meaning Connection Activity.

separate		separation		convulse	convulsion
fascinate	extinct	fascination	extinction	repulse	repulsion
educate	conduct	education	conduction	express	expression
complicate	affect	complication	affection	profess	profession
generate	act	generation	action		
navigate	contract	navigation	contraction		
vegetate		vegetation			

108. Assimilated Prefix Sort

com	ad	in
contest	allot	illegal
conform	affair	irresponsible
colleague	affront	immature
confront	assemble	irrational
context	affirm	immortal
correlate	arrange	illogical
constrain	acclaim	innumerable

Vowel Alternations

109. Vowel Alternations in Related Pairs
Sort words into two different alternation patterns.
Keep partners together.

Long-a to Short-a
cave/cavity
humane/humanity
nation/national
volcano/volcanic
grave/gravity
nature/natural
insane/insanity

Long-a to Schwa
major/majority
narrate/narrative
relate/relative
famous/infamous
able/ability
native/nativity
educate/educable

110. Vowel Alternations in Related Pairs
Sort words in two different alternation patterns.
Keep partners together.

Long-e to Short-e
serene/serenity
brief/brevity
proceed/procession
recede/recession
succeed/succession
conceive/conception
receive/reception

Long-e to Schwa
compete/competition
repeat/repetition
remedial/remedy

111. Vowel Alternations in Related Pairs
Sort words into two different alternation patterns.
Keep partners together.

Long-i to Short-i
resign/resignation
sign/signal
divine/divinity
divide/division
revise/revision
deride/derision

Long-i to Schwa
invite/invitation
define/definition
reside/resident
recite/recitation
deprive/deprivation
admire/admiration
inspire/inspiration

112. Vowel Alternations in Related Pairs
Sort words in two different alternation patterns.

Long-u to Short-u
induce/induction
seduce/seduction
misconstrue/misconstruction
conduce/conduction
reduce/reduction
produce/production

Long-o to Schwa
compose/composition
propose/proposition
impose/imposition
expose/exposition
harmonious/harmony

Sorting by Roots

113. Vowel Alternation Patterns in Related Words

Long to Short	Long to Schwa	Schwa to Short
divine/divinity	*compose/composition*	*metal/metallic*
prescribe/prescription	proclaim/proclamation	brutal/brutality
sage/sagacity	stable/stability	local/locality
profane/profanity	preside/president	spiritual/spirituality
criticize/criticism	adore/adoration	vital/vitality
telescope/telescopic	compete/competition	fatal/fatality
microscope/microscopic	repeat/repetition	total/totality
cone/conic	impose/imposition	normal/normality
flame/flammable		final/finality
arise/arisen		original/originality

114. Greek and Latin Science Vocabulary Sort

See the Greek and Latin Science Vocabulary Sort.

astro	astronomer, astronaut, astrology, astrolabe
bio	biology, biome, biosphere, biotic
chlor	chlorophyll, chloroplast, chlorine, chlorella
eco	ecology, economy, ecosystem, ecotype
hydro	hydrophobia, hydrology, hydrogen
hypo	hypodermis, hypodermic, hypothermia, hypotension
photo/phos	phosphorescent, photography, telephoto
vor	voracious, omnivore, carnivore

115. Greek Roots

autograph	*telegram*
automatic	telepathy
autobiography	telegraph
autonomy	televise
automobile	telephone
autonomous	teleconference

116. Latin Roots

Sort words by Latin root.

jud	*tract*	*spec*
judge	contract	spectator
adjudicate	attract	inspect
judgment	intractable	respect
judicial	subtraction	spectacular
prejudice	tractor	inspector
judicious	contraction	spectacles
prejudicial	protractor	disrespect
judiciary	distraction	

117. Latin Roots

See Joined at the Roots.

visual	transplant	geology	portable	photo
visionary	transportation	geographic	porter	photogenic
vision	transaction	geometry	opportunity	photosensitive
vista	transfer	geologist	portfolio	photographer
	transparent	geography	export	photosynthesis
		geometric	import	

WORD LISTS

The following lists of words are organized by features starting with the word families and then vowel sounds and patterns for each vowel. Under each feature the words are sometimes grouped by frequency and complexity. For example, under short *-a*, the early part of the list contains words most likely encountered by first graders (*am, ran, that*). The latter part of the list contains words which may be obscure in meaning and spelled with blends or digraphs (*yam, brass, tramp*).

These words can be transferred to a word sheet to create your own customized lessons. Many people have found it easy to create the word sheets you have seen throughout the book by making a table in a word processing program. Set the margins all around at zero, and create a table that is three columns by six to eight rows. Select a large font and save it as a template that you use each time before you fill it in. After creating each sort by typing in the words you want, simply save it using a name that defines the features such as "Short Vowels: a, o, e."

Here are three reminders and tips about creating word sorts:

1. Create sorts which will help your students form their own generalizations about how words work. Use a collection of 15 to 25 words so that there are plenty of examples to consider.
2. Contrast at least two and up to four features in a sort. There are many sample sorts here in the Appendix to give you ideas about how to do this. You can contrast sounds, spelling patterns, word endings, prefixes, root words, and so on.

Examples of sound sorts:
   Contrast short -o and long -o.
   Contrast the sound of *ear* in *learn* and in *hear*.
   Contrast the sound of *g* in *guest* and *gym*.
Examples of pattern sorts:
   Contrast long -o spelled with *oa*, *o-e*, and *ow*.
   Contrast words that end with *or*, *er*, and *ar*.
   Contrast words that double before *-ing* with those that do not.
Examples of meaning sorts:
   Contrast words derived from *spect* and *port*.
   Contrast words with prefixes *sub, un,* and *trans*.
The most elegant sorts are those that combine a sound sort with a pattern sort. For example, a long -o and short -o sort can begin with a picture sort and then proceed to a sort by patterns—CVVC and CVCe.

3. In most sorts, include up to three words that have the same sound or pattern but are not consistent with the generalization that governs the other words. Sometimes the oddballs you include will be true exceptions such as *said* but other times the oddballs may represent a less common spelling pattern such as *ey* representing long -a in *prey* and *grey*.

   The following lists include possible exceptions that can be added to sorts. For example, in a long -o sort, with words sorted by the *oa, o-e,* and *ow* patterns, the exceptions might include the words *now* and *love* since they are high frequency words which look like they would have the long -o sound but do not.

A Families

at	ad	ag	an	ap	ab	am	all
cat	bad	bag	can	cap	cab	dam	ball
bat	dad	rag	fan	lap	dab	ham	call
fat	had	sag	man	gap	jab	ram	fall
hat	mad	wag	pan	map	nab	jam	hall
mat	pad	nag	ran	nap	lab	clam	mall
pat	sad	flag	tan	rap	tab	slam	tall
rat	rad	brag	van	yap	blab	cram	wall
sat	glad	drag	plan	tap	crab	wham	small
that	lad	shag	than	zap	scab	swam	stall
flat		snag	clan	clap	stab	yam	
brat		lag	scan	flap	grab	gram	
chat		tag		slap	slab		
gnat				trap	stab		
				chap			
				snap			
				wrap			
				strap			

ar	art	and	ash	ang	ack	ank	amp
bar	cart	band	bash	bang	back	bank	camp
car	dart	hand	cash	fang	pack	sank	damp
far	mart	land	dash	hang	jack	tank	lamp
jar	part	sand	gash	sang	rack	yank	ramp
par	tart	brand	hash	rang	lack	blank	champ
star	start	grand	mash	clang	sack	plank	clamp
	chart	stand	rash		tack	crank	cramp
	smart	strand	sash		black	drank	stamp
			flash		quack	prank	tramp
			trash		crack	spank	scamp
			crash		track	thank	
			smash		shack		
			slash		snack		
			clash		stack		

Words Their Way Appendix © 2004 by Prentice-Hall, Inc.

E Families

et	en	ed	ell	eg	eck	est	end	ent
bet	den	bed	bell	beg	deck	best	bend	bent
get	hen	fed	cell	peg	neck	nest	lend	dent
let	men	led	fell	leg	peck	pest	mend	cent
met	ten	red	jell	keg	wreck	rest	send	lent
net	pen	wed	sell		speck	test	tend	rent
pet	then	bled	tell		check	vest	blend	sent
set	when	fled	well			west	spend	tent
wet	wren	sled	shell			chest	trend	vent
vet	Ben	shed	smell			quest		went
fret	Ken	shred	spell					scent
jet			swell					spent
yet			dwell					

I Families

it	id	ig	in	ill	ip	ick	ink	ing	im
bit	did	big	bin	bill	dip	lick	link	king	dim
kit	hid	dig	fin	dill	hip	kick	mink	ping	him
fit	lid	fig	pin	fill	lip	pick	pink	sing	Jim
hit	rid	jig	tin	hill	nip	sick	sink	ring	Kim
lit	slid	pig	din	kill	rip	tick	rink	wing	rim
pit	skid	rig	win	gill	sip	slick	wink	sling	Tim
sit		wig	grin	mill	tip	quick	blink	bring	brim
wit		zig	thin	pill	zip	trick	drink	sting	slim
quit		twig	twin	till	whip	chick	stink	swing	swim
skit			chin	will	clip	flick	think	thing	trim
spit			shin	drill	flip	brick	clink	spring	whim
slit			spin	grill	slip	stick	shrink	string	skim
				chill	skip	thick		cling	grim
				skill	drip	click		fling	
				spill	trip	prick		wring	
				still	chip				
				thrill	ship				
				quill	snip				
					strip				

O Families

ot	ob	og	op	ock	ong	oss
cot	bob	dog	cop	cock	bong	boss
dot	cob	bog	hop	dock	gong	toss
got	job	fog	pop	lock	long	moss
hot	rob	hog	mop	mock	song	gloss
jot	gob	jog	top	rock	strong	loss
lot	mob	log	slop	sock	throng	cross
not	sob	clog	flop	tock		
pot	snob	frog	drop	block		
blot	blob		shop	clock		
slot	glob		stop	flock		
plot	knob		crop	smock		
shot	throb		plop	shock		
spot			prop	stock		
knot						
trot						

U Families

ut	*ub*	*ug*	*um*	*un*	*uck*	*ump*	*ung*
but	cub	bug	bum	bun	buck	bump	sung
cut	hub	dug	gum	fun	duck	jump	rung
gut	rub	hug	hum	gun	luck	dump	hung
hut	tub	jug	drum	run	suck	hump	lung
nut	club	mug	plum	sun	tuck	lump	swung
rut	grub	rug	slum	spun	yuck	pump	clung
shut	snub	tug	scum	stun	pluck	rump	strung
	stub	slug	chum		cluck	plump	slung
	scrub	plug			truck	stump	sprung
	shrub	drug			stuck	thump	wrung
		snug					flung
							stung

uff	*unk*	*ush*	*ust*
buff	bunk	gush	bust
cuff	hunk	hush	dust
huff	junk	mush	gust
muff	sunk	rush	just
bluff	chunk	blush	must
puff	drunk	brush	rust
fluff	flunk	crush	crust
stuff	shunk	flush	trust
snuff	shrunk	slush	
scuff	stunk		
gruff	slunk		
	trunk		

Short-a Words *(See also word family lists.)*

CVC	CVCC					Exceptions:
ax	ant	batch	mass	draft	past	what
wax	ask	glass	mast	shaft	patch	was
gal	fast	grass	raft	branch	path	saw
pal	last	calf	staff	catch	ranch	laugh
gas	match	graph	vast	fact	shall	
tax	math	plant	bask	half	brass	
has	scratch	grasp	cramp	mask	grant	
yak	snatch	bath		pant	hatch	
	task	lash		pass	lamb	
	class	latch				

Short-e *(See also word family lists.)*

CVC	CVCC				
step	next	nest	knelt	bless	wept
them	best	rest	guess	clench	debt
yes	chest	slept	less	crest	drench
stem	desk	stretch	mend	elm	etch
web	dress	test	rent	flesh	jest
hem	egg	west	self	lend	pelt
gem	help	fetch	shelf	lens	stress
pep	held		swept	lest	tempt
	kept		tenth	sketch	wretch
	left		fresh	vest	
	melt				
	neck				

Short-i (*See also word family lists.*)

CVC

if	twig
in	whiz
is	
it	
fix	
him	
his	
mix	
six	
this	
crib	

CVCC

fish	kiss	film	hitch	disc
miss	lift	fist	inn	tilt
which	milk	gift	limb	frisk
wind	print	hint	mint	glint
wish	quilt	inch	risk	hint
sixth	rich	limp	shift	switch
dish	cliff	mitt	shrimp	sift
hiss	crisp	pinch	twist	
	drift	pitch	squint	
	fifth	brisk	stiff	
		ditch	swift	
			swish	
			chimp	

Short-o (*See also word family lists.*)

CVC

on	ox
box	sod
fox	con
mom	pox
god	prod
plod	
rod	

CVCC

doll	notch	frost	*Exceptions:*
fond	romp	gloss	from
odd	lost	loft	of
bond	off	moss	son
gosh	boss	moth	front
prompt	cloth	broth	won
stomp	cost	golf	
blond	cross	loss	
	soft	long	
	toss	lost	
		bong	

Short-u (*See also word family lists.*)

CVC

up	
bus	
mud	
cup	
bud	
huh	
plus	
strut	
stud	
sum	
thud	
thus	
jut	
nub	
strum	
pup	

CVCC

lunch	crunch	brusk	husk	*ul*	*Exceptions:*
much	dull	butt	plumb	bulge	push
bunch	dumb	crumb	ruff	bulk	put
fuzz	dusk	grunt	scuff	gulf	bush
stuff	fuss	hunch	shucks	gulp	truth
such	gruff	mutt	stunt	sulk	
thumb	munch	numb		pulse	
hunt	punch	tuft			
	gull	tusk			

Long-a Lists
CVCe

a-e

ate	shade	lace
bake	shake	lane
cake	shape	male
came	skate	mate
cave	space	pace
face	stage	pale
gave	state	rage
lake	strange	range
made`	tape	scale
make	taste	tale
place	wake	tame
same	wave	trace
care	ache	trade
take	bathe	wade
age	blame	waste
base	blaze	whale
cage	brake	ape
chase	cape	babe
gate	crane	cane
hate	fake	crate
late	fame	date
page	flame	daze
paste	gaze	drape
race	grace	fade
safe	grape	flake
sale	grade	
	change	
	plane	
	plate	

CVCe

ai

gape	paint
grave	rain
graze	tail
jade	train
lame	mail
mane	main
rate	nail
sake	pail
slate	rail
slave	sail
stale	aid
drake	bait
fate	braid
grate	brain
haste	fail
haze	grain
pane	maid
phase	pain
quake	waist
vane	wait
vase	claim
	gain

Exceptions:

have	praise
dance	straight
chance	strait
	vain

CVVC

ea

aide
ail
faith
quaint
stain

Exceptions:

said
aisle
plaid

CVV

ay

break	day
great	jay
steak	may
	play
ei	say
eight	stay
neigh	way
rein	clay
weigh	gray
weight	pray
eighth	tray
freight	slay
reign	
veil	
sleigh	*ey*
weigh	prey
beige	grey
	they
	hey

Long-e Lists
CVCe   CVVC

e-e

eve	
scene	
scheme	
theme	
these	

ea

bean	reach	peace	cease
clean	read	peach	crease
each	scream	peak	ease
eat	sneak	plead	feat
leave	stream	seal	grease
mean	tea	squeak	plea
real	team	steal	seam
sea	bead	steam	
seat	beak	treat	*Exceptions:*
teach	beam	weak	great
beach	beast	weave	break
beat	cream	flea	steak
breathe	creak	heal	
dream	deal	knead	
east	feast	league	
lead	heap	leak	
lean	least	leash	
meat	meal	squeal	
pea	neat	bleat	

ee

bee	green	seek	peel	kneel
beet	need	sheet	reed	preen
feed	sheep	teeth	speech	reef
feel	sleep	weed	speed	sleek
feet	street	wheel	steel	thee
see	three	beep	steep	wee
seed	tree	bleed	sweep	breed
seen	breeze	cheek	sleeve	fee
seem	cheese	creek	sneeze	flee
week	free	creep	deed	freeze
beef	geese	greed	eel	keen
peep	knee	greet	fleet	reel
deep	queen	heel	glee	seep
meet				

Exception:

been

388

CV

e	ie	
he	chief	*Exceptions:*
be	field	friend
me	piece	fierce
she	thief	pier
we	belief	else
	grief	seize
	brief	vein
	shriek	they
		hey
		weird
		brief

Long-i Lists

CVCe

i-e		
bike	quite	whine
bite	prize	wipe
dime	shine	crime
fine	size	fife
hide	slide	file
kite	strike	lice
like	stripe	mite
line	vine	prime
live	wide	spike
nice	wife	spite
ride	wise	stride
side	write	chime
smile	glide	lime
time	guide	scribes
while	hike	site
white	hive	spice
dive	knife	thrive
drive	pine	
five	price	*Exceptions:*
ice	pride	live
life	ripe	give
mice	rise	prince
mile	slice	since
mine	spine	ridge
nine	tide	
pile	tribe	
pipe	twice	

CV

ie	y/ye
lie	cry
pie	fly
tie	my
die	sky
	try
Exceptions:	why
buy	by
guy	dry
	shy
	sly
	bye
	dye
	lye
	rye

iCC

igh	
high	find
light	kind
might	child
night	climb
right	mind
bright	wild
fight	blind
sigh	grind
tight	hind
flight	sign
fright	bind
sight	wind
slight	
thigh	

Long-o Lists
CVCe

o-e

close	wove	joke
drove	doze	lone
hole	froze	stove
lone	globe	whole
nose	lone	woke
note	robe	wrote
rope	role	
stone	slope	*Exceptions:*
those	sole	come
broke	cove	gone
chose	dome	love
clothe	lope	move
choke	pose	some
code	quote	done
cone	rove	lose
home	yoke	none
mole	zone	one
owe	phone	once
poke	pole	prove
shone	ode	dove
stole	smoke	glove
stroke	spoke	whose
throne	hope	shove
tone	hose	
vote		

CVVC

oa

boat	oat
coat	roam
float	roast
goat	soak
moan	throat
road	cloak
soap	goal
toad	loaf
toast	loaves
coach	whoa
coal	boast
coast	coax
croak	loan
groan	
foam	*Exceptions:*
load	broad
moat	sew
oak	

CV

o

go
no
so
ho
yo-yo

CVV

ow

grow
know
show
slow
snow
blow
bowl
crow
grown
low
own
throw
blown
flow
flown
glow
sow
tow

VCC

oCC

cold
gold
hold
most
old
told
both
fold
roll
scold
bolt
folk
ghost
post
sold
bold
colt
host
mold
stroll
volt
jolt
poll
scroll

Ambiguous Vowels ô *sound*

al	au	aw	o	w + a
tall	caught	draw	on	watch
wall	fault	saw	off	want
small	pause	crawl	dog	wash
talk	sauce	paw	frog	wand
walk	taught	straw	log	wasp
salt	haunt	claw	fog	watt
calm	launch	dawn	bog	swap
chalk		drawn	hog	swat
halt	*Exceptions:*	law	lost	
palm	aunt	lawn	cost	
stalk	laugh	shawl	frost	
stall		squawk	boss	
bald		yawn	cross	
		awe	toss	
		bawl	gloss	
		hawk	moss	
		raw	loss	
		caw	cloth	
		fawn	moth	
		gnaw	broth	
		sprawl	long	
		thaw	strong	
			throng	
			loft	
			soft	
			golf	

Words Their Way Appendix © 2004 by Prentice-Hall, Inc.

Ambiguous Vowels

ow	ou	oo	oo = u	ou	ough	oi	/u/	/u/ o-e
brown	cloud	book	food	could	thought	coin	from	come
clown	found	cook	room	would	ought	join	of	love
cow	ground	good	school	should	bought	oil	does	some
down	out	look	soon		brought	point	son	done
how	pound	took	too		trough	soil	front	none
now	shout	wood	zoo		cough	boil	rough	once
town	proud	brook	bloom		fought	coil	ton	one
bow	round	foot	boot			foil	touch	glove
growl	sound	shook	cool			joint	won	dove
howl	count	stood	fool			hoist	young	shove
owl	mount	wool	moo			moist	tough	
crowd	loud	crook	moon			toil		
crown	mount	hood	noon			broil		
drown	bound	hook	pool					
frown	hound	hoof	roof			*oi-e*		
gown	wound	soot	roost			voice		
plow	couch		root			noise		
sow	crouch		shoot			choice		
wow	doubt		smooth					
bow	mound		spoon			*oy*		
prowl	ouch		tool			boy		
scowl	pouch		zoom			toy		
fowl	scout		boom			joy		
vow	snout		gloom			enjoy		
	sprout		loom					
	stout		loop					
	drought		mood					
	foul		pooh					
	mouth		proof					
			scoop					
			spook					
			tooth					
			stool					
			troop					
			whoop					
			goof					
			brood					

Exceptions:
poor
blood

Long-u Lists

CVCe		CVVC	CVV	CVV	

u-e		*ui*	*ue*	*ew*	
dune	prune	fruit	blue	new	brew
flute	cute	suit	sue	grew	shrewd
rude	use	bruise	clue	chew	strewn
rule	huge	cruise	glue	drew	whew
tube	June	juice	due	few	
tune	cube		flue	flew	
chute	mule	*Exceptions:*	hue	knew	
dude	fume	build	true	threw	
duke	muse	built		crew	
nude	mute	guide	*Exceptions:*	grew	
crude			cruel	stew	
plume	*Exception:*		fuel	dew	
prude	truth			screw	

R-influenced Vowels

ar		are	air	Exceptions:	ear	eer	/ur/ear
bark	yard	care	chair	are	near	cheer	heard
car	scarf	bare	hair	bear	clear	deer	earth
dark	shark	scare	pair	wear	dear	peer	learn
far	yarn	share	stair	swear	fear	steer	earn
part	arch	stare	flair	pear	tear	queer	search
star	dart	dare	lair	where	year	jeer	pearl
start	hard	flare		there	beard	sneer	yearn
arm	lark	glare		their	gear	steer	
art	mar	mare		heart	spear		/ur/er-e
bar	scar	rare		ar + e			nerve
card	snarl	square		carve	Exceptions:		verse
cart	barb	snare		large	bear		swerve
charm	harp	blare		starve	heart		
harm		fare		barge	wear		
jar		hare			pear		
arch					swear		
sharp							

er	ur	ir	ire	or	ore	our	oar	w + or
her	burn	bird	fire	for	more	your	roar	word
fern	hurt	first	tire	born	store	course	hoarse	work
herd	turn	girl	wire	corn	shore	four	soar	world
jerk	curl	chirp	hire	forth	bore	pour	boar	worm
perch	purr	dirt	sire	horn	chore	court	coarse	worth
clerk	burst	shirt		north	score	fourth		worse
germ	church	third	ure	porch	sore	mourn		
herb	churn	birth	cure	short	wore	source		w + ar
per	curb	firm	pure	storm	tore	gourd		warm
perk	hurl	stir		worn	swore			war
stern	burr	swirl		cord		Exceptions:		ward
term	blurt	thirst		cork	oor	our		wharf
	lurch	whirl		nor	door	flour		quart
	lurk	squirt		chord	poor	hour		
	spur	twirl		ford	floor	scour		
	surf	fir		fort		sour		
				lord	ōor			
				pork	lure			
				torch	sure			
				scorn				
				force				
				horse				
				forge				
				gorge				

Words Their Way Appendix © 2004 by Prentice-Hall, Inc.

Complex Consonants

ch	*tch*	*Cch*	*ge*	**Hard-g**	**Soft-g**	**y-words**	
teach	catch	lunch	stage	dog	huge	**/i/**	**/e/**
reach	patch	watch	rage	get	magic	try	funny
beach	stretch	bench	huge	good	orange	cry	county
peach	clutch	branch	page	go	page	fly	family
coach	fetch	bunch		gave	stage	spy	party
screech	hatch	march		pig	age	fry	story
couch	match	porch	*dge*	gone	cage	pry	baby
crouch	pitch	stretch	edge	tiger	giant	terrify	berry
pouch	witch	birch	ledge	frog	village	identify	body
	scratch	church	bridge	got	strange	rely	carry
	batch	munch	judge	girl	gym	classify	copy
	ditch	perch	budge	game	danger	reply	marry
	clutch	pinch	dodge	bug	gem	supply	study
	latch	punch	hedge	gain	gentle	July	worry
	sketch	search	lodge	dragon	engine		pony
	stitch	clench	nudge	egg	giraffe		puppy
	switch	hunch	ridge	gate	legend		twenty
	twitch	torch	trudge	gear	general		army
		haunch	wedge	geese	pigeon		hobby
		drench	smudge	ghost	rage		ferry
		lurch	bulge	goat	germ		entry
		gulch		gold	dungeon		trophy
		starch	*Cge*	guilt	gesture		injury
		drench	charge	gulp	geology		envy
		arch	change	guess	ginger		gravity
			strange	drug	oxygen		glory
			range	gust	angel		pantry
			barge	gum	genuine		city
			forge	gun	genius		
			surge	golf			
			gorge	guy			
			large	goof			
				gag			
				gas			
				gift			
				rug			
				gill			
				sugar			
				giggle			
				gorilla			
				angle			

Compound Words by Common Base Words

We have limited the list here to words that have base words across a number of compound words.

aircraft	childbirth	eyeglasses	handball
airline	blackberry	eyelash	handbook
airmail	blackbird	eyelid	handcuffs
airplane	blackboard	eyesight	handmade
airport	blackmail	eyewitness	handout
airtight	blacksmith	shuteye	handshake
anybody	blacktop	firearm	handspring
anymore	bookcase	firecracker	handstand
anyone	bookkeeper	firefighter	handwriting
anyplace	bookmark	firefly	backhand
anything	bookworm	firehouse	firsthand
anywhere	checkbook	fireman	secondhand
backboard	cookbook	fireplace	underhand
backbone	scrapbook	fireproof	headache
backfire	textbook	fireside	headband
background	buttercup	firewood	headdress
backpack	butterfly	fireworks	headfirst
backward	buttermilk	backfire	headlight
backyard	butterscotch	bonfire	headline
bareback	doorbell	campfire	headlong
feedback	doorknob	football	headmaster
flashback	doorman	foothill	headphones
hatchback	doormat	foothold	headquarters
paperback	doorstep	footlights	headstart
piggyback	doorway	footnote	headstrong
bathrobe	backdoor	footprint	headway
bathroom	outdoor	footstep	airhead
bathtub	downcast	footstool	blockhead
birdbath	downhill	barefoot	figurehead
bedrock	download	tenderfoot	racehorse
bedroom	downpour	grandchildren	sawhorse
bedside	downright	granddaughter	homeland
bedspread	downsize	grandfather	homemade
bedtime	downstairs	grandmother	homemaker
flatbed	downstream	grandparent	homeroom
hotbed	downtown	grandson	homesick
sickbed	breakdown	haircut	homespun
waterbed	countdown	hairdo	homestead
birthday	sundown	hairdresser	homework
birthmark	touchdown	hairpin	horseback
birthplace	eyeball	hairstyle	horsefly
birthstone	eyebrow	handbag	horseman

Words Their Way Appendix © 2004 by Prentice-Hall, Inc.

horseplay
horsepower
horseshoe
houseboat
housefly
housewife
housework
housetop
birdhouse
clubhouse
doghouse
greenhouse
townhouse
landfill
landlady
landlord
landmark
landscape
landslide
dreamland
farmland
homeland
highland
wasteland
wonderland
lifeboat
lifeguard
lifejacket
lifelike
lifelong
lifestyle
lifetime
nightlife
wildlife
lighthouse
lightweight
daylight
flashlight
headlight
moonlight
spotlight
sunlight
mailman
doorman
snowman
fireman

gentleman
handyman
policeman
salesman
nightfall
nightgown
nightmare
nighttime
overnight
outbreak
outcast
outcome
outcry
outdated
outdo
outdoors
outfield
outfit
outgrow
outlaw
outline
outlook
outnumber
outpost
outrage
outright
outside
outsmart
outwit
blowout
carryout
cookout
handout
hideout
workout
lookout
overall
overboard
overcast
overcome
overflow
overhead
overlook
overview
playground
playhouse

playmate
playpen
playroom
playwright
rainbow
raincoat
raindrop
rainfall
rainstorm
roadblock
roadway
roadwork
railroad
sandbag
sandbar
sandbox
sandpaper
sandpiper
sandstone
seacoast
seafood
seagull
seaman
seaport
seasick
seashore
seaside
seaweed
snowball
snowflake
snowman
snowplow
snowshoe
snowstorm
somebody
someone
someday
somehow
someone
something
sometime
somewhere
undergo
underground
undergrowth
underline

undermine
understand
underwater
watercolor
waterfall
watermelon
waterproof
saltwater
windfall
windmill
windpipe
windshield
windswept
downwind
headwind

Homophones

be/bee	hey/hay	serial/cereal	Mary/mary/merry	bred/bread
blue/blew	made/maid	cheap/cheep	great/grate	tred/tread
I/eye/aye	male/mail	days/daze	seem/seam	guessed/guest
no/know	nay/neigh	dew/do/due	knew/new	rest/wrest
here/hear	oh/owe	doe/dough	stair/stare	beech/beach
to/too/two	pail/pale	gray/grey	hour/our	real/reel
hi/high	pair/pear/pare	heel/heal	rough/ruff	peel/peal
new/knew/gnu	peek/peak/pique	horse/hoarse	poor/pour	team/teem
see/sea	reed/read/Reid	ho/hoe	haul/hall	leak/leek
there/they're/their	so/sew/sow	in/inn	piece/peace	sees/seas
bear/bare	root/route	need/kneed/knead	ant/aunt	sheer/shear
by/buy/bye	shone/shown	lone/loan	flair/flare	feet/feat
deer/dear	aid/aide	we/wee	mist/missed	hymn/him
ate/eight	add/ad	ring/wring	mane/main	whit/wit
for/four/fore	break/brake	peddle/petal/pedal	wail/whale/wale	scents/cents/sense
our/hour	cent/sent/scent	straight/strait	died/dyed	tents/tense
red/read	flee/flea	pole/poll	manor/manner	gilt/guile
lead/led	creak/creek	earn/urn	pier/peer	knit/nit
meat/meet	die/dye	past/passed	Ann/an	tic/tick
plane/plain	fair/fare	sweet/suite	tacks/tax	sight/site/cite
rode/road/rowed	hair/hare	ore/or	cash/cache	rye/wry
sail/sale	heard/herd	rain/reign/rein	rap/wrap	style/stile
stare/stair	night/knight	role/roll	maze/maize	might/mite
we'd/weed	steel/steal	sole/soul	air/heir	climb/clime
we'll/wheel	tail/tale	seller/cellar	bail/bale	fined/find
hole/whole	thrown/throne	shoo/shoe	ail/ale	side/sighed
wear/ware/where	fir/fur	soar/sore	prays/praise	tide/tied
one/won	waist/waste	steak/stake	base/bass	vice/vise
flower/flour	week/weak	some/sum	faint/feint	awl/all
right/write	we've/weave	tow/toe	wade/weighed	paws/pause
your/you're	way/weigh	vein/vane/vain	wave/waive	born/borne
lye/lie	wait/weight	medal/metal/meddle	knave/nave	chord/cord
its/it's	threw/through	wrote/rote	whet/wet	foul/fowl
not/knot	Vail/veil/vale	forth/fourth	sell/cell	mall/maul
gate/gait	aisle/I'll/isle	tea/tee	bell/belle	mourn/morn
jeans/genes	ball/bawl	been/bin	bowled/bold	rot/wrought
time/thyme	beat/beet	sox/socks	bough/bow	bomb/balm
son/sun	bolder/boulder	board/bored		bald/balled
boy/buoy	course/coarse			browse/brows

Use these words to play Homophone Rummy.

Plurals and Changes from *y* to *i*

Plurals With *es*

arches	crashes	kisses
beaches	crosses	lunches
bonuses	dishes	notches
bosses	flashes	passes
boxes	foxes	peaches
bushes	gases	pushes
brushes	guesses	
classes	inches	

Change *y* to *i*

babies	fries
berries	guppies
bodies	ladies
bunnies	parties
cities	pennies
copies	ponies
counties	supplies
fairies	trophies
flies	

Words Their Way Appendix © 2004 by Prentice-Hall, Inc.

Verbs for Inflected Ending Sorts

VVC	VCe	E-drop	Two-Syllable	CVC Words That Double		Two-Syllable Words That Do Not Double	Two-Syllable Words That Double	Miscellaneous Verbs
help	need	lie	arrive	stop	drip	admit	level	see/saw
jump	wait	time	escape	pat	fan	begin	edit	fall/fell
want	boat	live	excuse	sun	flop	commit	enter	feel/felt
ask	shout	name	nibble	top	grin	control	exit	find/found
back	cook	bake	rattle	hop	grip	excel	limit	grow/grew
talk	head	care	refuse	plan	mop	forbid	suffer	know/knew
call	meet	close	amuse	pot	plod	forget	appear	sing/sang
thank	peek	love	ignore	shop	rob	omit	complain	sleep/slept
laugh	bloom	move	retire	trip	shrug	permit	explain	tell/told
trick	cool	smile		bet	sip	rebel	repeat	draw/drew
park	cheer	use		cap	skin	refer	attend	drink/drank
pick	clear	hate		clap	skip		collect	feed/fed
plant	dream	hope		slip	slam			hear/heard
rock	float	ice		snap	slap			hold/held
start	flood	joke		spot	snip			keep/kept
bark	fool	paste		tag	sob			stand/stood
work	oil	phone		thin	strip			blow/blew
walk	join	prove		trap	wrap			break/broke
yell	lean	race		trot	zip			bring/brought
wish	mail	scare		tug	brag			build/built
guess	nail	share		wag	char			buy/bought
turn	moan	skate		drop	chug			lay/laid
smell	scream	stare		drum	hem			pay/paid
track	pour	taste		fit	jog			send/sent
push	sail	wave		flap	mob			speak/spoke
miss	trail	blame		flip	plot			wear/wore
paint	zoom	carve		grab	prop			
act		dance		hug	scar			
add		glance		jam	skim			
crash		hike		kid	slug			
crack		hire		log	stab			
block		serve		map	throb			
bowl		score		nap	whiz			
count		solve		nod	blot			
brush		sneeze		pin	chat			
bump		trace		pop	scan			
burn		trade		bob	slop			
climb		vote		rub	strum			
camp		drape		beg	swap			
curl		fade		blur	swat			
dash		graze		bud				
dust		praise		chip	*Exceptions:*			
farm		scrape		chop	box			
fold		shave		crop	fix			
growl		shove		dim	wax			
hunt		snare		dip	row			
kick		adore			chew			
land		cease						
learn		pose						
nest		quote						
lick		rove						
lock								
melt								
point								
print								
quack								
reach								
rest								
touch								
wash								
wink								

Two Syllable Words to Explore Syllable Junction and Stress

VCCV			VCCV Doublet	V/CV	V/CV	V/CV	VCCCV
First Syllable Accent	pilgrim	**Second Syllable Accent**	**First Syllable Accent**	**First Syllable Accent**	**First Syllable Accent**	**Second Syllable Accent**	**Constant**
after	picture	absorb	attic	baby	cabin	around	dolphin
artist	plastic	admire	better	hoping	planet	because	laughter
border	powder	admit	blizzard	writer	finish	before	pilgrim
carpet	problem	although	blossom	basic	robin	believe	instant
chapter	public	complete	button	even	magic	beyond	complain
chimney	pumpkin	compose	cabbage	waving	limit	decide	hundred
dentist	reptile	confess	copper	bacon	cousin	demand	monster
elbow	rescue	confuse	cottage	chosen	prison	event	orchard
current	seldom	contain	dipper	moment	habit	hotel	orphan
canyon	sentence	disturb	fellow	raking	punish	prepare	public
harvest	signal	enjoy	foggy	human	cover	pretend	purchase
barber	sister	forget	follow	pilot	manage	prevent	mumble
basket	subject	ignore	common	silent	medal	remain	paddle
cactus	Sunday		funny	season	promise	repair	sample
canyon	temper		happen	navy	closet	resist	battle
capture	thunder		mammal	music	camel	return	candle
carpet	trumpet		message	female	cavern	select	pickle
center	turkey		office	stolen	comet		bubble
chapter	twenty		pattern	robot	dozen		bottle
children	umpire		sudden	crater	finish		nozzle
chimney	under		tennis	climate	habit		
compass	walnut		traffic	duty	honest		**VV**
contest	welcome		tunnel	famous	level		create
costume	whimper		valley	female	lever		riot
dentist	window		village	fever	lizard		liar
dolphin	winter		hollow	final	modern		fuel
doctor	wonder			flavor	never		poem
fabric	plastic		**Second Syllable Accent**	humid	oven		diary
garden	organ		attack	labor	palace		area
harvest	lumber		balloon	legal	panel		trial
hammer	carpet		dessert	local	panic		radio
helmet	perfect			music	rapid		cruel
husband	master			pirate	robin		diet
injure	thirty			private	shovel		variety
insect	fellow			program	solid		neon
lumber	enter			recent	stomach		video
market	harvest			rumor	timid		meteor
champion	index			siren	topic		violin
master	insect			solar	travel		annual
monster	problem			spiral	vanish		casual
morning	rescue			vacant	visit		
napkin	seldom				volume		
number	sentence				wagon		
orbit	signal				weather		
order	thunder						
pardon	turkey						
pencil	velvet						
person	welcome						
picnic							

Words Their Way Appendix © 2004 by Prentice-Hall, Inc.

Final Unstressed Syllables

al	il/ile	el	le	
central	April	angel	able	hurdle
crystal	civil	barrel	ample	hustle
cymbal	council	bagel	angle	juggle
dental	evil	bushel	ankle	jungle
fatal	fossil	camel	apple	kettle
feudal	gerbil	cancel	battle	knuckle
final	lentil	channel	beagle	little
focal	nostril	chapel	beetle	maple
formal	pencil	diesel	bottle	middle
global	peril	flannel	bramble	needle
journal	pupil	funnel	bridle	noodle
legal	stencil	gravel	bubble	noble
mammal	tonsil	hazel	buckle	paddle
medal	docile	jewel	bundle	pebble
mental	facile	kennel	bugle	people
metal	fertile	kernel	candle	pickle
nasal	fragile	label	castle	purple
naval	futile	level	cattle	puzzle
neutral	hostile	model	cable	riddle
normal	missile	morsel	chuckle	saddle
oval	mobile	nickel	circle	sample
pedal	sterile	novel	cradle	scribble
petal		panel	cripple	settle
plural		parcel	cuddle	single
rascal		quarrel	cycle	steeple
rival		ravel	dimple	struggle
royal		satchel	doodle	stumble
rural		sequel	double	tackle
sandal		shovel	eagle	tickle
scandal		shrivel	fable	title
signal		squirrel	fiddle	triple
spiral		swivel	freckle	trouble
tidal		tinsel	fumble	twinkle
total		towel	gamble	turtle
vandal		travel	gargle	waffle
vital		tunnel	gentle	whistle
vocal		vessel	grumble	wrinkle
		vowel	handle	

er	*er-comparative*	*ar*	*or*	*et*	*it*	
banner	manner	beggar	actor	basket	magnet	audit
barber	peddler	burglar	anchor	blanket	midget	bandit
blister	plumber	cellar	author	bucket	planet	credit
border	poster	cedar	armor	budget	poet	digit
cancer	printer	cheddar	color	carpet	puppet	edit
cider	racer	collar	cursor	closet	racket	exit
clover	ranger	cougar	director	comet	scarlet	habit
cluster	shower	dollar	doctor	cricket	secret	hermit
crater	shopper	grammar	donor	faucet	skillet	limit
dreamer	skater	hangar	editor	fidget	sonnet	merit
fiber	soldier	lunar	error	gadget	tablet	orbit
founder	speaker	molar	equator	hatchet	target	profit
freezer	timber	mortar	favor	helmet	thicket	rabbit
grocer	toaster	pillar	governor	hornet	toilet	spirit
jogger	trooper	scholar	honor	jacket	trumpet	summit
ledger	trouser	sugar	horror	locket	velvet	unit
liter	usher	calendar	juror		wallet	visit
litter	voter	circular	humor			vomit
lumber	composer	muscular	mayor			
	consumer	peculiar	meteor			
	employer		mirror			
	officer		motor			
	cylinder		neighbor			
	disaster		razor			
	bigger		rumor			
	cheaper		sailor			
	cleaner		scissors			
	farther		senior			
	gentler		splendor			
	quicker		sponsor			
	younger		tailor			
	cleaner		terror			
	flatter		tractor			
	lighter		traitor			
	blacker		tremor			
	older		tutor			
			vapor			
			visitor			

Spelling the /er/ Sound in Stressed and Unstressed Syllables

First Syllable Accent				*Second Syllable Accent*	*First Syllable Accent*	*Second Syllable Accent*
certain	birdbath	burglar	jury	alert	northern	surprise
merchant	birthday	bursting	plural	emerge	western	perhaps
mermaid	circle	curly	purchase	exert	eastern	surround
nervous	chirping	cursor	purpose	prefer	southern	pursue
person	dirty	curtain	sturdy	reverse	expert	survive
serpent	firmly	turtle	surface	reserve	lantern	
service	girlfriend	during	surgeon	observe	concert	
version	thirsty	purple	Thursday		modern	
	whirlwind	further	turkey		govern	
		burrow	current			
		furnace	hurry			
		furnish	purring			
		gurgle	burro			
		hurdle				

Unaccented Final /n/ Syllables

ain	*an*	*en-verb*	*en-noun*	*en-adj*	*in*	*on*	
captain	human	frighten	chicken	golden	basin	apron	bacon
certain	organ	listen	children	often	cabin	button	carton
curtain	orphan	sharpen	garden	open	cousin	cannon	cotton
fountain	slogan	shorten	kitten	rotten	margin	common	gallon
mountain	urban	sweeten	mitten	spoken	pumpkin	dragon	lemon
villain	woman	thicken	women	sunken	raisin	gallon	lesson
bargain		widen		swollen	robin	pardon	prison
				wooden	dolphin	person	poison
					muffin	reason	ribbon
					penguin	season	weapon
					satin	salmon	
						wagon	

ure

/ch r/		/shoor/	/j r/	/yoor/	/zh r/	/cher/ (for contrast)
culture	nurture	assure	conjure	endure	leisure	archer
capture	rapture	ensure	injure	failure	measure	butcher
creature	sculpture	insure	procedure	obscure	closure	catcher
denture	stature	pressure		secure	pleasure	marcher
feature	stricture	fissure		manicure	treasure	poacher
fixture	texture	brochure		insecure		preacher
fracture	tincture	enclosure				rancher
future	torture	exposure				scorcher
gesture	venture	reassure				stretcher
juncture	adventure	composure				teacher
lecture	departure	disclosure				bleacher
mature	furniture					pitcher
mixture	indenture					
moisture	premature					
picture	signature					
pasture	immature					
posture	miniature					
puncture	overture					
nature	aperture					

Use these lists in You're Up/Password Game.

Prefixes and Suffixes

mis	*pre*	*re*	*un*	*dis*	*in*	*non*	*en*
misbehave	precook	rebound	unable	disable	incomplete	nonsense	enable
misconduct	predate	recall	unafraid	disagreeable	incorrect	nonstop	endanger
miscount	prefix	recapture	unarmed	disappear	indecent	nonfiction	enact
misdeed	pregame	recharge	unbeaten	disarm	indirect	nonfat	enclose
misfit	preheat	reclaim	unbroken	discharge	inexpensive	nonprofit	encourage
misgivings	prejudge	recopy	uncertain	disclose	inflexible	nondiary	enforce
misguide	premature	recount	unclean	discolor	informal	nonstick	enjoy
misjudge	prepay	recycle	unclear	discomfort	inhuman	nonviolent	enslave
mislay	preschool	reelect	uncommon	discontent	injustice		enlarge
mislead	preset	refill	uncover	discover	insane		enlist
mismatch	preteen	refinish	undone	dishonest	invalid		enrage
misplace	pretest	reform	unequal	disinfect	invisible		enrich
misprint	preview	refresh	unfair	dislike			enroll
misspell	prewash	relearn	unkind	disloyal			entrust
mistake	predict	remind	unlike	disobey			encircle
mistreat	precede	remodel	unlock	disorder			enform
mistrust	prehistoric	renew	unpack	displace			entrust
misuse	prepare	reorder	unreal	disregard			
misspell	prevent	repay	unripe	disrespect			
	precaution	reprint	unselfish	distaste			
		research	unstable	distrust			
		restore	unsteady				
		retrace	untangle				
		return	untie				
		review	unwrap				
		rewrite					

uni	*bi*	*tri*	*ly*	*y*	*er/est*	*less*	*ful*	*ness*
unicorn	biceps	triangle	badly	breezy	blacker/blackest	ageless	careful	awareness
unicycle	bicycle	triathalon	barely	bumpy	bigger/biggest	breathless	cheerful	closeness
uniform	bifocals	triceps	bravely	chilly	bolder/boldest	careless	colorful	coolness
unify	bilingual	triceratops	closely	choppy	braver/bravest	ceaseless	fearful	darkness
union	binoculars	tricycle	coarsely	cloudy	calmer/calmest	endless	graceful	firmness
unique	bisect	trilogy	constantly	dirty	closer/closest	helpless	graceful	goodness
unison	biweekly	trio	costly	dusty	cheaper/cheapest	homeless	harmful	openness
universal		triple	cowardly	easy	cleaner/cleanest	lawless	hopeful	ripeness
universe		triplets	cruelly	floppy	cooler/coolest	painless	lawful	sickness
		tripod	deadly	frosty	colder/coldest	powerless	peaceful	sharpness
		triad	directly	gloomy	dirtier/dirtiest	priceless	playful	stiffness
		trivet	eagerly	greasy	easier/easiest	reckless	powerful	stillness
			finally	grouchy	fewer/fewest	spotless	tasteful	thinness
			frequently	injury	finer/finest	tasteless	thoughtful	weakness
			loudly	noisy	funnier/funniest	painless	truthful	
			loyally	rainy	harder/hardest		useful	
			proudly	sandy	hotter/hottest		wasteful	
			really	soapy	juicier/juiciest		wonderful	
			smoothly	snowy	lazier/laziest		youthful	
			angrily	stormy	lighter/lightest		beautiful	
			busily	sweaty	louder/loudest		armful	
			easily	thirsty	larger/largest		dreadful	
			happily	windy	meaner/meanest		respectful	
			kindly	dressy	nearer/nearest			
			nicely	shinny	newer/newest			
			nightly	speedy	noisier/noisiest			
				floppy	prettier/prettiest			
			safely	gritty	quicker/quickest			
					sadder/saddest			
					smaller/smallest			
					thinner/thinnest			

Words Their Way Appendix © 2004 by Prentice-Hall, Inc.

Word List of Accented Syllables

First Syllable

anything	cantaloupe
somebody	comedy
beautiful	customer
families	engineer
grandfather	evidence
January	forestry
libraries	generator
Wednesday	improvise
wonderful	iodine
populate	meteorite
acrobat	navigator
amateur	average
aptitude	camera
architect	carpenter
artery	everything
avalanche	colorful
calculator	gasoline
	everywhere
	hamburger

Second Syllable

December	asparagus
November	attorney
October	computer
September	election
uncommon	endurance
unusual	executive
unwanted	erosion
protection	ignition
reduction	judicial
romantic	mechanic
unable	banana
providing	department
vacation	important
whoever	deliver
accountant	remember
agility	whenever
amphibian	tomorrow
apprentice	abilities
	apartment
	companion
	condition

Third Syllable

constitution
population
planetarium
Sacramento
Tallahassee
understand
imitation
regulation
California
definition
diagnosis
hippopotamus
irrigation
Mississippi
declaration
exclamation

This list is used in Stressbusters.

Silent Consonant	Sounded Consonant
bomb	bombard
column	columnist
condemn	condemnation
crumb	crumble
debt	debit
damn	damnation
design	designate
fasten	fast
hasten	hast
hymn	hymnal
malign	malignant
moisten	moist
muscle	muscular
resign	resignation
sign	signal
soften	soft

ant	*ance*	*ancy*	*other*
attendant	attendance		attend
assistant	assistance		assist
important	importance		import
defiant	defiance		defy
arrogant	arrogance		arrogate
dominant	dominance		dominate
ambulant	ambulance		ambulate/tory
ignorant	ignorance		ignore
vigilant	vigilance		vigil
significant	significance		signify
elegant	elegance	elegancy	
hesitant	hesitance	hesitancy	hesitate
reluctant	reluctance	reluctancy	reluct
expectant	expectance	expectancy	expect
radiant	radiance	radiancy	radiate
abundant	abundance	abundancy	abound
resistant	resistance	resistancy	resist

ary, ery, and ory

ary	ery	ary	ery	ory	ory
customary	cemetery	anniversary	artery	allegory	compulsory
fragmentary	stationery	boundary	bribery	auditory	cursory
extraordinary		documentary	celery	category	directory
hereditary		elementary	discovery	dormitory	memory
imaginary		glossary	gallery	explanatory	satisfactory
legendary		salary	grocery	inventory	theory
literary		summary	imagery	observatory	victory
military			machinery	territory	
missionary			mystery		
necessary			nursery		
ordinary			scenery		
revolutionary			surgery		
secretary					
solitary					
stationary					
temporary					
vocabulary					

Vowel Alternations

long to short	long to schwa	short to schwa
cave cavity	able ability	legality legal
flame flammable	famous infamous	locality local
grave gravity	major majority	metallic metal
nature natural	native nativity	personality personal
athlete athletic	prepare preparation	vitality vital
please pleasant	relate relative	celebrate celebrity
crime criminal	stable stability	democrate democracy
decide decision	compete competition	excel excellent
revise revision	combine combination	perfection perfect
wise wisdom	define definition	critic criticize
know knowledge	divide division	habit habitat
episode episodic	invite invitation	mobility mobile
assume assumption	recite recitation	prohibit prohibition
produce production	reside resident	geometry geometric
	compose composition	periodic period
	expose exposition	
	custodian custody	
	pose position	
	social society	

These lists can be used to play Which Suffix?

TEMPLATES FOR SORTS AND GAMES

TEMPLATE FOR PICTURE SORTS

Words Their Way Appendix © 2004 by Prentice-Hall, Inc.

SAMPLE WORD SORTS

Words Their Way Appendix © 2004 by Prentice-Hall, Inc.

Within Word Pattern Sort 1			Short-e CVC Long-e CVVC EE Long-e CVVC EA 1 pair of homophones
feel	fell	see
meat	fed	tree
leak	bee	read
seen	leap	sled
sea	jeep	free
bleed	seat	neck
treat	feet	mess
help	team	sweet

Word Family Sort for *et* and *en*		
pet	wet	jet
ten	pen	net
hen	men	vet

Within Word Pattern Sort 2

Long-a CVVC *ai*
Long-a CVV *ay*
L-controlled *al*
1 oddball

rain	may	call
small	pail	pain
play	say	mail
tail	hay	said
wall	clay	gray
day	tall	talk
walk	stay	sail
fall	snail	train

Words Their Way Appendix © 2004 by Prentice-Hall, Inc.

Syllables & Affixes Sort

Sort by *ic* and *ick*
Sort by Syllables and Compounds

brick	panic	picnic
music	limerick	flick
cowlick	trick	basic
homesick	arctic	attic
quick	classic	chopstick
comic	fabric	drastic
fantastic	yardstick	garlic
gimmick	magic	Pacific

GAMEBOARDS

Figures A-7 through A-13 are gameboard templates that can be used to create some of the games described throughout the book. Note that there are two sides for each gameboard. When the two sides are placed together they form a continuous track or path. These games can be adapted for many different features and for many different levels. Here are some general tips on creating the games.

1. The gameboards can be photocopied and mounted on manila file folders (colored ones are nice), making them easy to create and store. All the materials needed for the game, such as spinners, word cards, or game markers, can be put in plastic bags or envelopes labeled with the name of the game and stored in the folder. You might mark the flip side of word cards in some way so that lost cards can be returned to the correct game. Rubber stamp figures work well.

2. When mounting a gameboard in a folder, be sure to leave a slight gap (about an eighth of an inch) between the two sides so that the folder will still fold. If you do not leave this gap the paper will buckle. Trim the gameboards to line up neatly or cut out the entire path.

3. A variety of things can be used for game markers or pawns that the children will move around the board such as buttons, plastic discs, coins, and bottle caps. Flat objects store best in the folders or you may just want to put a collection of game markers, dice, and spinners in a box. This box can be stored near the games, and students can take what they need.

4. Add pizazz to the games with pictures cut from magazines or old workbooks, stickers, comic characters, clip art, and so on. Rubber stamps, your drawings, or children's drawings can be used to add interest and color. Create catchy themes such as Rabbit Race, Lost in Space, Through the Woods, Mouse Maze, Rainforest Adventure, and so forth.

5. Include directions and correct answers (when appropriate) with the game. They might be stored inside along with playing pieces or glued to the game itself.

6. Label the spaces around the path or track according to the feature you want to reinforce, and laminate for durability. If you want to create open-ended games that can be adapted to a variety of features, laminate the path before you label the spaces. Then you can write in letters or words with a washable overhead pen and change them as needed. Permanent marker can also be used and removed with hairspray or fingernail polish remover.

7. Add interest to the game by labeling some spaces with special directions (if you are using a numbered die or spinner) or add cards with special directions to the deck of words. Directions might offer the students a bonus in the form of an extra turn or there might be a penalty such as lose a turn. These bonus or penalty directions can tie in with your themes. For example, in the Rainforest Adventure the player might forget a lunch and be asked to go back to the starting space. Keep the reading ability of your children in mind as you create these special directions.

SPINNERS

Many of the word study games described in this book use a game spinner. Figure A-14 provides simple directions for making a spinner.

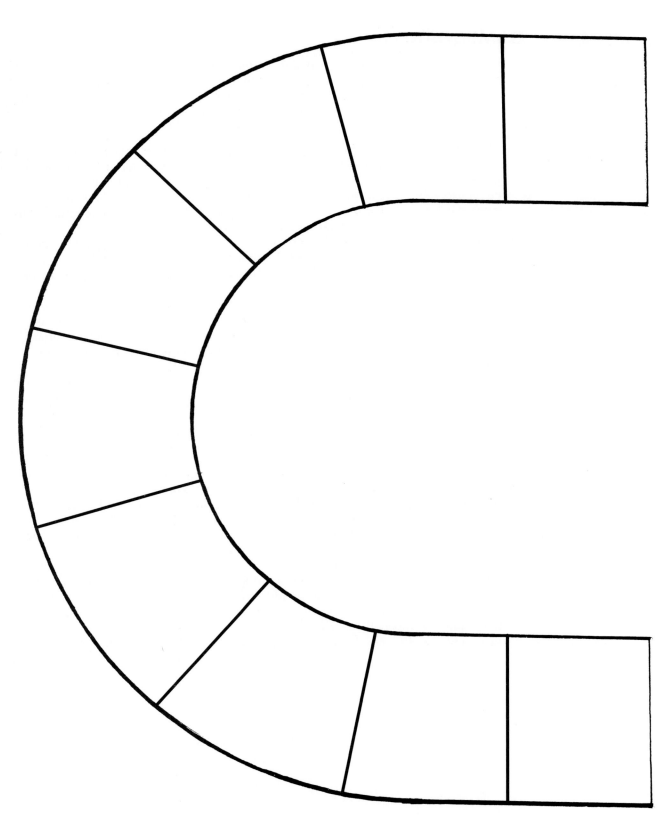

FIGURE A-7   Racetrack Gameboard (left and right)

Words Their Way Appendix © 2004 by Prentice-Hall, Inc.

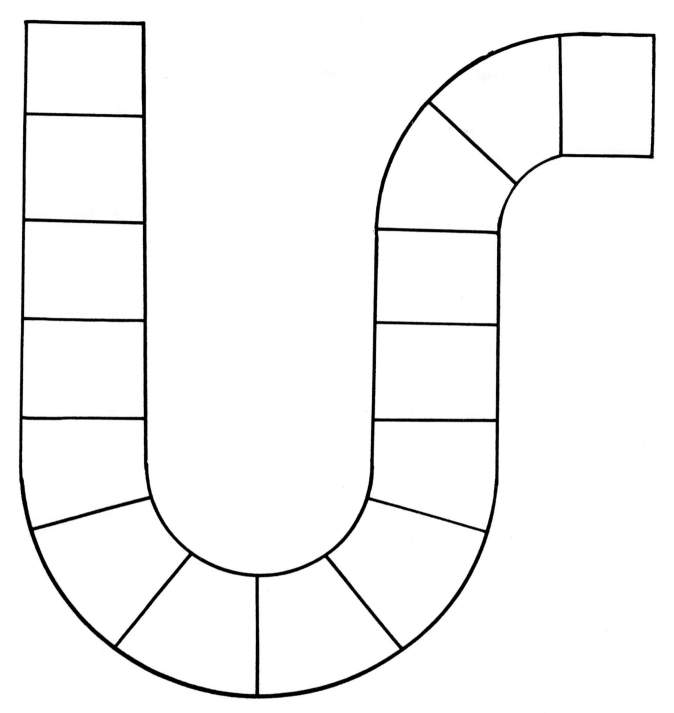

FIGURE A-8 U-gameboard (left)

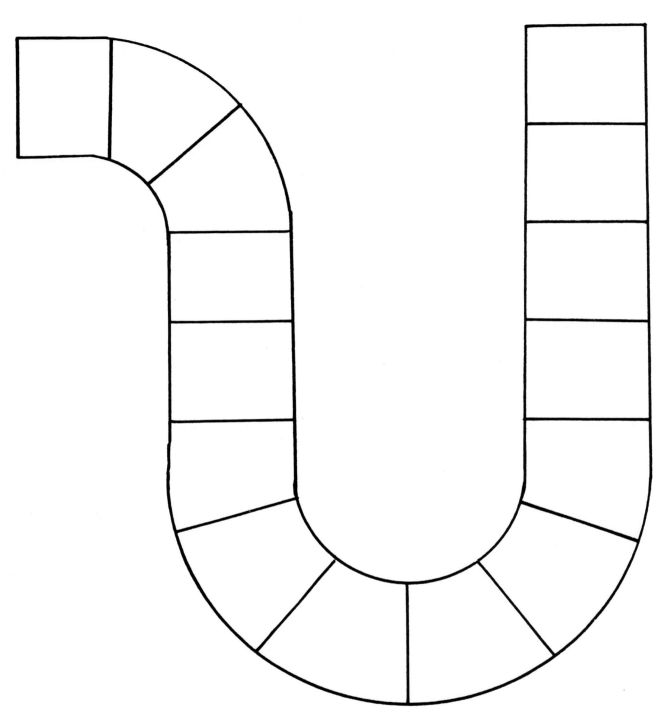

FIGURE A-9 U-gameboard (right)

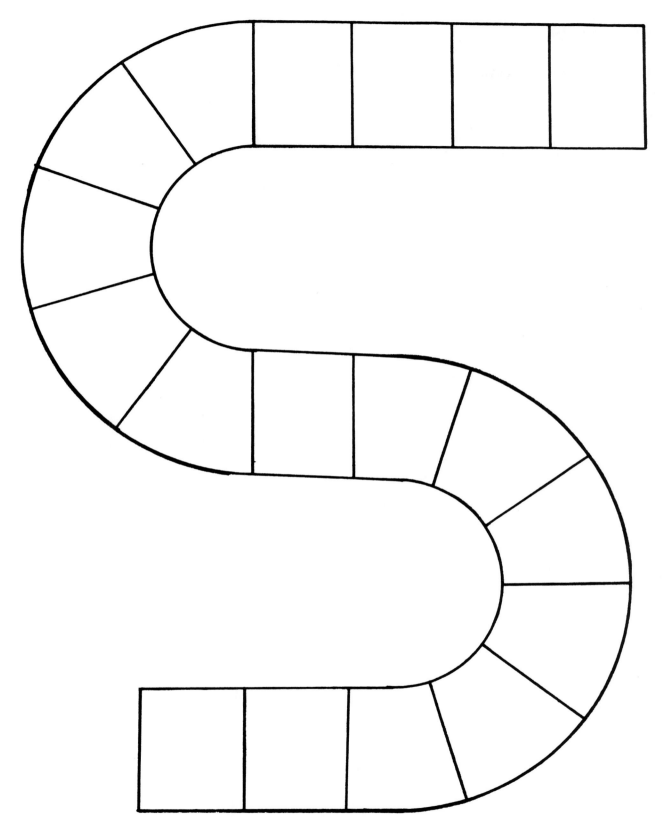

FIGURE A-10 S-gameboard (left)

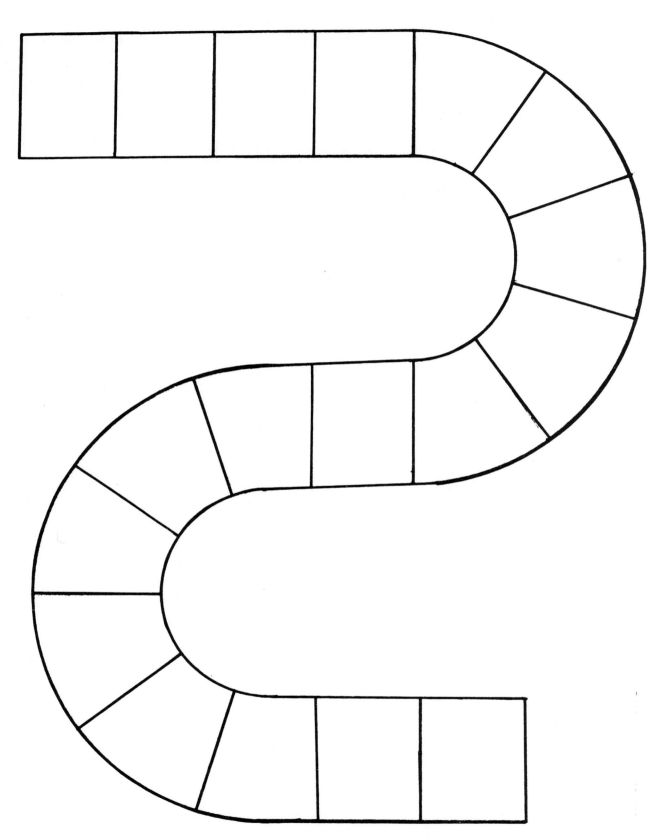

FIGURE A-11   S-gameboard (right)

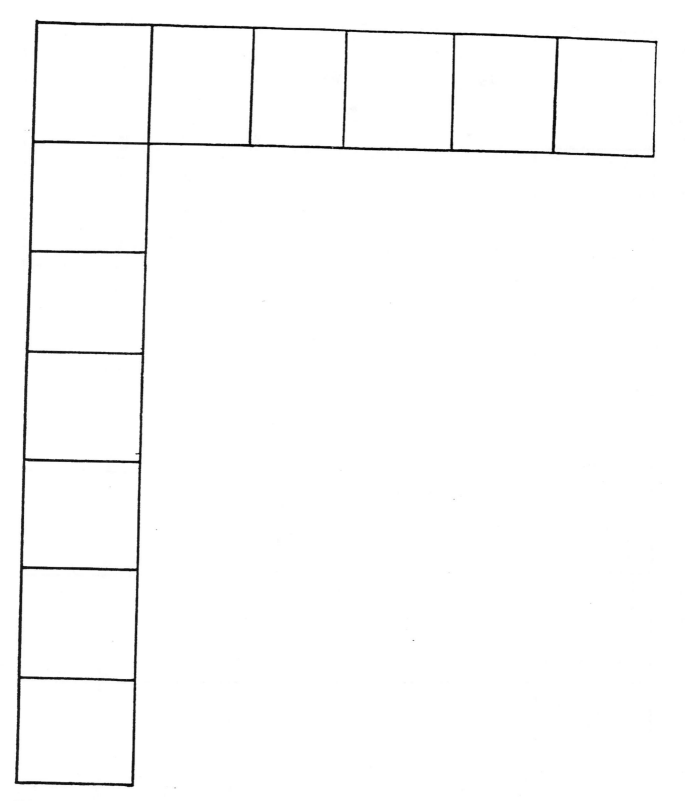

FIGURE A-12 Rectangle Gameboard (left)

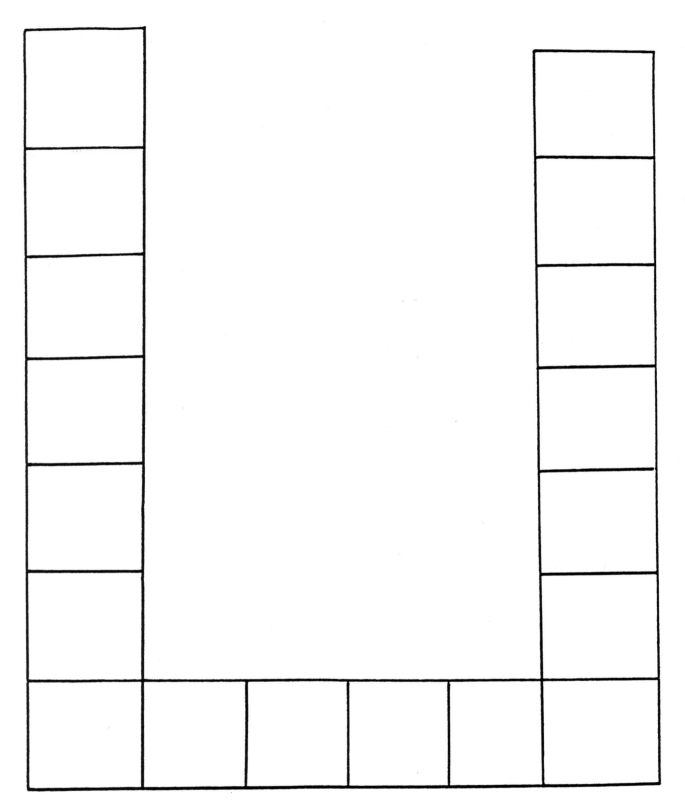

FIGURE A-13 Rectangle Gameboard (right)

Words Their Way Appendix © 2004 by Prentice-Hall, Inc.

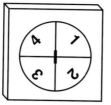

1. Glue a **circle** (patterns or cutouts to the right) onto a square of **heavy cardboard** that is no smaller than 4" x 4". Square spinner bases are easier to hold than round bases.

2. Cut a narrow slot in the center with the point of a sharp pair of scissors or a razor blade.

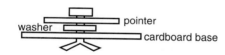

pointer pattern

3. Cut the pointer from **soft plastic** (such as a milk jug) and make a clean round hole with a **hole punch**.

4. A **washer,** either a metal one from the hardware store or one cut from cardboard, helps the pointer move freely.

washer — pointer — cardboard base

5. Push a **paper fastener** through the pointer hole, the washer, and the slot in the spinner base. Flatten the legs, leaving space for the pointer to spin easily.

FIGURE A-14 Directions for Making a Game Spinner

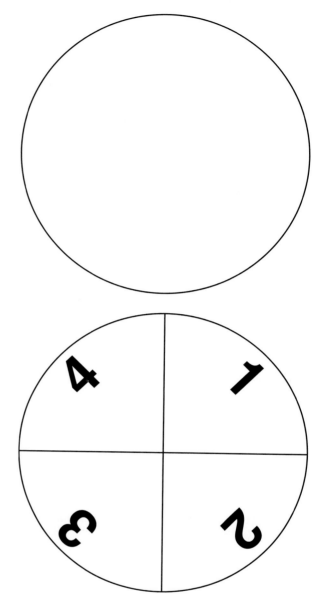

RESOURCES

Children's Literature*

Asimov, I. (1960). *Words from the myths.* Boston: Houghton Mifflin.

Barchas, S. E. (1975). *I was walking down the road.* New York: Scholastic.

Bauer, M. D. (1986). *On my honor.* New York: Clarion.

Blume, J. (1980). *Superfudge.* New York: Dell Publishers.

Blume, J., (1988). *Blubber.* Santa Barbara, CA: ABC-CLIO.

Blume, J., & Lisker, S. O. (1978). *Freckle juice.* New York: Dell Publishers.

Carle, E. (1974). *My very first book of shapes.* New York: HarperCollins.

Carle, E. (1987). *Have you seen my cat?* Picture Books LTD.

Christelow, E. (1989). *Five little monkeys jumping on the bed.* Boston: Clarion Books.

Cleary, B. (1981). *Ramona Quimby, age 8.* New York: Morrow.

Cleary, B. (1996). *Ramona the pest.* New York: Dell Publishers.

Dahl, R. (1982). *The BFG.* New York: Trumpet Club.

Dahl, R. (1988). *Fantastic Mr. Fox.* New York: Puffin Books.

Dahl, R. (1998). *Matilda.* London: Puffin

Dahl, R. (1998). *Witches.* London: Puffin

D'Aulaire, I., & D'Aulaire, E. (1980). *D'Aulaires' book of Greek myths.* New York: Doubleday.

Fisher, L. (1984). *The Olympians: Great gods and goddesses of ancient Greece.* New York: Holiday.

Galdone, P. (1973). *The three billy goats gruff.* New York: Clarion Books.

Gates, D. (1974). *Two queens of heaven: Aphrodite and Demeter.* New York: Viking.

Heller, R. (1993). *Chickens aren't the only ones.* New York: Putnam.

Hoban, T. (1978). *Is it red? Is it yellow? Is it blue?* New York: Greenwillow Books.

Hoffman, P. (1990). *We play.* Illustrated by Sara Wilson. New York: Scholastic.

Jacques, B. (1998). *Redwall.* Ace Books.

Langstaff, J. (1974). *Oh, a hunting we will go.* New York: Atheneum.

Lionni, L. (1969). *Alexander and the wind-up mouse.* New York: Pantheon.

Martin, B. (1983). *Brown bear, brown bear, what do you see?* New York: Henry Holt.

Martin, B., & Archambault, J. (1989). *Chicka chicka boom boom.* New York: Simon & Schuster.

McLenighan, V. (1982). *Stop-go, fast-slow.* Chicago: Children's Press.

O'Dell, S. (1989). *Black star, bright dawn.* Boston: Houghton Mifflin.

Parish, P. (1981). *Amelia Bedelia.* New York: Avon.

Pullman, P. (2002). *His dark materials trilogy: The golden compass, the subtle knife, the amber spyglass.* Knopf.

Raffi. (1976). *Singable songs for the very young.* Universal City, CA: Troubadour Records.

Raffi. (1985). *One light, one sun.* Universal City, CA: Troubadour Records.

Scieska, J. (2001). *The time warp trio series.* New York: Viking.

Seuss, Dr. (1974). *There's a wocket in my pocket.* New York: Random House.

Sharmat, M. (1980). *Gregory the terrible eater.* New York: Four Winds Press.

Shaw, N. (1986). *Sheep in a jeep.* Boston: Houghton Mifflin.

Shaw, N. (1992). *Sheep on a ship.* Boston: Houghton Mifflin.

Slepian, J., & Seidler, A. (1967). *The hungry thing.* New York: Follet.

Slepian, J., & Seidler, A. (1987). *The cat who wore a pot on her head.* New York: Scholastic.

Slepian, J., & Seidler, A. (1990). *The hungry thing returns.* New York: Scholastic.

Sobol, D. (2002). *Encyclopedia Brown Series.* New York: Skylark.

Steig, W. (1978). *Amos and Boris.* New York: Farrar, Straus and Giroux.

Straus, B., & Friedman, H. (1987). *See you later alligator: A first book of rhyming word play.* New York: Trumpet Club.

Taylor, T. (1993). *Timothy of the cay.* San Diego, CA: Harcourt Brace.

Wallner, J. (1987a). *City mouse–country mouse.* New York: Scholastic.

Wallner, J. (1987b). *The country mouse and the city mouse and two more mouse tales from Aesop.* New York: Scholastic.

Wells, N. (1980). *Noisy Nora.* New York: Dial Press.

White, E. B. (1945). *Stuart Little.* New York: Harper Row.

*See Chapter 4 for rhyme and ABC books.

Bibliography of Word Study Books

Allen, M. S., & Cunningham, M. (1999). *Webster's new world rhyming dictionary.* New York: Simon & Schuster.

Almond, J. (1995). *Dictionary of word origins: A history of the words, expressions, and cliches we use.* New Jersey: Carol Publishing Group.

Asimov, I. (1959). *Words of science, and the history behind them.* Boston: Houghton Mifflin.

Asimov, I. (1961). *Words from the myths.* Boston: Houghton Mifflin.

Asimov, I. (1962). *Words on the map.* Boston: Houghton Mifflin.

Ayers, D. M. (1986). *English words from Latin and Greek elements* (2nd ed.). Tucson: University of Arizona.

Ayto, J. (1990). *Dictionary of word origins.* New York: Arcade Publishing.

Black, D. C. (1988). *Spoonerisms, sycophants and sops: A celebration of fascinating facts about words.* New York: Harper & Row.

Byson, B. (1990). *The mother tongue: English and how it got that way.* New York: Morrow.

Byson, B. (1994). *Made in America: An informal history of the English language in the United States.* New York: Morrow.

Ciardi, J. (1980). *A browser's dictionary: A compendium of curious expressions and intriguing facts.* New York: Harper & Row.

Collis, H. (1981). *Colloquial English.* New York: Regents Pub.

Collis, H. (1986). *101 American English idioms.* New York: McGraw Hill.

Cummings, D. W. (1988). *American English spelling.* Baltimore: Johns Hopkins University Press.

Folsom, M. (1985). *Easy as pie: A guessing game of sayings.* New York: Clarion.

Franlyn, J. (1987). *Which is witch?* New York: Dorset Press.

Funk, C. E. (1948). *A hog on ice and other curious expressions.* New York: Harper & Row.

Funk, C. E. (1955). *Heavens to Betsy and other curious sayings.* New York: Harper & Row.

Funk, W. (1954). *Word origins and their romantic stories.* New York: Grosset & Dunlap.

Gwynne, F. (1970). *The king who rained* (homophones). New York: Simon & Schuster.

Gwynne, F. (1976). *A chocolate moose for dinner* (homophones). New York: Simon & Schuster.

Gwynne, F. (1980). *A sixteen hand horse* (homophones). New York: Simon & Schuster.

Gwynne, F. (1988). *A little pigeon toad* (homophones). New York: Simon & Schuster.

Harrison, J. S. (1987). *Confusion reigns.* New York: St. Martin's Press.

Heacock, P. (1989). *Which word when?* New York: Dell Pub.

Heller, R. (1987). *A cache of jewels and other collective nouns.* New York: Grosset & Dunlap.

Heller, R. (1988). *Kites sail high.* New York: Grosset & Dunlap.

Heller, R. (1989). *Many luscious lollipops: A book about adjectives.* New York: Grosset & Dunlap.

Heller, R. (1990). *Merry-go-round: A book about nouns.* New York: Grosset & Dunlap.

Heller, R. (1991). *Up, up and away: A book about adverbs.* New York: Grosset & Dunlap.

Heller, R. (1995). *Behind the mask: A book about prepositions.* New York: Grosset & Dunlap.

Hoad, T. F. (1986). *The concise Oxford dictionary of English etymology.* New York: Oxford University Press.

Jones, C. F. (1999). *Eat your words: A fascinating look at the language of food.* New York: Delacorte Press.

Kennedy, J. (1996). *Word stems.* New York: Soho Press.

Kingsley, C. (1980). *The heroes.* New York: Mayflower.

Lewis, N. (1983). *Dictionary of correct spelling.* New York: Harper & Row.

Maestro, G. (1983). *Riddle romp.* New York: Clarion.

Maestro, G. (1984). *What's a frank frank? Easy homograph riddles.* New York: Clarion.

Maestro, G. (1985). *Razzle-dazzle riddles.* New York: Clarion.

Maestro, G. (1986). *What's mite might? Homophone riddles to boost your word power.* New York: Clarion.

Maestro, G. (1989). *Riddle roundup: A wild bunch to beef up your word power.* New York: Clarion.

Partridge, E. (1984). *Origins: A short etymological dictionary of modern English.* New York: Greenwich House.

Pei, M. (1965). *The story of language.* Philadelphia: Lippincott and Company.

Presson, L. (1996). *What in the world is a homophone?* Hauppauge, NY: Barron's.

Presson, L. (1997). *A dictionary of homophones.* New York: Barrons.

Randall, B. (1992). *When is a pig a hog? A guide to confoundingly related English words.* New York: Prentice Hall.

Room, A. (1992). *A NTC's dictionary of word origins.* Lincolnwood, IL: National Textbook.

Safire, W. (1984). *I stand corrected: More on language.* New York: Avon.

Sarnoff, J., & Ruffins, R. (1981). *Words: A book about word origins of everyday words and phrases.* New York: Charles Scribner's Sons.

Schleifer, R. (1995). *Grow your own vocabulary: By learning the roots of English words.* New York: Random House.

Scragg, D. G. (1974). *A history of English spelling.* Manchester, England: Manchester University Press.

Shipley, J. T. (1967). *Dictionary of word origins.* Lanham, MD: Rowman & Littlefield.

Shipley, J. (1984). *The origins of English words.* Baltimore: Johns Hopkins University Press.

The Oxford English Dictionary on CD-ROM. (1994). Oxford: Oxford University Press.

The American heritage book of English usage: A practical and authoritative guide to contemporary English. (1996). Boston: Houghton Mifflin.

The Scholastic dictionary of synonyms, antonyms, homonyms. (1965). New York: Scholastic.

The Scholastic rhyming dictionary. (1994). New York: Scholastic.

Terban, M. (1982). *Eight ate: A feast of homonym riddles.* New York: Clarion.

Terban, M. (1983). *In a pickle and other funny idioms.* New York: Clarion.

Terban, M. (1984). *I think I thought and other tricky verbs.* New York: Clarion.

Terban, M. (1986). *Your foot's on my feet! and other tricky nouns.* New York: Clarion.

Terban, M. (1987). *Mad as a wet hen! and other funny idioms.* New York: Clarion.

Terban, M. (1988a). *The dove dove: Funny homograph riddles.* New York: Clarion.

Terban, M. (1988b). *Guppies in tuxedoes: Funny eponyms.* New York: Clarion.

Terban, M. (1988c). *Too hot to hoot: Funny palindrome riddles.* New York: Clarion.

Terban, M. (1991). *Hey, hay! A wagonful of funny homonym riddles.* New York: Clarion.

Terban, M. (1992). *Funny you should ask: How to make up jokes and riddles with wordplay.* New York: Clarion.

Venezky, R. L. (1999). *The American way of spelling: The structure and origins of American English orthography.* New York: Guilford Press.

Webster's dictionary of word origins. (1992). New York: Smithmark.

Weiner, S. (1981). *Handy book of commonly used American idioms.* New York: Regents Pub.

Glossary

advanced readers Highly skilled readers and writers capable of reading different genres of texts for different purposes with speed, accuracy, and comprehension. Advanced readers acquire an advanced Greek- and Latin-derived vocabulary particular to specific fields of study. See also *specialized readers* or *derivational relations spelling stage*.

affix Most commonly a suffix or prefix attached to a base word, stem, or root.

affixation The process of attaching a word part, such as a prefix or suffix, to a base word, stem, or root.

affricate A speech sound produced when the breath stream is stopped and released at the point of articulation, usually where the tip of the tongue rubs against the roof of the mouth just behind the teeth when pronouncing the final sound in the word *clutch* or the beginning sound in the word *trip*.

alliteration The occurrence in a phrase or line of speech of two or more words having the same beginning sound.

alphabetic A writing system containing characters or symbols representing individual speech sounds.

alphabetic layer of instruction The first layer of word study instruction focusing on letters and letter-sound correspondences.

alphabetic principle The concept that letters and letter combinations are used to represent phonemes in orthography. See *phoneme; orthography*.

alternation patterns The regular pattern of change in moving from one form of a word to another. *Admire/admiration, perspire/perspiration*, and *declare/declaration* form a consistent pattern of change in moving from one form of the word to another.

ambiguous vowels A vowel sound represented by a variety of different spelling patterns, or vowel patterns that represent a wide range of sounds.

analytic Word study that divides words into their elemental parts through phonemic and orthographic analysis.

articulation How sounds are shaped in the mouth during speech. The ways sounds are articulated guides some invented spellings. Some confusions are made in spelling based on similarities in articulation (e.g., *tr* for *dr*).

assimilated/absorbed prefixes The spelling and sound of the consonant in a prefix has been assimilated into the same spelling and sound at the beginning of the base or root to which the prefix is affixed (e.g., *ad + tract = attract*).

automaticity Refers to the speed and accuracy of word recognition and spelling. Automaticity is the goal of word study instruction. Achieving automaticity in the mechanics reading and writing frees cognitive resources for comprehension.

base word A word to which prefixes and/or suffixes are added. For example, the base word of *unwholesome* is *whole*.

beat-the-teacher speed sorts Students practice their word sorts all week to increase the speed of their categorization processes. Their speed and accuracy are "tested" by trying to beat the teacher who also sorts the same set of words into the same categories. Beat-the-teacher speed sorts encourage automaticity. See *automaticity; speed sorts*.

beginning period of literacy development A period of literacy development that begins when students have a concept of word and can make sound-symbol correspondences. This period is noted for disfluent reading and writing, and letter name–alphabetic spelling.

blends An orthographic term referring to consonant blends. Consonant blends are made of two- or three-letter sequences that are blended together. There are *l* blends (*bl, cl, fl, gl, pl, sl*), *r*-blends (*br, cr, dr, fr, gr, pr, tr*), and *s*-blends (*sc, scr, sk, sp, st, squ, sw*). Although the letter sounds are blended together quickly, each one is pronounced. A two-letter blend represents two sounds; a three-letter blend represents three sounds. Consonant blends occurring at the beginning of words are *onsets*, and as such, are treated orthographically as a unit. See *onset*.

center time/center work Work completed independently in prepared areas within a classroom.

checklist A form, available in the Appendix, used for conducting feature analyses of spelling samples. See *feature analysis*.

choral reading Oral reading done in unison with another person or persons.

circle time See *circle work*.

circle work Group work conducted under the teacher's direction.

classroom composite   A classroom profile that organizes children into instructional groups by spelling stage and by features to be taught within each stage.

closed sorts   Word sorts that classify words into predetermined categories.

closed syllable   A closed syllable ends with or is "closed" by a consonant sound. In polysyllabic words, a closed syllable contains a short vowel sound that is closed by two consonants (*rabbit, racket*). See *open syllable*.

cloze   An activity in which children supply a single missing word in the middle or end of a sentence, as in, "the cat sat on the _____." Usually the omitted word can be predicted by the recurring rhyming pattern and/or by supplying the initial consonant sound, as in, "the cat sat on the m_____."

cognates   Words that are related in origin such as certain words in different languages are derived from the same root. See *derivational relations spelling stage*.

complex consonant patterns   Consonant units occurring at the end of words that correspond to the vowel sound in the middle of the word. Final *tch* corresponds to the short vowel sound in the middle of *fetch* and *scotch*, while final *ch* corresponds to the long-vowel sound in the middle of *peach* and *coach*. Other complex consonant patterns include final *ck* (*pack* vs. *peak*) and final *dge* (*badge* vs. *cage*).

compound words   Words made up of two or more smaller words. A compound word may or may not be hyphenated, depending on its part of speech.

concept of word   The ability to match spoken words to printed words as demonstrated by the ability to point to the words of a memorized text while reading. This demonstration must include one or more two-syllable words.

concept sorts   A categorization task in which pictures, objects, or words are grouped by shared attributes or meanings. A concept and vocabulary development activity.

connotation/connotative   The associative meaning of words—what words suggest to an individual and how they make an individual feel. For example, the word *sick* to a particular individual may suggest extreme discomfort and depression; to another, the word may suggest bad taste, as in a "sick" joke. See *denotation/denotative*.

consonant alternation   The process in which the pronunciation of consonants changes in the base or root of derivationally related words, while the spelling does not change. For example, the silent-to-sounded pattern in the words *sign* and *signal*; the /k/ to /sh/ pattern in the words *music* and *musician*.

consonant blend   See *blends*.

consonant digraph   See *digraph*.

consonant-vowel-consonant (CVC)   Refers to the pattern of consonants and vowels within a syllable. The spelling pattern for the word *mat* would be represented as a *CVC* pattern while the spelling

pattern for the word *mail* would be represented as a *CVVC* pattern.

consonants   Students often learn what consonants are by what they are not: they are not vowels (*a, e, i, o,* and *u*). Where vowel sounds are thought of as musical with resonance, consonant sounds are known for their noise and the way in which air is constricted as it is stopped and released or forced through the vocal tract, mouth, teeth, and lips.

continuant sound   A consonant sound, such as /s/ or /m/, that can be prolonged as long as the breath lasts without distorting the sound quality.

cut-and-paste activities   A variation of picture sorting in which students cut out pictures from magazines or catalogs and paste them into categories.

denotation/denotative   The literal meaning of words; what words refer to. For example, the word *sick* refers to or denotes the condition of not being well. See *connotation/connotative*.

derivational relations spelling stage   The last stage of spelling development in which spellers learn about derivational relationships preserved in the spelling of words. *Derivational* refers to (a) the process by which new words are created from existing words, chiefly through affixation; and (b) the development of a word from its historical origin. *Derivational constancy* refers to spelling patterns that remain the same despite changes in pronunciation across derived forms. *Bomb* retains the *b* from *bombard* because of its historical evolution.

developmental classroom profiles   A class roster arranged by developmental spelling stages. These profiles are used to plan small group word study activities.

developmental level   One of five stages of spelling development: emergent, letter name–alphabetic, within word pattern, syllables and affixes, or derivational relations.

digraph   Two letters that represent one sound. There are consonant digraphs and vowel digraphs, though the term most commonly refers to consonant digraphs. Common consonant digraphs include *sh, ch, th,* and *wh*. Consonant digraphs at the beginning of words are *onsets*.

diphthong   A complex speech sound beginning with one vowel sound and moving to another within the same syllable. The *oy* in *boy* is a diphthong as is the *oi* in *noise*.

directed reading-thinking activities (DRTAs)   A strategy for developing comprehension processes during reading. The strategy is a variation of a predict-read-prove routine.

directionality   The left-to-right direction used for reading and writing English.

draw and label activities   A variation of picture sorting in which students draw pictures of things that begin with the sounds under study. The pictures are drawn in the appropriate categories and labeled with the letter(s) corresponding to that sound.

echo reading   Oral reading in which the student echoes or imitates the reading of the teacher or buddy. Echo reading is used with very beginning readers as a form of support and as a default option when the text is too hard. Echo reading can also be used to model fluent reading.

emergent   A period of literacy development ranging from birth to beginning reading. This period precedes the letter name–alphabetic stage of spelling development.

eponyms   Places, things, and actions that are named after an individual.

error guide   A sample of spelling errors arranged by spelling stages that enables teachers to place children in instructional groups.

etymology   The study of the origin and historical development of words.

familiarity   The degree to which a student already knows something about a text to be read. Familiarity comes from prior experience with the text, or with an event described in the text. Familiarity is also defined by the closeness of match between the language of the text and the language of the child.

feature analysis   More than scoring for just right and wrong, feature analyses provide a way of interpreting children's spelling errors by taking into account their knowledge of specific orthographic features such as consonant blends or short vowels. Feature analyses inform teachers what spelling features to teach to whom.

feature guide   A tool used to classify students' errors within a hierarchy of orthographic features. Used to score spelling inventories to assess students' knowledge of specific spelling features at their particular stage of spelling development and to plan word study instruction to meet individual needs.

fingerpoint reading   Refers to the kind of reading that emergent and beginning readers do, using a finger to point to each word as it is spoken.

frustration level   A dysfunctional level of instruction where there is a mismatch between instruction and what an individual is able to grasp. This mismatch precludes learning and often results in frustration.

generative   An approach to word study that emphasizes processes that apply to many words, as opposed to an approach that focuses on one word at a time.

homographs   Words that are spelled alike, but have different pronunciations and different meanings, e.g., "*tear* a piece of paper" and "to shed a *tear*"; "*lead* someone along" and "the element *lead.*"

homonyms/homophones   Words that sound alike, are spelled differently, and have different meanings, e.g., *bear* and *bare, pane* and *pain,* and *forth* and *fourth.*

independent level   That level of academic engagement in which an individual works independently, without need of instructional support. Independent-level behaviors demonstrate a high degree of accuracy, speed, ease, and fluency.

instructional level   A level of academic engagement in which instruction is comfortably matched to what an individual is able to grasp. See *zone of proximal development.*

intermediate readers   Intermediate readers are fluent readers and writers whose word recognition of one- and two-syllable words is automatic. Intermediate readers are grappling with a more advanced vocabulary involving meaning units such as prefixes and suffixes. Intermediate readers negotiate unfamiliar genres and expository texts typical of the upper elementary and middle grades. Intermediate readers are spellers learning about syllables and affixes.

invariance   Spelling features that do not vary, but remain constant.

juncture   Syllable juncture refers to the transition from one syllable to the next. Frequently this transition involves a spelling change such as consonant doubling or dropping the final -*e* before adding *ing.*

key pictures   Pictures placed at the top of each category in a picture sort. Key pictures act as headers for each column and can be used for analogy.

key words   Words placed at the top of each category in a word sort. Key words act as headers for each column and can be used for analogy.

language experience   An approach to the teaching of reading in which students read about their own experiences recorded in their own language. Experience stories are dictated by the student to a teacher who writes them down. Dictated accounts are reread in unison, in echo fashion, and independently. Known words are lifted out of context and grouped by various phonic elements.

lax   Lax vowels are commonly known as the short-vowel sound.

letter name–alphabetic spelling stage   The second stage of spelling development in which students represent beginning, middle, and ending sounds of words with phonetically accurate letter choices. Often the selections are based on the sound of the letter name itself, rather than abstract letter-sound associations. The letter name *h* (aitch), for example, produces the /ch/ sound, and is often selected to represent that sound rather than the abstract /huh/.

liquids   The consonant sounds for /r/ and /l/ are referred to as liquids because, unlike other consonant sounds, they do not obstruct air in the mouth. The sounds for /r/ and /l/ are more vowel-like in that they do not involve direct contact between the lips, tongue, and the roof of the mouth as other consonants do. Instead, they sort of roll around in the mouth, as if liquid.

long vowels   Every vowel (*a, e, i, o,* and *u*) has two sounds, commonly referred to as "long" and "short." The long-vowel sound "says its letter name." The vocal cords are tense when producing the long-vowel sound. Because of this, the linguistic term for the long-vowel sound is *tense.*

meaning layer of information   The third layer of English orthography including meaning units such as prefixes, suffixes, and word roots. These word elements were acquired primarily during the Renaissance when English was overlaid with many words of Greek and Latin derivation.

meaning sorts   A type of word sort where the categories are determined by semantic categories or by spelling-meaning connections that remain constant across related words.

memory reading   An accurate recitation of text accompanied by fingerpoint reading. See *fingerpoint reading.*

metaphor   A word or phrase that means one thing is used, through implication, to refer to something else. For example, "His remark created a blizzard of controversy." See *simile.*

mock linear   Writing characteristic of the emergent stage of spelling development in which the linear arrangement of written English is mimicked in long rows of letterlike shapes and squiggles.

morphemic   Refers to morphemes, or meaning units in the spelling of words, such as the suffix *-ed* which signals past tense, or the root *graph* in the words *autograph* or *graphite.*

nasals   A sound produced when the air is blocked in the oral cavity but escapes through the nose. The first consonants in the words *mom* and *no* represent nasal sounds.

no-peeking sorts   A picture or word sort done with a partner; A type of no-peeking sort in which students who are responsible for sorting cannot see the word but must instead "blindly" rely upon their memory of the spelling pattern and the sounds they hear to determine the category as labeled by the key word displayed. See *key words.*

no-peeking writing sort   A variant of a no-peeking sort in which one student (or teacher) names a word without showing it to another student who must write it in the correct category under a key word. See *key words.*

oddballs   Exception words that do not fit the targeted letter-sound or pattern feature.

onset   The onset of a single syllable or word is the initial consonant(s) sound. The onset of the word *sun* is /s/. The onset of the word *slide* is /sl/.

open sorts   A type of picture or word sort in which the categories for sorting are left open. Students sort pictures or words into groups according to the students' own judgment. Open sorts are useful for determining what word features are salient for students.

open syllable   An open syllable ends with a long-vowel sound (*labor, reason*). See *closed syllable.*

orthography/orthographic   Refers to the writing system of a language, specifically, the correct sequence of letters, characters, or symbols.

pattern   Letter sequences that function as a unit and are related to a consistent category of sound. Frequently these patterns form rhyming families, as in the *ain* of *Spain, rain,* and *drain.*

pattern layer of information   The second layer or tier of English orthography in which patterns of letter sequences, rather than individual letters themselves, represent vowel sounds. This layer of information was acquired during the period of English history following the Norman Invasion. Many of the vowel patterns of English are of French derivation.

pattern sort   A word sort in which students categorize words according to similar spelling patterns.

personal readers   Individual books of reading materials that beginning readers can read with good accuracy. Group experience charts, dictations, and rhymes comprise the majority of the reading material.

phoneme   The smallest unit of speech that distinguishes one word from another. For example, the *t* of *tug* and the *r* of *rug* are two English phonemes.

phoneme segmentation   The process of dividing a spoken word into the smallest units of sound within that word. The word *bat* can be divided or segmented into three phonemes: [b] [æ] [t].

phonemic awareness   Refers to the ability to consciously separate individual phonemes in a spoken language. Phonemic awareness is often assessed by the ability to tap, count, or push a penny forward for every sound heard in a word like *cat:* [c] [a] [t].

phonetic   Representing the sounds of speech with a set of distinct symbols (letters), each denoting a single sound. See *alphabetic principle.*

phonics   The systematic relationship between letters and sounds.

phonics readers   Beginning reading books that are leveled in difficulty and contain recurring phonics elements.

phonograms   Often called *word families,* phonograms end in high frequency rimes that require only a beginning consonant sound to make a word. For example, *ack, ight, aw,* and *all* are all high frequency phonograms.

phonological awareness   An awareness of various speech sounds such as syllables, rhyme, and individual phonemes.

picture sort   A categorization task in which pictures are sorted into categories of similarity and difference. Pictures may be sorted by sound or by meaning. Pictures cannot be sorted by pattern.

picture-sorting activities   Various categorization games and routines using picture cards. Picture-sorting activities are all variations on the process of compare and contrast.

prephonetic   Writing that bears no correspondence to speech sounds; literally, "before sound." Prephonetic writing occurs during the emergent stage and typically consists of random scribbles, mock linear writing, or hieroglyphic-looking symbols. See *mock linear.*

preconsonantal nasals   Nasals that occur before consonants, as in the words *bump* or *sink.* The vowel is nasalized as part of the air escapes through the nose during pronunciation. See *nasals.*

predictability   The degree to which a story, text passage, or word sort may be anticipated or foretold based on familiarity and/or prior knowledge.

prefix   An affix attached at the beginning of a base word or word root.

preliterate stage   Henderson (1990) called the emergent stage the preliterate because students are not yet reading or writing conventionally. Students in the preliterate stage have not discovered the alphabetic principle. (See *alphabetic principle.*)

pretend reading   A paraphrase or spontaneous retelling told by children as they turn the pages of a familiar story book.

prosody/prosodic   The musical qualities of language, including intonation, expression, stress, and rhythm.

rimes   A rime unit is composed of the vowel and any following consonants within a syllable. For example, the rime unit in the word *tag* would be *ag.*

r-influenced vowels   In English, when an *r* colors the way the preceding vowel is pronounced. For example, compare the pronunciation of the vowels in *bar* and *bad.* The vowel in *bar* is influenced by the *r.*

root word/roots   Often used as a synonym for *base word;* refers to Greek roots or word parts of Greek origin that are often combined with other roots to form words such as *telephone* (*tele* and *phone*).

salient sounds   A prominent sound in a word or syllable that stands out because of the way it is made or felt in the mouth, or because of idiosyncratic reasons such as being similar to a sound in one's name. Salient sounds often correspond to syllable boundaries. See *articulation.*

scaffold   A form of support. The familiar structures of oral language offer a form of support for beginning readers.

schwa   A vowel sound in English that often occurs in an unstressed syllable, such as the /uh/ sound in the first syllable of the word *above.*

seat work   School work that is completed independently at the student's own desk. Students are already familiar with whatever seat work is assigned. Seat work is usually on a student's independent level and is usually assigned for practice. See *independent level.*

semiphonetic   Writing that demonstrates *some* awareness that letters represent speech sounds. Literally, "part sound." Beginning and/or ending consonant sounds of syllables or words may be represented but medial vowels are usually omitted (ICDD for *I see Daddy*). Semiphonetic writing occurs at the end of the emergent stage or the very outset of the early letter name–alphabetic stage when children are developing a concept of word. See *concept of word.*

short-term word banks   Words that are not consistently recognized out of context; words are promoted to word bank status when consistently recognized out of

context or, conversely, are discarded if they remain problematic. Compare with *word bank.*

short vowels   Every vowel (*a, e, i, o,* and *u*) has two sounds, commonly referred to as "long" and "short." The vocal cords are more relaxed when producing the short-vowel sound, as opposed to the long-vowel sound. See *long vowels.* Because of this, short-vowel sounds are often referred to as *lax.* The short-vowel sound for /a/ is the same sound you hear at the beginning of *apple.* The short-vowel sound for /e/ is the same sound you hear at the beginning of *Ed.* The short-vowel sound for /i/ is the same sound you hear at the beginning of *igloo.* The short-vowel sound for /o/ is the same sound you hear at the beginning of *octopus.* The short-vowel sound for /u/ is the same sound you hear at the beginning of *umbrella.*

sight words   Words recognized and pronounced immediately "at first sight." The term *sight words* does not necessarily mean high frequency words, phonetically irregular words, or lists of words. A sight word is simply any *known* word, regardless of its frequency or phonetic regularity.

simile   Two unlike things are explicitly compared, usually with the words *like* or *as.* For example, "Her tousled hair was like an explosion in a spaghetti factory." See *metaphor.*

sound   See *sound sort.*

sound board   Charts used by letter name–alphabetic spellers that contain pictures and letters for the basic sound-symbol correspondences (e.g., the letter *b,* a picture of a bell, and the word *bell*). Individual copies of sound boards are given to students for easy reference, and sound board charts are posted so students can refer to them as they write. Sound boards are provided in the Appendix.

sound sort   Sorts that ask students to categorize pictures or words by sound as opposed to visual patterns.

specialized readers   Proficient readers whose reading speeds exceed 250 to 300 words per minute and vary thereafter according to interest and background knowledge. Specialized readers encounter derivational vocabulary of Greek and Latin origin. Vocabulary growth begins to specialize according to academic discipline, personal interest, or profession.

spectrograph   An acoustic record of sound levels present in speech. We can see how speech is organized in contours through a spectrograph.

speed sorts   Pictures or words that are sorted under a timed condition. Students try to beat their own time.

spelling-by-stage classroom organization chart   Another form of a classroom composite sheet that places children in a developmental spelling stage.

spelling-meaning connections   Words that are related in meaning often share the same spelling despite changes in pronunciation from one form of the word to the next. The word *sign,* for example, retains the *g* from *signal* even though it is not pronounced, thus "signaling" the meaning connection through the spelling.

stems   Word parts, usually of Latin origin, that cannot stand alone, but are used in combination with other word parts in words related in meaning. Latin stems carry consistent though abstract meanings and can appear in various positions in words. For example, the Latin stem *spect* means roughly "to look at" or "to watch" and occurs at the beginning of the word *spectator,* the end of the word *inspect,* and the middle of the word *respectable.*

suffix   An affix attached at the end of a base word or word root.

syllable patterns   The alternating patterns of consonants (C) and vowels (V) at the point where syllables meet. For example, the word *rabbit* follows a VCCV syllable pattern at the point where the syllables meet.

syllables   Units of spoken language that consist of a vowel that may be preceded and/or followed by several consonants. Syllables are units of sound and can often be detected by paying attention to movements of the mouth. Syllabic divisions indicated in the dictionary are not always correct since the dictionary will always separate meaning units regardless of how the word is pronounced. For example, the proper syllable division for the word *naming* is *na-ming*; however, the dictionary divides this word as *nam-ing* to preserve the *ing.*

syllables and affixes stage   The fourth stage of spelling development which coincides with intermediate reading. Syllables and affixes spellers learn about the spelling changes which often take place at the point of transition from one syllable to the next. Frequently this transition involves consonant doubling or dropping the final *-e* before adding *ing.* See *juncture.*

synchrony   Occurring at the same time. In this book, stages of spelling development are described in the context of reading and writing behaviors occurring at the same time.

synthetic   Word study that combines separate word elements to form whole words.

tense   A vowel sound that is commonly known as the long-vowel sound. Long-vowel sounds are produced by tensing the vocal cords.

tracking   The ability to fingerpoint read a text, demonstrating concept of a word.

transitional stage of literacy development   A period of literacy development when learners are becoming fluent in reading easy materials. Silent reading becomes the preferred mode of reading. There is some expression in oral reading. This stage is between the beginning and intermediate stages of literacy development. The transitional period corresponds to the within word pattern stage of spelling development.

unaccented   Unstressed syllables. The final unstressed syllable in words such as *label* and *doctor* have no distinct vowel sound.

unvoiced   A sound that, when produced, does not necessitate the vibration of the vocal cords.

voiced   A sound that, when produced, vibrates the vocal cords. The letter sound *d,* for example, vibrates the vocal cords in a way that the letter sound *t* does not. See *unvoiced.*

vowel   A speech sound produced by the easy passage of air through a relatively open vocal tract. Vowels form the most central sound of a syllable. In English, vowel sounds are represented by the following letters: *a, e, i, o, u,* and sometimes *y.* See *consonants.*

vowel alternation   The process in which the pronunciation of vowels changes in the base or root of derivationally related words, while the spelling does not change. For example, the long-to-short vowel change in the related words *crime* and *criminal;* the long-to-schwa vowel change in the related words *impose* and *imposition.*

vowel digraphs   See *digraph.*

vowel marker   A silent letter used to indicate the sound of the vowel. In English, silent letters are used to form patterns associated with specific vowel sounds. Vowel markers are usually vowels themselves, as the *i* in *drain* or the *a* in *treat,* but they can also be consonants, as the *l* in *told.*

within word pattern spelling stage   The third stage of spelling development that coincides with the transitional period of literacy development. Within word pattern spellers have mastered the basic letter-sound correspondences of written English, and they grapple with letter sequences that function as a unit, especially long-vowel patterns. Some of the letters in the unit may have no sound themselves. These silent letters, such as the silent *-e* in *snake* or the silent *-i* in *drain,* serve as important markers in the pattern.

word   A unit of meaning. A word may be a single syllable or a combination of syllables. A word may contain smaller units of meaning within it. In print, a word is separated by white space. In speech, several words may be strung together in a breath group. For this reason, it takes a while for young children to develop a clear concept of word. See *concept of word.*

word bank   A collection of known words harvested from frequently read texts such as little leveled books, dictated stories, basal preprimers, and primers. Word bank words are *sight words.*

word cards   Known words are written on 2-by-1-inch pieces of cardstock. Words students can recognize with ease are used in word study games and word sorts.

word families   Phonograms or words that share the same rime (ex: *fast, past, last, blast,* all share the *ast* rime). In the derivational relations stage word families refer to words that share the same root or origin, as in *spectator, spectacle, inspect, inspector.* See *rime, phonogram,* and *cognates.*

word hunts   A word study activity in which students are sent back to texts they have previously read to hunt for other words that follow the same spelling features examined during the word or picture sort.

word root   A Greek or Latin element to which affixes are attached, for example, *cred, dict, fract, phon.* A word root usually cannot stand alone as a word. See *stems.*

word sort   A basic word study routine in which students group words into categories. Word sorting involves comparing and contrasting within and across categories. Word sorts are often cued by key words placed at the top of each category. See *key words.*

word study   A learner-centered, conceptual approach to instruction in phonics, spelling, word recognition, and vocabulary.

word study notebooks   Notebooks in which students write their word sorts into columns and add other words that follow similar spelling patterns throughout the week. Word study notebooks are organized around the orthographic features students are studying. Within word pattern students have sections of their notebooks dedicated to long-vowel sounds and patterns. Students in the syllables and affixes stage have sections dedicated to lists of different prefixes and suffixes (e.g., *es* words and *tion* words). Derivational relations students collect words by their common meanings (e.g., words that have *ter* in them: *terrain, terrestrial*).

writing sorts   A writing sort often follows a word sort. Students write key words as headings of columns.

zone of proximal development (ZPD)   A term coined by the Russian psychologist Vygotsky referring to the ripe conditions for learning something new. A person's ZPD is that zone which is neither too hard nor too easy. The term is similar to the concept of *instructional level.*

References

Adams, M. J. (1990). *Beginning to read: Thinking and learning about print.* Cambridge, MA: MIT Press.

Adams, M. J., Foorman, B. R., Lundberg, L., & Beeler, T. (1998). The elusive phoneme: Why phoneme awareness is so important and how to help children develop it. *American Educator, 22,* 18–29.

Anders, P., & Bos, C. (1986). Semantic feature analysis: An interactive strategy for vocabulary development and text comprehension. *Journal of Reading, 29,* 610–616.

Armbruster, B. B., Lehr, F., & Osborn, J. (2001). *Put reading first: The research building blocks for teaching children to read.* Washington, DC: The Partnership for Reading.

Ashton-Warner, S. (1963). *Teacher.* New York: Simon & Schuster.

Ball, E. W., & Blachman, B.A . (1988). Phoneme segmentation training: Effect on reading readiness. *Annals of Dyslexia, 38,* 208–225.

Baretta-Lorton, M. L. (1968). *Math their way.* Reading, MA: Addison-Wesley.

Barone, D. (1989). Young children's written responses to literature: The relationship between written response and orthographic knowledge. In S. McCormick & J. Zutell (Eds.), *Cognitive and social perspectives for literacy research and instruction* (pp. 371–380). Chicago: National Reading Conference.

Barone, D. (1990). The written responses of young children: Beyond comprehension to story understanding. *The New Advocate, 3*(1), 49–56.

Bear, D. (1982). *Patterns of oral reading across stages of word knowledge.* Unpublished manuscript, University of Virginia, Charlottesville.

Bear, D. (1991a). Copying fluency and orthographic development. *Visible Language, 25*(1), 40–53.

Bear, D. (1991b). "Learning to fasten the seat of my union suit without looking around": The synchrony of literacy development. *Theory into Practice, 30*(3), 149–157.

Bear, D. (1992). The prosody of oral reading and stage of word knowledge. In S. Templeton & D. Bear (Eds.), *Development of orthographic knowledge and the foundations of literacy: A memorial Festschrift for Edmund H. Henderson* (pp. 137–186). Hillsdale, NJ: Lawrence Erlbaum.

Bear, D., & McIntosh, M. (1990). Directed reading-thinking activities to promote reading and study habits in social studies. *Social Education, 54*(6), 385–388.

Bear, D., Invernizzi, M., Templeton, S., & Johnston, F. (2001). *Words Their Way CD.*

Bear, D., & Cathey, S. (1989, November). *Reading fluency in beginning readers and expression in practiced oral reading: Links with word knowledge.* Paper presented at National Reading Conference, Austin, TX.

Bear, D., Templeton, S., & Warner, M. (1991). The development of a qualitative inventory of higher levels of orthographic knowledge. In J. Zutell & S. McCormick (Eds.), *Learner factors/teacher factors: Issues in literacy research and instruction: Fortieth yearbook of the National Reading Conference* (pp. 105–110). Chicago: National Reading Conference.

Bear, D., Truex, P., & Barone, D. (1989). In search of meaningful diagnoses: Spelling-by-stage assessment of literacy proficiency. *Adult Literacy and Basic Education, 13*(3), 165–185.

Bear, D., & Barone, D. (1998). *Developing literacy: An integrated approach to assessment and instruction.* Boston: Houghton Mifflin.

Bear, D., & Templeton, S. (1998). Explorations in developmental spelling: Foundations for learning and teaching phonics, spelling and vocabulary. *The Reading Teacher, 52,* 222–242.

Bear, D., Templeton, S., Helman, L., & Baren, T. (2003). Orthographic development and learning to read in different languages. In G. Garcia (Ed.), *English learners: Reaching the highest level of English literacy* (pp. 71–95). Newark, DE: International Reading Association.

Beck, I. L., McKeown, M. G., & Kucan, L. (2002). *Bringing words to life: Robust vocabulary instruction.* New York: Guilford.

Beck, I. L., & McKeown, M. (1991). Conditions of vocabulary acquisition. In R. Barr, M. L. Kamil, P. Mosenthal, & P. D. Pearson (Eds.), *Handbook of reading research* (Vol. 2, pp. 789–814). White Plains, NY: Longman.

Biemiller, A. (1970). The development of the use of graphic and contextual information as children learn to read. *Reading Research Quarterly, 6,* 1, 75–96.

Blachman, B. A. (1994). What we have learned from longitudinal studies of phonological processing and reading, and some unanswered questions: A response to Torgeson, Wagner, and Rashotte. *Journal of Learning Disabilities, 27,* 287–291.

Bloodgood, J. R. (1996). *What's in a name? The role of name writing in children's literacy acquisition.* Unpublished doctoral dissertation, University of Virginia, Charlottesville.

Bryant, P., Nunes, T., & Bindman, M. (1997). Backward readers' awareness of language: Strengths and weaknesses. *European Journal of Psychology of Education, 12*(4), 357–372.

Button, K., Johnson, M. J., & Furgeson, P. (1996). Interactive writing in a primary classroom. *The Reading Teacher, 49,* 446–454.

Cantrell, R. J. (2001). Exploring the relationship between dialect and spelling for specific vocalic features in Appalachian first-grade children. *Linguistics and Education, 12*(1), 1–23.

Carlisle, J. F. (2000). Awareness of the structure and meaning of morphologically complex words: Impact on reading. *Reading and Writing: An Interdisciplinary Journal, 12,* 169–190.

Caserta-Henry, C., Bear, D. R., Del Porto, C. (1997). *Reading buddies manual.* Center for Learning and Literacy, MS 288, University of Nevada, Reno, NV 89557.

Cathey, S. S. (1991). *Emerging concept of word: Exploring young children's abilities to read rhythmic text.* Doctoral dissertation, University of Nevada. Reno, UMI #9220355.

Chall, J. S. (1983). *Stages of reading development.* New York: McGraw-Hill.

Chomsky, C. (1970). Reading, writing, and phonology. *Harvard Educational Review, 40*(2), 287–309.

Chomsky, C. (1971). Write first read later. *Childhood Education, 47,* 296–299.

Clarke, L. K. (1988). Invented versus traditional spelling in first graders' writing: Effects on learning to spell and read. *Research in the Teaching of English, 22,* 281–309.

Clay, M. (1975). *What did I write?* Exeter, NH: Heinemann.

Clay, M. M. (1991). Introducing a new storybook to young readers. *The Reading Teacher, 45,* 264–273.

Crystal, D. (1987). *The Cambridge encyclopedia of language.* New York: Cambridge University Press.

Cummings, D. (1988). *American English spelling.* Baltimore: Johns Hopkins University Press.

Cunningham, P. (1995). *Phonics they use: Words for reading and writing.* Boston: Allyn & Bacon.

Delpit, L. D. (1988). The silenced dialogue: Power and pedagogy in educating other people's children. *Harvard Educational Review, 58,* 280–298.

Ehri, L. (1992). Review and commentary: Stages of spelling development. In S. Templeton & D. Bear (Eds.), *Development of orthographic knowledge and the foundations of literacy: A memorial Festschrift for Edmund H. Henderson* (pp. 307–332). Hillsdale, NJ: Lawrence Erlbaum.

Ehri, L., & McCormick, S. (1998). Phases of word learning: Implications for instruction with delayed and disabled readers. *Reading and Writing Quarterly: Overcoming Learning Difficulties, 14,* 135–164.

Ehri, L. C. (1997). Learning to read and learning to spell are one and the same, almost. In C. A. Perfetti, L. Rieben, & M. Fayol (Eds.), *Learning to spell: Research, theory, and practice across languages* (pp. 237–269). Mahwah, NJ: Lawrence Erlbaum.

Ehri, L. C. (1998). Grapheme-phoneme knowledge is essential for learning to read words in English. In J. L. Metsala & L. C. Ehri (Eds.), *Word recognition in beginning literacy* (pp. 3–40). Mahwah, NJ: Lawrence Erlbaum Associates.

Ehri, L. C., & Wilce, L. S. (1980). Do beginning readers learn to read function words better in sentences or lists? *Reading Research Quarterly, 15,* 675–685.

Elkonin, D. B. (1973). U.S.S.R. In J. Downing (Ed.), *Comparative reading.* New York: Macmillan.

Estes, T. (1998). *Spanish spelling inventory.* http://www.curry.edschool.Virginia.EDU/curry/centers/ciera/p4.html.

Ferreiro, E., & Teberosky, A. (1982). *Literacy before schooling.* Portsmouth, NH: Heinemann.

Frith, U. (1985). Beneath the surface of developmental dyslexia. In K. Patterson, J. Marshall, & M. Coltheart (Eds.), *Surface dyslexia: Neuropsychological and cognitive studies of phonological reading* (pp. 301–330). London: Lawrence Erlbaum Associates.

Fry, B. E., Kress, J. E., & Fountoukidis, D. L. (2000). *The reading teacher's book of lists* (4th ed.). Jossey-Bass.

Ganske, K. (1994). Developmental spelling analysis: A diagnostic measure for instruction and research (University of Virginia). *Dissertation Abstracts International, 55*(05), 1230A.

Ganske, K. (1999). The developmental spelling analysis: A measure of orthographic knowledge. *Educational Assessment, 6,* 41–70.

Ganske, K. (2000). *Word journeys.* New York: Guilford.

Gelb, I. J. (1963). *A study of writing* (2nd ed.). Chicago: University of Chicago Press.

Gibson, E. J. (1965). Learning to read. *Science, 148,* 1006–1072.

Gibson, J. J., & Yonas, P. M. (1968). A new theory of scribbling and drawing in children. In *The analysis of reading skill: A program of basic and applied research* (Final Report, Project No. 5-1213,

Cornell University and the U.S. Office of Education, pp. 335–370). Ithaca, NY: Cornell University.

Gill, J., & Bear, D. (1988). No book, whole book, and chapter DR-TAs: Three study techniques. *Journal of Reading, 31*(5), 444–449.

Gill, J., & Bear, D. (1989). *Directions for upper level word study.* Unpublished paper.

Gillet, J. W., & Kita, M. J. (1979). Words, kids, and categories. *The Reading Teacher, 32,* 538–542.

Goswami, U. (1990). A special link between rhyming skill and the use of orthographic analogies by beginning readers. *Journal of Child Psychiatry, 31,* 301–311.

Gough, P.B., & Hillenger, M. L. (1980). Learning to read: An unnatural act. *Bulletin of the Orton Society, 20,* 179–196.

Hall, M. (1980). *Teaching reading as a language experience.* Columbus, OH: Merrill.

Henderson, E. (1981). *Learning to read and spell: The child's knowledge of words.* DeKalb: Northern Illinois Press.

Henderson, E. (1990). *Teaching spelling* (2nd ed.). Boston: Houghton Mifflin.

Henderson, E., & Beers, J. (Eds.), (1980). *Developmental and cognitive aspects of learning to spell.* Newark, DE: International Reading Association.

Henderson, E., Estes, T., & Stonecash, S. (1972). An exploratory study of word acquisition among first graders at midyear in a language experience approach. *Journal of Reading Behavior, 4,* 21–30.

Henderson, E. H. (1985). *Teaching spelling.* Boston: Houghton Mifflin.

Henderson, E. H., & Templeton, S. (1986). The development of spelling ability through alphabet, pattern, and meaning. *Elementary School Journal, 86,* 305–316.

Henry, M. (1988). Beyond phonics: Integrated decoding and spelling instruction based on word origin and structures. *Annals of Dyslexia, 38,* 258–275.

Horn, E. (1954). *Teaching spelling.* Washington, DC: National Education Association.

Invernizzi, M. (1985). *A cross-sectional analysis of children's recognition and recall of word elements.* Unpublished manuscript, University of Virginia, Charlottesville.

Invernizzi, M. (1992). The vowel and what follows: A phonological frame of orthographic analysis. In S. Templeton & D. Bear (Eds.), *Development of orthographic knowledge and the foundations of literacy: A memorial Festschrift for Edmund H. Henderson* (pp. 106–136). Hillsdale, NJ: Lawrence Erlbaum.

Invernizzi, M. (2002). Concepts, sounds, and the ABCs: A diet for a very young reader. In D. M. Barone & L. M. Morrow (Eds.), *Literacy and young children.* New York: Guilford Publications.

Invernizzi, M., Abouzeid, M., & Gill, T. (1994). Using students' invented spellings as a guide for spelling instruction that emphasizes word study. *Elementary School Journal, 95*(2), 155–167.

Invernizzi, M. & Meier, J. (2002). *Phonological Awareness Literacy Screening 2001–2002.* Charlottesville, VA: The Rector and the Board of Visitors of the University of Virginia.

Invernizzi, M., Meier, J., Swank, L., & Juel, C. (1998). *Phonological awareness literacy screening: Teacher's manual.* Charlottesville, VA: University of Virginia Printing Services.

James, W. (1958). *Talks to teachers on psychology and to students on some of life's ideals.* New York: Norton. (Original work published 1899).

Johnston, F., Invernizzi, M., Bear, D., & Templeton, S., (2003). *Words Their Way: Word Sorts for Letter-Name Alphabetic Spellers.* Columbus, OH: Prentice Hall.

Johnston, F. R. (1998). The reader, the text, and the task: Learning words in first grade. *The Reading Teacher, 51,* 666–675.

Johnston, F. R. (2001). The utility of phonic generalizations: Let's take another look at Clymer's conclusions. *The Reading Teacher, 55,* 132–43.

Johnston, F. R., Invernizzi, M., & Juel, C. (1998). *Book Buddies: Guidelines for volunteer tutors of emergent and beginning readers.* New York: Guilford Press.

Juel, C. (1991). Beginning reading. In R. Barr, M. Kamil, P. Mosenthal, & P. D. Pearson (Eds.), *Handbook of reading research* (Vol. II, pp. 759–788). New York: Longman Press.

Juel, C., & Minden-Cupp, C. (2000). Learning to read words: Linguistic units and instructional strategies. *Reading Research Quarterly, 35,* 458–492.

Juel, C., & Roper-Schneider, D. (1985). The influence of basal readers on first grade reading. *Reading Research Quarterly, 18,* 306–327.

Kress, J. E. (2002) *The ESL teacher's book of lists.* John Wiley & Sons.

Leong, C. K. (2000). Rapid processing of base and derived forms of words and grades 4, 5, and 6 children's spelling. *Reading and Writing: An Interdisciplinary Journal, 12,* 277–302.

Liberman, I., & Shankweiler, D. (1991). Phonology and beginning reading: A tutorial. In L. Rieben & C. Perfetti (Eds.), *Learning to read: Basic research and its implication.* Hillsdale, NJ: Lawrence Erlbaum.

Lundberg, I., Frost, J., & Peterson, O. (1988). Effects of an extensive program for stimulating phonological awareness in preschool children. *Reading Research Quarterly, 23,* 267–284.

Mahony, D., Singson, M., & Mann, V. (2000). Reading ability and sensitivity to morphological relations. *Reading and Writing: An Interdisciplinary Journal, 12,* 191–218.

Malinowski, B. (1952). The problem of meaning in primitive languages. In C. K. Ogden & I. A. Richards (Eds.), *The meaning of meaning* (10th ed.). New York: Harcourt.

MatchWord. (2001). Bothell, WA: Wright Group/McGraw- Hill.

McBride-Chang, C. (1999). The ABCs of the ABCs: The development of letter-name and letter-sound knowledge. *Merrill Palmer Quarterly Journal of Developmental Psychology, 45,* 285–308.

McIntosh, M., & Bear, D. (1993, December). *The development of content-specific orthographic knowledge: A look at vocabulary in geometry.* Paper presented at the 43rd Annual National Reading Conference, Charleston, SC.

McKenzie, M. G. (1985). Shared writing: Apprenticeship in writing. *Language Matters, 1–2.* 1–5.

Morais, J., Cary, L., Alegria, J., & Bertelson, P. (1979). Does awareness of speech as a sequence of phonemes arise spontaneously? *Cognition, 7,* 323–331.

Morris, D. (1980). Beginning readers' concept of word. In E. Henderson & J. Beers (Eds.), *Developmental and cognitive aspects of learning to spell* (pp. 97–111). Newark, DE: International Reading Association.

Morris, D. (1981). Concept of word: A developmental phenomenon in the beginning reading and writing process. *Language Arts, 58*(6), 659–668.

Morris, D. (1982). "Word sort": A categorization strategy for improving word recognition ability. *Reading Psychology, 3,* 247–259.

Morris, D. (1999). *The Howard Street tutoring manual.* New York: Guilford Press.

Morris, D., Blanton, L., Blanton, W., & Perney, J. (1995). Spelling instruction and achievement in six elementary classrooms. *The Elementary School Journal, 96,* 145–162.

Morris, D., Bloodgood, J., Lomax, R., & Perney, J. (2001). Developmental steps in learning to read: A longitudinal study in kindergarten and first grade. (Submitted for review.)

Morris, D., Nelson, L., & Perney, J. (1986). Exploring the concept of "spelling instructional level" through the analysis of error-types. *Elementary School Journal, 87,* 181–200.

Morris, D., & Perney, J. (1984). Developmental spelling as a predictor of first-grade reading achievement. *The Elementary School Journal, 84,* 441–457.

Murray, B. A. (1998). Gaining alphabetic insight: Is phonemic manipulation skill or identity knowledge causal? *Journal of Educational Psychology, 90,* 461–475.

Nessel, D., & Jones, M. (1981). *The language-experience approach to reading.* New York: Teachers College Press.

Perfetti, C., Beck, I., Bell, L., & Hughes, C. (1987). Phonemic knowledge and learning to read are reciprocal. *Merrill-Palmer Quarterly, 33,* 283–319.

Phenix, J. (1996). *The spelling teacher's book of lists.* Ontario: Pembroke.

Pressley, M. (1998). *Reading instruction that works: The case for balanced teaching.* New York: Guilford Publications.

Purcell, T. (2002). *Linguistic influences on letter sound learning: Considering manner, place, and voicing.* Unpublished Doctoral Dissertation. University of Virginia, Charlottesville.

Raphael, T. E., Pardo, L. S., Highfield, K., & McMahon, S. I. (1997). *Book Club: A literature-based curriculum.* Littleton, MA: Small Planet Communications, Inc.

Read, C. (1971). Pre-school children's knowledge of English phonology. *Harvard Educational Review, 41*(1), 1–34.

Read, C. (1975). *Children's categorization of speech sounds in English.* Urbana, IL: NCTE Research Report No. 17.

Roberts, B. S. (1992). The evolution of the young child's concept of word as a unit of spoken and written language. *Reading Research Quarterly, 27*(2), 125–138.

Sawyer, D. J., Lipa-Wade, S., Kim, J., Ritenour, D., & Knight, D. F. (1997). *Spelling errors as a window on dyslexia.* Paper presented at the 1997 annual convention of the American Educational Research Association, Chicago.

Schlagal, R. (1992). Patterns of orthographic development into the intermediate grades. In S. Templeton & D. Bear (Eds.), *Development of orthographic knowledge and the foundations of literacy: A memorial Festschrift for Edmund H. Henderson* (pp. 31–52). Hillsdale, NJ: Lawrence Erlbaum.

Scragg, D. (1974). *A history of English spelling.* New York: Barnes & Noble Books, Manchester University Press.

Smith, M. L. (1998). Sense and sensitivity: An investigation into fifth-grade children's knowledge of English derivational morphology and its relationship to vocabulary and reading ability. University Microfilms No. AAM9830072. *Dissertation Abstracts International, 59* (4-A), 1111.

Smith, S. B., Simmons, D. C., & Kame'enui, E. J. (1995). *Synthesis of research on phonological awareness: Principles and implications for reading acquisition* (Tech. Rep. No. 21). Eugene, OR: University of Oregon, National Center to Improve the Tools of Educators.

Snow, C. E. (1983). Literacy and language: Relationships during the preschool years. *Harvard Educational Review, 53*(2), 165–189.

Snow, C. E., Burns, M. S., & Griffin, P. (Eds.), (1998). *Preventing reading difficulties in young children.* Washington, DC: National Academy Press.

Spear-Swerling, L., & Sternberg, R. J. (Contributor) (1997). *Off track: When poor readers become "learning disabled."* Boulder, CO: Westview Press.

Stahl, S. A., & McKenna, M. C. (2001, August). The concurrent development of phonological awareness, word recognition, and spelling. CIERA Technical Report No. 01-07. Available at http://www.ciera.org/library/archive/index.html.

Stanovich, K. (1986). Matthew effects in reading: Some consequences of individual differences in the acquisition of literacy. *Reading Research Quarterly, 21,* 360–406.

Stauffer, R. (1980). *The language-experience approach to the teaching of reading* (2nd ed.). New York: Harper & Row.

Strickland, D., & Morrow, L. (1989). Environments rich in print promote literacy behavior during play. *Reading Teacher, 43,* 178–179.

Sulzby, E. (1986). Writing and reading organization. In W. H. Teale & E. Sulzby (Eds.), *Emergent literacy: Writing and reading* (pp. 50–89). Norwood, NJ: Abex.

Taft, M. (1991). *Reading and the mental lexicon.* London: Lawrence Erlbaum Associates.

Templeton, S. (1976, December). *The spelling of young children in relation to the logic of alphabetic orthography.* Paper presented at the 26th annual convention of the National Reading Conference, Atlanta, GA.

Templeton, S. (1979). Spelling first, sound later: The relationship between orthography and higher order phonological knowledge in older students. *Research in the Teaching of English, 13,* 255–264.

Templeton, S. (1980). Logic and mnemonics for demons and curiosities: Spelling awareness for middle- and secondary-level students. *Reading World, 20,* 123–130.

Templeton, S. (1983). Using the spelling/meaning connection to develop word knowledge in older students. *Journal of Reading, 27*(1), 8–14.

Templeton, S. (1989). Tacit and explicit knowledge of derivational morphology: Foundations for a unified approach to spelling and vocabulary development in the intermediate grades and beyond. *Reading Psychology, 10,* 233–253.

Templeton, S. (1992). Theory, nature, and pedagogy of higher-order orthographic development in older children. In S. Templeton & D. Bear (Eds.), *Development of orthographic knowledge and the foundations of literacy: A memorial Festschrift for Edmund H. Henderson* (pp. 253–278), Hillsdale, NJ: Lawrence Erlbaum.

Templeton, S. (1997). *Teaching the integrated language arts* (2nd ed.). Boston: Houghton Mifflin.

Templeton, S. (2003). Spelling. In J. Flood, D. Lapp, J. R. Squire, & J. M. Jensen (Eds.), *Handbook of research on teaching the English language arts* (2nd ed., pp. 738–751). Mahwah, NJ: Lawrence Erlbaum Associates.

Templeton, S., & Bear, D. (Eds.). (1992a). *Development of orthographic knowledge and the foundations of literacy: A memorial Festschrift for Edmund H. Henderson.* Hillsdale, NJ: Lawrence Erlbaum.

Templeton, S., & Bear, D. (1992b). Teaching the lexicon to read and spell. In S. Templeton & D. Bear (Eds.), *Development of orthographic knowledge and the foundations of literacy: A memorial Festschrift for Edmund H. Henderson* (pp. 333–352). Hillsdale, NJ: Lawrence Erlbaum.

Templeton, S., & Morris, D. (1999). Questions teachers ask about spelling. *Reading Research Quarterly, 34,* 102–112.

Templeton, S., & Morris, D. (2000). Spelling. In M. Kamil, P. Mosenthal, P. D. Pearson, & R. Barr (Eds.), . *Handbook of reading research: Vol. 3* (pp. 525–543). Mahwah, NJ: Lawrence Erlbaum Associates.

Templeton, S., & Scarborough-Franks, L. (1985). The spelling's the thing: Older students' knowledge of derivational morphology in phonology and orthography. *Applied Psycholinguistics, 6,* 371–389.

Templeton, S., & Spivey, E. M. (1980). The concept of "word" in young children as a function of level of cognitive development. *Research in the Teaching of English, 14*(3), 265–278.

Torgesen, J., Davis, C. (1996). Individual differences variables that predict response to training in phonological awareness. *Journal of Experimental Child Psychology, 63,* 1, 1–21.

Treiman, R. (1985). Onsets and rimes as units of spoken syllables: Evidence from children. *Journal of Educational Psychology, 77*(4), 417–427.

Treiman, R. (1991). The role of intrasyllabic units in learning to read. In L. Rieben & C. A. Perfetti (Eds.), *Learning to read: Basic research and its implications.* (pp. 149–160). Hillsdale, NJ: Lawrence Erlbaum.

Tunmer, W. E. (1991). Phonological awareness and literacy acquisition. In L. Rieben & C. A. Perfetti (Eds.), *Learning to read: Basic research and its implications* (pp. 105–120). Hillsdale, NJ: Lawrence Erlbaum Associates.

Vallins, G. H. (1954). *Spelling.* Andre Deutsch.

Venesky, R. (1970). *The structure of English orthography.* The Hague: Mouton.

Viise, N. (1996). A study of the spelling development of adult literacy learners compared with that of classroom children. *Journal of Literacy Research, 28*(4), 561–587.

Vygotsky, L. S. (1962). *Thought and language.* Cambridge, MA: MIT Press.

Wildsmith, B. (1982). *The cat on the mat.* New York: Oxford Press.

Worthy, J., & Viise, N. (1993). *Can we know what we know about children in teaching adults to read?* Unpublished paper.

Worthy, M. J., & Invernizzi, M. (1989). Spelling errors of normal and disabled students on achievement levels one through four: Instructional implications. *Bulletin of the Orton Society, 40,* 138–149.

Wylie, R. E., & Durrell, D. D. (1970). Teaching vowels through phonograms. *Elementary English, 47,* 787–791.

Yopp, H. K., & Yopp, R. E. (2000). *Oo-pples and Boo-noo-noos.* Posrtsmouth, NH: Heineman.

Young, S. (1994). *Scholastic rhyming dictionary.* New York: Scholastic.

Zutell, J. (1994). Spelling instruction. In A. C. Purves, L. Papa, & S. Jordan (Eds.), *Encyclopedia of English studies and language arts* (Vol. 2, pp. 1098–1100). New York: Scholastic.

Zutell, J. (1996). The directed spelling thinking activity (DSTA): Providing an effective balance in word study instruction. *The Reading Teacher, 50,* 98–107.

Zutell, J., & Rasinski, T. (1989). Reading and spelling connections in third and fourth grade students. *Reading Psychology, 10,* 137–156.

Index